THE ILLUSTRATED

THE ILLUSTRATED
Kitchen Bible

Editor-in-chief
Victoria Blashford-Snell

Penguin Random House

Produced for Dorling Kindersley by **Carroll & Brown Limited**,
20 Lonsdale Road, London, NW6 6PD
www.carrollandbrown.co.uk

For Dorling Kindersley
Project Editor Laura Nickoll
Senior Art Editor Susan Downing
Senior Jacket Creative Nicola Powling
Managing Editor Dawn Henderson
Managing Art Editor Christine Keilty
Senior Production Editor Jenny Woodcock
Senior Production Controller Wendy Penn
Creative Technical Support Sonia Charbonnier

First American Edition, 2008
This edition published in the United States in 2016 by DK Publishing
345 Hudson Street, New York, New York 10014

Copyright © 2008, 2016 Dorling Kindersley Limited
DK, a Division of Penguin Random House LLC
10 9 8 7 6 5 4 3 2 1
001–294016–Aug/2016

A catalog record for this book is available from the Library of Congress
ISBN 978-1-4654-5155-2

DK books are available at special discounts when purchased in bulk for sales promotions,
premiums, fund-raising, or educational use. For details, contact: DK Publishing Special
Markets, 345 Hudson Street, New York, New York 10014
SpecialSales@dk.com.

All butter is unsalted, unless otherwise indicated. All herbs are fresh, unless otherwise
indicated. Some recipes in this book are made with raw eggs, which may contain harmful
bacterium and should not be served to the young or elderly, pregnant, ill, or anyone with a
compromised immune system.

Printed and bound in China

All images © Dorling Kindersley Limited
For further information see: www.dkimages.com

A WORLD OF IDEAS:
SEE ALL THERE IS TO KNOW

www.dk.com

Contents

STARTERS AND LIGHT BITES 14

Foreword

I am passionate about cooking and eating, and thoroughly enjoy all that goes with it. Reading about food, researching and purchasing ingredients, choosing recipes old and new, thumbing through magazines and books, and talking to fellow enthusiasts are among my favorite activities. I enjoy experimenting with much-loved family dishes, finding new ways for them to "hit the spot," but I do love to make something different when I have friends around.

I run a catering business, teach, and write about food, and like many, have a family to look after, so although I would be happy to be puttering about in the kitchen all day, I do not have all that much time to spare, so organization is essential in planning my menus, especially if I want to include something to please everyone. There can be as many as seven people most days for lunch in our home, so I need to feed everyone quickly.

For these reasons and many others, I am thrilled to be involved with the creation of this book, as I believe it is essential for helping other modern busy people like myself. The book makes it easy for us to prepare nutritious and healthy meals simply by following clearly laid-out recipes, each accompanied by a tempting photograph. There are hundreds of superb ideas for everyday family food, and others for more formal entertaining, a comprehensive collection of recipes from all over the world includes the classics of fine dining, and modern variations to spice up one's everyday repertoire.

The book is so full of special features, that it is certain to please every level of cook, from the beginner, to the more adventurous. The wealth of cooking expertise on display is truly exceptional. Enjoy!

Victoria Blashford-Snell

Introduction

Becoming a confident cook is all about producing delicious meals consistently. This book has been designed to help you do just that.

As you become familiar with the contents of this book, you will benefit hugely from the range of recipes that will enable you to create a multitude of imaginative and delicious meals. Whatever the occasion—from everyday sandwich lunches to elegant party fare—and whatever it is you want to achieve—from serving up healthy everyday dinner dishes cooked in as little time as possible, to mastering the classic dishes of international cuisine—this book will enable you to achieve great results. It contains a marvelous collection of recipes from the ever-more familiar world of international cookery. Recipes that were once only eaten in exotic restaurants can now be served successfully at home alongside family favorites. Furthermore, many recipes have variations, which means that having mastered one, you can very easily make another along similar lines.

Most lives today are busy ones, so all the recipes have preparation and cooking times and, where applicable, instructions on preparing ahead and freezing. Any requirements for special equipment and/or advance preparation are flagged, and when a dish is low fat or low GI, there is an icon to point it out, making this book unusually helpful.

Recipe Choosers with photographic galleries of dishes suitable for specific occasions make your meal planning easier. At a glance, you'll be able to see many different possibilities for main meals under 30 minutes, meat-free dishes, or a weekend brunch or dinner party.

Special Features look more closely at the preparation of certain key dishes, such as roasting the most flavorful chicken, making different types of omelets, cooking the perfect steak, and perfecting your pastry skills.

Techniques demonstrate step-by-step how to work with a wide range of ingredients including vegetables, fruits, nuts, eggs, seafood, pasta, and rice.

Plan

Leafing through the pages of this book, there's no doubt that your appetite will be whetted to try out various dishes, simply because they look so delicious. However, the choice of what to cook can arise from a number of other things. You may choose to cook a dish because of its main ingredient—you liked the look of fresh fish in the market, or a neighbor gave you some freshly picked vegetables. Or, you may want to cater for a specific occasion, such as a breakfast or lunch. Sometimes there will be particular circumstances—you've invited vegetarian friends over for brunch or you are hosting a cocktail party. Time or equipment may be other factors; what can you get on the table in under an hour, is there something you can prepare the night before, and what tastes good grilled outdoors?

Your budget and how many are eating needs to be considered. You may decide to splurge on lobster for an intimate dinner for two, but a casserole will be a cheaper and easier choice when cooking for a large number of guests (see Cook for a Crowd, far right).

Another consideration when menu planning should be to provide varied textures, colors, and tastes—all of which work well together. This will come with practice; the more you cook, the faster you will learn what works with what, and why. These days it is not usually necessary to serve a three course meal. For everyday dining, a substantial main course with a salad and/or vegetables could be followed by fruit or a simple dessert, and this book helps you to choose with Recipe Choosers in each main section, and an image for every recipe in the book.

Shop

Shopping, rather than being a chore, should be about buying the freshest ingredients available without having to visit too many different shops, therefore not having to take a lot of time and travel. Consider shopping at good-quality stores to avoid the disappointment of aisles of limp, colorless vegetables or tired old fish, and whenever possible, shop locally. The choice of ingredients may be smaller, but their freshness and quality will make up for it. Always attempt to buy meat from a good quality butcher, and fish from similar fishmonger; supporting small local shops is essential to the future of quality ingredients. To save time, know how many you're cooking for, make a list, and pre-order important ingredients.

Tips for Quantities

There are times when a recipe does not yield the right quantity of food for the number of people you plan to serve, and altering the quantities can become confusing. When halving, doubling, or serving more than one course, consider the following weights before shopping for ingredients:

- **6oz (175g) per person** when serving one meat or fish main course dish
- **4oz (115g) per dish per person** when serving two courses
- **3oz (85g) per dish per person** when serving three courses

Store

Once the shopping is done, it is important to store the ingredients properly to avoid food spoiling. Be careful not to place tender lettuce and herbs at the back of the refrigerator where they are at risk of over chilling and possibly freezing. All dried, canned, and boxed products should be stored in a cool and dark place. Root vegetables should be stored in a cool, well-ventilated place, but not necessarily the refrigerator. Certain foods, like tomatoes, are best kept in the light, i.e., a basket or bowl on the windowsill.

Soft fruit, such as berries, will keep for several days if kept dry and cool. Store hard fruit, such as apples, pears, or pineapple, for up to a week in a cool place out of direct sunlight, which will keep them from becoming overripe.

Meat and fish should be stored on a plate, loosely covered with plastic wrap, in the refrigerator for 1–2 days. Be careful not to store any meat or fish that may drip above dairy foods or vegetables.

Dairy products such as cream, butter, and yogurt need to be refrigerated, but soft cheeses must be kept at room temperature to ripen before serving. Hard cheeses can be kept in a cool place or chilled. Eggs should be kept in a cool place, pointed end downward, to keep the yolk central in the white.

Freeze

If you are not planning to use ingredients right away, they should be frozen when fresh, and as quickly as possible. Freezing is useful to preserve leftovers for last minute meals.

Keep a thermometer in your freezer, to maintain the temperature at 17°F (8°C).

For even freezing, keep the freezer only three-quarters full.

Make sure all food is properly covered, labeled, and sealed before freezing to keep the food from drying out and becoming ruined or unidentifiable at a later time.

Milk and cream do not freeze well, as they often curdle when defrosted.

Don't freeze dishes that contain mayonnaise or raw eggs.

Never refreeze defrosted food.

Defrost food slowly, ideally in the refrigerator or overnight somewhere cool, never near direct heat.

Cook for a Crowd

Many cooks find cooking for a large number of people daunting. The important thing is to keep things simple. Do not over-stretch yourself; plan around what space you have to store dishes, as well as the facilities you have to prepare them in. Here are some tips for success:

When multiplying a recipe, be careful not to over-season, add too much liquid, or over-cook.

A casserole for six people and one for twelve will take approximately the same amount of time to cook, even though you may have doubled the weight of the ingredients.

Preparing too little food can be embarrassing, while a lot of uneaten dishes can ruin the success of a party. Figure out quantities carefully in advance of the event.

When catering, remember that if you are providing a number of different dishes, people will only have a little of each.

Guests will eat less if it is a stand-up party, rather than a sit-down meal.

Serve

The appearance of the food you serve and eat is very important. We are not suggesting everything be served garnished with a tomato rose, but by simply ensuring the plates are clean, drops of sauce are wiped away from the rim, and adding a wedge of lemon or lime with certain dishes, or adding a scattering of fresh herbs on savory recipes, will enhance a dish greatly. Keep the following tips in mind, and your presentation will always be successful:

Serve hot food straight from the oven, therefore avoiding skin forming on the juices, which never looks attractive.

Try to choose textures and colors that complement each other—crisp green beans alongside mashed potatoes, puréed carrots with stir-fried broccoli, or peas with roasted parsnips.

Do not dress a salad too early, but rather just before serving, if possible, so that the leaves stay crisp.

Searing meat not only gives a better color for presentation, but it also improves the flavor.

Avoid fussy garnishes on the plate that are not edible.

Desserts, cakes, and pastries served with a quick dusting of confectioner's sugar will always look more appealing to the eye.

A Guide to Symbols

The recipes in this book are accompanied by symbols that alert you to important information.

🍴 Tells you how many people the recipe serves, or how much is produced.

🕐 Indicates how much time you will need to prepare and cook a dish. Next to this symbol, you will also find out if additional time is required for such things as marinating, standing, rising, or cooling. You will have to read the recipe to find out exactly how much extra time is needed.

✅ Points out nutritional benefits, such as low fat or low GI.

❗ This is especially important, because it alerts you to what has to be done before you can begin to cook the recipe. For example, you may need to soak some beans overnight.

📦 This denotes that special equipment is required, such as a deep-fat fryer or skewers. Where possible, alternatives are given.

❄️ This symbol accompanies freezing information.

Roasting Meat

As all cuts of meat can vary, these times are intended as a general guide. When calculating timings, add an extra 1lb (450g) of weight to your joint if it weighs less than 3lb (1.35kg). Be sure to preheat the oven before cooking your meat, use a meat thermometer (inserted into the thickest part of the cut, away from any bones) for an accurate internal temperature, and always allow the meat to rest for 15–30 minutes before carving.

MEAT		OVEN TEMPERATURE	COOKING TIME	INTERNAL TEMPERATURE
Beef	Rare	350°F (180°C)	15 mins per 1lb (450g)	140°F (60°C)
	Medium	350°F (180°C)	20 mins per 1lb (450g)	160°F (70°C)
	Well-done	350°F (180°C)	25 mins per 1lb (450g)	175°F (80°C)
Veal	Well-done	350°F (180°C)	25 mins per 1lb (450g)	175°F (80°C)
Lamb	Medium	350°F (180°C)	20 mins per 1lb (450g)	160°F (70°C)
	Well-done	350°F (180°C)	25 mins per 1lb (450g)	175°F (80°C)

Roasting Poultry

Use these times as a guide, bearing in mind that the size and weight of each bird varies. Be sure to preheat the oven before cooking your bird(s), and always check that the bird is fully cooked before serving.

MEAT		OVEN TEMPERATURE	COOKING TIME
Poussin		375°F (190°C)	12 mins per 1lb (450g) plus 12 mins
Chicken		400°F (200°C)	20 mins per 1lb (450g) plus 20 mins
Duck		350°F (180°C)	20 mins per 1lb (450g) plus 20 mins
Goose		350°F (180°C)	20 mins per 1lb (450g) plus 20 mins
Pheasant		400°F (200°C)	50 mins total cooking
Turkey	7–9lb (3.5–4.5kg)	375°F (190°C)	2½–3 hrs total cooking
	10–12lb (5–6kg)	375°F (190°C)	3½–4 hrs total cooking
	13–17lb (6.5–8.5kg)	375°F (190°C)	4½–5 hrs total cooking

Refrigerator and Freezer Storage Guide

FOOD	REFRIGERATOR	FREEZER
Raw poultry, fish, and meat (small pieces)	2–3 days	3–6 months
Raw minced beef and poultry	1–2 days	3 months
Cooked whole roasts or whole poultry	2–3 days	9 months
Cooked poultry pieces	1–2 days	1 month (6 months in stock or gravy)
Bread	-	3 months
Ice cream	-	1–2 months
Soups and stews	2–3 days	1–3 months
Casseroles	2–3 days	2–4 weeks
Cookies	-	6–8 months

Oven Temperature Equivalents

FAHRENHEIT	CELSIUS	GAS	DESCRIPTION
225°F	110°C	¼	Cool
250°F	120°C	½	Cool
275°F	140°C	1	Very Low
300°F	150°C	2	Very Low
325°F	170°C	3	Low
350°F	180°C	4	Moderate
375°F	190°C	5	Moderately Hot
400°F	200°C	6	Hot
425°F	220°C	7	Hot
450°F	230°C	8	Very Hot

Volume Equivalents

IMPERIAL	METRIC	IMPERIAL	METRIC
1fl oz	25ml	7fl oz (⅓ pint)	200ml
2fl oz	50ml	8fl oz	225ml
2fl oz	75ml	9fl oz	250ml
3fl oz	100ml	10fl oz (½ pint)	300ml
4fl oz	125ml	12fl oz	350ml
5fl oz (¼ pint)	150ml	14fl oz	400ml
6fl oz	175ml	18fl oz	500ml

Basic Kitchen Equipment

There is no need to spend a fortune on gadgets to cook well, since good food comes from the ingredients and the cook, but certain tools of the trade will make the job more enjoyable:

Food processor
Citrus juicer – hand-held
Knives – 1 large chopping,
    1 small serrated, 1 bread, and
    1 carving knife
Vegetable peeler
Cheese grater
Fruit zester
Large cutting board
Salad spinner
Roasting trays – for meat
Flat baking sheets – for baking
Electric hand whisk
Hand-held balloon whisk
Large fine sieve
Garlic press

Colander
Pastry brush
Rolling pin
Food weighing scales
Wooden spoons
Ladle
Ice cream scoop
Slotted spoon
Spatula
Fish slice
Mixing bowls
Good nonstick frying pan
Saucepans with lids in varying sizes
Kitchen scissors
Measuring jug
Oven mitts

Recipe Terms

Just as in any other activity, cooking has its own specialized vocabulary. Although in this book, recipes are written without unnecessary jargon, it can help to know exactly what is meant by specific terms.

FOOD PREPARATION

Drizzle refers to pouring a liquid, such as olive oil, slowly back and forth in a fine stream.

Fold refers to incorporating a light, airy mixture into a heavier mixture.

Marinate means to let a food soak in a liquid that will add flavor and/or tenderize it.

Pinch is an amount of a dry, powdery ingredient that you can hold between your thumb and forefinger.

Purée is both an action and product, results in a smooth mixture when food is processed in a food processor, blender, or food mill.

Zest is both the action and product of removing the rind of a citrus fruit. Avoid zesting the bitter white pith.

Dice describes small, uniform cubes of approximately ¼in (5mm). To cut dice, first cut the food into matchsticks then, bundling the sticks together, cut crosswise into uniform cubes.

Julienne are matchsticks that are thin and about 2in (5cm) long. To cut julienne, cut first to length, then stack the slices and cut lengthwise into ⅛in (3mm) wide sticks.

Chop means to cut food into small, irregular, pea-size pieces. The best way to do this is to coarsely cut up the food first, then place the pieces in a pile. Holding the tip and handle of a chef's knife and using a rocking motion, chop the pieces. "Finely chopped" indicates pieces, cut as described above, that are less than ⅛in (3mm) thick.

COOKING

Browning means cooking food quickly so it colors all over and keeps the juices sealed. It can be done in oil or butter on the stove top, under the grill, or in the oven.

Boiling occurs when a liquid reaches 212°F (100°C), and produces large bubbles that continuously rise and break the surface.

Simmering also produces bubbles, but these rise in a steady stream, are much smaller, and are just visible on the surface.

Reducing means to boil a liquid rapidly so that a proportion evaporates leaving a deeper, more concentrated sauce.

STARTERS AND LIGHT BITES

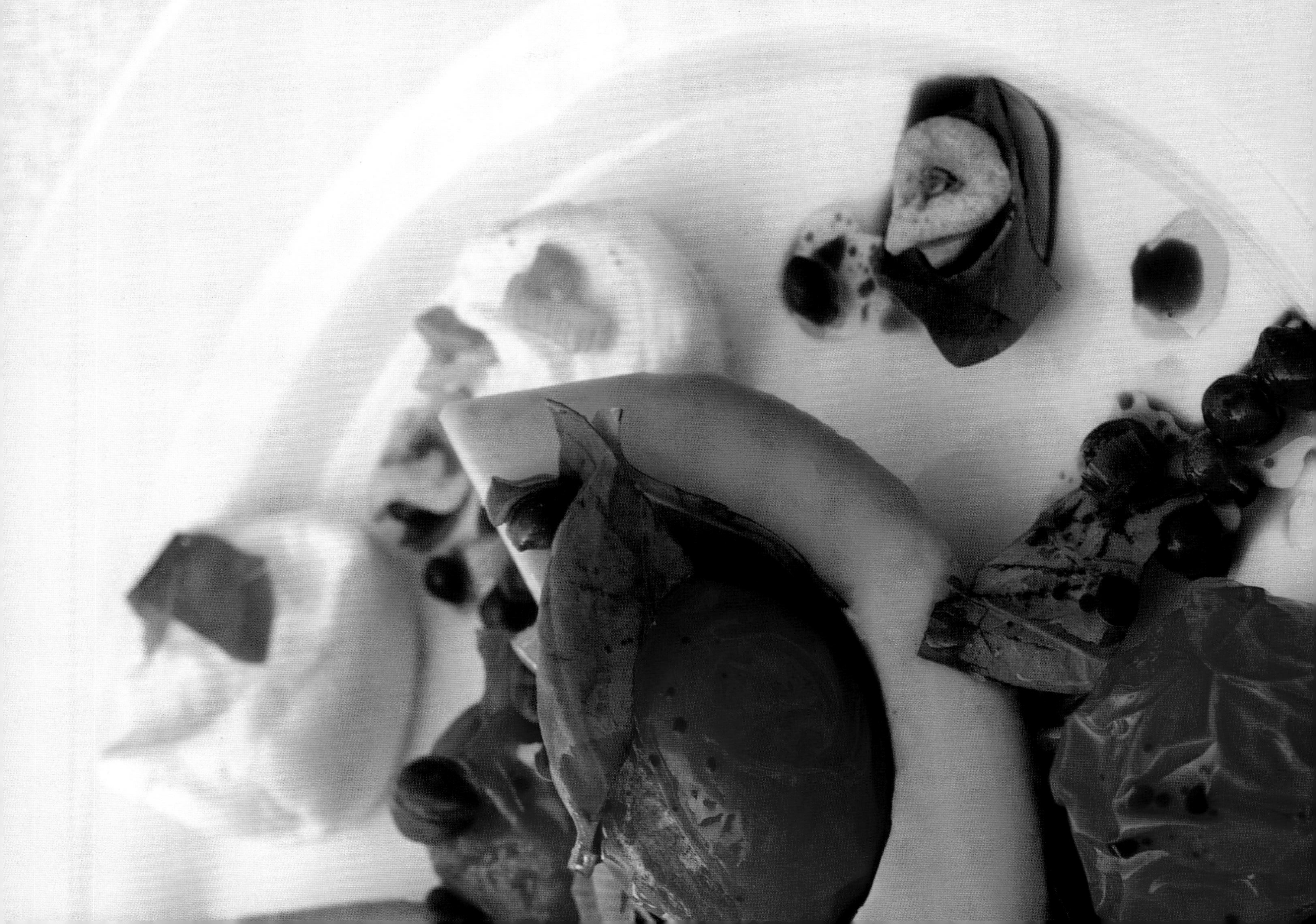

Seafood Starters

Smoked Fish Spread
Horseradish brings out the smokey flavor of the fish in this creamy spread

🕐 10 mins ❄ 1 month **page 29**

Salmon Rillettes
This piquant pâté from France should have a fairly rough texture

🕐 15 mins ❄ 1 month **page 30**

Taramasalata
Made with smoked cod's roe, this is a popular Middle Eastern dip

🕐 15 mins **page 31**

Grilled Scallops with Prosciutto and Lime
Perfect for entertaining when served in the shell

🕐 15 mins **page 39**

Marinated Salmon
Allow 2 days for marinating, but the flavors that develop are worth the wait

🕐 10 mins **page 39**

Smoked Salmon Potato Cakes
This popular starter is easy to make at home

🕐 20 mins **page 40**

Marinated Anchovies
Boquerones en Vinagre are a Spanish speciality, wonderful served with crusty pieces of bread or as a part of a tapas spread

🕐 24 hrs **page 42**

Shrimp with Parmesan Cream
Shrimp dressed in a creamy, rich sauce

🕐 25 mins **page 41**

Shrimp cocktail, Mexican-style
A Mexican twist to this perennial favorite

🕐 20 mins **page 41**

Fried Whitebait
Deep-frying is the best way to cook these tiny fish, which are eaten whole

🕐 35 mins **page 43**

Shrimp with Mint, Chile, and Ginger
Quick, easy, and ideal for a dinner party

🕐 10 mins **page 45**

Herbed Fish Goujons
Fish sticks for grown-ups

🕐 35 mins **page 46**

Seafood Ceviche
Lightly pickled, this dish is crisp and refreshing

🕐 20 mins **page 46**

Snacks on Toast

Anchovies on Toast
Choose any canned anchovies to your taste

🕐 15 mins   page 42

Crostini with Green Olive Tapenade
An easy dish made into an attractive starter

🕐 10 mins   page 47

Smoked Salmon and Pancetta Crostini
The smoky flavor of the salmon is perfectly balanced by the cream and slightly salty pancetta

🕐 25 mins   page 48

Scallop and Pesto Crostini
These stylish canapés also can be served as a simple appetizer

🕐 15–20 mins   page 49

Sesame Shrimp Toasts
A combination of fresh Thai flavors on savory fried toasts

🕐 30 mins   page 50

Fava Bean, Garlic, and Herb Crostini
Vibrant in color, these look and taste great

🕐 30 mins   page 54

Eggplant and Goat Cheese Crostini
Crisp crostini with a substantial savory topping

🕐 30 mins   page 56

Croque Monsieur
In France, these toasted cheese and ham sandwiches are very popular

🕐 25 mins   page 88

Welsh Rarebit
This simple recipe can make a meal out of cheese on toast

🕐 15 mins   page 157

Anchovy and Olive Bruschette
These canapés are lovely passed around at a cocktail party

🕐 15 mins   page 49

Weekend Brunch

Seven Grain Bread
A healthy bread with seven different grains

🕐 1 hr ❄ 6 months **page 68**

Walnut Bread
In France, this savory bread is a traditional accompaniment to the cheese course

🕐 1 hr 5 mins ❄ 6 months **page 69**

Savory Onion Tart
Anchovies give a salty kick to this mild onion tart

🕐 1hr 30 mins ❄ 3 months **page 57**

Brioche
A sweet morning bread that is best served warm

🕐 55 mins – 1 hr **page 70**

English Muffins
Homemade English muffins are a real treat

🕐 1 hr 5 mins **page 76**

Croissants
Time-consuming to make, but the delicate and buttery texture makes them worth the wait

🕐 1 hr 15 mins **page 79**

Buttermilk Biscuits
These are favorites from the American South and are best served straight from the oven

🕐 25–30 mins **page 80**

Scotch Pancakes
These thick little pancakes are delicious drizzled with sweet maple syrup

🕐 25 mins ❄ 1 month **page 81**

Smoked Salmon and Cream Cheese Bagels
An American-style brunch sandwich

🕐 10 mins **page 86**

Pizza Bianca
This tasty pizza is made without tomato sauce, but piled with fresh tomatoes, figs, and prosciutto

🕐 55 mins **page 99**

Tarte Flambé
This thin-crusted tart from Alsace has both sweet and savory toppings
🕐 1 hr 10 mins **page 101**

Spanish Vegetable Tortilla
This variation of a traditional thick Spanish omelet includes broccoli and peas
🕐 1 hr **page 136**

Herb and Goat Cheese Frittata
This popular Italian dish is lighter than a tortilla
🕐 30 mins **page 137**

Eggs Benedict
The smooth and rich Hollandaise sauce makes this a truly indulgent breakfast or brunch
🕐 20 mins **page 138**

Scrambled Eggs with Smoked Salmon
The ultimate feel-good weekend brunch recipe
🕐 20 mins **page 139**

French Toast
Syrupy toasts make a very satisfying dish
🕐 25 mins **page 144**

Parsi Eggs
This Indian dish has its origins in ancient Persia
🕐 45 mins **page 145**

Quiche Lorraine
A French classic, this egg and bacon tart is the original and the best
🕐 1 hr 10 mins **page 146**

Poached Eggs with Frisée
A French favorite, the egg adds a twist to a crunchy salad
🕐 35 mins **page 147**

Baked Eggs in Cream
A simple way to prepare eggs with rich cream and fresh chives
🕐 35 mins **page 148**

Piperade
The filling makes this brunch dish savory, filling, and satisfying
🕐 25 mins **page 150**

Omelet Arnold Bennett
A popular omelet, created in London
🕐 25 mins **page 151**

Ricotta and Bacon Tart
A simple tart with a light cheese filling
🕐 1 hr 10 mins ✱ 3 months **page 163**

Healthy Snacks

Hummus
This chickpea and tahini dip is one of the most widely recognized of all Middle Eastern dishes
🕐 10 mins page 32

Fava Bean Dip
This dip is savory, but surprisingly fresh
🕐 1 hr 35 mins page 32

Artichoke and Scallion Dip
A delicious dip, made in a few minutes
🕐 5 mins page 34

Stuffed Grape Leaves
Greek *dolmadakia* are filling, fresh snacks full of Mediterranean flavors
🕐 1 hr 35 mins page 37

Herbed Shrimp and Goat Cheese Wraps
Serve these as a light meal
🕐 15 mins page 44

Melon and Nectarines with Parma Ham
Sweet and savory, and simple to make
🕐 15 mins page 67

Gazpacho
A savory, chilled Spanish soup
🕐 1 hr 15 mins ❄ 1 month page 104

Warm Chicken Salad
This French *salade tiède*, or warm salad, is quick to cook and easy to assemble
🕐 18 mins page 119

Tzatziki
This simple Greek yogurt and cucumber dip is perfect to serve anytime with a selection of crudités
🕐 40 mins page 28

Watercress and Toasted Walnut Salad
Try this dish served alongside savory tarts
🕐 25 mins page 123

Vietnamese Salad of Broiled Shrimp with Papaya
Full of the fresh flavors of Vietnamese cuisine
🕐 18 mins page 124

Shrimp, Grapefruit, and Avocado Salad
A great combination of ingredients
🕐 15 mins page 124

Tabbouleh
This Lebanese speciality, packed with parsley and mint, is bright and refreshing
🕐 35 mins page 125

Roasted Beets with Bresaola

Imparting an unmistakeable deep pink color and an earthy flavor, beets never tasted so good

🕐 25 mins page 126

Asian Cucumber Salad with Smoked Salmon

Freshly sliced cucumber is perfect with salmon

🕐 10 mins page 127

Carrot and Orange Salad

This is a light and colorful salad, perfect on its own or alongside a sandwich

🕐 20 mins page 128

Shaved Fennel Salad

Thinly sliced fennel adds a crisp crunch to this leafy salad

🕐 10 mins page 129

Spinach, Pear, and Endive Salad

Fresh pears are lovely with the spinach leaves

🕐 10 mins page 129

Avocado, Tomato, and Mozzarella Salad

Only a light drizzle of oil and vinegar is needed

🕐 20 mins page 130

Warm Green Bean Salad

This crunchy, nutty salad is great served cold

🕐 25 mins page 131

Red Pepper Salad

In this Spanish dish, sweet red peppers are gently stewed, then served cold

🕐 35 mins page 131

Greek Tomato and Feta Salad

A popular salad ideal for healthy meals outside

🕐 20 mins page 133

Crab Salad with Mango Dressing

Crab works well with fruity flavors

🕐 15 mins page 129

Party Bites

Shrimp Spring Rolls
Savory little bites that are delicious served with sweet chile sauce
🕐 40 mins   **page 40**

Smoked Salmon Blinis
Elegant snacks that can be served on a platter with other little bites
🕐 40 mins   **page 44**

Onion Bhajis
These crisp, onion fritters are made with chickpea flour
🕐 30 mins   **page 50**

Vegetable Samosas
Serve these Indian pastries hot or cold
🕐 1 hr 25 mins   ❄ 1 month   **page 51**

Boreks
These cheese pastries from Turkey are traditionally made in cigar-shapes
🕐 35–40 mins   **page 53**

Cheese Straws
This classic, quick, and easy appetizer can be served with drinks on any occasion
🕐 35 mins   **page 55**

Mushroom Vol-au-vents
Puff pastry cases enclosing a savory mushroom filling
🕐 35 mins   **page 55**

Smoked Trout Tartlets
Lovely tartlets to pass around at formal parties
🕐 1 hr   ❄ 1 month   **page 56**

Pizzette
Bite-sized pizzas with endless topping variations
🕐 35 mins   **page 100**

Salted Roasted Almonds
Popular to serve with drinks at a cocktail party
🕐 20–25 mins   **page 60**

Chicken Livers in Sherry
These livers, sweetened by the sherry, will entice more mature palates
🕐 10–15 mins   **page 60**

Baked BBQ Wings
A variation on Buffalo wings, these are served with a blue cheese dip
🕐 45 mins   **page 61**

Chicken Satay
Ideal for a crowd, these can easily be eaten with the fingers
🕐 25 mins   **page 62**

Devils on Horseback
These spicy savories are often served as pre-dinner canapés

🕐 25–30 mins **page 63**

Classic Chinese Wontons
Healthy and easy to have ready in the freezer

🕐 30 mins ❄ 1 month **page 63**

Smoked Salmon Rolls
Simple to assemble, this is elegant finger food, great served with drinks

🕐 30 mins **page 64**

Asian Meatballs with Peanut Sauce
Sweet peanut sauce is perfect for dipping

🕐 35 mins **page 65**

Crab Croustades
Lightly spiced crabmeat in a crispy case, these are versatile enough to be served before any meal

🕐 10 mins **page 59**

Grissini
Italian-style breadsticks, perfect served alongside antipasti

🕐 35–40 mins ❄ 2 months **page 84**

Nachos
Quick and simple, these are always satisfying

🕐 15 mins **page 52**

Figs with Prosciutto
Sophisticated canapé of sweet figs, salty prosciutto, and tangy arugula

🕐 10 mins **page 64**

Cheese Nuggets
Savory cheese snacks everyone will enjoy

🕐 1hr 45 mins ❄ 3 months **page 155**

Spicy Feta Squares
Cheesy finger food for casual snacks

🕐 35 mins **page 159**

Lunch Box Ideas

Guacamole
Popular as a dip for tortilla chips, or served with tacos and sandwiches
🕐 15 mins   **page 28**

Smoked Chicken and Spinach Filo Triangles
These parcels are delicious served hot or cold
🕐 45 mins   ❄ 1 month   **page 53**

Sausage Rolls
Bite-sized rolls are perfect packing food
🕐 45-50 mins   ❄ 3 months   **page 66**

Ham Croissants
Easy croissants made with ready-made dough
🕐 20-25 mins   **page 79**

Pan Bagnat
The traditional worker's sandwich in France
🕐 20 mins   **page 87**

Coronation Chicken Rolls
Synonymous with British summer picnics and garden parties
🕐 20 mins   **page 89**

Focaccia Sandwich with Tomatoes and Peppers
This vegetarian sandwich is savory and filling
🕐 40 mins   **page 94**

Deluxe Peanut Butter Sandwiches
A "dressed-up" version of the popular sandwich
🕐 10 mins   **page 97**

Reuben Sandwich
This substantial sandwich is a delicatessen standard
🕐 20-25 mins   **page 97**

Tarte Flambé
This thin-crusted tart from Alsace has both sweet and savory toppings
🕐 1 hr 10 mins   **page 101**

Potato Salad with Prosciutto
A hearty salad that is full of flavor
🕐 35 mins   **page 117**

Smoked Trout and Pancetta Salad
Smoked fish on light and crisp, bitter leaves
🕐 20 mins   **page 123**

Crab Salad with Mango Dressing
Crab and avocado are tasty summer treats
🕐 15 mins   **page 129**

Ensaladilla Rusa
A filling salad, widely enjoyed with tapas
🕐 40 mins   **page 130**

Scotch Eggs
Crumb coated sausage wrapped eggs are delicious served with your favorite chutney
🕐 40 mins   **page 139**

Pasta and Tuna Niçoise Salad
This easy summer dish is made with shell pasta
🕐 35 mins   **page 117**

Hearty Soups

White Bean Soup
This thick soup from northern Italy is guaranteed to keep out the winter chills

🕐 30 mins   **page 108**

Watercress and Pear Soup
An unusual combination that goes down well

🕐 25 mins   **page 104**

Porcini Mushroom Soup
This hearty Italian country soup is full of deep, earthy flavor

🕐 1 hr 20 mins ❄ 3 months   **page 108**

Fish Soup with Saffron and Fennel
A rustic, Mediterranean-style fish soup

🕐 1 hr 10 mins   **page 110**

Hungarian Goulash Soup
Warming flavors make this traditional soup a rich and satisfying meal

🕐 2 hrs 15 mins   **page 111**

Tuscan Bean Soup
This soup is thick, filling, and nutritious

🕐 1 hr 35 mins   **page 111**

French Onion Soup
This Parisian classic is given extra punch with a spoonful of brandy in each bowl

🕐 80 mins ❄ 1 month   **page 112**

New England Clam Chowder
An American favorite, often served with crushed saltine crackers

🕐 50 mins   **page 113**

Minestrone
A substantial soup, this makes a great lunch or supper dish, and you can add whatever vegetables are fresh in season

🕐 2 hrs 5 mins ❄ 1 month   **page 112**

Bouillabaisse
The ocean's bounty in a bowl

🕐 1 hr 5 mins   **page 114**

Meat-free Starters

Baba Ganoush
No Middle Eastern meze table is complete without a bowl of this creamy dip
🕐 40 mins   **page 30**

Avocado Mousse with Lime
This smooth-textured mousse can be served as a starter or light lunch
🕐 15 mins   **page 31**

Tapenade
A full-flavored olive spread, popular in the Mediterranean
🕐 15 mins   **page 34**

Zucchini Sticks
These crisp morsels make a lovely vegetarian party snack
🕐 30 mins   **page 35**

Grilled Mushrooms with Goat Cheese
Warm cheese in savory mushroom cups
🕐 35 mins   **page 36**

Artichoke Salad
The delicate and distinctive flavor of artichokes are balanced with peppery arugula
🕐 35 mins   **page 36**

Pan-Grilled Asparagus with Hollandaise
Asparagus made into something special
🕐 20 mins   **page 37**

Stuffed Grape Leaves
Making your own stuffed grape leaves is fun. Jarred grape leaves are sold at supermarkets
🕐 1 hr 35 mins   **page 37**

Wild Mushroom Tartlets
These appetizers are a tasty meat-free option
🕐 1 hr 20 mins   **page 52**

Borscht
Thickly textured and satisfying, this classic Russian soup can be enjoyed on any occasion
🕐 1 hr 45 mins   **page 105**

Marinated Goat Cheese Salad
This recipe makes a great dinner-party starter
🕐 20 mins   **page 120**

White Bean Soup
This thick soup from northern Italy is guaranteed to keep out the winter chills
🕐 2 hrs 30 mins   **page 108**

Carrot and Orange Soup
A light, refreshing soup with a hint of spice, this is the perfect start to a summer meal
🕐 50 mins   **page 107**

Bibb Lettuce Salad
Contrast the sweet Bibb lettuce with this piquant, creamy Parmesan dressing
🕐 30–35 mins   **page 120**

Roasted Tomato Salad with Lemon and Crème Fraîche
Sweet roasted tomatoes with a creamy dressing
🕐 2 hrs 15 mins   **page 121**

Waldorf Salad
A classic salad named after the prestigious Waldorf-Astoria Hotel in New York
🕐 50 mins   **page 121**

Grilled Zucchini and Pepper Salad with Cilantro and Cumin
A mix of vegetables topped with vinaigrette
🕐 40 mins   **page 122**

Eggplant and Goat Cheese Salad
This crunchy salad is best with sweet tomatoes
🕐 35 mins   **page 128**

Spinach Timbales
These vegetable molds are served with a salad
🕐 40 mins ❄ 3 months   **page 144**

Spinach and Mushroom Crêpes
Savory crêpes are great to begin any meal
🕐 1 hr 40 mins ❄ 3 months   **page 148**

Egg Fu Yung
Light and tasty, these can be made with shrimp and stir-fried vegetables
🕐 35 mins   **page 149**

Cheese Soufflé
The most popular savoury soufflé is this simple cheese one
🕐 1 hr 5 mins   **page 150**

Twice-baked Cheese Soufflés
This foolproof recipe can be prepared several hours in advance
🕐 30–35 mins ❄ 3 months   **page 153**

Ricotta and Arugula Roulade
This makes a sumptuous first course
🕐 45 mins   **page 161**

Feta Filo Pie
Crisp pastry encases a delicious blend of spinach, feta, and pine nuts
🕐 1 hr 30 mins   **page 158**

Warm Halloumi with Herbs
Halloumi is made from sheep and goat's milk
🕐 10 mins   **page 162**

Authentic Swiss Fondue
A luscious way to serve melted cheese
🕐 25 mins   **page 163**

Tandoori Paneer Kebabs
Paneer is a firm Indian cheese that takes up the flavor of other ingredients
🕐 30 mins   **page 165**

Gruyère Tart
This vegetarian tart, with crisp, thyme-flavored pastry, is equally delicious served warm or cold
🕐 1 hr 10 mins   **page 165**

Tzatziki

This simple Greek dip makes a good start to a casual meal,
served with a selection of crudités

 makes 4 servings

prep 10 mins, plus 30 mins standing

1 cucumber, peeled and coarsely grated

salt

1½ cups Greek yogurt

3 garlic cloves, crushed, or more to taste

2 tbsp chopped dill or mint

2 tbsp extra virgin olive oil

1 tbsp red wine vinegar

● **Prepare ahead** The dip can be refrigerated for up to one day; stir before serving.

1 **Put the cucumber** in a bowl, sprinkle with salt, and let stand for 30 minutes.

2 **Rinse the cucumber** well to remove the excess salt. A handful at a time, squeeze out the excess liquid, putting the cucumber in a bowl.

3 **Add the yogurt** and stir. Add the garlic, mint, olive oil, and vinegar and mix well. Cover with plastic wrap and chill until needed.

● **Good with** warmed pita bread and a variety of vegetables, such as carrot, celery, fennel, and pepper slices, for dipping.

● **Leftovers** will keep covered in the refrigerator for a day.

Guacamole

This popular dip, which has its origins in Mexico, can also be
used as a condiment for grilled meats and seafood

 makes 6 appetizer servings, 12 condiment servings

prep 15 mins

3 large, ripe avocados

juice of ½ lime

½ onion, finely chopped

1 medium tomato, seeded and minced

1 or 2 fresh hot red chiles, seeded and finely chopped

2 tbsp chopped cilantro, plus a few sprigs to garnish

salt

2 tbsp sour cream (optional)

● **Prepare ahead** Chop the onions, tomato, garlic, and chiles in advance but do not combine with the avocado until just before serving.

1 **Pit and skin the avocados.** Place the flesh in a medium bowl and combine with a fork or potato masher until the mixture is mashed but somewhat chunky.

2 **Add the lime juice** then the onion, tomato, and chiles. Mix well, then stir in the cilantro. Season with salt to taste.

3 **Fold in the sour cream,** if using. Mound the guacamole into a serving bowl, garnish with cilantro sprigs, and serve immediately. If you cannot serve the guacamole immediately, cover it with plastic wrap, pressing it directly on the surface of the guacamole.

● **Good with** tortilla chips.

Chicken Liver Pâté

Red wine adds flavor to this spread and cuts through the richness of the liver

- makes 4 servings
- prep 10 mins, plus cooling and chilling • cook 15 mins
- the pâté can be frozen for up to 6 months

12oz (350g) **chicken livers**

8 tbsp **butter**

⅔ cup hearty **red wine**

2 tbsp chopped **chives**, plus more for garnishing

¼ tsp dried **thyme**

salt and freshly ground **pepper**

sprigs of fresh **thyme**, to garnish

● **Prepare ahead** The pâté is best refrigerated for 2 days before serving to develop the flavors.

1 Rinse the livers and pat dry with paper towels. Trim away any sinew or greenish portions from the livers with kitchen scissors, then cut each in half.

2 Melt 4 tbsp butter in a large frying pan over medium heat. Add the livers and cook, stirring occasionally, for about 4 minutes, or until browned.

3 Add the wine, chives, and thyme to the pan. Bring to a boil. Cook, stirring occasionally, for 4 minutes, or until the liquid is reduced by about half and the livers are just cooked through when sliced open.

4 Remove the pan from the heat and let cool for 10 minutes. Transfer the contents of the pan to a food processor. Process until smooth. Season with salt and pepper. Spoon the pâté into a serving bowl, pressing it down with the back of the spoon after each addition so that it is firmly packed.

5 Melt the remaining butter over medium heat. Pour it over the top of the pâté. Refrigerate, uncovered, for at least 2 hours. Garnish with sprigs of fresh thyme and serve.

● **Good with** plenty of toasted French breach slices and small sour pickles (cornichons).

Smoked Fish Spread

Once you have the smoked fish, which is available at the local delicatessen, this appetizer can be prepared in minutes

- makes 4–6 servings
- prep about 10 mins, plus chilling
- food processor
- freeze for up to 1 month without garnishes

9oz (250g) **smoked trout** or **hot-smoked salmon**, filleted and skinned

6oz (170g) **whipped cream cheese**

1 tbsp **fresh lemon juice**

1 tsp **prepared horseradish**, or more to taste

freshly ground **pepper**

pinch of **paprika**, for garnishing

● **Prepare ahead** The spread can be refrigerated for up to one day. Add the garnishes when ready to serve.

1 Cut the smoked fish into 1in (2.5cm) pieces. Place in a food processor and add the cheese, lemon juice, and horseradish. Pulse until smooth. Season with pepper and more horseradish if you wish. Cover and refrigerate until chilled, at least 1 hour and up to 24 hours.

2 Transfer to a serving bowl and sprinkle with paprika.

● **Good with** melba toast, toasted slices of whole-grain bread, or chunks of baguette.

VARIATION

Smoked Eel Spread

Try making the spread with smoked eel, a traditional Dutch delicacy.

Salmon Rillettes

This piquant spread from France should have
a fairly rough texture

 makes 4 servings

 prep 15 mins

freeze for up to 1 month

4 tbsp **butter**, softened

9oz (250g) **hot-smoked salmon**,
skinned

¼ cup plain **low-fat yogurt**,
preferably Greek-style

grated zest and juice of ½ **lemon**

2 tbsp chopped **chives**

one 1¾oz (50g) jar **salmon caviar**

watercress sprigs, to garnish

lemon wedges, to garnish

● **Prepare ahead** The rillettes
can be refrigerated for up to 1 day
before serving.

1 Beat the butter in a medium
bowl with a wooden spoon until
smooth. Break up the salmon into
small pieces, add to the butter, and
mash with a fork.

2 Add the yogurt, lemon zest
and juice, and chives and stir
until evenly combined. Cover and chill
for at least 1 hour.

3 Spoon on to serving plates and
top with caviar. Garnish with
watercress sprigs and lemon wedges.

● **Good with** small rounds of
pumpernickel to make tasty and
attractive canapés.

VARIATION

Poached Salmon Rillettes

Use the same quantity of poached
fresh salmon fillet, removing the skin
after the fish has been cooked.

Baba Ganoush

No Middle Eastern meze table is complete
without a bowl of this creamy dip

 makes 6 servings

prep 10 mins, plus standing
• cook 25–30 mins

2lb (900g) **eggplants**, cut in
half lengthwise

3 tbsp **tahini**, plus more to taste

2 tbsp fresh **lemon** juice, plus more
to taste

2 tbsp **extra virgin olive oil**

2 tbsp **plain yogurt**

2 large **garlic cloves**, crushed

salt and freshly ground **black pepper**

cilantro sprigs, to garnish

● **Prepare ahead** The dip can be
refrigerated up to 1 day before
serving. Bring to room temperature
before serving.

1 Preheat the oven to 425°F
(220°C). Lightly oil a baking
sheet. Make a deep lengthwise
incision, without cutting through the
skin, down the center of the cut side
of each eggplant half. Place on the
baking sheet, skin side up. Bake for
25–30 minutes, or until the flesh is
thoroughly softened and collapsing.

2 Transfer the eggplant halves
to a colander on a plate. Let
stand for 15 minutes, or until they
are cool enough to handle.

3 Scoop the eggplant flesh
into a food processor. Add the
tahini and lemon juice with the olive
oil, yogurt, and garlic, and process
until smooth. Taste and adjust the
tahini and lemon juice as needed,
then season with salt and pepper.
Sprinkle with cilantro, and serve.

● **Good with** warmed pita bread,
cut into strips.

● **Leftovers** can be kept in the
refrigerator, covered, for 2 days.

> **PREPARE BY HAND**
> Preheat the broiler and set the
> pan about 8in (20cm) from the
> source of heat. Broil the scored
> eggplant halves, cut-sides down,
> about 10 minutes, until
> thoroughly softened and
> collapsing. Instead of using a
> food processor, the ingredients
> can be mashed together to a
> paste using a large pestle and
> mortar or in a large bowl using
> a sturdy wooden spoon.

Avocado Mousse with Lime

This creamy textured mousse can be served as a starter or a light lunch

- 🍴 makes 4 servings
- 🕐 prep 15 mins, plus chilling
- ▦ four 4oz (100ml) ramekins

2 large ripe **avocados**

grated zest of 1 **lime**

2 tbsp fresh **lime** juice

3½oz (100g) **low-fat cream cheese**, softened

salt and freshly ground **black pepper**

2 tsp unflavored **powdered gelatin**

1 **egg white** (optional)

● **Prepare ahead** The mousse can be made up to 12 hours in advance.

1 Pit and peel the avocados and scoop the flesh into a blender or food processor. Add the lime zest and juice, and process until really smooth.

2 Add the cream cheese and blend until completely combined. Season with salt and pepper. Transfer to a bowl.

3 Sprinkle the gelatin over 2 tbsp of water in a small heatproof bowl. Let stand about 5 minutes until the mixture looks spongy. Place the bowl in a skillet of barely simmering water and stir constantly until the gelatin dissolves.

4 Drizzle the dissolved gelatin over the avocado mixture, and stir well. If using, beat the egg white until soft peaks form. Fold the egg white into the avocado mixture.

5 Spoon into four 4oz (100ml) ramekins. Cover with plastic wrap and refrigerate 2 hours, or until chilled and set. Serve chilled.

● **Good with** a topping of fruit salsa and tortilla chips.

Taramasalata

To make this wonderful dip of smoked roe, look for *tarama* at Mediterranean markets

- 🍴 makes 4–6 servings
- 🕐 prep 15 mins, plus chilling
- ❗ soak the bread crumbs for 15 mins before starting

¾ cup fresh **bread crumbs**

9oz (250g) piece **smoked cod's roe**

2 tbsp fresh **lemon** juice

⅓ cup **extra virgin olive oil**

1 small **onion**, grated

sweet paprika, to garnish

● **Prepare ahead** The taramasalata can be covered and refrigerated for up to 2 days.

1 Soak the bread crumbs with 3 tbsp water for 15 minutes. Split the roe down the center using a sharp knife and carefully peel away the skin. Process the roe, lemon juice, and soaked bread crumbs in a blender until well combined.

2 With the blender running, very slowly add the oil in a thin steady stream until the mixture resembles smooth mayonnaise.

3 Spoon into a small serving dish and mix in the onion. Cover and chill for at least 30 minutes. Serve sprinkled with paprika.

● **Good with** olives, Greek or Turkish breads, and crunchy vegetable crudités.

VARIATION

For a lighter version, omit the bread crumbs and oil. Process the roe and lemon juice with 6oz (175g) reduced-fat cream cheese.

Hummus

This chickpea bean and tahini dip is one of the most widely recognized of all Middle Eastern dishes

- makes 4 servings
- prep 10 mins

15oz (420g) can **chickpeas**

6 tbsp fresh **lemon** juice

3 tbsp **tahini**

3 **garlic** cloves, chopped

½ tsp **salt**

paprika, for garnish

● **Prepare ahead** Make the dip up to 24 hours in advance. Store in the refrigerator, covered with plastic wrap. Remove the hummus from the refrigerator at least 30 minutes before serving.

1 Drain the chickpeas, reserving about 5 tbsp of the canning liquid in a small bowl. Carefully rinse the chickpeas under cold running water. Drain well and transfer to a food processor or a blender along with half of the reserved canning liquid.

2 Add the lemon juice, tahini, and garlic and blend until smooth and creamy, adding a little more of the canning liquid as needed.

3 Season to taste with salt. Transfer the hummus to a small serving bowl, sprinkle with paprika, and serve at room temperature.

● **Good with** warm pita bread and sticks of carrot, cucumber, and sweet pepper. For a traditional finish, drizzle with olive oil in addition to the paprika garnish.

VARIATION

Red Pepper Hummus

Position a broiler rack about 6in (15cm) from the source of heat and preheat the broiler. Cut in half lengthwise and seed a small red pepper. Grill, skin side up, until lightly charred. Cool, peel, and roughly chop the pepper. Add to the blender along with the chickpeas. If the pepper is juicy, add less canning liquid. Add 1 tsp ground cumin for a spicier flavor.

Fava Bean Dip

Look for skinless dried fava beans at Middle Eastern and Latino grocers

- makes 6–8 servings
- prep 20 mins, plus soaking ● cook 1¼ hrs
- ✓ low fat
- ! soak the beans overnight in cold water

9oz (250g) skinless **dried fava beans**, soaked overnight in cold water to cover

3 **onions**

6 **garlic** cloves

⅓ cup chopped **cilantro**, plus more to garnish

⅓ cup chopped **parsley**, chopped, plus more to garnish

2 tbsp chopped **mint**

1 tsp ground **cumin**

salt and freshly ground **black pepper**

3 tbsp **olive oil**

juice of 1 **lemon**

● **Prepare ahead** The dip can be covered with plastic wrap and refrigerated for up to 2 days. Serve at room temperature.

1 Drain the beans. Place them in a large saucepan and add enough fresh water to cover. Coarsely chop 1 of the onions and 3 of the garlic cloves and add to the pan. Bring to a boil, skimming off any foam. Reduce the heat and cover. Simmer 1 hour, or until the beans are soft.

2 Drain the beans and vegetables, reserving the cooking liquid. Transfer the mixture to a food processor and add the cilantro, parsley, mint, and cumin. Purée, adding enough of the reserved cooking liquid to moisten the mixture. Season with salt and pepper. Transfer to a dish and keep warm.

3 Meanwhile, slice the remaining onions. Heat 1 tbsp oil over medium-high heat. Add the onions and cook, stirring often, for about 12 minutes, or until they are dark golden and slightly caramelized. Chop the garlic, stir into the onions, and cook for 1 minute more.

4 Spread the fried onions and garlic over the purée and drizzle with the lemon juice and remaining oil. Garnish with additional cilantro and parsley and serve.

Duck Confit

For this classic French dish, look for duck fat online or render duck skin and fat purchased at an Asian butcher

- 🍴 makes 4 servings
- 🕐 prep 15 mins, plus chilling and curing • cook 1½ hrs, plus curing
- ▭ ovenproof baking dish
- ❄ freeze for up to 6 months

4 duck legs

1 cup kosher or sea salt

4 garlic cloves, peeled and crushed

1 tbsp whole white peppercorns

1 tsp coriander seeds

5 juniper berries

1 tbsp chopped thyme

2½lb (1kg) duck fat, melted

● **Prepare ahead** Make the confit up to 4 weeks in advance. Keep in the refrigerator until needed. To give you plenty of time, start the confit at least 1 day before you plan to serve it.

1 Dry the duck legs on paper towels. Process the salt, garlic, peppercorns, coriander seeds, juniper berries, and thyme in a food processor until a rough paste forms. Transfer to a glass or ceramic baking dish. Add the duck legs, and rub with and bury in the salt mixture. Cover with plastic wrap and refrigerate for 12 hours.

2 Preheat the oven to 275°F (140°C). Rinse the duck well and pat dry. Transfer to a baking dish just large enough to hold the duck in a single layer, and add the duck fat.

3 Cook the duck for 1½ hours, or until very tender when tested with the tip of a knife.

4 Remove from the oven and let the duck cool completely in the fat. Transfer the confit and the fat to a zippered plastic bag and refrigerate for up to 5 days or freeze for up to 3 months.

5 When ready to serve, heat the duck with a thin layer of clinging fat in a skillet over medium heat, turning occasionally, about 12 minutes, until browned and heated through. Serve immediately.

● **Good with** mesclun salad and roasted root vegetables.

Brandade de Morue

This appetizer of creamed salt cod is popular in the South of France, where it is traditionally served on Christmas Eve

- 🍴 makes 4–6 servings
- 🕐 prep 20 mins, plus soaking and standing • cook 20 mins
- ❗ start soaking the cod at least 24 hrs before cooking the dish

1lb (450g) salt cod

2 garlic cloves, crushed and peeled

¾ cup olive oil, as needed

½ cup whole milk, brought to a boil, as needed

2 tbsp chopped parsley

freshly ground black pepper

bread triangles, fried in olive oil

black olives

1 Place the salt cod in a large bowl and add enough cold water to cover. Refrigerate for 24 hours, changing the water from time to time.

2 Drain the salt cod. Place in a shallow frying pan and cover with fresh cold water. Bring to a simmer. Cook over low heat for 10 minutes. Remove from the heat and let stand 10 minutes more. Drain well.

3 Remove the skin and bones from the fish. Flake the flesh into a food processor. Add the garlic and process until smooth.

4 Transfer to a saucepan. Heat the brandade over low heat, whisking in enough of the oil and milk, a tablespoon at a time, to make a creamy mixture that holds its shape.

5 Transfer the hot brandade to a serving bowl. Garnish with the parsley, a drizzle of olive oil, and a grinding of pepper. Serve hot with the fried bread and black olives.

MAKING THE SAUCE

The oil and milk must be beaten very gradually into the cod or the mixture will separate. Should this happen, transfer to a bowl and whisk vigorously to bring it back together.

Rustic Meat Terrine

Full of flavor and texture, this pâté is extremely versatile

- 🍴 makes 8 appetizer servings
- 🕐 prep 30 mins
  - cook 1½ hrs, plus pressing
- ⬚ 6 cup terrine mold or loaf pan
- ❄ can be frozen for up to 1 month

12oz (350g) sliced bacon

9oz (250g) chicken livers, trimmed

1lb (450g) ground veal

12oz (300g) ground pork

8 tbsp butter, melted and cooled

½ cup dry sherry

1 onion, finely chopped

2 garlic cloves, minced

1 tsp dried oregano

½ tsp ground allspice

salt and freshly ground black pepper

● **Prepare ahead** After pressing, the unmolded terrine can be wrapped and refrigerated for up to 5 days.

1 **Preheat the oven** to 350°F (180°C). Line a 6 cup terrine mold or loaf pan with the bacon slices, letting the ends of the bacon hang over the sides of the dish.

2 **Pulse the chicken livers** in a food processor until finely chopped. Transfer to a bowl. Add the veal, pork, butter, sherry, onion, garlic, oregano, and allspice and season well with salt and pepper. Mix with your hands until combined.

3 **Transfer the meat** mixture to the terrine mold and fold the bacon ends over the top. Cover tightly with the lid or aluminum foil. Place the dish in a roasting pan and add enough hot water to come halfway up the sides of the dish.

4 **Bake** for 1½ hours, until a meat thermometer inserted in the center reads 165°F (74°C). Transfer the terrine in its mold to a baking sheet. Replace the foil with a fresh sheet. Place another pan to fit inside the terrine, and fill with heavy cans of food. Refrigerate for 24 hours. Unmold, slice, and serve.

● **Good with** slices of warm crusty bread or toast, and plenty of Dijon mustard and cornichon pickles.

Tapenade

A full-flavored olive spread, popular in the Mediterranean

- 🍴 makes 4–6 servings
- 🕐 prep 15 mins

9oz (250g) Mediterranean black olives, pitted

1½ tbsp nonpareil capers, drained and rinsed

2 large garlic cloves

4 anchovy fillets in olive oil, drained

1 tsp chopped thyme

1 tsp chopped rosemary

2 tbsp fresh lemon juice

2 tbsp extra virgin olive oil

1 tsp Dijon mustard

¼ tsp crushed hot red pepper

● **Prepare ahead** The tapenade can be refrigerated, stored in an airtight container, and filmed with a thin layer of olive oil, for up to 2 weeks. Stir well before serving.

1 **Pulse the olives**, capers, garlic, anchovies, thyme, and rosemary in a food processor or blender until finely chopped.

2 **Add the lemon juice**, olive oil, mustard, and hot pepper and process to form a thick paste. Serve in a small bowl with slices of toasted French bread.

● **Good with** crudités and a selection of Mediterranean appetizers.

Artichoke and Scallion Dip

This heavy and delicious dip can be made in minutes

- 🍴 makes 6 servings
- 🕐 prep 5 mins

one 14oz (390g) can artichoke hearts, drained

3 scallions, white and green parts, coarsely chopped

1 garlic clove, halved

¼ cup mayonnaise

salt and freshly ground black pepper

● **Prepare ahead** The dip can be made up to 24 hours in advance, covered with plastic wrap, and chilled until ready to serve.

1 **Place the artichokes**, scallions, garlic, and mayonnaise in a food processor or blender and process to form a smooth purée.

2 **Season to taste** with salt and pepper, then spoon into a serving bowl, cover, and refrigerate until ready to serve.

● **Good with** pita bread, vegetable crudités, or bread sticks, or spread on baguette slices and broil until lightly browned.

Zucchini Sticks

These crisp morsels make a lovely vegetarian party snack

- makes 6 servings
- prep 15 mins • cook 15 mins
- deep-frying thermometer

3 large **zucchini**

1¾ cups fresh **bread crumbs**

1 cup freshly grated **Parmesan**

3 tbsp finely chopped **parsley**

grated zest of ½ **lemon**

2 large **eggs**

¾ cup **all-purpose flour**

salt and freshly ground **black pepper**

vegetable oil, for deep-frying

● **Prepare ahead** The coated zucchini can be stored at room temperature for up to 2 hours before frying.

1 **Preheat the oven** to 200°F (95°C). Wash and dry the zucchini. Cut them into sticks about 3 x ½in (7.5cm x 13mm).

2 **Mix the bread crumbs**, cheese, parsley, and lemon zest well in a shallow bowl. Beat the eggs in a second bowl. Spread the flour in a third bowl and season.

3 **In batches**, coat the zucchini in the flour, then the egg, and then the bread crumbs. Transfer to a wax paper-lined baking sheet.

4 **Half-fill a deep** frying pan with oil and heat over high heat to 350°F (170°C). In batches, add the zucchini and cook about 3 minutes, or until golden brown. Transfer to a paper towel-lined baking sheet and keep warm in the oven while frying the remaining zucchini. Serve hot.

Stuffed Mushrooms

Portobello mushrooms make great bases for savory goat cheese and pine nut fillings

- makes 4 servings
- prep 15 mins • cook 20 mins

8 **portobello mushrooms**

2 tbsp **olive oil**, plus more for greasing

4 **shallots**, finely chopped

2 **garlic cloves**, minced

¾ cup **pine nuts**, toasted

¼ cup roughly torn **basil**

¼ cup finely chopped **parsley**

salt and freshly ground **black pepper**

6oz (170g) firm **goat cheese**, cut into 8 slices

8 slices **pancetta**, unrolled into strips

● **Prepare ahead** The stuffed mushrooms can be prepared in advance and refrigerated for up to 8 hours before baking.

1 **Preheat the oven** to 375°F (190°C). Place the mushrooms on a lightly oiled baking sheet.

2 **Heat the oil** in a large frying pan over medium heat. Add the shallots and cook for 2 minutes, stirring frequently, until softened. Add the garlic and cook for 1 minute. Stir in pine nuts, basil, and parsley and season with salt and pepper.

3 **Spoon the mixture** into the mushrooms. Top each with a slice of goat cheese. Wrap a pancetta strip around each mushroom, tucking the ends underneath.

4 **Bake for 15-20 minutes**, or until the mushrooms are tender and the pancetta is crisp. Serve immediately.

● **Good with** mixed green salad and a drizzle of balsamic vinegar.

Grilled Mushrooms with Goat Cheese

Ideally, the toasted bread should be about the same size as the mushrooms, so choose a loaf of the appropriate size

🍴 makes 6 servings

🕐 prep 20 mins • cook 15 mins

For the dressing

¼ cup extra virgin olive oil

2 tbsp balsamic vinegar

2 tsp chopped thyme

1 tsp Dijon mustard

1 garlic clove, minced

12 black olives, pitted and chopped

baguette or rustic-style loaf

olive oil

6 portobello mushrooms

5oz (130g) goat cheese

1 tbsp balsamic vinegar

salt and freshly ground black pepper

● **Prepare ahead** The dressing and mushrooms can be prepared the day before and refrigerated.

1 Preheat the oven to 350°F (180°C). To make the dressing, whisk together all the ingredients and set aside.

2 Cut the bread diagonally into ¼in (6mm) slices. Brush both sides with olive oil and arrange on a baking sheet. Bake for 10 minutes, or until crisp and golden brown.

3 Remove the stems from the mushrooms. Slice the goat cheese into rounds. Place a slice in each mushroom cap. Position the broiler rack about 6in (15cm) from the source of heat and preheat the broiler. Place the mushrooms on the broiler rack. Drizzle with a little olive oil and the balsamic vinegar, then season with salt and pepper. Grill for about 5 minutes, or until the cheese is bubbling and the mushrooms are tender.

4 To serve, top each toast with a mushroom, and drizzle with the dressing.

● **Good with** a salad of peppery arugula, sliced endive, and radicchio.

VARIATION

Blue Cheese Mushrooms

Use a mild blue cheese, such as Roquefort or gorgonzola, instead of goat cheese. Omit the olives from the dressing.

Artichoke Salad

Delicately flavored artichokes combine well with peppery arugula

🍴 makes 4 servings

🕐 prep 25 mins, plus cooling • cook 10 mins

3 lemons

4 globe artichokes

1 large bunch of arugula

¼ cup freshly grated Parmesan cheese

freshly ground pepper

2 tbsp extra virgin olive oil

1 tbsp balsamic vinegar

1 Add the juice and rinds of 2 lemons to a large bowl of cold water. Pull the tough, dark green leaves from each artichoke to reveal the pale green core of leaves. Cut off the cones at the indentation just above the artichoke bottom. Dig out the hairy choke with a teaspoon. With a paring knife, trim away the thick green skin and immediately place the artichoke bottom in the lemon water.

2 Bring a saucepan of lightly salted water with the juice of 1 lemon to a boil. Cook the artichoke bottoms for 10 minutes, or until tender. Drain well and let cool.

3 Quarter the artichokes. Divide the arugula and artichokes among 4 plates. Sprinkle with cheese and pepper, and drizzle with the olive oil and balsamic vinegar.

Stuffed Grape Leaves

This meze dish is delicious warm or cold. Jarred grape leaves are sold at supermarkets and Middle Eastern delicatessens

- makes 4–6 servings
- prep 45 mins • cook 50 mins
- soak preserved grape leaves in hot water then rinse several times to remove the brine; fresh grape leaves should be blanched for 5 minutes.
- frying pan, large saucepan

2 onions, finely chopped

2 tbsp olive oil

1 cup long-grain rice

½ tsp ground allspice

2¼ cups vegetable stock

3 ripe tomatoes, skinned, seeded, and chopped

1 tbsp chopped dill

1 tbsp chopped mint

salt and freshly ground black pepper

40 grape leaves

2 tbsp fresh lemon juice

1 **Cook the onions** in the oil until softened but not browned.

Stir in the rice and allspice, and cook for 2 minutes more.

2 **Pour in the stock** and bring to a boil. Reduce the heat and simmer for about 15 minutes, until the rice is tender and has absorbed the liquid. Stir in the tomatoes, herbs, and season with salt and pepper.

3 **Spoon** some of the rice in the center of each grape leaf, shiny side down. Fold in the sides and roll into a parcel.

4 **Pack the grape leaves** tightly in a large saucepan; add the lemon juice and enough cold water to just cover. Place a heatproof plate on top so they don't unravel. Bring to a boil then reduce the heat; simmer for 30 minutes, adding water if necessary. Carefully drain then serve.

VARIATION

Vine Leaves with Lamb
Brown 9oz (250g) lean ground lamb with the onions in step 1. Reduce the rice to ¾ cup and the stock to 1¾ cups.

Pan-Grilled Asparagus with Hollandaise

Rich and tangy hollandaise sauce and fresh asparagus is a time-honored partnership

- makes 4 servings
- prep 10 mins • cook 10 mins
- ridged grill pan

1 lb (450g) fresh asparagus

1 tbsp olive oil

For the sauce

2 tbsp white wine vinegar

4 large egg yolks

8 tbsp butter, melted

1 tbsp lemon juice

salt and freshly ground black pepper

1 **Snap off** the woody ends from the asparagus spears. Brush a ridged grill pan with the oil and heat over medium-high heat until the pan is very hot. Cook the asparagus, turning once, for about 6 minutes, until the asparagus has grill marks and is just tender (thick spears may take longer, so reduce the temperature as needed so the asparagus cooks without charring).

2 **Meanwhile**, make the sauce. Boil the vinegar until reduced by half. Remove from the heat, and add 2 tbsp water. One at a time, whisk in the egg yolks.

3 **Return the saucepan** to a very low heat and whisk until the mixture is thick and pale. Remove from the heat and gradually whisk in the melted butter. Stir in the lemon juice. Season with salt and pepper.

4 **Divide the asparagus** between serving plates. Spoon the sauce over the asparagus, and serve at once.

Potato Skins with Cheddar and Bacon

Presented this way, these baked potatoes are a real treat

 makes 4 servings

prep 50 mins • cook 25 mins

4 medium **baking potatoes**, scrubbed

7oz (200g) **bacon**, rind removed, cut into sticks

2 **shallots**, finely chopped

scant ½ cup **whole milk**

2 tbsp **butter**

¾ cup shredded **Cheddar cheese**

2 tbsp chopped **parsley**

salt and freshly ground **black pepper**

1 Preheat the oven to 400°F (200°C). Prick the potato skins all over with a fork. Bake in the oven for about 45–50 minutes, until tender. Reduce the oven temperature to 350°F (180°C).

2 Meanwhile, cook the bacon in a frying pan over medium-high heat about 4 minutes until golden. Add the shallots and cook until they soften, about 1 minute more.

3 Slice off the top third of each potato, horizontally. Using a spoon, scoop out the flesh into a large bowl. Reserve the hollowed-out skins and place in a lightly oiled baking dish.

4 Mash the potato with a potato masher. Add the milk and butter, and beat until smooth. Stir in the Cheddar and bacon mixture along with the parsley. Season with salt and pepper.

5 Spoon the mixture back into the potato skins and bake for 20–25 minutes, or until the filling is heated through and golden on top. Serve hot with extra chopped parsley sprinkled on top, if desired.

VARIATIONS

Potato Skins with Crab

Mix the mashed potato with a 16oz (168g) can crabmeat, drained, 3 chopped scallions, 1 chopped fresh small red chile, ¼ cup crème fraîche, and 2 tbsp chopped cilantro. Spoon back into the skins and bake as above.

Potato Skins with Chorizo

Mix the mashed potato with 5oz (145g) chopped smoked chorizo, 1 ripe tomato, seeded and diced, 5oz (145g) mozzarella, diced, and 1 tbsp chopped oregano. Spoon back into the skins and bake as above.

Grilled Scallops with Prosciutto and Lime

A delicious, elegant starter

 makes 6 servings

prep 10 mins • cook 5 mins

6 scallop shells or ramekins

18 sea scallops

salt and freshly ground black pepper

2 limes

2 tbsp butter, melted

2 garlic cloves, chopped

3 tbsp chopped basil, parsley, and/or chives, plus more for garnish

2oz (55g) thinly sliced prosciutto, cut into strips

1 Trim the small white muscle from the side of each scallop. Place 3 scallops in each of 6 scallop shells or ramekins. Season with salt and pepper.

2 Cut 1 lime into 6 wedges and set aside. Combine the butter, the juice of the remaining lime, the garlic, and basil. Divide evenly among the scallops. Sprinkle with the prosciutto strips.

3 Preheat the broiler. Broil the scallops in the shells for about 5 minutes, until they turn opaque. Sprinkle with additional herbs. Serve immediately with the lime wedges.

● **Good with** warm crusty bread.

Marinated Salmon

Marinated in the Scandinavian fashion, serve this as a brunch dish, or with vodka cocktails

 makes 6–8 servings

prep 10 mins, plus chilling

the salmon needs to be prepared at least 48 hours before required

2 salmon fillets with skin, 5oz (140g)

3 tbsp coarse sea salt

3 tbsp sugar

1 tbsp coarsely crushed black peppercorns

3 tbsp aquavit or vodka

4 tbsp chopped dill

lemon wedges, to garnish

For the mustard sauce

¼ cup Dijon mustard

¼ cup vegetable oil

3 tbsp sugar

2 tbsp distilled white vinegar

1 tsp sour cream

pinch of salt

2 tbsp chopped dill

● **Prepare ahead** The salmon must be marinated for at least 1 and up to 2 days before serving.

1 Score each fillet with several diagonal shallow cuts on the skin side, about ⅛in (3mm) deep.

2 Combine the salt, sugar, and peppercorns. Sprinkle a quarter of the mixture on the bottom of a shallow nonmetallic dish. Place one fillet, skin-side down, in the dish and sprinkle with half the aquavit and another quarter of the salt mixture. Spread 2 tbsp of the dill in an even layer over the fillet.

3 Sprinkle the flesh side of the second fillet with another quarter of the dry mixture. Place it, skin-side up, on top of the first fillet. Rub the remaining salt-and-sugar mixture over the skin and sprinkle with the remaining aquavit.

4 Cover the salmon with a sheet of wax paper. Top with a large flat plate or cutting board, and weigh it down with cans of food.

Refrigerate for 24 hours, checking the salmon every 6 hours and draining off accumulated liquid from the dish. Turn the salmon over and refrigerate for another 24 hours, turning and weighing the salmon every 6 hours or so.

5 To make the mustard sauce, thoroughly whisk the mustard, oil, sugar, vinegar, sour cream, and salt in a bowl. Cover and refrigerate until chilled, at least 1 hour. Just before serving, add the dill.

6 To serve, scrape the seasonings and dill from the salmon. Place the salmon, skin-side down, on a cutting board. Slice the fish thinly on the slant, away from the skin. Sprinkle with the remaining dill. Serve with the mustard sauce and lemon wedges.

● **Good with** dark rye or whole wheat bread.

Shrimp Spring Rolls

These get their name because they were served to commemorate the first day of Spring in the Chinese calendar

 makes 12

prep 25 mins • cook 15 mins

8oz (225g) medium shrimp, peeled, deveined, and chopped

1 cup bean sprouts

½ red bell pepper, cored, seeded, and finely chopped

4oz (115g) shiitake mushrooms, stemmed and chopped

4 scallions, green and white parts, thinly sliced

¾in (2cm) piece of fresh ginger, peeled and grated

1 tbsp rice wine or cider vinegar

1 tbsp soy sauce

2 tbsp vegetable oil, plus more for deep-frying

1 cup chopped cooked chicken

6 napa cabbage leaves, tough stalks cut away

1 tbsp cornstarch, plus more for the baking sheet

12 spring roll wrappers

sweet chile dipping sauce, to serve

1 In a bowl, mix together the shrimp, bean sprouts, red pepper, mushrooms, scallions, ginger, vinegar, and soy sauce.

2 Heat 2 tbsp oil in a frying pan over medium-high heat. Add the shrimp mixture and stir-fry for 3 minutes. Set aside to cool, then stir in the chicken.

3 In a bowl, mix the cornstarch with 4 tbsp cold water.

4 Dust a baking sheet with cornstarch. Lay a wrapper on a work surface. Top with half a cabbage leaf and 1 tbsp of the shrimp mixture. Brush the edges with the dissolved cornstarch and roll up around the filling, tucking in the sides and pressing together to seal. Place on the baking sheet. Repeat with the remaining wrappers and filling.

5 Line another baking sheet with paper towels. Preheat the oven to 200°F (100°C). Pour ¼in (5mm) oil into a large frying pan. In batches, add the rolls and fry, turning occasionally, about 4 minutes, or until golden. Transfer to paper towels to drain. Keep warm in the oven while frying the remaining rolls. Serve hot, with the chile sauce for dipping.

Smoked Salmon Potato Cakes

This popular restaurant appetizer is easy to make at home

 makes 6 servings

prep 10 mins • cook 10 mins

For the dill mayonnaise

2 egg yolks

1 tbsp Dijon mustard

1 tsp sugar

1 tbsp fresh lemon juice

¾ cup plus 2 tbsp vegetable oil

2 tbsp chopped dill

salt and freshly ground black pepper

1lb 2oz (500g) baking potatoes, such as russet

9oz (250g) smoked salmon, finely chopped

2 scallions, finely chopped

3 tbsp chopped parsley

1 large egg, beaten

grated zest of 1 lemon

⅔ cup dried plain bread crumbs

1 tbsp chopped dill

1 tbsp chopped parsley

½ cup vegetable oil

1 lemon, cut into wedges, to serve

● **Prepare ahead** The cakes can be made the day before, covered, and refrigerated. The mayonnaise can be made 2 days in advance.

1 Make the mayonnaise. Pulse the egg yolks, mustard, lemon juice, and sugar in a food processor until well combined. With the machine running, pour in the oil in a thin stream. Stir in the dill and season with salt and pepper. Transfer to a bowl, cover, and refrigerate.

2 Parboil the potatoes in boiling salted water for 5 minutes. Drain and cool. Peel and shred on a box grater.

3 Combine the grated potato, salmon, scallions, parsley, egg, and lemon zest in a medium bowl. Season with salt and pepper. In a shallow dish, combine the bread crumbs with the dill and parsley.

4 Shape the potato mixture into 6 cakes and coat in the bread crumbs. Heat the oil in a large nonstick frying pan over medium-high heat until shimmering. Add the cakes and fry, turning once, about 5 minutes, until golden on both sides. Transfer to paper towels to drain.

5 Serve hot, garnished with the lemon wedges, and serve the mayonnaise on the side.

Shrimp Cocktail, Mexican-style

Corn kernels and avocado give a south-of-the-border twist to this perennial favorite

 makes 4 servings

 prep 20 mins • cook 1–2 mins

 devein the shrimp through the back and remove the shells

9oz (250g) **large shrimp**

1 tbsp **olive oil**

1½ tbsp fresh **lime** juice

1 tsp **hot red pepper sauce**

¼ cup **mayonnaise**

2 tbsp **sour cream**

1 tbsp **sun-dried tomato paste**

1 tbsp chopped **cilantro**, plus sprigs to garnish

¼ head **iceberg lettuce**, shredded

1 **avocado**, pitted, peeled, and diced

2 tbsp fresh or thawed frozen **corn** kernels

● **Prepare ahead** Steps 1–3 can be completed several hours ahead.

1 Peel and devein the shrimp, leaving the last tail segment attached on 4 of the shrimp to use as a garnish.

2 Heat the olive oil in a large frying pan over medium-high heat. Add the shrimp and cook, stirring often, for 2 minutes until they turn pink. Transfer to a bowl, and toss with the lime juice. Add the hot sauce, and toss again. Let cool.

3 Mix the mayonnaise, sour cream, tomato paste, and chopped cilantro together in a small bowl. Cover and refrigerate for at least 1 hour to blend the flavors.

4 Divide the lettuce among 4 dessert glasses. Set aside the 4 shrimp with their tails. Add the avocado and corn to the remaining shrimp and mix gently, taking care not to break up the avocado. Spoon equal amounts of the shrimp mixture into the glasses.

5 Top with mayonnaise sauce and garnish with the reserved shrimp and cilantro sprigs.

Shrimp with Parmesan Cream

Large shrimp are cloaked in a cheese-flavored cream sauce

 makes 4 servings

prep 10 mins • cook 15 mins

2 tbsp **olive oil**

4oz (115g) **pancetta** or slab bacon, diced

4 **scallions**, white and green parts, sliced

2 **garlic cloves**, minced

24 **large shrimp**, peeled and deveined

¼ cup **crème fraîche** or heavy cream

2 tbsp fresh **lemon** juice

salt and freshly ground **black pepper**

3 tbsp freshly shredded **Parmesan cheese**, to garnish

baby spinach leaves, to garnish

1 Heat the olive oil in a large frying pan over medium heat.

Add the pancetta and cook for 5 minutes until beginning to brown. Add the scallions and garlic, and cook 3 minutes more, or until the scallions are just beginning to soften.

2 Add the shrimp and cook, stirring occasionally, for about 3 minutes, until they are almost completely opaque. Add the crème fraîche and bring just to a simmer. Stir in the lemon juice and season to taste with salt and pepper. Lower the heat and simmer until the shrimp are opaque throughout, about 1 minute.

3 Transfer to a serving dish. Sprinkle with the Parmesan and garnish with spinach. Serve hot.

VARIATION

Pasta with Shrimp
Turn this into a main dish for 4 by serving it as a sauce over spaghetti. Add a touch of spice with a dash of hot sauce.

Marinated Anchovies

Boquerones en Vinagre are a Spanish speciality,
ideal as tapas or as a lunchtime dish

 makes 4 servings

🕐 prep 20 mins, plus
24–48 hrs marinating

2lbs (900g) fresh **anchovies**

1 tbsp **salt**

½ cup **sherry vinegar** or white wine
vinegar, as needed

⅓ cup **extra virgin olive oil**

2 **garlic cloves**, sliced

3 tbsp chopped **parsley**

● **Prepare ahead** The anchovies
must soak in vinegar for at least 24
hours, then they can be dressed with
oil and refrigerated for up to 2 days.

1 **To fillet anchovies,** cut off
heads and tails. Cut a slit along
the underside of each fish and discard
the innards. Open out each fish and
remove the central bone by lifting the
tail end and pulling upwards. Wash
the anchovies and remove any stray
bones. Pat dry with paper towels.

2 **Place half the** anchovy fillets
in a single layer in a shallow dish.
Sprinkle with 1½ tsp salt. Arrange the
remaining anchovies at right angles
over the first layer. Sprinkle with the
remaining salt. Add enough vinegar
to barely cover them. Cover and
refrigerate for at least 24 hours.

3 **Pour off the vinegar,** rinse
the anchovies in cold water, and
pat dry with paper towels. Arrange the
anchovies in a shallow serving dish

and pour the olive oil over them.
Sprinkle with the garlic and parsley.
Serve chilled.

● **Good with** lightly toasted slices
of crusty bread, rubbed with a cut
garlic clove and drizzled with olive oil.

VARIATION

Lemon-marinated Anchovies

Cover the anchovies with the zest and
juice of 2 lemons and marinate for
2 hours, then continue with the
recipe from step 3.

Anchovies on Toast

Canned anchovies can be
turned into a quick snack

 makes 4–6 servings

🕐 prep 10 mins • cook 5 mins

1 baguette

4 large ripe **tomatoes**

3½oz (100g) can **anchovy fillets**
in oil, drained

2 tbsp **extra virgin olive oil**

1 **shallot**, finely chopped

2 tbsp chopped **parsley**

freshly ground **black pepper**

1 **Cut the baguette** in half
lengthways and lightly toast
on both sides.

2 **Cut 2 tomatoes** in half
crosswise. Rub the tomato
halves over the cut sides of the
toasted baguettes, squeezing out the
seeds and flesh onto the bread, and
discarding the skins. Top with half
the anchovy fillets.

3 **Thinly slice** the remaining
tomatoes. Arrange the tomatoes
over the anchovies. Drizzle with olive
oil on top, then sprinkle with the
shallot and parsley. Season with the
pepper. Top with the remaining
anchovies. Cut into thick slices and
serve at once.

● **Good with** a green salad, as
an appetizer or as a light lunch.

Smoked Haddock and Herb Fishcakes

Crisp fishcakes make a tasty starter, and are a good way to use up leftover mashed potato

 makes 6 servings

 prep 10 mins, plus cooling,
• cook 30 mins

10oz (300g) **smoked haddock fillet** (finnan haddie), skinned

1 cup **mashed potatoes**

2 **scallions**, white and green parts, minced

2 tbsp chopped **parsley**

grated zest and juice of ½ **lemon**

½ tsp **Dijon mustard**

salt and freshly ground **black pepper**

⅓ cup **all-purpose flour**

1 large **egg**, beaten

¾ cup dried **bread crumbs**

½ cup **vegetable oil**

● **Prepare ahead** The fishcakes can be refrigerated for up to 4 hours before frying.

1 Preheat the oven to 375°F (190°C). Place the smoked haddock in a baking dish with 3 tbsp water. Cover with aluminum foil. Bake for 15 minutes, until heated through. Uncover and let cool, then flake into pieces.

2 Mix the flaked haddock, mashed potato, scallions, parsley, lemon zest and juice, and mustard together in a bowl. Season with salt and pepper.

3 Divide the mixture into 12 cakes. Place the flour in a small dish, the beaten egg in another, and the bread crumbs in a third dish. Roll each fishcake in the flour, then dip into the egg, and coat with the bread crumbs.

4 Heat the oil in a large frying pan over medium heat. In batches, add the cakes and cook about 5 minutes, turning once, until golden brown. Transfer to paper towels to drain. Serve hot.

● **Good with** a salad of arugula and watercress, and homemade mayonnaise, rouille, or tartare sauce.

Fried Whitebait

Deep-frying is the perfect way to cook these tiny fish, which are eaten whole

 makes 4 servings

 prep 15 mins • cook 20 mins

vegetable oil, for deep-frying

⅓ cup **all-purpose flour**

1 tsp **cayenne pepper**

1 tsp **salt**

1lb (450g) **whitebait** or smelt

lemon wedges, to serve

1 Preheat the oven to 200°F (95°C). Pour enough oil to come halfway up the sides of a large deep saucepan. Heat the oil over high heat until 350°F (180°C) on a deep-frying thermometer.

2 Mix the flour, cayenne, and salt together in a large bowl.

3 Toss the whitebait in the seasoned flour, making sure they are evenly coated. Place in a large sieve and shake off the excess flour.

4 Line a baking sheet with paper towels. In three batches, deep-fry the whitebait for 2–3 minutes, until they turn lightly golden. Transfer to the paper towels and keep warm in the oven until all the fish are fried.

5 Serve immediately, with the lemon wedges.

● **Good with** chilled potato salad.

> **FRYING FISH**
>
> Frying the whitebait in small batches will prevent them from clumping together and turning soggy.

Smoked Salmon Blinis

These bite-sized treats are perfect party food

 makes 20 blinis

 prep 20 mins, plus cooling • cook 20 mins

scant 1 cup **buckwheat flour**

¼ tsp **baking powder**

¼ tsp **salt**

½ cup **milk**

1 large **egg**, separated

vegetable oil, for the pan

½ cup **crème fraîche**

4 oz (115g) **smoked salmon**, cut into 20 strips

freshly ground **black pepper**

20 small **dill sprigs**

1 **lemon**, cut into wedges

1 Sift the flour, baking powder, and salt together into a bowl. Make a well in the center. Add the milk and egg yolk. Whisk until smooth.

2 Beat the egg white until it forms soft peaks. Fold the beaten white into the batter.

3 Brush a large nonstick frying pan with a little oil and heat over medium heat. Add well-spaced teaspoons of the batter to the pan. Cook about 2 minutes, or until bubbles appear on the surface. Flip the blinis and cook for about 2 minutes more, or until the undersides are browned.

4 Top each blini with a spoonful of crème fraîche, a twirl of smoked salmon, a pinch of pepper, and a sprig of dill. Arrange on a platter and serve, with lemon wedges for squeezing.

VARIATION

Smoked Salmon Corn Cakes

Substitute this mixture for the blini batter: sift ½ cup all-purpose flour, ¼ cup yellow cornmeal, ½ tsp baking powder, ¼ tsp salt, and a pinch of cayenne together into a bowl. Add ⅔ cup heavy cream and 2 large egg yolks and whisk until smooth. Add 1 cup fresh or thawed frozen corn kernels, 2 tbsp melted butter, and 2 tbsp chopped chives. Mix well, cover, and let stand for 30 minutes. Cook as above.

Herbed Shrimp and Goat Cheese Wraps

Serve these as a light meal or with wine before dinner

 makes 18 pieces

 prep 15 mins

6 oz (175g) rindless **goat cheese**, at room temperature

2 tbsp chopped **dill**, **chives**, and/or **chervil**, plus sprigs of herbs for garnish

grated zest of 1 **lemon**

salt and freshly ground **black pepper**

3 large flour **tortillas**

8 oz (225g) small cooked **shrimp**

● **Prepare ahead** The wraps can be refrigerated for up to 2 hours.

1 Mix the goat cheese, dill, and lemon zest together. Season with salt and pepper.

2 Spread the cheese over the tortillas. Sprinkle with the shrimp. Tightly roll up each tortilla. Refrigerate until ready to serve.

3 Thirty minutes before serving, cut each wrap at a slight diagonal into 6 pieces. Garnish with the herbs and serve.

Smoked Trout and Goat Cheese Bites

A delicious blend of smoked trout and herbed goat cheese in a tortilla wrap

 makes 28 appetizers

prep 15 mins

6 oz (165g) rindless **soft goat cheese**

2 tbsp chopped **dill** or chervil

grated zest of 1 **lemon**

salt and freshly ground **black pepper**

4 large **flour tortillas**

2 **red bell peppers**, roasted, peeled, and sliced into thin strips

1 cup flaked skinless **smoked trout** fillet

● **Prepare ahead** The rolled tortillas can be refrigerated for up to 8 hours; slice just before serving.

1 Mix the goat cheese, dill, and lemon zest together and season with salt and pepper.

2 Spread the tortillas with equal amounts of the cheese mixture. Arrange the peppers and smoked trout over the cheese. Roll up each tortilla as tightly as possible. Wrap each in plastic wrap and refrigerate at least 1 hour, until chilled. Cut each wrap diagonally into 7 pieces. Serve chilled.

VARIATION

Smoked Salmon Bites

Substitute 4oz (115g) hot-smoked salmon for the smoked trout.

Shrimp with Mint, Chile, and Ginger

Easy and quick to prepare, this is an ideal starter for an informal dinner party

 makes 6 servings

prep 10 mins, plus marinating

For the marinade

¼ cup **olive oil**

3 tbsp torn **mint leaves**

2 tbsp fresh **lime** juice

2 tbsp peeled and finely grated fresh **ginger**

3 fresh **hot red chiles**, seeded and minced

1 **garlic clove**, minced

salt

1½ lb (750g) large cooked **shrimp**

12 Belgian **endive leaves**

bunch of **watercress**

1 **lime**, cut into wedges

1 To make the marinade, whisk the oil, mint, lime juice, ginger, chiles, and garlic. Season with salt. Add the shrimp and mix. Refrigerate for at least 15 minutes and up to 1 hour.

2 To serve, divide the endive among 4 salad plates. Top with the shrimp and garnish with the watercress and lime wedges. Serve immediately.

Herbed Fish Goujons

These are fish sticks for grown-ups

- makes 4 servings
- prep 20 mins
  - cook 10–15 mins

1½ cups fresh **bread crumbs**

3 tbsp chopped **parsley**, plus sprigs for serving

½ tsp **smoked paprika**

salt and freshly ground **black pepper**

⅔ cup **all-purpose flour**

2 large **eggs**

12oz (325g) **white fish fillets**, such as haddock, cod, or flounder

vegetable oil, for frying

lemon wedges, to garnish

1 Mix the bread crumbs, parsley, and smoked paprika well into a bowl and season with salt and pepper.

2 Spread the flour in another bowl. Whisk the eggs and 2 tbsp water in another bowl.

3 Slice the fish into strips about ½in (1cm) wide. In batches, coat the fish in the flour. Dip in the egg, then coat with the bread crumbs. Spread them, without touching each other, on a baking sheet.

4 Add enough oil to come 1in (2.5cm) up the sides of a large, deep saucepan and heat over high heat to 350°F (180°C). In batches, add the fish and deep-fry, turning once, about 2 minutes, until golden. Using a slotted spoon, transfer to paper towels to drain. Transfer to a platter and garnish with the parsley. Serve hot, with the lemon wedges.

● **Good with** tartar sauce and a fresh tossed salad.

Seafood Ceviche

Ceviche lightly pickles raw fish to conserve freshness and bring out its true flavor

- makes 4 servings
- prep 20 mins, plus marinating
- ❄ wrap the fish in plastic wrap and put it in the freezer for 1 hour to firm up the flesh so that it will slice easily

1lb (450g) very fresh, **firm-fleshed fish**, such as salmon, snapper, tuna, or monkfish

1 **red onion**, thinly sliced

juice of 2 **limes**

1 tbsp **olive oil**

½ tsp **hot smoked paprika**

1 fresh hot **red** or **green chile**, finely chopped

salt and freshly ground **pepper**

2 tbsp finely chopped **cilantro**

1 With a sharp knife, thinly slice the fish.

2 Spread the sliced onion evenly in the bottom of a shallow nonreactive dish. Pour the lime juice over the onion, then sprinkle it with the oil, paprika, and chile.

3 Layer the fish on top, turning the slices to coat with the marinade.

4 Cover and refrigerate for at least 20 minutes or up to 2 hours. Season with salt and pepper. Sprinkle with the cilantro and serve chilled.

● **Good with** crusty bread or tortilla chips.

Stuffed Filo Tartlets

A stylish appetizer

 makes 6 servings

 prep 45 mins • cook 20 mins

 six 4in (10cm) tartlet tins

6 sheets thawed frozen **filo dough**

olive oil, as needed

3 **red** or **orange bell peppers**, seeded, and cut into quarters

10oz (300g) **firm smoked chorizo**, sliced

½ **red onion**, very finely sliced

5oz (140g) **goat cheese**, crumbled

1 Preheat the oven to 350°F (180°C). Brush 1 filo sheet with oil and cut into quarters. Place a filo quarter in a tartlet pan. Stack the remaining three sheets on top of the first, giving each a quarter turn before stacking. Fold the filo over the edge of the pan. Brush with oil and bake for 10 minutes, until crisp and golden.

2 To make the filling, broil the peppers, skin side up, until the skin is blackened and blistered. Cool. Peel and cut into thick slices.

3 Heat 1 tbsp oil in a frying pan and cook the chorizo until crisp and browned. Drain on paper towels.

4 Arrange the peppers, onion, and cheese on the tarts. Top with hot chorizo to serve.

Empanadas

These turnovers are found wherever Spanish is spoken

 makes 6 servings

 prep 45 mins, plus chilling • cook 40–50 mins

3½in (9cm) round cookie cutter

3¼ cups **all-purpose flour**

½ tsp **salt**

6 tbsp cold **butter**, diced

3 large **eggs**, beaten

1 tbsp **olive oil**

1 **onion**, finely chopped

⅓ cup canned **chopped tomatoes**, drained

2 tsp **tomato paste**

One 6oz (168g) can **tuna**, drained

2 tbsp finely chopped **parsley**

1 To make the pastry, sift the flour and salt into a large mixing bowl. Rub in the butter with your fingertips until it resembles fine bread crumbs. Beat 2 of the eggs with 2 tbsp water, add to the bowl, and stir until the dough holds together. Make a thick disk, cover with plastic wrap, and refrigerate for 30 minutes.

2 Meanwhile, heat the oil in a frying pan over medium heat. Cook the onion, stirring often, for about 5 minutes, or until translucent. Add the tomatoes and tomato paste, and simmer, stirring often, about 10 minutes, until thick. Remove from the heat and stir in the tuna and parsley. Season with salt and pepper.

3 Preheat the oven to 375°F (190°C). Roll out the dough to a thickness of ¹⁄₁₆in (2mm). Cut out 24 rounds with a 3½in (9cm) round cookie cutter. Fill each with a spoonful of the filling. Brush the edges with water, fold over, and press the edges closed with a fork.

4 Place the empanadas on an oiled baking sheet and brush with the remaining egg. Bake for about 15 minutes, or until golden. Serve warm.

VARIATION

Experiment with other fillings: replace the tuna with chopped cooked chicken or chorizo, or with diced cooked potato.

Crostini with Green Olive Tapenade

This easy-to-make dish is great as an appetizer or snack

 makes 12–16 crostini

prep 10 mins

⅔ cup pitted **green olives**

1 **garlic clove**, peeled

grated zest of ½ **lemon**

2 tsp **olive oil**

4 **basil leaves**

freshly ground **black pepper**

12 **baguette slices**, toasted

6 **yellow** or **red cherry tomatoes**, roasted, to garnish (optional)

1 Purée the olives, garlic, lemon zest, oil, and basil into a food processor. Season with pepper.

2 Spread the tapenade over the baguette slices. Garnish each one with a roasted cherry tomato half (if using).

● **Good with** pre-dinner drinks, and especially Champagne.

Smoked Salmon and Pancetta Crostini

Crostini and bruschette can be made in many variations.
Tangy-buttery crème fraîche lightens this savory bite.

🍴 makes 12 crostini

🕐 prep 10 mins • cook 15 mins

12 slices of French (baguette)
bread

3 tbsp olive oil

6 slices of pancetta

¾ cup crème fraîche
or sour cream

2 tbsp whole grain mustard

3 tbsp capers, rinsed

1 tsp fresh lemon zest

1 tsp fresh lemon juice

freshly ground black pepper

7 oz (200 g) smoked salmon, cut
into strips

12 whole chives, snipped into 1 in
(2.5cm) lengths to garnish

● **Prepare ahead** The bread slices can be baked up to 2 hours ahead. The crème fraîche mixture can be made 24 hours in advance. Assemble the crostini just before serving.

1 Preheat the oven to 400°F (200°C). Brush both sides of the bread slices with olive oil, and place them on a baking sheet. Bake for 10 minutes, or until crisp and golden. Cool completely.

2 Preheat the broiler and position the broiler rack 6 in (15cm) from the source of heat. Broil the pancetta for about 5 minutes until crisp on both sides. Drain on paper towels. Cut into thin strips.

3 Mix the crème fraîche with the mustard, the capers, the lemon zest, and juice, and black pepper to taste.

4 Place the bread slices on a serving plate, spread with the crème fraîche mixture, and top with strips of smoked salmon, pieces of pancetta, and chives to garnish.

VARIATION

Classic Italian Crostini

Remove the smoked salmon, replace the crème fraîche mixture with slices of fresh mozzarella, and use fresh basil instead of chives. Brush the bread slices with garlic and olive oil, then lightly pepper the mozzarella. Place a piece of basil on each piece of mozzarella, then wrap it in half a slice of prosciutto. Place the crostini under the broiler for 3—5 minutes, until the cheese melts.

PANCETTA

Pancetta is widely available from delicatessens and supermarkets, but if you cannot find any, use thinly sliced bacon instead. Prepared horseradish can be used instead of mustard; the flavor goes very well with the salmon and pancetta.

Anchovy and Olive Bruschette

These simple canapés are ideal with pre-dinner drinks

🍴 makes 12 appetizers

🕐 prep 10 mins • cook 5 mins

12 slices **Italian bread**, such as ciabatta, about ¾in (2cm) thick

1 **garlic clove**, peeled

extra virgin **olive oil**

½ cup store-bought **marinara sauce**

salt and freshly ground **black pepper**

4oz (115g) **mozzarella cheese**, drained and cut into 12 thin slices

1 tsp dried **Italian herbs**

12 **anchovy fillets** in olive oil, drained and cut in half crosswise

6 pitted **Kalamata olives**, sliced

● **Prepare ahead** Steps 1 and 2 can be done in advance with the bruschette broiled just before serving.

1 **Preheat the broiler** and position the rack 6in (15cm) from the heat. Broil the bread slices until toasted golden on both sides. Rub 1 side of each slice with the garlic clove. Brush the garlic side of each slice with about 2 tsp olive oil.

2 **For each bruschetta**, spread the toasted bread with about 2 tsp marinara sauce and sprinkle with salt and pepper to taste. Put 1 slice of mozzarella on each, sprinkle with the herbs, and top with 2 pieces of anchovy in a criss-cross pattern.

3 **Broil** for 2–3 minutes, or until the mozzarella has melted. Serve hot, sprinkled with the olives.

● **Good with** a chilled glass of sparkling Prosecco.

Scallop and Pesto Crostini

These stylish canapés can also be served as a simple appetizer

🍴 makes 12 crostini

🕐 prep 10 mins • cook 7 mins

12 slices **Italian bread**, such as ciabatta, about ¾in (2cm) thick

½ **garlic clove**

3 tbsp **olive oil**

6 **sea scallops**

1 tbsp fresh **lemon** juice

salt and freshly ground **black pepper**

2 tbsp store-bought **pesto**

2 tbsp sun-dried **tomato paste**

12 fresh **basil leaves**, to garnish

● **Prepare ahead** Step 1 can be done in advance.

1 **Preheat the broiler** and position the broiler rack about 6in (15cm) from the source of heat.

Broil the bread slices in the broiler until toasted golden on both sides. Rub one side of each slice with the garlic clove. Brush the garlic side of each slice with about 2 tsp olive oil.

2 **Heat the remaining oil** in a large frying pan over medium heat. Add the scallops, sprinkle with the lemon juice, and salt and pepper to taste. Cook for 2 minutes on each side, or until cooked through and tender; keep hot.

3 **Spread one half** of each toasted bread slice with pesto and the other half with tomato paste.

4 **Cut each scallop** in half horizontally and put 1 scallop half on top of each crostini. Grind black pepper over the top. Serve hot, garnished with basil leaves.

● **Good with** a dry white wine.

Onion Bhajis

These crisp vegetable fritters are made with chickpea flour, also known as gram flour, which can be found in Indian food shops

 makes 4 servings

prep 15 mins • cook 15 mins

deep-fat fryer or large saucepan, deep-frying thermometer

1½ cups chopped **onions**

¾ cup **chickpea flour**

2 tsp **cumin seeds**

1 tsp **ground coriander**

½ tsp **ground turmeric**

1 fresh **hot green** or **red chile**, seeded and minced

vegetable oil, for frying

● **Prepare ahead** The batter can be made and covered several hours in advance. If the batter becomes too thick, add a little more water.

1 **In a large bowl**, mix together the onions, chickpea flour, cumin seeds, coriander, turmeric, and chile. Add enough cold water (about ½ cup) to make a thick batter.

2 **Pour enough oil** into a large, deep saucepan to reach 2in (5cm) up the sides, and heat to 350°F (180°C). In batches, carefully add spoonfuls of batter (about the size of golfballs) to the oil. Deep-fry, about 3 minutes, turning occasionally, until golden.

3 **Using a** slotted spoon, transfer the bhajis to paper towels to drain.

4 **Just before serving**, return the bhajis to hot oil and deep-fry again until crisp and golden-brown. Drain briefly on paper towels and serve hot.

● **Good with** a simple raita of plain yogurt mixed with chopped mint and a squeeze of lemon juice.

VARIATION

Vegetable Bhajis

Replace one-third of the onion with finely shredded spinach or grated carrot.

Sesame Shrimp Toasts

These Thai-style toasts make warm and savory mouthfuls

makes 12 toasts

prep 15 mins • cook 15 mins

deep-fat fryer or large saucepan, deep-frying thermometer

9oz (250g) **medium shrimp**, peeled and coarsely chopped

2 **scallions**, roughly chopped

one ½in (1cm) piece of **fresh ginger**, peeled and shredded

1 tsp **soy sauce**

½ tsp **sugar**

½ tsp **Asian sesame oil**

1 large **egg white**, beaten

⅛ tsp freshly ground **black pepper**

3 large slices firm **white sandwich bread**, crusts trimmed

2 tbsp **sesame seeds**

vegetable oil, for deep-frying

fresh cilantro, to garnish

● **Prepare ahead** The toasts can be prepared to the end of step 2 up to 4 hours in advance, ready to be fried just before serving.

1 **Combine the shrimp** and scallions, white and green parts, in a food processor and process until they form a paste. Transfer to a bowl and stir in the ginger, soy sauce, sugar, sesame oil, and enough egg white to bind the mixture together. Season with the pepper.

2 **Spread the bread** thickly with the shrimp paste. Cut each slice into four triangles. Sprinkle the sesame seeds evenly over the top.

3 **Pour enough oil** into a deep-fryer or skillet to come halfway up the sides, and heat to 350°F (180°C). In batches, add the toasts, shrimp sides down, and deep-fry for 2 minutes, until the shrimp paste is puffed. Carefully turn them over and deep-fry until the toasts are crisp and golden brown.

4 **Using a slotted spoon**, transfer the toasts to paper towels and drain briefly. Serve hot, garnished with coriander.

● **Good with** sweet chile sauce and chilled sake or a cold beer.

Vegetable Samosas

Serve these Indian pastries hot or cold. In India, they would be fried in ghee,
a clarified butter that can be heated to a high temperature, but oil works equally well

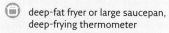 makes 16 samosas

prep 45 mins, plus resting and cooling • cook 35–40 mins

deep-fat fryer or large saucepan, deep-frying thermometer

freeze uncooked samosas up to 1 month, defrost and pat dry with paper towels before frying

For the pastry

2½ cups all-purpose flour, plus more for rolling the dough

½ tsp salt

6 tbsp vegetable oil, plus more for deep-frying

1 cup warm water, as needed

For the filling

3 baking potatoes (1lb/450g)

2 cups cauliflower florets

3 tbsp vegetable oil

2 shallots, sliced

1 cup thawed frozen peas

2 tbsp curry powder

2 tbsp chopped cilantro

1 tbsp fresh lemon juice

● **Prepare ahead** The samosas can be prepared up to 2 hours ahead, stored at room temperature, and fried just before serving.

1 **To make** the pastry, sift the flour and salt into a bowl. Stir in the oil. Gradually stir in the warm water until the dough comes together.

2 **Knead the dough** on a floured surface until smooth. Wrap in plastic wrap and let stand at room temperature for at least 30 minutes.

3 **To make the filling**, cook the unpeeled potatoes until tender, about 25 minutes. Drain and cool. Peel and cut into small dice.

4 **Cook the cauliflower** in a saucepan of lightly salted, boiling water for 2–3 minutes, or until just tender. Drain.

5 **Heat the oil** in a large, deep frying pan over medium heat. Add the shallots and cook for 3–4 minutes, stirring frequently, until tender. Add the potatoes, cauliflower, peas, curry powder, cilantro, and lemon juice. Reduce the heat to low and cook, stirring occasionally, until heated through, about 3 minutes. Let cool.

6 **Divide the dough** into 8 equal balls. Roll out each into a 7in (18cm) round. Cut each round in half, one at a time, and shape into a cone, moistening the edges of the cone to seal. Spoon a little of the filling into a cone, moisten the top edge, and press down over the filling to enclose it. Transfer to a wax paper lined baking sheet.

7 **Pour in enough oil** to come halfway up the sides of a large, heavy saucepan, and heat to 350°F (180°C). In batches, fry the samosas for 3–4 minutes, or until golden brown on both sides. Transfer to paper towels to drain. Serve warm or at room temperature.

VARIATION

Meat Samosas

Replace 8oz (225g) potatoes with an equal amount of ground lamb. Cook the lamb with the shallots until well browned and drain off any excess fat before combining with the other ingredients.

Wild Mushroom Tartlets

Earthy mushroom tartlets get an elegant accent with chive hollandaise sauce

 makes 6 servings

 prep 40 mins, plus chilling • cook 40 mins

 six 4in (10cm) tart pans with removable bottoms, baking beans

For the filling

½ cup boiling water

½oz (15g) dried porcini mushrooms

2 tbsp butter

14oz (400g) cremini mushrooms, sliced

1 small onion, finely chopped

1 tbsp fresh lemon juice

4oz (115g) cream cheese

salt and freshly ground black pepper

6 tbsp chive hollandaise sauce

chopped fresh chives, for garnish

For the pastry

1¼ cups all-purpose flour, plus extra for dusting

6 tbsp butter, chilled and diced

1 egg yolk mixed with 2 tbsp water

1 To make the filling, soak the dried mushrooms in the boiling water for 20 minutes to soften. Drain and chop the soaked mushrooms. Heat the butter in a frying pan over medium-high heat. Add the mushrooms and onion and cook 5 minutes, until the mushrooms are softened. Add the soaked mushrooms and cook about 5 minutes more, until the mushrooms are sizzling. Stir in the lemon juice. Let cool. Pulse the mushroom mixture and cream cheese in a food processor until combined. Season with salt and pepper.

2 Meanwhile, make the pastry. Pulse the flour and butter in a food processor until it resembles coarse bread crumbs. Add the egg mixture and pulse just until it clumps together. Gather into a disk, wrap in plastic wrap, and refrigerate for 30 minutes.

3 Have ready the tart pans with removable bottoms. Divide the dough into 6 portions, and roll out each on a lightly floured work surface into a ⅛in (3mm) thick round. Line each pan with a round, trimming the excess dough. Prick the dough with a fork. Refrigerate for 30 minutes.

4 Preheat the oven to 400°F (200°C). Line each tart pan with parchment paper and fill with baking beans. Bake for 10 minutes. Remove the paper and beans and bake until the crusts are lightly browned, about 5 minutes more. Remove the pans from the oven. Reduce the oven temperature to 375°F (190°C).

5 Spread the mushroom mixture in the pastry shells. Top each with 1 tbsp hollandaise sauce. Bake for 10 minutes, until the hollandaise glazes. Remove the tarts from the pans and transfer to plates. Sprinkle with chives and serve hot.

> **LEFTOVER HOLLANDAISE**
> You will have leftover hollandaise sauce. Refrigerate the sauce for up to 1 day. Spoon the cold sauce over hot food, and the warmth of the food will heat and melt the sauce.

Nachos

Quick to make—and great for sharing

 makes 4 servings

prep 10 mins • cook 5 mins

7oz (200g) tortilla chips

1 cup canned chopped tomatoes, drained

4 scallions, white and green parts, finely chopped

3 tbsp drained and chopped pickled jalapeño slices

1 cup shredded Monterey Jack or Cheddar cheese

1 avocado, pitted, peeled, and diced

2 tbsp chopped cilantro

1½ cups sour cream

1 Position the broiler rack about 8in (20cm) from the source of heat and preheat.

2 Spread the tortilla chips on a large heatproof platter. Sprinkle the tomatoes, scallions, jalapeños, and cheese over the chips.

3 Broil for about 4 minutes, until the cheese is melted.

4 Sprinkle with avocado and cilantro. Serve hot, with sour cream passed on the side.

Boreks

These small cigar-shaped cheese pastries from Turkey are seen on Middle Eastern menus all over the world

🍴 makes 24

🕐 prep 25 mins • cook 10-12 mins

6oz (175g) **feta cheese**, finely crumbled

1 tsp **dried mint** or 1 tbsp chopped fresh mint

pinch of **ground nutmeg**

freshly ground **black pepper**

8 thawed frozen **filo sheets**

4 tbsp **butter**, melted

● **Prepare ahead** The pastries can be prepared up to 24 hours in advance of baking.

1 **Preheat the oven** to 350°F (180°C). Combine the feta, mint, and nutmeg, and season with black pepper.

2 **Lay the filo sheets** on top of each other and cut into 3 long strips, 4in (10cm) wide.

3 **Taking one strip** of pastry at a time, brush with butter.

4 **Place a heaping** teaspoon of the cheese mixture at one end. Roll up the pastry into a cylinder, stopping after rolling one-third to fold over the long sides of the filo to completely enclose the filling, then finish rolling. Make sure the ends are tightly sealed. Transfer to the baking sheet and cover with a damp paper towel. Do not let the pastries touch each other.

5 **Lightly brush** another baking sheet with the butter. Arrange the pastries on the sheet and brush with the remaining butter. Bake for 10-12 minutes, or until crisp and golden. Serve hot or warm.

● **Good with** Middle Eastern dishes as part of a meze platter.

VARIATION

Spinach Boreks

Substitute the cheese filling for the following mixture: Sauté 2 chopped scallions in 1 tbsp olive oil. Stir in 5oz (140g) baby spinach leaves; cook until wilted. Drain, cool, then chop finely. Mix in ½ cup crumbled feta cheese and 1 tbsp chopped dill. Season with salt and pepper.

Smoked Chicken and Spinach Filo Triangles

These flaky parcels are delicious served hot or cold as an appetizer

🍴 makes 6 servings

🕐 prep 25 mins • cook 20 mins

❄ suitable for freezing before baking

1 tsp **olive oil**

8oz (225g) fresh **spinach**, washed, tough stems removed

4 **scallions**, white and green parts, finely chopped

4oz (115g) **smoked chicken**

1⅓ cup **crème fraîche** or heavy cream

1 tbsp chopped **tarragon**

1 tsp **Dijon mustard**

grated zest of 1 large **lemon**

½ cup toasted **pine nuts**

freshly ground **black pepper**

4 thawed frozen **filo sheets**

4 tbsp **butter**, melted

¼ cup **Parmesan cheese**, grated

● **Prepare ahead** The triangles can be covered and refrigerated for up to 1 day.

1 **Preheat the oven** to 350°F (180°C). Heat the oil in a medium saucepan over medium heat. Add the spinach, cover, and cook about 5 minutes, until tender. Drain well and let cool. Pulse the spinach, scallions, smoked chicken, crème fraîche, tarragon, mustard, and lemon zest in a food processor until coarsely chopped. Stir in the pine nuts and season with pepper.

2 **Line a baking sheet** with wax paper. Place 1 filo sheet on the work surface, with the short side running horizontally. Cover the remaining filo with a damp paper towel to prevent drying. Brush the filo sheet with melted butter. Top with a second sheet and brush again with butter. Cut the filo pastry into three 4in (10cm) strips. Place a heaping spoonful of the chicken mixture about ½in (13mm) below the top of a strip. Fold the right corner of the strip diagonally to the left to form a triangle that covers the filling. Fold the triangle with the filling down, and repeat folding down and over until you reach the end of the strip. Brush with butter and place on the baking sheet. Repeat with the other 3 strips, then with 2 more filo sheets and the remaining filling. Sprinkle with the Parmesan.

3 **Transfer to** a lightly oiled baking sheet. Bake for 20 minutes, until golden brown. Serve hot or warm.

Cheesy Spinach Squares

Spanakopita, the Greek spinach pie, can be cut into small diamonds or squares and served as an appetizer

 makes 12 servings

prep 35 mins, plus cooling • cook 1½ hrs

11½ x 8in (29 x 20cm) baking or roasting pan

4 tbsp **olive oil**

1 **onion**, peeled and chopped

8 **scallions**, white and green parts, chopped

2lb (900g) **spinach**, rinsed and shredded, but nor dried

3 tbsp chopped **dill**

3 tbsp chopped **parsley**

4 large **eggs**

8oz (225g) **feta cheese**, finely crumbled

freshly ground **black pepper**

10 tbsp **butter**, melted

14 sheets thawed frozen **filo dough**

● **Prepare ahead** The filling can be prepared through step 2, and refrigerated for up to 1 day.

1 Heat the olive oil in a large saucepan over medium heat. Add the onion and scallions and cook, stirring occasionally, about 5 minutes, until softened.

2 Stir in the spinach, and cover. Cook, stirring occasionally, about 8 minutes, or until wilted. Stir in the dill and parsley, and increase the heat to medium-high. Cook, uncovered, stirring frequently, for about 15 minutes, until the liquid evaporates and the mixture starts to stick to the bottom of the saucepan. Transfer to a colander lined with paper towels, and let cool.

3 Beat the eggs in a large bowl. Add the spinach and feta cheese and season with plenty of pepper.

4 Preheat the oven to 325°F (170°C). Generously brush the pan with some melted butter. Line the pan with a sheet of filo dough, carefully pressing it into the sides and corners of the pan. Repeat with 6 more filo sheets.

5 Spread the spinach mixture into the pan. Repeat layering and buttering the remaining 7 filo sheets. Using kitchen scissors, trim away excess dough, and tuck the filo edges into the pan. Brush the top with any remaining butter. Bake for 1 hour, or until the pastry is crisp and golden brown all over.

6 Cut into squares and serve hot or warm.

● **Good with** other Greek or Middle Eastern appetizers, such as hummus and taramasalata, as a mezze platter.

VARIATION

Creamy Spinach Pie
Delete the cheese. After half of the filo has been layered, spread half of the spinach mixture into the pan. Spread with 2 cups cold béchamel sauce and 2 chopped hard-boiled eggs, then the remaining spinach mixture. Finish layering with the remaining filo.

Fava Bean, Garlic, and Herb Crostini

Ideal for parties or as an appetizer with drinks

 makes 12 crostini

prep 15 mins • cook 15 mins

12 **baguette slices**

3 tbsp **extra virgin olive oil**

salt and freshly ground **black pepper**

1 cup **fava beans**, shelled

1 small **shallot**

1 **garlic clove**

6 sprigs **tarragon**, leaves only

1 Preheat the oven to 300°F (150°C). Brush both sides of each slice of baguette with 2 tbsp olive oil. Season with salt and pepper. Spread on a baking sheet. Bake for 15 minutes, or until crisp and golden.

2 Meanwhile, cook the fava beans in boiling water for 2 minutes. Drain and rinse under cold running water. Reserve a few beans for garnish. Purée the remaining beans in a food processor with the shallot, garlic, the remaining 1 tbsp olive oil, and the tarragon leaves. Season to taste with salt and pepper.

3 Just before serving, spread the fava bean paste onto the prepared crostini. Garnish with the reserved beans and a sprinkling of black pepper.

Cheese Straws

This classic, quick, and easy appetizer can be served with drinks at any occasion

🍴 makes approx 40

🕐 prep 20 mins • cook 15 mins

one 17.3oz (484g) package thawed frozen **puff pastry** (2 sheets)

all-purpose flour, for dusting

2 tbsp **Dijon mustard**

1 cup grated **sharp Cheddar cheese**

½ cup freshly grated **Parmesan cheese**

1 large **egg yolk**

1 tbsp **whole milk**

butter, for the baking sheets

● **Prepare ahead** The straws can be made a day in advance and kept chilled until ready to bake.

1 Preheat the oven to 375°F (190°C). One sheet at a time, roll out the thawed puff pastry on a lightly floured surface into a 14x10in (35x25cm) rectangle, trimming the edges to neaten.

2 Combine the cheeses. Spread 1 tbsp mustard over the top half of each pastry sheet, leaving a ½in (12mm) border, then top with half of the grated cheeses.

3 Mix together the egg yolk and milk, then brush lightly around the exposed borders on the pastries.

4 Fold over the pastries and press together, sealing the edges. Lightly roll over the top to compress.

5 Cut the pastries into 20 strips about ½in (12mm) wide. Holding both ends, twist strips into a spiral and place, well spaced, on lightly greased baking sheets.

6 Bake for 12–15 minutes, or until puffed and golden. Transfer to a wire rack and let cool.

VARIATION

Blue Cheese Straws

Replace the cheeses with 1 cup blue cheese and ½ cup finely chopped walnuts.

Mushroom Vol-au-vents

Vol-au-vents or "puffs of wind" are little puff pastry cases enclosing a savory filling, such as creamy mushrooms

🍴 makes 20

🕐 prep 20 mins • cook 15 mins

▣ baking sheet • 2½in (6cm) and 1¾in (4.5cm) round pastry cutters

20 medium **button mushrooms**

¼ cup **olive oil**

2 tbsp chopped **lemon thyme leaves**

salt and freshly ground **black pepper**

2 tbsp **tapenade**

2 tbsp **crème fraîche**

all-purpose flour, for dusting

one 17.3oz (484g) package thawed frozen **puff pastry** (2 sheets)

1 **egg yolk**, lightly beaten with 1 tsp water

1 Preheat the oven to 400°F (200°C). Put the mushrooms, olive oil, lemon thyme, and salt and pepper in a bowl and mix together. In another bowl, stir together the tapenade and crème fraîche.

2 Unroll the pastry onto a lightly floured work surface. Stamp out 20 circles using the larger pastry cutter. Use the smaller pastry cutter to cut a shallow circle inside each round, making sure you don't cut all the way through.

3 Transfer the circles to the baking sheet. Spoon tapenade mixture in the center of each round and place a mushroom on top.

4 Lightly brush the edges of the pastry circles with the yolk mixture. Bake for about 15 minutes until golden and puffed up. Serve hot or warm.

VARIATIONS

Chicken and Pesto Vol-au-vents

Omit the mushrooms. Substitute 3 tbsp pesto for the tapenade. Top with equal amounts of ¾ cup finely diced cooked chicken, then sprinkle with 2 tbsp pine nuts.

Smoked Salmon and Ricotta Vol-au-vents

Omit the tapenade mixture and mushrooms. Substitute 5oz (150g) hot-smoked salmon, flaked, with 4 tbsp ricotta cheese and 2 tbsp dill.

Eggplant and Goat Cheese Crostini

Crisp crostini with a deliciously savory topping

 makes 12 crostini

 prep 10 mins • cook 20 mins

12 slices baguette

2 tbsp olive oil

1 garlic clove, cut in half

1 firm eggplant

2 tbsp chopped mint

1 tbsp balsamic vinegar

salt and freshly ground black pepper

2oz (60g) soft goat cheese

1 Preheat the oven to 350°F (180°C). Brush the bread on both sides with olive oil, then toast for 10 minutes, turning once, or until crisp. Cut the garlic in half and rub the cut side over each slice.

2 Preheat the broiler. Slice the eggplant into ¼in (5mm) thick rounds, brush each side with olive oil, then broil on both sides until tender.

3 Halve or quarter the eggplant slices, and transfer to a bowl. Add the remaining olive oil, mint, and balsamic vinegar, toss, and season with salt and pepper.

4 Spread the crostini with goat cheese, top with slices of eggplant, and serve.

Mushroom Bruschetta

A quick winter appetizer

 makes 12 bruschetta

 prep 10 mins • cook 20 mins

12 slices rustic bread

3 tbsp olive oil

3 tbsp butter

1lb (450g) cremini mushrooms, sliced

4 shallots, finely chopped

2 garlic cloves, finely chopped

½ cup dry Marsala

½ cup heavy cream

salt and freshly ground black pepper

3 tbsp freshly grated Parmesan

2 tbsp chopped parsley

1 Preheat the oven to 350°F (180°C). Brush the bread slices with the oil. Place on baking sheets and bake for 10 minutes, turning once, until crisp.

2 Melt the butter in a pan. Cook the mushrooms, stirring often, around 5 minutes, until wilted. Add the shallots and garlic and cook about 3 minutes more. Add the Marsala, and boil about 5 minutes until the wine is reduced to a glaze.

3 Add the cream, and boil for 3 minutes, until reduced. Season with salt and pepper and add the Parmesan and parsley. Spoon the mixture over the toasts to serve.

Smoked Trout Tartlets

These tartlets are perfect for a light supper or picnic

 makes 6 tartlets

prep 30 mins, plus chilling • cook 30 mins

six 4in (10cm) tartlet pans, baking beans

freeze for up to 1 month

For the pastry

1 cup all-purpose flour

6 tbsp cold butter, diced

1 large egg yolk

For the filling

½ cup crème fraîche

3 large egg yolks, beaten

2 tbsp chopped dill

1 tsp prepared horseradish

2 tsp drained nonpareil capers

½ tsp fresh lemon juice

grated zest of ½ lemon

7oz (200g) skinless smoked trout fillet, flaked

salt and freshly ground black pepper

1 To make the pastry, pulse the flour, butter, and salt in a food processor until the mixture resembles coarse bread crumbs. Add the egg and pulse until it clumps together. Gather into a disk, wrap in plastic wrap, and refrigerate for 30 minutes.

2 Divide the pastry into six portons, and roll out each into a ⅛in (3mm) thick round. Line each pan with a round, trimming the excess dough. Prick the dough with a fork. Refrigerate for 30 minutes.

3 Preheat the oven to 400°F (200°C). Line the tart pans with parchment paper and fill with baking beans. Bake for 10 minutes. Remove the paper and weights and bake until lightly browned, about 10 minutes. Remove from the oven, and reduce the temperature to 375°F (190°C).

4 Mix the crème fraîche, egg yolks, dill, horseradish, capers, and lemon juice and zest. Add the trout and season with salt and pepper. Divide among the tart pans.

5 Bake about 15 minutes, until the filling sets. Cool 5 minutes, remove sides of the pan, and serve hot.

Vegetarian Enchiladas

Serve these right out of the pan with sour cream and salsa

 makes 4 servings

prep 10 mins • cook 30 mins

8 flour tortillas

For the sauce

2 tbsp **olive oil**, plus more for the dish

1 large **onion**, chopped

2 **garlic cloves**, minced

1 tbsp **chili powder**

1 tsp **ground cumin**

1¼ cups **chicken** or beef stock

⅓ cup **tomato paste**

salt and freshly ground **black pepper**

For the filling

1 tbsp **olive oil**

1 **red onion**, finely chopped

1 **red pepper**, seeded and chopped

2 cups shredded **Monterey Jack**

1 To make the sauce, heat the olive oil in a saucepan over medium heat. Cook the onion about 8 minutes, until golden. Stir in the garlic, then the chili powder and cumin. Add the stock and tomato paste and simmer for 5 minutes. Season with salt and pepper.

2 Preheat the oven to 350°F (180°C). To prepare the filling, heat the oil in a frying pan over medium heat. Cook the onion and red pepper for 5 minutes, until tender.

3 Lightly oil a 2qt (2 liter) baking dish. Spread each tortilla with a spoonful of sauce. Top with equal amounts of the filling and about 3 tbsp cheese. Roll up each tortilla and place in the dish.

4 Spread the remaining sauce over the tortillas, and sprinkle with the remaining cheese. Bake for 20 minutes, or until the sauce is bubbling and the cheese has melted.

VARIATION

Chicken Enchiladas

In step 3, add some shredded, seasoned chicken onto the sauce.

Savory Onion Tart

Anchovies give a salty kick to this mild onion tart

 makes 4–6 servings

prep 15 mins, plus chilling • cook 1 hr 15 mins

8in (20cm) tart pan with removable bottom

freeze, without the anchovies, for up to 3 months

⅓ package **refrigerated pie dough**

3 tbsp **olive oil**

1lb (450g) **onions**, thinly sliced

3oz (85g) **farmer's cheese**

2 large **eggs**

½ cup **half and half**

1 tsp **caraway** or cumin seeds, crushed

salt and freshly ground **black pepper**

one 2oz (60g) can **anchovy fillets in oil**, drained and rinsed

● **Prepare ahead** The tart can be baked a few hours in advance then reheated in a 350°F (180°C) oven for 15 minutes, until hot.

1 Roll out the pie dough on a lightly floured work surface, and use to line the tart pan. Chill for 30 minutes.

2 Heat the oil in a large saucepan over low heat. Add the onions and cover. Cook, stirring occasionally, about 20 minutes, until the onions are meltingly tender. Uncover and cook for 4–5 minutes more, or until golden. Let cool.

3 Meanwhile, preheat the oven to 400°F (200°C). Line the tart crust with parchment paper and fill with pie weights. Bake about 10 minutes, until set. Remove the paper and weights and bake until beginning to brown, about 10 minutes more.

4 Reduce the oven to 350°F (180°C). Spread the onions in the shell. Whisk together the cheese, eggs, half and half, and caraway seeds. Season with salt and pepper and pour over the onions. Arrange the anchovies on top. Bake for 25 minutes, or until the filling is set. Cool slightly then remove the sides of the pan. Serve warm.

Goat Cheese Croustades

Versatile, crisp croustade baskets can host a wide range of different fillings, such as this delicious combination of goat cheese, mint, and tomato

 makes 12 croustades

⏱ prep 10 mins • cook 30 mins

🍳 2in (5cm) round cookie cutter, 12-cup mini-muffin pan

For the croustade baskets

4 slices of thin slice **white** or whole-wheat **bread** sandwich bread

1 tbsp melted **butter** or olive oil

For the filling

6 cherry tomatoes

olive oil, to drizzle

salt and freshly ground **black pepper**

3oz (85g) rindless **goat cheese**

mint leaves, for garnish

● **Prepare ahead** The croustade baskets can be stored in an airtight container for up to 1 week. The roasted tomatoes can be refrigerated for up to 3 days.

1 Preheat the oven to 350°F (180°C). Trim the crusts from the bread. Flatten the slices with a rolling pin, and brush with the melted butter.

2 Using a 2in (5cm) round cookie cutter, stamp out 3 pieces from each slice of bread. Push the bread, butter-side down, firmly into a 12-cup mini-muffin pan. Bake for about 12 minutes, or until well crisped. Remove the croustades from the pan and let cool on a wire rack.

3 Cut each cherry tomato in half. Spread on a baking sheet. Drizzle with oil and season with salt and pepper. Roast for 25 minutes, until the tomatoes are shriveled. Let cool.

4 Divide the goat cheese among the croustades. Top each with a tomato half, and garnish with mint leaves. Serve immediately.

Rich Smoked Salmon Croustades

Horseradish gives this smooth, creamy filling a little bite

🍴 makes 12 croustades

⏱ prep 10 mins, plus chilling • cook 30 mins

½ cup **crème fraîche** or sour cream

1 tbsp prepared **horseradish**

salt and freshly ground **black pepper**

12 **croustade baskets** (see Goat Cheese Croustades, left)

3oz (60g) **smoked salmon**

1oz (25g) red lumpfish caviar

1oz (25g) black lumpfish caviar

1 Mix the crème fraîche and horseradish. Season with salt pepper. Refrigerate for 30 minutes.

2 Fill each croustade basket with a spoonful of the crème fraîche mixture, twist a swirl of smoked salmon on top, and top that with a little caviar. Serve within 1 hour.

> **VARIATION**

Salmon and Tarragon Cream Croustades

Mix ½ cup crème fraîche, 5oz (140g) finely chopped smoked salmon, 1 tbsp chopped tarragon, and the grated zest of ½ a lemon with freshly ground pepper to taste. Chill for 30 minutes, then spoon into croustade baskets and serve within 1 hour.

Soybean Croustades

You'll find shelled frozen soybeans at natural food stores

 makes 12 croustades

⏱ prep 10 mins

½ cup frozen shelled **soy beans**

1 small **shallot**, coarsely chopped

2 tbsp chopped **basil**, plus 12 small leaves for garnish

1 tbsp **olive oil**

1 **garlic clove**, chopped

salt and freshly ground **black pepper**

12 **croustade baskets** (see Goat Cheese Croustades, far left)

● **Prepare ahead** The soybean pesto can be refrigerated for 1 day before serving.

1 Cook the frozen beans in a saucepan of lightly salted boiling water about 5 minutes, until tender. Drain, rinse in cold water, and drain again.

2 Coarsely purée the beans, shallot, basil, oil, and garlic in a blender or food processor. Season with salt and pepper.

3 Divide the bean pesto among the croustades and top each with a basil leaf. Serve immediately.

Chicken Croustades

Tarragon and chicken is a popular combination

 makes 12 croustades

prep 15 mins

1 cooked **chicken breast**, skin removed

2 tbsp **mayonnaise**

1 tsp chopped **tarragon**, plus sprigs, to garnish

1 tsp **whole-grain mustard**

1 tsp fresh **lemon** juice

salt and freshly ground **black pepper**

12 **croustade baskets** (see Goat Cheese Croustades, far left)

● **Prepare ahead** The chicken filling can be refrigerated for several hours before using.

1 **Shred the chicken** into small pieces.

2 **Mix the mayonnaise**, tarragon, mustard, and lemon juice together in a bowl. Add the chicken and mix again. Season with salt and pepper.

3 **Divide the mixture** among the croustades. Garnish each one with a tarragon sprig. Serve immediately.

Roast Beef Croustades

Roast beef with a creamy mustard mayo combine in this party dish

🍴 makes 12 croustades

🕐 prep 15 mins

3 tbsp **olive oil**

8oz (225g) **fillet mignon**

salt and freshly ground **black pepper**

12 **cherry tomatoes**

1 tsp **sugar**

12 **croustade baskets** (see Goat Cheese Croustades, far left)

1 tbsp chopped **chives**, to garnish

For the mustard mayonnaise

⅓ cup **mayonnaise**

2 tbsp **Dijon mustard**

1 **Preheat the oven** to 400°F (200°C). Heat 2 tbsp olive oil in an ovenproof frying pan over high heat. Season the beef with salt and pepper. Place in the pan and cook, turning once, for about 3 minutes, until seared on both sides. Transfer the pan to the oven and roast for about 10 minutes, until an instant-read thermometer inserted in the center of the roast reads 130°F (55°C). Let cool. Carve the beef into small strips.

2 **Meanwhile**, place the tomatoes, cut-side up, on a baking sheet. Sprinkle with the remaining 1 tbsp oil, sugar, and some salt and pepper. Roast for 30 minutes.

3 **To make** the mustard mayonnaise, combine the mayonnaise and the mustard in a bowl and mix well.

4 **To assemble** the croustades, spoon the mayonnaise mustard into the croustade baskets. Top each with the beef and 2 cherry tomato halves. Sprinkle with chives and serve immediately.

Crab Croustades

Lightly spiced crabmeat in a crispy case

🍴 makes 12 croustades

🕐 prep 10 mins

3 tbsp **mayonnaise**

1 **scallion**, finely chopped

2 tsp peeled and grated fresh **ginger**

grated zest and juice of 1 **lime**

1 tbsp chopped **cilantro**

8oz (230g) **crabmeat**

salt and freshly ground **black pepper**

12 **croustade baskets** (see Goat Cheese Croustades, far left)

1 fresh **red chile**, seeded and cut into thin strips, to garnish

● **Prepare ahead** The crab filling can be refrigerated for several hours before using.

1 **In a bowl**, mix the mayonnaise, scallion, ginger, lime zest and juice, and cilantro. Add the crabmeat and mix again. Season with salt and black pepper.

2 **Divide** the mixture among the croustades. Garnish each with a strip of red chile. Serve immediately.

Fava Beans with Ham

Spanish *habas con jamón* is a popular snack dish of soft beans and chewy, salty cured ham

- serves 6 as a tapas dish, or 4 as an appetizer
- prep 10 mins • cook 30 mins

2lb 2oz (900g) fresh **fava beans**, removed from their pods

2 tbsp **olive oil**

1 **onion**, finely chopped

7oz (200g) **Serrano ham** or prosciutto, diced

2 **garlic cloves**, minced

½ cup **dry white wine**

1 cup **chicken** or vegetable **stock**

● **Prepare ahead** The dish can be prepared up to 2 days in advance. The flavors improve with reheating.

1 **In a saucepan** of lightly salted, boiling water, cook the beans until the skins loosen, about 2 minutes. Drain and rinse under cold running water. Slip off the skins.

2 **Heat the oil** in a frying pan over medium heat. Add the onion and cook, stirring often, about 4 minutes, or until translucent. Add the ham and garlic, increase the heat to medium-high, and cook for about 2 minutes more, or until the ham begins to brown.

3 **Add the beans** and the wine. Cook, stirring occasionally, until the wine is almost completely reduced, about 8 minutes. Stir in the stock and simmer over medium-low heat for about 10 minutes, until the stock is reduced by half. Serve hot.

Salted Roasted Almonds

Almendras tostadas are served with drinks in Spain

- makes about 8 servings
- prep 5 mins • cook 15–25 mins

2 cups **blanched whole almonds**

1 tbsp **salt**, preferably fine sea salt

2 tsp sweet, hot, or smoked **paprika**

1 **Preheat the oven** to 350°F (175°C).

2 **Spread the almonds** on a baking sheet. Sprinkle them with a little water and toss on the sheet. (The water will help the salt and paprika cling to the nuts.) Sprinkle the nuts with the salt and the paprika, tossing to ensure that they are all evenly coated. Spread out the nuts in an even layer.

3 **Place in the oven** and roast the almonds, stirring occasionally, for 15 to 20 minutes. Transfer to a bowl and serve warm or cooled to room temperature.

VARIATION

Spiced Nuts

Any of your favorite nuts can be used. Try cashews, skinned hazelnuts, or Brazils. Paprika comes in sweet, hot, and smoked varieties, so use whichever you prefer.

Chicken Livers in Sherry

In *higaditos al Jeréz*, the sweet sherry perfectly offsets the intense richness of the livers

- makes 4 appetizer servings
- prep 5 mins • cook 8 mins

1 cup **sweet sherry**

2 tsp **olive oil**

1 **garlic clove**, crushed

8oz (225g) **chicken livers**, trimmed

salt and freshly ground **pepper**

2 tbsp chopped **parsley**, to garnish

1 **Boil the sherry** in a small saucepan over a high heat until it is reduced to about 2 tbsp.

2 **Heat the oil** in a large frying pan over medium heat. Add the garlic and cook for 1 minute. Increase the heat to medium-high, and add the chicken livers. Cook, stirring often, for 3–4 minutes, or until the livers are dark brown and crusty but still slightly pink on the inside. Season with salt and pepper.

3 **Transfer to a serving dish**. Pour the reduced sherry on top, sprinkle with the parsley, and serve hot.

● **Good with** small pieces of toast, or speared on skewers, as an appetizer.

Peas with Ham

Guisantes con jamón is a classic tapas dish with delicious sweet and savory flavors

- makes 6–8 servings
- prep 5 mins • cook 15 mins

2 tbsp **olive oil**

1 **onion**, finely diced

7oz (200g) **Serrano ham** or prosciutto, diced

¾ cup **canned crushed tomatoes**

1 tsp **sweet paprika**

one 1lb (450g) bag **frozen baby peas**, thawed

1 **garlic clove**, crushed

1 tbsp finely chopped **parsley**

salt and freshly ground **black pepper**

⅔ cup **dry white wine**

1 Heat the oil in a frying pan. Cook the onion for 5 minutes, stirring frequently, until translucent.

2 Increase the heat. Add the ham and cook for about 3 minutes until it begins to brown. Stir in the tomatoes and paprika. Bring to a boil, then simmer for 3 minutes, stirring frequently. Mix in the peas.

3 Mash the garlic, parsley, and ½ tsp salt together, then stir in the wine. Add to the pan, and season with pepper. Simmer for 5 minutes more, and serve hot.

Baked BBQ Wings with Blue Cheese Dip

A variation on Buffalo wings, these sticky chicken wings are served with a tangy dip

- makes 4 servings
- prep 20 mins, plus marinating • cook 25 mins
- blender

2 lb (900g) **chicken wings**

salt and freshly ground **black pepper**

2 tbsp **olive oil**

2 tbsp **tomato paste**

1 tbsp dried **oregano**

2 tsp **light brown sugar**

1 **shallot**, finely chopped

1 **garlic clove**, crushed

½ tsp **hot red pepper sauce**

For the dip

⅔ cup **sour cream**

½ cup crumbled **blue cheese**, such as Roquefort or Danish blue

2 tbsp snipped **chives**

1 tbsp fresh **lemon juice**

● **Prepare ahead** The chicken can be coated in the tomato mixture and refrigerated for up to 6 hours.

1 Season the wings with salt and pepper. Process the oil, tomato paste, oregano, brown sugar, shallot, garlic, and hot pepper sauce in a blender until smooth. Combine the wings and sauce in a large self-sealing plastic bag, and coat the wings with the sauce. Let stand at room temperature for no more than 90 minutes.

2 Preheat the oven to 375°F (190°C). Spread the chicken on an oiled baking sheet. Bake for 20 minutes. Turn the wings and bake for 15 minutes more, until the wings show no sign of pink when pierced at the bone.

3 Meanwhile, mix the dip ingredients in a bowl. Serve the chicken wings hot, with the dip on the side, and a bowl to collect the bones.

Chicken Satay

The authentic version is made with Indonesian soy sauce, *kecap manis*, but Chinese or Japanese soy sauce can also be used

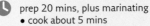
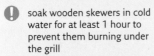

- makes 6 servings
- prep 20 mins, plus marinating • cook about 5 mins
- soak wooden skewers in cold water for at least 1 hour to prevent them burning under the grill
- wooden or thin metal skewers

3 boneless and skinless **chicken breasts**

2 tbsp **kecap manis** (available at Asian grocers) or **soy sauce**

4 tsp **light** or **dark brown sugar**

1 tbsp fresh **lime** juice

¾in (2cm) piece fresh **ginger**, peeled and shredded

2 **garlic cloves**, crushed

2 tsp **ground coriander**

1 tsp minced **lemongrass**

½ tsp **ground cumin**

vegetable oil

For the satay sauce

1 cup (250g) smooth or chunky **peanut butter**

2 **garlic cloves**, finely chopped

¾ cup well shaken **coconut milk**

1 tbsp **soy sauce**, preferably dark

1 tbsp **dark brown sugar**

½in (1cm) piece fresh **ginger**, peeled and shredded

1 tbsp fresh **lemon** juice

⅛ tsp **cayenne pepper**

salt and freshly ground **pepper**

lime wedges, for serving

● **Prepare ahead** The marinating chicken and the sauce can be refrigerated for up to 1 day.

1 **Cut the chicken** into thin strips across the grain of the

meat. Spread the strips out in a shallow, nonmetallic dish.

2 **In a small bowl**, mix kecap manis, brown sugar, lime juice, ginger, garlic, coriander, lemongrass, cumin, salt, and 2 tsp vegetable oil. Pour over the chicken and toss to coat. Cover the dish with plastic wrap and marinate in the refrigerator for at least 4 hours.

3 **To make the satay sauce**, put the peanut butter with half of the garlic in a small saucepan and cook over low heat for 2 minutes. Add the coconut milk, soy sauce, brown sugar, and ginger, and cook, stirring, for 2 minutes, or until heated through.

4 **Add the lemon juice** and remaining garlic, and season to taste with cayenne pepper, salt, and pepper. Let the sauce cool, cover with plastic wrap, and refrigerate.

5 **When ready to cook**, thread the chicken on soaked and drained wooden skewers. In a pan over low heat, reheat the satay sauce, stirring frequently.

6 **Brush the chicken** with oil and broil or grill on an outdoor grill for 5 minutes, turning over once or twice, until the chicken is opaque throughout. Garnish with lime wedges and serve hot with satay sauce.

VARIATION

Beef Satay

1lb 20oz (500g) beef, trimmed of any extra fat and cut into strips, then used in the recipe above, make a delicious alternative to chicken.

Falafel

These chickpea fritters can be enjoyed tucked into pita bread

- makes 12 falafels
- prep 25 mins, plus overnight soaking and 30 mins to set aside • cook 15 mins

1 heaping cup **dried chickpeas**, soaked overnight in cold water

2 tbsp finely chopped **parsley**

2 tbsp fresh **lemon** juice

1 tbsp **tahini**

1 **garlic clove**, minced

1 tsp **ground cumin**

1 tsp **ground turmeric**

1 tsp **ground coriander**

1 tsp **salt**

½ tsp **cayenne pepper**

vegetable oil, for deep-frying

1 **Drain the soaked chickpeas**. Process the chickpeas with the other ingredients until finely chopped but not puréed.

2 **Transfer to a bowl**. Let stand for at least 30 minutes (or up to 8 hours), covered in the refrigerator.

3 **Pour enough oil** into a large saucepan to come 2in (5cm) up the sides and heat over high heat to 350°F (170°C).

4 **Moisten your hands** with water and shape the mixture into 12 slightly flat balls. In batches, deep-fry in the oil about 3 minutes, or until golden. Transfer to paper towels to drain. Serve hot.

Classic Chinese Wontons

Wontons are healthy and great to have ready in the freezer

- 🍴 makes 20
- 🕐 prep 20 mins • cook 10 mins
- 📇 steamer, bamboo preferred, and a wire rack
- ❄️ uncooked wontons can be frozen for up to 1 month

6oz (175g) ground pork

2 scallions, white and green parts, finely chopped

4oz (115g) shiitake mushrooms, stemmed and finely chopped

½in (1cm) piece fresh ginger, peeled and shredded

½ tsp Asian sesame oil

1 tbsp chopped cilantro

1 tbsp soy sauce

freshly ground pepper

1 large egg, beaten

20 wonton wrappers

cornstarch, for the baking sheet

lettuce or napa cabbage

● **Prepare ahead** The wontons can be covered with plastic wrap and refrigerated several hours in advance.

1 Mix the pork, scallions, mushrooms, ginger, sesame oil, cilantro, soy sauce, and pepper.

2 Spoon a teaspoon of the pork mixture into the center of a wrapper. Brush the edges lightly with egg, fold the wrapper in half, and crimp the edges to seal. Transfer to a cornstarch-dusted baking sheet.

3 Fill a large saucepan about one-fourth full of water and bring to a boil. Line a steamer with lettuce and add the wontons. Place the steamer on a rack so it sits above the water. Cover and steam the dumplings for 10 minutes or until cooked through. Serve at once.

● **Good with** soy sauce or your favorite dipping sauce.

VARIATION

Wonton Soup
Instead of steaming the wontons, cook them in a rich chicken broth, along with such vegetables as sliced bok choy, baby corn, or chopped Chinese broccoli. Simmer 10 minutes or until wontons are cooked.

Devils on Horseback

Everyone enjoys these popular cocktail party treats

- 🍴 makes 16 appetizers
- 🕐 prep 15 mins • cook 12 mins
- 📇 wooden toothpicks

3 tbsp mango chutney

1 tsp dry mustard

pinch of cayenne pepper, plus more for garnish

salt and freshly ground pepper

16 pitted dried plums (prunes)

8 bacon strips, each cut in half crosswise

4 slices of firm white sandwich bread

butter for spreading

● **Prepare ahead** Place the wrapped dried plums on a baking sheet, and refrigerate for up to 4 hours before baking.

1 Preheat the oven to 425°F (220°C). Mix the chutney, mustard, and cayenne, seasoning to taste with salt and pepper.

2 Make a small slit in each dried plum and stuff with a little of the chutney mixture. Wrap each with a bacon strip and secure with a toothpick. Place the wrapped dried plums on an oiled baking sheet.

3 Bake for 10–12 minutes, turning them after 5 minutes, until the bacon is crisp.

4 Meanwhile, toast the bread. Remove the crusts, and using a 2in (5cm) cookie cutter, cut out 12 rounds. Butter the toast rounds and top each one with a bacon-wrapped plum. Sprinkle each with a little cayenne pepper and serve warm.

VARIATION

Angels on Horseback
Replace the prunes with 16 shucked oysters, and leave out the chutney. Lightly season the oysters with black pepper, then wrap a strip of bacon around each, securing it with a toothpick. Place on a baking sheet, and bake for 5–7 minutes, taking care not to overcook the oysters. Add a squeeze of fresh lemon juice, and serve hot.

Smoked Salmon Rolls

These easy party appetizers can be served with drinks or as a first course alongside a salad

- makes 16 rolls
- prep 30 mins
- low GI

(12oz) 350g **smoked salmon** slices

1 **cucumber**

4oz (110g) **cream cheese**, softened

2 tbsp **mayonnaise**

grated zest of ½ **lemon**

1 tsp chopped **dill**

1 tsp prepared **horseradish**

dill sprigs and **lemon** wedges, to serve

● **Prepare ahead** If making ahead, stand the rolls on end on a large plate and cover tightly with plastic wrap to prevent them from drying out. Chill until ready to serve.

1 **Cut the smoked salmon** into 16 strips about 5 x 1½in (12cm x 4cm). Cut the cucumber into sticks measuring 1½in (4cm) by ¼in (5mm).

2 **Combine** the cream cheese, mayonnaise, lemon zest, dill, and horseradish together in a bowl and mash together until ingredients are fully combined.

3 **Lay the smoked salmon** strips on the work surface. Spread with the cheese mixture, leaving 1in (2.5cm) empty at one short end. Lay a cucumber stick about ½in (1cm) from the cheese-spread end, and roll up tightly.

4 **Arrange the rolls** on a serving platter. Garnish with dill sprigs and lemon wedges, and serve chilled.

VARIATIONS

Smoked Salmon and Asparagus Rolls

Replace the cucumber sticks with 16 thin asparagus spears, cut about 1½in (4cm) long. Boil until just tender, toss with 2 tbsp vinaigrette, and let cool.

Smoked Salmon and Shrimp Rolls

Replace the cream cheese mixture and cucumber sticks with 16 cooked shrimp. Mix 3 tbsp mayonnaise, 2 tsp tomato ketchup, 1 tsp fresh lemon juice, and a dash of hot red pepper sauce. Toss the shrimp in the mayonnaise and roll in the smoked salmon strips.

Smoked Salmon and Egg Rolls

Replace the cream cheese mixture with 4 chopped hard-boiled eggs mixed with 2 tbsp mayonnaise and 1 tsp Dijon mustard.

Inside-out Smoked Salmon Rolls

Peel wide strips of cucumber using a vegetable peeler. Lay the strips out and spread the cream cheese mixture over each one. Scatter over finely chopped smoked salmon and roll up.

Figs with Prosciutto

The sweet figs contrast with salty prosciutto and the peppery tang of arugula in these one-bite party snacks

- makes 24
- prep 10 mins
- 24 wooden skewers

12 ripe **figs**

6 large slices of **prosciutto**

24 **arugula** leaves

freshly ground **black pepper**

Parmesan cheese shavings

● **Prepare ahead** The wrapped figs can be refrigerated up to 4 hours before servings.

1 **Cut each fig** in half and each slice of ham into 4 long strips.

2 **Thread** 1 fig half, 1 prosciutto strip, and 1 arugula leaf onto a wooden skewer. Season with pepper.

3 **Scatter** with Parmesan shavings and arugula leaves and serve.

VARIATION

Cantaloupe with Prosciutto

Substitute cubes of cantaloupe, or other juicy, ripe melon for the figs.

Kibbeh

Serve these crisp-fried dumplings with a yogurt dip

- makes 12 kibbeh
- prep 30 mins, plus chilling • cook 25 mins
- soak the bulgur wheat for 20 mins in cold water, then drain, and squeeze out excess water before using
- deep-frying thermometer

For the filling

2 tbsp **olive oil**

1 small **onion**, finely chopped

3oz (85g) **ground sirloin** or ground lamb

1 tbsp **pine nuts**, lightly toasted

½ tsp **ground cinnamon**

salt and freshly ground **black pepper**

For the shells

1 cup **bulgur** (cracked wheat), soaked in cold water, drained, and pressed

9oz (250g) **ground sirloin** or ground lamb

½ tsp **ground allspice**

salt and freshly ground **black pepper**

vegetable oil, for deep-frying

1 **To make the filling**, heat the oil in a frying pan over medium heat. Add the onion and cook about 6 minutes, until golden. Add the ground sirloin and cook, breaking up the meat, about 5 minutes, until lightly browned. Stir in the pine nuts and cinnamon and season with salt and pepper. Let cool.

2 **Purée the onion** in a food processor. Add the bulgur, raw beef, and allspice and season with salt and pepper. Process until the mixture can be kneaded like a dough.

3 **Moisten your hands** with water. Flatten an egg-sized piece of the shell mixture to about ¼in (5mm) thickness. Top with a portion of the filling and enclose the filling with the shell mixture. Shape the ends into points. Continue with the remaining shell mixture and filling to make a total of 12 kibbeh. Cover and refrigerate for at least 1 hour.

4 **Halfway fill** a large frying pan with oil and heat over high heat to 350°F (170°C). In batches, add the kibbeh and deep-fry about 3 minutes, until golden brown. Drain on paper towels and serve hot.

Asian Meatballs with Peanut Sauce

The sweet peanut sauce is a perfect accompaniment to these savory bites

- makes 6–8 servings
- prep 15 mins • cook 20 mins

For the peanut sauce

1 tbsp **vegetable oil**

1 tsp **Thai red curry paste**

2 tbsp **crunchy peanut butter**

1 tbsp **light brown sugar**

1 tbsp fresh **lemon** juice

1 cup well-stirred **canned coconut milk**

For the meatballs

1lb (450g) **ground sirloin** or pork, or a combination of both

1 tbsp chopped **cilantro**

1 tbsp **Thai red curry paste**

1 tbsp fresh **lemon** juice

1 tbsp **Thai fish sauce**

1 tsp minced tender **lemongrass**

1 large **egg**

1 **garlic clove**, minced

salt and freshly ground **black pepper**

rice flour, for dusting

vegetable oil, for deep-frying

lime wedges, for garnish

● **Prepare ahead** The uncooked, uncoated meatballs can be covered and refrigerated for up to 1 day.

1 **To make the peanut sauce**, heat the vegetable oil in a small saucepan over medium heat. Add the curry paste and cook for 30 seconds, until fragrant. Stir in the peanut butter, brown sugar, and lemon juice, then gradually stir in the coconut milk. Bring to a boil, reduce the heat to low, and simmer for 5 minutes, or until thickened. If it becomes too thick, stir in a little water. Keep warm.

2 **For the meatballs**, combine the ground beef, cilantro, curry paste, lemon juice, fish sauce, lemongrass, egg, and garlic, and season with salt and pepper. Roll the mixture into small balls about the size of a walnut. Dust each meatball with the rice flour.

3 **Heat enough oil** to come halfway up the sides of a large frying pan and heat over high heat until the oil shimmers. In batches, fry the meatballs for about 3 minutes, until browned and cooked through. Using a slotted spoon, transfer to paper towels to drain. Serve hot, with the warm peanut sauce and lime wedges.

Sausage Rolls

Serve these at a cocktail party—they are a sure bet to disappear

- makes 24 rolls
- prep 40 mins, plus chilling • cook 10–12 mins
- freeze, unbaked, for up to 3 months

½ package thawed frozen **puff pastry**

1½ lb (675g) bulk **pork sausage**

1 **onion**, finely chopped

1 tbsp chopped **thyme**

grated zest of 1 **lemon**

1 tsp Dijon **mustard**

1 large **egg** plus 1 large **egg yolk**

salt and freshly ground **black pepper**

1 Preheat the oven to 400°F (200°C). Line a baking sheet with parchment paper.

2 Roll the puff pastry on a lightly floured work surface into a 12in (30cm) square. Cut in half.

3 Combine the sausage, onion, thyme, lemon zest, mustard, and egg yolk, and season with salt and pepper.

4 Beat the egg. Form half of the sausage mixture into a 12in (30cm) long sausage shape. Place in the center of one pastry strip. Brush the pastry with beaten egg, roll up to enclose the sausage, and pinch the seam closed. Repeat with the remaining pastry and sausage mixture. Cut each roll crosswise into 12 pieces.

5 Place the rolls, seam down, on the baking sheet. Using kitchen scissors, snip 2 cuts in the top of each roll. Brush with beaten egg. Bake for 10–12 minutes, or until golden brown. Serve warm.

● **Good with** a spicy mustard dipping sauce.

Smoked Chicken Mousse on Endive

Simple to make, these elegant hors d'oeuvres look wonderful and taste great

- makes 12 servings
- prep 10 mins

8oz (225g) smoked **chicken breasts**

3 tbsp **mayonnaise**

2 tbsp Dijon **mustard**

1 tbsp chopped **tarragon**

zest and juice of ½ **lemon**

sea salt and freshly ground **black pepper**

2 Belgian **endive**

1 red Belgian endive

chopped **chives**, to garnish

1 Discard the skin and bone from the smoked chicken. Dice the smoked chicken meat. Combine the chicken, mayonnaise, mustard, lemon zest and juice, and tarragon in a food processor and process until very finely chopped. Season with salt and pepper.

2 To serve, separate the endive leaves. Place spoonfuls of the mousse onto the ends of the wide ends of the endive leaves, and sprinkle with the chives. Serve immediately.

● **Prepare ahead** The mousse can be refrigerated for up to 1 day. The filled endive leaves should be served within 1 hour.

Melon and Nectarines with Parma Ham

Prosciutto is the Italian word for ham, Parma ham being a type of air-cured ham

 makes 8–12 servings

🕐 prep 15 mins

🍱 wooden toothpicks

½ small **honeydew melon**

4 **nectarines**, stoned

8oz (225g) thinly sliced **Parma ham**

freshly ground **black pepper**

● **Prepare ahead** These canapés can be made several hours in advance. Chill until required.

1 **Cut the melon** into 16 wedge-shaped slices. Cut off the rind. Cut each nectarine into wedges.

2 **Cut the Parma ham** into thin strips. Thread a strip of ham and a piece of fruit on to toothpicks.

3 **Arrange on a serving** platter and season with a little pepper.

VARIATION

Melon, Fig, and Prosciutto Salad

Arrange arugala leaves on 4 plates. Cut the melon into 16 wedge-shaped slices, as above, and divide between the serving plates. Cut 4 figs in quarters but not through the base. Open out the figs and place one in the center of each plate. Cut 8 prosciutto slices in half lengthways and arrange between the melon slices. Sprinkle with pepper and drizzle with balsamic vinegar. Using a potato peeler, shave 3½oz (100g) Pecorino cheese over the top.

Seven Grain Bread

Full of healthful goodness, this chewy bread includes seven grains, but there is some flexibility. If you don't have one of the grains, you can replace it with others that you have at hand

- makes 2 loaves
- prep 20 mins, plus 2 risings • cook 35–40 mins
- 9 x 5in (23 x 13cm) loaf pans
- can be frozen up to 6 months

½ cup **bulgur (cracked) wheat**

⅓ cup **polenta** or **stone-ground yellow cornmeal**

¼ cup **millet**

¼ cup **quinoa**

1¾ cups **boiling water**

1¼ cups **whole milk**

¼ cup **maple syrup** or **honey**

½ cup cold **water**

2 tbsp **vegetable oil**, plus more for the bowl

2 tsp **salt**

3¼ cups **bread flour**

⅔ cup **old-fashioned (rolled) oats**

⅔ cup **rye, wheat, barley**, or **triticale flakes**

two ¼oz (7g) envelopes **instant yeast**

1¾ cups **whole wheat flour**, as needed, plus more for kneading

⅓ cup cooked **rice**, preferably brown rice (optional)

1 Combine the bulgur, polenta, millet, and quinoa in a large bowl. Add the boiling water and stir. Let stand, stirring often, for about 20 minutes.

2 Add the milk and honey to the cooled grain mixture, along with the cold water, the oil, and salt. Stir in the bread flour, oats, rye flakes, and yeast.

3 Stir in enough of the whole wheat flour to make a heavy and sticky dough that is difficult to stir. Dust the work surface with whole wheat flour and turn out the dough. Knead for 5 minutes, adding more flour as necessary (whole grain dough will remain a little sticky). Add the cooked rice, if using, and knead 5 minutes more or until the dough is supple and tacky.

4 Coat the inside of a bowl with oil. Shape the dough into a ball, place in the bowl, and turn to coat with oil. Cover the bowl with plastic wrap. Let stand in a warm place about 1 hour, or until the dough doubles in volume.

5 Lightly oil two 9 x 5in (23 x 13cm) loaf pans. Knead the dough on the floured work surface for 1 minute. Cut the dough into 2 pieces and form each into a ball. Working with one ball at a time, use a floured rolling pin to roll the dough into a 9in x 10in (23cm x 26cm) rectangle. Starting at a short side, roll up the dough, and pinch the long seam to seal. Place, seam side down, in the pan, and press to fill the pan with dough. Cover with a clean kitchen towel. Let rise in a warm place about 30 minutes, or until the dough reaches the tops of the pans.

6 Preheat the oven to 425°F (220°C). Gently brush the tops of the loaves with oil. Bake for 10 minutes. Reduce the heat to 375°F (190°C) and continue baking for 25 to 30 minutes or until the unmolded loaves sound hollow when tapped on the bottom. Cool briefly, then remove the loaves from the pans and cool completely on wire racks.

VARIATION

Seven Grain Rolls
Cut the risen dough into rolls and follow the rest of step 5. Bake for 20 minutes or until they sound hollow when tapped on the base.

Walnut Bread

In France, this savory bread is a traditional accompaniment to the cheese course

 makes 2 loaves

prep 20 mins, plus 2 risings • cook 35–45 mins

can be frozen up to 6 months

1¾ cups tepid **water**

1 tbsp **walnut oil**, plus a little extra for the bowl

1½ tsp **salt**

1 tsp **sugar**

2⅓ cups whole wheat flour

one ¼oz (7g) envelope **instant yeast**

1⅓ cups **bread flour**, as needed, plus more for kneading

1¼ cups **coarsely chopped walnuts**

1 **Combine the water**, walnut oil, salt, and sugar. Stir in the whole wheat flour, yeast, then enough of the bread flour to make a dough that is difficult to stir.

2 **Knead the dough** on a floured surface for 5–8 minutes, adding more flour when necessary, until the dough is smooth and elastic. Shape the dough into a ball.

3 **Coat the inside** of a large bowl with oil. Add the dough, and turn to coat with oil. Cover with plastic wrap and let stand in a warm place about 1 hour, or until doubled in volume.

4 **Punch down the dough**, turn it out onto a floured surface, and knead for 1 minute. Pat the dough into a rectangle and sprinkle with the walnuts. Roll the dough, and knead until the nuts are distributed.

5 **Lightly flour** a large baking sheet. Cut the dough in half and form each into a ball. Transfer to the baking sheet and flatten lightly. Loosely cover with plastic wrap, and let rise for 15 minutes, until puffy.

6 **Preheat the oven** to 425°F (220°C). Lightly dust the balls of dough with flour. Cut a square, no more than ¼in (5cm) deep, in the top of each. Bake for 10 minutes. Reduce the temperature to 375°F (190°C) and bake for 25–35 minutes or until the bases sound hollow when tapped. Transfer to a wire rack and cool.

Herb and Olive Bread

Bursting with Mediterranean flavors, this bread is delicious dipped in olive oil

makes 2 loaves

prep 15 mins, plus rising • cook 25–30 mins

2 cups tepid **water**

2 tbsp **extra virgin olive oil**, plus extra for brushing

1½ tsp **salt**

4 cups **unbleached flour**, as needed

one ¼oz (7g) envelope **instant yeast**

1 cup pitted and coarsely chopped **Kalamata olives**

4 tbsp finely chopped **herbs**, such as **marjoram**, **parsley**, **rosemary**, or **thyme**

1 **Combine the** water with the oil and salt in a large bowl. Stir in 3 cups of the flour and the yeast, then enough of the remaining flour to make a stiff dough.

2 **Turn out** the dough onto a lightly floured surface. Knead, adding more flour as needed, for 10 minutes, until the dough is smooth and supple. Pat and stretch the dough into a thin rectangle. Sprinkle the olives and herbs over the dough. Roll the dough into a cylinder, then knead for a few more minutes until the ingredients are evenly distributed. Shape the dough into a ball.

3 **Lightly oil** a bowl. Add the dough and turn to coat with oil. Cover with plastic wrap and let stand in a warm place about 1¼ hours, or until doubled in volume.

4 **Dust a large** baking sheet with flour. Punch down the dough, turn it out on to a lightly floured surface and knead for 1 minute. Cut the dough in half. Shape each into a log about 10in (25cm) long and pinch the seams closed. Transfer the logs to the baking sheet and press down lightly. Cover with plastic wrap and let stand about 30 minutes, or until puffy.

5 **Preheat the oven** to 425°F (220°C). Lightly brush the loaves with oil. Use a sharp knife to score 5 shallow slits on top of each. Bake for 25 minutes, or until the tops are golden brown and the bottoms sound hollow when tapped. Transfer to a wire rack and cool completely.

Braided Fruit Bread

This rich fruit bread makes a lovely afternoon treat—and it's also great toasted

- makes 1 large loaf
- prep 35 mins, plus rising • cook 40 mins

one ¼oz (7g) envelope **instant yeast**

2 tbsp warm (110°F/38°C) **water**

1 cup **heavy cream**

½ cup **sugar**

2 tsp **pure vanilla extract**

grated zest of 1 **lemon**

2 tsp **salt**

3 large **eggs**

3 cups **unbleached flour**, as needed, plus more for kneading

vegetable oil, for greasing

1⅓ cup **raisins**

2 tsp **whole milk**

1 **To make the dough**, sprinkle the yeast over the warm water in a small bowl. Let stand 5 minutes, then stir to dissolve. Pour into a large bowl. Add the cream, sugar, vanilla, lemon zest, and salt. Separate one of the eggs, and cover and refrigerate the yolk. Add the egg white and 2 whole eggs to the bowl and whisk until combined with the other ingredients.

2 **Stir in enough** of the flour to make a soft, slightly sticky dough. Turn out onto a lightly floured work surface and knead for about 8 minutes, or until the dough is smooth and supple. (The dough can also be mixed and kneaded in a heavy-duty electric mixer.) Gather into a ball, place in an oiled bowl, and turn to coat the dough. Cover the bowl with plastic wrap. Let stand in a warm place about 1½ hours until doubled in volume.

3 **Line a baking sheet** with parchment paper. Punch the dough. Transfer to the work surface and knead in the raisins. Take two-thirds of the dough and make 3 long ropes, each about 16in (40cm) long. Braid them together and place on the baking sheet. Using your fingertips, press a gutter lengthwise down the center of the braid.

4 **Beat together** the reserved egg yolk and milk. Brush the gutter with a little of the egg mixture. Divide the remaining dough into 3 equal portions. Roll into thin ropes, about 14in (35cm) long and braid. Place the smaller braid into the gutter on the larger braid. Cover loosely with plastic wrap and let stand in a warm place about 40 minutes, until almost doubled in volume.

5 **Preheat the oven** to 350°F (180°C). Uncover and brush the loaf with the egg glaze. Bake about 35 minutes or until golden brown and the loaf sounds hollow when tapped on the bottom. Transfer to a wire rack and cool.

● **Good with** a little butter and good strawberry jam.

Brioche

The ideal morning bread

- makes 12 individual brioche
- prep 35-45 mins, plus rising • cook 15-20 mins
- 12 x 3in (7.5cm) brioche molds

3 cups **bread flour**

¼ cup **sugar**

one ¼oz (7g) envelope **instant yeast**

2 tsp **salt**

scant ½ cup tepid **whole milk**

4 large **eggs**, at room temperature

12 tbsp **butter**, softened, plus more for the bowl and molds

1 **Mix** the first 4 ingredients in the bowl of an electric mixer fitted with the dough hook. Add the milk. Mix on medium speed. One at a time, add 3 of the eggs. Add the butter 1 tbsp at a time, letting it incorporate before adding more. Knead the dough for about 8 minutes. Cover with plastic wrap and let stand in a warm place until doubled. Deflate the dough and refrigerate, covered, overnight.

2 **Butter** the molds. Knead the dough; divide into 12 pieces, and cut a quarter off each. Form 12 large and 12 small balls. Place a large ball in a mold. Make a hole in the center with a floured wooden spoon handle. Fit a small ball in the hole. Repeat with the other balls.

3 **Cover and let stand** in a warm place about 2 hours. Preheat the oven to 375°F (190°C). Lightly brush with the remaining beaten egg. Bake for 15-20 minutes. Let cool on a wire rack.

Focaccia

This traditional Italian-style flatbread is easy to make

- makes 6-8 servings
- prep 15 mins, plus rising • cook 40 mins
- freeze for up to 2 months

3½ cups **bread flour**

one ¼oz (7g) envelope **instant yeast**

1 tsp **salt**

1¼ cups tepid **water**, as needed

¼ cup **regular** or extra virgin **olive oil**

3 tbsp **extra virgin olive oil**

½–1 tbsp **coarse sea salt**

1 Mix the flour, yeast, and salt in a large bowl. Make a well in the center and add the water and olive oil. Stir to make a soft dough, adding more water as needed. Knead for 8-10 minutes on a lightly floured work surface until smooth and elastic. Shape into a ball. Transfer to an oiled bowl, turn to coat with oil, and cover with plastic wrap. Let stand in a warm place about 1½ hours, until doubled.

2 Roll the dough out to a rectangle of about 10 x 16in (25 x 40cm). Brush 1½ tbsp of the extra virgin olive oil over half of the dough. Brush water around the edges of the other half and fold the dough in half, to make a rectangle of about 10 x 8in (25 x 20cm). Transfer to a large baking sheet. Press the dough with your knuckles to dimple the surface. Cover the dough with plastic wrap and let stand for about 30-40 minutes, until puffy.

3 Preheat the oven to 400°F (200°C). Drizzle the remaining 1½ tbsp olive oil over the dough, letting it pool in the dimpled dough. Sprinkle with the sea salt. Bake for 30-35 minutes, or until risen and golden.

4 Slide the focaccia onto a wire rack and let cool. Serve the bread the day it is baked, either warm or cooled, cut into chunks.

● **Good with** antipasti.

Crusty White Loaf

This is a basic white bread that has countless uses

- makes 1 large loaf
- prep 35 mins plus rising • cook 40 mins
- 9 x 5in (23 x 13cm) loaf pan
- freeze for up to 3 months

3 cups **bread flour**

1½ tsp **instant yeast**

1¼ tsp **salt**

1 tsp **sugar**

1 tbsp **vegetable** or **olive oil**

1⅔ cups tepid **water**, as needed

1 Stir the flour, yeast, salt, and sugar together in a large bowl. Make a well in the center and pour in the oil. Stir in as much of the water as needed to make a soft dough.

2 Knead on a lightly floured work surface about 8 minutes, until smooth and elastic. Shape into a ball. Turn into a large oiled bowl, and turn to coat. Cover with plastic wrap. Let stand in a warm place about 1 hour, or until doubled in volume.

3 Oil and flour the inside of a 9 x 5in (23 x 13cm) loaf pan, and tap out the excess flour. Punch down the dough. Shape it into a rough rectangle to fit the pan and place in the pan. Cover with plastic wrap and let stand about 30 minutes, or until almost doubled in volume.

4 Preheat the oven to 425°F (220°C). Dust the top of the loaf with flour. Cut a shallow slash down the center of the loaf. Bake for 20 minutes. Reduce the oven temperature to 400°F (200°C) and bake for 20 minutes more until the loaf sounds hollow when removed from the pan and tapped on the bottom. Transfer to a wire rack and let cool.

● **Good with** butter and jam or marmalade for breakfast, or to make a tasty sandwich.

Sourdough Bread with Fennel Seeds

To make this bread, the starter must be prepared a couple of days in advance. Despite the need for forward planning, it is easy to make and the leftover starter can be used to make more loaves

 makes 1 large loaf

 prep 40 mins, plus standing and rising • cook 35 mins

❄ freeze for up to 1 month

For the starter

1½ cups bread flour

one ¼oz (7g) envelope instant yeast

2¼ cups tepid water

For the dough

4¾cups bread flour, plus more for dusting

one ¼oz (7g) envelope instant yeast

1 tbsp sugar

1 tbsp fennel seeds

1 tsp salt

1½ cups tepid water

● **Prepare ahead** Make the sourdough starter 2 days in advance.

1 To make the starter, mix the flour and yeast together in a large bowl. Using a wooden spoon, gradually stir in the water to make a smooth batter. Cover with plastic wrap. Let stand in the kitchen (not necessarily in a warm place) for 2 days, stirring daily. The finished starter will look separated and have a sharp aroma.

2 For the bread, mix the flour, yeast, sugar, fennel, and salt together in a large bowl. Make a well in the center. Stir the starter well. Add ¼ cup of the starter and the water to the flour mixture.

3 Stir until the dough comes together, adding a little more water if needed. Knead on a lightly floured work surface for 8–10 minutes, until the dough is smooth and elastic. Shape into a ball. Transfer to a clean bowl and cover with plastic wrap. Let stand in a warm place until doubled in volume.

4 Oil a large baking sheet. Punch down the dough and knead briefly on a lightly floured surface. Shape into a ball and flatten the top. Transfer to the baking sheet. Cover with plastic wrap and let stand in a warm place until doubled.

5 Preheat the oven to 425°F (220°C). Lightly dust the loaf with flour then, using a sharp knife, slash the top in a diamond pattern. Bake for 15 minutes. Lower the oven temperature to 375°F (190°C) and bake for 20–25 minutes, or until the bread sounds hollow when tapped underneath. Transfer to a wire rack and let cool.

● **Leftover** starter dough can be kept indefinitely, if used once a week and maintained with regular additions of flour and water to invigorate it. Refrigerate the leftover starter in a covered container for up to a week. The day before using, stir in ⅔ cup bread flour and a generous ⅓ cup water, and let stand at room temperature, covered with plastic wrap and not the lid, for 8 hours.

VARIATION

German Sourdough Bread (Bauernbrot)

Replace 2 cups of the bread flour in the dough with rye flour.

Morning Rolls

Easy-to-make soft white rolls that are ideal for breakfast

🍴 makes 16 rolls

🕐 prep 40 mins, plus rising • cook 20 mins

❄ freeze for up to 3 months

3⅔ cups bread flour

one ¼oz (7g) envelope instant yeast

2 tsp light brown sugar

2 tsp salt

1 cup plus 2 tbsp tepid water

1 Combine the flour, yeast, brown sugar, and salt in a large bowl. Make a well in the center and pour in the water. Stir to make a soft dough. Knead well on a lightly floured work surface about 10 minutes, until smooth and elastic. Place in an oiled bowl and turn to coat. Cover with plastic wrap and let stand in a warm place for 1 hour, until doubled.

2 Punch down the dough. Divide into 16 pieces and shape into balls. Arrange 2in (5cm) apart on two lightly oiled baking sheets. Cover loosely with plastic wrap and let stand until puffy, about 30 minutes.

3 Preheat the oven to 400°F (200°F). Bake for 20 minutes, or until they are golden brown and sound hollow when tapped on the bottom.

Crumpets

Yeasty, spongy crumpets are cooked on top of the stove.
Crumpet rings are available online

 makes 8 crumpets

prep 10 mins, plus resting • cook 15 mins

four 4in (10cm) crumpet or English muffin rings

freeze for up to 1 month

scant 1 cup **all-purpose flour**

scant 1 cup **bread flour**

½ tsp **instant yeast**

¾ cup tepid **milk**

¾ cup plus 2 tbsp tepid **water**

½ tsp **baking soda**

½ tsp **salt**

vegetable oil, for brushing

1 Whisk the bread and all-purpose flours and yeast together. Stir in the milk and ¾ tepid water. Cover and let stand in a warm place until the mixture has risen and begun to deflate. Dissolve the baking soda and salt in the remaining tepid water and whisk into the batter.

2 Heat a large griddle over medium heat. Have ready four 4in (10cm) crumpet rings. Lightly oil the pan with oiled paper towels. Put the rings in the pan.

3 Pour the batter into a glass measuring cup. Pour enough batter into each ring to come about ½–¾in (1–2cm) up the sides. Cook for about 8 minutes, or until the batter has set all the way through and the top is covered in holes. If no bubbles appear the batter is too dry; stir a little water into the remaining batter.

4 Lift the rings off the crumpets. Turn the crumpets and cook for about 3 minutes more, or until just golden. Repeat with the remaining batter. Serve warm. (If desired, cool the crumpets, split and toast them.)

Stottie Cakes

Stott means "to bounce" in northeastern British dialect, and these squat rolls are delectably chewy

makes 8 rolls

prep 20 mins, plus rising • cook 15–20 mins

freeze for up to 3 months

3⅔ cups **bread flour**, plus more as needed

1¾ tsp **instant yeast**

1 tsp **sugar**

1½ tsp **salt**

3 tbsp **butter**, at room temperature

¾ cup tepid **water**

⅔ cup tepid **whole milk**

1 Mix the flour, yeast, sugar, and salt in a large bowl. Add the butter and rub it in with your fingertips. Make a well in the center and pour in the tepid water and milk. Stir with a wooden spoon to make a stiff dough. Turn out onto a floured work surface and knead for about 5 minutes, adding more flour as needed, until smooth. Place in an oiled bowl, and turn to coat with oil. Cover with plastic wrap and let stand in a warm place for about 1 hour, or until doubled in volume.

2 Lightly flour 2 large baking sheets. Knead the dough on a work surface until smooth. Divide it into 8 equal balls. Roll each into a flat round about 4in (10cm) wide. Poke a hole through the center of each with the handle end of a wooden spoon. Place on the baking sheet and prick lightly with a fork. Cover with plastic wrap and let stand in a warm place for about 20 minutes until puffy.

3 Preheat the oven to 425°F (220°C). Bake for about 15 minutes, or lightly golden. Transfer the breads to a wire cake rack and cool.

● **Good with** sweet or savory fillings as sandwiches.

● **Leftovers** can be made into bread crumbs for stuffings or toppings. Stottie cakes make great bread pudding.

Whole Wheat Bread

This recipe uses a blend of white and whole wheat flour to make a light, but full-flavored, loaf

 makes 1 loaf

 prep 35 mins, plus rising • cook 40 mins

 9 x 5in (23 x 13cm) loaf pan

1⅔ cups **bread flour**, plus more for kneading

1⅔ cups **whole wheat flour**, plus more to dust

1½ tsp **instant (fast-rising) yeast**

1 tsp **salt**

¾ cup hot **water**

¾ cup **whole milk**

1 tbsp **vegetable oil**, plus more for the bowl

1 tbsp **honey**

1 large **egg**, beaten, to glaze

1 **Mix the bread flour**, whole wheat flour, yeast, and salt in a large bowl. Make a well in the center. Stir the hot water, milk, oil, and honey together and pour into the well. Mix to form a slightly sticky dough. Cover with plastic wrap and let stand for 10 minutes.

2 **Knead the dough** on a lightly floured work surface for 8-10 minutes, or until it is smooth and elastic. (The dough will remain slightly tacky—do no add too much flour.) Shape into a ball, place in a large oiled bowl, and turn to coat with oil. Cover loosely with plastic wrap and let stand in a warm place for 1 hour, or until doubled in size.

3 **Oil and flour** a 9 x 5in (23 x 13cm) loaf pan, and tap out the excess flour. Briefly knead the dough on the work surface. Press the dough into a rough rectangle and place in the pan. Cover loosely with oiled plastic wrap. Let stand in a warm place about for 30 minutes, or until doubled in size.

4 **Preheat the oven** to 425°F (220°C). Brush the egg over the loaf to glaze it, and sprinkle with a little whole wheat flour. Slash a few diagonal slits in the top of the loaf. Bake for 20 minutes. Reduce the oven temperature to 400°F (200°C) and bake for 20 minutes, or until the loaf sounds hollow when tapped on the bottom. Let cool on a wire rack for 10 minutes. Invert and unmold onto the rack and cool completely.

● **Good with** butter and jam.

Moroccan Spiced Flatbreads

Best eaten on the day they are made, these breads can be baked in the oven or cooked on a ridged grill pan

 makes 8 flatbreads

prep 25 mins, plus rising • cook 15 mins

1½ tsp **cumin seeds**, plus more for garnish

1½ tsp **ground coriander**

3¼ cups **bread flour**, plus more for kneading

1 tsp **instant yeast**

1 tsp **salt**

½ cup drained and crushed canned **chickpeas**

2 tbsp chopped **cilantro**

1¼ cups tepid **water**

⅔ cup **plain low-fat yogurt**

1 tbsp **olive oil**, plus more for the bowl and brushing

1 **Toast the cumin seeds** and coriander in a dry pan over medium heat for 1 minute, or until fragrant. Transfer to a large bowl and cool. Add the flour, yeast, and salt and stir. Mix in the chickpeas and cilantro. Make a well in the center, add the water and yogurt, and stir to make a sticky dough. Cover with plastic wrap and let stand for 10 minutes.

2 **Knead the dough** on a lightly floured work surface about 8 minutes, until smooth and elastic. Shape into a ball. Place in an oiled bowl and turn to coat. Cover tightly with plastic wrap and let stand in a warm place about 1 hour, or until doubled in size.

3 **Lightly dust** 2 large baking sheets with flour. Preheat the oven to 425°F (220°C). Turn the dough out onto a floured surface and cut into 8 equal pieces. Using a rolling pin, flatten out into ovals about ¼in (5mm) thick. Place on the baking sheets. Brush each with oil and sprinkle with cumin seeds. Bake for 15 minutes, or until the breads are golden and puffed.

● **Good with** lamb koftas, black olive tapenade, hummus, and salads.

Fougasse

Fougasse is French flatbread similar to Italian focaccia. This version has bacon and onion blended into the dough before cooking

🍴 makes 3 small loaves

🕐 prep 30-35 mins, plus rising
• cook 15 mins

2⅔ cups **bread flour**

one ¼oz (7g) envelope **instant yeast**

1 tsp **salt**

5 tbsp **olive oil**, plus more for the bowl and brushing

1 **onion**, finely chopped

2 slices **bacon**, finely chopped

coarse **sea salt**, for sprinkling

1 At least 6 hours before baking the fougasse, make a starter. Stir 1⅓ cups of the flour, the yeast, and ⅔ cup water together in a bowl. Cover with plastic wrap. Let stand in a warm place for at least 4 hours, until the starter rises, then falls.

2 Add 1⅓ cups flour, the salt, ⅔ cup water, and 4 tbsp olive oil to the starter and stir to make a soft dough. Knead on a lightly floured work surface until the dough is smooth and elastic. Shape into a ball. Place in an oiled bowl, turn to coat, then cover again. Let stand for about 1 hour, until doubled.

3 Meanwhile, heat the remaining 1 tbsp oil in a frying pan over medium heat. Add the onion and bacon and cook about 6 minutes, until the bacon is browned. Transfer to a plate and cool.

4 Turn out the dough on a floured work surface and knead in the bacon mixture. Divide the dough into 3 balls. Cover with plastic wrap and let stand for 10 minutes. Roll each ball into a round about ½in (1cm) thick.

5 Line 3 baking sheets with parchment paper. Put each round on a baking sheet. Cut each round twice down the center, then cut 3 diagonal slits on either side of the center cuts. Cut all the way through the dough, but not through the edges. Brush with olive oil and cover loosely with plastic wrap. Let stand for about 45 minutes, or until doubled.

6 Preheat the oven to 450°F (230°C). Bake for 15 minutes, until golden. Let cool on wire racks before serving.

Rustic Italian Loaf

A fermented starter gives this rustic loaf bread a lovely sour flavor

🍴 makes 1 loaf

🕐 prep 30 mins, plus rising
• cook 40 mins

For the starter

1 cup **bread flour**

¼ tsp **instant yeast**

⅓ cup tepid **water**

1½ cups tepid **water**

3¼ cups **bread flour**

2 tsp **olive oil**, plus more for brushing

1½ tsp **instant yeast**

1 tsp **salt**

● **Prepare ahead** Make the starter the day before using.

1 For the starter, stir the flour, yeast, and water in a bowl until the mixture forms a ball. Transfer to a lightly oiled bowl, coat with oil, and cover. Let stand in a warm place for at least 12 hours, until it triples in volume and has an acidic aroma.

2 The next day, combine the starter and water in a large bowl. Add the flour, oil, yeast, and salt and stir until the dough comes together. It will be very wet and sticky. Fold the dough over on itself in the bowl for a few minutes, until it begins to pull away from the sides of the bowl.

3 Cover tightly with plastic wrap. Let stand in a warm place until doubled in volume, about 2 hours.

4 Preheat the oven to 425°F (220°C). Lightly oil a baking sheet. Punch down the dough. Knead the dough on a floured work surface until smooth and elastic. Mold the dough into an oval shape. Bake for 10 minutes. Reduce the oven temperature to 375°F (190°C) and bake for 30 minutes more, or until the loaf sounds hollow when tapped underneath. Let cool on a wire rack.

● **Good with** soup, Italian cheeses, or simply dipped into oil with a meal.

Onion and Herb Bread

This loaf is made savory with herbs and lots of caramelized onions

 makes 1 loaf

 prep 35 mins, plus rising time • cook 50 mins

4 cups **bread flour**, plus more for kneading and sprinkling

1 tsp **instant yeast**

⅓ cup plus ½ tsp **olive oil**

1 tbsp finely chopped **rosemary**, plus 1 tsp whole **rosemary leaves**

1¼ tsp **salt**

1 large **egg**, beaten, for glazing

For the filling

2 tbsp extra virgin **olive oil**

2 **onions**, sliced

½ tsp **salt**

½ tsp coarsely crushed **peppercorns**

3 tbsp **light brown sugar**

1 tbsp **balsamic vinegar**

1 tbsp **rosemary**, finely chopped

1 Stir 1⅔ cups of the flour, the yeast, and 1¼ cups tepid water in a bowl. Cover with plastic wrap and let stand 1 hour in warm place, until bubbling. Stir in ⅓ cup oil, the rosemary, and salt and enough of the flour to make a sticky dough. Cover and let stand for 10 minutes. Knead on a floured work surface about 8 minutes, until smooth and elastic.

2 Shape into a ball. Place in an oiled bowl and turn to coat. Cover with plastic wrap and leave in a warm place for 1 hour, to double.

3 Meanwhile, heat the oil in a frying pan over medium heat. Add the onions, salt, and pepper and cook, stirring, until tender, about 10 minutes. Stir in the brown sugar, vinegar, and rosemary, and cook 3 minutes more. Let cool.

4 Lightly flour a large baking sheet. Knead the dough on the work surface. Press into a 15 x 13in (37.5 x 32.5cm) rectangle and spread with the onions, leaving a 1in (2.5cm) border. Fold the shorter sides in by 1in (2.5cm), then fold the bottom third up, and the top third down. Pinch the seams closed, then transfer to the baking sheet, seams down. Shape into an oblong shape with pointed ends. Cover with a clean kitchen towel and let stand in a warm place for 30 minutes, or until puffy.

5 Preheat the oven to 425°F (220°C). Brush the dough with the egg and sprinkle with flour. Cut 3 slashes in the top of the loaf. Toss the rosemary leaves with ½ tsp oil, and sprinkle over. Bake for 20 minutes. Reduce the temperature to 400°F (200°C) and bake for 20 minutes more, until deep golden.

Whole Wheat Rolls

Ideal with lunch or dinner

 makes 16 rolls

 prep 20-25 mins, plus rising • cook 15-20 mins

1⅔ cups **bread flour**, plus more for kneading

1⅔ cups **whole wheat flour**

one ¼oz (7g) envelope **instant yeast**

1 tsp **salt**

¾ cup plus 2 tbsp tepid **whole milk**

⅔ cup tepid **water**

1 tbsp **vegetable oil**

1 tbsp **honey**

1 large **egg**, beaten, to glaze

rolled oats, to sprinkle

1 Mix the flours, yeast, and salt in a large bowl. Stir the milk, water, oil, and honey together, then pour into a well in the flours. Stir until slightly sticky. Cover with plastic wrap and leave for 10 minutes.

2 Knead the dough on a floured work surface for 8 minutes, until elastic. The dough will remain slightly sticky. Shape into a ball, place in an oiled bowl, and turn to coat. Cover and leave for 1 hour, until doubled.

3 Lightly oil a baking sheet. Punch down the dough and knead. Divide into 16 balls and place on the sheet. Cover with oiled plastic wrap and leave for 30 minutes.

4 Preheat the oven to 400°F (200°C). Brush the egg over the rolls and sprinkle with oats. Bake for 15-20 minutes. Cool on a wire rack.

English Muffins

Homemade English muffins are a real treat

 makes 10 muffins

prep 25-30 mins, plus rising • cook 30 mins

3 cups **bread flour**, plus more for kneading

1 tsp **instant yeast**

1 tsp **salt**

1¼ cups tepid **water**

2 tbsp **butter**, melted

2 tbsp **semolina**

1 Mix the flour, yeast, and salt in a bowl. Make a well in the center, and pour in the water and butter. Stir to make a slightly sticky dough.

2 Knead the dough on a floured work surface for about 8 minutes, until smooth and elastic. Shape into a ball, place in an oiled bowl, and turn to coat. Cover with plastic wrap. Let stand for 1 hour in a warm place until doubled.

3 Line a baking sheet with a kitchen towel and sprinkle with most of the semolina. Turn the dough out onto a floured surface and knead. Divide into 10 balls. Place the balls on the towel and press into thick disks. Sprinkle with the rest of the semolina. Cover with another towel. Leave for 20-30 minutes, until risen.

4 Heat a frying pan with a lid. In batches, place the muffins in the pan and cover. Reduce heat to low and cook for 10-12 minutes, until they puff up. Flip and cook for 3-4 minutes, until golden.

Spiced Fruit Buns

These delicious sweetened rolls make a perfect snack

 makes 12 buns

 prep 30 mins, plus rising
• cook 15-20 mins

3⅔ cups bread flour

6 tbsp granulated sugar

one ¼oz (7g) envelope instant yeast

1 tsp pumpkin pie spice

1 tsp salt

½ tsp ground nutmeg

4 tbsp cold butter, sliced

1 cup tepid milk, as needed

1 cup chopped mixed dried fruit

2 tbsp confectioner's sugar

¼ tsp pure vanilla extract

1 Mix the flour, sugar, yeast, spice, and salt. Add the butter and rub it in with your fingertips until the mixture looks crumbly. Stir in enough milk to make a soft dough. Knead on a floured work surface for 10 minutes. Place in an oiled bowl, turn to coat, and cover with plastic wrap. Let stand in a warm place about 1 hour, until doubled.

2 Punch down the dough. Knead in the dried fruit. Divide the dough into 12 pieces and roll into balls place. Place, spaced well apart, on an oiled baking sheet. Cover with plastic wrap and let stand in a warm place for 30 minutes until doubled.

3 Preheat the oven to 400°F (200°C). Bake for 15 minutes, or until the buns sound hollow when tapped. Transfer to a wire rack and let cool. Mix the confectioner's sugar, vanilla, and 1 tbsp cold water until smooth. Brush over the buns to glaze them, and cool completely.

VARIATION

Maple and Pecan Buns
Substitute maple syrup for the granulated sugar, and chopped pecans for the fruit. Use only about ¾ cup milk to make the dough.

Rye Bread

Breads made with rye flour are very popular in central and eastern Europe

 makes 1 large loaf

prep 25 mins, plus rising
• cook 50 mins

For the starter

1 cup tepid water

1 cup rye flour

¾ cup plain yogurt

1 tbsp unsulfured molasses

1 tsp instant yeast

1 tsp caraway seeds, lightly crushed

For the dough

1 cup rye flour

2 tsp salt

1¾ cups bread flour, as needed

1 large egg, beaten, to glaze

1 tsp caraway seeds, for the crust

● **Prepare ahead** Make the starter the day before making the loaf.

1 Whisk the starter ingredients together in a medium bowl. Cover with plastic wrap and let stand for 8-12 hours, until bubbly.

2 Transfer to a large bowl. Stir in the rye flour and salt. Stir in enough of the bread flour to make a stiff dough. Knead on a lightly floured work surface, adding more flour as needed, about 8 minutes, until the dough is smooth and elastic, but slightly sticky—do not add too much flour. Shape the dough into a ball, and turn in an oiled bowl. Cover with plastic wrap and let stand in a warm place until the dough doubles, about 1 hour.

3 Punch down the dough and form into a 9in (23cm) long football shape. Transfer to a floured baking sheet, cover with plastic wrap, and let stand until almost doubled, about 30 minutes.

4 Preheat the oven to 425°F (220°C). Brush the loaf with beaten egg and sprinkle with caraway seeds. Cut a shallow slash down the center of the loaf. Bake for 20 minutes. Reduce the oven temperature to 400°F (200°C) and continue baking until the dough sounds hollow when tapped on the bottom. Cool on a wire rack.

● **Good with** smoked salmon.

Cheese and Garlic Stromboli

A stuffed loaf filled with Italian flavors

🍴 makes 1 loaf

🕐 prep 30 mins, plus rising
• cook 40–45 mins

3⅔ cups **bread flour**, as needed

1 tbsp **sugar**

1½ tsp **salt**

one ¼oz (7g) envelope **instant yeast**

2 tbsp **olive oil**

1¾ cups shredded **mozzarella**

8 **scallions**, white and green parts, thinly sliced

4 **garlic cloves**, chopped

¼ cup loosely packed shredded **basil**

1 tbsp **butter**, melted

1 **Combine the flour**, sugar, salt, and yeast in a large bowl. Make a well in the center and add 1 cup tepid water and the oil. Stir to make a soft dough. Knead on a lightly floured work surface, adding more flour as needed, about 8 minutes, until smooth and elastic. Place in an oiled bowl and turn to coat. Cover with plastic wrap. Let stand in a warm place until doubled, about 1 hour.

2 **Lightly oil** a baking sheet. Punch down the dough. Transfer to a lightly oiled work surface and roll into a 14 x 9in (35 x 23cm) rectangle. Combine the mozzarella, scallions, basil, and garlic. Spread the mixture over the dough, leaving a 1in (2.5cm) border along all sides.

3 **Starting from** a short end, roll up tightly. Pinch the seams closed. Place the loaf, seam side down, on the baking sheet. Cover loosely with oiled plastic wrap. Let stand in a warm place about 45 minutes, until doubled.

4 **Preheat the oven** to 400°F (200°C). Bake for about 40 minutes, or until golden and the loaf sounds hollow when tapped on the underside. Transfer to a wire rack, brush the top with melted butter, and let cool completely.

● **Good with** salads as part of a buffet table.

Sesame Seed Rolls

These little bread rolls can be served with dinner, or used for sandwiches

🍴 makes 8 rolls

🕐 prep 30 mins, plus 1½ hrs rising • cook 20 mins

3¼ cups **bread flour**, plus extra for kneading

1 tsp **salt**

1 tsp **instant yeast**

1 tbsp **vegetable oil**

1 **large egg**, beaten, for glazing

4 tsp **sesame seeds**

1 **Stir the flour**, salt, and yeast together in a large bowl. Make a well in the center. Mix 1½ cups tepid water with the oil, and pour into the well. Stir to make a soft dough. Cover and let stand for 10 minutes.

2 **Knead the dough** on a lightly floured work surface for about 8 minutes, until smooth and elastic. Shape into a ball. Place in an oiled bowl, turning to coat the dough. Cover with plastic wrap and let stand in a warm place about 1 hour, or until doubled in size.

3 **Lightly dust** a baking sheet with flour. Knead the dough briefly on a lightly floured work surface. Divide the dough into 8 equal pieces, and shape each into a ball. Place onto the baking sheet, well separated. Cover with plastic wrap and let stand in warm place about 30 minutes, until puffy.

4 **Preheat the oven** to 400°F (200°C). Lightly brush the rolls with the beaten egg and sprinkle each with ½ tsp sesame seeds. Bake for 20 minutes, or until golden brown. Transfer to a wire rack and let cool.

● **Good with** beef burgers and salad.

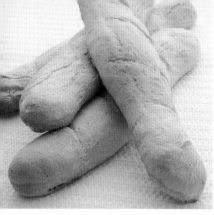

Ficelles

These are very thin baguettes with a light, crisp crust

 makes 4 loaves

 prep 15 mins, plus rising • cook 20 mins

3½ cups **bread flour**

one ¼ oz (7g) envelope **instant (fast-acting) yeast**

4 tsp **salt**

1½ cups tepid **water**

⅔ cup boiling **water**

1 Mix the flour, yeast, and 1 tsp of the salt in a large bowl. Add the tepid water and stir to make a soft dough. Knead on a lightly floured work surface for 8–10 minutes, or until smooth and elastic.

2 Divide the dough into four equal portions. Roll each into a 12in (30cm) rope. Place 2 ficelles on each of 2 large baking trays. Cover the loaves with oiled plastic wrap. Let stand in a warm place for 30 minutes, until doubled in size.

3 Preheat the oven to 425°F (220°C). Dissolve the remaining 3 tsp salt in the boiling water. Brush the salted water over the loaves. Use a sharp knife to make 4 diagonal slashes in the top of each loaf. Bake for 15–20 minutes, until light gold. After 10 minutes, switch the positions of the baking sheets from top to bottom to ensure even baking.

4 Transfer to a wire rack. Serve warm, with lots of butter.

Croissants

These take some time to make, but much of that is taken up chilling the dough and the final result is well worth the effort

 makes 16 croissants

prep 1 hr, plus chilling and resting • cook 15 mins

2 cups **bread flour**

3½ tsp **instant yeast**

2 tbsp **sugar**

1 tsp **salt**

¾ cup tepid **water**

1 cup cold **butter**, thinly sliced

1 large **egg**, beaten

1 Place the flour, yeast, sugar, and salt in a large bowl and make a well in the center. Add the water and stir make a soft dough. Knead on a floured surface for 8 minutes, until smooth and elastic Transfer to a buttered bowl, turn to coat, and cover with plastic wrap. Leave in a warm place for 1 hour, until doubled.

2 Place the butter in a bowl. Work with your knuckles and fingers until malleable but cool. Roll out the dough on a floured surface to a 12 x 6in (30 x 15cm) rectangle. Shape the butter into a 6 x 5in (15 x 13cm) rectangle. Place on one side of the dough and fold the dough over to encase the butter, pinching the seams closed. Roll the dough into a 12 x 6in (30 x 15cm) rectangle. Fold the dough into thirds. Repeat the rolling and folding. Wrap and chill for 20 minutes.

3 Roll out the dough on a floured surface to a 30 x 15cm (12 x 6in) rectangle. Fold the right third over to the center, then fold the left third over the top so you have 3 layers. Chill for 1 hour, until firm. Repeat the process (rolling and folding twice, with a 20-minute refrigerated rest) two more times. Wrap and chill for 4–24 hours.

4 Line 2 baking sheets with parchment paper. Roll out the dough on a floured surface into a 14 x 14in (35 x 35cm) square. Cut into four 7in (18cm) squares. Cut each square diagonally into quarters to make 16 triangles. Gently pull and elongate the center point of each triangle. Roll up, ending with the center point on the top of the croissant. Place on the baking sheet, point facing up, curving the triangle into a crescent. Repeat with all the triangles, leaving space between them on the baking sheets. Cover with plastic wrap and leave in a warm place for 1½ hours, until doubled.

5 Preheat the oven to 450°F (230°C). Brush the croissants with the egg. Bake for 10 minutes. Reduce the temperature to 375°F (190°C) and bake for 10 minutes more, until golden. Cool on a rack.

Ham Croissants

Easy croissants made with ready-made dough

 makes 6

prep 10 mins • cook 10–12 mins

one 10.1oz (283g) tube refrigerated **croissant dough**

2 tbsp **whole-grain mustard**

1 tsp **honey**

salt and freshly ground **black pepper**

6 slices **cooked ham**

1 **egg yolk**, beaten with 1 tsp water, to glaze

1 Preheat the oven to 400°F (200°C). Lightly butter a baking sheet. Unroll the croissant dough and separate the triangles.

2 Mix the mustard and honey together in a small bowl, and season with salt and pepper. Spread over one side of each triangle.

3 Place a slice of ham over each triangle. Don't worry too much if it doesn't fit the triangle, as the dough will expand during baking. Roll up each triangle, from its wide side up towards the point.

4 Arrange the triangles point side down, on the baking sheet, spacing them well apart. Brush the tops with the yolk mixture.

5 Bake for 10–12 minutes, or until the croissants are puffed up and golden. Serve immediately.

Buttermilk Biscuits

Light and fluffy, these American favorites are best served straight from the oven with plenty of butter

 makes 12 biscuits

 prep 12 mins • cook 15 mins

 2⅔in (6cm) round cookie or biscuit cutter

2⅓ cups **all-purpose flour**, plus more for kneading

1½ tbsp **sugar**

2 tsp **baking powder**

¾ tsp **baking soda**

¾ tsp **salt**

6 tbsp **butter** chilled, cut into thin slices

1 cup plus 2 tbsp **buttermilk**, plus more for glazing the tops

1 Preheat the oven to 425°F (220°C). Have an unbuttered 10in (25cm) round cake pan ready.

2 Sift the flour, sugar, baking powder, baking soda, and salt into a large bowl. Use your fingertips to rub in the butter until the mixture resembles fine crumbs (or cut in the butter with two knives).

3 Add the buttermilk and stir, adding a little more buttermilk if needed, to make a soft dough.

4 Turn the dough out onto a lightly floured work surface. Knead once or twice, then gently shape into a rectangle about 1in (2.5cm) thick. Using a 2½in (6cm) round cookie cutter, cut out the biscuits and place them in the cake pan with the sides of the biscuits touching. Gather up the scraps, knead together gently, and cut out the remaining biscuits, discarding any scraps.

5 Brush the tops with buttermilk. Bake for 15–20 minutes, or until the biscuits are risen and the tops are golden.

● **Good with** plenty of butter and strawberry jam.

● **Another time**, use the biscuits to make strawberry shortcakes: Cut each biscuit in half. Top each with lots of sliced, sweetened strawberries and whipped cream.

Irish Soda Bread

A true quick bread that requires no yeast, this loaf gets its tender crumb from buttermilk

 makes 6 servings

prep 10 mins • cook 30–35 mins

3¼ cups **bread flour**, plus extra for dusting

2 tsp **baking soda**

2 tsp **cream of tartar**

1 tsp **salt**

4 tbsp **butter** or lard, diced

1¼ cups **buttermilk** or 1¼ cups whole milk mixed with 1 tsp cider vinegar

1 Preheat the oven to 425°F (220°C). Dust a baking sheet with flour. Sift the flour, baking soda, cream of tartar, and salt together into a bowl. Add the butter and rub in with your fingertips to form fine crumbs.

2 Make a well in the center. Pour in the buttermilk and then mix to form a soft dough. Knead briefly on a lightly floured work surface. Shape into a ball, then roll on the work surface to smooth the surface.

3 Place on the baking sheet, and lightly flatten the top. Using a floured knife, cut into 6 equal wedges, without completely cutting all the way through the dough.

4 Bake for 30–35 minutes, or until golden brown and the bread sounds hollow when tapped on the bottom. Transfer to a wire rack and let cool.

● **Good with** a bowl of hot soup or with a wedge of sharp Cheddar cheese and cooked ham.

● **Leftovers** will become dry after a day, but make good toast and croutons for soup. Or, make bread crumbs for using in other dishes, and freeze until needed.

VARIATION

Brown Irish Soda Bread

Replace 1½ cups of the bread flour with whole wheat flour.

BUTTERMILK

Look for buttermilk in the dairy section, or make a substitute by stirring 1 tsp lemon juice or cider vinegar into 1 cup milk and letting it stand for 5 minutes.

Potato Scones

These smooth potato pancakes are addictive, especially topped with lots of butter. In Scotland, they are called "tattie scones"

 makes 8 scones

prep 30 mins • cook 18 mins

freeze layered between sheets of wax paper for up to 6 months

1 lb (450g) **baking potatoes**, such as Burbank or russet, peeled and diced

⅓ cup **all-purpose flour**

½ tsp **baking powder**

½ tsp **salt**

vegetable oil, for the griddle

1 Boil the potatoes in lightly salted water about 20 minutes, until tender. Drain and pat dry with paper towels. Then place in a bowl and mash until smooth using a potato masher.

2 Sift the flour, baking powder, and salt into the warm mashed potatoes, and mix well to make a pliable dough.

3 Turn onto lightly floured work surface and knead briefly until smooth. Pat the dough into a 7in (18cm) square. Cut the dough into quarters, then cut each in half diagonally to make 8 triangles.

4 Brush a griddle pan lightly with oil and heat until hot. Add the scones and cook, turning halfway through, about 4 minutes, until golden brown. Serve hot or warm.

 Good with soft garlic and herb cheese and a chive garnish; butter and jam; or as a side dish for main courses to replace mashed potatoes or rice. They also make a hearty accompaniment to soups and stews.

VARIATION

Savory Potato Scones
Add finely chopped fried onion, dried mixed herbs, or even curry powder to the mashed potato dough before rolling out.

Scotch Pancakes

These thick little pancakes are also called drop scones, as drops of the batter are cooked on a hot griddle

 makes 12 pancakes

prep 10 mins • cook 15 mins

freeze for up to 1 month

1⅔ cups **all-purpose flour**

4 tsp **baking powder**

1 cup **whole milk**

1 large **egg**

2 tsp **golden** or **light corn syrup**

vegetable oil, for the griddle

1 Heat a griddle over medium heat. Place a folded clean kitchen towel on a baking sheet.

2 Sift the flour and baking powder together into a bowl. Make a well in the center and add the milk, egg, and golden syrup. Whisk well until the batter is smooth and the consistency of thick cream. If the mixture is too thick, beat in a little more milk.

3 To test the griddle, sprinkle a little flour on the surface; it should brown slowly. If it burns quickly, cool the pan. Carefully dust off the flour and lightly oil the griddle.

4 Using a soup spoon, scoop out the batter, cleaning the back of the spoon on the edge of the bowl. Pour the batter from the tip of the spoon onto the hot pan to make a round shape. Repeat, leaving enough room between the pancakes for them to rise and spread.

5 Cook until bubbles appear on the surface of the pancakes and they begin to burst. Carefully flip the pancakes with a metal spatula. Lightly press the spatula on each pancake to ensure even browning, and cook until the other sides are browned. Tuck the pancakes inside the folds of the towel to keep warm. Repeat with the remaining batter, oiling the griddle before each batch. Serve immediately, while the pancakes are still warm.

Good with butter, maple syrup, honey, or jam.

Chapatis

These thin, flat, unleavened breads can be easily prepared at home in a cast-iron frying pan

- makes 8 breads
- prep 30 mins, plus resting • cook 10 mins
- heavy frying pan, preferably cast-iron

1¾ cups **whole wheat flour**, plus more for dusting

1 tsp **salt**

scant ¾ cup **water**, as needed

ghee (clarified butter) or melted butter, to serve

1 Sift the flour and salt into a bowl and discard any bran left in the sieve. Make a well in the center. Add 3 tbsp cold water and mix. Stir in enough of the remaining water to make a soft dough.

2 Knead the dough in the bowl until firm, elastic, and less sticky.

3 Cover the bowl with a clean kitchen towel, and let stand about 30 minutes until the dough is a little more firm and less sticky.

4 Dust your hands with flour. Divide the dough into 8 balls. On an unfloured work surface, roll each ball into a round about 7in (18cm) in diameter.

5 Heat an ungreased frying pan over medium-high heat until hot. One at a time, cook the chapatis for about 30 seconds on each side, until golden and speckled with brown patches. Transfer to a plate, brush with ghee, and cover with another towel to keep warm while cooking the remaining breads. Serve warm.

Pita Bread

These Middle Eastern flat breads are best served warm. They are essential for serving with salads and dips such as hummus

- makes 8 breads
- prep 20 mins, plus resting • cook 10 mins
- cool, wrap and freeze for up to 3 months

1¼ cups tepid **water**

¼ cup **olive oil**, plus more for brushing

1 tsp **sugar**

1 tsp **salt**

3½ cups **bread flour**, plus more for rolling the dough

1 tsp **instant yeast**

1 Combine the water, oil, sugar, and salt in a large bowl.

2 Stir in ½ cup of the flour and the yeast. Add the remaining flour, ½ cup at a time, to make a soft dough. Knead on a lightly floured work surface for 5 minutes, adding more flour as necessary, until the dough is smooth. Shape into a ball.

3 Place the dough in a lightly oiled bowl. Cover with plastic wrap and let stand about 1 hour in a warm place until doubled in volume.

4 Briefly knead the dough until smooth. Cut the dough into 8 pieces. Roll each into a thin oval shape, about 8in (20cm) long. Brush 2 large baking sheets with oil. Place 4 ovals onto each sheet. Cover with oiled plastic wrap and let stand in a warm place for about 20 minutes until the dough has risen slightly.

5 Preheat oven to 425°F (220°C). Brush the tops of the ovals lightly with oil. Bake for about 10 minutes, until puffed and golden. Transfer to a wire rack to cool slightly. Serve warm.

VARIATION

Spiced Pitas

Before baking, sprinkle with lightly crushed coriander, cumin, or fennel seeds for a fragrant version, or add 2 tbsp toasted sesame seeds to the dough during the second kneading.

Whole Wheat Pooris

These deep-fried puffed Indian breads are ideal served with curries; chapati flour is available from Asian grocers

🍴 makes 8 breads

🕐 prep 15 mins plus standing • cook 16 mins

½ cup tepid **water**

2 tsp **vegetable oil**, plus more for deep-frying

1 tsp **black onion seeds**

1 tsp **salt**

½ tsp **cumin seeds**

½ tsp **sugar**

1¾ cups **chapati** or **whole wheat flour**, as needed

● **Prepare ahead** The dough can be refrigerated for up to 3 hours; punch down, roll out, cover with plastic wrap, and let stand for 30 minutes before frying.

1 Mix the water with 2 tsp oil, onion seeds, salt, cumin, and sugar in a bowl. Stir in flour to make a stiff dough. Knead on a floured work surface for 5 minutes, or until smooth. Wrap in plastic wrap and let stand for 45 minutes.

2 Divide the dough into 8 equal balls. On an unfloured work surface, flatten and roll out each ball into a 5in (12.5cm) round. Cover with plastic wrap and let stand while heating the oil.

3 Pour enough oil into a large deep saucepan to come halfway up the sides and heat the oil over high heat to 350°F (180°C). One at a time, deep-fry the dough rounds for about 2 minutes, turning once, until puffed up and golden. Transfer to paper towels to drain. Serve hot.

Naan Bread

This Indian flat bread is traditionally cooked in a clay oven called a tandoor, but a hot home oven works just as well

🍴 makes 4 breads

🕐 prep 20 mins, plus resting • cook 9 mins

❄ cool, wrap, and freeze for up to 3 months

¾ cup tepid **water**

½ cup **plain full-fat yogurt**

4 tbsp **butter**, melted

1½ tsp **salt**

1 tsp **sugar**

3½ cups **bread flour**, plus more for rolling the dough

1¼ tsp **instant yeast**

2 tsp **black onion seeds**

50g (2oz) **ghee** or butter, melted

1 Combine the water, yogurt, melted butter, salt, and sugar in a large bowl.

2 Stir in ½ cup of the flour and the yeast, then enough of the flour to make a soft dough. On a lightly floured work surface, knead the dough for 5 minutes, adding more flour as necessary, but keeping the dough soft, until the dough is smooth. During the last minute or so, knead in the onion seeds and shape into a ball.

3 Place the dough in a lightly oiled bowl and turn to coat with the oil. Cover with plastic wrap and let stand in a warm place until doubled in volume, about an hour.

4 Place two large baking sheets in the center and top third of the oven and preheat to 500°F (260°C). Knead the dough for a minute until smooth. Cut dough into 4 equal pieces and roll each into an oval about 10in (24cm) long.

5 Carefully transfer the breads to the baking sheets in the oven. Bake for 6 minutes, until puffed. Transfer to a wire rack. Position a broiler rack about 6in (15cm) from the heat and preheat the broiler. One at a time, broil the breads 30 seconds on each side until blistered and browned lightly. Serve warm.

Grissini

Baked until dry, these Italian-style bread sticks are often served with antipasti

 makes 20–24 bread sticks

 prep 25 mins, plus rising
• cook 12–15 mins

 freeze for up to 2 months

1¾ cups **bread flour**

1 tbsp **olive oil**

1 tsp **sugar**

1 tsp **salt**

½ tsp **instant yeast**

1 **egg**, beaten, to glaze

sesame seeds, to sprinkle

coarse sea salt, to sprinkle

● **Prepare ahead** The bread sticks can be stored in an airtight container for 2 weeks.

1 Mix the flour, oil, sugar, salt, and yeast together in a large bowl. Add ½ cup water and stir to make a soft dough. Knead the dough on a lightly floured work surface for 10 minutes. Place in a lightly oiled bowl, turn to coat, and cover tightly with plastic wrap. Let stand in a warm place about 1 hour, until doubled.

2 Lightly grease 2 baking sheets. Preheat the oven to 425°F (220°C). Briefly knead the dough on a lightly floured work surface. Break off pieces of the dough about the size of a walnut and roll each piece into a long stick about the thickness of a pencil. Place the grissini about ½in (1cm) apart on the baking sheets.

3 Brush the bread sticks with the beaten egg and sprinkle them liberally with sesame seeds and coarse sea salt. Do not let the dough rise after shaping. Bake the grissini for 12–15 minutes, or until golden and crisp. The sticks should snap easily when broken and not be doughy in the middle.

4 Transfer to a wire rack and leave until completely cooled.

● **Good with** pre-dinner drinks or with creamy dips, such as sour cream and chive.

Cornbread

A golden quick bread, delicious straight from the oven

 makes 1 loaf

 prep 5 mins • cook 30 mins

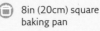 8in (20cm) square baking pan

vegetable oil, for the pan

1¼ cups **yellow cornmeal**

½ cup **all-purpose flour**

1½ tbsp **sugar**

1 tsp **baking powder**

1 tsp **salt**

1¼ cups **whole milk**

2 tbsp **butter**, melted

1 large **egg**, beaten

1 Preheat the oven to 375°F (190°C). Lightly oil the insides of an 8in (20cm) square baking pan.

2 Whisk the cornmeal, flour, sugar, baking powder, and salt in a large bowl. Make a well in the center. Pour in the milk, butter, and egg to the well and stir with a wooden spoon just until combined. Do not overmix. Spread the cornbread mixture evenly in the pan.

3 Bake for 25–30 minutes, or until the cornbread is browned around the edges and a wooden toothpick inserted into the center comes out clean.

4 Cut the cornbread into squares and serve warm.

● **Good with** chile butter.

Easy Flatbread

A simple yeast bread cooked in a frying pan

 makes 8 flatbreads

 prep 10 mins, plus rising
• cook 40 mins

3⅔ cups **bread flour**

one ¼oz (7g) envelope **instant yeast**

2 tsp **salt**

1¼ cups **tepid water**

3 tbsp **olive oil**

1 Mix the flour, yeast, and salt in a bowl. Make a well in the center and add the water and oil. Stir to make a soft dough. Knead on a lightly floured work surface 8–10 minutes. Place in a lightly oiled bowl, turn to coat the dough with oil, and cover tightly with plastic wrap. Let stand in a warm place for 45 minutes, until doubled.

2 Briefly knead the dough on a lightly floured work surface. Cut into 8 equal pieces. Flatten each into a round about ½in (1cm). Use a rolling pin to make them a little thinner. Place on lightly floured baking sheets, cover with plastic wrap, and let stand about 10 minutes, until puffy.

3 Heat a large frying pan over medium heat. One at a time, add a flatbread. Cook about 3 minutes, until the underside is browned. Turn and cook about 2 minutes to brown the other side. Transfer to a wire rack to cool. Serve warm.

Waffles

Perfect for breakfast or a dessert, these waffles are easy to make

 makes 6-8 waffles

 prep 10 mins
• cook 20-25 mins

waffle iron

freeze for up to 1 month

1 cup plus 2 tbsp **all-purpose flour**

2 tbsp **sugar**

1 tsp **baking powder**

1¼ cups **whole milk**

5 tbsp **butter**, melted

2 **large eggs**, separated, at room temperature

1 tsp **pure vanilla extract**

● **Prepare ahead** Although best eaten as fresh as possible, you can make waffles up to 24 hours in advance and reheat in a toaster.

1 **Preheat a waffle maker**. Preheat the oven to 200°F (95°C). Whisk the flour, sugar, and baking powder together in a bowl to combine. Make a well in the center. Whisk the milk, melted butter, egg yolks, and vanilla in another bowl. Pour into the well and whisk, until just combined. Do not overbeat.

2 **Beat the egg whites** until soft peaks form. Fold the whites into the batter.

3 **Following** the manufacturer's instructions, ladle the batter into the center of the waffle iron and close the lid. Cook until the waffles are golden and the batter stops steaming. Serve waffles immediately, or transfer to a baking sheet and keep warm in the oven while making the remaining waffles.

● **Good with** fresh maple syrup and butter for breakfast, or topped with whipped cream and mixed berries for dessert.

VARIATIONS

Buttermilk Waffles

Substitute buttermilk for the milk and add another 1 tsp baking powder.

Spiced Waffles

Add 2 tsp pumpkin pie spice to the dry ingredients.

Scones

There is nothing better for afternoon tea than freshly baked flaky scones

 makes 8 scones

 prep 25 mins
• cook 20 mins

2½in (7cm) diameter cookie cutter

1⅔ cups **all-purpose flour**, plus more for rolling

2 tbsp **sugar**

1½ tsp **baking powder**

½ tsp **salt**

4 tbsp **cold butter**, diced

¼ cup **raisins**

⅔ cup **whole milk**

1 **large egg**, beaten, for glazing

1 **Preheat the oven** to 425°F (220°C). Sift the flour, sugar, baking powder, and salt into a large bowl. Add the butter and rub it in with your fingertips until the mixture resembles coarse bread crumbs. Stir in the raisins and make a well in the center. Pour in the milk and stir quickly to make a soft dough.

2 **Gently and briefly** knead the dough on a lightly floured work surface until it is smooth. Pat into a round about 1in (2.5cm) thick.

3 **Cut rounds from the dough** using a 2½in (7cm) diameter cookie cutter and place on a baking sheet. Gather up the scraps, pat out, and cut out more scones until all of the dough is used.

4 **Brush the tops** lightly with the beaten egg. Bake for 12-15 minutes, or until golden in color. Transfer to a wire rack and serve warm.

● **Good with** fruit preserves and butter, clotted cream, or thickly whipped heavy cream and berries.

> **SHAPING SCONES**
> When cutting out the dough, make clean cuts so the scones rise evenly. Press the cutter straight down and do not twist it.

Club Sandwich

Here is a hearty sandwich of chicken, bacon, tomatoes, and lettuce, layered between slices of toasted bread, guaranteed to satisfy those hunger pangs

🍴 makes 4 servings

🕐 prep 15 mins, plus marinating
• cook 15 mins

---

1 tsp **dried Italian herbs**

2 tbsp **olive oil**

1 small **garlic clove**, crushed

salt and freshly ground **black pepper**

3 boneless and skinless **chicken breasts**

16 slices **bacon**

12 slices **white sandwich bread**

⅓ cup **mayonnaise**

1 tsp **whole grain mustard**

4 ripe **tomatoes**, sliced

½ head **romaine lettuce**, shredded

8 small **sour pickles** (cornichons)

● **Prepare ahead** The recipe can be made through step 5 up to 2 hours in advance.

1 Mix together the herbs, 1 tbsp olive oil, and garlic in a bowl and season with salt and pepper. Add the chicken breasts, toss to coat, and set aside for 30 to 90 minutes.

2 Meanwhile, heat the remaining oil in a large frying pan over medium heat. In batches, cook the bacon for about 5 minutes, until crisp and golden. Using a slotted spatula, transfer to paper towels, leaving the fat in the pan.

3 Add the chicken breasts to the pan and cook for about 5 minutes on each side until the flesh feels firm when pressed in the center. Transfer to a plate.

4 Meanwhile, toast the bread. Arrange the slices on a large cutting board. Trim the crusts if desired. Cut the bacon slices in half.

5 In a small bowl, mix together the mayonnaise and mustard. Spread the toast with the mayonnaise mixture. Slice the chicken breasts against the grain. Arrange half of the chicken on four of the toasted bread slices. Top the chicken with half of the bacon, tomato slices, and lettuce. Top each with a slice of toast. Repeat with the remaining chicken, bacon, tomatoes, and lettuce, then top with the remaining 4 slices of toast, mayonnaise-side down.

6 Cut each sandwich in half, diagonally. Push a cocktail toothpick through the center of each triangle to hold it together, and top each with a pickle.

● **Great with** sweet or dill gherkins and other pickles on the side.

● **Substitute** fresh slices of turkey for the chicken, if desired.

▒▒ **VARIATION** ▒▒

Fish Club Sandwich

Replace the chicken with pan-fried white fish fillets, such as cod or haddock. And, use tartar sauce on the toast instead of the mustard-mayonnaise mixture.

Smoked Salmon and Cream Cheese Bagels

A big breakfast or a true brunch dish for long, lazy Sundays

🍴 makes 4 servings

🕐 prep 10 mins

---

4 **bagels** (plain, poppy seed, or sesame seed)

8oz (230g) **cream cheese**

1 tbsp finely chopped **dill**

1 tsp prepared **horseradish**

6oz (175g) sliced **smoked salmon**

freshly ground **black pepper**

lemon wedges, to serve

---

1 Split each bagel in half crosswise with a knife, and toast.

2 Mash the cream cheese, dill, and horseradish in a bowl.

3 Spread the bottom halves of the bagels with the cream cheese mixture. Top with the smoked salmon slices.

4 Grind the pepper over the salmon and cover with the top halves. Serve immediately, with the lemon wedges.

Fried Mozzarella Panini

Served hot, this is a truly indulgent snack

 makes 4 servings

prep 10 mins • cook 6 mins

8 slices of **sourdough bread**

2 tbsp **olive oil**, plus more as needed

5oz (150g) thinly sliced **mozzarella**

12 **sun-dried tomatoes**, coarsely chopped

16 large **basil leaves**, torn

salt and freshly ground **black pepper**

4oz (112g) **arugula leaves**, to serve

1 tbsp **balsamic vinegar**

1 Preheat the oven to 200°F (95°C). Drizzle the bread on both sides with the oil.

2 Top four bread slices with the mozzarella, tomatoes, and basil. Season with salt and pepper.

3 Top with the remaining bread and compress with your hands, making sure none of the filling is sticking out.

4 Heat a heavy frying pan over high heat. Add 1 tbsp oil and tilt to coat the bottom of the pan. Carefully add 2 sandwiches. Cook, turning once, about 5 minutes, until golden on both sides. Transfer to a baking sheet and keep warm while frying the remaining sandwiches in the remaining 1 tbsp oil.

5 Toss the arugula with the vinegar in a medium bowl. Slice each sandwich in half and transfer each to a plate. Add equal amounts of the salad, and serve immediately.

Pan Bagnat

Essentially a Salade Niçoise sandwich, this Provençale worker's sandwich roughly translates as "wet bread"

 makes 4 servings

prep 20 mins, plus chilling

4 round **crusty rolls**

2 **garlic cloves**, cut in half

4 tbsp **olive oil**

1 tbsp **white wine vinegar**

salt and freshly ground **black pepper**

one 6oz (168g) can **tuna in oil**, drained

½ **green pepper**, seeded and sliced

2 **scallions**, sliced

¼ **cucumber**, thinly sliced

½ cup **green beans**, cooked

8 pitted **Kalamata olives**

1 **hard-boiled egg**, sliced

2 large **tomatoes**, sliced

12 **anchovy fillets**

8 **basil leaves**

● **Prepare ahead** The pan bagnat is best made at least 1 hour ahead.

1 Cut each roll in half and pull out most of the soft crumbs. Rub the insides of the rolls with the cut sides of the garlic. Mix the oil and vinegar and season with salt and pepper. Drizzle over the cut surfaces of the rolls.

2 Mix together the tuna, green pepper, scallions, cucumber, green beans, and olives. Divide the tuna mixture among the bottom halves of the rolls. Top each with equal amounts of the sliced egg and tomatoes, then 3 anchovy fillets and 2 basil leaves. Cover with the top of the rolls.

3 Wrap each in plastic wrap and refrigerate for at least 1 hour. Serve chilled or at room temperature.

Tuna Melt

This version of the diner classic is enlivened with the tangy flavors of red pepper, lemon, and ketchup

🍴 makes 4 servings

🕐 prep 15 mins • cook 10 mins

4 English muffins

1 tbsp **olive oil**

1 **red bell pepper**, seeded and finely chopped

4 **scallions**, white and green parts, thinly sliced

2 **shallots**, finely chopped

2 x 6oz (170g) cans **albacore tuna**, drained

2 tbsp **ketchup**

6 tbsp **mayonnaise**

grated zest of 1 **lemon**

4 large, thin slices of **sharp Cheddar cheese**, halved diagonally

1 Position a broiler rack 6in (15cm) from the heat and preheat. Split the muffins and toast.

2 Heat the oil in a small frying pan over medium heat. Add the red pepper, scallions, and shallots. Cook, stirring often, about 3 minutes. Add the tuna, breaking up the chunks with a fork. Cook for about 1 minute, until the tuna is heated through. Remove the pan from the heat and stir in the ketchup, 2 tbsp of the mayonnaise, and the lemon zest.

3 Spread the remaining mayonnaise over the cut sides of the muffins. Spread 4 muffin halves with the tuna mixture and arrange the cheese triangles on top.

4 Grill until the cheese melts. Top with the remaining 4 muffin halves. Serve at once.

● **Good with** a selection of your favorite pickles.

Croque Monsieur

In France, these toasted cheese and ham sandwiches are very popular

🍴 makes 4 sandwiches

🕐 prep 15 mins • cook 10 mins

14oz (400g) **Gruyère cheese**, grated

4 tbsp **butter**, plus softened butter for spreading

2 tbsp **all-purpose flour**

⅔ cup **whole milk**

2 tsp **Dijon mustard**

8 slices **white sandwich bread**

8 thin slices of **ham**

● **Prepare ahead** Steps 1 and 2 can be completed 2 hours ahead.

1 Cut 4oz (115g) of the cheese into thin slices and shred the rest.

2 Melt the butter in a medium saucepan over low heat. Whisk in the flour and let bubble without browning for 1 minute. Whisk in the milk. Simmer, whisking often, until smooth and thick. Add the shredded cheese and mustard and stir until the cheese is melted.

3 Position a broiler rack 6in (15cm) from the heat and preheat the broiler. Toast the bread slices on 1 side only. Spread the untoasted sides lightly with butter, then top 4 slices with the ham and sliced cheese. Press the remaining 4 bread slices on top, toasted sides up, and spread with the cheese mixture.

4 Broil about 2 minutes until the sauce is bubbling and golden brown. Serve at once.

● **Good with** a green salad and French fries or potato chips.

VARIATION

Croque Madame

To make Croque Madames, top each serving with a fried or poached egg.

Coronation Chicken Rolls

These rolls are synonymous with British summer picnics and garden parties

- 🍽 makes 8 sandwiches
- 🕐 prep 15 mins, plus cooling
  • cook 5 mins

1 tbsp **vegetable oil**

1 **shallot**, finely chopped

1 tsp **curry powder** (either mild or hot, according to taste)

1 tbsp **tomato paste**

dash of **Worcestershire sauce**

½ cup (115g) **mayonnaise**

6 canned **apricot halves** in juice

2 cups diced **cooked chicken**

8 **small rolls**, preferably oval, split and spread with softened butter or left plain

2 tbsp chopped **parsley**

● **Prepare ahead** The chicken salad can be refrigerated up to 1 day in advance, then spooned on to the rolls an hour or two before serving.

1 Heat the oil in a small frying pan over medium-low heat. Add the shallot and cook for about 2 minutes until softened but not browned. Add the curry powder and stir for 1 minute until fragrant. Stir in the tomato paste and Worcestershire sauce. Remove from heat and let cool.

2 Process the shallot mixture, mayonnaise, and drained apricot halves in a food processor until smooth and creamy. Transfer to a bowl and stir in the chicken. Cover and refrigerate until needed.

3 Spoon the chicken salad onto the rolls, and sprinkle with the chopped parsley.

VARIATION

Egg Salad Rolls

Substitute 4 chopped, hard-boiled eggs for the chicken. If desired, add the grated zest of 1 lemon.

Cucumber Sandwiches

These traditional dainty sandwiches are an essential part of an English tea party

- 🍽 makes 4 servings
- 🕐 prep 15 mins, plus 30 mins standing

1 **cucumber**, lightly peeled

½ tsp **salt**

2 tsp **white wine vinegar**

8 thinly sliced **white** or **wheat bread**

softened **butter**, for spreading

freshly ground **black pepper**

tiny **watercress leaves**, or microgreens, to garnish

● **Prepare ahead** Step 1 can be completed 1 hour in advance, and the cucumber slices stored in the refrigerator.

1 Using a sharp knife, carefully slice the cucumber into rounds, no thicker than ⅛in (2mm). Place the cucumber slices in a colander and sprinkle with the salt. Let stand for 20-30 minutes to allow the excess liquid to drain off. When ready to use, sprinkle the slices with the vinegar.

2 Spread each slice of bread with some softened butter. Arrange the cucumber slices in an even layer over 4 slices of bread. Season with pepper, then top with the remaining bread slices, buttered sides down.

3 Cut off the crusts from each sandwich, then cut each sandwich into squares, triangles, or rectangles. Arrange the sandwiches on a serving plate. Sprinkle with watercress, and serve at once.

VARIATION

Cheese and Cucumber Sandwiches

As an alternative to butter, spread the bread with cream cheese or soft goat cheese.

Sandwiches

When you are in a hurry for good food fast, make a sandwich. Whether it's for lunch, supper, a snack, or even breakfast, there are many types of sandwiches to choose from. Let your creativity run wild, and see what fantastic flavor combinations you can come up with.

Types of Sandwiches

The great thing about making sandwiches is that there are no rules. You can make them hot or cold, light and delicate, or hearty and filling. Place roasted vegetables inside a whole grain pita with fresh goat cheese, or fill a crusty baguette with sliced duck breast and a sweet fruit preserve. When in need of inspiration, see the suggestions on page 92.

Open-faced Sandwiches
Originally from Scandinavia, these are unique among sandwiches in that they are made with 1 slice of bread. Use a dense bread, such as pumpernickel, so you can pick it up easily.

Tips for Packing

- Keep sandwiches fresh by wrapping them in paper, foil, or plastic bags as soon as they are assembled.
- Use crisp lettuce leaves to act as a barrier between the bread and watery ingredients, such as tomatoes.
- Never leave sandwiches with meat, poultry, or dairy fillings unrefrigerated for more than 2 hours.

Heros
Also called hoagies, grinders, subs, and poor boys, these 2-handed sandwiches are small Italian or French loaves stuffed with a selection of thinly sliced meats, vegetables, and pickles.

TYPES OF BREAD

Great bread makes a great sandwich—branch out and try one of these:

Baguettes The versatile French favorite.

Sourdough Made popular in San Francisco, perfect with seafood, cheese, or pâtés.

Pita Greek pockets, ideal for filling with a variety of salads.

Ciabatta Individual-sized Italian loaves make lovely paninis.

Mixed grain Dense and chewy, great to balance cured meats, smoked fish, and richly flavored spreads.

Paninis
Often made with ciabatta bread, paninis are toasted sandwiches from Italy. Add a quick-melting cheese for extra flavor.

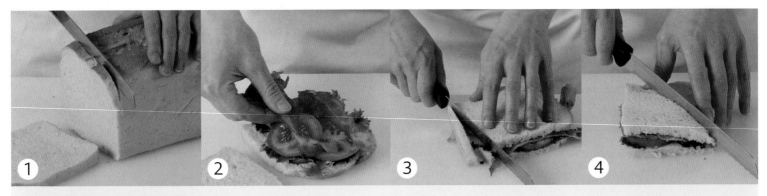

Sliced Bread Sandwich

1 **If you are using** an unsliced loaf, hold it firmly with one hand, while using a sawing motion with a serrated bread knife to cut 2 equal-sized slices. Spread one slice of bread with mayonnaise.

2 **Cook some bacon** until crisp, then leave on paper towels to drain. Place lettuce leaves on one slice of bread, then add tomato slices and bacon.

3 **Spread mayonnaise** on the second slice and place on top. Using the bread knife, carefully remove the crusts from the sandwich, while holding the stack firmly with your other hand.

4 **Cut the sandwich** diagonally into equal halves using the bread knife.

Grilled Sandwich

1 **Butter both sides** of 2 slices of bread and add cheese, tomato slices, and basil leaves. Top with a second slice of bread.

2 **Heat a frying pan** over medium-high heat. Add the sandwich and toast the first side for 2–3 minutes, or until the underside is browned.

3 **Using a spatula**, turn the sandwich over to cook the second side for 2–3 minutes, or until the bread is toasted and the cheese is melted.

4 **Carefully remove** the sandwich, place it on a cutting board, and use a serrated knife to cut it in half.

Thin Layered Sandwich

1 **To cut thin slices** without tearing the bread, spread cream cheese over the end of an uncut loaf, before slicing with a bread knife.

2 **Place a slice of bread** on the work surface and cover with smoked salmon. Sprinkle with snipped chives, then top with a second slice of bread, cream-cheese-side down. Repeat for any remaining sandwiches.

3 **Stack 2 sandwiches** on top of each other on a cutting board. Using the bread knife, cut the crusts off the sandwiches, holding the stack firmly with your other hand.

4 **Using the bread knife**, cut the stack of sandwiches in half diagonally, then cut in half again to make triangles.

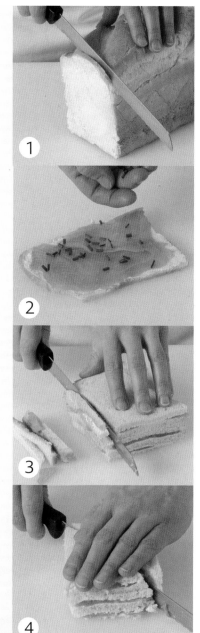

Alternatively...

You can also make tempting grilled cheese sandwiches by using a toaster oven or a sandwich maker. Preheat the toaster oven to its highest setting, then toast the sandwich on both sides until golden brown and the cheese has melted. Or, make your sandwich using an electric sandwich maker, following the manufacturer's instructions.

Alternatively...

To make party pinwheels, cover each bread slice with smoked salmon and chives, then cut off and discard the crusts. Tightly roll each Swiss-roll style. Wrap each roll tightly in plastic wrap, twisting the ends, and chill for up to a day. When ready to serve, unwrap each roll, and use a bread knife to cut into ¼in (5mm) slices.

Sandwiches

Cheese and Chutney
Try these ingredients on toasted slices of crusty baguette.

Cheddar cheese, sliced

apple chutney

butter, softened

Avocado and Bacon
Use mixed grain bread. Spread both slices of bread with mayonnaise, then top one with the lettuce, avocado, and bacon. Place the second slice spread-side down, and press the sandwich together.

mayonnaise

romaine lettuce

avocado, peeled, pit removed, and sliced

bacon slices, cooked until crisp, and drained well

Hummus Special
Spread whole grain slices of bread with hummus, then top with the vegetables, lettuce, and a second slice of bread.

hummus

red pepper, sliced

carrot, grated

tomatoes, sliced

mixed salad leaves

Toasted Fish
Split open a soft bun, spread with tartar sauce, and add the lettuce leaves. Top with the hot fish sticks, then slices of cheese. Add the top of the bun and press together.

tartar sauce

romaine lettuce, shredded

fish sticks, cooked

Cheddar cheese, sliced

Ham and Cheese
For a French classic, butter a slice of baguette, then add the ham and cheese.

butter, softened

Parma ham, sliced

Emmental cheese, sliced

Mediterranean Eggplant Panini
Slice a large piece of ciabatta bread in half. Spread with the pesto sauce, then add the eggplant, tomato, cheese, and arugula leaves. Top with the other half of ciabatta, and toast under a grill.

pesto sauce

grilled eggplant, sliced

tomatoes, sliced

provolone cheese, sliced

arugula leaves

Pâté Tartine
Spread a toasted slice of sourdough bread with pâté, then top with sliced gherkins.

chicken liver pâté

gherkins, sliced

Tuna-sweetcorn
Put the tuna in a bowl and stir in the mayonnaise. Add the sweetcorn and parsley, and season to taste with salt and freshly ground pepper. Spread on to whole grain bread, then top with a second slice of bread.

canned tuna, drained and flaked

mayonnaise

canned sweetcorn, drained

chopped fresh parsley

salt and pepper

Mozzarella Panini
Cut open ciabatta bread and brush with oil. Add the remaining ingredients and toast.

olive oil

mozzarella cheese, sliced

sun-dried tomatoes

basil leaves

Greek Pockets
Toast whole wheat pita bread, then split open and add the fillings.

leftover cooked lamb

feta cheese, crumbled

red pepper, diced

cucumber, diced

All-day Breakfast
Toast a soft roll, then add the eggs, sausage, and tomato.

scrambled eggs

broiled sausages, sliced

tomato, sliced

Chicken Wrap
Mix the yogurt with the lime zest, and spread over a soft flour tortilla. Add the other ingredients and tightly roll the tortilla.

thick plain yogurt

zest of lime

roasted chicken, sliced

cucumber, sliced

arugula leaves

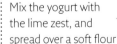

STACKS OF SANDWICHES
For a meal on the run it's hard to beat a simple but nutritious sandwich. With numerous combinations of breads and fillings (see left), the choice is yours.

Focaccia Sandwich with Tomatoes and Peppers

Buy a thick focaccia at your bakery and use it to make these Italian-style vegetarian sandwiches

 makes 4 sandwiches

prep 20 mins, plus cooling • cook 20 mins

2 **orange** or **yellow bell peppers**, or 1 of each

1 large **focaccia**, preferably with garlic and rosemary

4 tbsp **sun-dried tomato paste**

8 ripe **tomatoes**, halved

2 tbsp **extra virgin olive oil**

salt and freshly ground **black pepper**

8oz (225g) fresh **mozzarella**, thinly sliced

about 16 large **basil leaves**

1 Preheat the broiler. Line the broiler pan with aluminum foil. Grill the peppers, turning occasionally, until their skins are blackened and blistered. Leave the broiler on.

2 Wrap the foil around the peppers, folding over the edges to make a tightly sealed parcel. Let cool.

3 Slice the focaccia in half vertically with a long serrated knife. Cut the focaccia into quarters. Toast in the broiler on both sides. Spread the cut sides with the sun-dried tomato paste.

4 Line the broiler pan again with foil. Place the tomatoes on the pan, cut sides up, and drizzle with the olive oil. Season with the salt and pepper. Broil for about 5 minutes, or until the tomatoes have softened but are not falling apart.

5 Meanwhile, peel and seed the peppers, and cut the flesh into thick strips. Arrange the tomato halves and pepper slices on the focaccia bottoms. Top with the mozzarella and a few basil leaves, whole or torn, and drizzle over any oil and juices from the broiler pan. Place the remaining focaccia halves on top and serve immediately.

TIME SAVER

If you are short on time, use roasted peppers from the delicatessen instead of grilling your own.

BLT

The key to making this classic sandwich is to use the very best bacon and bread

 makes 4 sandwiches

prep 10 mins • cook 10 mins

12 slices **bacon**

8 slices **white sandwich bread**

½ cup **mayonnaise**

2 cups shredded **iceberg lettuce**

2 ripe **tomatoes**, sliced

freshly ground **black pepper**

1 Cook the bacon in a large frying pan over medium heat, turning once, about 6 minutes, until crisp and brown. Transfer to paper towels to drain.

2 Lightly toast the bread on both sides.

3 To assemble the sandwich, spread one side of each bread slice with the mayonnaise. Place 4 slices, mayonnaise side up, on the work surface. Top each with equal amounts of the lettuce and tomatoes and 3 bacon slices. Season with the pepper. Top each with the one of the remaining bread slices, mayonnaise-side down. Cut each sandwich in half and serve immediately.

Quesadillas with Salsa Mexicana

Quesadillas may have already overtaken the grilled cheese sandwich in popularity. These are served with a chunky salsa

 makes 8 servings

prep 10 mins • cook 20 mins

For the salsa

2 large ripe **tomatoes**, seeded and finely chopped

½ **onion**, finely chopped

3 tbsp chopped **cilantro**

1 fresh **hot green chile**, seeded and minced

1 **garlic clove**, minced

juice of ½ **lime**

salt

8 **flour tortillas**

2 cups shredded **sharp Cheddar**

guacamole, to serve

1 **To make the salsa**, combine all the ingredients in a bowl. Season with the salt. Set aside for about 1 hour to blend the flavors.

2 **Preheat the oven** to 200°F (95°C). Heat a heavy frying pan over medium heat. Place 1 tortilla in the pan and heat for 30 seconds. Flip over and sprinkle ¼ cup of the cheese over the surface. Fold in half and press down lightly with a spatula.

3 **Cook, turning once**, until the quesadilla is lightly toasted on both sides and the cheese has melted. Transfer to a baking sheet and keep warm in the oven while making the remaining quesadillas.

4 **To serve**, cut each quesadilla in half and serve immediately with the Salsa Mexicana and guacamole.

VARIATION

BBQ Chicken and Cheese Quesadillas

Toss 1 cup shredded cooked chicken with 2 tbsp barbecue sauce, and mix in 1 cup shredded Monterey jack cheese instead of Cheddar. Serve with sour cream instead of guacamole.

Steakhouse Sandwich

Great for lunch, this filling East Coast-style sandwich will keep you going through the afternoon

 makes 4 servings

 prep 15 mins • cook 10 mins

ridged grill pan

2 **sirloin steaks**, 10oz (250g) each

1 tbsp **oil**

salt and freshly ground **black pepper**

4oz (115g) **cream cheese**, softened

4oz (115g) crumbled **Roquefort**, or other blue cheese

2 tsp prepared **horseradish**

4 **crusty white rolls** split in half, toasted

2 **tomatoes**, sliced

1 **onion**, thinly sliced into rings

8 **dill pickle** slices

4 **lettuce** leaves

Dijon mustard, for serving

1 **Heat a ridged** grill pan over high heat until very hot. Cut each steak in half crosswise. Brush the steaks with oil and season with salt and pepper. In batches, add the steaks to the pan and cook, turning once, for about 3 minutes on each side for medium-rare.

2 **Meanwhile**, mash the cream cheese, blue cheese, and horseradish together. Spread on the toasted rolls.

3 **Place a steak** on the bottom half of each roll. Top each with tomato slices, onion rings, 2 pickle slices, and a lettuce leaf. Replace the roll tops and secure with wooden toothpicks. Serve at once, with the mustard passed on the side.

Open-faced Sandwiches

A variety of colorful sandwiches

 makes 4 servings

 prep 10 mins

12 slices of **bread**, a mixture of white, whole wheat, and whole grain

¼ cup **mayonnaise**

4 tsp Dijon mustard

To serve

hard-boiled **egg**, peeled and sliced

store-bought grilled **eggplant**

mozzarella

lemon slices

tomato slices

mixed salad leaves

cooked shrimp

3 ham slices

salt and freshly ground black pepper

1 Lay the bread slices on a work surface. Mix the mayonnaise and mustard together in a bowl and spread on the bread. Cut the egg, eggplant, mozzarella, lemon, and tomato into slices.

2 Top each of 3 bread slices with ham, sliced egg and a few salad leaves. Top 3 more slices with equal amounts of the shrimp, lettuce leaves, and a lemon slice. Layer the eggplant, mozzarella, and tomato over the 3 remaining bread slices.

3 Transfer to a serving platter and let everyone help themselves.

Deluxe Peanut Butter Sandwiches

A "dressed-up" version of the popular peanut and jelly sandwich, makes a nutritious, delicious sandwich

- makes 4 servings
- prep 10 mins

½ cup creamy or chunky **peanut butter**

2 tbsp orange **marmalade**

3 ripe medium **bananas**

8 slices **whole wheat bread**, toasted

1 **In a small bowl**, combine the peanut butter and marmalade until well mixed. Peel the bananas and cut them in half lengthwise, and then crosswise in half to make 12 pieces total.

2 **Spread the peanut butter** equally over 4 slices of toast. Top each with 3 pieces of banana, and top with remaining toast.

3 **Cut each sandwich** in half diagonally, if you like.

- **Good with** sliced apple or pear.

Reuben Sandwich

This substantial sandwich, a delicatessen standard, could very well have been invented in Omaha, and not New York

- makes 4 sandwiches
- prep 10 mins • cook 8–12 mins

8oz (225g) **sauerkraut**

8 slices **rye bread**

½ cup store-bought **Russian salad dressing**

12oz (340g) sliced **corned beef**

4oz (115g) sliced **Swiss cheese**

4 tbsp **butter**

1 **Rinse the sauerkraut** in a colander. Place a plate on top and let drain in the sink for 15 minutes.

2 **Spread the bread slices** with the dressing. Divide the corned beef, Swiss cheese, and sauerkraut over 4 slices. Top each with a bread slice, dressing side down.

3 **Melt 1 tbsp** of butter in a very large frying pan over medium heat. Add 2 of the sandwiches and top each with a small heatproof plate. Cook for about 2 minutes, or until the underside is golden brown.

4 **Flip the sandwiches** over, removing and replacing the plates. Add 1 tbsp of butter and cook another 2 minutes, or until the other side is golden brown. Transfer to a platter and tent with aluminium foil. Repeat with the remaining sandwiches and butter. Serve hot.

- **Good with** sour dill pickles.

Tacos

Tacos are popular with kids and are great party food, too

- makes 4–6 servings
- prep 15 mins • cook 25 mins

2 tbsp **olive oil**

1 **onion**, finely chopped

1 **garlic clove**, minced

1lb 2oz (500g) **ground round**

2 tbsp **chili powder**

1 tsp dried **oregano**

3 tbsp **tomato paste**

12 crisp **taco shells**

shredded **iceberg lettuce**, shredded **Cheddar**, **tomato salsa**, **jalapeño peppers**, and **sour cream**, to serve

1 **Heat the oil** in a frying pan. Add the onion and garlic and cook, stirring, for 3 minutes. Add the beef and brown, about 8 minutes. Drain off fat. Stir in the chili powder and oregano, tomato paste, and ½ cup water. Simmer until thickened, for 10 minutes. Season.

2 **Meanwhile**, preheat the oven to 300°F (150°C). Bake the shells on a sheet for 4 minutes. Spoon the meat into the shells. Serve with bowls of lettuce, Cheddar, salsa, jalapeños, and sour cream.

Basic Pizza Dough

The starting point for countless great recipes

🍴 makes 4 servings

🕐 prep 15 mins, plus rising • cook 20-25 mins

3⅔ cups **bread flour**

two ¼oz (7g) envelopes **instant yeast**

½ tsp **salt**

1½ cups tepid **water**

2 tbsp **olive oil**, plus more for the bowl

● **Prepare ahead** The dough can be refrigerated in an airtight container for up to 1 day. Let stand in a warm place about 2½ hours, until doubled, and knead briefly before using.

1 **Combine the flour**, yeast, and salt in a large bowl. Make a well in the center, add the water and oil, and stir to make a soft dough. Knead on a lightly floured work surface about 10 minutes, until smooth and elastic.

2 **Roll the dough** into a ball. Place in a lightly oiled bowl and turn to coat the dough. Cover tightly with plastic wrap. Let stand in a warm place until doubled in size.

● **Good with** a variety of vegetables, meats, and cheeses to make a wide range of pizzas.

Pissaladière

Essentially an onion-and-olive pizza with lots of anchovies, you can certainly omit the anchovies

🍴 makes 4 main-course or 8 appetizer servings

🕐 prep 20 mins, plus rising • cook 1 hr 25 mins

▭ 13 x 9in (33 x 23cm) rimmed baking sheet

❄ freeze for up to 3 months; thaw at room temperature and reheat in a warm oven

1⅔ cups **bread flour**, plus more for kneading

1 tsp **instant yeast**

1 tsp **brown sugar**

1 tsp **salt**

⅔ cup tepid **water**

1 tbsp **olive oil**

For the topping

¼ cup **olive oil**

2lb (900g) **onions**, finely sliced

3 **garlic cloves**, sliced

1 tsp **herbes de Provence**

1 sprig **thyme**

1 **bay leaf**

two 2oz (56g) cans **anchovies in oil**

12 pitted **Kalamata olives**

salt and freshly ground **black pepper**

1 **To make the dough**, stir the flour, yeast, brown sugar, and salt together in a bowl. Make a well in the center and add the water and oil. Stir to make a soft dough, adding more water if needed.

2 **Knead on a floured** work surface for about 8 minutes, until smooth and elastic. Shape into a ball. Place in an oiled bowl and turn to coat with oil. Cover with plastic wrap and let stand in a warm place for about 1 hour, until doubled.

3 **For the topping**, heat the oil in a large, heavy-bottomed casserole over low heat. Add the onions, garlic, herbs, thyme, and bay leaf. Cover and cook, stirring occasionally, adding a little water if the onions begin to stick, for about 45 minutes, until very tender. Drain in a sieve, discarding the thyme and bay leaf. Let cool.

4 **Preheat the oven** to 350°F (180°C). Lightly oil a 13 x 9in (33 x 23cm) rimmed baking sheet. Knead the dough briefly on a floured work surface. Roll into a rectangle to fit the baking sheet, and transfer to the pan. Prick all over with a fork.

5 **Spread the onions** over the dough. Drain the anchovies, reserving 3 tbsp oil. Arrange the anchovy fillets in a crisscross pattern over the onions, and garnish with the olives. Drizzle with the reserved anchovy oil, and sprinkle with pepper.

6 **Bake for about** 25 minutes, until the crust is brown. Let cool slightly. Cut into serving pieces and serve warm, or cool completely.

Pizza Bianca

Crisp pizza dough makes the perfect base for light, fresh toppings such as prosciutto, figs, arugula, and tangy blue cheese

 makes 4 individual pizzas

 prep 25 mins
• cook 25–30 mins

2 large or 4 smaller baking sheets

Basic Pizza Dough (p98)

4 tbsp **extra virgin olive oil**, plus more for the baking sheets

5oz (140g) **Gorgonzola cheese**, crumbled

4 slices of **prosciutto** torn into strips

4 **figs**, each cut into 8 wedges and peeled

2 **tomatoes**, seeded and diced

4oz (115g) **arugula**

freshly ground **black pepper**

1 **Preheat the oven** to 400°F (200°C). Lightly oil 2 large baking sheets. Divide the dough into 4 equal portions. Roll each on a very lightly floured work surface into an 8in (20cm) round. Arrange 2 rounds on each sheet. Brush with 2 tbsp of the oil and sprinkle with the Gorgonzola.

2 **Bake for 15 minutes**, or until the dough is just beginning to brown.

3 **Remove from the oven**, top with the prosciutto, figs, and tomatoes, and continue baking about 6 minutes, or until the pizzas are golden brown.

4 **Divide the arugula** over each pizza and grind a generous amount of pepper on top. Drizzle with the remaining olive oil and serve at once.

VARIATION

Gruyère Pizza Bianca
Substitute Gruyère cheese for the Gorgonzola and sprinkle with Fontina.

Pizza Four Seasons

On these pizzas, the toppings are arranged separately to represent the four seasons

 makes 4 small pizzas

prep 15 mins • cook 20 mins

Basic Pizza Dough (p98)

1⅓ cups canned **crushed tomatoes**

6oz (175g) **mozzarella cheese**, thinly sliced

4oz (115g) **white mushrooms**, thinly sliced

2 **roasted red peppers**, sliced into thin strips

16 **anchovy fillets** in oil

4oz (115g) **pepperoni**, thinly sliced

2 tbsp **capers**

8 **marinated artichokes hearts**, drained and halved

12 pitted **Kalamata olives**

4 tbsp **extra virgin olive oil**

1 **Preheat the oven** to 400°F (200°C). Lightly oil 2 large baking sheets. Divide the dough into 4 equal portions. Roll each on a very lightly floured work surface into an 8in (20cm) round. Arrange 2 rounds on each sheet. Spread each with ⅓ cup tomato sauce, leaving a 1in (2.5cm) border. Divide the mozzarella evenly over the pizza tops.

2 **For each pizza**, arrange the mushroom slices on one quarter of the pizza round. Arrange the red peppers and 4 anchovy fillets on another quarter of the round. Cover a third quarter with the pepperoni and capers, and finally top the fourth quarter with 4 artichoke pieces and 3 olives. Drizzle the oil evenly over the pizza.

3 **Bake for 20-25 minutes**, until the edges of the dough are crisp and golden brown. Serve hot.

Pizzette

These are mini party pizzas. Try the toppings below, or create your own favorite combinations

- makes 24 pizzettes
- prep 20 mins, plus rising • cook 12–15 mins
- 3in (7.5cm) plain pastry cutter
- freeze the baked pizzettes for up to 1 month

Basic Pizza Dough (p98)

3 tbsp **pesto**, homemade or store-bought

3 tbsp **sun-dried tomato paste**

2oz (60g) sliced **salami** or pepperoni, cut into strips

6 pitted **Kalamata olives**, halved

2oz (60g) **mozzarella**, cut into small slices

½ cup packed, coarsely chopped **arugula leaves**

2 tbsp **pine nuts**

extra virgin olive oil, to drizzle

● **Prepare ahead** The pizzettes can be baked up to 24 hours in advance. Reheat to serve.

1 Preheat the oven to 425°F (220°C). Lightly oil 2 or 3 large baking sheets.

2 Knead the pizza dough on a lightly floured surface. Roll out into a thin rectangle ¼in (5mm) thick. Using a 3in (7.5cm) round cookie cutter, cut out 24 rounds, gathering up the dough trimmings and re-rolling as required. Transfer the rounds to the baking sheets.

3 Spread 12 rounds with the pesto and half with the sun-dried tomato paste. Top the pesto rounds with salami, olives, and mozzarella. Top the sun-dried tomato rounds with the arugula and pine nuts. Brush with olive oil, cover loosely with a clean paper towel, and let stand for 20 minutes, or until puffy.

4 Bake for 12–15 minutes, until golden brown. Serve warm.

> ### FREEZING TIP
> These little bites make a good snack to keep in the freezer. Batch freeze them in small quantities, then reheat in a hot oven before serving.

Pizza Florentina

An eye-catching pizza with spinach and a whole egg

- makes 4 small pizzas
- prep 15 mins • cook 20 mins

Basic Pizza Dough (p98)

1⅓ cups store-bought **tomato pizza** or **pasta sauce**

8oz (225g) **spinach**, cooked, drained well, and chopped

1 tsp **thyme leaves**

¼ tsp freshly grated **nutmeg**

6oz (175g) **mozzarella**, sliced

4 small **eggs**

4 tbsp grated **Parmesan cheese**

1 Preheat the oven to 400°F (200°C). Lightly oil 2 large baking sheets. Divide the dough into 4 equal portions. Roll each on a lightly floured work surface into an 8in (20cm) round. Arrange 2 rounds on each sheet. Spread each with ⅓ cup tomato sauce, leaving a 1in (2.5cm) border.

2 Top each pizza with spinach, then sprinkle with the thyme and nutmeg. Divide the mozzarella overtop. Crack an egg in the center of each, and sprinkle with the Parmesan.

3 Bake for 20–25 minutes, until the edges of the dough are crisp and golden brown.

Tarte Flambé

This thin-crusted tart from Alsace is topped with sweet onions and crisp smoky bacon

 makes 4 servings

 prep 20 mins, plus cooling • cook 50 mins

 two 13 x 9in (33 x 23cm) rimmed baking sheets

2 tbsp **vegetable oil**

2 tbsp **butter**

4 large **onions**, thinly sliced

1 cup **fromage blanc** (or cottage cheese rubbed through a sieve)

2 large **eggs**

2 tbsp **cornstarch**

1 tbsp **crème fraîche**

Basic Pizza Dough (p98)

4oz (115g) **thick-sliced bacon**, chopped

1 Heat the oil and butter in a large saucepan over medium-low heat. Add the onions and cover. Cook 10 minutes, until softened. Uncover and cook, stirring often, 15 minutes, until golden. Let cool.

2 Beat the fromage blanc, eggs, and cornstarch until smooth. Stir in enough crème fraîche until the mixture is spreadable.

3 Preheat the oven to 400°F (200°C). Lightly oil two 13 x 9in (33 x 23cm) rimmed baking sheets. Cut the dough in half and stretch and press each portion into a baking sheet. Spread an equal amount of the cheese mixture over each, leaving a 1in (2.5cm) border, and top with equal amounts of the onion and bacon. Bake for 30 minutes, until the crust is golden brown. Serve hot.

Calzone

These folded pizzas have a tasty chicken, pancetta, and vegetable filling

 makes 4 calzones

prep 20 mins, plus cooling • cook 25–30 mins

3 tbsp **olive oil**, plus more for the baking sheets

6 slices **pancetta**, chopped

1 boneless skinless **chicken breast**, cut into small pieces

1 **green bell pepper**, seeded and chopped

¼ cup **sun-dried tomato paste**

Basic Pizza Dough (p98)

7oz (200g) **mozzarella cheese**, sliced

¼ cup chopped **parsley**

freshly ground **black pepper**

1 large beaten **egg**, to seal

1 Heat 1 tbsp of the oil in a frying pan over medium-high heat. Add the pancetta, chicken, and green pepper and cook until the chicken is opaque throughout, about 5 minutes. Transfer to a bowl and let cool.

2 Preheat the oven to 400°F (200°C). Divide the dough into four equal portions. Roll out each on a lightly floured work surface into a 9in (23cm) round.

3 Spread the tomato paste over the lower half of each dough round, leaving a ½in (13mm) border. Divide the filling evenly over the paste, then top with equal amounts of the mozzarella and parsley. Season generously with the pepper.

4 Brush the exposed edges of the dough with the beaten egg. Fold over to enclose the filling, pressing the edges together firmly with your fingers or a fork to seal.

5 Brush with the remaining olive oil. Bake for 20–25 minutes or until the edges are crisp and golden brown. Serve hot.

● **Good with** a green salad.

VARIATION

Spicy Calzone

Fry 1–2 tsp of dried chile flakes in the mix in step 1 for added heat.

Brown Meat Stock

This rich stock is made from raw bones: use either beef or lamb bones, not a mixture of the two

🍴 makes about 2½ qts (2½ liters)

🕐 prep 10 mins
• cook 3½–4½ hrs

❄ freeze for up to 6 months

3lb (1.35kg) **beef bones**

2 **onions**, unpeeled and cut in half

2 **carrots**, cut in half

vegetable trimmings, such as mushroom peelings, celery tops, or tomato skins

bouquet garni, made with 1 celery stick, 1 bay leaf, a few sprigs of thyme and parsley, tied together with

kitchen twine

1 tbsp **black peppercorns**

⬤ **Prepare ahead** The stock can be cooled, covered, and refrigerated for up to 2 days. Scrape off any residual fat from the surface.

1 **Preheat the oven** to 400°F (200°C). Combine the beef bones, onions, and carrots in a roasting pan. Roast, turning the ingredients occasionally, about 40 minutes, until well browned.

2 **Transfer the bones**, onions, and carrots into a large

saucepan, adding any vegetable trimmings, the bouquet garni, and the peppercorns.

3 **Pour in enough** cold water to cover by 1in (2.5cm). Bring to a boil over high heat, skimming off any foam that rises to the surface. Reduce the heat to low and simmer 3-4 hours, until well flavored.

4 **Strain the stock** into a large bowl. Let stand 10 minutes, then skim the fat from the surface. Use immediately, or cool completely and refrigerate or freeze.

Vegetable Stock

It is worth making a double batch of this stock to use in other soups and casseroles

🍴 makes about 5 cups

🕐 prep 10 mins • cook 1 hr

❄ freeze for up to 6 months

3 large **carrots**, coarsely chopped

3 large **onions**, coarsely chopped

3 large **celery stalks** with leaves, coarsely chopped

2 **leeks**, white and pale green parts only, chopped and rinsed

10 whole **black peppercorns**, lightly crushed

10 large sprigs **parsley**

2 **bay leaves**

½ tsp **salt**

⬤ **Prepare ahead** The cooled stock can be refrigerated for up to 2 days.

1 **Combine the carrots**, onions, celery, and leeks in a large saucepan with 7 cups water. Bring to a boil over high heat, skimming off any foam that rises to the surface. Reduce the heat to low. Add the peppercorns, parsley, bay leaves, and salt. Partially cover the saucepan and simmer for 45 minutes, or until the stock is well-flavored.

2 **Strain the stock** into a large bowl. Use immediately, or cool completely to refrigerate or freeze.

Fish Stock

A tasty, delicate stock that is quick and easy to make

 makes about 1 quart

prep 10 mins • cook 20 mins

freeze for up to 2 months

1½lb (675g) miscellaneous **fish trimmings** (heads, bones, tails), gills removed and any blood rinsed off

2 **onions**, coarsely chopped

1 **celery** stalk

few sprigs **thyme**

few sprigs **parsley**

1 **bay leaf**

¼ tsp each **salt** and **whole black peppercorns**

⬤ **Prepare ahead** The stock can be cooled and refrigerated for up to 2 days.

1 **Bring the fish trimmings**, onions, celery, and 7 cups water just to a boil in a large saucepan over high heat, skimming off any foam that rises to the surface.

2 **Add the thyme**, parsley, bay leaf, salt, and peppercorns. Partially cover the pan, reduce the heat to medium-low, and simmer for about 20 minutes.

3 **Strain the stock** into a large bowl. Use immediately, or cool and refrigerate.

OILY FISH

Do not use bones from oily fish, such as mackerel, or the stock will be too cloudy and strongly flavored.

Chicken Stock

Endlessly versatile, it is worthwhile to make your own chicken stock

 makes about 2 qts (2 liters)

prep 10 mins • cook 1 hr

freeze for up to 6 months

3lb (1.3kg) **chicken wings**, chopped at the joints

2 **celery** stalks, roughly chopped

2 **onions**, quartered

8 sprigs **parsley**

4 sprigs **thyme**

1 **bay leaf**

1 tsp **salt**

10 **whole black peppercorns**, lightly crushed

⬤ **Prepare ahead** The stock can be cooled, covered, and refrigerated for up to 2 days. Scrape any residual fat from the surface.

1 **Combine the chicken**, celery, and onion in a large saucepan with 2 qts (2 liters) cold water. Bring just to a boil over high heat. Using a large spoon, skim off any foam that rises to the surface. Reduce the heat to low and add the parsley, thyme, bay leaf, salt, and peppercorns. Partially cover the saucepan. Simmer for at least 1 and up to 3 hours.

2 **Strain the stock** into a large bowl. Let stand 10 minutes, then skim the fat from the surface. Use immediately, or cool completely and refrigerate or freeze.

 **VARIATION**

Turkey Stock

Substitute 2 turkey wings for the chicken wings. Add the neck and giblets (but not the liver) from 1 turkey, if available.

Gazpacho

This chilled, no-cook Spanish soup is always popular when temperatures are hot outside

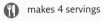 makes 4 servings

prep 15 mins, plus at least 1 hr for chilling

can be frozen for up to 1 month without the garnishes

2¼lb (1 kg) **tomatoes**, plus extra for serving

1 small **cucumber**, peeled, seeded, and chopped, plus extra for serving

1 small **red pepper**, seeded and finely chopped, plus extra for serving

¼ cup **sherry vinegar**

2 **garlic cloves**, crushed and peeled

salt and freshly ground **pepper**

½ cup **extra virgin olive oil**, plus more for serving

1 **hard-boiled egg**, white and yolk separated, finely chopped, for serving

● **Prepare ahead** The soup can be chilled for up to 2 days.

1 Place the tomatoes in a heatproof bowl, add enough boiling water to cover, and let stand for 20 seconds or until the skins split. Drain and rinse under cold running water to cool. Gently peel off the skins. Cut the tomatoes in half, and use a teaspoon to remove the cores and seeds. Chop the flesh.

2 Purée the tomato flesh, cucumber, red pepper, vinegar, garlic, and salt and pepper to taste in a food processor. Pour in the olive oil and process again. Dilute with a little water if too thick. Transfer the soup to a serving bowl, cover with plastic wrap, and chill for at least 1 hour.

3 Serve the gazpacho with bowls of the tomatoes, cucumber, red pepper, egg yolk and white, and a cruet of olive oil, to add as garnishes.

Watercress and Pear Soup

For extra flavor, serve this velvety soup with shredded Parmesan cheese

 makes 4 servings

prep 10 mins • cook 15 mins

the soup, without the cream, can be frozen up to 3 months. Add the cream after reheating.

2 tbsp **butter**

1 **onion**, finely chopped

6oz (175g) **watercress**

3 ripe **pears**, peeled, cored, and roughly chopped

1qt (liter) **chicken stock**

salt and freshly ground **black pepper**

¾ cup **heavy cream**

1 tbsp fresh **lemon** juice

olive oil, to drizzle

● **Prepare ahead** The soup can cooled, covered, and refrigerated up to one day.

1 Melt the butter in a large saucepan over medium-low heat. Add the onion and cover. Cook, stirring occasionally, about 10 minutes, or until tender.

2 Meanwhile, trim the watercress and pluck off the leaves. Add the watercress stems to the pot with the pears and stock. Bring to a boil over high heat.

3 Cover and simmer gently for 15 minutes, or until the pears are tender. Season with salt and pepper. Reserving a few watercress leaves for garnish, purée the soup and watercress leaves in a blender. Add the cream and lemon juice, and adjust the seasoning.

4 Serve hot, garnished with watercress leaves.

VARIATION

Spinach Soup

Substitute spinach leaves for the watercress and omit the pears. Substitute ¾ cup canned coconut milk for the cream. Serve warm.

CHILLED SOUP
Let cool and chill in the refrigerator. To serve; pour the soup into chilled bowls, top with crushed ice, and drizzle with a little olive oil.

Curried Parsnip Soup

Gentle spices perk up this earthy-flavored soup

🍴 makes 4 servings

🕐 prep 10 mins • cook 50 mins

3 tbsp **butter**

1 **onion**, chopped

11oz (300g) **parsnips**, chopped

1 **carrot**, chopped

1 **baking potato**, peeled and chopped

2 tbsp **all-purpose flour**

2 tbsp **mild curry powder**

4½ cups **chicken** or **vegetable stock**

salt and freshly ground **black pepper**

crème fraîche, for serving

chopped **parsley**, for serving

1 Melt the butter in a saucepan over a medium heat. Add the onion and cook, stirring frequently, until softened. Add the parsnips, carrot, and potato. Sprinkle in the flour and curry powder and stir for 2 minutes.

2 Gradually stir in the stock. Turn up the heat and bring to a boil. Reduce the heat to low. Cover and simmer gently for 40 minutes, or until the vegetables are tender.

3 Turn the heat off, uncover, and allow the soup to cool slightly. Purée the soup into a blender or food processor. Season with salt and pepper. Pour back into the pot and reheat before serving.

4 To serve, ladle into bowls. Top each with a swirl of crème fraîche and a sprinkle of chopped parsley.

● **Good with** crusty bread or cheese scones.

Borscht

Hearty and satisfying, this Russian beet and vegetable soup can be enjoyed at any time of year, either hot or chilled

🍴 makes 6 servings

🕐 prep 15 mins • cook 1½ hrs

▦ small piece of cheesecloth

2 large **beets**

1 **onion**

1 **carrot**

1 **celery stalk**

2 tbsp **vegetable oil**

one 14.5oz (110g) can **chopped tomatoes**

1 **garlic clove**, chopped

6 cups **vegetable stock**

2 **bay leaves**

4 whole **cloves**

2 tbsp fresh **lemon** juice

salt and freshly ground **black pepper**

sour cream, for serving

1 Roughly shred the beets, onion, carrot, and celery.

2 Heat the oil in a large saucepan over medium-low heat. Add the beets, onion, carrot, and celery, and cook, stirring occasionally, for 5 minutes, or until just softened.

3 Stir in the tomatoes with their juices and the garlic. Cook, stirring often, for 2–3 minutes. Stir in the stock and return to a boil.

4 Tie the bay leaves and cloves in a small piece of rinsed cheesecloth. Add to the pot. Reduce the heat to low and cover. Simmer for 1¼ hours.

5 Discard the cheesecloth packet. Stir in the lemon juice and season with salt and pepper.

6 Top each serving with a dollop of sour cream.

VARIATION

Lite Borscht

For a lighter soup, blend until smooth and add a little more stock. Serve hot or chilled, garnished with a swirl of natural yogurt and a sprinkle of chopped parsley.

Vichyssoise

Despite its French name, this iced soup originates from America. It can also be served hot, with a few cooked shrimp on top

 makes 6 servings

 prep 15 mins • cook 30 mins

 the soup, without the cream, can be frozen up to 3 months; thaw, then reheat, stir in the cream, and serve warm or chilled

2 tbsp **vegetable oil** (or butter, if the soup is served hot)

3 large **leeks**, cleaned, white and pale green parts only, finely sliced

4¾ cups fresh **vegetable stock**

1 large **baking potato**, such as russet or Burbank, peeled and chopped

1 **celery** stalk, roughly chopped

salt and freshly ground **black pepper**

⅔ cup **heavy cream**, plus more to garnish

2 tbsp finely chopped **chives**, to serve

1 Heat the oil in a large heavy saucepan over medium heat. Add the leeks and cover. Cook, gently shaking the pot from time to time, for about 15 minutes, or until the leeks are softened and golden.

2 Add the stock, potato, and celery and bring to a boil, stirring often. Season with salt and pepper. Cover, reduce the heat to medium-low, and simmer for 30 minutes, until the vegetables are tender.

3 Remove the pan from the heat and let cool slightly. In batches, purée in a blender with the lid ajar. Season with salt and pepper and cool completely. Stir in the cream. Cover and refrigerate at least 3 hours, or until well chilled.

4 Ladle into soup bowls, sprinkle with chives and black pepper, and add a drizzle of cream. Serve chilled.

Tomato Soup

Easy to make using canned tomatoes, this delicious soup can be enjoyed all year round

 makes 6-8 servings

 prep 20 mins • cook 55 mins

 low fat

1 tbsp **olive oil**

1 **onion**, chopped

2 **celery** stalks, sliced

1 **garlic clove**, sliced

1 **carrot**, sliced

1 **baking potato**, peeled and chopped

one 28oz (784g) can **plum tomatoes** in juice

3 cups **vegetable or chicken stock**

1 tsp **sugar**

1 **bay leaf**

salt and freshly ground **black pepper**

● **Prepare ahead** The soup can be cooled and refrigerated for up to 2 days.

1 Heat the oil in a large saucepan over medium-low heat. Add the onion, celery, and garlic. Cook, stirring frequently, until softened but not colored.

2 Add the carrot and potato and stir for 1 minute. Add the tomatoes with their juice, the stock, sugar, and bay leaf. Season to taste with salt and pepper. Bring to a boil over high heat, then return the heat to medium-low. Cover and simmer for 45 minutes, or until the vegetables are very tender.

3 Let cool slightly. In batches, purée in a blender with the lid ajar. Adjust the seasoning. Reheat gently and serve hot.

● **Good with** a swirl of heavy cream, crème fraîche, or yogurt, or a garnish of celery leaves.

VARIATION

Roasted Red Pepper and Tomato Soup

Omit the potato. Broil 2 whole red peppers, turning occasionally, until the skin blackens. Place in a bowl, cover with plastic wrap, and let stand until cool enough to handle. Peel off the blackened skin and remove the seeds and ribs. Add the red peppers and ½ tsp smoked paprika to the soup just before puréeing it.

Mushroom Soup

Using a selection of both wild and cultivated mushrooms will produce a soup that is bursting with flavor

- 🍴 makes 6 servings
- 🕐 prep 10 mins • cook 45 mins
- ❄ can be frozen for up to 3 months

2 tbsp **butter**

1 **onion**, finely chopped

2 **celery** ribs, finely chopped

1 **garlic clove**, crushed

1lb (450g) mixed **mushrooms**, cleaned and coarsely chopped

1 quart **vegetable** or **chicken stock**

7oz (200g) **baking potatoes**, peeled and cubed

2 tbsp finely chopped **parsley**

salt and freshly ground **black pepper**

⬤ **Prepare ahead** The soup can be cooled, covered, and refrigerated for up to 2 days. Reheat before serving.

1 Melt the butter in a large saucepan over medium heat. Add the onion, celery, and garlic and cook for about 3–4 minutes, or until softened.

2 Stir in the mushrooms and cook for 5-6 minutes more. Add the stock and potatoes and bring to a boil. Reduce the heat and simmer gently for 30 minutes.

3 In batches, process in a blender or food processor with the lid ajar until coarsely puréed.

4 Sprinkle in the parsley and season with salt and pepper. Serve hot.

EXTRA FLAVOR

As an extra flavor, add a spoonful of prepared horseradish to each bowl of soup.

Carrot and Orange Soup

A light, refreshing soup with a hint of spice, this is the perfect start to a summer meal

- 🍴 makes 4 servings
- 🕐 prep 10 mins • cook 40 mins
- ⬤ low fat

1lb (450g) **carrots**, sliced

1 **leek**, white and pale green parts only, sliced

2 tsp **olive oil**

1 small **baking potato**, about 4oz (115g), peeled and chopped

½ tsp **ground coriander**

pinch of **ground cumin**

10fl oz (300ml) **orange** juice

2 cups **vegetable** or **chicken stock**

1 **bay leaf**

salt and freshly ground **black pepper**

2 tbsp chopped **cilantro**, to garnish

⬤ **Prepare ahead** The soup can be made up to 2 days in advance.

1 Combine the carrots, leek, and oil in a large saucepan and cook over low heat, stirring frequently for 5 minutes, or until the leeks have softened. Stir in the potato, coriander, and cumin. Add the stock, orange juice, and bay leaf and stir well.

2 Increase the heat to high and bring to a boil. Return the heat to low and cover. Simmer about 40 minutes, until the vegetables are very tender.

3 Allow the soup to cool slightly, then transfer to a blender or food processor and process until smooth, working in batches if necessary.

4 Let cool slightly. In batches, purée in a blender with the lid ajar. Return to the saucepan and season with salt and pepper. If the soup is too thick, thin with a little water. Ladle into soup bowls, garnished with the cilantro.

⬤ **Good with** a spoonful of low-fat plain yogurt or a swirl of cream.

VARIATION

Sweet Potato Soup

Substitute orange-fleshed sweet potatoes for some or all of the carrots. Use apple juice instead of orange juice, and replace the ground coriander and cumin with 1 tsp sweet paprika.

Porcini Mushroom Soup

This hearty Italian country soup is full of deep, earthy goodness

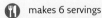 makes 6 servings

 prep 20 mins, plus soaking • cook 1 hr, plus standing

low fat, low GI

freeze, without the bread, for up to 3 months

1oz (30g) **dried porcini mushrooms**

1⅓ cups boiling **water**

3 tbsp **extra virgin olive oil**, plus more for drizzling

2 **onions**, finely chopped

2 **celery stalks** with leaves, finely chopped

4oz (115g) **cremini mushrooms**, sliced

2 **garlic cloves**, thinly sliced

2 tsp chopped **rosemary**

1 tsp chopped **thyme**

3 cups **vegetable stock**

one 14.5oz (411g) can **chopped tomatoes**, drained

salt and freshly ground **black pepper**

4 cups diced day-old **crusty bread**

● **Prepare ahead** The soup can be made through step 3, then cooled, covered, and refrigerated for up to 2 days. Reheat, then add the bread.

1 **Combine the dried porcini** and boiling water in a small bowl. Let stand for 30 minutes. Drain through a fine sieve, reserving the soaking liquid. Coarsely chop the soaked mushrooms.

2 **Heat the oil** in a large saucepan over medium-low heat. Add the onions and cook about 5 minutes, until softened. Add the celery and cook 5 minutes more, until the celery is tender. Stir in the mushrooms, garlic, rosemary, and thyme and cook until the mushrooms soften, about 5 minutes more.

3 **Add the stock**, tomatoes, and the soaked mushrooms and their liquid. Bring to a boil over high heat. Return the heat to medium-low and simmer for 45 minutes.

4 **Stir in the bread**. Season with salt and pepper. Remove from the heat, cover, and let stand for 10 minutes. Stir well so the bread can break up and thicken the soup. Spoon into deep bowls, drizzle each serving with olive oil, and serve hot.

● **Good with** bowls of spiced olives, and crusty bread.

VARIATION

Fresh Porcini Soup

Replace the dried porcini with 4oz (115g) fresh porcini. Do not soak them; instead, slice and add them to the soup along with the cremini mushrooms. You will need an extra cup of vegetable stock.

White Bean Soup

This thick soup from northern Italy is guaranteed to keep out the winter chills

makes 4–6 servings

prep 30 mins, plus soaking • cook 2 hrs

! soak the beans overnight to rehydrate them

8oz (225g) **dried cannellini beans**

3 tbsp **olive oil**

2 **onions**, finely chopped

2 **garlic cloves**, minced

5 cups **chicken** or **vegetable stock**

1 **celery stalk**, chopped

3 or 4 **parsley stems**

1 **bay leaf**

1 tbsp **lemon** juice

salt and freshly ground **black pepper**

To serve

2oz (60g) **pancetta**, chopped (optional)

3 **shallots**, thinly sliced

3oz (85g) **Italian fontina** or taleggio

● **Prepare ahead** The soup can be cooled, covered, and refrigerated for up to 2 days. Add stock to thin.

1 **Soak the beans** in cold water to cover overnight. Drain.

2 **Heat 2 tbsp** oil in a saucepan over medium-low heat. Add the onions and cook, stirring, for 8 minutes, until translucent. Add the garlic and cook for 1 minute.

3 **Add the drained beans**, stock, celery, parsley, and bay leaf. Bring to a boil over high heat. Cover and simmer about 1½ hours, stirring, or until the beans are very tender. Stir in the lemon juice.

4 **Remove the bay leaf.** In batches, with the lid ajar, purée the soup in a blender. Return to the pan and season. Keep warm.

5 **Heat the remaining** 1 tbsp oil in a small frying pan over medium heat. Add the pancetta and cook, stirring, 5 minutes, until browned. Stir in the shallots and cook 3 minutes, until softened.

6 **Trim off any rind** from and dice the cheese. Stir into the soup. Ladle into bowls, and sprinkle with the pancetta mixture. Serve hot.

Lobster Bisque

Bisque, an elegant creamy shellfish soup, is thought to have originated in the Spanish Biscay region

 makes 6–8 servings

 prep 45 mins
• cook 1 hr 10 mins

 freeze for up to 3 months; thaw at room temperature and reheat

1 cooked **lobster**, about 2¼ lb (1kg)

3 tbsp **butter**

1 **onion**, finely chopped

1 **carrot**, finely chopped

2 **celery stalks**, finely chopped

1 **leek**, white and pale green part only, finely chopped

½ **fennel bulb**, finely chopped

2 **garlic cloves**, minced

1 **tarragon** sprig

1 bay leaf

7 cups **fish stock**

½ cup **Cognac** or brandy

½ cup **dry white wine** or vermouth

4 ripe **tomatoes**, coarsely chopped

¼ cup **tomato paste**

¼ cup **long-grain rice**

½ cup **heavy cream**

2 tbsp fresh **lemon** juice

cayenne pepper

salt and freshly ground **black pepper**

crème fraîche and chopped **chives**, to garnish

● **Prepare ahead** The bisque can be prepared through step 5 several hours in advance; refrigerate the lobster until ready to serve.

1 Split the lobster in half. Twist off the claws and legs, break the claw apart at the joints, and crack the shells. Remove all meat from the lobster, chop the meat into small pieces, cover, and refrigerate. Chop the shell into rough pieces.

2 Heat the butter in a large saucepan over medium heat. Add the onion, carrot, celery, leek, fennel, garlic, tarragon, and bay leaf. Cook, stirring occasionally, for about 10 minutes, until tender.

3 Add the lobster shells. Stir in the fish stock, Cognac, wine, tomatoes, tomato paste, and rice. Bring to a boil, then simmer for 1 hour.

4 Let cool. In batches, pulse the stock mixture in a blender to chop the shell into small pieces.

5 Strain through a coarse sieve, pressing through as much liquid as possible. Strain again through a fine sieve to be sure that no shell remains in the soup.

6 Return the soup to a boil. Stir in the cream and lemon juice, and season with cayenne, salt, and pepper. Stir in the lobster and heat through. Ladle into bowls, garnish with crème fraîche and chives, and serve hot.

VARIATION

Crab Bisque

Substitute 1 cooked Dungeness crab for the lobster. Pull off the top shell, remove and discard the gills and grit sac. Pull off the legs and crack the claws. Remove all of the available meat from the crab, chop, and refrigerate. Reserve the crab shells to use in step 3. Cook 2 tbsp peeled and chopped fresh ginger with the vegetables in step 2.

Andalucian Soup

A refreshing chilled soup

 makes 4 servings

 prep 15 mins, plus soaking and chilling

4oz (115g) day-old **rustic bread**, crusts removed

3 tbsp **olive oil**, plus more to garnish

2 tbsp **red wine vinegar**

4 ripe large **tomatoes**, skinned and seeded

1 **cucumber**, peeled, seeded, and chopped

1 **red bell pepper**, seeded and quartered

1 **onion**, roughly chopped

3 **garlic cloves**

salt and freshly ground **black pepper**

2 **hard-boiled eggs**, peeled and chopped

2 slices **Serrano ham** or prosciutto, cut into thin strips

1 Break the bread into pieces and place in a bowl. Add the oil and vinegar, mix well, let stand for about 10 minutes, until softened.

2 Purée the tomatoes, cucumber, red pepper, onion, and garlic with ½ cup water in a food processor. Add the bread and process. Season.

3 Transfer to a bowl and chill at least 2 hours. Ladle into bowls and top each with hard-boiled eggs, ham, and a drizzle of olive oil.

Fish Soup with Saffron and Fennel

A robust soup of assorted fish and shellfish partnered with Mediterranean flavorings

 makes 6–8 servings

🕐 prep 10 mins • cook 1 hr

3 tbsp **butter**

2 tbsp **olive oil**

1 large **fennel bulb**, finely chopped

1 small **leek**, white and pale green part only, thinly sliced

2 **garlic cloves**, crushed

4 ripe **tomatoes**, skinned, seeded, and chopped

¼ tsp **saffron threads**, soaked in 1 tbsp hot water

7 cups **fish stock** or bottled clam juice

3 tbsp **brandy**

grated **zest** of ½ orange

1 **bay leaf**

¼ cup **dry white wine**

2lb (900g) **mussels**, scrubbed and debearded if necessary

1lb (500g) **firm white fish fillets**, cut into bite-sized pieces

12 large **shrimp**, peeled and deveined

salt and freshly ground **pepper**

parsley, chopped, to garnish

1 **Heat the butter** with 1 tbsp of the oil in a large saucepan over medium-low heat. Add the fennel, leek, and garlic. Cook, stirring frequently, for 5 minutes, or until the fennel is tender and pale gold.

2 **Stir in the tomatoes** and soaked saffron and cook for 3 minutes. Stir in the stock, brandy, orange zest, and bay leaf. Bring to a boil and skim the surface. Reduce heat to medium-low and simmer for 30 minutes.

3 **In a separate large** saucepan, heat the remaining 1 tbsp oil with the wine over high heat until the wine boils. Add the mussels and cover. Cook for about 3 minutes, or until all the mussels have opened. Transfer the mussels to a bowl and strain the cooking liquid into the soup.

4 **Add the fish and shrimp** to the soup. Simmer gently for about 5 minutes, until they are just opaque. Season with salt and pepper. Ladle into deep soup bowls and add equal amounts of the mussels to each.

5 **Sprinkle with** chopped parsley, and serve hot.

Stracciatella with Pasta

A simple combination of chicken broth with eggs

 makes 4–6 servings

🕐 prep 10 mins • cook 20 mins

6 cups **chicken stock**, preferably homemade

salt and freshly ground **black pepper**

1 cup **small pasta**, such as ditalini or broken spaghetti

4 large **eggs**

½ tsp freshly grated **nutmeg**

1 tbsp chopped **parsley**

1 tbsp **butter**

1 **Bring the stock** to a steady boil. Season with salt and pepper. Add the pasta and cook according to package instructions.

2 **Beat the eggs** with the nutmeg, and season with salt and pepper. Add the parsley.

3 **Reduce the heat** to low. Add the butter to the stock. Stir the simmering stock with a whisk so the stock swirls in a vortex. In a steady stream, add the eggs. Cook about 1 minute, until the egg strands look set. Do not let the stock return to a boil. Remove from the heat and let stand for 3 minutes. Serve hot.

Tuscan Bean Soup

This soup, *ribollita*, is thick, filling, nutritious, and delicious. It is even wonderful at room temperature

 makes 8 servings

 prep 15 mins
• cook 1 hr 20 mins

¼ cup **extra virgin olive oil**, plus more for serving

1 **onion**, chopped

2 **carrots**, sliced

1 **leek**, white and pale green parts only, sliced

2 **garlic cloves**, chopped

1 quart (1 liter) **chicken stock**

one 14.5oz (411g) can **chopped tomatoes**

1 tbsp **tomato paste**

one 15oz (420g) can **white kidney (cannellini) beans**, drained and rinsed

9oz (250g) **spinach**, sliced

salt and freshly ground **black pepper**

8 slices **Italian bread**

2 tbsp grated **Parmesan** (optional), for serving

● **Prepare ahead** This soup is best made ahead and reheated.

1 Heat the oil in a soup pot over medium-low heat. Add the onion, carrots, and leek and cook until softened but not colored. Add the garlic and cook for 1 minute. Add the stock, tomatoes and their juices, and tomato paste.

2 In a bowl, mash half the beans with a fork and stir into the pot. Bring to a boil over high heat. Return the heat to medium-low and simmer for 30 minutes.

3 Add the remaining beans and spinach and simmer for 30 minutes more.

4 Place a slice of bread in each soup bowl. Ladle in the soup, and, if you like, top with a sprinkling of Parmesan.

● **Good with** a dollop of pesto placed on top and olive oil passed on the side.

Hungarian Goulash Soup

Full of warming flavors, this traditional soup makes a rich and satisfying meal

 makes 6–8 servings

prep 15 mins
• cook 2 hrs

½ cup **olive oil**

3 large **onions**, sliced

1½lb (680g) **boneless beef chuck**, cut into 1½in (4cm) cubes

salt and freshly ground **pepper**

2 tbsp **sweet paprika**

1 tsp **caraway seeds**

½ tsp **cayenne pepper**

4 whole **cloves**

4 tbsp **tomato paste**

1 quart (1 liter) **beef** or chicken **stock**

sour cream, to serve

1 Heat 3 tbsp of the oil in a large saucepan over medium heat. Add the onions and cook about 12 minutes, or until tender and golden.

2 Meanwhile, heat the remaining oil in a large frying pan. In batches, add the beef and cook, turning occasionally, until browned. Transfer to a plate and season with salt.

3 Add the beef, paprika, caraway seeds, cayenne, and cloves to the onions, then stir in the tomato paste. Cook, stirring occasionally, for 2 minutes, until the mixture is very fragrant. Stir in the stock and bring to a boil. Reduce the heat to medium-low.

4 Simmer gently for 1½ hours, or until the meat is very tender. Season with salt and pepper. Serve, topping each portion with a dollop of sour cream.

VARIATION

Goulash Dumplings

To make this traditional accompaniment, mix 2 cups flour, 4 tsp baking powder, ½ tsp salt and enough water to form a smooth, elastic dough. Divide into 12 portions and, with floured hands, roll into balls. Place the dumplings in the soup for the last 25–30 minutes of cooking.

French Onion Soup

This Parisian classic is given extra punch with a few spoonfuls of brandy

- 🍴 makes 4 servings
- 🕐 prep 10 mins • cook 1 hr
- 🍲 flameproof soup bowls
- ❄️ the soup, without the bread or cheese, can be frozen for up to 1 month

2 tbsp **butter**

1 tbsp **vegetable oil**

1½lb (675g) **onions**, thinly sliced

1 tsp **sugar**

salt and freshly ground **pepper**

½ cup **dry red wine**

2 tbsp **all-purpose flour**

6 cups hot **beef stock**

¼ cup **brandy**

1 **garlic clove**, cut in half

4 slices French **baguette**, about ¾in (2cm) thick, toasted

½ cup **Gruyère** or Emmenthal **cheese**, grated

1 Melt the butter with the oil in a large, heavy saucepan over low heat. Stir in the onions and sugar, and season with salt and pepper. Press a round of wax paper over the surface. Cook for 40 minutes, uncovering and stirring occasionally, until the onions are a rich, dark brown. Watch carefully to avoid scorching.

2 Remove the wax paper and stir in the wine. Increase the heat to medium and boil, stirring often, for 5 minutes, or until the wine reduces to a glaze. Sprinkle in the flour and cook, stirring often, for 2 minutes. Stir in the stock and bring to a boil. Reduce the heat to low, cover, and simmer for 30 minutes. Stir in the brandy and season to taste.

3 Meanwhile, place the broiler rack 8in (20cm) from the heat, and preheat the broiler. Divide the soup among 4 flameproof bowls. Rub the garlic clove over the toast and place 1 slice in each bowl. Sprinkle with the cheese and broil for 2–3 minutes, or until the cheese is bubbling and golden. Serve at once.

● **Prepare ahead** Steps 1 and 2 can be completed up to a day ahead.

Minestrone

This hearty soup makes a great lunch or dinner. Feel free to add whatever vegetables are in season

- 🍴 makes 4–6 servings
- 🕐 prep 20 mins, plus soaking the beans • cook 1¾ hrs
- ❗ soak the beans in advance
- ❄️ up to 1 month before the pasta is added in step 3

½ cup **dried white cannellini (white kidney) beans**

2 tbsp **olive oil**

2 **celery stalks**, finely chopped

2 **carrots**, finely chopped

1 **onion**, peeled and finely chopped

6 cups **chicken stock** or vegetable stock

one 14.5oz (400g) can **chopped tomatoes**

salt and freshly ground **black pepper**

½ cup **elbow macaroni** or ditalini

4 tbsp chopped **parsley**

½ cup freshly grated **Parmesan cheese**

1 Put the beans in a large bowl, cover with cold water, and let soak overnight. Drain the beans and place in a large saucepan. Cover with fresh cold water and bring to a boil over high heat. Skim the surface as necessary. Boil for 10 minutes. Reduce the heat to low, partially cover the pan, and simmer for 1 hour or until just tender. Drain well and set aside.

2 In a large saucepan, heat the oil over medium heat. Add the celery, carrots, and onion, and cook, stirring occasionally, for 5 minutes or until tender. Stir in the beans, stock, tomatoes with their juice, and salt and pepper to taste. Bring to a boil, stirring occasionally. Reduce the heat, cover, and simmer for 20 minutes.

3 Add the pasta and simmer for 10–12 minutes longer, or until tender. Stir in the parsley and half the cheese. Season to taste. Pour into a warmed tureen, and sprinkle with the remaining Parmesan cheese. Serve hot.

● **Prepare ahead** Steps 1 and 2 can be done up to a day ahead.

● **Good with** a dollop of pesto, stirred in before adding the cheese in step 3.

New England Clam Chowder

Serve this rich, creamy soup with plenty of saltines or crusty bread

 makes 4–6 servings

 prep 15 mins • cook 35 mins

cook clams on day of purchase

36 littleneck clams

1 tbsp oil

4 strips bacon, sliced

1 onion, finely chopped

2 baking potatoes, such as russet, peeled and cut into ½in (1cm) cubes

2 tbsp all-purpose flour

2½ cups whole milk

salt and freshly ground black pepper

½ cup heavy cream

2 tbsp finely chopped parsley

● **Prepare ahead** Steps 1 and 2 can be completed several hours in advance; keep the clams refrigerated until ready to use.

1 Place the clams and ¼ cup water in a large saucepan. Cover and cook over high heat, shaking the pan, until the clams open. Using tongs, transfer the clams to a bowl. Strain the liquid through a wire sieve lined with paper towels to remove grit. Add enough water to measure 2 cups. Remove the clams from the shells. Coarsely chop the clams, cover, and chill.

2 Heat the oil in a large, heavy pan over medium heat. Add the bacon and cook until crispy. Using a slotted spoon, transfer to paper towels to drain.

3 Add the onion and potatoes to the pan. Cook for 5 minutes, or until the onion has softened. Stir in the flour and cook for 2 minutes.

4 Stir in the clam juice and milk and season with salt and pepper. Cover, reduce the heat, and simmer for 20 minutes or until the potatoes are tender. Stir in the cream and clams, and heat through without boiling. Season and serve hot, topped with the bacon and parsley.

VARIATION

Manhattan Clam Chowder
Delete the milk and cream. Add one 28oz (794g) can chopped tomatoes with their juice to the pot with the clam juice. Substitute chopped thyme for the parsley.

Cock-a-Leekie Soup

In days past, this soup involved the slow simmering of a whole chicken, but today it is prepared with less time and effort

 makes 4 servings

 prep 10 mins • cook 1½ hrs

 low fat

 freeze for up to 3 months

1lb (450g) chicken breasts and/or thighs, skinned

1 quart (1 liter) chicken stock

2 bay leaves

⅓ cup long-grain rice

2 leeks, white and pale green parts only, cleaned and thinly sliced

2 carrots, shredded

pinch of ground cloves

salt and freshly ground pepper

1 tbsp chopped parsley

1 Combine the chicken, stock, and bay leaves in a large saucepan and bring to a boil over high heat, skimming off any foam. Reduce the heat to medium-low and cover. Simmer, skimming occasionally, for 30 minutes.

2 Add the rice, leeks, carrots, and cloves, and season with salt and pepper. Return to a boil over high heat, then reduce the heat to medium-low, and cover again. Simmer about 30 minutes more, until the chicken shows no sign of pink at the bone.

3 Discard the bay leaves. Transfer the chicken to a carving board, cool, remove the meat from the bones, chop it into bite-size pieces, and return it to the soup.

4 Ladle the soup into bowls and sprinkle with parsley. Serve hot.

● **Good with** warm crusty bread.

VARIATION

Traditional Cock-a-Leekie Soup
Traditionally, pitted prunes were included in this soup, and they add a delicious sweetness. Add a few with the vegetables in step 2. You can also make the soup with turkey instead of chicken, and add other vegetables such as peas, grated turnips, or potatoes.

Bouillabaisse

Originally nothing more than a humble fisherman's soup using the remains of the day's catch, bouillabaisse has evolved into one of the great dishes

makes 4 servings

prep 20 mins • cook 45 mins

¼ cup **olive oil**

1 **onion**, thinly sliced

2 **leeks**, thinly sliced

1 small **fennel bulb**, thinly sliced

2–3 **garlic cloves**, finely chopped

4 **tomatoes**, skinned, seeded, and chopped

1 cup **dry white wine**

1 tbsp **tomato paste**

6 cups hot **fish** or **chicken stock**

1 **bouquet garni** with 1 celery stalk, 4 thyme springs, and 1 bay leaf

pinch of **saffron threads**

1 strip of **orange** zest

1 tbsp **chopped parsley**

salt and freshly ground **pepper**

3lb (1.35kg) mixed **fish fillets** and **shellfish**, such as red snapper, cod, bluefish, clams, mussels, and shrimp, prepared as necessary

2 tbsp **Pernod** (optional)

salt and freshly ground **black pepper**

8 thin slices **day-old French bread**, toasted, for serving

For the Rouille

½ cup **mayonnaise**

1 small, fresh **hot red chile**, seeded and roughly chopped

4 **garlic cloves**, roughly chopped

1 tbsp **tomato paste**

½ tsp **salt**

● **Prepare ahead** The rouille can be made and chilled for up to 2 days.

1 Heat the oil in a large saucepan over a medium heat. Add the onion, leeks, fennel, and garlic and cook, stirring frequently, for 5–8 minutes, or until the vegetables are softened but not colored. Add the tomatoes, wine, and tomato paste and stir until blended.

2 Add the stock, bouquet garni, saffron, orange zest, and salt and pepper to taste. Bring to a boil. Reduce the heat, partially cover the pan. Simmer for 30 minutes, or until the soup is reduced slightly, stirring occasionally.

3 To make the rouille, place all ingredients in a food processor and process until smooth. Transfer to a bowl, cover with plastic wrap, and refrigerate until needed.

4 Cut the fish into bite-sized chunks. Remove the orange zest and bouquet garni from the stock, and add the shellfish. Reduce the heat to low and simmer for 3 minutes. Add the fish fillets and simmer for a 2–3 minutes more or until the fish flakes easily. Stir in the Pernod, if using, and season with salt and pepper.

5 To serve, spread each piece of toast with rouille and put 2 slices in the bottom of each bowl. Ladle in the soup,. including a good selection of fish and shellfish.

● **Good with** a crisp, dry white wine or a Côtes de Provence rosé. Serve leftover rouille as a spread on a sandwich or as a dip.

Winter Vegetable Soup

Some people call this "Penny Soup," because the vegetable pieces resemble coins

 makes 4 servings

prep 15 mins • cook 25 mins

4 small red-skinned **new potatoes**

4 large **carrots**

1 medium **sweet potato**

1 **leek**, white and pale green parts only

1 tbsp **butter**

1 tbsp **olive oil**

2½ cups **vegetable stock**

salt and freshly ground **black pepper**

● **Prepare ahead** The soup can be made 1 day ahead, cooled, covered, and refrigerated, or frozen for up to three months.

1 **Slice the potates**, carrots, sweet potato, and leek crosswise into rounds about ⅛in (2–3cm) thick. The potatoes can be peeled or unpeeled. Rinse the leeks well.

2 **Melt the butter** with the oil in a large saucepan over medium-low heat. Add the leeks and cook, stirring occasionally, for 3–4 minutes, until beginning to soften. Add the potatoes, carrots, and sweet potato, and stir for 1 minute.

3 **Pour in the stock**, and bring to a boil over high heat. Reduce the heat to medium-low and simmer for 20 minutes, or until the vegetables are tender but not falling apart.

4 **Transfer about one-third** of the vegetables to a blender or food processor with the cooking liquid. Purée then return to the pan. Season with salt and pepper and serve hot.

Sopa de Tortilla

Fresh lime juice, cilantro, and ancho chiles add an unmistakable Mexican flavor to this tomato soup

makes 4 servings

prep 15 mins • cook 50 mins

5 tbsp **vegetable oil**

½ **onion**, finely chopped

2 large **garlic cloves**, finely chopped

1 lb (450g) ripe **tomatoes**, skinned and seeded

6 cups **chicken** or **vegetable stock**

1 or 2 dried **ancho chiles**, seeded

2 **corn tortillas**, cut into strips

3 tbsp chopped **cilantro**

2 tbsp fresh **lime** juice

salt and freshly ground **black pepper**

¾ cup shredded **queso fresco** or **ricotta salata** cheese

2 **limes**, cut into wedges, for serving

● **Prepare ahead** Steps 1–4 can be prepared up to a day ahead. Store the crisp tortilla strips in an airtight container.

1 **Heat 1 tbsp of the oil** in a large saucepan over medium heat. Add the onion and cook, stirring, for 5 minutes, until softened. Add the garlic and stir for 30 seconds.

Transfer to a blender, add the tomatoes, and process until smooth.

2 **Return the purée** to the pan and simmer for 8–10 minutes, stirring constantly, until reduced by one-third. Stir in the stock and bring to a boil. Reduce the heat, partially cover the pan, and simmer gently for 15 minutes.

3 **Place a nonstick** frying pan over medium heat. Add the chiles, and press them flat with a spatula until they begin to blister, then turn them and repeat for the other side. Transfer to a plate and cool. Cut into small pieces and set aside.

4 **Heat the remaining** 4 tbsp oil in a frying pan until hot but not smoking. Add the tortilla strips in batches and fry just until crisp. Remove with a slotted spoon, and drain on paper towels.

5 **When ready to serve**, add the chiles to the soup and bring to a boil. Simmer for 3 minutes, or until the chiles are soft. Stir in the cilantro, lime juice, and salt and pepper to taste. Ladle the soup into bowls, top with the tortillas and cheese, and serve with the limes.

Mexican Chicken Noodle Soup

This spicy Mexican soup has thin *fideo* noodles—similar to angel hair pasta—and makes a substantial meal

- 🍴 makes 4 servings
- 🕐 prep 20 mins • cook 15 mins
- ❗ if using dried chiles, soak for 30 mins beforehand
- ✓ low fat

2 large ripe tomatoes, skinned and seeded

1 small onion, roughly chopped

2 canned chipotle chiles *en adobo* or 2 dried chipotle chiles, soaked

2 garlic cloves

3 tbsp vegetable oil

2 boneless and skinless chicken breasts, cut into bite-sized pieces

3¾ cups chicken stock

8oz (225g) Mexican *fideos* or angel hair pasta

To serve

¼ cup sour cream

1 avocado, peeled, pitted, and cubed

● **Prepare ahead** The soup can be refrigerated for up to 3 days.

1 **Purée the tomatoes**, onion, chiles, and garlic in a blender.

2 **Heat 2 tbsp of the oil** in a large saucepan over medium-high heat. Add the chicken and stir-fry for 2–3 minutes, or until just cooked. Using a slotted spoon, transfer to a plate.

3 **Add the remaining** 1 tbsp oil to the pan and heat. Reduce the heat to medium-low. Add the noodles and cook, turning once, about 2 minutes, until golden.

4 **Add the tomato purée** and stir until the noodles are coated. Stir in the stock and return the chicken to the saucepan. Return the heat to high and cook until the noodles are tender.

5 **Ladle the soup** into bowls and top each serving with a dollop of sour cream and some avocado cubes. Serve hot.

VARIATION

Chinese Chicken Noodle Soup

Soak 6 dried Chinese mushrooms in 1¼ cup boiling water for 30 minutes. Strain the soaking water into a large saucepan and add 2½ cups chicken stock. Slice the mushrooms and cut 2 boneless, skinless chicken breasts into thin strips. Break up 6oz (175g) rice vermicelli into short lengths, stir into the stock, and bring to a simmer. Cook for 2 minutes, then add the mushrooms, chicken, and ¾ cup fresh or thawed frozen corn. Simmer until the noodles are tender, about 2 minutes more. Spoon into bowls and serve at once.

Lentil Soup

This hearty vegetarian soup has just a touch of spice certain to warm you up

- 🍴 makes 4–6 servings
- 🕐 prep 20 mins • cook 35 mins
- ✓ low fat

1 tbsp olive oil

2 onions, finely chopped

2 celery stalks, finely chopped

2 carrots, finely chopped

2 garlic cloves, crushed

1–2 tsp curry powder

5½ cups vegetable stock

¾ cup red lentils

½ cup tomato or multi-vegetable juice

salt and freshly ground black pepper

1 **Heat the oil** in a large saucepan set over medium heat. Add the onions, celery, and carrots. Cook, stirring frequently, for about 5 minutes, or until the onions are translucent.

2 **Add the garlic** and curry powder and cook, stirring, for 1 minute more. Add the stock, lentils, and tomato juice.

3 **Bring to a boil**. Reduce the heat to medium-low and cover. Simmer for 25 minutes, or until the lentils are tender. Season to taste with salt and pepper and serve hot.

● **Good with** a spoonful of plain yogurt and crusty bread.

Potato Salad with Prosciutto

With the addition of salty ham and fragrant caraway seeds,
this hearty salad is full of flavor

 makes 6 servings

prep 10 mins • cook 25 mins

1½lb (675g) small **new potatoes**

salt

1 tbsp **caraway seeds**

6 slices **prosciutto**, cut into thin
strips

3 tbsp chopped **parsley**

For the dressing

⅔ cup **sour cream**

2 **shallots** or scallions, finely chopped

1 tbsp **red wine vinegar**

1 tsp **Dijon mustard**

1 **garlic clove**, minced

3 tbsp **olive oil**

salt and freshly ground **black pepper**

● **Prepare ahead** The salad can
be made up to 8 hours ahead.

1 **Place the potatoes** in a large
saucepan, cover with lightly
salted cold water, and bring to a boil
over high heat. Reduce the heat to
medium and cover. Simmer for about
15 minutes, or until tender. Drain
and let cool.

2 **Meanwhile**, heat a small
frying pan over medium-high
heat. Add the caraway seeds and
cook, stirring almost constantly, for
1–2 minutes, or until lightly toasted.
Transfer to a plate.

3 **To make the dressing**, whisk
the sour cream, shallots, vinegar,
mustard, and garlic in a small bowl.
Slowly whisk in the oil and season
with salt and pepper.

4 **Cut each potato** in half and
put in a large bowl. Add the
caraway seeds, prosciutto, 2 tbsp of
the parsley, and the dressing. Toss
gently to combine. Transfer to a
serving platter and scatter with the
remaining chopped parsley.

Pasta and Tuna Niçoise Salad

This easy summer dish is great for summer
lunches and dining alfresco

 makes 4–6 servings

prep 20 mins • cook 15 mins

For the dressing

¼ cup plus 2 tbsp **extra virgin olive oil**

1 tbsp fresh **lemon** juice

1 tbsp **balsamic vinegar**

1 tsp **whole-grain mustard**

1lb (450g) dried **shell-shaped pasta**

6oz (140g) **green beans**, trimmed

2 **tuna steaks**, 1lb (450g) total

olive oil, for the pasta and for
brushing

salt and freshly ground **black pepper**

2 hard-boiled **eggs**, peeled and
quartered

1 **Bibb lettuce**, leaves separated

8oz (225g) **cherry tomatoes**,
halved

12 canned **anchovy fillets**, rinsed

⅔ cup pitted **Kalamata olives**

● **Prepare ahead** The salad,
without the lettuce and dressing,
can be covered and refrigerated for
several hours before serving. Just

before serving, add the lettuce and
dressing and lightly toss to combine.

1 **To make the dressing**, whisk
the oil, lemon juice, vinegar, and
mustard until combined.

2 **Cook the pasta** in a large pot
of lightly salted water over high
heat according to the package
instructions until tender. Drain, rinse
under cold running water, and drain
well. Transfer to a large bowl and toss
with a little olive oil.

3 **Meanwhile**, cook the beans
in a saucepan of salted boiling
water for 4–5 minutes, or until
crisp-tender. Drain, rinse under cold
water, and pat dry. Add to the pasta.

4 **Preheat a ridged grill pan**
over high heat. Brush the tuna
lightly with oil and season with salt
and pepper. Place on the grill pan
and cook, turning once, for about
4 minutes, until seared but rare inside.

5 **Cut the tuna** into bite-sized
pieces and add to the pasta.
Add the eggs, lettuce, tomatoes,
anchovies, and olives. Just before
serving, add the dressing and toss
well. Season with salt and pepper.
Serve at once.

Caesar Salad

Anchovies help to give this classic salad its traditional flavor, but they can be omitted from the dressing if preferred

🍴 makes 6 servings

🕐 prep 10 mins • cook 2 mins

For the dressing

2 garlic cloves, minced into a purée

2 anchovy fillets in olive oil, drained and finely chopped

½ cup extra virgin olive oil

2 tbsp fresh lemon juice

1 tsp Worcestershire sauce

freshly ground black pepper

2 small heads of romaine lettuce

1 cup croûtons

2 large eggs

½ cup Parmesan cheese, shaved or grated

1 **To make the dressing**, mash the garlic and anchovies together to make a thick paste. Scrape into a screw-top jar, add the olive oil, lemon juice, Worcestershire sauce, and pepper to taste. Shake until well blended and thick. Set aside.

2 **To assemble the salad**, tear the lettuce into bite-sized pieces and toss with the croûtons in a salad bowl. Bring a small saucepan of water to a boil over high heat. Reduce the heat to medium, add the eggs, and boil gently 2 minutes, no longer. Drain and rinse well with cold water.

3 **Crack open the eggs**, scoop over the lettuce and toss. Shake the dressing well, pour over the salad, and toss again. Sprinkle with the Parmesan and serve at once.

● **Good with** all barbecued meats. It is also good served as a first course or lunch with chunks of French bread.

VARIATION

Chicken Caesar Salad

For a more substantial dish, add chunks or shreds of chicken. To make your own croûtons, toss cubed French bread with olive oil, spread on a baking sheet, and bake in a preheated 350°F (180°C) oven about 12 minutes, or until golden.

Arugula Salad with Parmesan

Quick to prepare, this makes an excellent first course or side salad

🍴 makes 4 servings

🕐 prep about 10 mins

½ cup extra-virgin olive oil

¼ cup fresh lemon juice

½ tsp salt

6oz (175g) arugula, rinsed and spun dry

chunk of Parmesan cheese about 1½oz (45g)

freshly ground black pepper

● **Prepare ahead** Many supermarkets sell rinsed, ready-to-use arugula, in bags or in bulk.

1 **Whisk together** the olive oil, lemon juice, and salt in a large non-metallic bowl. Add the arugula and toss together.

2 **Arrange the arugula** in a serving bowl. Use a vegetable peeler to shave curls of the Parmesan over the arugula. Add a generous amount of freshly ground pepper and serve.

● **Good with** barbecued meat or seafood, or as a light first course with bread and olives.

VARIATION

Watercress Salad

Other peppery leaves would work well in this recipe, in place of arugula. Try using watercress, endive, or radicchio, or a colorful combination, depending upon what is in season.

Layered Marinated Herring Salad

For convenience and speedy cooking, buy marinated herring fillets at the supermarket

 makes 6-10 servings

🕐 prep 15 mins, plus 15 mins soaking and at least 5 hrs chilling

1 **sweet onion**, thinly sliced

1 cup **sour cream**

½ cup **plain yogurt**

1 tbsp fresh **lemon** juice

¼ tsp **sugar**

2 **tart apples**, such as Granny Smith, peeled, cored, and thinly sliced

2 **small sour pickles** (cornichons), chopped

salt and freshly ground **black pepper**

10oz (280g) **marinated herring fillets**, drained

2 **cooked potatoes**, sliced (optional)

1 **small cooked beet**, peeled, if necessary, and diced (optional)

1 tbsp **chopped dill**, to garnish

● **Prepare ahead** The salad can be assembled up to 2 days in advance and chilled until required.

1 **Soak the onion** in a bowl of cold water for 15 minutes. Drain well, then toss with the sour cream, yogurt, lemon juice, and sugar. Stir in the apples and pickles, and season with salt and pepper.

2 **Place half the herring** in a serving dish and top with the potatoes and beets, if using. Cover with half the sour cream mixture. Layer the remaining herring, potatoes, and beets on top, then spread with the remaining sauce.

3 **Cover the dish** tightly with plastic wrap and refrigerate for at least 5 hours. Sprinkle with dill just before serving.

● **Good with** chunks of sourdough bread or slices of pumpernickel.

Warm Chicken Salad

Quick to cook, and easy to assemble, this warm salad is hearty, but refreshing at the same time

 makes 4 servings

🕐 prep 10 mins ● cook 8 mins

4 tbsp **extra virgin olive oil**

4 skinless, boneless **chicken breasts**, about 5½oz (150g) each, cut into ½in (1cm) wide strips

⅓ cup drained and thinly sliced **sun-dried tomatoes** in olive oil

1 **garlic clove**, finely chopped

salt and freshly ground **black pepper**

1 small head **radicchio**, torn into small pieces

9oz (250g) **asparagus spears**, trimmed and each cut into 3 pieces

2 tbsp **raspberry vinegar**

½ tsp **sugar**

1 **Heat 2 tbsp of the oil** in a large non-stick frying pan over medium-high heat. Add the chicken, sun-dried tomatoes, and garlic. Season with salt and pepper. Cook, stirring often, for 5 minutes, or until the chicken is opaque when pierced with the tip of a knife.

2 **Meanwhile, put the** radicchio in a large serving bowl. Using a slotted spoon, add the chicken mixture to the radicchio.

3 **Add the asparagus** pieces to the fat remaining in the pan and stir-fry for 1–2 minutes, or until they are crisp-tender. Transfer to the bowl with the chicken.

4 **Whisk together** the remaining 2 tbsp oil, the vinegar, and sugar in a bowl, then pour into the pan, and stir over high heat until hot. Pour the vinaigrette over the salad, and toss quickly to combine. Serve immediately.

● **Good with** thick slices of crusty French bread.

Bibb Lettuce Salad

Sweet Bibb lettuce contrasts well with a piquant, creamy Parmesan dressing

- 🍴 makes 6 servings
- 🕐 prep 20 mins • cook 10–15 mins

12 thin **baguette** slices

3 tbsp **olive oil**

salt and freshly ground **black pepper**

3 heads **Bibb lettuce**

Parmesan shavings, to garnish

For the dressing

1 large **egg**

1½ tbsp fresh **lemon juice**

1 tsp **Dijon mustard**

1 tsp **Worcestershire sauce**

2 **anchovies in oil**, rinsed and drained

1 **garlic clove**, peeled

⅔ cup **vegetable oil**

½ cup freshly grated **Parmesan**

● **Prepare ahead** The croutons can be stored in an airtight container for up to 1 week. Refrigerate the dressing for up to 3 days.

1 **Preheat the oven** to 350°F (180°C). To make croutons, cut the sliced bread into quarters. Transfer to a bowl and toss with the olive oil, salt, and pepper. Spread on a baking sheet. Bake for 10–15 minutes, or until crisp. Let cool.

2 **To make the** dressing, process the egg, lemon juice, mustard, Worcestershire sauce, anchovies, and garlic in a blender. With the machine running, drizzle in the oil. Transfer to a bowl and stir in the Parmesan. Season with salt and pepper. Stir in a little water if the dressing is too thick. Cover and refrigerate until serving.

3 **Wash and dry** the lettuce. Tear the lettuce into bite-sized pieces and place in a large bowl. Drizzle with the dressing and toss gently. Serve, topping each serving with the croutons and Parmesan shavings, if desired.

● **Good with** crisp cooked pancetta, or bacon, or strips of prosciutto scattered on top.

Marinated Goat Cheese Salad

This simple bistro-style recipe makes a great dinner-party starter

- 🍴 makes 6 servings
- 🕐 prep 15 mins, plus 24 hrs marinating • cook 5 mins

⅔ cup **olive oil**, plus more for brushing

¼ cup packed **basil leaves**, shredded

2 **garlic cloves**, chopped

grated **zest** of 1 large **lemon**

1 small fresh **hot red chile**, seeded and finely chopped

salt and freshly ground **black pepper**

6 individual **goat cheeses** (*crottins*)

1 **baguette**

2 heads **Belgian endive**, leaves separated

1 bunch **watercress**, washed and dried

½ cup **Kalamata olives**, halved

● **Prepare ahead** The toasts can be made 2 days ahead and stored in an airtight container.

1 **At least one day** before serving, marinate the cheeses: Whisk the oil, basil, garlic, lemon zest, and chile in a bowl. Season with salt and pepper.

2 **Place the goat cheeses** in a shallow nonmetallic dish. Pour the marinade over the cheeses. Cover and refrigerate for 24 hours.

3 **When ready** to serve, preheat the oven to 350°F (180°C). Cut the baguette into 12 thick slices. Brush the bread with olive oil. Spread on a baking sheet and bake about 12 minutes, until crisp and golden.

4 **To serve,** position the broiler rack about 6in (15cm) from the source of heat and preheat. Remove the goat cheeses from the marinade, reserving the marinade. Cut each cheese in half crosswise and place on a baking sheet. Broil about 3 minutes or until just melting. Divide the endive, watercress, and olives among 6 plates. Place 2 pieces of toast on each plate and top each with a round of cheese. Drizzle with the reserved marinade, and serve immediately.

Roasted Tomato Salad with Lemon and Crème Fraîche

Slow-roasting tomatoes intensifies their sweet flavor, which is well matched with a creamy dresssing

 makes 4 servings

prep 15 mins • cook 2 hrs

6 large **plum tomatoes**

2 tbsp **olive oil**

salt and freshly ground **black pepper**

2 bunches of **scallions**

⅔ cup **crème fraîche**

lemon-infused olive oil or a fruity extra virgin olive oil

● **Prepare ahead** The tomatoes can be roasted a day ahead and the spring onions wilted 1 hour before.

1 Preheat oven to 275°F (140°C). Halve and core the tomatoes and place, cut side up, on a baking sheet. Drizzle with 1 tbsp olive oil and season with salt and pepper. Roast about 2 hours, until very tender. Let cool.

2 Trim the scallions, and cut each one in half crosswise, then lengthwise. Heat the remaining oil in a large skillet over medium heat. Add the scallions and cook about 3 minutes, until wilted. Season with salt and pepper. Let cool.

3 Arrange 3 tomato halves and a tangle of scallions on each plate.

Add a dollop of crème fraîche and drizzle with lemon oil. Serve at room temperature.

● **Good with** herbed rustic bread, olives, and roasted peppers.

VARIATION

Balsamic Tomatoes
Drizzle the warm roasted tomatoes with balsamic vinegar. Cool, and serve with whole grain toast.

Waldorf Salad

A classic salad named after the prestigious Waldorf–Astoria Hotel in New York

 makes 4 servings

 prep 20 mins, plus at least 30 mins chilling

1 lb (450g) crisp, **red-skinned apples**, cored and diced

2 tbsp fresh **lemon** juice

4 **celery stalks**, sliced

½ cup **mayonnaise**

salt and freshly ground **black pepper**

3oz (85g) **walnuts**, toasted and coarsely chopped

1 Toss the diced apples and lemon juice well in a medium bowl.

2 Add the celery and mayonnaise, and mix. Season with salt and pepper. Cover with plastic wrap and refrigerate.

3 Stir in the walnuts. Transfer to a serving dish and serve well chilled.

Grilled Zucchini and Pepper Salad with Cilantro and Cumin

Use a grill pan if the weather isn't cooperating

- makes 6 servings
- prep 30 mins • cook 10 mins
- ridged grill pan

For the vinaigrette

2 lemons

2 tbsp toasted **cumin seeds**

1 tbsp **honey**

2 **garlic cloves**, chopped

⅔ cup **olive oil**

3 tbsp chopped **cilantro**

6 **zucchini**, trimmed and cut lengthwise into ½in (6mm) slices

olive oil for brushing

3 red or yellow **bell peppers**, quartered and seeded

4 **scallions**, thinly sliced

4 **plum tomatoes**, cut into wedges

● **Prepare ahead** The vinaigrette can be made 3 days ahead.

1 To make the dressing, zest 1 lemon and whisk this and the juice of both lemons, the cumin, honey, and garlic in a small bowl. Gradually whisk in the oil then add the cilantro. Season.

2 Oil the grate on an outdoor grill (or indoors, oil a grill pan). Lightly oil the zucchini. Grill the zucchini, turning once, about 3 minutes, or until seared with marks on both sides. Transfer to a plate. Grill the peppers, skin side down, until the skins are blackened and blistered, about 8 minutes. Transfer to a bowl. When cool enough to handle, peel and cut into strips.

3 Combine the zucchini, peppers, scallions, and tomatoes. Toss gently with the vinaigrette, and serve at room temperature.

Tuscan Bread Salad

Stale crusty bread doesn't have to go to waste when you know how to make this substantial salad, known as *panzanella*

- makes 4 servings
- prep 25 mins, plus 40 mins marinating

½ loaf **day-old crusty bread**, such as ciabatta, cut into bite-sized pieces

14oz (400g) small, ripe **plum tomatoes**, quartered or cut into chunks

½ **red onion**, thinly sliced

½ **cucumber**, peeled and cut into chunks

3 tbsp **extra virgin olive oil**

1 tbsp **red wine vinegar**

salt and freshly ground **black pepper**

¼ tbsp chopped **parsley**

8 **basil leaves**, torn into small pieces

● **Prepare ahead** The salad should be made 30–40 minutes in advance, to allow the dressing and tomato and cucumber juices to soften the bread; add the herbs just before serving.

1 Combine the bread, tomatoes, onion, and cucumber in a large serving bowl. Whisk together the oil and vinegar and sprinkle over the bread mixture. Season with salt and pepper, then mix well. Let stand for 30–40 minutes, mixing thoroughly once or twice to ensure the bread pieces evenly soak up all the juices.

2 Sprinkle the parsley and basil over the salad and serve.

● **Good with** cold meats or a cheese platter.

┌─────────────────────────────┐
BREAD PIECES
If you do not have ciabatta, any good quality, country-style bread will do.
└─────────────────────────────┘

Smoked Trout and Pancetta Salad

The bitter leaves and radishes combine well with the salty fish and cheese in this light dish

🍴 serves 6

🕐 prep 10 mins • cook 10 mins

For the dressing

1 tbsp red wine vinegar

1½ tsp fresh lemon juice

1 tsp Dijon mustard

⅓ cup plus 1 tbsp extra virgin olive oil

salt and freshly ground pepper

12oz (350g) smoked trout

12 thin slices pancetta

2 bunches watercress, washed

2 Belgian endive, leaves separated

5oz (140g) feta cheese, diced

5 small radishes, finely sliced

2 shallots, finely sliced

1 **To make the dressing**, whisk the vinegar, lemon juice, and mustard together in a small bowl. Gradually whisk in the oil and season with salt and pepper.

2 **Remove the** bones and skin from the trout. Cook the pancetta about 5 minutes, until crisp.

Drain on paper towels. Divide the watercress and endive among 4 plates. Scatter trout, feta, pancetta, radishes, and shallots over each. Drizzle with the dressing.

 VARIATION

Smoked Mackerel Salad
Omit the trout and radishes. Use flaked fillets of peppered smoked mackerel in place of the smoked trout.

Watercress and Toasted Walnut Salad

Try serving this dish alongside savory tarts

🍴 makes 6 servings

🕐 prep 15 mins • cook 10 mins

1 cup walnut pieces

2 bunches watercress, washed and dried

2 shallots, finely chopped

For the dressing

1 tbsp red wine vinegar

1 tsp Dijon mustard

1 tsp light brown sugar

¼ cup walnut oil

salt and freshly ground black pepper

1 **Preheat the oven** to 350°F (180°C). Spread the walnuts in a single layer on a baking sheet. Bake, stirring occasionally, for 10 minutes, or until nicely browned, watching closely so they don't burn. Let cool, and crush lightly with your hands.

2 **To make the dressing**, whisk the vinegar, mustard, and sugar in a bowl. Gradually whisk in the oil. Season with salt and pepper.

3 **Combine the watercress**, shallots, and walnuts in a large bowl. Toss with the dressing, and serve immediately.

Vietnamese Salad of Broiled Shrimp with Papaya

Vietnamese cuisine is noted for its fresh, clean flavors: lime, mint, chiles, and fish sauce are all widely used

 makes 4 servings

prep 15 mins • cook 2-3 mins

low fat

vegetable oil, for oiling the rack and shrimp

12 large shrimp, peeled and deveined

2 tbsp Asian fish sauce

1 tbsp fresh lime juice

1 tsp rice wine vinegar

1 tsp sugar

1 small fresh hot red chile, seeded and minced

2 garlic cloves, minced into a paste

1 green papaya, peeled, deseeded, quartered lengthwise, and cut into julienne strips

½ cucumber, peeled, deseeded, and cut into julienne strips

1 tbsp chopped mint, plus sprigs to garnish

● **Prepare ahead** Steps 1 and 2 can be completed several hours in advance and stored, covered, in the refrigerator.

1 **Position a broiler rack** 4in (10cm) from the source of heat. Preheat the broiler. Line the rack with aluminum foil and lightly oil. Spread the shrimp on the foil and brush with oil. Broil for 2–3 minutes, turning once, until the shrimp turn opaque.

2 **Meanwhile, whisk** the fish sauce, lime juice, vinegar, sugar, chile, garlic, and 6 tbsp cold water together in a bowl until the sugar dissolves. Add the shrimp to the bowl and stir. Let stand until cooled.

3 **Add the papaya**, cucumber, and chopped mint, and toss together. Transfer the salad to a serving platter, and arrange the shrimp on top. Garnish with the mint sprigs and serve at once.

GREEN PAPAYA
is crunchier and much less sweet than the ripe, orange-fleshed fruit.

Shrimp, Grapefruit, and Avocado Salad

A tangy salad to satisfy seafood lovers, this is simple enough for a weekend brunch, but special enough to serve to dinner guests

makes 6 servings

prep 15 mins

For the dressing

3 tbsp Asian fish sauce

3 tbsp fresh lime juice

2 tbsp sugar

2 tbsp avocado or olive oil

30 large shrimp, cooked, peeled, and deveined

2 large pink grapefruit, segmented

3 red radishes, thinly sliced

2 avocados, peeled, pitted, and cut into chunks or slices

3 scallions, thinly sliced

6 oz (175g) baby salad greens (mesclun)

bunch of watercress, thick stems discarded

6 sprigs of mint leaves, stems discarded, leaves torn

● **Prepare ahead** The dressing can be made several days in advance and refrigerated.

1 **Make the dressing**. Combine all of the ingredients together in a jar, and shake until blended.

2 **Pat the shrimp** dry with paper towels, and place in a bowl. Add 2 tbsp of the dressing and toss.

3 **Toss the grapefruit**, radishes, avocados, scallions, greens, watercress, and mint leaves in a large bowl. Divide among 6 dinner plates. Arrange 5 shrimp on top of each, and drizzle with the remaining dressing. Serve immediately.

VARIATION

Lobster and Crab Salad
Substitute chunks of lobster or lump crab meat for the shrimp.

Coleslaw

Homemade coleslaw is so much better than the store-bought kind, and it is worth making extra to have on hand. Prepare in a food processor for the fastest results

 makes 4 servings

prep about 15 mins

grater, mandoline, or food processor with grater attachment

¼ head **green cabbage**, cored

2 large **carrots**, coarsely grated

2 **celery** stalks, finely sliced

2 **scallions**, thinly sliced

½ cup **mayonnaise**

4 tsp **whole milk**

2 tbsp fresh **lemon** juice

2 tbsp chopped **parsley**

1 tbsp snipped **chives**

salt and freshly ground **black pepper**

● **Prepare ahead** The coleslaw can be made a couple of hours in advance;and refrigerated in a covered container for up to 2 days.

1 **Slice the cabbage** as finely as possible. Transfer to a large bowl and add the carrots, celery, and scallions. Mix well.

2 **In a small bowl**, mix together the mayonnaise and milk, then the lemon juice, parsley, and chives. Pour over the vegetables and mix well. Season with salt and pepper. Cover and refrigerate for at least 2 hours. Serve chilled.

● **Good with** grilled sausages or with a sandwich for lunch.

VARIATION

Fruit and Nut Coleslaw

For extra sweetness and crunch, add ½ cup chopped toasted walnuts or pecans, and ½ cup golden raisins just before serving.

Tabbouleh

This Lebanese specialty of parsley, mint, tomatoes and bulgur is refreshing all year round

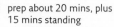 makes 4 servings

prep about 20 mins, plus 15 mins standing

¾ cup **bulgur** (cracked wheat)

boiling water, as needed

⅓ cup **extra-virgin olive oil**

¼ cup fresh **lemon** juice

salt and freshly ground **black pepper**

4 **scallions**, finely chopped

½ cup chopped **parsley**

¼ cup chopped **mint**

small **lettuce leaves**

2 ripe **tomatoes**, seeded, and finely diced

1 **Put the bulgur** in a large bowl. Pour in enough boiling water to cover. Let stand about 10 minutes, or until the grains are swollen and

tender. Drain in a fine wire sieve, rinse in cold water, and drain again.

2 **Whisk the oil** and lemon juice in a large bowl. Stir in bulgur. Season with salt and pepper.

3 **Just before serving**, mix in the scallions, parsley, and mint.

4 **Arrange lettuce leaves** on a serving dish. Spoon portions of tabbouleh into the leaves, scatter the diced tomatoes over the top and serve at room temperature.

VARIATION

Fruit Tabbouleh

Replace the chopped tomatoes with 2–3 tbsp pomegranate seeds or the same quantity of toasted pine nuts.

Salad Niçoise

This well-known classic French salad is made here with fresh tuna for a main-course serving

 makes 4 servings

🕐 prep 50 mins

9oz (250g) green beans, trimmed

4 tuna steaks, 5oz (140g) each

¾ cup extra virgin olive oil

salt and freshly ground pepper

3 tbsp white wine vinegar

1½ tbsp fresh lemon juice

2 tsp Dijon mustard

1 garlic clove, finely chopped

2 romaine lettuce hearts, trimmed and torn into bite-sized pieces

8–10 basil leaves

9oz (250g) plum tomatoes, quartered lengthways

12 Kalamata olives

8 anchovy fillets in olive oil, drained

1 small red onion, finely sliced

4 large, hard-boiled eggs, peeled and quartered

1 Cook the green beans in gently boiling water, for 3–4 minutes, or until crisp-tender. Drain the beans, rinse well under cold water, and pat dry with paper towels.

2 Heat a ridged grill pan over medium-high heat. Brush the tuna steaks with 1 tbsp olive oil and season with salt and pepper. Sear the tuna for 2 minutes on each side; the centers should be slightly pink.

3 To make the vinaigrette, whisk together the vinegar, lemon juice, mustard, and garlic. Slowly whisk in the remaining olive oil. Season with salt and pepper.

4 Combine the lettuce, basil, green beans, tomatoes, olives, anchovies, and onion in a large bowl. Drizzle with the vinaigrette and gently toss.

5 Divide the salad among 4 plates. Cut each tuna steak in half crosswise and arrange both halves on top of the salad. Garnish with the eggs.

VARIATION

Grilled Chicken Salad

Grill 4 chicken breasts instead of tuna. Both versions are good with the addition of boiled new potatoes that have been chilled and thickly sliced, and a sprinkle of capers .

Roasted Beets with Bresaola

Bresaola, air-dried beef from Northern Italy, adds a salty contrast to sweet roasted beets in a spicy horseradish dressing

 makes 6 servings

🕐 prep 15 mins • cook 45 mins

18 very small beets, preferably baby beets

2 sprigs of thyme

3 tbsp extra virgin olive oil

salt and freshly ground pepper

2 tbsp red wine vinegar

6oz (165g) arugula

12 thin slices bresaola

chives, to garnish

For the dressing

1 lemon

5 tbsp crème fraîche or sour cream

1 tbsp freshly grated or prepared horseradish

1 tsp white wine or rice vinegar

● **Prepare ahead** The dressing can be made several days in advance and the beets cooked the day before.

1 Preheat the oven to 400°F (200°C). Place the beets on a large piece of heavy-duty aluminum foil with the thyme and olive oil, and season to taste. Fold the foil into a packet, sealing the edges. Place on a baking sheet and bake for 45 minutes, or until the beets are easily pierced with a knife.

2 Unwrap the beets and let cool. Peel, trim, and cut the beets into rounds. Transfer to a bowl and sprinkle with the vinegar.

3 To make the dressing, grate the zest and squeeze the juice from the lemon. Mix with the crème fraîche, horseradish, and vinegar.

4 Divde the arugula among 6 plates, and drizzle with dressing. Top with beets and bresaola. Garnish with the chives and serve.

TIP

When you rub the skins from the beets, wear rubber gloves to prevent staining your hands pink.

Asian Cucumber Salad with Smoked Salmon

Cucumber slices combine well with the flavor of smoked salmon

 makes 6 servings

prep 10 mins

For the dressing

¼ cup **white wine vinegar**

2 tbsp **vegetable oil**

2 tbsp chopped **cilantro**

1 tbsp **Asian fish sauce**

1 tbsp **Thai sweet chili dipping sauce**

1 **garlic clove**, chopped (optional)

2 large **cucumbers**

salt and freshly ground **black pepper**

14oz (400g) **smoked salmon**, cut into long strips

1 **lime**, cut into 12 wedges, to garnish (optional)

1 **To make the dressing**, shake the vinegar, oil, cilantro, fish sauce, chili sauce, and garlic in a jar.

2 **With a vegetable peeler**, slice the cucumber lengthwise into ribbons, discarding the center core of seeds. Place in a bowl.

3 **10 minutes before serving**, pour the dressing over the cucumber and season with salt and pepper.

4 **Mound equal amounts** of cucumber on individual plates, and arrange the smoked salmon strips on top. Sprinkle with black pepper and garnish with lime wedges (if using).

Carrot and Orange Salad

This light, multicolored salad is good as an accompaniment to hot or cold meats, or served alongside a sandwich

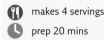 makes 4 servings

prep 20 mins

2 large **carrots**

2 large **navel oranges**

1 **fennel bulb**

1 bunch **watercress**

For the dressing

3 tbsp fresh **orange** juice

1 tbsp fresh **lemon** juice

1 tsp **honey**

3 tbsp **olive oil**

3 tbsp **vegetable oil**

salt and freshly ground **black pepper**

2 tsp **sesame seeds**, lightly toasted

● **Prepare ahead** The salad can be refrigerated in a covered bowl for up to 6 hours. Toss the fennel in a lemon juice to prevent discoloration Dress and toss just before serving.

1 Trim and peel the carrots. Use a vegetable peeler to make long, thin strips of the entire carrot.

2 Cut away the peel and pith from the oranges. Working over a bowl, cut between the membranes to release the orange segments. Trim the fennel and thinly slice. Remove any tough stalks from the watercress. Combine the carrot, orange, fennel, and watercress in a serving bowl.

3 To make the dressing, whisk together the juices and honey. Gradually whisk in the oils. Season with salt and pepper. Pour the dressing over the salad mixture, sprinkle with the sesame seeds, and serve.

Eggplant and Goat Cheese Salad

Serve this crunchy, creamy, and zesty salad by itself or with roast lamb

 makes 6 servings

prep 15 mins • cook 20 mins

For the dressing

2 tbsp fresh **lemon** juice

1 **garlic clove**, crushed

¼ tbsp **walnut oil**

salt and freshly ground **pepper**

2 **eggplants**, peeled

½ cup crumbled **goat cheese**

½ cup toasted and coarsely chopped **walnuts**

2 ripe **tomatoes**, seeded and diced

1 small **red onion**, finely diced

3 tbsp chopped **parsley**

salt and freshly ground **black pepper**

1 tbsp **sesame seeds**, lightly toasted

1 To make the dressing, whisk the lemon juice and garlic in a small bowl. Whisk in the walnut oil. Season with salt and pepper.

2 Cut the eggplants into ¾in (2cm) cubes. Steam until tender, about 10 minutes. Drain and let cool.

3 Gently squeeze out excess water. Combine the eggplant, goat cheese, walnuts, tomato, red onion, and parsley in a large bowl with the dressing. Season with salt and pepper. Sprinkle the sesame seeds on top. Serve at room temperature.

VARIATION

Eggplant Salad with Feta and Pine Nuts

Replace the cheese and sesame seeds with feta and pine nuts for a change.

Crab Salad with Mango Dressing

This lovely summer lunch proves how well crab matches with fruit

 makes 4 servings

🕐 prep 15 mins

❗ purchase the crab on the day you intend to make the salad

For the dressing

1 ripe **mango**, peeled, pitted, and diced

3 tbsp **olive oil**

zest and juice of ½ **lime**

1 **shallot**, finely chopped

2 tbsp chopped **cilantro**

1 tbsp chopped **mint leaves**

5oz (140g) **mixed salad greens**

1lb (450g) fresh **crabmeat**, picked over

1 ripe **avocado**, peeled, pitted, and sliced lengthwise

1 **To make the dressing**, purée the mango, oil, lime zest, and juice in a food processor or blender. Season with salt and pepper, adding a little water if too thick.

2 **Toss the** shallot, cilantro, and mint with the salad greens in a large bowl. Add a few spoonfuls of dressing and toss again. Divide among 4 plates and top each with equal amounts of crab and avocado. Serve at once, passing the rest of the dressing on the side.

⬤ **Good with** slices of freshly baked Irish soda bread.

⬤ **Leftovers** are perfect for piling on top of mixed salad leaves or used as a filling for vol-au-vents.

Shaved Fennel Salad

This is a fantastic salad to serve as an appetizer, a side dish, or with cheese

🍴 makes 6 servings

🕐 prep 10 mins, plus marinating

1 **fennel bulb**

3 tbsp **extra virgin olive oil**

½ tbsp aged **balsamic vinegar**

salt and freshly ground **black pepper**

1 **garlic clove**, crushed

6oz (170g) **mixed baby greens** (mesclun)

1 **Peel and discard** the tough outer layer of the fennel. Cut out the hard core. Use a serrated knife to slice the fennel crosswise as thinly as possible. Transfer to a large bowl. Whisk the oil and vinegar in a small bowl, and season with salt and pepper. Add 1 tbsp of the dressing to the fennel with the garlic, toss, and let stand for 1 hour.

2 **Toss the** mixed greens with the remaining dressing and season with salt and pepper. Divide the greens among 6 plates, then top with equal amounts of the fennel salad, and serve.

⬤ **Good with** shavings of Parmesan and pitted Kalamata olives scattered over the salad.

Spinach, Pear, and Endive Salad

An ideal salad to serve alongside Asian-style duck or grilled meat

🍴 makes 6 servings

🕐 prep 10 mins

For the vinaigrette

2 tbsp **red wine vinegar**

1 tbsp **honey**

½ tbsp **Dijon mustard**

⅓ cup plus 1 tbsp **olive oil**

salt and freshly ground **black pepper**

7oz (200g) **baby spinach leaves**, washed and dried

2 **Belgian endive**, leaves separated, cut into bite-sized pieces

2 firm, ripe **pears**, peeled and sliced

3 **shallots**, finely sliced

1 **Shake the vinegar**, honey, mustard, and oil in a jar until blended. Season with salt and pepper.

2 **Place the spinach**, endive, pears, and shallots in a large bowl. Drizzle with the vinaigrette and toss gently.

Avocado, Tomato, and Mozzarella Salad

Red, white, and green are the colors of the Italian flag and are echoed in this Italian dish

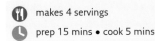

makes 4 servings

prep 15 mins • cook 5 mins

4 small **plum tomatoes**, halved

¼ cup **extra virgin olive oil**

salt and freshly ground **black pepper**

2 **garlic cloves**, thinly sliced

2 **scallions**, white and green parts, finely chopped

6oz (150g) small **buffalo mozzarella balls**, torn in half

2 tbsp **balsamic vinegar**, plus more for serving

2 tbsp nonpareil **capers**, drained and rinsed

basil leaves, roughly chopped

2 ripe **Hass avocados**, pitted, skinned, and quartered

1 **Position a rack** 6in (15cm) from the source of heat and preheat the broiler. Arrange the tomatoes, cut sides up, on a baking sheet. Season with salt and pepper, and sprinkle with the garlic and scallions. Drizzle 1 tbsp of the oil over the tomatoes.

2 **Broil the tomatoes** for 4–5 minutes, or until they just begin to soften and the garlic is golden brown.

3 **Place the hot tomatoes**, garlic, scallions, and all cooking juices in a bowl. Add the mozzarella, remaining 3 tbsp oil, vinegar, capers, and basil and toss gently.

4 **Place 2 avocado quarters** on each of 4 plates. Divide the tomato mixture evenly over the avocados and drizzle with balsamic vinegar. Serve immediately.

Ensaladilla Rusa

Russian salad always consists of vegetables in mayonnaise, but the Spanish version includes tuna and red peppers

makes 4 servings

prep 15 mins • cook 25 mins

1lb (450g) red-skinned **potatoes**, scrubbed

1 **carrot**, finely diced

1 cup **frozen peas**

one 6oz (168g) can **tuna** in oil, drained

2 **roasted red peppers** in brine, drained and cut into thin strips

6 tbsp **mayonnaise**

salt and freshly ground **black pepper**

2 hard-boiled **eggs**, cut into quarters

2 tbsp chopped **parsley**, to garnish

● **Prepare ahead** The potatoes, carrots, and peas can be prepared a day ahead, covered, and refrigerated. The salad is best served within an hour after it is made.

1 **Boil the potatoes** in salted water in a large saucepan over medium-high heat for about 20 minutes, until tender. Drain and let cool slightly. Peel and cut into ½in (13mm) cubes.

2 **Meanwhile, in another** saucepan of lightly salted water over medium-high heat, boil the carrot for about 4 minutes, until almost tender. Add the peas, return to a boil, and cook for about 3 minutes more, until the peas are tender. Drain, rinse under cold running water, drain well, and pat dry with paper towels.

3 **Mix the potatoes**, carrots, peas, tuna, and most of the roasted pepper strips together with the mayonnaise in a bowl. Season with salt and pepper.

4 **Spoon into** a serving dish, add the eggs and reserved pepper strips. Sprinkle with parsley and serve chilled or at room temperature.

Warm Green Bean Salad

This crunchy, nutty salad is also a great vegetable side dish

 makes 6 servings

prep 15 mins • cook 10 mins

3 tbsp **sesame seeds**

1lb (450g) **green beans**, preferably *haricots verts*, trimmed

9oz (250g) **snow peas**, trimmed

1 tbsp **soy sauce**

2 tsp peeled and grated fresh **ginger**

1 **garlic clove**, minced

1½ tsp Asian **sesame oil**

1½ tsp **honey**

3 **scallions**, white parts only, finely chopped

salt and freshly ground **black pepper**

● **Prepare ahead** The green beans and snow peas can be blanched and the dressing prepared up to 4 hours ahead; reheat the vegetables in boiling water for 1 minute, drain, and add the dressing.

1 **Toast the sesame seeds** in a frying pan over medium heat, stirring often, until toasted. Transfer to a plate.

2 **Cook the green beans** in a large saucepan of lightly salted boiling water for 3 minutes. Add the snow peas and cook about 1 minute more, until both vegetables are crisp-tender. Drain well in a colander.

3 **Mix the soy sauce**, ginger, garlic, sesame oil, and honey in a large bowl. Add the green beans, snow peas, and scallions and toss well. Season with salt and pepper. Sprinkle with the sesame seeds and serve.

Red Pepper Salad

In this Spanish salad, sweet red peppers are gently stewed, then combined with a fresh tomato sauce

 makes 4 servings

prep 10 mins • cook 25 mins

3 tbsp **olive oil**

6 **red bell peppers**, seeded and cut into thick strips

2 **garlic cloves**, finely chopped

2 ripe medium **tomatoes**, peeled, seeded, and chopped

2 tbsp chopped **parsley**

salt and freshly ground **black pepper**

1 tbsp **sherry vinegar**

● **Prepare ahead** The salad can be refrigerated for up to 2 days. Serve at room temperature.

1 **Heat the oil** in a large frying pan over medium-low heat. Add the red peppers and garlic and cook, stirring frequently, over low heat for 5 minutes, until the peppers soften. Add the tomatoes and bring to a simmer over high heat. Return the heat to medium-low and cover. Simmer for 12–15 minutes, until the tomatoes have broken down.

2 **Stir in the parsley**, season well with salt and pepper, and cook for 2 minutes more, until the tomato juices thicken slightly.

3 **Using a slotted spoon**, remove the peppers from the pan and arrange on a serving platter.

4 **Add the vinegar** to the tomatoes, increase the heat to medium-high, and cook for 5–7 minutes, or until the tomatoes have thickened.

5 **Pour the sauce** over the peppers and let cool.

VARIATION

Red Pepper Dressing

Process the salad in a food processor until smooth. Whisk in enough olive oil to make a dressing and use to coat a mix of green leaves.

Lobster Salad with Watercress

A very special summer salad, ideal for outdoor dining

 serves 4

prep 20 mins

For the dressing

1 large **egg**

1 large **egg yolk**

2 tsp Dijon mustard

zest and juice of 1 **lemon**

1¾ cups **vegetable oil**

3 tbsp chopped **dill** and/or **chives**

salt and freshly ground **black pepper**

½ **red onion**, very thinly sliced

1 tsp **red wine vinegar**

4 cooked **lobster tails**

1 large bunch of **watercress**, tough stalks removed

½ **fennel bulb**, very thinly sliced

8 **sun-dried tomatoes** in oil, drained and chopped

chervil, dill, or chives, to garnish

1 **To make the dressing**, combine the egg, egg yolk, mustard, and lemon zest and juice in a food processor. Slowly add the oil. Add the dill and season. Transfer to a bowl, cover, and refrigerate.

2 **Combine the red onion** and vinegar in a bowl. Let stand for 10 minutes. Drain well.

3 **Remove the lobster** meat from the shell, and chop it in large chunks.

4 **Divide the watercress** among 4 plates, and add the fennel, onion, tomatoes, and lobster; drizzle with the dressing. Serve with more dressing served on the side.

Spinach and Bacon Salad with Blue Cheese Dressing

A delicious steakhouse salad that is full of flavor and textures

 makes 4 servings

prep 15 mins
• cook 10-12 mins

Blue Cheese Dressing

½ cup crumbled **blue cheese**

3 tbsp **olive oil**

2 tbsp **red wine vinegar**

2 tsp **Dijon mustard**

2 tsp finely chopped **shallot**

pinch **sugar**

salt and freshly ground **black pepper**

8 slices of **bacon**

8 oz (225g) **baby spinach leaves**

8oz (225g) **white mushrooms**, sliced

2 **scallions**, white and green parts, sliced

● **Prepare ahead** The dressing can be refrigerated up to 2 days before serving.

1 **To make the dressing**, shake the cheese, oil, vinegar, mustard, shallots, and sugar in a jar until well combined. Season with salt and pepper, and shake again.

2 **Cook the bacon** in a large frying pan over medium heat about 6 minutes, until crisp. Transfer to paper towels. Let cool. Crumble the bacon.

3 **Toss the spinach**, mushrooms, scallions and crumbled bacon together in a large bowl. Add the dressing and toss again. Serve immediately.

● **Good with** grilled meat.

Greek Tomato and Feta Salad

Juicy tomatoes, cool crisp cucumber, and salty feta cheese are a winning combination

 makes 4-6 servings

prep 20 mins

1 lb 5oz (600g) ripe **plum tomatoes**

1 **cucumber**

7oz (200g) **feta cheese**

½ cup pitted **Kalamata olives**

juice of ½ **lemon**

¼ cup **extra virgin olive oil**

salt and freshly ground **black pepper**

8 large **basil leaves**, torn into pieces

● **Prepare ahead** The salad can be made through step 2, stored at room temperature, for up to 2 hours. Add the basil just before serving.

1 **Cut the tomatoes** into chunks. Peel away about half of the cucumber skin. Quarter the cucumber lengthwise, scoop out the seeds, then chop the cucumber. Arrange the tomatoes and cucumber on a serving platter.

2 **Drain the feta** and cut into small cubes. Sprinkle the feta and olives over the vegetables. Sprinkle the lemon juice over the salad and drizzle with the oil. Season with salt and pepper and toss.

3 **Add the basil**, toss again, and serve.

Vinaigrette Dressing

This versatile dressing is suitable for almost any salad

- 🍴 makes about ¾ cup
- 🕐 prep 5 mins

3 tbsp **wine vinegar**

1 tbsp **Dijon mustard**

⅔ cup **extra virgin olive oil**

salt and freshly ground **black pepper**

1 Whisk the vinegar and mustard in a medium bowl.

2 Using a balloon whisk, gradually whisk in the oil to make a thick, smooth vinaigrette. Season with salt and pepper.

VARIATION

Garlic Vinaigrette Dressing
Add 1 garlic clove, crushed to a paste with a little salt, in step 1.

> **PERFECT VINAIGRETTE**
> If you follow the recipe exactly, mixing the mustard and vinegar first, then adding the oil and whisking with a balloon whisk, you will achieve a thick emulsion that will not separate, even when stored.

Blue Cheese Dressing

Drizzle this creamy, tangy dressing over your favorite greens

- 🍴 makes about 1 cup
- 🕐 prep 10 mins

¾ cup plus 2 tbsp **sour cream**

4oz (100g) **Roquefort cheese**, crumbled

1 **garlic clove**, crushed

2 tbsp **white wine vinegar**

1 tsp **Dijon mustard**

1 tbsp finely snipped **chives**

salt and freshly ground **black pepper**

● **Prepare ahead** The dressing can be made well ahead of time and refrigerated until ready to use.

1 Place the sour cream, cheese, garlic, vinegar, and mustard with 3 tbsp of water in a food processor, and blend until smooth. Transfer to a bowl, and stir in the chives. Season with salt and pepper.

2 Pour into a serving bowl, cover, and refrigerate until ready to serve.

● **Good with** green salads, or as a dressing for steamed new potatoes.

VARIATION

Cheese Dressing
If you prefer, use another blue cheese, such as Danish blue or Gorgonzola or the same quantity of crumbled Cheddar cheese will make an equally creamy dressing.

Thousand Island Dressing

There is no need to limit this dressing to salads—it goes particularly well with seafood

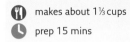

- makes about 1⅓ cups
- prep 15 mins

⅔ cup **mayonnaise**

⅓ cup finely chopped **red bell pepper**

1 **shallot**, finely chopped

3 tbsp finely chopped **sweet pickles**

2 tbsp **ketchup**

1 tbsp finely chopped **parsley**

1 tsp **Worcestershire sauce**

few drops of **hot red pepper sauce**

● **Prepare ahead** The dressing can be made 2 days in advance, covered and refrigerated.

1 Combine the mayonnaise, bell pepper, shallot, pickles, ketchup, parsley, and Worcestershire sauce in a bowl, and mix well. Season with the hot pepper sauce.

2 Cover and refrigerate until serving.

● **Good with** shrimp cocktails or salads containing shrimp, crabmeat, or avocado.

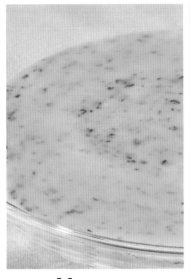

Yogurt Dressing

If made with fat-free yogurt, this is a healthy alternative to mayonnaise

- makes about ¾ cup (5–7fl oz) (150–200ml)
- prep 10 mins

¾ cup **plain low-fat yogurt**

1 tbsp finely chopped **parsley**

1 tbsp finely chopped **dill**

1 tbsp finely chopped **preserved stem ginger**

1 tsp **preserved ginger syrup**, from the jar

zest and juice of 1 small **lemon**

salt and freshly ground **black pepper**

● **Prepare ahead** The dressing can be covered and refrigerated for up to 4 days.

1 Mix the yogurt, parsley, dill, ginger, ginger syrup, lemon zest, and juice in a small bowl. Season with salt and pepper.

2 Cover with plastic wrap and refrigerate until ready to serve.

● **Good with** falafel or grilled meat, such as lamb.

Mayonnaise

Making your own mayonnaise is easy and allows you to choose your own flavorings

- makes 1½ cups
- prep 10 mins
- to prevent curdling, all the ingredients should be at room temperature before you start

2 large **egg yolks**

2 tbsp **white wine vinegar**

1 tsp **Dijon mustard**

1¼ cups **olive oil** (not extra virgin)

1 tbsp fresh **lemon** juice

● **Prepare ahead** The mayonnaise can be stored in the refrigerator.

1 Place the egg yolks, vinegar, and mustard in a food processor. Process for about 1 minute, until pale and creamy. (Or whisk by hand.)

2 With the machine running, slowly pour in the oil through the feed tube in a thin, steady stream, processing until the mayonnaise is thick and creamy. (If making by hand, dribble in the oil.)

3 Add the lemon juice and pulse briefly (or stir) to combine. Season with salt and pepper.

VARIATIONS

Substitute 3 tbsp of a flavored oil (hazelnut, walnut, basil, or lemon) for an equal amount of the olive oil. Or stir Chinese chile paste, chopped sun-dried tomatoes, crushed garlic, or chopped fresh herbs into the finished mayonnaise to taste.

Spanish Vegetable Tortilla

In Spain, a tortilla is a thick, frittata-like dish, often made with just potatoes. This version includes broccoli and peas

 makes 4 servings

 prep 15 mins • cook 45 mins

9in (23cm) nonstick frying pan

½ cup **fresh** or frozen **peas**

1 cup small **broccoli florets**

6 tbsp **olive oil**

12oz (350g) **baking potatoes**, such as russet or Burbank, peeled and cut into ¾in (2cm) cubes

1 medium **red onion**, finely chopped

6 large **eggs**, beaten

salt and freshly ground **black pepper**

● **Prepare ahead** The tortilla can be made a day in advance.

1 Bring a large saucepan of lightly salted water to a boil over high heat. Add the peas and boil for 5 minutes, or until just tender. Use a wire sieve to transfer the peas to a bowl of cold water. Return the pan to a boil, add the broccoli, and boil for 4 minutes, or until just tender. Transfer the broccoli to the peas and cool. Drain the vegetables together and pat dry with paper towels.

2 Heat 4 tbsp of the oil in a 9in (23cm) nonstick frying pan over medium heat. Add the potatoes and onion. Cook, stirring occasionally, for 10–15 minutes, or until the potatoes are tender. Let cool slightly.

3 Beat the eggs in a large bowl, and season with salt and pepper.

4 Use a slotted spoon to transfer the potatoes and onions to the eggs. Add the peas and broccoli and gently stir. Wipe out the pan with paper towels.

5 Heat the remaining 2 tbsp oil in the pan over high heat. Pour in the egg mixture, reduce the heat to low, and smooth the surface. Cook gently for 20–25 minutes or until the top begins to set and the underside is golden brown.

6 Carefully, slide the tortilla on to a plate. Place a second plate on top and invert both together so that the cooked side is on top. Slide the tortilla back into the pan and cook for 5 minutes, until the underside is golden brown.

7 Let stand for at least 5 minutes. Invert onto a serving platter. Serve warm or cooled, cut in wedges.

● **Good with** a dressed salad of mixed greens.

VARIATION

Quick Tortilla

For simple tortilla, omit the peas and broccoli. Substitute red-skinned potatoes, cut into matchsticks, and cook for about 10 minutes.

Egg Mayonnaise

Here is a near-perfect egg salad, which makes a classic sandwich filling for a summer's lunch

 makes 4 servings

 prep 10 mins • cook 7 mins

4 tbsp **mayonnaise**

2 **scallions**, finely sliced

1 tbsp chopped **chives**

4 large **eggs**, hard boiled

salt and freshly ground **black pepper**

1 Mix the mayonnaise, scallions, and chives in a small bowl.

2 Peel and slice the eggs. Add to the mayonnaise. Using a fork, mash the eggs. Season with salt and pepper.

● **Good with** salad greens or when served in lettuce cups as an appetizer.

> **PEELING EGGS**
> Cool the eggs rapidly after cooking, or a dark ring will form around the yolk. Peel the eggs in the cold water and the shells will slip off easily.

Devilled Eggs

Perfect party food, make them hot as the devil with spicy paprika and hot mustard, or keep them mellow with milder condiments

🍴 makes 4–6 servings

🕐 prep 10 mins • cook 10 mins

6 large **eggs**

3 tbsp **mayonnaise**

1 tsp hot or Dijon **mustard**

1 tsp **hot** or sweet **paprika**, plus more for garnish

salt and freshly ground **black pepper**

3 **cherry tomatoes**, cut in quarters

1 tbsp finely chopped **chives**

1 Simmer the eggs for 8 minutes. Rinse briefly under cold water. Lightly crack the eggs and soak them in ice water until cooled. Peel the eggs. Cut each in half lengthwise.

2 Remove the yolks and place them in a small bowl. Add the mayonnaise, mustard, and paprika, and mash with a fork. Season with salt and pepper.

3 Fill the egg white halves with the yolk mixture. Top each one with a cherry tomato quarter, a sprinkle of chives, and a dusting of paprika.

● **Prepare ahead** The eggs can be made up to 24 hours ahead, covered and refrigerated.

● **Good with** rounds of buttered toast and a few salad leaves.

Herb and Goat Cheese Frittata

Thinner than a Spanish tortilla, this popular Italian dish is ideal for lunch or a light supper

🍴 makes 4–6 servings

🕐 prep 10 mins • cook 20 mins

▣ 23cm (9in) nonstick frying pan with a lid and flameproof handle

6 large **eggs**

4 **sage** or basil **leaves**, finely chopped

salt and freshly ground **black pepper**

3 tbsp **olive oil**, plus extra for brushing

1 **shallot**, chopped

10 **cherry tomatoes**, halved

4oz (120g) rindless **goat cheese**, crumbled

1 Preheat the broiler and position the rack 6in (15cm) from the heat. Beat the eggs in a bowl with the sage, season with salt and pepper, and set aside.

2 Heat the oil in a 9in (23cm) nonstick frying pan with a lid and flameproof handle over medium-low heat. Add the shallot and cook, stirring constantly, for 3 minutes, or until just softened but not browned.

3 Add the eggs to the pan and stir gently to combine. Cover and cook gently for 2–3 minutes; the frittata should remain moist on top.

4 Arrange the tomatoes and goat cheese over the surface and lightly brush with olive oil. Place the pan in the broiler for 5 minutes or until the frittata is set and lightly browned. Let stand for 5 minutes. Slide onto a serving platter and cut into wedges. Serve hot, warm, or at room temperature.

● **Good with** plenty of Italian bread and a tomato salad.

VARIATION

Red Pepper and Salami Frittata

In step 2 add 1 red pepper, seeded and cut into strips, and 4 thin slices of salami, rind removed, cut into strips, to the shallot. Replace the goat cheese and tomatoes with ½ cup of shredded Cheddar cheese.

Curried Quail Eggs

This quick recipe uses dainty quail eggs, and the mild curry sauce tops the whole dish off perfectly

 makes 4 appetizer servings

prep 15 mins • cook 3 mins

4 quail eggs

2 slices of whole wheat bread

4 tbsp low-fat plain yogurt

2 tbsp mayonnaise

2 tbsp chopped cilantro

1 tsp mild curry powder

salt and freshly ground black pepper

To serve

1 tsp fresh lemon juice

1 tsp vegetable oil

½ cup loosely packed cilantro and parsley leaves

● **Prepare ahead** The eggs and the sauce can be refrigerated several hours in advance.

1 Place a bowl of iced water near the stove. Bring a small pan of water to a boil over high heat and add the eggs. Cook for 2½ minutes. Using a slotted spoon, transfer the eggs to the iced water. Let cool, then peel the eggs.

2 Lightly toast the bread and, using a 2in (5cm) cookie cutter, cut 2 circles or ovals from each slice. Divide the toasts among 4 plates.

3 Combine the yogurt, mayonnaise, cilantro, and curry powder in a small bowl. Season with salt and pepper.

4 Whisk the lemon juice and oil together in a medium bowl, then add the cilantro and parsley leaves, and toss.

5 Cut each egg in half and arrange 1 egg on each toast. Spoon the curry sauce over the top. Serve immediately, garnished with the dressed herbs.

● **Leftovers** of both the eggs and curry sauce can be gently reheated and used to top cooked spinach for a quick and spicy variation of the classic Eggs Florentine.

> **HEN'S EGGS**
> This recipe works equally well with 4 hard-boiled hen's eggs. Boil for 6 minutes, peel, then cut into quarters.

Eggs Benedict

The smooth buttery sauce makes a truly indulgent breakfast or brunch

 makes 4 servings

prep 10 mins • cook 11 mins

8 large eggs

2 tbsp distilled white vinegar

4 English muffins

butter, for spreading

1 cup warm hollandaise sauce

1 Fill a large frying pan with water to a depth of 2in (5cm). Add the vinegar and bring to a simmer over medium heat. When tiny bubbles appear at the bottom of the pan, carefully crack 4 eggs, one by one, into each pan.

2 Cook for 1 minute. Remove from the heat and let stand for exactly 6 minutes. Remove the eggs, using a slotted spoon, and drain on paper towels.

3 Meanwhile, split each muffin in half and toast.

4 Butter each muffin half and place 2 on each serving plate. Top each half with a poached egg and spoon the hollandaise over the top.

● **Good with** ham or crisp grilled bacon on the side.

Scrambled Eggs with Smoked Salmon

This is the ultimate feel-good Sunday brunch recipe

 makes 4 servings

prep 10 mins • cook 10 mins

6 large **eggs**

2 tbsp **whole milk**

salt and freshly ground **black pepper**

1 tbsp **butter**

8oz (225g) **smoked salmon**, cut into thin strips, or hot smoked salmon, flaked

2 tbsp finely chopped **chives**

4 **English muffins**, split and toasted

1 Beat the eggs with the milk, and season with salt and pepper.

2 Heat the butter in a medium nonstick frying pan over medium heat until foaming. Add the eggs and stir with a wooden spoon until almost set. Stir in the smoked salmon and cook until just set.

3 Sprinkle with the chives. Spoon over the toasted muffin halves and serve hot.

VARIATIONS

Scrambled Eggs with Mushrooms

Cook 8oz (225g) mixed mushrooms, whole or sliced, in butter, and add in place of the salmon.

Scrambled Eggs with Green Peppers and Tomatoes

Cook 1 seeded and chopped green pepper in olive oil until just tender. Add 3 tomatoes, skinned, seeded, and chopped. Use instead of salmon.

Scotch Eggs

Great for picnics and packed lunches, serve these with a spoonful of your favorite chutney

 makes 4 servings

prep 25 mins • cook 15 mins

10oz (300g) **ground pork**

2 **scallions**, white and green parts, finely chopped

2 tsp dried **Italian herbs**

pinch of crushed **red hot pepper**

salt and freshly ground **black pepper**

4 **hard-boiled eggs**, peeled

⅓ cup **all-purpose flour**

vegetable oil, for deep frying

1 large **egg**, beaten

¾ cup plain dried **bread crumbs**

1 In a large bowl, mix the pork, scallions, herbs, and hot pepper. Season with salt and pepper.

2 Coat the eggs in flour. Divide the pork mixture into 4 equal portions. Working with one portion at a time, flatten the pork into a thick disk. Place an egg in the center and gather up the pork to completely enclose the egg.

3 Pour enough oil to come halfway up the sides of a large, deep saucepan and heat to 350°F (180°C). Beat the eggs in a shallow dish Spread the bread crumbs in another dish. Dip each pork-wrapped egg into the beaten egg to coat, then roll in the bread crumbs.

4 Carefully place the eggs in the hot oil and fry for 3–4 minutes, or until golden. Serve hot or cold.

VARIATION

Vegetarian Scotch Eggs

Omit the ground pork. Substitute 1 drained 15oz (420g) can of white kidney (cannellini) beans, puréed in a food processor with 2oz (60g) soft goat cheese. Transfer to a bowl, and mix in the scallions, herbs, hot pepper, and 3 tbsp of dried bread crumbs.

Omelets

Although cooks around the world make different omelets, they are all similar in that they make quick meals at any time of the day—you can even enjoy omelets for dessert!

Quail Egg
Tiny and speckled, these are best hard-boiled.

Bantam Chicken Egg
Bantams are small chickens, so these eggs are smaller than average.

Brown Leghorn Chicken Egg
This breed lays both white and brown eggs.

Welsummer Chicken Egg
Originally from Holland, these large eggs are dark reddish-brown.

Burford Browns Chicken Egg
These large eggs are recognized by their thick, dark brown shells.

Old Cotswold Legbar Chicken Egg
This breed lays eggs in pretty pastel colors.

Duck Egg
Larger than most chicken eggs, these have a richer flavor.

Goose Egg
These large eggs taste stronger than chicken eggs.

Choosing Eggs

The essential ingredient of any great-tasting omelet is fresh eggs. Many types of eggs can be used in omelets, and farmers' markets and supermarkets offer a large choice of chicken and other eggs.

When you are buying eggs, the box gives you information about the quality and types of eggs inside. The USDA grade shield or mark means that the eggs were graded for quality and weight. Look for a best-before date stamped on the shells, as well as on the box. Eggs sold as "free-range" come from birds with continuous daylight access to runs and a variety of vegetation.

- "Organic" eggs are from free-range hens fed an organic diet on farms approved by one of the several organic certification bodies.
- US eggs sold for domestic use are graded as Grade AA (the highest quality), Grade A, and Grade B.
- Check the condition of the eggs inside the box before you buy to ensure none are cracked.

Storing

- Store eggs in the refrigerator, not at room temperature.
- Egg shells are porous so, ideally, keep eggs in their box or in a closed compartment in the refrigerator door, which prevents them from absorbing other smells.
- When transferring eggs to a rack in the refrigerator, be sure to put them pointed-end down, to keep the yolk centered.
- Observe the best-before date.

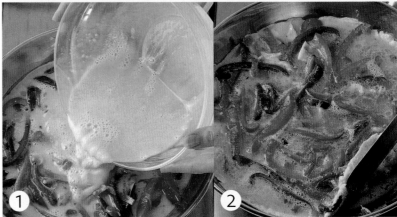

HOW DO I KNOW IT'S FRESH?

Always check the best-before date on the box. Or you can use this simple test if you have thrown the box away and have eggs without a best-before date: immerse the egg in water and see if it rises. A stale egg contains much more air and less liquid than a fresh one, so it will float. Do not use a stale egg.

Fresh   Borderline   Stale

Folded Omelet

1 **To make a 3-egg** omelet, melt 1–2 tbsp butter in an 8in (20cm) nonstick frying pan over high heat until foaming but not browning. Pour in the beaten eggs and shake the pan to distribute evenly. Stir with a fork, keeping the rounded side of the fork flat. Stop stirring after 20–30 seconds, or when the eggs are set but still soft.

2 **Using the fork**, fold the side of the omelet nearest you halfway over itself, like you are folding a letter. Grasp the handle of the pan from underneath, and lift the pan to a 45 degree angle. Sharply tap the top of the handle closest to the pan, to encourage the omelet to curl over the folded portion. Use the fork to fully "close the letter."

3 **Bring a warmed** serving plate to the omelet, then tilt the pan so the omelet falls on to the plate. Serve immediately.

Flat Omelet

1 **Cook the filling ingredients** in an 8–10in (20–25cm) frying pan with a flameproof handle until they are all tender. Pour over the seasoned beaten eggs and stir to combine all the ingredients. Leave the omelet to cook, undisturbed, or until most of the egg is set and the base is golden brown. Meanwhile, preheat the broiler.

2 **Test that the omelet** is set underneath by lifting the edge with a palette knife. Put the omelet under the broiler for 2–3 minutes, or until the top is set.

3 **Remove the pan** from the heat and sprinkle cheese or any other ingredients over the top. Place under the broiler until the cheese is melted and lightly browned and any other ingredients are cooked as required. If serving hot, transfer to a warmed serving plate, otherwise set aside and leave to cool completely to serve cold.

Soufflé Omelet

1 **Separate 2 eggs**. Beat the yolks with 1 tbsp sugar, 1 tbsp water, and ½ tsp vanilla extract. Beat the whites until stiff peaks form, then fold into the yolks. Preheat the oven to its highest setting. Melt 1–2 tbsp clarified butter in a 7–8in (18–20cm) nonstick frying pan over a high heat until foaming.

2 **Reduce the heat** to medium, add the egg mixture, spread out, and cook for 30–45 seconds, or until the eggs are set underneath. Place under the broiler and cook for 1 minute, or until the top is set. Quickly spread any filling, such as Cherry and Almond (p142), over half the omelet, then use a palette knife to fold the other half over.

3 **Slide the omelet** on to a warmed serving plate and dust with confectioner's sugar. The omelet is now ready to serve, or you can decorate the top by using a red-hot skewer to scorch the sugar. Serve at once.

Simple Omelet Flavorings

Be inventive. Almost anything you have in the kitchen will add extra flavor and variety to folded and flat omelets. Add any of these ingredients to the beaten eggs, with seasoning to taste, just before starting to cook.

Cheese Grated mature Cheddar, Parmesan, Gruyère, and Emmental, or crumbled feta, make flat omelets more filling.

Spices Stir in a pinch of cayenne pepper, paprika, mustard powder, or mild curry powder for heat, or turmeric for a rich golden color.

Bottled Sauces Add a splash of soy, Worcestershire, or chile-hot Tabasco sauce.

Vegetables For flat omelets, add several crushed garlic cloves lightly sautéed with a finely chopped onion; several finely chopped scallions; 1 tbsp seeded and chopped green chile; 1 thinly sliced skinned red pepper bottled in olive oil.

Herbs For a garden-fresh taste, add 1 tbsp chopped chervil, chives, parsley, or tarragon—or a mixture of two or more herbs. When fresh herbs are not available, stir in 1 tsp dried mixed herbs.

Beat the eggs *with salt and pepper and other flavorings, before cooking.*

Omelets

Folded Omelet Fillings

Spinach, Cheddar, and Bacon
Cook the omelet, then spoon on the spinach. Sprinkle over the bacon and cheese and season to taste with salt and pepper just before folding and sliding out of the pan.

2oz (60g) cooked, chopped **spinach**, kept hot

2–4 slices **bacon**, cooked until crisp, drained, crumbled, and kept hot

1oz (30g) **Cheddar cheese**, grated

salt and **black pepper**

Smoked Ham and Mustard
Beat the mustard into the eggs in the omelet recipe before adding to the pan. Cook the omelet, then sprinkle in the ham just before folding and sliding out of the pan.

1 tbsp **whole grain mustard**

1oz (30g) **smoked ham**, thinly sliced

Soufflé Omelet Fillings

Cherry and Almond
Melt the jam and stir in the kirsch. Spread over half the cooked soufflé omelet and sprinkle with the almonds just after folding.

4 tbsp **cherry jam**

½ tbsp **kirsch**

1oz (30g) **blanched almonds**, coarsely ground

Apricot and Vanilla
Melt the jam and stir in the vanilla extract. Spread over half the cooked soufflé omelet just after folding, then dust with confectioner's sugar.

4 tbsp **apricot jam**

2–3 drops **pure vanilla extract**

1 tbsp **confectioner's sugar**

Flat Omelet Fillings

Zucchini and Feta

Cook the onion and red pepper in the olive oil for 3 minutes. Add the zucchini with salt and pepper to taste and continue cooking for 3–5 minutes, or until the vegetables are tender. Pour the eggs from the omelet recipe over the top and cook until set underneath. Put under a preheated broiler until the eggs are set on top. Sprinkle with the cheese and return to the oven until the cheese is soft and lightly browned.

1 **onion**, diced

1 **red pepper**, diced

1 tbsp **olive oil**

2 **zucchini**, diced

salt and **black pepper**

2oz (60g) drained and crumbled **feta cheese**

Tomato and Asparagus

Cook the asparagus and onion in the oil until tender. Pour the eggs from your omelet recipe over the top and cook until the omelet is set. Sprinkle with cheese, tomato, and salt and pepper, then place in the oven.

4oz (115g) **asparagus tips**, chopped

1 **onion**, sliced

1 tbsp **olive oil**

2oz (60g) grated **Emmental cheese**

1 **tomato**, cut into wedges

salt and **black pepper**

PERFECT OMELETS

- It is easiest to make an omelet per person, rather than trying to make a larger omelet to serve two people. Use 3 eggs for an omelet to serve one. A 2-egg soufflé omelet serves one or two people.

- Use a nonstick or well-seasoned omelet or frying pan.

- A 7–8in (18–20cm) frying pan (measured across the base) is the best size to use for a 3-egg omelet. A sloping side enables the omelet to slide out more easily.

- Using clarified butter for soufflé omelets is recommended so the bottom does not brown before the top is set.

- Beat the eggs in a bowl using a fork until the yolks and whites are well blended. Season to taste with salt and pepper and add any flavorings, such as herbs. Take a look at the suggestions on p141 (or above) for more inspiration.

- Have a warmed serving plate ready before you start cooking.

World Omelets

Tortilla

This variation of a traditional, thick Spanish omelet includes broccoli and peas along with the more usual potatoes and onion.

🕐 1 hr　　　　　　　　**page 136**

Herb and Goat Cheese Frittata

Thinner than a Spanish tortilla, this popular Italian flat omelet makes a great hot or cold lunch or light supper.

🕐 30 mins　　　　　　　**page 137**

Omelet Arnold Bennett

Originally created at London's Savoy Hotel, this traditional breakfast omelet is flavored with chunky flakes of smoked haddock.

🕐 25 mins　　　　　　　**page 151**

Spinach Timbales

These vegetable molds can be served as a light main course or appetizer with the salad, or serve them on their own to accompany roast lamb

- 🍴 makes 4 servings
- 🕐 prep 10 mins • cook 30 mins
- 🗄 individual timbale molds or ramekins
- ❄ freeze for up to 3 months; to serve, reheat in a low oven

3 tbsp **butter**, plus more for the molds

1 **onion**, finely chopped

1 **garlic clove**, minced

1¼ cups **half-and-half**

5oz (150g) firm **goat cheese**, crumbled

5oz (150g) **spinach**

5 large **eggs**

⅓ cup fresh **bread crumbs**

½ tsp freshly grated **nutmeg**

salt and freshly ground **black pepper**

For the salad

2 tbsp **extra virgin olive oil**

1 tbsp **balsamic vinegar**

1 **garlic clove**, minced to a paste

salt and freshly ground **black pepper**

2oz (60g) **frisée**

½ **seedless cucumber**, cut into sticks

1 Preheat the oven to 350°F (180°C). Lightly butter 4 timbale molds. Melt 1 tbsp butter in a saucepan over low heat. Add the onion and garlic, cover, and cook for about 10 minutes, or until translucent but not browned.

2 Add the half-and-half, and bring to a simmer. Remove from the heat, add the goat cheese, and stir until melted.

3 In another saucepan, melt the remaining 2 tbsp butter over medium heat. Add the spinach and cook until it is wilted and tender. Add to the cream mixture. Whisk in the eggs and bread crumbs. Season with nutmeg, salt, and pepper. Purée in a blender. Divide the mixture among the timbale molds. Place the molds in a roasting pan and add enough hot water to come halfway up the sides of the molds.

4 Bake for 15–20 minutes, or until they have risen and are just firm to touch.

5 Meanwhile, prepare the salad. Whisk the oil, vinegar, and garlic together. Season with salt and pepper. Divide the frisée and cucumbers among 4 plates. Drizzle with the dressing. Unmold a timbale onto each plate and serve immediately.

French Toast

This makes a hot, satisfying breakfast or brunch

- 🍴 makes 4 servings
- 🕐 prep 5 mins • cook 20 mins

1¼ cups **whole millk**

1¼ cups **half-and-half** or more milk

3 large **eggs**

2 tsp **sugar**

1 tsp **pure vanilla extract**

8 slices of **white bread**, preferably day-old

4 tbsp **butter**

maple syrup, to serve

1 Preheat the oven to 200°F (95°C). In a shallow dish, beat together the milk, half-and-half, eggs, sugar, and vanilla.

2 Melt 1 tbsp butter in a large frying pan over medium heat. In batches, submerge each bread slice in the egg mixture until just saturated but not soaked. Add to the frying pan and cook, turning once, until golden on both sides. Transfer to a baking sheet and keep warm in the oven while cooking the remaining bread.

3 Cut the toasts in half diagonally and arrange 4 pieces on each serving plate. Drizzle with maple syrup and serve.

● **Good with** a few summer berries or a spoonful of yogurt.

Buckwheat Galettes

Popular in Brittany, in northwest France, where the local cuisine is defined by rich, rustic flavors

 makes 4 servings

 prep 25 mins, plus 2 hrs standing • cook 30 mins

8in (20cm) nonstick frying pan

the unfilled pancakes can be frozen for up to 3 months

½ cup buckwheat flour

½ cup all-purpose flour

2 large eggs, beaten

1 cup plus 2 tbsp milk

vegetable oil, for frying

For the filling

2 tbsp vegetable oil

2 red onions, thinly sliced

7oz (200g) smoked ham, chopped

1 tsp chopped thyme

4oz (115g) Brie, cut into small pieces

½ cup crème fraîche

● **Prepare ahead** The batter can be prepared a few hours in advance and left at room temperature.

1 To make the pancakes, sift the flours into a large mixing bowl. Make a well in the center and add the eggs. Gradually mix the eggs into the flours using a wooden spoon, adding the milk and and a scant ½ cup water to make a smooth batter. Cover and let stand for 2 hours.

2 To make the filling, heat the oil in a small frying pan over medium heat. Add the onions and cook, stirring occasionally, until softened. Add the ham and thyme. Remove from the heat.

3 Preheat the oven to 300°F (150°C). Heat an 8in (20cm) nonstick frying pan over medium heat. Grease lightly with oil. Spoon in 2 tbsp of the batter and swirl to coat the base. Cook for about 1 minute, or until lightly browned underneath. Flip over and cook for 1 minute more, or until lightly browned on the other side. Repeat with the remaining batter, re-greasing the pan as necessary. Make 8 pancakes in total.

4 Stir the Brie and crème fraîche into the filling. Evenly divide among the pancakes then fold in the pancake edges to form "parcels." Place on a baking sheet. Bake for 10 minutes until hot.

Parsi Eggs

This Indian dish has its origins in ancient Persia

 makes 4 servings

prep 10 mins • cook 30 mins

4 tbsp butter

4 scallions, thinly sliced

1 tsp peeled, grated fresh ginger

1 large fresh hot red or green chile, seeded and minced

2 tsp curry powder

4 tomatoes, seeded and chopped

8 large eggs

2 tbsp whole milk

salt and freshly ground black pepper

2 tbsp chopped cilantro

● **Prepare ahead** The ingredients can be prepared ahead, but the dish should be cooked just before serving.

1 Melt 2 tbsp butter in a large nonstick frying pan over low heat. Add the scallions, ginger, and chile and cook, stirring occasionally, for 2 minutes.

2 Stir in the curry powder. Add the tomatoes and cook for 1 minute. Transfer to a plate.

3 Add the remaining 2 tbsp butter to the pan and melt. Whisk the eggs and milk together, and season with salt and pepper. Pour into the pan and stir until scrambled and almost set. Add the vegetables, stir well, and cook until just set. Sprinkle with cilantro and serve at once.

● **Good with** salad leaves, light toasted naan bread, or chapatis.

VARIATION

Parsi Turkey Bacon and Eggs

Add 4oz (115g) cooked diced turkey bacon to the pan in step 1.

Quiche Lorraine

A French classic, this egg and bacon tart is the original and the best

 makes 8 servings

 prep 35 mins, plus chilling • cook 35 mins

 9in (23cm) tart pan with a removable bottom, baking beans

For the dough

1½ cups **all-purpose flour**, plus more for rolling out

8 tbsp **butter**, chilled and cubed

1 large **egg yolk**

3 tbsp **ice water**, as needed

For the filling

7oz (200g) **bacon**

1 **onion**, finely chopped

⅔ cup shredded **Gruyère cheese**

4 large **eggs**, lightly beaten

⅔ cup **heavy cream**

⅔ cup **whole milk**

freshly ground **black pepper**

● **Prepare ahead** Refrigerate the cooled, baked quiche for up to 2 days; reheat at 325°F (160°C) for 15–20 minutes.

1 **To make the dough**, pulse the flour and butter in a food processor until the mixture resembles fine crumbs. Mix the yolk and water. Transfer the flour mixture to a bowl and stir in enough of the water mixture until the dough clumps together. Gather in a disk and wrap in plastic wrap. Refrigerate 30 minutes. On a lightly floured surface, roll out the dough ⅛in (3mm) thick. Line a 9in (23cm) tart pan with a removable bottom with the dough, trimming any excess. Refrigerate for 30 minutes.

2 **Preheat the oven** to 375°F (190°C). Prick the dough with a fork, and line with parchment paper and beans. Place on a baking sheet and bake 15 minutes. Remove the parchment paper and beans and bake another 10 minutes, until golden.

3 **Meanwhile**, cook the bacon in a large frying pan over medium heat about 4 minutes, until golden. Add the onion and cook 2–3 minutes, until softened. Spread in the pastry shell, then sprinkle with the Gruyère.

4 **Whisk together** the eggs, cream, milk, and season with pepper. Pour into the shell. Bake for 25–30 minutes, or until golden and just set. Serve hot, warm, or cold.

 VARIATION

Mushroom Quiche

Omit the onion, bacon, and Gruyère. Cook 1 large red onion, finely chopped, with 2 tbsp olive oil in a pan over medium heat for 2–3 minutes. Add 10oz (300g) of sliced mixed mushrooms and 1 minced garlic clove. Cook for another 6 minutes. Spoon into the pastry and sprinkle with 4 tbsp freshly grated Parmesan cheese and 3 tbsp chopped parsley. Add the custard and bake as above.

Poached Egg Muffins

A simple, satisfying breakfast that anyone can make

 makes 4 servings

 cook 4–6 mins

4 large, very fresh **eggs**

1 tbsp fresh **lemon** juice or cider vinegar

4 **English muffins**, split and toasted

1 **Bring a large** frying pan of water to a gentle simmer, so small bubbles are just breaking at the surface. Add the lemon juice. Bring a second frying pan of water to a simmer, and turn off the heat.

2 **Crack one egg** on to a plate. Stir the water with a large, slotted spoon, then slip the egg into the water, letting the edge of the plate touch the water so it does not splash. Repeat with the other eggs.

3 **Cook gently** for about 3 minutes just until the white is set (or for a few extra minutes if you prefer a fully set yolk). Using a slotted spoon, lift out each egg, dip into the frying pan of water, then place on a plate lined with paper towels.

4 **Trim any loose strands** of egg white and serve immediately with the toasted muffins.

Buckwheat Galettes

Popular in Brittany, in northwest France, where the local cuisine is defined by rich, rustic flavors

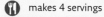
- makes 4 servings
- prep 25 mins, plus 2 hrs standing • cook 30 mins
- 8in (20cm) nonstick frying pan
- the unfilled pancakes can be frozen for up to 3 months

½ cup **buckwheat flour**

½ cup **all-purpose flour**

2 large **eggs**, beaten

1 cup plus 2 tbsp **milk**

vegetable oil, for frying

For the filling

2 tbsp **vegetable oil**

2 **red onions**, thinly sliced

7oz (200g) **smoked ham**, chopped

1 tsp chopped **thyme**

4oz (115g) **Brie**, cut into small pieces

½ cup **crème fraîche**

● **Prepare ahead** The batter can be prepared a few hours in advance and left at room temperature.

1 **To make the pancakes**, sift the flours into a large mixing bowl. Make a well in the center and add the eggs. Gradually mix the eggs into the flours using a wooden spoon, adding the milk and and a scant ½ cup water to make a smooth batter. Cover and let stand for 2 hours.

2 **To make the filling**, heat the oil in a small frying pan over medium heat. Add the onions and cook, stirring occasionally, until softened. Add the ham and thyme. Remove from the heat.

3 **Preheat the oven** to 300°F (150°C). Heat an 8in (20cm) nonstick frying pan over medium heat. Grease lightly with oil. Spoon in 2 tbsp of the batter and swirl to coat the base. Cook for about 1 minute, or until lightly browned underneath. Flip over and cook for 1 minute more, or until lightly browned on the other side. Repeat with the remaining batter, re-greasing the pan as necessary. Make 8 pancakes in total.

4 **Stir the Brie** and crème fraîche into the filling. Evenly divide among the pancakes then fold in the pancake edges to form "parcels." Place on a baking sheet. Bake for 10 minutes until hot.

Parsi Eggs

This Indian dish has its origins in ancient Persia

- makes 4 servings
- prep 10 mins • cook 30 mins

4 tbsp **butter**

4 **scallions**, thinly sliced

1 tsp peeled, grated **fresh ginger**

1 large fresh **hot red** or green **chile**, seeded and minced

2 tsp **curry powder**

4 **tomatoes**, seeded and chopped

8 large **eggs**

2 tbsp **whole milk**

salt and freshly ground **black pepper**

2 tbsp chopped **cilantro**

● **Prepare ahead** The ingredients can be prepared ahead, but the dish should be cooked just before serving.

1 **Melt 2 tbsp butter** in a large nonstick frying pan over low heat. Add the scallions, ginger, and chile and cook, stirring occasionally, for 2 minutes.

2 **Stir in the curry powder.** Add the tomatoes and cook for 1 minute. Transfer to a plate.

3 **Add the remaining** 2 tbsp butter to the pan and melt. Whisk the eggs and milk together, and season with salt and pepper. Pour into the pan and stir until scrambled and almost set. Add the vegetables, stir well, and cook until just set. Sprinkle with cilantro and serve at once.

● **Good with** salad leaves, light toasted naan bread, or chapatis.

Parsi Turkey Bacon and Eggs

Add 4oz (115g) cooked diced turkey bacon to the pan in step 1.

Quiche Lorraine

A French classic, this egg and bacon tart is the original and the best

- makes 8 servings
- prep 35 mins, plus chilling • cook 35 mins
- 9in (23cm) tart pan with a removable bottom, baking beans

For the dough

1½ cups **all-purpose flour**, plus more for rolling out

8 tbsp **butter**, chilled and cubed

1 large **egg yolk**

3 tbsp **ice water**, as needed

For the filling

7oz (200g) **bacon**

1 **onion**, finely chopped

⅔ cup shredded **Gruyère cheese**

4 large **eggs**, lightly beaten

⅔ cup **heavy cream**

⅔ cup **whole milk**

freshly ground **black pepper**

● **Prepare ahead** Refrigerate the cooled, baked quiche for up to 2 days; reheat at 325°F (160°C) for 15–20 minutes.

1 To make the dough, pulse the flour and butter in a food processor until the mixture resembles fine crumbs. Mix the yolk and water. Transfer the flour mixture to a bowl and stir in enough of the water mixture until the dough clumps together. Gather in a disk and wrap in plastic wrap. Refrigerate 30 minutes. On a lightly floured surface, roll out the dough ⅛in (3mm) thick. Line a 9in (23cm) tart pan with a removable bottom with the dough, trimming any excess. Refrigerate for 30 minutes.

2 Preheat the oven to 375°F (190°C). Prick the dough with a fork, and line with parchment paper and beans. Place on a baking sheet and bake 15 minutes. Remove the parchment paper and beans and bake another 10 minutes, until golden.

3 Meanwhile, cook the bacon in a large frying pan over medium heat about 4 minutes, until golden. Add the onion and cook 2–3 minutes, until softened. Spread in the pastry shell, then sprinkle with the Gruyère.

4 Whisk together the eggs, cream, milk, and season with pepper. Pour into the shell. Bake for 25–30 minutes, or until golden and just set. Serve hot, warm, or cold.

VARIATION

Mushroom Quiche

Omit the onion, bacon, and Gruyère. Cook 1 large red onion, finely chopped, with 2 tbsp olive oil in a pan over medium heat for 2–3 minutes. Add 10oz (300g) of sliced mixed mushrooms and 1 minced garlic clove. Cook for another 6 minutes. Spoon into the pastry and sprinkle with 4 tbsp freshly grated Parmesan cheese and 3 tbsp chopped parsley. Add the custard and bake as above.

Poached Egg Muffins

A simple, satisfying breakfast that anyone can make

- makes 4 servings
- cook 4–6 mins

4 large, very fresh **eggs**

1 tbsp fresh **lemon** juice or cider vinegar

4 **English muffins**, split and toasted

1 Bring a large frying pan of water to a gentle simmer, so small bubbles are just breaking at the surface. Add the lemon juice. Bring a second frying pan of water to a simmer, and turn off the heat.

2 Crack one egg on to a plate. Stir the water with a large, slotted spoon, then slip the egg into the water, letting the edge of the plate touch the water so it does not splash. Repeat with the other eggs.

3 Cook gently for about 3 minutes just until the white is set (or for a few extra minutes if you prefer a fully set yolk). Using a slotted spoon, lift out each egg, dip into the frying pan of water, then place on a plate lined with paper towels.

4 Trim any loose strands of egg white and serve immediately with the toasted muffins.

Poached Eggs with Frisée

This is a favorite appetizer or light lunch dish in rural France

- makes 4 servings
- prep 15 mins • cook 20 mins
- low GI

For the dressing

2 tbsp cider vinegar

1 tsp whole grain mustard

1 tbsp chopped tarragon

6 tbsp extra virgin olive oil

salt and freshly ground black pepper

6oz (175g) thick-sliced bacon, coarsely chopped

1 head frisée

8 cherry tomatoes, cut in half

¼ seedless cucumber, sliced

¾ cup coarsely chopped walnuts

4 hot poached eggs

● **Prepare ahead** The dressing can be stored in a jar for up to 5 days. Shake well before using.

1 **To make the dressing**, whisk together the vinegar, mustard, and tarragon. Gradually whisk in the oil. Season with salt and pepper.

2 **Cook the bacon** in a nonstick frying pan over medium heat about 8–10 minutes, until crispy and brown.

3 **Meanwhile**, break up the frisée into small leaves. Divide among four serving plates, and top with the cherry tomatoes, cucumber slices, and walnuts.

4 **Place a hot poached egg** in the center of each salad, and sprinkle the hot bacon on top. Drizzle with equal amounts of the dressing and serve immediately.

Eggs Florentine

This classic brunch dish of poached eggs on a bed of spinach is also good for lunch or dinner

- makes 4 servings
- prep 15 mins • cook 10 mins
- 4 flameproof serving dishes

4 tbsp butter

3 tbsp all-purpose flour

1½ cups whole milk

salt and freshly ground black pepper

2 large egg yolks

2 tbsp heavy cream

1 cup shredded Gruyère cheese

2 shallots, chopped

1lb (450g) fresh spinach, well rinsed but not dried

4 hot poached eggs

4 slices buttered toast, to serve

1 **Melt 2 tbsp** of the butter in a small saucepan over medium-low heat. Whisk in the flour and let bubble for 1 minute. Gradually beat in the milk. Cook, whisking often, until boiling and thickened. Season with salt and pepper. Whisk egg yolks and cream together, then whisk into the sauce. Stir in ¾ cup of the Gruyère. Keep warm.

2 **Meanwhile**, melt the remaining 2 tbsp butter in a large saucepan over medium heat. Add the shallots and cook, stirring often, about 2 minutes, until softened. Add the rinsed spinach, cover, and cook about 5 minutes, until the spinach has wilted. Drain well.

3 **Position a broiler rack** about 6in (15cm) from the source of heat and preheat the broiler. Divide the spinach among four flameproof ramekins. Using a slotted spoon, place a poached egg in each ramekin, then top with the sauce and sprinkle with the remaining Gruyère. Broil until the cheese is melted and golden. Serve hot, with the toast.

Spinach and Mushroom Crêpes

Savory crêpes are great for lunch, supper, or brunch

- makes 4 servings
- prep 30 mins plus standing • cook 1 hr 10 mins
- freeze, unbaked, for up to 3 months

For the crêpes

1¼ cups **whole milk**

scant 1 cup **all-purpose flour**

1 large **egg** plus 1 large **egg yolk**

1 tbsp **light olive oil** or melted butter, plus extra for frying

pinch of **salt**

For the filling

2 tbsp **butter**

7oz (200g) **mushrooms**, chopped

one 10oz (280g) box **frozen chopped spinach**

thawed 1¾ cups **béchamel sauce**

pinch of grated **nutmeg**

salt and freshly ground **black pepper**

¾ cup shredded sharp **Cheddar**

½ tsp **dry mustard**

2 ripe **tomatoes**, sliced

3 tbsp grated **Parmesan cheese**

● **Prepare ahead** The crêpes and the filling can be made and refrigerated for up to 8 hours before rolling and baking.

1 **To make the crêpes**, process all of the ingredients in a blender until smooth. Let the mixture stand for 30 minutes.

2 **Lightly grease** the frying pan with melted butter. Add about 3 tbsp of the batter to the pan, and tilt and swirl the pan so the batter covers the bottom. Cook until the underside is golden brown. Turn the crêpe and cook until the other side is golden. Transfer to a plate. Repeat with the remaining batter, buttering the pan as needed. You should have 12 crêpes. Separate the crêpes with pieces of wax paper.

3 **To make the filling**, melt the butter in a frying pan over medium heat. Add the mushrooms and cook 6 minutes. Transfer to a bowl. Add the spinach and ¼ cup of the béchamel sauce. Season with nutmeg, salt, and pepper.

4 **Preheat the oven** to 375°F (190°C). Divide the filling among the crêpes. Roll them up and place in a shallow buttered baking dish. Stir the Cheddar and mustard into the remaining sauce and season with salt and pepper. Spread over the crêpes. Arrange the tomato on top and sprinkle with the Parmesan. Bake for 30 minutes, or until bubbling and browned.

VARIATION

Spinach and Ricotta Crêpes

Replace the mushrooms with 10oz (300g) ricotta cheese. Add to the cooked spinach and fill the pancakes.

Baked Eggs in Cream

A simple and satisfying dish

- makes 4 servings
- prep 10 mins, plus cooling • cook 25 mins
- four 6oz (180ml) ramekins

2 tbsp **olive oil**

4 small **shallots**, finely chopped

2 **garlic cloves**, minced (optional)

1 tbsp chopped **tarragon**

¾ cup **heavy cream** or crème fraîche

4 large **eggs**

3 tbsp shredded **Gruyère**

1 tbsp dry **bread crumbs**

1 tbsp finely chopped **chives**

freshly ground **black pepper**

1 **Preheat the oven** to 325°F (160°C). Heat the oil in a frying pan over medium-low heat. Add the shallots and garlic and cook, stirring, until the shallots are golden. Stir in the tarragon and 2 tbsp of the cream.

2 **Spread equal amounts** of the mixture in 4 x 6oz (180ml) ramekins, making a slight well in each portion of the shallots. Crack an egg into each dish. Divide the remaining cream among the ramekins.

3 **Mix together** the Gruyère, bread crumbs, and chives, and season with pepper. Sprinkle in the ramekins. Place the ramekins on a baking sheet and bake for 10–15 minutes, or until the eggs are cooked to your liking. Serve at once.

Spinach Soufflés

These soufflés are deliciously golden and puffy once cooked, and taste every bit as good as they look

 makes 4 servings

 prep 20 mins • cook 20 mins

four 7oz (200ml) ramekins

8oz (225g) **spinach**, rinsed but not dried

4 tbsp **butter**, plus extra for the ramekins

⅓ cup all-purpose **flour**

1½ cups **whole milk**

⅔ cup grated **Parmesan cheese**

pinch of freshly grated **nutmeg**

salt and freshly ground **black pepper**

4 large **eggs**, separated

1 Place the spinach with any clinging water in a large saucepan over medium heat. Cover and cook for 3 minutes, or until tender. Drain and let cool. A handful at a time, squeeze out the excess liquid.

2 Preheat the oven to 400°F (200°C). Butter four ramekins and place on a baking sheet.

3 Melt the butter in a medium saucepan over low heat. Whisk in the flour and let bubble for 1 minute. Whisk in the milk and bring to a boil over medium heat. Return the heat to low and simmer for about 3 minutes. Stir ½ cup of the Parmesan cheese and the nutmeg into the saucepan. Season with salt and pepper. Transfer the sauce to a large bowl.

4 Roughly chop the spinach and stir into the cheese mixture. Cover with plastic wrap pressed on the surface and let cool to room temperature. Stir in the yolks.

5 Beat the egg whites until stiff peaks form. Stir about one-quarter of the whites into the spinach mixture, then fold in the remainder.

6 Divide the mixture among the ramekins. Using a knife, make a shallow circle around the ramekins about ¼in (6mm) from the edge. Sprinkle with the remaining Parmesan cheese. Bake about 20 minutes, until puffed and golden. Serve at once.

Egg Fu Yung

Light and tasty, these are made with shrimp and stir-fried vegetables

 makes 4 servings

 prep 15 mins • cook 20 mins

wok

vegetable oil, as needed

3 **shallots**, thinly sliced

1 **green pepper**, seeded and diced

1 **celery stalk**, chopped

2 **garlic cloves**, minced

1 cup **bean sprouts**

4oz (115g) small **shrimp**, peeled and deveined

5 **eggs**, beaten

¾ cup **vegetable stock**

1 tbsp **oyster sauce**

1 tbsp **soy sauce**

1 tbsp **Chinese rice wine** or sherry

2 tsp **cornstarch**

boiled **rice**, to serve

1 Heat 2 tbsp oil in a wok over high heat. Add the shallots, bell pepper, celery, and garlic and stir-fry for 3 minutes. Add the bean sprouts, stir-fry for 1 minute, then add the shrimp and stir-fry for 1 minute, or until the shrimp turn pink. Transfer to a bowl and let cool.

2 Add the beaten eggs, stirring until well combined. Wash the wok and wipe dry with paper towels.

3 Return the wok to high heat and pour in 2in (5cm) oil. When the oil is hot, ladle ¼ of the mixture into the oil. Fry about 2 minutes, until the underside is lightly browned, spooning a little of the hot oil over the eggs so the top starts to set.

4 Carefully turn the egg cake over and cook 1 minute, until lightly browned on the other side. Transfer to paper towels to drain. Keep warm in a 200°F (95°C) oven while making the remaining cakes.

5 Meanwhile, mix the stock, oyster sauce, soy sauce, and rice wine in a saucepan. Dissolve the cornstarch in 2 tbsp cold water, and stir into the stock mixture. Bring to a boil over high heat, stirring constantly until thickened; simmer for 1 minute. Serve the cakes with the sauce and rice.

Cheese Soufflé

Soufflés are not challenging at all, and actually quite easy.
There are many options beyond the basic cheese version

 makes 4 servings

 prep 20 mins
• cook 30–35 mins

 6 cup soufflé dish

3 tbsp **butter**

3 tbsp **all-purpose flour**

1 cup **whole milk**

salt and freshly ground **black pepper**

1 cup shredded **Cheddar** or Gruyère

½ tsp **Dijon mustard**

4 **large eggs**, separated, plus 1 large egg white, at room temperature

1 tbsp freshly grated **Parmesan**

● **Prepare ahead** The sauce in step 1 can be prepared up to 4 hours ahead, covered to prevent a skin from forming; reheat gently.

1 Preheat the oven to 375°F (190°C). Melt the butter in a saucepan over medium heat. Whisk in the flour and cook for 1 minute. Whisk in the milk and bring to a boil, whisking constantly, until thickened and smooth.

2 Remove the pan from the heat. Stir in the cheese and mustard and season with salt and pepper. Add the egg yolks into the cheese mixture one at a time, stirring until combined.

3 Beat the 5 egg whites until stiff peaks form. Stir about one fourth of the whites into the cheese mixture, then fold in the remainder.

4 Pour the mixture into a 6 cup soufflé dish. Sprinkle with the Parmesan. Place the dish on a baking sheet. Bake for 25–30 minutes, or until the soufflé is puffed and golden brown. Serve at once.

● **Good with** a green salad and plenty of crusty bread.

VARIATIONS

Mushroom Soufflé

Replace the cheese and mustard with 6oz (175g) very finely chopped mushrooms, cooked until tender with 1 finely chopped shallot in 1 tbsp butter. Drain the cooked mushrooms well, and stir in 2 tbsp chopped parsley.

Watercress Soufflé

Replace the cheese and mustard with ¾ cup loosely packed, chopped watercress leaves and 2 tsp finely chopped chives.

Carrot Soufflé

Replace the grated cheese and mustard with ½ cup boiled and puréed carrots and the grated zest of ½ orange.

Piperade

This savory scrambled egg dish is from the Basque region of southwest France

 makes 4 servings

 prep 5 mins • cook 20 mins

2 tbsp **olive oil**

1 large **onion**, chopped

1 **red bell pepper**, seeded and chopped

1 **green bell pepper**, seeded and chopped

2 **garlic cloves**, minced

3oz (85g) **Serrano ham** or prosciutto, chopped

4 ripe medium **tomatoes**, peeled, seeded, and chopped

8 **large eggs**

salt and freshly ground **black pepper**

2 tbsp chopped **parsley**

1 Heat the oil in a large frying pan over medium heat. Add the onion and cook about 3 minutes, until beginning to soften. Add the red and green peppers and garlic and cook, stirring occasionally, until the peppers soften, about 5 minutes.

2 Add the ham and cook for 2 minutes. Add the tomatoes and cook for about 7 minutes, or until the juices evaporate.

3 Beat the eggs and season with salt and pepper. Pour into the pan and cook until scrambled, stirring often. Sprinkle with parsley and serve.

Soufflé Omelet

Beaten egg whites give this omelet
a light and fluffy texture

- makes 1 serving
- prep 10 mins • cook 5 mins
- 7in (18cm) nonstick frying pan

2 large eggs, separated

salt and freshly ground black pepper

1 tbsp butter

¼ cup shredded sharp Cheddar

¼ cup shredded Gruyère

1oz (30g) sliced ham, cut into strips

chopped chives, for garnish

1 Preheat the broiler. Whisk the egg whites in a bowl until soft peaks form. Whisk the egg yolks in a bowl until pale and lightly thickened. Whisk in 2 tbsp water and season with salt and pepper. Add the whites to the yolks. Add 2 tbsp each of the Cheddar and Gruyère and fold together with a rubber spatula just until combined.

2 Heat the butter in an 7in (18cm) nonstick frying pan over medium heat until the butter is foaming. Add the egg mixture and spread evenly. Cook for about 1 minute, until the eggs look set around the edges. Run a heatproof spatula around the edge of the omelet to loosen it.

3 Sprinkle with the remaining Cheddar and Gruyère and the ham. Broil about 1 minute, until the top of the omelet is set. Run the spatula around the edge of omelet. Fold the omelet almost in half and slide onto the plate. Sprinkle with the chives and serve hot.

● **Good with** toast and grilled tomatoes.

Omelet Arnold Bennett

This famous dish was specially created for the Victorian novelist by the chefs at the Savoy Grill, London

- makes 4 servings
- prep 5 mins • cook 20 mins

12oz (350g) smoked haddock fillet (finnan haddie)

8 large eggs, separated

½ cup half-and-half

4 tbsp freshly grated Parmesan

freshly ground black pepper

4 tbsp butter

1 Place the fish in a saucepan and add enough cold water to cover. Bring to a simmer over medium heat, and simmer about 7 minutes, until the fish is hot and flakes easily. Drain. Remove the skin and bones and flake the fish.

2 Whisk the egg whites in a bowl until soft peaks form. Beat the yolks with 2 tbsp of the half-and-half in another bowl. Fold in the whites. Add the fish and 2 tbsp of the Parmesan. Season with pepper.

3 Preheat the broiler. Melt the butter in a large nonstick frying pan over medium heat. When foaming, add the egg mixture. Cook, lifting up the sides of the omelet as they set with a rubber spatula, allowing the uncooked egg mixture to run underneath the cooked portion, about 3 minutes, or until the omelet is almost set but the top is uncooked.

4 Sprinkle the remaining 2 tbsp of Parmesan over the omelet. Pour the remaining half-and-half over the top. Broil until the top of the omelet is set and lightly browned. Serve immediately, straight from the pan.

> ### SHOPPING FOR FISH
> Finnan haddie (British smoked haddock) is used in many savory dishes. Available at specialty fish markets, it is usually bright yellow, but you may find uncolored versions as well.

Ranch-style Eggs with Refried Beans

Serve this filling dish for breakfast, and you won't have
to be concerned about what to make for lunch

 makes 4 servings

prep 25 mins • cook 35 mins

For the refried beans

two 15oz (420g) cans pinto beans

3 tbsp lard or vegetable oil

1 onion, chopped

3 garlic cloves, chopped

1 vegetable stock cube, crumbled,
or salt to taste

For the sauce

4 small dried hot red pequín chiles

¼ cup boiling water

1½lb (750g) ripe tomatoes, peeled

1 onion, chopped

2 garlic cloves, chopped

1 tbsp olive oil

2 tbsp white wine vinegar

2 tbsp tomato paste

1 tsp ground cumin

1 tsp dried oregano

½ tsp sugar

4 corn tortillas

6 tbsp vegetable oil

4 large eggs

1 avocado, pitted, peeled, and sliced

1 tbsp chopped cilantro

1 To make the beans, drain the
beans, reserving some of the
liquid from the can. Rinse the beans.
Heat the lard in a frying pan over
medium heat. Add the onion and
garlic and cook about 7 minutes,
until the onion is golden. Increase the
heat to medium high. In batches, add
the beans and stir and mash them
with a wooden spoon, adding some
of the bean liquid, as needed, to
make a coarse purée. Add the stock
cube and reduce the heat to low.
Cook, stirring often, until thick.

2 To make the sauce, combine
the chiles and boiling water in a
small bowl and soak for 15 minutes.
Drain, discarding the liquid. Purée the
tomatoes, chiles, onion, and garlic in
a blender. Heat the oil in a large frying
pan over medium heat. Add the
tomato mixture and cook, stirring
frequently, about 5 minutes. Add
the vinegar, tomato paste, cumin,
oregano, and sugar and simmer over
medium-low heat for 10 minutes.

3 To assemble, heat 4 tbsp of
the oil in a frying pan over high
heat until shimmering. Fry each
tortilla for approximately 30 seconds
on each side, until hot but not crisp.
Transfer to paper towels. Add the
remaining 2 tbsp oil to the pan.
Add the eggs and fry according to
your taste.

4 To serve, place each tortilla on
a dinner plate and top with an
egg. Spoon some of the tomato
sauce over each, and garnish with the
avocado slices and cilantro. Add a
spoonful of the beans to each tortilla,
and serve hot.

Yorkshire Puddings

Similar to popovers,
these are the traditional
accompaniment to
roast prime rib of beef

 makes 4 servings

prep 10 mins, plus resting
• cook 20–25 mins

muffin pan

¾ cup all-purpose flour

pinch of salt

1 large egg

1¼ cups whole milk

¼ cup beef drippings or melted
butter, for the pan

1 Sift the flour and salt into
a large bowl. Make a well in the
center. Crack the egg into the well
and add about one-third of the milk.
Beat the egg and milk together with
a wooden spoon, gradually drawing in
the flour from the sides of the bowl.

2 Stir in half of the remaining
milk. Change to a whisk, and
whisk in the remaining milk. Let stand
for 30 minutes.

3 Preheat the oven to
425°F (220°C). Generously
grease the muffin cups with the
drippings. Place the pan in the oven
for about 3 minutes, or until the pan
is very hot. Pour equal amounts of
the batter into the muffin cups.
Bake for 20–25 minutes, until the
puddings are golden brown and crisp.
Serve immediately.

Cheese Puffs

These small cream puffs are filled with a blend of cheese, herbs, and spices

 makes 16 puffs

 prep 10 mins • cook 50 mins

 freeze empty cheese puffs for up to 1 month

4 tbsp **butter**, plus more for the baking sheet

½ cup **all-purpose flour**, sifted, plus more for the baking sheet

pinch of **salt**

2 large **eggs**, beaten

¼ cup freshly grated **Parmesan**

For the filling

5oz (140g) **low fat cream cheese** with garlic and herbs

2 tbsp low fat **milk**

1 tsp fresh **lemon** juice

pinch of **cayenne**

freshly ground **black pepper**

¼ cup freshly grated **Parmesan** or sharp **Cheddar**, or crumbled blue cheese

1 Preheat the oven to 400°F (200°C). Bring the butter and ½ cup water to a boil in a medium saucepan. Remove from the heat and quickly beat in the flour and salt with a wooden spoon. Return to very low heat and stir until the dough is smooth and very lightly films the bottom of the pan.

2 Remove from the heat and cool 5 minutes. Gradually stir in the beaten egg until the dough is glossy and thick. Stir in the cheese.

3 Butter and flour a baking sheet. Using 2 dessert spoons, drop 16 balls of the dough, spaced well apart, on the baking sheet. Bake for 20–25 minutes, or until puffed and golden.

4 Remove from the oven and use a sharp knife to make a slit in the side of each puff to allow the hot steam to escape. Transfer the puffs onto a wire cake rack and let cool.

5 For the filling, mix the ingredients until combined. Split each puff open and fill with a teaspoon of the mixture. Serve at room temperature.

Twice-baked Cheese Soufflés

This foolproof recipe can be prepared several hours in advance, so is ideal for serving at a dinner party

 makes 4 servings

 prep 20 mins • cook 45 mins

 four 5oz (150ml) ramekins, parchment paper

 freeze the soufflés at the end of step 4 for up to 3 months; thaw at room temperature, then complete the recipe

2 tbsp **butter**, plus more for the ramekins and baking sheet

3 tbsp **all-purpose flour**

1 cup **whole milk**

2 large **eggs**, separated, at room temperature

4oz (125g) **rindless goat cheese**, crumbled

salt and freshly ground **black pepper**

scant 1 cup **heavy cream**

1 tbsp **Dijon mustard**

3 tbsp freshly grated **Parmesan**

● **Prepare ahead** The soufflés can be prepared up to the end of step 4 several hours ahead of time.

1 Preheat the oven to 350°F (180°C). Lightly butter the ramekins and line the bottoms with circles of parchment paper.

2 Melt the butter in a medium saucepan over medium-low heat. Whisk in the flour and cook for 1 minute. Whisk in the milk. Cook, whisking often, until the sauce comes to a boil and thickens. Let cool slightly.

3 Beat in the egg yolks and goat cheese. Season generously with salt and pepper. Beat the egg whites until soft peaks form. Stir about one-fourth of the whites into the cheese mixture, then fold in the remainder. Spoon into ramekins.

4 Place the ramekins in a roasting pan and add enough hot water to come halfway up the sides of the ramekins. Bake for 15 minutes, or until firm to the touch. Remove from the pan and let cool. Run a dinner knife around the edge of each soufflé and turn out onto an oiled baking sheet; remove the paper.

5 Increase the oven temperature to 400°F (200°C). Bring the cream, mustard, and pepper to a boil in a saucepan. Simmer over medium heat about 12 minutes, until reduced by half. Top the soufflés with equal amounts of the cream mixture and sprinkle with the Parmesan. Bake for 20–25 minutes, until golden. Serve immediately.

Cheese and Pepper Jalousie

Quick to make, this "peek-a-boo" vegetarian pastry makes the most of store-bought ingredients

makes 4 servings

prep 20 mins • cook 25 mins

one 17.3oz (484g) box thawed frozen **puff pastry**

all-purpose flour, for dusting

3 tbsp **sun-dried tomato paste**

1 cup shredded **sharp Cheddar**

one 10oz (280g) jar sliced **roasted peppers**, drained

4oz (115g) **mozzarella**, thinly sliced

freshly ground **black pepper**

beaten **egg** or milk, to glaze

1 Preheat the oven to 425°F (220°C). Dampen a large baking sheet. Roll out one sheet of the pastry on a lightly floured surface. Trim into a 10 x 6in (30 x 15cm) rectangle. Place the pastry on the baking sheet. Roll out and trim the remaining pastry to a 10 x 7in (30 x 18cm) rectangle. Lightly dust it with flour, then fold in half lengthwise. Make cuts ½in (1cm) apart along the folded edge to within 1in (2.5cm) of the outer edge; unfold.

2 Spread the tomato paste over the pastry on the baking

tray, leaving a 1in (2.5cm) border. Top with the Cheddar. Pat the pepper slices dry with paper towels, then arrange them on the Cheddar. Sprinkle with the mozzarella and season with pepper.

3 Brush the edges of the pastry with water. Carefully place the remaining pastry over the filling and press the edges together to seal, trimming excess pastry. Brush with beaten egg. Bake for 25 minutes, or until golden brown and crisp. Let cool for 5 minutes, then slice and serve.

● **Good with** a green salad.

VARIATION

Goat Cheese and Red Onion Jalousie

Omit the Cheddar and pepper and replace with this mixture: Cook 2 thinly sliced red onions in 1 tbsp each butter and olive oil over low heat, stirring often, about 10 minutes, or until tender. Stir in 1 tbsp balsamic vinegar, a pinch of sugar, and a pinch of Italian dried herbs, and stir another minute. Transfer to a bowl and let cool. Mix in 4oz (115g) crumbled goat cheese.

Stilton Rarebit with Pear and Walnuts

This is a more sophisticated recipe of the supper dish, Welsh rarebit, which is a comforting meal of cheese sauce over toast

makes 4 servings

prep 10 mins • cook 20 mins

4 slices crusty **walnut bread**

⅓ cup **hard cider**

1 **shallot**, finely chopped

2 tbsp **butter**

2 tbsp **all-purpose flour**

⅔ cup **whole milk**

¾ cup crumbled **Stilton** or other blue cheese

½ cup shredded sharp **Cheddar**

2 large **egg yolks**

1 tsp **dry mustard**

4oz (115g) **watercress**, tough stems removed

2 ripe **pears**, cored and sliced

½ cup coarsely chopped **walnuts**

2 tbsp **extra virgin olive oil**

1 tbsp **balsamic vinegar**

freshly ground **black pepper**

● **Prepare ahead** The toasts can be prepared several hours ahead of time to the end of step 3, and broiled just before serving.

1 Toast the bread. Boil the cider and shallots in a small saucepan over medium heat until the cider is almost completely evaporated. Transfer to a small bowl.

2 Wipe out the saucepan. Add the butter and melt over medium-low heat. Whisk in the flour and let bubble without browning for 1 minute. Whisk in the milk. Cook, whisking often, until simmering and thickened. Add the Stilton and Cheddar cheeses and whisk until melted. Remove from the heat and whisk in the egg yolks, mustard, and shallots. Spread the cheese mixture generously on to each toasted bread slice.

3 Position a broiler rack about 6 in (15cm) from the source of heat and preheat the broiler. Arrange the toasts on a broiler pan and broil for 1-2 minutes, until the tops are golden and bubbling.

4 Toss the watercress, pears, walnuts, oil, and vinegar, in a bowl, and season with pepper. Divide among serving plates. Place the toasts on the side and serve at once.

Fresh Cheese

It's fun and easy to make this fresh yogurt cheese, called *labna*

- makes 4 servings
- prep 5 mins, plus 12 hrs draining
- cheesecloth, kitchen twine

2½ cups thick low-fat or whole milk Greek-style yogurt

½ tsp salt

1 Stir the yogurt and salt together. Spoon onto a large piece of rinsed and squeezed dry cheesecloth. Gather together the four corners and tie the top of the bundle with a long length of kitchen twine to make a bag.

2 Tie the bag on a faucet or cabinet knob and suspend over a bowl. Let the whey drain from yogurt for at least 12 hours.

3 Remove the thickened yogurt from the cheesecloth, shape into a ball, and place on a platter.

● **Good with** herbs sprinkled on top along with toasted pita bread.

Cheese Nuggets

These crispy and spicy snacks would be great with a cold glass of beer

- makes 4 servings
- prep 45 mins, plus chilling • cook 1 hr
- the nuggets can be frozen, cooked or uncooked, for up to 3 months

6 tbsp butter

⅓ cup plus 1 tbsp all-purpose flour, plus extra for dusting

2½ cups milk

2 large eggs, beaten, plus 3 large egg yolks

2 cups grated Emmental or Swiss cheese

salt and freshly ground black pepper

pinch of freshly grated nutmeg

1 cup fresh breadcrumbs

⅔ cup oil

For the spicy pepper dip

1 tbsp olive oil

1 red pepper, seeded and chopped

1 fresh hot red chile, seeded and chopped

1 garlic clove, crushed

one 14.5oz (411g) can chopped tomatoes

1 tsp sugar

½ cup heavy cream

● **Prepare ahead** The cheese mixture (without breading) and dip can made 1 day ahead and stored, covered, in the refrigerator.

1 To prepare the nuggets, melt the butter in a saucepan over low heat. Whisk in the flour and cook without browning for 1 minute. Whisk in the milk, increase the heat to medium, and bring to a boil, whisking often, until smooth and thick. Return the heat to low and simmer gently, whisking often, for 5 minutes.

2 Remove the saucepan from the heat and beat in the egg yolks, one at a time. Sir in the cheese, then season with salt, pepper, and nutmeg. Spread out the mixture in a shallow rectangular dish in a layer about ¾in (2cm) deep, smoothing the top. Cover with plastic wrap and refrigerate for at least 8 hours.

3 Cut the mixture into pieces about ¾ x 2in (2 x 5cm), then shape into nuggets. Roll in flour, dip in beaten egg, then roll in the bread crumbs until coated. Chill on wax paper for 1 hour.

4 To make the dip, heat the oil in a frying pan over medium heat. Add the red pepper, chile, and garlic and cook, stirring often, about 4 minutes, until softened, Add the tomatoes and sugar, cover, and simmer for 30 minutes. Purée in a blender, then add the cream.

5 Heat the vegetable oil in a frying pan over high heat until shimmering. In batches, fry the nuggets, turning often, about 3 minutes, until golden brown. Transfer to paper towels to drain. Serve hot or warm, with the dip.

● **Good with** pre-dinner drinks or as part of a buffet.

VARIATION

Herbed Cheese Nuggets

Stir in 2 tablespoons chopped parsley, chives, and/or thyme with the cheese. Substitute Gruyère or sharp Cheddar for the Emmental, if you wish.

Cheese and Corn Pudding

This savory baked dish is a wonderful way of celebrating fresh corn when it is in season

- makes 4–6 servings
- prep 10 mins • cook 45 mins
- 5–6 cup ovenproof serving dish

5 ears of **fresh corn**, kernels cut from cob, or 2 cups frozen corn kernels, thawed

2 cups shredded **sharp Cheddar** or Monterey Jack

2 large **eggs**

¼ cup **all-purpose flour**

2 tbsp **butter**, melted, plus more for the dish

2 tbsp **sugar**

¼ tsp **salt**

pinch of **cayenne pepper**

1 Preheat the oven to 325°F (160°C) and lightly butter a 5–6 cup ovenproof serving dish. Purée 1½ cups of the corn in a blender. Add 1¾ cups of the cheese, the eggs, flour, melted butter, sugar, salt, and cayenne. Process until blended.

2 Pour the corn mixture into the dish. Sprinkle with the remaining corn, and stir gently. Smooth the surface. Sprinkle the remaining cheese on top.

3 Bake for 45 minutes, until set and golden. Cool for 5 minutes, then serve hot from the dish.

● **Good with** roast chicken, turkey, or ham. Leftovers can be covered, refrigerated, and reheated.

● **Prepare ahead** The assembled dish can be refrigerated for several hours for last-minute cooking; top with the cheese just before baking.

Paneer and Peas

This Indian restaurant favorite is easy to make at home. If you can't find paneer, farmer's cheese is a good substitute

- makes 4 servings
- prep 15 mins • cook 15 mins

6 tbsp **vegetable oil**

1 large **onion**, thinly sliced

2 large **garlic cloves**, coarsely chopped

1 **fresh hot green chile**, seeds and ribs removed and chopped

one ½in (1cm) piece fresh **ginger**, peeled and coarsely chopped

2 tsp **garam masala**

salt and freshly ground **black pepper**

one 14.5oz (411g) can **crushed tomatoes**

one 1lb (450g) bag **frozen peas**

8oz (225g) **paneer**, cut into bite-sized cubes

1 Heat 3 tbsp of the oil in a large nonstick frying pan over medium-high heat. Add the onion and reduce the heat to medium-low. Cook, stirring frequently for 8–10 minutes or until the onions are dark golden brown; do not burn.

2 Meanwhile, combine the garlic, chile, and ginger in a blender and process into a thick paste. Add the garam masala and season with salt and pepper.

3 Add the spice mixture to the fried onions and cook, stirring, for 1–2 minutes. Transfer to a large, heavy-bottomed saucepan. Stir in the tomatoes and ⅔ cup water. Bring to a boil, stirring often. Reduce the heat to low and simmer, stirring often, until lightly thickened.

4 Gently stir the frozen peas into the sauce, increase the heat to medium, and return the sauce to a simmer. Cover and cook for about 5 minutes, or until the peas are hot.

5 Wash and dry the frying pan. Add 3 tbsp oil and heat over high heat. In batches, add the paneer in a single layer. Cook, turning occasionally with a slotted spatula, about 3 minutes or until golden brown. Transfer the fried paneer to the hot tomato sauce. Continue with the remaining paneer, adding more oil as needed.

Welsh Rarebit

Often pronounced as Welsh "rabbit," this simple recipe makes a meal out of Cheddar or Lancashire cheese

 makes 4 servings

prep 10 mins • cook 6 mins

the cheese sauce is runny, so line the baking sheet with aluminum foil before baking

4 slices **white** or **whole-wheat bread**

2 tbsp **butter**

2 cups (8oz/225g) shredded **sharp Cheddar** or **Lancashire cheese**

3 tbsp **dark ale, porter,** or **lager**

1 tbsp **dry mustard**

Worcestershire sauce

1 **Line a baking sheet** with aluminum foil. Position the broiler rack 4in (10cm) from the heat, and preheat. Toast the bread on both sides until golden brown. Transfer the toast to the baking sheet.

2 **Melt the butter** in a saucepan over low heat. Add the cheese, ale, and mustard and cook, stirring often, until the cheese is melted and smooth.

3 **Pour the sauce** over the toast. Splash a few drops of Worcestershire sauce on each. Return the cheese-covered toast to the broiler for a few minutes, or until the cheese is bubbling and golden. Cut each slice in half and serve.

● **Good with** salad. If desired, put cooked ham under the cheese sauce before grilling.

VARIATION

Golden Bucks

Prepare the recipe as above, preferably using Lancashire cheese instead of Cheddar. Add a poached or fried egg to the top of each toast, just before serving.

Gorgonzola with Figs and Honey

Grilling figs enhances their natural sweetness and the addition of blue cheese makes a great flavor contrast

makes 4 servings

prep 10 mins • cook 10 mins

vegetable oil, for the pan

12 **ripe figs,** halved

6oz (180g) **Gorgonzola cheese,** crumbled

honey, to serve

1 **Lightly oil** a ridged grill pan over medium-high heat. Grill the figs, cut-side down, for 4 minutes, or until browned.

2 **When the figs** are browned, gently turn them and cook on the other side for 3–4 minutes.

3 **Remove the figs** from the pan and place them in a shallow dish. Sprinkle with Gorgonzola, drizzle with honey, and serve immediately.

● **Good with** pre-dinner drinks, or served after a meal.

VARIATION

Savory Fig Salad

For a sweet and savory salad, delete the honey and serve the salad with thinly sliced proscuitto and ricotta.

Feta Filo Pie

Crisp pastry encases a delicious blend of spinach, feta, and pine nuts in this classic Middle Eastern dish

 makes 6 servings

 prep 30 mins, plus cooling and standing • cook 1 hr

 8in (20cm) springform pan

2lb (900g) **spinach**, rinsed

4 tbsp **butter**

2 **red onions**, finely chopped

1 tsp ground **cumin**

1 tsp ground **coriander**

1 tsp ground **cinnamon**

⅓ cup finely chopped **dried apricots**

½ cup toasted **pine nuts**

salt and freshly ground **black pepper**

6 sheets thawed frozen **filo**

10oz (300g) **feta cheese**, crumbled

parsley sprigs, to garnish

strips of **lemon** zest, to garnish

1 Rinse the spinach leaves, shake off the excess water, and pack into a large saucepan. Cover and cook over medium heat for 8–10 minutes, turning occasionally, until just wilted. Drain well in a colander, pressing the spinach to extract as much water as possible. Let cool in the colander.

2 Meanwhile, melt 2 tbsp of butter in a large skillet over low heat. Add the onion and spices and cook 7–8 minutes, stirring occasionally, until softened but not browned. Stir in the apricots and pine nuts and set aside to cool. Preheat the oven to 400°F (200°C).

3 To assemble the pie, melt the remaining 2 tbsp butter. Lightly brush an 8in (20cm) springform pan with melted butter. Line the pan with a filo sheet, letting the edges hang over the edge, and brush with butter. Repeat with 5 more sheets, brushing with butter each time and letting the excess hang over.

4 Blot the cooled spinach with paper towels, then chop finely. Stir into the cooked onion mixture, and season with salt and pepper. Spread half of the spinach into the filo-lined pan. Sprinkle with the feta, then cover with the remaining spinach mixture.

5 Piece by piece, fold the overhanging filo over the spinach, brushing with butter as you go. Brush the top with any remaining butter and place the pan on a baking sheet. Bake for 35–40 minutes, until crisp and golden. Let stand for 10 minutes, then carefully remove the sides of the pan.

6 Serve hot or warm, cut into wedges, and garnish with parsley and strips of lemon zest.

● **Good with** a crisp salad or a selection of seasonal vegetables.

VARIATION

Blue Cheese Filo Pie

Substitute crumbled blue cheese, such as Stilton, for the feta, if desired. For a meat version of this pie, replace the cheese with 2 cups chopped cooked chicken or cooked ground lamb.

Herbed Goat Cheese Spread

Delicious on toast, this spread is also a great sandwich filling

 makes 4 servings

prep 10 mins, plus chilling

5oz (150g) soft rindless **goat cheese**

3 tbsp **sour cream**

1 tbsp chopped **parsley**

1 **sun-dried tomato** in oil, finely chopped

1 tsp chopped fresh **thyme**

1 tsp finely chopped **chives**, plus more to garnish

1 **garlic clove**, crushed through a press (optional)

pinch of grated **nutmeg**

freshly ground **black pepper**

● **Prepare ahead** The spread can be prepared up to 3 days ahead, covered, and refrigerated.

1 Mash the goat cheese and sour cream together in a bowl with a rubber spatula until smooth.

2 Add the parsley, sun-dried tomato, thyme, chives, garlic (if using), and season with nutmeg and black pepper and mix until well combined.

3 Transfer to a serving bowl. Cover and refrigerate. Remove the bowl from the refrigerator 1 hour before serving. Garnish the spread with chives and serve.

Spicy Feta Squares

These crunchy little snacks are packed with the rich and salty flavors of Greek feta cheese

 makes about 75 squares

 prep 10 mins • cook 25 mins

❄ freeze for up to 3 months

9 tbsp **unsalted butter**, softened, plus more for the baking sheets

½ cup **extra virgin olive oil**

9oz (250g) **feta cheese**, crumbled

¼ cup **whole milk**

1½ tsp **baking powder**

scant 3 cups **all-purpose flour**

1 tbsp **poppy seeds**

1 tsp **cayenne pepper**

● **Prepare ahead** The squares can be stored in an airtight container for up to 1 week. Reheat in a 350°F (150°C) oven for about 10 minutes.

1 **Preheat the oven** to 350°F (180°C). Butter 2 large baking sheets. Process the butter in a food processor until soft and smooth. With the machine running, slowly add the olive oil. Add the feta cheese, milk, and baking powder and pulse 2 or 3 times until combined.

2 **Add half the flour** and pulse until evenly blended. Add the remaining flour and pulse again. Turn out onto a clean work surface and knead briefly until the dough is smooth and soft. (If you do not have a food processor, beat the olive oil and milk into the butter with an electric hand mixer. Stir in the cheese, then work in the flour and baking powder with your hands.)

3 **Divide the mixture** in half. Press each portion into a large square about ⅛in (3mm) thick. Sprinkle with poppy seeds and cayenne pepper. Using a sharp knife, cut the dough into 1in (2.5cm) squares. Transfer to the baking sheets, about ¾in (20mm) apart.

4 **Bake** for about 20 minutes, or until the tops are lightly browned. Transfer the squares to a wire cake rack. Serve warm or let cool.

Baked Ricotta with Roasted Tomatoes

This dish is all about balance. Match the mild ricotta with full-flavored olive oil, ripe tomatoes, and sharp black pepper

 makes 4 appetizer servings

prep 15 mins • cook 25 mins

1 large **red pepper**

2 tbsp **extra virgin olive oil**, plus more for the pan and for drizzling

7 ripe **cherry tomatoes**, cut in half

salt and freshly ground **black pepper**

8oz (220g) fresh **ricotta cheese**, drained to remove excess whey

2 tbsp freshly grated **Parmesan cheese**

● **Prepare ahead** The dish is best served hot, but it can also be baked up to 4 hours in advance and served at room temperature.

1 **Position a broiler rack** 6in (15cm) from the source of heat and preheat the broiler. Place the red pepper on the rack and broil, turning occasionally, about 10 minutes, until the skin is charred and blistered. Transfer to a plate and cool. Peel and discard the ribs and seeds. Cut the pepper into thin strips.

2 **Preheat the oven** to 425°F (220°C). Lightly oil a small baking dish. Reserve 2 tomato halves and place the remaining tomato halves in the dish, cut sides up. Drizzle with 2 tbsp olive oil and sprinkle with salt and pepper. Bake for 7–10 minutes until the tomatoes soften. Remove the dish from the oven and set aside.

3 **Cut the ricotta cheese** in half crosswise. Remove the tomatoes from the dish. Place the bottom half of the ricotta, cut side up, in the dish and season lightly with salt and pepper. Arrange the pepper strips on top, then the tomatoes. Drizzle with olive oil and top with the remaining ricotta, cut side down.

4 **Sprinkle** with the Parmesan and drizzle with a little extra oil. Return to the oven and bake for 15 minutes until the cheese is hot and the top is golden.

● **VARIATION**

Substitute sun-dried tomatoes in oil for the roasted cherry tomatoes and pimiento del piquillo (preserved Spanish peppers) for the red peppers.

Goat Cheese Mousse with Grilled Peppers

A delicious cold dish for a summer's lunch or brunch

3 **red, yellow, and green bell peppers**, each seeded and quartered lengthwise

2 tbsp **olive oil**, plus more for the ramekins

2 tsp **balsamic vinegar**

2 tbsp chopped **basil**

1 **garlic clove**, finely chopped

salt and freshly ground **black pepper**

1 cup **heavy cream**

3 large **eggs**

4oz (115g) **rindless goat cheese**

¼ cup freshly grated **Parmesan**

a few gratings of **nutmeg**

● **Prepare ahead** The mousses must be refrigerated for at least 4 hours and up to 2 days before serving.

1 **Preheat** the broiler. Lightly oil four 6oz (180ml) ramekins.

2 **Place the peppers** on the broiler rack, skin sides up, and broil about 4–5 minutes, until the skins are blackened. Place in a bowl, cover, and let stand until cool enough to handle. Peel off the skins. Slice the peppers into strips and transfer to a bowl. Add the oil, vinegar, basil, and garlic, and mix. Season with salt and pepper and let stand for 1 hour.

3 **Meanwhile**, preheat the 350°F (180°C). Process the cream, eggs, goat cheese, Parmesan, and nutmeg in a food processor until smooth. Season with salt and pepper. Pour into the ramekins.

4 **Place the ramekins** in a roasting pan. Pour in enough hot water to come halfway up the sides of the ramekins. Bake for 30–40 minutes, or until set. Remove from the pan. Let cool. Cover and refrigerate for at least 5 hours.

5 **To serve**, run a dinner knife around the inside of each ramekin. Invert and unmold each mousse onto a plate. Divide the peppers among the plates and drizzle with the dressing.

● **Good with** warm crusty bread or Melba toast.

Fonduta

Soft polenta topped with cheese sauce is a dish that hails from northern Italy, where polenta is often favored over pasta

1½ cups **polenta** or yellow cornmeal

salt

2 tbsp **butter**

1½ cups shredded **Italian fontina cheese**

½ cup **whole milk**

3 large **egg yolks**

pinch ground **white pepper**

8 **button mushrooms**, thinly sliced

1 **Bring 1 quart** (1 liter) water to a boil in a medium saucepan over high heat. In a bowl, whisk the polenta and 1 cup water until smooth. Whisk the polenta mixture into the boiling water. Reduce the heat to medium. Cook, stirring constantly, about 5 minutes, or until thickened. Reduce the heat to low, cover, and cook 20 minutes, until soft. Season lightly with salt.

2 **Meanwhile**, place a heatproof bowl over a saucepan of gently simmering water. Add the butter and let it melt. Add the cheese and milk and cook, stirring often, until the cheese melts. Beat in the egg yolks and cook until the cheese sauce is lightly thickened. Season with pepper.

3 **Divide the polenta** among 4 bowls, and make an indentation with a spoon in the center of each. Top each with the cheese sauce, then the raw sliced mushrooms. Serve hot.

● **Good with** steamed green beans and carrots.

COOKING OVER HOT WATER

When cooking with a bowl over a pan of simmering water, make sure the bottom of the bowl does not touch the water. This ensures very gentle cooking without direct heat, which is ideal for melting chocolate, cooking egg sauces, and (as in this case) melting cheese without over-cooking it. Over-cooking the cheese would toughen it and prevent it combining with the other ingredients to form a smooth sauce.

Ricotta and Arugula Roulade

This makes a sumptuous first course or light lunch, served warm or at room temperature

 makes 4-6 servings

 prep 20 mins • cook 25 mins

9 x 13in (23 x 33cm) baking sheet

4 tbsp **butter**, plus more for the baking sheet

⅓ cup **all-purpose flour**

1¼ cups **whole milk**

¾ cup freshly grated **Parmesan cheese**

2 tsp **Dijon mustard**

salt and freshly ground **black pepper**

4 large **eggs**, separated

1 cup **ricotta cheese**

1 packed cup coarsely chopped **arugula**

● **Prepare ahead** The roulade can be prepared through step 4 a few hours in advance of baking. The baked roulade can be refrigerated for up to 24 hours.

1 Preheat the oven to 375°F (190°C). Butter a 9 x 13in (23 x 33cm) baking sheet and line with parchment paper.

2 Melt the butter in a large saucepan over medium-low heat. Whisk in the flour and let bubble for 1 minute. Gradually whisk in the milk and cook, whisking often, until the sauce comes to a boil. Remove from the heat again and stir in half of the Parmesan. Add the mustard and season with salt and pepper. Allow to cool slightly, then beat in the egg yolks.

3 Beat the egg whites in a bowl until they form soft peaks. Stir one-fourth of the whites into the cheese mixture to lighten it, then fold in the remaining whites. Spread evenly into the prepared pan.

4 Bake for about 20 minutes, or until golden and the top springs back when pressed. Turn out on to a large piece of wax paper dusted with the remaining Parmesan.

5 Peel away the parchment paper and trim off the crispy edges from the roulade. Spread the surface with the ricotta, leaving a 1in (2.5cm) border at the short sides. Cover the ricotta with the arugula. Roll up the roulade lengthwise, using the paper as an aide. Cut into slices, and serve.

● **Good with** a mesclun salad.

Sun-dried Tomato and Spinach Cheese Roulade
Mix a pinch of nutmeg into the ricotta before spreading over the roulade. Replace the arugula with spinach and add 3oz (85g) roughly chopped sun-dried tomatoes before rolling in step 5.

Feta and Pumpkin Pastries

Popular Middle Eastern snacks, these tasty filo pastries are filled with a sweet-savory mixture

makes 24

prep about 20 mins, plus cooling • cook 30 mins

one 4oz (115g) piece **pumpkin** or winter squash, peeled and seeded

4oz (115g) **feta cheese**, finely crumbled

3 tbsp chopped **raisins**

½ tsp ground **cinnamon**

freshly ground **black pepper**

8 sheets thawed frozen **filo dough**

all-purpose flour, for dusting

4 tbsp **butter**, melted, plus extra for the baking sheet

● **Prepare ahead** The pastries can be refrigerated up to 24 hours before baking.

1 Cut the pumpkin flesh into very small dice and place in a small saucepan. Pour in enough water to barely cover, and bring to a boil. Reduce the heat to low, cover, and simmer for 5 minutes, or until tender. Drain and let cool.

2 Preheat the oven to 350°F (180°C). Mix the pumpkin, feta cheese, raisins, and cinnamon, and season with the pepper.

3 Stack the filo sheets on top of each other and cut the stack into 4 long strips, about 3in (7.5cm) wide for a total of 24 strips. Cover the strips with moistened paper towels.

4 Lightly dust a baking sheet with flour. Working with 1 strip at a time, brush the strip with butter. Place a heaping teaspoonful of the pumpkin and cheese mixture about 1in (2.5cm) from the bottom end. Fold over a corner of the strip diagonally to cover the filling and form a triangular pocket of filled pastry. Working upward, keep folding diagonally, from one side to the other, to retain the triangular shape, until all the pastry is folded, making sure any gaps in the pastry are pressed closed. Transfer the triangle to the baking sheet and cover with a damp paper towel. Repeat with the remaining ingredients.

5 Butter another large baking sheet. Arrange the triangles on the buttered sheet. Brush with the remaining melted butter. Bake for about 20 minutes, or until crisp and golden. Serve hot or warm.

● **Good with** other Greek or Middle Eastern dishes as part of a mezze selection.

VARIATION

Cheese and Potato Pastries

Substitute finely diced potato or sweet potato for the pumpkin.

Warm Halloumi with Herbs

Halloumi is made from sheep and goat's milk

makes 4–6 servings

prep 5 mins • cook 3–5 mins

rinse the halloumi cheese before using to rid it of excess salt; dry well on paper towels

8oz (450g) **halloumi cheese**

all-purpose flour, for dusting

½ cup **olive oil**, plus extra for drizzling

1 tbsp chopped **thyme** or oregano

juice of 2 **lemons**

1 **lemon**, cut into wedges, to serve

1 Cut the halloumi cheese into ½in (1cm) thick slices and lightly dust with flour. Heat the oil in a nonstick frying pan over high heat. Fry the cheese slices for 2–3 minutes on each side, or until golden brown.

2 Sprinkle with the thyme and lemon juice. Serve immediately with a little extra oil drizzled with oil and garnished with the lemon wedges.

● **Good with** pita bread, and a spinach and red onion salad.

Ricotta and Bacon Tart

A simple, stylish tart with a light cheese filling

 makes 6–8 servings

 prep 35 mins, plus chilling • cook 35 mins, plus baking blind

9in (23cm) tart pan

freeze for up to 3 months, wrapped in cling film

For the pastry

1¼ cups all-purpose flour, plus extra for rolling out

¼ tsp salt

6 tbsp butter, diced

4 tbsp ice water, as needed

For the filling

1 tbsp butter

1 onion, chopped

4oz (115g) sliced bacon, chopped

1 cup ricotta cheese

2 large eggs

⅓ cup whole milk

3 tbsp grated Parmesan cheese

1 tbsp finely chopped chives

1 tbsp finely chopped thyme

salt and freshly ground black pepper

1 **Preheat the oven** to 400°F (200°). Make the pastry: Sift the flour and salt into a large bowl. Add the butter and cut into the flour with a pastry blender until it resembles coarse bread crumbs. Stir in enough water to make a firm dough. Wrap and chill for 30 minutes. Roll out on a floured work surface into an ⅛in (3mm) thick round. Line the tart pan with the pastry and trim any excess. Refrigerate for 30 minutes.

2 **Put the pan** on a baking sheet. Line the tart shell with parchment paper, fill with baking beans, and bake 15 minutes, until the dough looks set. Remove the paper and beans and bake another 5 minutes, until the pastry starts to brown. Transfer to a wire rack to cool. Reduce the oven to 350°F (180°C).

3 **Meanwhile**, melt the butter in a frying pan over medium-low heat. Add the onion and cover. Cook, stirring, for 10 minutes, until tender. Add the bacon and increase the heat to medium-high. Cook, uncovered, stirring, about 5 minutes.

4 **Meanwhile**, mix the ricotta, eggs, and milk. Stir in the Parmesan, chives, and thyme. Season with salt and pepper. Stir in the bacon and onion and pour into the pastry shell. Bake for 35 minutes or until the filling has set. Let cool in the pan. Transfer to a serving platter and serve.

Authentic Swiss Fondue

"Fondue" means melted in French, and there never was a more luscious way to serve melted cheese

makes 4 servings

prep 15 mins • cook 10 mins

fondue set

1 large garlic clove, cut in half

1½ cups dry white wine

1 tbsp fresh lemon juice

7oz (200g) shredded Gruyère cheese

7oz (200g) shredded Emmental cheese

2 tsp cornstarch

3 tbsp kirsch or brandy

freshly ground black pepper

1 large day-old baguette, cut into bite-sized pieces

1 **Rub the cut side** of the garlic clove inside the fondue pot and discard the garlic. Add the wine and lemon juice to the pot and bring it to a boil on the stove over medium heat. Reduce the heat to low. Toss the Gruyère and Emmental cheeses in a bowl with the cornstarch. One handful at a time, stir the cheeses into the wine, mixing until the cheeses melt before adding more.

2 **Cook**, stirring constantly, until the fondue just comes to a simmer. Stir in the kirsch, and season with pepper.

3 **If the fondue** is too thin, add more cheese or stir in cornstarch dissolved in wine. If too thick, stir in a little warmed white wine.

4 **To serve**, transfer the pot to its stand on the table. Spear the bread cubes onto fondue forks and dunk into the cheese.

Goat Cheese Tartlets

Oats give the tartlet pastry an interesting texture and flavor that complements the light goat cheese and yogurt filling

- makes 4 tartlets
- prep 25 mins, plus chilling • cook 35–40 mins
- four 4in (10cm) tartlet pans with removable bottoms, parchment paper, baking beans

For the oat pastry

¾ cup **all-purpose flour**, plus more for rolling

pinch of **salt**

¼ cup **rolled (old-fashioned) oats**

4 tbsp cold **butter**, diced

3–4 tbsp iced **water**

For the filling

⅔ cup **whole milk**

⅓ cup **Greek-style yogurt**

2 large **eggs**

2 tbsp finely chopped **chives**

salt and freshly ground **black pepper**

3oz (85g) crumbled **goat cheese**

● **Prepare ahead** Refrigerate the lined tartlet pans up to 1 day in advance. The baked tartlets can be covered and refrigerated for up to 1 day; serve at room temperature.

1 **To make the pastry**, sift the flour and salt into a bowl. Stir in the oats. Add the butter and rub it in with your fingertips until the mixture looks like coarse bread crumbs. Stir in enough of the water for the dough to hold together. Gather into a disk, wrap in plastic wrap, and refrigerate for 30 minutes.

2 **Have ready** four 4in (10cm) tart pans with removable bottoms. Divide the dough into 6 portions, and roll out each on a lightly floured work surface into a ⅛in (3mm) thick round. Line each pan with a round, trimming the excess dough. Prick the dough with a fork. Refrigerate for 30 minutes.

3 **Preheat the oven** to 400°F (200°C). Line each tart pan with parchment paper and fill with baking beans. Bake for 10 minutes. Remove the paper and beans and bake until the crusts are lightly browned, about 5 minutes more. Remove the pans from the oven. Reduce the oven temperature to 350°F (180°C).

4 **Whisk the milk**, yogurt, eggs, and chives in a large glass measuring cup, and season with salt and pepper. Divide the cheese evenly among the pastry shells, and carefully pour in the milk mixture. Bake for 20–25 minutes, until the filling is lightly set and beginning to brown.

● **Good with** salad leaves sprinkled with toasted pine nuts.

VARIATION

Sun-dried Tomato and Goat Cheese Tartlets

Add some chopped sun-dried tomatoes to the pastry shells with the goat cheese. Or spread each pastry shell with 1 tbsp store-bought tomato chutney before adding the cheese.

Goat Cheese in Herbed Oil

Use individual cheeses or a whole cheese for this recipe

- makes 4 servings
- prep 10 mins
- 1 pint (500ml) screw-top glass jar

8oz (225g) **goat cheese**, cut into 4 slices, or 4 small individual goat cheeses

2 **garlic cloves**, halved

1 tbsp **mixed white, black, and pink peppercorns**

2–3 sprigs **rosemary**

4–5 sprigs **thyme**

2 dried **red chiles**

about 1½ cups **extra virgin olive oil**

● **Prepare ahead** The goat cheese can be refrigerated for up to 3 months.

1 **Carefully place** the goat cheese slices in a clean 1-pint (500ml) glass jar. Arrange the garlic cloves, peppercorns, herbs, and chiles around the cheese.

2 **Pour in enough** olive oil to completely cover all the ingredients. Close the jar.

3 **Store at room temperature** for a few hours, then refrigerate overnight. Let stand at room temperature for 1 hour before serving.

● **Good with** bread or crackers, or chopped and placed on pieces of toast as a canapé. Label and decorate the jar to make a lovely gift.

Tandoori Paneer Kebabs

You will find *paneer* (a firm Indian cheese) and tandoori paste at Indian markets

- 🍴 makes 4 servings
- 🕐 prep 20 mins, plus 6-24 hrs marinating • cook 10 mins
- ❗ soak the wooden skewers in cold water for 30 mins before using to prevent them from burning
- 🎛 wooden skewers

¾ cup **plain yogurt**

1 tbsp **tandoori paste** or powder

1 tbsp fresh **lemon** juice

9oz (250g) **paneer**, cut into 1in (2.5cm) cubes

1 **red bell pepper**, seeded and cut into 1in (2.5cm) pieces

12 white **mushrooms**

1 large **zucchini**, cut into ½in rounds

2 tbsp **vegetable oil**

1 Mix the yogurt, tandoori paste, and lemon juice together in a nonreactive bowl. Add the paneer and stir gently to coat. Cover and refrigerate for at least 6 and up to 24 hours.

2 Thread the paneer cubes, red pepper, mushrooms, and zucchini onto the soaked skewers. Brush with the oil.

3 Broil or grill the kebabs for about 10 minutes, until the paneer is tinged with brown. Serve hot, with lemon wedges, if desired.

Gruyère Tart

This vegetarian tart, with crisp, thyme-flavored pastry, is equally delicious warm or cold

- 🍴 makes 6 servings
- 🕐 prep 25 mins, plus resting • cook 45 mins
- 🎛 14 x 5in (35 x 12cm) tart pan, or 9in (23cm) round tart pan

For the pastry

1 cup **all-purpose flour**, plus more for rolling

⅓ cup **whole wheat flour**

9 tbsp cold **butter**, diced

1 tsp chopped **thyme**

4-5 tbsp iced **water**

For the filling

1 tbsp **butter**

1 tbsp **olive oil**

1 large **onion**, thinly sliced

1 tsp **sugar**

pinch of freshly grated **nutmeg**

1 cup shredded **Gruyère cheese**

¾ cup **half-and-half**

3 large **eggs**

1 tsp **Dijon mustard**

salt and freshly ground **black pepper**

● **Prepare ahead** The pastry dough, wrapped in plastic wrap, and the onion mixture, stored in an airtight container, can be refrigerated for up to 1 day. Let the dough stand at room temperature for 15 minutes before rolling out.

1 To make the dough, stir the flours together. Add the butter and rub it with your fingertips until it resembles coarse bread crumbs. Stir in enough of the water until the dough holds together. Shape into a thick disk, wrap in plastic wrap, and refrigerate for 30 minutes.

2 On a lightly floured surface, roll the dough into a ⅛in (3mm)

round circle and use to line a 9in (23cm) tart pan with a removable bottom. Prick it lightly all over with a fork. Chill for 30 minutes.

3 Preheat the oven to 400°F (200°C). Line the dough with parchment paper and fill with baking beans. Bake for 10 minutes. Remove the paper and beans and bake for 10 minutes more, until the crust is golden and crisp. Remove from the oven. Reduce the oven temperature to 375°F (190°C).

4 Meanwhile, to make the filling, heat the butter and oil in a large frying pan. Add the onion and cook over low heat, stirring frequently for 15 minutes, until tender. Stir in the sugar and nutmeg and cook for about 3 minutes more, until golden. Transfer to a plate and cool.

5 Stir half the Gruyère into the cooled onion mixture, then spread in the pastry shell. Sprinkle with the remaining cheese. Whisk the

half-and-half, eggs, and mustard together and season with salt and pepper. Pour into the shell. Bake for 30 minutes, until lightly set.

6 Let cool on a wire rack for 10 minutes. Remove the sides of the pan and serve warm or cooled.

● **Good with** an arugula or watercress salad with sliced plum tomatoes and black olives, tossed in a lemon-flavored dressing.

VARIATION

Roquefort and Walnut Tart

Add ½ cup toasted and very finely chopped walnuts to the flour in the pastry dough. Substitute 2 leeks, white and pale green parts, finely sliced, for the onion, and Roquefort for the Gruyère.

Fresh Mango Relish

Be sure the mangoes are fully ripened—they should yield slightly when squeezed

- makes 4 servings
- prep 15 mins
- low fat, low GI

2 ripe **mangoes**, peeled, pitted, and finely diced

1 fresh **hot red chile**, seeded and minced

4 tsp **canola or olive oil**

2 tsp **light brown sugar**

2 tsp **white wine vinegar**

½ tsp **ground coriander**

salt and freshly ground **black pepper**

1 tbsp chopped **mint**

● **Prepare ahead** The chutney is best made up to 3 days ahead so the flavors develop.

1 Combine the mangoes, chile, oil, brown sugar, white wine vinegar, and coriander in a small mixing bowl. Season with salt and pepper.

2 Cover and refrigerate for at least 2 and up to 8 hours to develop the flavor. Just before serving, stir in the mint.

● **Good with** hot and cold meats, and cheeses.

VARIATION

Mango-cilantro Sauce

Prepare the chutney through step 1. Purée in a food processor with 1 tbsp desiccated coconut and 1 tbsp chopped fresh cilantro, and a little water if needed, until the mixture is the thickness of heavy cream. Serve at once, garnished with a few torn cilantro leaves. Serve the sauce with seared salmon.

Pickled Vegetables

This recipe is an exciting combination of crunchy seasonal vegetables, pickled in an herb and spice vinegar

- makes 5 1pt (450g) jars
- prep 20 mins, plus standing
- large stainless steel saucepan, five 1pt (450g) canning jars with lids

2lb (900g) mixed **seasonal vegetables** such as small cucumbers, small onions, cauliflower, trimmed green beans, and small green tomatoes

¼ cup kosher **salt**

For the vinegar

1qt (1 liter) **malt vinegar** or white wine vinegar

1 tbsp whole **black peppercorns**

1 tbsp **allspice berries**

1 tsp crushed **hot red pepper**

One ½in (13mm) slice fresh **ginger**, crushed

4 **bay leaves**

8 whole **cloves**

● **Prepare ahead** Make the pickles at least 1 month before serving.

1 Cut your chosen vegetables into bite-sized pieces. Place the vegetables in a large nonreactive bowl, and toss with the salt. Cover and let stand in a cool place for 24 hours.

2 For the vinegar, combine the vinegar, peppercorns, allspice, hot pepper, ginger, bay leaves, and cloves in a large nonreactive saucepan. Heat over low heat just until the vinegar is hot. Do not simmer or boil. Remove from the heat and let cool completely.

3 Have ready five hot, sterilized 1pt (450g) glass canning jars and lids. Drain the vegetables thoroughly, but do not rinse. Pack the vegetables into the jars. Strain the vinegar and discard the solids. Cover the vegetables with the spiced vinegar. Cover the jars with their lids. Let stand in a cool, dark place for at least 1 month before serving. After opening, store in the refrigerator and eat within 1 week.

● **Good with** hot and cold meats, cheese, and salads, and sandwiches and burgers.

Apple and Pear Chutney

Make this fruity, spicy chutney at harvest time and you will have a good supply to last for months

- makes 5 qts (5 liters)
- prep 1 hr • cook 40 mins
- large non-aluminum saucepan, five 1qt (1 liter) glass canning jars with lids, canning funnel

2¼lb (1kg) Granny Smith or other **tart apples**, peeled, quartered, and cored

1lb (450g) Bosc or other **firm pears**, peeled, quartered, and cored

3 cups **golden raisins**

1½ cups **raisins**

1 **onion**, quartered

1 **lemon**, quartered and seeded

one 2in (5cm) piece fresh **ginger**, peeled and chopped

4 **garlic cloves**, chopped

1 hot fresh **chile**, seeded and minced

2½ cups **malt vinegar**

2¼ cups packed **light brown sugar**

1 tbsp **yellow mustard seeds**

2 tsp **salt**

1 In batches, pulse the apples, pears, golden raisins, raisins, onion, lemon, ginger, garlic, and chile in a food processor until coarsely chopped. Transfer to a large saucepan and add the vinegar, brown sugar, mustard, and salt.

2 Bring to a boil, stirring constantly. Reduce the heat to medium-low and simmer, stirring occasionally, for 40 minutes, until the juices are syrupy.

3 Have ready five hot, sterilized, 1qt (1 liter) glass canning jars and lids.

4 Using tongs or oven mitts, transfer the jars to a baking sheet. Carefully fill the hot jars with the hot chutney, then cover with the lids. Let stand to cool completely.

5 Wipe the jars clean. Store in a cool dark place for at least a few weeks before opening.

Lime Pickle

These pungently spiced preserved limes will enhance curries or pilafs, are wonderful with fish or chicken, and are easy to make

- makes 2 qts (2 liters)
- prep 20 mins, plus standing • cook 5 mins
- two 1qt (1 liter) glass canning jars

2½ cups **olive oil**

1 tbsp **cumin seeds**

1 tbsp **black peppercorns**

1 tbsp **coriander seeds**

1 tbsp **crushed hot red pepper**

10 **limes**, washed and cut into quarters

3 tbsp fine **sea salt**

3 **garlic cloves**, crushed

1 tsp **ground ginger**

a few **whole cloves**

2 **bay leaves**

● **Prepare ahead** The pickle must be made at least 4 weeks before serving.

1 Heat the oil in a saucepan until very hot but not smoking. Remove from the heat and set aside to let cool completely.

2 Coarsely crush the cumin seeds, peppercorns, and coriander seeds with a mortar and pestle. Mix in the hot pepper.

3 Put the limes in a shallow bowl and sprinkle with the ground spices. Add the salt, garlic, ginger, cloves, and bay leaves and stir well. Let stand for 30 minutes.

4 Have ready two hot, sterilized, 1qt (1 liter) glass canning jars with lids. Divide the limes among the jars and add cooled oil to cover. Cover each jar with cheesecloth. Place in a sunny place (or near a warm stove); let stand for 6 days, stirring each day.

5 Cover each jar with its lid. Store in a cool, dark place for at least 4 weeks to develop the flavors and soften the rinds. The pickle can be stored up to 6 months, although the color may change. Refrigerate after opening.

VARIATION

Pickled Lemons and Oranges

You can make similar pickles using lemons or oranges instead of limes.

Green Tomato Chutney

Apple, ginger, and mild onion make this chutney especially sweet, rather than spicy

- 🍴 makes 6 qts (6 liters)
- 🕐 prep 30 mins
  - cook 2½ hrs
- 🍲 extra large stainless steel saucepan, 5–6 x 1lb (450g) glass canning jars

2¼lb (1kg) **green tomatoes**, washed and chopped

1½lb (675g) **red** or yellow **onions**, chopped

2¼lb (1kg) tart **apples**, cored and chopped

2½ cups packed **light brown sugar**

2½ cups **malt vinegar**

1 tbsp **ground ginger**

1 tbsp **black** or mixed **peppercorns**

1 Mix the tomatoes, onions and apples together in a large, heavy-bottomed saucepan. Add the brown sugar, vinegar, ginger, and peppercorns, and mix again.

2 Bring to a boil over medium-high heat, stirring almost constantly to dissolve the sugar. Reduce the heat to low and simmer about 1¾ hours, stirring often to discourage scorching, until the chutney is thick and pulpy.

3 Have ready 6 hot, sterilized 1 quart (1 liter) glass canning jars. Screw the lids on the hot jars. Let stand until cooled.

4 Wipe the jars clean and label. Store in a cool dark place. Once opened, store in the refrigerator and eat within a week.

VARIATION

Banana and Green Tomato Chutney

Substitute peeled, thickly sliced bananas for the apples and 1 tbsp curry powder, 1 tsp ground allspice, and 1 tsp ground ginger for the ginger and peppercorns. Replace the apples with bananas and the spices with 1 tbsp mild curry powder, 1 heaped tsp allspice and 1 tsp ground ginger.

Corn Relish

A refreshing cross between a salsa and a true cooked relish

- 🍴 makes 4 servings
- 🕐 prep 15 mins, plus standing
  - cook 10 mins, plus chilling

olive or canola **oil**

1 **red onion**, finely chopped

8oz (225g) **cherry tomatoes**

1 small fresh **hot red chile**, seeded and minced

1 tsp **light brown sugar**

¼ tsp **cayenne pepper**

1 tbsp **ketchup**

2 tsp **white wine vinegar**

2 cups cooked fresh or thawed frozen **corn kernels**

salt and freshly ground **black pepper**

chopped **cilantro**, for serving

1 Heat 2 tsp of oil in a saucepan over medium heat. Add the onion and cook, stirring often, for 2 minutes, until beginning to soften.

2 Add the cherry tomatoes, chile, brown sugar, and cayenne and stir well to mix. Reduce the heat to low and cover. Cook 5 minutes, until the tomatoes soften.

3 Transfer to a bowl and cool. Stir in the corn, ketchup, and vinegar. Season with salt and pepper. Cover and refrigerate overnight.

4 Just before serving, stir in the cilantro. Serve chilled or at room temperature.

VARIATIONS

Warm Egyptian Corn Relish

Substitute 2 tsp *ras-al-hanout* (North African spice mixture) for the chile and cayenne. Serve warm.

Crunchy and Colorful Relish

Add ½ cup finely diced red, green, and yellow pepper with the cilantro.

Piccalilli

This is a modern version of a traditional Indian pickle called *peccalillo*

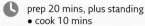 makes 5 x 8oz (225g) jars

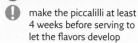 prep 20 mins, plus standing • cook 10 mins

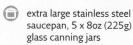 low fat, low GI

make the piccalilli at least 4 weeks before serving to let the flavors develop

extra large stainless steel saucepan, 5 x 8oz (225g) glass canning jars

2lb (900g) mixed fresh **seasonal vegetables**, such as: cauliflower, shallots, cucumber, young kidney beans, carrots and French beans

2½ tbsp **salt**

For the piccalilli sauce

2¼ cups **malt vinegar**

15 small dried whole **chiles**, rinsed

scant 1 cup **granulated sugar**

3 tbsp **cornstarch**

3 tbsp **dry mustard**

1 tbsp **turmeric**

1 Prepare the vegetables of your choice and cut them into small bite-sized pieces. Toss with the salt in a large glass bowl. Cover and let stand overnight in a cool place.

2 The following day, drain the vegetables well. Bring the vinegar and chiles to a boil in a nonreactive saucepan and cook for 2 minutes. Let stand for 30 minutes. Strain the vinegar, discarding the chiles.

3 Mix together the sugar, cornstarch, mustard, and turmeric in a bowl. Stir in enough of the vinegar to make a smooth paste. Return the remaining vinegar to its saucepan, and return to a boil. Whisk the hot vinegar into the paste, then return to the saucepan. Bring to a boil, stirring constantly. Simmer for 3 minutes. Stir in the vegetables.

4 Pack into five sterilized, hot 8oz (225g) glass jars and seal immediately while still hot. Let stand until cool. Wipe clean and label. Store the jars in a cool dark place for at least 4 weeks before serving. Once opened, store in the refrigerator and eat within 1 week.

● **Good with** crusty bread and a robust sharp cheese, and with cold meats and pork pies.

Plum Chutney

A mild-tasting but very enjoyable fruit relish that is particularly good with cold meats and cheeses

 makes 5 x 1qt (1 liter) jars

prep 15 mins • cook 1 hr 15 mins

large non-aluminum pot, canning glass jars with 2-piece lids

3lb (1.35kg) **plums**, pitted and cut into quarters

2 **apples**, peeled, cored, and chopped

2 **onions**, chopped

1 tbsp **ground ginger**

1 tbsp **ground cinnamon**

1 tbsp **ground allspice**

2 tsp **salt**

1¾ cups plus 2 tbsp **cider vinegar**

1¾ cups packed **light brown sugar**

● **Prepare ahead** Chutney should be made several weeks ahead for the best flavor.

1 Combine all of the ingredients into a large non-aluminum pot. Bring to a boil over medium heat, stirring almost constantly to dissolve the sugar.

2 Reduce the heat to medium-low. Simmer for 1 hour, stirring often, or until the chutney is soft and thickened. Taste and adjust the seasoning if needed.

3 While the chutney is simmering, wash the jars well and sterilize them in a hot water bath for 10 minutes or in a 350°F (180°C) oven for 20 minutes.

4 Using tongs or oven mitts, transfer the jars to a baking sheet. Carefully fill the hot jars with the hot chutney.

5 Cover with the lids and screw on the rings. Let stand to cool completely.

6 Wipe the jars clean. Label, date, and store in a cool dark place, ideally for a few weeks, before opening.

> ### Transferring to Jars
> The best way to transfer a hot mixture to a jar is with a wide-mouthed canning funnel.

Hot Mains in 30 Minutes or Less

Pasta alla Carbonara
A satisfying and filling dish with its unique combination of eggs and crispy pancetta

🕐 20 mins   page 202

Spaghetti, Roman-style
Quick to prepare and cook, this is a great meal when time is short

🕐 25 mins   page 190

Singapore Noodles
This dish combines Chinese, Indian, and Malaysian flavors

🕐 25 mins   page 191

Orecchiette with Pancetta
A light pasta dish with bright colors

🕐 20 mins   page 196

Fettucine Alfredo
An unsurpassable pasta when made with the best ingredients

🕐 20 mins   page 192

Linguine with Tomato Clam Sauce
A popular classic pasta and shellfish dish

🕐 25 mins   page 188

Grilled Halibut with Green Sauce
A fresh-tasting dish that cooks in minutes

🕐 10–15 mins   page 264

Chinese-style Steamed Bass
A restaurant-style dish that brings out the clean flavors of the fish and is easy to prepare

🕐 30 mins   page 270

Leaf-wrapped Asian Sole
Gently steamed fish makes a healthy, tasty supper

🕐 25 mins   page 272

Tuna with Warm Cucumber and Fennel Salad
Tuna is often cooked with Asian flavors, but here the profile is Mediterranean

🕐 20–25 mins   page 270

Seafood Curry

This quick curry is flavored with chiles, coconut, and lime

🕐 25–30 mins **page 274**

Shrimp Diavolo

Quick and easy shrimp in a spicy tomato sauce

🕐 25 mins **page 275**

Mussels in White Wine Sauce

The classic way to cook mussels

🕐 30 mins **page 275**

Thai Green Chicken Curry

Use Thai curry paste to make this quick and flavorful dish

🕐 20 mins **page 288**

Devilled Turkey

Serve these spicy stir-fried turkey strips as a healthy lunch or supper

🕐 25 mins **page 308**

Steak au Poivre

This restaurant classic can easily be made at home

🕐 20–25 mins **page 320**

Veal Scaloppine

This popular Italian dish uses a classic method to prepare veal

🕐 15–20 mins **page 321**

Danish Meatballs

This dish incorporates the fresh flavors of thyme and lemon

🕐 25 mins ❄ 3 months **page 336**

Filet Mignons with Walnut Pesto

A great dish for autumn, when walnuts are at their peak. The bright green color of the walnut pesto comes from fresh tarragon and parsley

🕐 20–30 mins **page 334**

Pork Chops with Green Peppercorn Sauce

Mild peppercorns add gentle spice

🕐 25 mins **page 337**

Pork Chops with Blue Cheese Stuffing

Pecans add a crunchy texture to the stuffing

🕐 25–30 mins **page 337**

Lamb with Blueberries

Tender lamb noisettes (filet mignons) are a special treat

🕐 20–25 mins **page 340**

Sauté of Liver, Bacon, and Shallots

A quick dish with a rich, savory sauce

🕐 20 mins **page 351**

Meat-free Mains

Butternut Squash Penne
Sweet roasted squash with a savory cheese sauce makes for a filling main dish
🕐 55 mins   **page 194**

Ravioli with Ricotta and Spinach
Spinach and Ricotta make a perfect-tasting pair
🕐 40–45 mins   **page 195**

Spinach and Ricotta Manicotti
This stuffed baked pasta dish has two sauces
🕐 1 hr   **page 195**

Penne and Vegetable Salad
This classic dish is a celebration of the best of spring flavors
🕐 45 mins   **page 197**

Mushroom Risotto
Choose a dark, richly flavored mushroom to make this risotto
🕐 50 mins   **page 207**

Mediterranean Lasagna
A simple baked vegetarian pasta dish full of Italian flavors
🕐 1 hr 30 mins   **page 203**

Quinoa Tabbouleh
Whole grain quinoa makes a tasty and healthful summer salad
🕐 30 mins   **page 208**

Puy Lentils with Goat Cheese, Olives, and Fresh Thyme
Goat cheese brightens the earthy lentils
🕐 40 mins   **page 209**

Kasha Pilaf
A refreshing change from rice, this makes a tasty side dish
🕐 30 mins   **page 211**

Cabbage Rolls
These vegetarian cabbage rolls are lighter than the traditional version
🕐 1 hrs 50 mins   **page 220**

Chile Tofu Stir-fry
This quick and easy dish takes advantage of tofu's ability to take on other flavors
🕐 25 mins   **page 221**

Chiles en Nogada
Heart-shaped green poblano chiles are traditionally used for this recipe
🕐 1 hr   ❄ 1 month   **page 222**

Parmesan Cheese and Walnut Tart
A lovely tart for lunch or part of a light supper
🕐 1 hr 10 mins   **page 223**

Stuffed Eggplants
A popular Turkish meze of cold and spicy stuffed eggplants

🕐 90 mins ❄ 1 month

page 226

Vegetable Curry
Cardamom, cloves, coriander, and cumin seeds add warming flavor to this Indian favorite

🕐 1 hr 5 mins ❄ 3 months **page 224**

Potato and Fennel Pancakes with Mushrooms
A delicious way to use flavorful mushrooms

🕐 1 hr 45 mins **page 225**

Tofu and Mushroom Stroganoff
Traditional stroganoff with a vegetarian twist

🕐 35 mins **page 225**

Olive, Thyme, and Onion Tart
This savory tart is easier to prepare than most

🕐 1 hr 10 mins **page 226**

Eggplant Parmigiana
This is one of Italy's most popular dishes and a great choice for vegetarians

🕐 1 hr 10 mins ❄ 1 month **page 228**

Vegetable Biryani
A satisfying dish that both vegetarians and meat eaters will enjoy

🕐 1 hr 15 mins **page 227**

Vegetable Moussaka
Lentils replace the lamb, and yogurt is a light alternative to béchamel sauce

🕐 1 hr 50 mins **page 227**

Leek and Cheese Tart
This savory puff pastry tart can be served for brunch, lunch, or supper

🕐 1 hr 15 mins ❄ 1 month **page 229**

Squash and Gorgonzola Tart
This works well with either a creamy or firm Gorgonzola cheese

🕐 1 hr 50 mins ❄ 1 month **page 229**

Meat-free Sides

Kasha Pilaf
A tasty side dish to serve with Middle Eastern-style dishes

🕐 30 mins   **page 211**

Risotto Balls
Crispy on the outside and soft and creamy on the inside

🕐 40 mins   ❋ 2 months   **page 216**

Rice and Peas
A Caribbean staple dish, the "peas" are known as gungo peas in Jamaica and pigeon peas in Trinidad

🕐 55 mins   **page 216**

Thai Coconut Rice
Coconut and kaffir lime leaves flavor this popular Asian rice dish

🕐 1 hr 5 mins   **page 215**

Rice Timbales
Lightly spiced rice pressed into ramekins

🕐 40 mins   **page 218**

Spiced Pilaf
Subtly spiced, this versatile rice dish can be served hot or cold

🕐 30 mins   **page 211**

Potato Gnocchi
Light-as-air potato dumplings, served with a simple sage and butter sauce

🕐 55 mins   **page 218**

Braised Red Cabbage with Apple
Cabbage cooked in a sweet-sour sauce

🕐 1 hr 50 mins   **page 234**

Deep-Fried Zucchini
Crisp and delicious fritters

🕐 30 mins   **page 235**

Grilled Vegetables
A herby blend of bell peppers, zucchini, eggplant, and fennel

🕐 55 mins   **page 235**

Brussels Sprouts with Orange
Citrus flavors bring a burst of sunshine

🕐 20–25 mins   **page 237**

Roasted Acorn Squash
A naturally sweet flavor accented by the glaze

🕐 45 mins   **page 237**

Ratatouille
This popular Mediterranean dish is delicious hot or cold

🕐 55 mins   **page 236**

Belgian Endive with Thyme
Slow-cooking reduces endive's bitterness

🕐 35 mins   **page 238**

Glazed Shallots with Red Wine
Sweet-and-sour tender shallots

🕐 50 mins   **page 240**

Bok Choy with Oyster Sauce
A lovely leafy accompaniment to any main dish

🕐 15 mins   **page 239**

Mixed Root Vegetable Gratin
A creamy, warming cheese-topped dish

🕐 1 hr 10 mins   **page 241**

Roast Artichokes with Tomato and Garlic
A very colorful and tasty simpe dish

🕐 1 hr 5 mins   **page 242**

Potato Gratin
This baked potato dish is rich with cream and fragrant with garlic and nutmeg

🕐 1 hr 50 mins   **page 242**

Roast Sweet Potato with Sesame Glaze
Honey and soy sauce-infused potato cubes

🕐 1 hr   **page 243**

Potato and Parmesan Cakes
These little cakes make a nice change from mashed potatoes

🕐 40 mins   **page 245**

Sweet Potato and Sage Gratin
An out-of-the-ordinary sweet potato dish for holiday entertaining

🕐 1 hr 20 mins   **page 241**

Grilled Eggplant with Pomegranate Vinaigrette
Pomegranate seeds enliven this warm dish

🕐 20 mins   **page 245**

Potato Pancakes
Crispier than *latkes*, served with sour cream and apple sauce

🕐 50 mins   **page 246**

Sweet Potato Purée with Horseradish
Intensely sweet and full of flavor

🕐 1 hr 20 mins ❄ 3 months   **page 247**

Creamed Spinach with Pine Nuts
A rich and crunchy dish

🕐 15 mins   **page 247**

Light Lunches

Singapore Noodles
This popular dish combines Chinese, Indian, and Malay flavors
🕐 25 mins   **page 191**

Lentil Salad with Lemon and Almonds
A mix of the fragrant and the crisp
🕐 25–30 mins   **page 205**

Egg Noodles with Lemongrass and Herbs
Fresh lemon and herb dressing on egg noodles
🕐 25 mins   **page 212**

Roast Beet and Feta Salad
Deep magenta with accents of white and green, this is a very colorful salad
🕐 1 hr 25 mins   **page 221**

Baked Salmon with Cucumber Dill Sauce
Equally good using salmon steaks or fillets, this light dish is quick to make, very healthy, and tastes delicious
🕐 20 mins   **page 257**

Chilli Tofu Stir-fry
Vegetable and tofu cubes in a spicy sauce
🕐 25 mins   **page 221**

Vegetable Biryani
A satisfying curry dish served over rice
🕐 1 hr 15 mins   **page 227**

Squash and Gorgonzola Tart
A rich vegetable and cheese tart to serve with a green salad
🕐 1 hr 55 mins ❄ 1 month   **page 229**

Salmon Fishcakes
Flavored salmon cakes with a crispy bread crumb coating
🕐 1 hr ❄ 1 month   **page 255**

Mackerel with Cucumber Salad
A simple grilled fish and salad combo
🕐 40 mins   **page 265**

Seafood Salad
Suitable for lunch, a picnic, or a light supper in the back yard, this is an ideal summer dish
🕐 45 mins   **page 268**

Leaf-wrapped Asian Sole
Gently steamed fish in bok choy makes a healthy, tasty lunch
🕐 25 mins   **page 272**

Calamari Salad with Mint and Dill
A warm salad of fresh herbs and grilled seafood
🕐 25 mins   **page 274**

Low-fat Dishes

Chicken and Chickpea Pilaf
This one-pot rice dish is full of flavor and is easy to make

🕐 55 mins   **page 205**

Clams in White Wine
Almejas al vino blanco is a popular dish throughout the Mediterranean

🕐 25 mins   **page 276**

Chicken Cacciatore
This Italian dish translates as "hunter-style chicken," and is traditionally served with polenta

🕐 55 mins–1 hr   **page 298**

Chicken in Balsamic Vinegar
A cold chicken dish with a hint of sweetness

🕐 1 hr 10 mins   **page 299**

Chicken Jalfrezi
A spicy chicken curry

🕐 45 mins ✳ 3 months   **page 310**

Roast Quail with Apple and Calvados
Wrapping in pancetta keeps the flesh moist

🕐 35–40 mins ✳ 3 months   **page 317**

Balsamic Beef Salad
Colorful and filling, this makes a substantial summer salad

🕐 1 hr 25 mins   **page 324**

Herb-baked Swordfish
Rosemary is not usually used with fish, but perfectly complements the meaty flavor of this dish

🕐 35–40 mins   **page 272**

Beef Salad with Caramelized Walnuts
A hearty salad served warm or cold

🕐 1 hr 5 mins   **page 333**

Lamb Kebabs
Melt-in-the-mouth marinated lamb cubes with baby vegetables

🕐 35 mins   **page 343**

Kitchen-staple Dishes

Tuna and Pasta Bake
This one-dish meal, using dried pasta and canned tuna, is ideal at the end of a busy day

⏱ 50 mins **page 190**

Potato Gnocchi
These light-as-air dumplings, make a simple, but filling dish from potatoes, flour, and eggs

⏱ 55 mins **page 218**

Macaroni and Three Cheeses
Quick to make with elbow macaroni and fresh cheese on hand

⏱ 55 mins **page 191**

Fettucine Alfredo
An unsurpassable pasta made with a few good quality ingredients

⏱ 15–20 mins **page 192**

Spaghetti with Puttanesca
Canned anchovies, olives, and capers add fresh Mediterranean flavor to this spicy pasta dish

⏱ 20–25 mins **page 201**

Lentil Salad with Lemon and Almonds
Preserved lemons add a bright flavor

⏱ 25–30 mins **page 205**

Egg Fried Rice
This popular Chinese-style rice dish is an excellent way to use up leftover rice

⏱ 15 mins **page 212**

Rice and Peas
The ingredients are easy to keep on hand for this perfect last-minute side dish

⏱ 55 mins **page 216**

Linguine with Tomato Clam Sauce
Made with thin dried linguine and canned clams

⏱ 25 mins **page 188**

Polenta
Smooth and unctuous, soft polenta is served in northern Italy with meaty sauces

⏱ 20 mins **page 214**

One-pot Meals

Tuna and Pasta Bake
This simple recipe uses mostly kitchen staples to make a satisfying meal

🕐 50 mins   **page 190**

Chicken and Noodle Stir-fry
A variety of vegetables add color and texture to the noodles in this easy Chinese favorite

🕐 30 mins   **page 204**

Seafood Paella
Cooked on the stove, this version of the classic Spanish rice dish contains a mixture of seafood

🕐 40 mins   **page 206**

Hoppin' John
In the American South this is a traditional dish of ham hocks, rice, and black-eyed beans

🕐 3 hrs 45 mins   **page 206**

Vegetable Biryani
A curry that both vegetarians and meat eaters will enjoy. Fresh vegetables and frozen peas are combined with basmati rice and flavored with ground spices and curry powder

🕐 1 hr 15 mins   **page 227**

Kedgeree
Salmon is added to this Anglo-Indian rice dish along with the traditional smoked haddock

🕐 40 mins   **page 209**

Jambalaya
This spicy meal captures the authentic flavors of cooking along the Louisiana bayous

🕐 1 hr 15 mins   **page 210**

Chicken in a Pot
Cooking the chicken and vegetables in hard apple cider and stock creates a wonderful flavor

🕐 2 hrs   ❄ 3 months   **page 289**

Arroz con Pollo
This colorful chicken and rice meal is served wherever there are Spanish-speaking cooks

🕐 1 hr 5 mins   **page 294**

Chicken Chow Mein
This popular Chinese dish contains noodles with a colorful mix of chicken and vegetables

🕐 30 mins   ❄ 3 months   **page 296**

Chicken Stew with Herb Dumplings
Hearty and filling, this is a good winter casserole

🕐 1 hr 5 mins   **page 302**

Chicken Biryani
Often served for special occasions, this subtly spiced dish combines chicken and basmati rice

🕐 50 mins   **page 305**

Roast Lamb with White Beans
Perfect to cook for a Sunday roast

🕐 1 hr 45 mins   **page 343**

Family Favorites

Baked Ziti with Sausage and Tomatoes
A rich, meaty sauce makes this a hearty dish
🕐 1 hr 10 mins   **page 189**

Macaroni and Three Cheeses
This easy dish makes a family meal that can be assembled in advance for last-minute cooking
🕐 55 mins   **page 191**

Eggplant Parmigiana
This is one of Italy's most popular dishes and a great choice for vegetarians
🕐 1 hr 10 mins   ❄ 3 months   **page 228**

Irish Stew
Lamb, potatoes, and carrots are cooked slowly for maximum flavor and tenderness
🕐 1 hr 50 mins   **page 342**

Fish and Chips
Make this British classic at home with a yeast batter that remains crisp
🕐 50 mins   **page 252**

Cod in Tomato Sauce
The tomatoes and wine add sweetness to this Spanish dish
🕐 40 mins   **page 263**

Grilled Halibut with Green Sauce
A fresh-tasting dish that is easy to prepare
🕐 10–15 mins   **page 264**

Salmon en Papillote
Individual packets ensure that the cooking juices are retained and the fish moist
🕐 40 mins   **page 268**

Tandoori Chicken
As tender and flavorful as the classic restaurant dish, this version has a more natural color
🕐 35–50 mins   **page 294**

Southern Fried Chicken
From America's deep South, this succulent dish is served with a smooth cream gravy
🕐 45 mins   **page 295**

Chicken Korma
This popular restaurant curry, with its fragrant, mild, creamy sauce, is easy to make at home
🕐 1 hr 5 mins   **page 297**

Chinese-style Lemon Chicken
Delectable citrus flavor sealed in a crisp skin
🕐 50 mins   **page 297**

Chicken Croquettes
These golden, savory nuggets are crunchy outside and meltingly soft inside
🕐 50 mins   ❄ 3 months   **page 299**

Meat Loaf
This recipe is great served hot for a weekday meal, or cold in a packed lunch or sandwich
🕐 50 mins   **page 322**

Sausages with Lima Beans
This satisfying supper dish is especially good on a cold winter evening
🕐 40 mins   ❄ 3 months   **page 352**

Sausage, Bacon, and Egg Pie
This pie transports well and can be eaten from your hand just as well as off a plate
🕐 1 hr 5 mins   **page 353**

Chicken Pinwheels with Pasta
Little rolls of flavorful stuffed chicken breast

🕐 1 hr ❄ 1 month **page 302**

Chicken Breasts in Garlic Sauce
The garlic flavor will mellow during cooking

🕐 50 mins ❄ 3 months **page 307**

Roast Turkey with Spiked Gravy
Turkey and stuffing are perfect for any occasion

🕐 4 hrs 15 mins ❄ 3 months **page 312**

Chicken Tikka Masala
A creamy Indian dish gets extra flavor from its marinade

🕐 45 mins ❄ 3 months **page 314**

Duck Breasts with Cherries
Seared duck with fresh cherries, when in season, is a treat for an elegant dinner party

🕐 35 mins **page 311**

Autumn Game Casserole
A mix of different game makes a wonderfully rich-flavored dish

🕐 1 hr 50 mins ❄ 3 months **page 317**

Swedish Meatballs
Regarded as a Swedish national dish, but popular in every home

🕐 50 mins ❄ 3 months **page 321**

Thai Red Beef Curry
Bird's-eye chillies in the curry paste make this dish delicious, and fiery

🕐 35 mins **page 324**

Roast Rib of Beef
Sunday roast doesn't come any better than this

🕐 1 hr 50 mins – 2 hrs 20 mins **page 333**

Hungarian Goulash
This warming winter stew makes a great main course for entertaining

🕐 2 hrs 55 mins ❄ 3 months **page 326**

Roast Lamb with White Beans
The beans make a tasty change to potatoes

🕐 1 hr 55 mins **page 343**

Shepherd's Pie
Traditionally a recipe to use up meat and potatoes from a roast lamb

🕐 1 hr **page 344**

Rabbit Provençale
A French bistro dish that makes the most of this healthy and easy-to-cook meat

🕐 1 hr 30 mins **page 356**

Great on a Grill

Vegetable Kebabs
Colorful and nutritious, these kebabs are equally good grilled or broiled
🕐 30 mins   **page 223**

Pan-grilled Eggplant and Zucchini Salad
Serve at room temperature so the flavors merge
🕐 45 mins   **page 244**

Swordfish Skewers with Arugula Salad
Serve hot, straight from a grill or broiler
🕐 20–25 mins   **page 262**

Honey Mustard Barbecued Chicken
Chicken legs with a delicious glaze
🕐 35 mins   **page 284**

Saffron Chicken Brochettes
Perfect for a summer barbecue
🕐 20 mins   **page 286**

Indian Garlic Chicken
Based on the Indian classic *Murg Massalam*, this dish can be left to cool and taken on a picnic
🕐 1 hr 10 mins   ❄ 1 month   **page 298**

Chicken Piri-Piri
Flavored with chiles and paprika, this chicken is suitable for barbecuing as well as roasting
🕐 1 hr 35 mins   **page 314**

Lamb Kebabs
Skewered pieces of lamb served hot with a fresh tomato vinaigrette
🕐 20 mins   **page 348**

Grilled Quail with Ginger Glaze
Sour and sweet birds great for the grill
🕐 30 mins   ❄ 1 month   **page 316**

Hamburgers
These are pan-fried, but can also be grilled for an outdoor meal
🕐 25 mins   ❄ 3 months   **page 322**

Beef Kebabs with Lime, Ginger, and Honey
Marinating ensures tender beef
🕐 25–30 mins   **page 335**

Barbecued Spare Ribs
Popular with adults and children alike, these sticky ribs are great for serving at parties
🕐 1 hr 35 mins   **page 339**

Turkey Kebabs
This is a great healthy dish for a barbecue
🕐 30–35 mins   **page 313**

Cooking for a Crowd

Macaroni Bake with Ham and Peppers
This makes a satisfying informal party dish
🕐 30–35 mins   **page 192**

Lasagna al Forno
A perfect dish for casual entertaining, this can be prepared in advance
🕐 2 hrs   **page 202**

Couscous Royale
This richly spiced dish makes a colorful Moroccan feast for a party
🕐 1 hr 30 mins   ❄ 1 month   **page 207**

Chicken Gumbo
The quantities in this recipe can easily be doubled or tripled
🕐 1 hr 10 mins   **page 301**

Turkey à la King
This is a time-honored way of using leftover turkey when entertaining after the holidays
🕐 30 mins   ❄ 3 months   **page 304**

Autumn Game Casserole
Either game birds or venison can be used for this richly flavored dish
🕐 1 hr 50 mins   ❄ 3 months   **page 317**

Hungarian Goulash
This stew makes a great main course for entertaining, as all the work is done in advance
🕐 2 hrs 55 mins   ❄ 3 months   **page 326**

Coq au Vin
Use a good-quality red wine for this French classic that tastes best when it is made in advance and reheated
🕐 1½hrs   ❄ 3 months   **page 315**

Boeuf Bourguignon
Another cook-ahead French classic, this can easily be made to feed any number of guests
🕐 2 hrs 55 mins   ❄ 3 months   **page 326**

Beef Daube with Wild Mushrooms
A stew with tender beef and plenty of rich sauce
🕐 3 hrs   ❄ 3 months   **page 327**

Chili con Carne
A Tex-Mex classic that is inexpensive and easy to make for large numbers
🕐 55 mins   ❄ 3 months   **page 332**

Cassoulet
This hearty bean and meat stew comes from southwest France
🕐 4 hrs 15 mins   **page 338**

Navarin of Lamb
Lighter than many stews, this is traditionally made with young spring vegetables
🕐 2 hrs   ❄ 3 months   **page 342**

Dinner Party Mains

Seafood Paella
This Spanish rice dish will both impress and satisfy your guests
🕐 40 mins   ❄ 3 months   **page 206**

Vegetable Tempura
Batter-covered vegetables lightly fried for a delicate, light dish
🕐 20–30 mins   **page 228**

Grilled Tuna with Tomato Salsa
Spicy salsa tops tuna steak
🕐 1 hr 20 mins   **page 253**

Baked Trout with Almonds
Delicate trout enhanced with citrus and a nutty texture
🕐 35 mins   **page 254**

Skate Wings with Brown Butter
The classic French dish
🕐 35 mins   **page 255**

Salmon in Puff Pastry
Baked salmon en croûte is moist and succulent
🕐 55 mins   **page 262**

Halibut with Chunky Romesco
A deliciously fresh but gutsy dish
🕐 40 mins   **page 266**

Salmon en Papillote
Tightly sealed paper ensures that the juices are retained and the cooked fish moist
🕐 40 mins   **page 268**

Tuna with Warm Cucumber and Fennel Salad
Here tuna is cooked with Mediterranean flavors
🕐 20 mins   **page 270**

Lobster Thermidor
Grilled lobster topped with a creamy sauce
🕐 45 mins   **page 273**

Mussels in White Wine Sauce
Cooking in wine, garlic, and herbs is easy
🕐 25 mins   **page 275**

Creamy Tarragon Chicken
Fresh tarragon and cream is a classic pairing in French cuisine
🕐 45 mins   ❄ 1 month   **page 288**

Chicken Schnitzels
Chicken breasts rolled in bread crumbs and quickly fried
🕐 32 mins   ❄ 3 months   **page 289**

Duck with Shallot Confit
Spices and melted honey lend comforting winter flavors to the duck
🕐 40 mins   **page 304**

Chicken Wrapped in Pancetta and Sage
A light and elegant main course
🕐 1 hr 35 mins   **page 306**

Guinea Hen with Spiced Lentils
A healthy, satisfying winter main course
🕐 1 hr 35 mins   **page 308**

Spicy Orange Duck
The flavor combination of rich duck and tangy orange gives a modern twist
🕐 40–50 mins   **page 310**

Roast Quail with Apple and Calvados
Petite game birds in an apple sauce
🕐 40 mins   ❄ 3 months   **page 317**

Braised Pheasant
This game bird is made flavorful and moist by braising in red wine
🕐 2 hrs 10 mins   **page 318**

Beef Wellington
Beef tenderloin topped with mushrooms and encased in pastry is impressive
🕐 1 hr 30 mins   **page 325**

Beef Strogonoff
A classic Russian dish of beef and mushrooms in a sour cream sauce
🕐 40 mins   **page 323**

Blanquette de Veau
A simple, delicately flavored French veal stew in white sauce
🕐 1 hr 45 mins   **page 325**

Ragout of Venison with Wild Mushrooms
A slowly simmering stew with rich, concentrated flavors
🕐 2 hrs 15 mins   ❄ 3 months   **page 357**

Roast Beef Tenderloin with Red Currant Jus
A sweet-tart sauce adds character to this dish
🕐 1 hr 40 mins   **page 335**

Osso Bucco
Veal shanks turn this stew into an extraordinary meal
🕐 2 hrs   ❄ 1 month   **page 327**

Braised Lamb
This dish packs plenty of flavor with its tomato, olive, and herb sauce
🕐 1 hr 50 mins   ❄ 1 month   **page 341**

Marinated Lamb Roast with Carrot Salsa
Marinated lamb slices with fresh-tasting salsa
🕐 35 mins   **page 345**

Rabbit Provençale
Rabbit benefits from braising in an herbed tomato sauce to keep it moist
🕐 1 hr 30 mins   **page 356**

Rabbit with Honey and Thyme
Chunks of lean meat braised in a flavorful liquid
🕐 55 mins   **page 357**

Linguine with Tomato Clam Sauce

Versions of this popular classic shellfish dish of thin linguine and clams are cooked all along the Italian Mediterranean and Adriatic coasts

🍴 makes 4 servings

🕐 prep 5 mins • cook 20 mins

2 tbsp **olive oil**

1 **onion**, finely chopped

2 **garlic cloves**, finely chopped

one 28oz (794g) can **chopped tomatoes**

two 6½ oz (184g) cans **clams in natural juice**, drained, juice reserved

¾ cup **dry white wine**

2 tbsp **tomato paste**

salt and freshly ground **black pepper**

1lb (450g) **dried linguine**

4 tbsp finely chopped **parsley**, plus more to garnish

● **Prepare ahead** The tomato sauce in step 1 can be made in advance and reheated before adding the clams and parsley in step 3.

1 Heat the oil in a large saucepan over medium heat. Add the onion and cook, stirring frequently, for 5 minutes, or until softened. Add the garlic and stir until fragrant, about 1 minute. Add the tomatoes with their juices, clam juices, wine, and tomato paste. Season with salt and pepper. Bring to a boil. Reduce the heat to low, partially cover the pan and simmer for 10–15 minutes, until the sauce thickens, stirring occasionally.

2 Meanwhile, bring a large pot of salted water to a boil over high heat. Stir in the linguine, and cook according to the package directions, or until *al dente*. Drain the pasta, and shake to remove any excess water.

3 When the pasta is almost done, add the clams and chopped parsley to the tomato sauce and continue to simmer for 1–2 minutes, until heated through. Add salt and pepper to taste.

4 Add the linguine to the sauce, and toss to combine all the ingredients, so the clams are well distributed throughout the pasta. Sprinkle with extra parsley and serve at once.

● **Good with** crusty Italian bread.

> **CANNED CLAMS**
> These are a great staple, but you could, of course, use 3 dozen fresh littleneck clams, well scrubbed. Add them to the tomato sauce in step 3, cover and simmer, shaking the pan occasionally, about 5 minutes, until the shells open. (You will not have clam juices for step 1.)

Tomato Sauce

Easy to make, this sauce is wonderfully versatile

🍴 makes about 2 cups

🕐 prep 5 mins • cook 30 mins

❄ can be frozen for up to 1 month

¼ cup **olive oil**

1 **onion**, chopped

1 **garlic clove**, chopped

one 28 oz (794g) can **chopped tomatoes**

¼ cup **tomato paste**

8 **basil leaves**, torn

salt and freshly ground **black pepper**

1 Heat the oil in a large heavy-bottomed saucepan over medium heat. Add the onion and garlic and cook, stirring occasionally, for 5–8 minutes until the onion is golden, but not browned.

2 Stir in the tomatoes with their juice, tomato paste, and half the basil leaves. Season with salt and pepper. Bring to a simmer. Reduce the heat to low, and simmer, uncovered, for about 20 minutes, or until the sauce is thick. Adjust the seasoning if necessary. Stir in the remaining basil.

VARIATION

Spicy Tomato Sauce
Add 1 minced fresh hot red chile pepper with the tomatoes.

Baked Ziti with Sausage and Tomatoes

Baked ziti in a hearty meat sauce is a great way to feed a hungry family; use either pork or turkey sausages

 makes 6 servings

 prep 20 mins • cook 50 mins

large, deep skillet; one large casserole dish or 6 individual casserole dishes

1 lb (450g) sweet or hot Italian sausages

2 tbsp olive oil

2 large onions, coarsely chopped

2 garlic cloves, finely chopped

One 28oz (794g) can chopped tomatoes

2 tbsp chopped basil

1 lb (450g) ziti

½ cup shredded mozzarella cheese

salt and freshly ground black pepper

1 Fill a deep skillet with water and bring it to a boil. Prick the sausages with a fork, add them to the pan, and simmer for 2 minutes, or until the casings turn pale. Drain the sausages, and let cool. Remove the casings and break up the meat.

2 Drain the skillet and return to the heat. Add the sausage and oil and cook for 5 minutes. Add the onions and garlic and cook for another 3 minutes, or until softened.

3 Stir in the tomatoes with their juices and the basil. Season with salt and pepper. Allow the sauce to simmer for 10 minutes, or until it has thickened, stirring occasionally.

4 Meanwhile, preheat the oven to 350°F (180°C). Bring a large pot of salted water to a boil, and add the ziti. Cook until *al dente*, about 3 minutes before the time recommended on the package. Drain and return the pasta to the pot.

5 Mix most of the sausage and tomato sauce with the ziti. Spread in the casserole(s), then spoon the reserved sauce over the top. Sprinkle with the mozzarella.

6 Bake for about 20 minutes, or until the sauce bubbles, and the cheese is melted and golden.

Linguine with Scallops

Succulent scallops with a hint of chile and lime make this a perfect pasta dish for lunch, dinner, or entertaining

 makes 4 servings

 prep 10 mins • cook 10 mins

large frying pan or ridged grill pan

1 lb (450g) dried linguine

2 limes

⅓ cup olive oil, plus extra for brushing

salt and freshly ground black pepper

1 fresh hot red chile, seeds removed, and finely chopped

12 large sea scallops

3 tbsp chopped cilantro

● **Prepare ahead** The dressing in step 2 can be made an hour ahead.

1 Cook the linguine in boiling, salted water according to package directions, or until *al dente*. Drain and keep warm.

2 While the pasta is cooking, grate the zest and squeeze the juice from 1 of the limes. Whisk the lime juice and olive oil together in a small bowl. Stir in the chile, and half of the cilantro. Season with salt and pepper. Toss the lime mixture with the linguine.

3 Heat a large, heavy frying pan, or ridged grill pan over high heat. Brush the scallops with olive oil, and season with salt and pepper. Add to the pan, and sear the scallops for 3 minutes, turning once.

4 Divide the linguine between 4 serving plates and arrange the scallops on top. Cut the remaining lime into wedges. Serve immediately, with lime wedges.

● **Good with** crusty bread and a side salad of arugula with shavings of Parmesan.

Tuna and Pasta Bake

Every cook should have a recipe for this quick one-dish meal, which is ideal at the end of a busy day

 makes 4–6 servings

prep 10 mins • cook 40 mins

8oz (230g) pasta shells

one 10.75oz (305g) can **condensed cream of mushroom soup**

I cup **whole milk**

one 6oz (170g) can **tuna in water**, drained and flaked

I cup **frozen corn**, thawed

1 **onion**, finely chopped

1 small **red bell pepper**, cored, seeded, and finely chopped

3 tbsp chopped **parsley**

pinch of **chili powder** (optional)

1 cup shredded **Cheddar cheese**

salt and freshly ground **black pepper**

● **Prepare ahead** The whole dish can be assembled, covered, and refrigerated several hours in advance. Remove the dish from the refrigerator at least 10 minutes before cooking.

1 **Bring a large** saucepan of salted water to a boil over high heat. Add the pasta, stir, and cook for 2 minutes less than the time on the package instructions.

2 **Meanwhile, preheat the** oven to 425°F (220°C). Butter an ovenproof casserole.

3 **Drain the pasta**. Bring the mushroom soup and milk to a simmer over low heat in the pasta pot. Add the tuna, corn, red pepper, parsley, chili powder, and half of the cheese, and mix. Stir in the cooked pasta. Season with salt and pepper.

4 **Spread the mixture** in the casserole. Sprinkle with the remaining cheese. Bake for about 30 minutes, or until the top is golden brown. Serve hot.

● **Good with** hot garlic bread and a green salad on the side.

● **Leftovers** can be reheated. If the sauce has thickened, thin with a little extra milk.

VARIATION

Chicken and Pasta Bake
Replace the tuna with 7oz (200g) cooked chicken breasts, chopped and mixed in before the cooked pasta.

Spaghetti, Roman-style

Quick to prepare and cook, this is a great meal when time is short

 makes 4 servings

prep 10 mins • cook 15 mins

¼ cup **olive oil**

1 **onion**, thinly sliced

6oz (175g) **pancetta**, cut into thin strips

¾ cup **dry white wine**

one 28oz (794g) can **chopped tomatoes**

salt and **crushed hot red pepper flakes**

1lb (450g) **dried spaghetti**

½ cup freshly grated **Pecorino Romano cheese**, plus more for serving

● **Prepare ahead** Steps 1 and 2 can be done a day in advance; reheat before mixing with the pasta.

1 **Heat the oil** in a large saucepan over medium heat. Add the onion and cook, stirring, for 3 minutes, or until softened. Add the pancetta and continue cooking, stirring often, for 5 minutes, or until the pancetta is lightly browned.

2 **Add the wine** and cook about 5 minutes, or until it evaporates by half. Stir in the tomatoes and their juices, reduce the heat to low, and simmer briskly for 15 minutes, or until thickened. Season with salt and red pepper flakes.

3 **Meanwhile**, bring a large pan of salted water to a boil over high heat. Stir in the spaghetti, and cook according to the package instructions, or until the pasta is al dente. Drain the spaghetti well. Add to the sauce and stir well. Remove from the heat and stir in the cheese. Serve hot, with additional cheese passed on the side.

Singapore Noodles

This popular dish combines the delicacy of Chinese cooking, the heat of Indian spices, and the fragrance of Malaysian herbs

 makes 4 servings

🕐 prep 15 mins • cook 10 mins

✓ low fat

❗ cook the shrimp on the day of purchase

🍳 wok

6oz (175g) thin **Asian egg noodles**

2 tbsp plus 1 tsp **vegetable oil**

5oz (140g) boneless skinless **chicken breast**, thinly sliced

5oz (140g) medium **shrimp**, peeled

1 **onion**, thinly sliced

½ **red bell pepper**, cored, seeded, and cut into strips

1 small head of **bok choy**, sliced

2 **garlic cloves**, finely chopped

1 fresh hot **red chile**, seeded and minced

4oz (115g) **bean sprouts**

2 tbsp **light soy sauce**

1 tbsp **curry powder**

2 large **eggs**, beaten

cilantro leaves, for garnish

⬤ **Prepare ahead** Slice the chicken, chop the vegetables, and peel the shrimp and refrigerate for up to 8 hours before cooking.

1 **Bring a large pot** of lightly salted water to a boil over high heat. Add the noodles and cook until tender. Drain and rinse under cold water. Toss with 1 tsp of the oil.

2 **Heat 1 tbsp oil** in a wok over high heat. Add the chicken and stir-fry for 1 minute. Add the shrimp and stir-fry for another 2 minutes. Transfer to a plate.

3 **Add 1 tbsp oil** to the wok and heat. Add the onion and stir-fry for 2 minutes. Add the pepper, bok choy, garlic, and chile, and stir-fry for 2 minutes more. Add the bean sprouts and stir-fry for 2 minutes.

4 **Add the soy sauce** and curry powder and stir-fry for 1 minute. Add the noodles, pour in the eggs, and toss together until the egg starts to set. Return the chicken and shrimp to the wok and stir-fry for 1 minute. Sprinkle with cilantro and serve hot.

Macaroni and Three Cheeses

This simple dish makes a nourishing family meal

🍽 makes 6-8 servings

🕐 prep 20 mins • cook 35 mins

1lb (450g) **elbow macaroni**

6 tbsp **butter**, plus more for the dish

1 cup fresh **bread crumbs**

¼ cup **all-purpose flour**

1 tsp **dry mustard**

pinch of ground **nutmeg**

1¾ cup **whole milk**, warmed

2 cups shredded sharp **Cheddar cheese**

4oz (115g) fresh **mozzarella cheese**, drained and finely diced

½ cup freshly grated **Parmesan cheese**

⬤ **Prepare ahead** The dish can be assembled up to a day in advance, covered, and refrigerated. Add the bread crumb and cheese topping just before baking.

1 **Bring a large pot** of lightly salted water to a boil over high heat. Add the macaroni and cook for 2 minutes less than the time on the package instructions. Drain well.

2 **Meanwhile**, preheat the oven to 400°F (200°C) and butter a 3qt (3 liter) ovenproof serving dish. Melt 2 tbsp of the butter in a frying pan. Add the bread crumbs, stir well until coated. Let cool.

3 **Melt 4 tbsp butter** in a large saucepan over medium heat. Whisk in the flour, and cook without browning for 30 seconds. Stir in the mustard and nutmeg. Remove the pan from the heat and slowly whisk in the milk. Return the pan to the heat and bring the mixture to the summer, whisking almost constantly. Cook for 3 minutes. Remove from the heat. Stir in the Cheddar cheese until melted. Stir in the macaroni and mozzarella. Transfer to the baking dish and smooth the surface.

4 **Stir the Parmesan cheese** into the bread crumbs. Sprinkle over the macaroni and cheese. Place the dish on a baking sheet. Bake for 25 minutes, or until heated through and golden brown on top. Let stand for 2 minutes. Serve straight from the dish.

⬤ **Good with** a green salad or garlic bread.

Macaroni Bake with Ham and Peppers

Quick to make and full of rich flavors, this pasta casserole makes a satisfying midweek meal or an informal dinner-party dish

- makes 6–8 servings
- prep 10 mins
  - cook 20–25 mins

1lb (450g) **elbow macaroni** or other tube-shaped pasta

1 tbsp **olive oil**

1 **red onion**, thinly sliced

1 **garlic clove**, crushed

1 **red bell pepper**, seeded and thinly sliced

one 14.5oz (411g) can **chopped tomatoes**

9oz (250g) **smoked ham**, diced

3 tbsp **dry white wine** or chicken stock

2 tsp dried **oregano**

salt and freshly ground **black pepper**

1 cup fresh **bread crumbs**

3 tbsp freshly grated **Parmesan**

2 tbsp **butter**, melted

● **Prepare ahead** Prepare through step 3; cool, cover with aluminum foil, and refrigerate for up to 1 day. Bake 15 minutes, remove the foil and bake 15 minutes more, until thoroughly heated.

1 Preheat the oven to 400°F (200°C). Bring a large saucepan of salted water to a boil over high heat. Add the macaroni and cook according to the package instructions, until barely tender. Drain well.

2 Meanwhile, heat the oil in a saucepan over medium heat. Add the onion, garlic, and red pepper, and cook, stirring occasionally, for about 5 minutes, or until softened but not browned.

3 Add the tomatoes, ham, wine, and oregano and bring to a boil. Simmer for 2–3 minutes to reduce slightly. Remove from the heat. Stir in the macaroni and season with salt and pepper. Spread in a 2 quart (2 liter) baking dish. Mix the bread crumbs, Parmesan, and butter, and sprinkle on top.

4 Place on a baking sheet and bake for 15–20 minutes, or until golden and bubbling. Serve hot.

● **Good with** a spinach salad.

Fettuccine Alfredo

An unsurpassable dish made with good-quality ingredients

- makes 4 servings
- prep 5 mins • cook 5–15 mins

1lb 5oz (600g) **fresh fettuccine**, or 1lb (450g) dried

8 tbsp **butter**, cubed

1 cup **heavy cream**

½ cup freshly grated **Parmesan**, plus more for serving

salt and freshly ground **black pepper**

1 Bring a large saucepan of lightly salted water to a boil over high heat. Add the fettuccine and cook according to the package instructions, just until *al dente*.

2 Meanwhile, melt the butter in a large saucepan over low heat. Add the cream and heat until steaming. Drain the fettuccine well, and add to the hot cream mixture. Add the Parmesan and toss well to coat. Season with salt and pepper.

3 Divide the pasta among warmed plates. Serve at once, with more grated Parmesan passed on the side, or shave curls from a chunk of Parmesan over each serving.

VARIATION

Pasta with Parmesan

For a lighter version of this dish, omit the butter and cream. Toss the hot pasta and Parmesan with ¼ cup extra virgin olive oil. Season with pepper.

Pappardelle with Ragù

This meaty, slow-simmered sauce goes well with pasta ribbons, but is also delicious served with tagliatelle or used in a lasagna

 makes 4 servings

 prep 15 mins • cook 2 hrs

❄ freeze the sauce for up to 3 months

For the ragù

2 tbsp **butter**

2 tbsp **olive oil**

4oz (125g) **pancetta**, diced

1 small **onion**, finely chopped

1 **celery stalk**, finely chopped

1 **carrot**, finely chopped

2 **garlic cloves**, minced

1lb (450g) **ground round**

one 14.5oz (411g) can **chopped tomatoes**

½ cup **beef stock**, as needed

2 tbsp **tomato paste**

salt and freshly ground **black pepper**

⅓ cup **whole milk**, heated

1lb (450g) **dried pappardelle**

freshly grated **Parmesan**, to serve

1 Melt the butter and the oil in a large saucepan over medium heat. Add the pancetta and cook 2 minutes, until it gives off some fat.

Add the onion, celery, carrot, and garlic and cook, stirring, 10 minutes, or until softened but not browned.

2 Stir in the ground round and cook 10 minutes, stirring and breaking it up with a spoon, until browned. Stir in the tomatoes and their juices, stock, and tomato paste, and season. Bring to a boil.

3 Reduce the heat and partially cover the saucepan. Simmer, stirring occasionally and adding more stock, if needed, for 1½ hours. Stir in the milk and simmer for 30 minutes more, until thick and well flavored.

4 Bring a saucepan of lightly salted water to a boil, add the pappardelle, and cook until *al dente*. Drain well. Transfer to a serving bowl and add the ragù. Toss and serve hot, with the Parmesan.

VARIATION

Pappardelle alla Bolognese

For a richer sauce, substitute 7oz (200g) ground round, 7oz (200g) ground pork, and 4oz (115g) chopped chicken livers for the ground round. Add ¼ cup red wine to the browned meats and boil until most of the wine has evaporated. Replace the milk with ⅓ cup heavy cream.

Spaetzle

When tossed with cheese and eggs, spaetzle, a homemade noodle from Switzerland, makes a delicious one-pot meal

 makes 4 servings

 prep 20 mins • cook 10 mins

3 cups **all-purpose flour**

6 large **eggs**

½ cup **whole milk**, as needed

½ tsp freshly grated **nutmeg**

4 tbsp **butter**

1 cup shredded **Gruyère cheese**

freshly ground **black pepper**

2 **scallions**, white and green parts, finely chopped

1 Sift the flour into a bowl. Lightly beat 4 eggs with ½ cup water, the milk, and nutmeg. Add to the flour, mixing to make a thick batter, adding more milk if necessary.

2 Bring a large saucepan of water to a boil over high heat. Transfer the batter to a colander with

large holes. Rub the batter through the holes with a rubber spatula, letting the batter drop into the hot water (be sure to protect your hands from the steam).

3 Cook for 2–3 minutes, or until all of the spaetzle are floating. Drain and rinse under cold running water.

4 Heat the butter in a large frying pan over medium-high heat. Add the spaetzle and cook, stirring occasionally, 3 minutes, until they are beginning to brown. Reduce the heat to low. Beat the remaining 2 eggs. Sprinkle in the cheese and eggs and stir for 1-2 minutes until the cheese melts and the eggs are set. Season with pepper. Sprinkle with the scallions and serve hot.

Spaghetti Frutti di Mare

The beauty of this pasta is variety—use whatever fresh seafood you like

 makes 4–6 servings

 prep 25 mins • cook 10 mins

tap the mussels and discard any that do not close

3 tbsp **olive oil**

1 small **onion**, finely chopped

2 **garlic cloves**, minced

2 cups **crushed tomatoes**

½ tsp crushed **hot red pepper**

1 lb (450g) **mussels**, scrubbed

¼ cup **dry white wine**

½ **lemon**, sliced

12 large **shrimp**, peeled and deveined

1 lb (450g) **baby squid**, cleaned, tubes sliced into rings

3 tbsp chopped **parsley**

salt and freshly ground **black pepper**

1 **Bring a large pot** of lightly salted water to a boil over high heat. Add the spaghetti and cook according to the package instructions until *al dente*.

2 **While the water** is coming to a boil, prepare the sauce. Heat the oil in a large saucepan over medium heat. Add the onion and garlic and cook, stirring often, for 3–4 minutes, or until softened. Add the crushed tomatoes and hot pepper. Simmer for 1 minute. Keep warm.

3 **Meanwhile**, combine the mussels, wine, and lemon in a large saucepan. Cover and bring to a boil over high heat. Cook for 3–4 minutes, shaking the pan occasionally, until the mussels have opened. Transfer the seafood to a bowl, discarding any unopened shells.

Strain the liquid through a fine sieve into the tomato sauce, discarding the lemons. Reserve a few mussels in their shells for garnish and remove the flesh from the remaining shells.

4 **Simmer the sauce** for 2–3 minutes, or until slightly reduced. Add the shrimp and squid to the sauce and simmer for 2 minutes, stirring, until just opaque. Add the reserved mussels to the sauce, stir in the parsley, and season with salt and pepper.

5 **Drain the pasta** thoroughly and return to the pan. Add the seafood sauce and toss. Transfer to deep bowls, topping each portion with a few mussels, and serve hot.

Butternut Squash Penne

The cheese complements the sweet roasted squash

makes 6 servings

prep 15 mins • cook 40 mins

1 **butternut squash**, about 2lb (900g), peeled and seeded

1 **red onion**, cut into eighths

3 tbsp **olive oil**, plus more for serving

2 tbsp **balsamic vinegar**

salt and freshly ground **black pepper**

2 **garlic cloves**, minced

1 lb (450g) **dried penne**

1 cup shredded **Gruyère**

⅓ cup **crème fraîche**

1 tbsp chopped **sage**

freshly grated **Parmesan**, to serve

1 **Preheat the oven** to 375°F (190°C). Peel the squash. Cut the squash into 1 in (2.5cm) cubes.

2 **Toss the squash**, onion, oil, and balsamic vinegar in a roasting pan. Season with salt and pepper. Roast for 40 minutes, stirring occasionally, or until tender. During the last few minutes, stir in the garlic.

3 **Meanwhile**, cook the pasta in a large saucepan of salted water over high heat until *al dente*. Drain and return to the saucepan. Add the roasted vegetables, Gruyère, crème fraîche, and sage, and stir. Season with salt and pepper. Serve in deep bowls, with olive oil and the Parmesan cheese passed on the side.

Spinach and Ricotta Manicotti

Stuffed pasta is a great way to feed a crowd. This version has two sauces to make it extra-special

 makes 6–8 servings

prep 25 mins • cook 35 mins

one 8oz (224g) box **manicotti** (14 each)

one 10oz (280g) box chopped **frozen spinach**, thawed

1 qt (1 liter) container **ricotta**

¾ cup freshly grated **Parmesan**

2 large **eggs**, lightly beaten

pinch of freshly grated **nutmeg**

salt and freshly ground **black pepper**

White Sauce (p518)

For the sauce

1 tbsp **extra virgin olive oil**

1 small **red onion**, finely chopped

1 **celery stalk**, finely chopped

2 **garlic cloves**, minced

2 cups canned **crushed tomatoes**

⅓ cup **vegetable stock** or water

⅓ cup chopped **basil**

1 **Cook the manicotti** shells in a large pot of lightly salted water according to the package instructions. Drain, rinse under cold running water, and drain again.

2 **Meanwhile**, drain the spinach well, pressing out any excess liquid. Mix the ricotta, ½ cup of the Parmesan, and the eggs in a bowl. Add the spinach and mix. Season with the nutmeg, salt, and pepper. Spoon the filling into the manicotti tubes. Arrange them in a lightly oiled 15 x 10in (38 x 25cm) baking dish.

3 **For the sauce**, heat the oil in a saucepan over medium-low heat. Add the onion and cook for 5 minutes, until softened. Add the celery and garlic and cook for another 2 minutes. Stir in the tomatoes and stock and simmer for 15 minutes, or until the sauce is slightly reduced. Stir in the basil.

4 **Preheat the oven** to 375°F (190°C). Pour the white sauce over the manicotti, then spoon the tomato sauce on top. Sprinkle with the remaining ¼ cup of Parmesan. Bake for 30–35 minutes, or until the top is golden and bubbling.

Ravioli with Ricotta and Spinach

In Italy, these little cheese and spinach-filled ravioli are often served on Christmas Eve

 makes 4 servings

prep 30 mins, plus standing • cook 10–15 mins

1½ cups **all-purpose flour**

pinch of **salt**

3 large **eggs**

1 tbsp **olive oil**

beaten egg, for brushing

For the filling

12oz (350g) **baby spinach leaves**, washed, but not dried

1 cup **ricotta**

⅓ cup freshly grated **Parmesan**

1 large **egg**, beaten, plus more for serving

¼ tsp freshly grated **nutmeg**

salt and freshly ground **black pepper**

olive oil or melted butter, to serve

1 **Sift the flour** and salt on to a work surface and make a well in the center. Beat 2 of the eggs and the oil together and pour into the well. Using your fingertips, draw the flour into the center, gradually incorporating all the liquid to form a rough, sticky dough. Knead the dough for about 10 minutes, adding more flour as needed, until the dough is smooth and elastic. Wrap in oiled plastic wrap and let stand for 30 minutes.

2 **To make the filling**, place the spinach in a heavy pan. Cover and cook over medium heat for 2 minutes, shaking occasionally, or until wilted. Drain, pressing out as much water as possible, then chop finely and transfer to a bowl. Add the ricotta, Parmesan, egg, and nutmeg and mix, seasoning with salt and pepper.

3 **Cut the pasta** in half. Keeping the other portion covered, roll out one portion on a very lightly floured work surface into a rectangle about ⅟₁₆in (1.5mm) thick.

4 **Using a teaspoon** for each, drop mounds of the filling on the pasta, spacing them 1½in (4cm) apart. Beat the remaining egg and brush it between the mounds. Roll out the second portion of dough to the same size as the first, and place it over the first rectangle. Use your fingertips to press the pasta between the mounds to seal.

5 **Cut squares around** the mounds with a pasta wheel or sharp knife. Place on a baking sheet lined with a floured kitchen towel and let stand for 1 hour to dry.

6 **Bring a large pot** of lightly salted water to a boil. In batches, add the ravioli and cook until floating. Transfer to a large warmed bowl and toss with melted butter. Grind pepper over the ravioli and serve hot.

Soba Salad with Shrimp and Avocado

This cool salad, with a base of full-flavored soba noodles, makes an extraordinary light meal

 makes 4 servings

 prep 15 mins, plus standing • cook 15 mins

8oz (230g) buckwheat soba noodles

2 tbsp **vegetable oil** or peanut oil

1½oz (45g) dried **wakame seaweed**

16 **large shrimp**, peeled, deveined, with tail segment intact

6 fresh **shiitake mushrooms**, stemmed and sliced

4 **cherry tomatoes**, halved

4 tbsp **mirin**

2 tbsp **rice vinegar**

2 tbsp **Japanese soy sauce**

2 tbsp rinsed and finely chopped **pickled ginger**

1 **avocado**, peeled, pitted, and sliced

2 tbsp black and/or white **sesame seeds**

2 tbsp chopped **cilantro leaves**

● **Prepare ahead** The various components of the salad can be prepared and refrigerated for a few hours before serving.

1 **Cook the noodles** in a large pot of boiling water according to the package directions, or until they are just tender. Drain and rinse under cold water until cool. Drain again (if not using immediately, toss with a little vegetable oil).

2 **Soak the wakame** in cold water about 5 minutes, or until soft. Drain and cut into strips.

3 **Heat the oil** in a large frying pan or wok over medium-high heat. Add the shrimp and shiitakes, and stir-fry for 1 minute. Add the cherry tomatoes and stir-fry for 1 minute, or until the shrimp turn opaque. Transfer to a plate and let cool.

4 **Whisk the mirin**, vinegar, soy sauce, and ginger in a large serving bowl. Add the noodles, shrimp mixture, and seaweed and toss gently. Add the avocado and toss again.

5 **Sprinkle** with the sesame seeds and cilantro. Serve immediately.

VARIATION

Soba Noodles with Tofu
Cut 8oz (230g) of firm tofu into 8 cubes. Cook the tofu on a hot grill pan, turning the pieces to brown evenly on each side. Add the cooked tofu pieces in place of the shrimp in step 3.

> **JAPANESE INGREDIENTS**
> Soba, wakame seaweed, pickled ginger, and mirin are available at natural food stores, Asian markets, and many supermarkets.

Orecchiette with Pancetta

A quick and light pasta dish

 makes 4–6 servings

 prep 10 mins • cook 10 mins

1lb (450g) dried **orecchiette pasta**

2 tbsp **olive oil**, plus more for drizzling

6oz (175g) **pancetta**, chopped

2 **zucchini**, diced

3 **garlic cloves**, chopped

½ crushed **hot red pepper**

1 cup thawed **frozen peas**

6 tbsp freshly grated **Parmesan**

3 tbsp chopped **parsley**

salt and freshly ground **black pepper**

1 **Cook the orecchiette** in a large pot of lightly salted boiling water according to the package instructions, until *al dente*.

2 **Meanwhile**, heat the oil in a large frying pan over medium heat. Add the pancetta and cook 5 minutes until lightly golden. Add the zucchini, garlic, and hot pepper and and cook for 3 minutes, until the zucchini is crisp-tender. Stir in the peas and cook about 2 minutes.

3 **Drain the pasta** and return to its pot. Add the pancetta mixture and stir over low heat until combined. Off the heat, stir in the Parmesan and parsley, and season with salt and pepper.

Penne and Vegetable Salad

Almost any spring vegetable can be used—for a change, try peas or diced zucchini

 makes 4–6 servings

 prep 20 mins • cook 25 mins

1lb (450g) **penne**

3 cups **broccoli** florets

2 cups **asparagus** tips

1 cup **snow peas**, trimmed

2 large **carrots**, cut into julienne

2 tbsp chopped **basil** or oregano

For the vinaigrette

⅓ cup **red wine vinegar**

1 tbsp **Dijon mustard**

1 **garlic clove**, minced

salt and freshly ground **black pepper**

½ cup **extra virgin olive oil**

1 Cook the penne in a large pot of lightly salted boiling water, according to the package instructions, until *al dente*.

2 Meanwhile, steam the borccoli and asparagus for 4 minutes. Add the snow peas and carrots and steam about 3 minutes more, until the vegetables are crisp-tender. Remove from the heat.

3 Whisk the vinegar, mustard, and garlic in a large bowl, then gradually whisk in the oil. Drain the pasta well and add to the bowl. Toss in the vegetables and basil. Season with salt and pepper. Serve warm.

● **Good with** hot crusty garlic rolls.

VARIATION

Creamy Pasta Primavera
In place of the vinaigrette, add ⅔ cup crème fraîche and 1 tsp whole-grain mustard to the vegetables and pasta. Thin with a little of the pasta cooking water if necesssary.

Spaghetti Mare e Monti

This pasta dish combines ingredients from the sea (mare) and from the mountains (monte)

 makes 4–6 servings

 prep 15 mins, plus soaking • cook 15 mins

 low in saturated fat

½oz (15g) **dried porcini mushrooms**, rinsed

⅔ cup **boiling water**

2 tbsp **extra-virgin olive oil**

6oz (175g) **white mushrooms**

2 **garlic cloves**, minced

1 **bay leaf**

6 ripe **plum tomatoes**, peeled, seeded, and chopped

⅔ cup dry **white wine**

8oz (225g) medium **shrimp**, peeled and deveined

salt and freshly ground **black pepper**

1lb (450g) dried **spaghetti**

1 Combine the porcini and boiling water in a bowl. Let stand for 30 minutes. Remove the mushrooms with a slotted spoon and chop them. Strain the soaking liquid through a fine sieve and reserve. Bring a large pot of salted water to a boil.

2 Heat the olive oil in a large frying pan over medium-high heat. Add the white mushrooms and cook, stirring often, about 5 minutes, until golden. Add the porcini and garlic and cook for 30 seconds. Pour in the porcini liquid, add the bay leaf, and simmer until the liquid is reduced to a glaze. Reduce the heat to low.

3 Add the tomatoes and wine and simmer for 7–8 minutes, until the liquid is slightly reduced and the tomatoes are beginning to break down. Remove the bay leaf. Add the shrimp and cook for 1 minute, or until just opaque. Season with salt and pepper.

4 When the sauce is almost done, cook the spaghetti in the boiling water according to the package directions until *al dente*. Drain well, then return to the pot. Add the sauce and toss well. Transfer to deep bowls and serve hot.

Crispy Rice Noodles with Beef

A combination of crunchy textures and Asian flavors

makes 4 servings

prep 20 mins • cook 15 mins

vegetable oil, as needed

5oz (140g) dried rice vermicelli

3 tbsp soy sauce

2 tbsp oyster sauce

1 tbsp light brown sugar

12oz (350g) sirloin steak or fillet mignon, thinly sliced

2 garlic cloves, thinly sliced

1 tsp peeled and shredded fresh ginger

12 thin asparagus spears, cut into 1in (2.5cm) lengths

6 scallions, white and green parts, cut into 1in (2.5cm) lengths

¼ cup chopped cashews

Asian sesame oil, for serving

1 **Heat** 2in (5cm) oil in a large saucepan over high heat. Break the vermicelli into 7 or 8 portions. In batches, add to the hot oil and cook for a few seconds until they turn white and become crisp. Transfer to paper towels. Keep warm.

2 **Mix the soy sauce**, oyster sauce, sugar, and 1 tbsp water. Heat 2 tbsp oil in a wok over high heat, stir-fry the beef for 2 minutes, until browned. Transfer to a plate.

3 **Add 1 tbsp oil**, and stir-fry the garlic and ginger for 30 seconds. Add the asparagus and scallions, stir-fry for 2 minutes, then add the sauce and beef to the pan. Stir-fry until the sauce is thick and boiling. Divide the rice vermicelli among 4 plates. Pile the stir-fry on top, top with cashews, drizzle with sesame oil, and serve immediately.

Fideua

Think of this as a seafood paella made with pasta instead of rice

 makes 4 servings

 prep 15 mins • cook 25 mins

✓ low fat

pinch of **saffron** threads

3 cups **fish stock**, heated, as needed

2 tbsp **olive oil**

1 **onion**, finely chopped

2 **garlic cloves**, minced

3 ripe **tomatoes**, skinned, seeded and chopped

1 tsp **sweet paprika**

10oz (300g) **spaghetti** or linguine, broken into 2in (5cm) lengths

8oz (225g) firm **white fish** fillets, such as cod, haddock, or monkfish, skinned and cut into ¾in (2cm) slices

8oz (225g) large **shrimp**, peeled and deveined

12 **mussels** or **clams**, scrubbed

8 small **scallops**, cut in half

1 cup **frozen peas**, thawed

salt and freshly ground **black pepper**

2 tbsp chopped **parsley**

1 Combine the saffron and 2 tbsp of the fish stock in a small bowl. Set aside.

2 Heat the oil in a large frying pan over medium heat. Add the onion and garlic and cook, stirring often, for about 5 minutes, until translucent. Add the tomatoes and paprika and cook for 5 minutes. Add the pasta, 2 cups of the remaining stock, and the soaked saffron. Bring to a boil. Cook for 5 minutes.

3 Add the fish, shrimp, mussels, scallops, and peas to the frying pan. Continue cooking until the pasta is tender, adding more stock as needed to keep the mixture moist. Season with salt and pepper. Sprinkle with the parsley and serve directly from the pan.

● **Good with** chunks of crusty bread to mop up the juices.

Tagliatelle all'Amatriciana

This fresh tomato pasta sauce is flavored with pancetta and hot red pepper

🍴 makes 4 servings

🕐 prep 10 mins • cook 25 mins

2 tbsp **extra virgin olive oil**

4oz (115g) **pancetta**, cubed

1 **onion**, finely chopped

1 **celery stalk**, finely chopped

2 **garlic cloves**, minced

¼ teaspoon crushed **hot red pepper**

2lb (900g) ripe **Roma (plum) tomatoes**, peeled, seeded and chopped, or one 28oz (784g) can chopped tomatoes with their juices

salt and freshly ground **black pepper**

1lb (450g) dried **tagliatelle** or fettuccine

freshly grated **Pecorino Romano**, to serve

1 Heat the oil in a large saucepan over medium-high heat. Add the pancetta and cook about 3 minutes, or until beginning to brown. Using a slotted spoon, transfer the pancetta to a plate.

2 Add the onion and celery and reduce the heat to medium-low. Cook, stirring often, about 6 minutes,

or until softened. Stir in the garlic and hot pepper and cook for 1 minute. Add the tomatoes and bring to a simmer. Simmer, stirring occasionally, for about 15 minutes, until the sauce is thick.

3 Meanwhile, cook the tagliatelle in a large pot of lightly salted water according the package instructions until *al dente*. Drain well.

4 Return the pasta to the pot. Add the pancetta and tomato sauce and stir well. Season with salt and pepper. Serve immediately, with the cheese passed on the side.

PEELING TOMATOES

Drop the tomatoes in a large saucepan of boiling water and cook just until the skins loosen. Drain and rinse under cold running water. Remove the skins with the help of a small, sharp knife. Cut each tomato in half through its equator, and squeeze lightly to extract the seeds.

Thai Noodle Stir-fry

A fragrant and colorful stir-fry with the flavors of Thailand

- 🍴 makes 4 servings
- 🕐 prep 20 mins • cook 15 mins
- ✓ low fat

6oz (75g) cellophane (mung bean) noodles

3 tbsp peanut or vegetable oil

3 skinless and boneless chicken breasts, cut into thin strips

1 onion, sliced

4oz (115g) shiitake mushrooms, sliced

1 red bell pepper, seeded and sliced

1 lemongrass stalk, peeled and bottom part minced

1 tsp peeled and finely grated fresh ginger

1 fresh hot Thai red chile, seeded and minced

1 head of bok choy, shredded

2 tbsp soy sauce

1 tbsp Asian fish sauce

1 tsp sweet chili sauce

1 **Soak the noodles** in a bowl of very hot water about 10 minutes, until softened. Drain well and rinse under cold running water. Cut into manageable lengths with kitchen scissors.

2 **Heat 2 tbsp** of the oil in a wok over high heat. Add the chicken and stir-fry about 3 minutes, or until lightly browned. Transfer to a plate.

3 **Reduce the heat** to medium and add the remaining 1 tbsp oil. Add the onion and stir-fry for 2 minutes. Add the mushrooms, bell pepper, lemongrass, ginger, and chili, and stir-fry about 2 minutes, or until the bell pepper softens.

4 **Add the bok choy** and stir-fry for about 2 minutes, or until wilted. Return the chicken to the pan and add the noodles. Pour in the soy sauce, fish sauce, and sweet chille sauce, and toss everything together over the heat for 2–3 minutes, or until piping hot. Serve hot.

Hokkien Noodles with Pork

Chinese barbecued pork (also called char-sui), pork loin cooked with a shiny scarlet glaze, and fresh Hokkien-style noodles can be purchased at Asian grocers

- 🍴 makes 4–6 servings
- 🕐 prep 20 mins, plus soaking • cook 10 mins

½ cup dried cloud ear (tree fungus) mushrooms

2 tbsp oyster sauce

2 tbsp soy sauce

1 tsp honey

2 tbsp vegetable oil

2 garlic cloves, minced

2 tsp peeled and finely grated fresh ginger

1 red bell pepper, seeded and thinly sliced

1 cup snow peas, each cut in half lengthwise

1lb (450g) thick fresh Hokkein-style egg noodles

12oz (350g) char-sui pork, thinly sliced

1 **Put the mushrooms** in a heatproof bowl, cover with boiling water, and set aside for 30 minutes to soak. Drain and cut the mushrooms into thin strips.

2 **Bring a large pot of water** to a boil over high heat. Mix the oyster sauce, soy sauce, and honey together in a small bowl.

3 **Heat the oil** in a wok or frying pan over high heat. Add the garlic and ginger and stir-fry for 15 seconds. Add the red pepper, stir-fry for 3 minutes, then add the snow peas, and stir-fry for 1 minute, until they turn bright green.

4 **Meanwhile**, add the noodles to the boiling water and cook for 1 minute. Add the pork to the wok, pour in the oyster sauce mixture and toss over the heat for 1 minute, until everything is heated. Drain the noodles, mix with the stir-fried pork and vegetables, and serve hot.

Spaghetti with Puttanesca

A spicy Sicilian pasta sauces gets its edge from capers and olives

 makes 4–6 servings

prep 10 mins • cook 10–15 mins

½ cup **extra virgin olive oil**

2 **garlic cloves**, finely chopped

½ fresh **hot red chile**, seeded and minced

1½lb (680g) ripe **tomatoes**, skinned, seeded, and chopped

1 cup pitted and chopped **Kalamata olives**

6 canned **anchovy fillets**, drained and finely chopped

3 tbsp **capers**, drained and rinsed

1lb (450g) **spaghetti**

2 tbsp chopped **parsley**

1 Heat the oil in a medium saucepan over low heat. Add garlic and chile and cook, stirring often, for 2 minutes, or until the garlic is pale gold. Add the tomatoes, olives, anchovies, and capers and bring to a boil over high heat.

2 Return the heat to low and simmer, stirring frequently, for about 15 minutes, or until the juices thicken.

3 Cook the spaghetti in a pot of lightly salted boiling water over high heat according to the package instructions until al dente. Drain.

4 Toss the spaghetti with the sauce and sprinkle with the parsley. Serve hot.

● **Good with** a glass of full-bodied red wine.

VARIATION

Arrabiata Sauce

Make as above, but omit the olives, capers and anchovies. Use 1 whole fresh hot red chile and replace the parsley with basil leaves.

Vietnamese Beef, Green Papaya, and Noodle Salad

Green, under-ripe papayas make a refreshing addition to many southeast Asian salads

makes 4 servings

prep 20 mins, plus standing • cook 10 mins

For the dressing

¼ cup fresh **lime** juice

2 tbsp **Asian fish sauce**

2 tbsp chopped **cilantro**

2 tbsp chopped **mint**

2 fresh hot **Thai red chiles**, seeded and minced

1 tsp finely minced **lemongrass**

1 tsp peeled and finely grated fresh **ginger**

1 tsp **light brown sugar**

12oz (350g) **fillet mignon**

salt and freshly ground **black pepper**

7oz (200g) **cellophane (mung bean) noodles**

9oz (250g) **green papaya**, peeled, seeded, and cut into matchsticks

¼ cup coarsely chopped unsalted **roasted peanuts**

● **Prepare ahead** If desired, broil the steak up to 2 hours in advance and slice it just before adding to the salad.

1 To make the dressing, mix together the lime juice, fish sauce, cilantro, mint, chiles, lemongrass, ginger, and brown sugar.

2 Preheat the broiler. Season the steak with salt and pepper. Broil for 3–4 minutes on each side, until medium-rare. Transfer to a carving board and let cool. Carve into thin slices.

3 Soak the noodles in a bowl of very hot water about 10 minutes, until softened. Drain well and rinse under cold running water. Cut into manageable lengths with kitchen scissors.

4 Heap the noodles, papaya, and steak in a platter. Add the dressing and peanuts and toss. Serve immediately.

Lasagna al Forno

The perfect dish for family meals or casual entertaining

 makes 6–8 servings

 prep 25 mins
• cook 1 hr 35 mins

 9 x 13in (23 x 33cm) baking dish

8oz (227g) oven-ready lasagna

½ cup freshly grated Parmesan

For the ragù sauce

1 tbsp olive oil

1 large onion, chopped

2 celery ribs, chopped

1 large carrot, chopped

2oz (50g) pancetta, diced

1lb (450g) ground beef round

one 14.5oz (411g) can chopped tomatoes

⅓ cup hearty red wine

1 tsp dried oregano

For the white sauce

4 tbsp butter

¼ cup all-purpose flour

2¼ cups whole milk

¾ cup ricotta

salt and freshly ground black pepper

¼ tsp freshly grated nutmeg

1 To make the ragù sauce, heat the oil in a large saucepan over medium heat. Add the onion, celery, carrot, and pancetta and cook for 5 minutes, until softened. Add the beef and cook, breaking up with the side of a spoon, about 10 minutes, until browned.

2 Add the tomatoes and their juices, the wine, and oregano. Bring to a boil, reduce the heat to low, and simmer for at least 40 minutes and up to 2½ hours.

3 Meanwhile, make the white sauce. Melt the butter in a saucepan over low heat, whisk in the flour, and cook for 1 minute. Whisk in the milk. Cook, whisking often, until the sauce boils. Stir in the ricotta. Season with salt, pepper, and nutmeg.

4 Preheat the oven to 375°F (190°C). Oil the baking dish. Spread ¼ cup of the white sauce in the dish. Arrange 3 lasagna in the dish. Top with one third of the ragù and ½ cup of the white sauce. Repeat twice with the lasagna, ragù, and white sauce. Top with 3 lasagna, the remaining white sauce, and the Parmesan.

5 Bake for 45 minutes, until the top is golden and bubbling. Let stand 10 minutes, then serve hot.

VARIATION

Vegetarian Lasagna

Replace the ragù with this vegetable sauce: Sauté 1 chopped onion and 2 chopped celery stalks in 2 tbsp olive oil. Add 2 zucchini, sliced, 1 red bell pepper, seeded and chopped, and 1 small eggplant, cut into small cubes. Sauté for about 20 minutes, until softened and beginning to brown. Add 2 tbsp sun-dried tomato paste, one 14.5oz (411g) can chopped tomatoes and their juices, 1 vegetable bouillon cube, and ¾ cup water. Simmer, partially covered, for 20 minutes.

Pasta alla Carbonara

A popular Italian classic

 makes 4–6 servings

prep 10 mins • cook 10 mins

1lb (450g) dried pasta, such as spaghetti or tagliatelle

4 tbsp olive oil

6oz (175g) pancetta, very finely chopped

2 garlic cloves, minced

5 large eggs

½ cup freshly grated Parmesan

½ cup freshly grated Romano, plus more to serve

freshly ground black pepper

1 Bring a large saucepan of salted water to the boil over high heat. Add the pasta, stir and cook according to the package instructions, until *al dente*.

2 Meanwhile, heat the oil in a large frying pan over medium heat. Add the pancetta and cook, stirring occasionally, about 6 minutes, until crispy. Add the garlic and cook for 1 minute.

3 Beat the eggs, Parmesan, and Romano together and season with pepper. Drain the pasta well and return to its saucepan. Add the egg mixture and the contents of the pan with the pancetta, including the fat, and mix quickly until the pasta is well coated. Serve immediately, with extra Romano passed on the side.

● **Good with** a simple salad.

Pad Thai

Once you have gathered the ingredients, this dish comes together quickly to create a fast weeknight supper

🍴 makes 4 servings

🕐 prep 20 mins • cook 10 mins

12oz (350g) flat rice noodles

4 tbsp vegetable oil

2 tbsp chopped cilantro

1 small hot red chile, seeded and finely chopped

9oz (250g) large shrimp, peeled and deveined

4 shallots, finely chopped

4 large eggs, beaten

1 tbsp sugar

2 tbsp oyster sauce

1 tbsp Thai fish sauce

2 tbsp fresh lime juice

9oz (250g) bean sprouts

4 scallions, white and green parts, sliced

1 cup unsalted roasted peanuts

1 lime cut into 4 wedges, to serve

1 **Soak the noodles** in a bowl of hot water to cover for about 15 minutes, or until soft. Drain.

2 **Meanwhile**, heat a wok or large frying pan over high heat. Add 2 tbsp of the oil, then the cilantro and chile. Immediately add the shrimp and stir-fry until the shrimp look opaque around the edges, about 1 minute. Transfer to a plate.

3 **Add the remaining oil** to the wok. Add the shallots and stir-fry for 1 minute. Add the eggs and sugar and cook, stirring, for 1 minute, until the eggs are scrambled.

4 **Stir in** the oyster sauce, fish sauce, and lime juice. Add the noodles, bean sprouts, and shrimp. Stir-fry for 2 minutes. Add the scallions and ½ cup of the peanuts, and stir-fry for 1 minute. Sprinkle with the remaining peanuts and garnish with lime wedges to serve.

⬤ **Good with** a fresh salad of bean sprouts and shredded carrot, tossed with lime juice.

Mediterranean Lasagna

A simple baked vegetarian pasta dish full of Italian flavors

🍴 makes 8 servings

🕐 prep 20 mins • cook 1 hr 10 mins

▭ 9 x 13in (23 x 33cm) baking dish

4 small eggplants

salt and freshly ground black pepper

1 large red bell pepper

4 large portobello mushrooms, stemmed

olive oil, for the dish

4 cups marinara sauce

8oz (227g) oven-ready lasagna

1lb (450g) mozzarella cheese, thinly sliced

15oz (420g) ricotta cheese

¼ cup freshly grated Parmesan

1 **Cut the eggplants** lengthwise ½in (13cm) thick. Place in a colander on a plate and toss with 1½ tbsp of salt. Let stand 30–60 minutes to draw out the bitter juices. Rinse well and pat dry with paper towels.

2 **Position** an oiled broiler rack 6in (15cm) from the heat and preheat the broiler. Broil the eggplant, peppers, and mushrooms for 5–10 minutes, or until they are softened but still hold their shape. Season to taste with salt and pepper.

3 **Preheat the oven** to 375°F (190°C). Lightly oil the baking dish and spoon in a ladleful of the marinara sauce. Top with a layer of pasta, some vegetables, another ladleful of sauce, then some of the mozzarella and ricotta. Repeat the layers, finishing with tomato sauce, topped with some vegetables. Sprinkle with the Parmesan.

4 **Cover the dish** tightly with aluminium foil and place on a baking sheet. Bake for 30 minutes. Remove the foil and bake for 15 minutes more to brown the top. Remove from the oven and let stand 15 minutes before serving.

Chicken and Noodle Stir-fry

A colorful Chinese favorite, packed with contrasting flavors and textures

- makes 4 servings
- prep 20 mins • cook 10 mins
- wok or large frying pan

12oz (350g) **fresh Asian egg noodles** or fresh fettucine

3 tbsp **vegetable oil**

2 **skinless boneless chicken breasts**, cut into bite-sized pieces

½ **red, green, and yellow** or orange **pepper**, seeded and sliced

4oz (115g) **shiitake mushrooms**, quartered

1 tbsp peeled and shredded **fresh ginger**

½ cup **chicken stock**

2 tbsp **ketchup**

2 tbsp **soy sauce**

1 tsp **cornstarch**

few drops of **Asian sesame oil**

2 tbsp **sesame seeds**, for garnish

1 Bring a saucepan of lightly salted water to a boil. Cook the noodles about 2 minutes, until barely tender. Drain and rinse under cold running water. Toss with 1 tbsp oil.

2 Heat 1 tbsp of the oil in a wok over high heat. Add the chicken and stir-fry for 3 minutes. Remove and set aside. Add the peppers, mushrooms, and ginger to the wok and stir-fry for 3 minutes.

3 Mix together the chicken stock, ketchup, soy sauce, and cornstarch. Return the chicken to the wok, add the noodles, and pour in the stock mixture. Stir-fry for 3 minutes, until the chicken is cooked through. Just before serving, drizzle with the sesame oil and sprinkle with the sesame seeds.

VARIATION

Vegetable and Noodle Stir-fry
Replace the peppers with 1 cup small broccoli florets, 1 sliced yellow squash, and 4 cherry tomatoes, halved. Add the broccoli and yellow squash with the ginger but add the tomatoes during the last minute of cook. Sliced onion, added with the broccoli, is also good.

Spaghetti with Clams

This light pasta dish has the classic sauce of white wine and garlic with toasted bread crumbs

- makes 4 servings
- prep 20 mins • cook 15 mins

3lbs (1.3kg) **littleneck clams**

6 tbsp **extra virgin olive oil**, plus more for serving

2 **garlic cloves**, thinly sliced

1 cup fresh **bread crumbs**

salt and freshly ground **black pepper**

1lb (450g) **spaghetti**

pinch crushed **hot red pepper**

½ cup **dry white wine**

¼ cup chopped **parsley**

1 Soak the clams in cold salted water for 1 hour. Drain, then scrub well, discarding any clams that do not close when tapped.

2 Bring a large pot of salted water to a boil over high heat. Meanwhile, heat 3 tbsp oil and 1 garlic clove in a large frying pan over medium heat. Add the bread crumbs and cook, stirring often, about 4 minutes until pale gold.

Season with salt and pepper and transfer to a bowl.

3 Cook the spaghetti in the boiling water according to package instructions until al dente.

4 Meanwhile, heat the remaining 5 tbsp olive oil in a large saucepan with the remaining garlic and the hot pepper over medium heat. Cook until the garlic turns gold. Add the clams and the wine. Cover and cook for about 5 minutes, shaking the pan often, until all the clams have opened. Remove the lid, increase the heat to high, and boil for 2 minutes. Stir in the parsley and season with salt and pepper.

5 Drain the spaghetti, add to the clams, and toss to combine. Transfer to individual bowls and sprinkle each with toasted bread crumbs. Serve hot, with more olive oil passed at the table.

Chicken and Chickpea Pilaf

This one-pot rice dish is full of flavor and is easy to make

- 🍴 makes 4 servings
- 🕐 prep 20 mins • cook 35 mins
- ✓ low fat

pinch of **saffron threads**

2 tbsp **vegetable oil**

6 skinless and boneless **chicken thighs**, cut into small pieces

salt and freshly ground **black pepper**

2 tsp **ground coriander**

1 tsp **ground cumin**

1 **onion**, sliced

1 **red pepper**, seeded and chopped

2 **garlic cloves**, peeled and crushed

1¼ cups **long-grain rice**

2½ cups hot **chicken stock**

2 **bay leaves**

one 15oz (420g) can **chickpeas**

⅓ cup **golden raisins**

½ cup **slivered almonds** toasted

3 tbsp chopped **parsley**

1 **Crumble the saffron** threads into a small bowl, add 2 tbsp boiling water, and set aside for at least 10 minutes.

2 **Meanwhile, heat 1 tbsp** oil in a large saucepan over medium heat. Season the chicken with salt and pepper and sprinkle with the coriander and cumin. In batches, cook the chicken, stirring often, for 3 minutes. Transfer to a plate. Add the remaining oil to the saucepan and heat. Add the onion, red pepper, and garlic and cook, stirring often, about 5 minutes, until softened.

3 **Stir in the rice**. Return the chicken to the saucepan and stir in the stock, along with the saffron and its liquid, ½ tsp salt, and the bay leaves. Bring to a boil over high heat. Reduce the heat to low and cover. Simmer for 15 minutes. Rinse and drain the chickpeas then stir in along with the raisins, and cook about 5 minutes, or until the rice is tender. Remove from the heat and let stand, covered, for 5 minutes. Transfer to a warm serving platter and serve hot, sprinkled with almonds and parsley.

Lentil Salad with Lemon and Almonds

Preserved lemons are available at Mediterranean grocers

- 🍴 makes 4 servings
- 🕐 prep 10 mins, plus standing • cook 15–20 mins

1¾ cups **French green (Puy) lentils**, rinsed and drained

2 tbsp **sherry vinegar**

6 tbsp **extra virgin olive oil**

1 cup loosely packed **cilantro leaves**

2 **preserved lemon quarters**, rinsed and finely chopped

1 **shallot**, minced

salt and freshly ground **black pepper**

3 tbsp **butter**

¾ cup **slivered almonds**

● **Prepare ahead** The salad can be prepared several hours in advance. Cover and refrigerate until required.

1 **Bring the lentils** with enough cold water to cover to a boil in a medium saucepan over high heat. Reduce the heat to medium-low and simmer about 15 minutes until tender. Drain, rinse under cold water, and let cool.

2 **Whisk the vinegar** and oil in a bowl. Add the lentils, ½ cup of cilantro, the preserved lemons, and half of the shallot. Season with salt and pepper.

3 **Melt the butter** in a small frying pan over medium heat. Add the almonds and cook, stirring often, until golden brown. Drain and cool on paper towels. Stir the almonds into the lentil salad. Let stand for 10 minutes or so to let the flavors blend.

4 **Scatter the** remaining onion and cilantro over the salad and serve at room temperature.

● **Good with** grilled lamb chops, or with firm oily fish, such as swordfish or mackerel.

Seafood Paella

This Spanish rice dish has many regional variations. This version contains a delicious mix of seafood

🍴 makes 4 servings

🕐 prep 10 mins • cook 30 mins

⚠ tap the mussels and discard any that do not close

5 tbsp **olive oil**

12 **jumbo shrimp**, peeled and deveined

8 **langoustines** or more **shrimp**

8oz (225g) **squid**, cleaned and sliced into rings

12-16 **mussels**, scrubbed

2 large **tomatoes**, peeled, seeded, and diced

pinch of **saffron**

2 cups **short-grain rice**

5 cups boiling **fish stock**

salt and freshly ground **black pepper**

2 tbsp chopped **parsley**

1 **lemon**, cut into 8 wedges

1 Heat 2 tbsp of the oil in a paella pan or a large frying pan over medium heat. Add the shrimp and cook about 2 minutes. Transfer to a plate. Add the langoustines to the pan, cover, and cook for 5 minutes, until the shells are red. Add to the shrimp. Add 1 tbsp oil to the pan, heat, and add the squid. Cook 1 minute, until barely opaque, and add to the plate. Add the mussels to the pan with ¼ cup water. Cover and cook about 4 minutes, or until they open. Transfer mussels and their juices to the plate.

2 Heat 2 tbsp oil in the pan. Add the tomatoes and saffron and cook for 1 minute. Stir in the rice, then the stock.

3 Simmer, uncovered, over medium-low heat for 15 minutes. Season with salt and pepper to taste. Nestle the shrimp, langoustines, squid, and mussels in the rice and let cook until the rice is just tender.

4 Remove from the heat and tent with aluminum foil. Let stand for 5 minutes. Garnish with the lemon and parsley and serve hot.

Hoppin' John

This is a traditional dish from the South

🍴 makes 4-6 servings

🕐 prep 12 mins • cook 3-3½ hrs

🍲 flameproof casserole with fitted lid, large heatproof bowl

2 smoked **ham hocks**, about 2¼lb (1.1kg)

1 fresh **bouquet garni**, with 1 celery rib, 4 thyme sprigs, and 1 bay leaf tied together with kitchen twine

2 large **onions**, chopped

¼ tsp **crushed hot red pepper**

1 tbsp **vegetable oil**

1 cup **long-grain rice**

2 cans (15.5oz/440g) **black-eyed beans**, drained and rinsed

hot pepper sauce, to serve

● **Prepare ahead** Step 1 can be prepared 1 day in advance. Chill the meat until ready to use.

1 Put the ham hock in a large saucepan and add enough cold water to cover. Slowly bring to a boil over high heat, skimming the surface as necessary. Reduce the heat to low, add the bouquet garni, half the onions and the hot pepper. Re-cover the pan again and simmer for 2½ hours, or until the meat is very tender when pierced with the tip of a knife.

2 Place a colander over a large heatproof bowl and strain the cooking liquid. Reserve the liquid and set the ham hock aside to cool.

3 Meanwhile, heat the oil in a large flameproof casserole over a medium heat. Add the remaining onions and cook for 5 minutes until softened but not browned, stirring occasionally. Stir in the rice.

4 Stir in 2 cups of the reserved cooking liquid, the beans and salt and pepper to taste. Bring to a boil, reduce the heat to low, cover tightly, and simmer for 20 minutes.

5 Meanwhile, remove the meat from the ham hock and cut into large chunks; discard skin and bones.

6 Remove the casserole from the heat and let stand for 5 minutes, covered. Use a fork to stir in the ham. Pile the mixture onto a large serving platter and serve with hot pepper sauce on the side.

Spicy Hoppin' John

Tomatoes make a good addition to the basic recipe and will make the dish go further. Simply add one 14.5oz (400g) can of chopped tomatoes, drained, in step 4. For extra spice, you can also add a good pinch of Cajun or Creole seasoning.

Couscous Royale

This richly spiced dish makes a colorful Moroccan feast

- 🍴 makes 6 servings
- 🕐 prep 10 mins
  • cook 1 hr 20 mins
- 🍲 large flameproof casserole
- ❄️ freeze for up to 1 month

2 tbsp **olive oil**

1lb 5oz (600g) **boneless leg of lamb**, cut into bite-sized chunks

6 **chicken legs**, about 3lb 3oz (1.5kg)

1 **red bell pepper**, seeded and diced

1 **eggplant**, cut into 1in (2.5cm) pieces

1 large **red onion**, sliced

2 **garlic cloves**, finely chopped

4 tsp **harissa** (hot Moroccan chile paste)

1 tbsp **sweet paprika**

1 tsp **ground turmeric**

2 medium **zucchini**, sliced

1 cup **chicken stock**

15oz (420g) can **chickpeas**, rinsed and drained

14.5oz (400g) can **chopped tomatoes**

6oz (175g) **chorizo**, thickly sliced

salt and freshly ground **black pepper**

large sprig of **thyme**

1 **bay leaf**

2¼ cups **couscous**

chopped **cilantro**, to garnish

1 Heat the oil in the casserole over medium-high heat. Add the lamb and chicken and cook, turning occasionally, about 6 minutes. Transfer to paper towels to drain.

2 Add the eggplant, red pepper, onion, and garlic to the casserole and cook, stirring occasionally, about 4 minutes. Stir in the harissa, paprika, and turmeric and cook for 1 minute.

3 Return the lamb and chicken to the casserole. Add the zucchini, stock, beans, tomatoes, and chorizo and season with salt and pepper. Bring to a boil. Reduce the heat to low and cover. Simmer about 1 hour, or until the meats are tender.

4 Strain the mixture in a colander set over a wide skillet. Transfer the meat and vegetables to a platter and cover to keep warm. Boil the strained liquid over high heat for about 5 minutes, or until slightly reduced. Season with salt and pepper.

5 Bring 3 cups water and ½ tsp salt to a boil in a large saucepan. Stir in the couscous and remove from the heat. Cover and let stand until the couscous is tender, about 5 minutes. Stir the meats and vegetables into the couscous. Pour the sauce on top and sprinkle with the cilantro. Serve hot.

Mushroom Risotto

For the best results, choose a dark, richly flavored mushroom, such as cremini or portobello, to make this risotto

- 🍴 makes 6 servings
- 🕐 prep 10 mins • cook 40 mins

4 tbsp **vegetable oil**

1 **onion**, chopped

2 cups **arborio** or **carnaroli rice**

6 cups **vegetable stock** or water, kept simmering

4 tbsp **butter**, diced

1lb (450g) **cremini mushrooms**, sliced

½ cup freshly grated **Parmesan**

1 Heat the oil in a large, heavy saucepan over medium heat. Add the onion and fry for 5 minutes or until golden, stirring occasionally. Add the rice and stir for 2 minutes.

2 Gradually add the stock, about ½ cup at a time, stirring constantly, waiting until it is absorbed before adding more. Continue in this manner for 25 minutes or until the rice is barely tender and has a creamy consistency, adding water if the stock has run out.

3 Meanwhile, melt the butter in a pan over a medium heat. Add the mushrooms and cook, stirring frequently, for 10 minutes or until the mushrooms have browned and the liquid evaporates.

4 Stir the mushrooms into the rice and turn off remove from the heat. Stir in the cheese and serve immediately.

● **Leftovers** can be shaped into patties, coated with fine bread crumbs and pan-fried.

VARIATION

Porcini Mushroom Risotto

Cover ¾oz (20g) dried porcini mushrooms with boiling water and let stand for 20 minutes, Strain through cheesecloth, stirring the soaking liquid into the vegetable stock. Use in addition to or in place of the cremini mushrooms. (Do not sauté the soaked dried mushrooms.)

Quinoa Tabbouleh

Whole grain quinoa makes a tasty and healthy summer salad. Be sure to rinse it well in a fine sieve before cooking

 makes 4 servings

prep 10 mins • cook 20 mins

1 cup **quinoa**

1 **cucumber**, peeled, seeded, and diced

1 small **red onion**, chopped

2 tbsp chopped **parsley**

2 tbsp chopped **mint**

salt and freshly ground **black pepper**

½ cup **olive oil**

2 tbsp fresh **lemon** juice

2oz (55g) **feta cheese**

½ cup pitted and coarsely chopped **Kalamata olives**

1 Rinse the quinoa well in a fine mesh sieve. Drain and place it in a medium heavy-bottomed pan. Stir constantly over a medium heat about 3 minutes, until the grains separate and begin to brown.

2 Add 2¼ cups water and ½ tsp salt and bring to a boil over high heat. Reduce the heat and cook for 15 minutes, or until the liquid is absorbed. Transfer to a bowl and let cool.

3 Add the cucumber, onion, parsley, and mint to the quinoa. Whisk together the oil and lemon juice in a small bowl. Pour over the quinoa and mix.

4 Sprinkle with the feta cheese and olives. Season with salt and pepper, and serve.

Kasha with Vegetables

Kasha, also called buckwheat groats, is a healthy and delicious whole grain cereal that can be prepared in a manner similar to risotto to make a hearty vegetarian main course

 makes 4–6 servings

prep 5 mins • cook 40 mins

2 tbsp **olive oil**

1 **onion**, finely chopped

1 **carrot**, finely chopped

2 **portobello mushrooms**, sliced

1 **celery stalk**, finely chopped

1 **garlic clove**, minced

⅓ cup **kasha (buckwheat groats)**

½ cup **dry white wine**

about 4 ¼ cups hot **vegetable stock** or **water**

1 **beet**, cooked until tender, chopped

2oz (55g) rindless **goat cheese**, crumbled

2 tbsp chopped **parsley**

1 Heat the oil in a large saucepan over medium heat. Add the onion, carrot, mushrooms, celery, and garlic, and cook, stirring often, for 8–10 minutes, or until lightly browned. Add the kasha and cook, stirring often, for 2–3 minutes more. Add the wine and stir until it has been absorbed.

2 Stir in ½ cup hot vegetable stock and reduce the heat to medium-low. Simmer, stirring, until the stock is absorbed. Stir in another ½ cup of stock and repeat. Continue cooking and adding more stock for about 20 minutes, or until the kasha is tender but still a bit chewy.

3 Stir in the beet and season with salt and pepper. Transfer to a serving bowl and sprinkle with cheese and parsley. Serve hot.

● **Good with** crusty bread, as a main meal.

Puy Lentils with Goat Cheese, Olives, and Fresh Thyme

French Puy lentils hold their shape during cooking, and lend an attractive look to rustic lentil recipes

 makes 4–6 servings

prep 10 mins • cook 30 mins

1⅔ cups **Puy lentils**, rinsed

1 **carrot**, peeled and diced

1 **shallot** or small onion, finely chopped

2 sprigs of **thyme**

1 **bay leaf**

¾ cup pitted and chopped **Kalamata olives**

3oz (85g) rindless **goat cheese**, crumbled

2 tbsp **extra virgin olive oil**

salt and freshly ground **black pepper**

6oz (170g) **mixed baby salad leaves**, to serve (optional)

 Prepare ahead The lentils can be cooked ahead in step 1 and reheated, or the dish can be served chilled as a salad.

1 **Place the lentils**, carrot, shallot, thyme, and bay leaf in a saucepan with 5 cups of water. Simmer for 15–20 minutes or until the lentils are tender.

2 **Drain the lentils** well, transfer to a serving bowl, and remove the thyme and bay leaf. Cool until lukewarm. Add the olives, goat cheese, and olive oil, and stir together. Season with salt and pepper and serve warm.

 Good with grilled spicy sausages, lamb chops, or pork chops.

VARIATION

Dressed Lentils

Leftovers are good served as a salad. Splash with balsamic vinegar, add extra olive oil, and sprinkle with lots of chopped parsley. If you wish, add sliced anchovy fillets.

Kedgeree

This Anglo-Indian brunch dish is traditionally made with smoked haddock, but you can use all fresh salmon if you wish

 makes 4 servings

prep 20 mins • cook 20 mins

10oz (280g) **smoked haddock**

10oz (280g) fresh **salmon fillets**

1 cup **basmati rice**

⅛ tsp crumbled **saffron**

salt and freshly ground **pepper**

4 tbsp **butter**

4 hard-boiled **eggs**

2 tbsp chopped **parsley**, plus more for garnish

1 **lemon**, cut into wedges

1 **Place the** haddock in a single layer in a large, deep frying pan. Add enough water to cover and heat over medium heat until just simmering. Reduce the heat to low, and simmer for 7 minutes. Using a

slotted spoon, transfer the fish to a plate and cool.

2 **Meanwhile**, bring the rice, 2 cups water, saffron, and ½ tsp salt to a boil in a medium saucepan. Reduce the heat to low and cover. Simmer about 15 minutes, until the rice is tender. Remove from heat and stir in the butter.

3 **Remove the yolks** from the hard-boiled eggs; chop finely, and set aside. Chop the egg whites and stir into the rice with the flaked fish and 2 tbsp chopped parsley.

4 **Spoon onto** heated plates, sprinkled with the chopped egg yolk and parsley, and serve with the lemon wedges.

 Good with triangles of buttered whole wheat toast.

Jambalaya

This one-pot meal captures the spicy flavors of Louisiana

makes 4–6 servings

prep 30 mins • cook 45 mins

large flameproof casserole

4 tbsp rendered **bacon fat** or vegetable oil

4 skinless and boneless **chicken thighs**, cut into bite-sized pieces

8oz (225g) **andouille** or **kielbasa sausage**, thickly sliced

1 **onion**, finely chopped

1 **red bell pepper**, seeded and finely chopped

1 **green bell pepper**, seeded and finely chopped

1 **celery stalk**, thinly sliced

2 **garlic cloves**, finely chopped

1 fresh **hot red chile**, seeded and chopped

1¾ cups **long-grain rice**

2 tbsp **tomato paste**

2 tsp dried **thyme**

1 tsp **salt**

½ tsp **sweet paprika**

¼ tsp **cayenne pepper**

2 **bay leaves**

pinch of **sugar**

freshly ground **black pepper**

2½ cups **chicken** or **vegetable stock**

one 14.5oz (411g) can **chopped tomatoes**

1 tsp **Worcestershire sauce**

12 large **shrimp**, peeled and deveined

chopped **parsley**, to garnish

hot red pepper sauce, to serve

1 Heat 2 tbsp of the bacon fat in a large flameproof casserole over high heat. In batches, add the chicken. Cook, stirring occasionally, for 10 minutes, or until the chicken is browned and opaque throughout. Using a slotted spoon, transfer the chicken to a plate.

2 Add the remaining bacon fat to the casserole and heat. Add the andouille and cook, stirring occasionally, for 5 minutes, or until browned. Remove the andouille with a slotted spoon and set aside with the chicken.

3 Add the onion, peppers, celery, garlic, and chile to the casserole. Cook, stirring often, for 5 minutes or until softened. Add the rice and cook, stirring often, for about 3 minutes. Add the tomato paste and stir for another minute.

4 Return the chicken and sausage to the casserole. Add the thyme, salt, paprika, cayenne, bay leaves, sugar, and pepper. Pour in the stock, the tomatoes with their juice, and the Worcestershire sauce. Bring to the boil over medium-high heat, stirring often. Reduce the heat to low and cover. Simmer for 12–15 minutes, or until the peppers are tender.

5 Add the shrimp and simmer, still covered, for 3-5 minutes, or until the rice is tender and the shrimp are pink (the jambalaya should be a little soupy). Transfer to a serving bowl and garnish with parsley. Serve hot, with a bottle of hot pepper sauce alongside.

● **Good with** cold beer to quell the spiciness.

German Bread Dumplings

This recipe is traditionally served with soups and stews

🍴 makes 8 dumplings

🕐 prep 20 mins • cook 50 mins

2 white bread rolls

1 tbsp vegetable oil

2 bacon strips, finely chopped

1 small onion, finely chopped

1 tbsp finely chopped parsley

1 tsp dried marjoram

½ cup whole milk

1 large egg

all-purpose flour, as needed

1 **Preheat the oven** to 275°F (140°C). Cut the rolls into small cubes. Spread on a baking sheet. Bake about 30 minutes, until crisp.

2 **Heat the oil** in a frying pan over medium heat. Add the bacon and onion and cook about 7 minutes. Stir in the herbs and let cool.

3 **Beat** the milk and egg together in a bowl. Add the bread cubes and bacon mixture and stir well. The dough should be firm enough to shape into dumplings; if it is too soft, stir in flour as needed.

4 **Bring a large saucepan** of water to a boil over high heat. With damp hands, form the dough into 8 dumplings. Add the dumplings to the water and cook about 10 minutes, or until cooked through. Drain carefully and serve hot.

Spiced Pilaf

Subtly spiced, this versatile rice dish can be served hot or cold

🍴 makes 4 servings

🕐 prep 5 mins • cook 25 mins

2 tsp vegetable oil

1 tsp black mustard seeds

1 small onion, finely chopped

1 tbsp butter

1 heaping cup basmati rice

1 tsp cardamom seeds

1 tsp ground coriander

2¼ cups vegetable or chicken stock

¼ tsp salt

1 tbsp chopped cilantro

1 **Heat the oil** in a large saucepan over medium-high heat. Add the mustard seeds and cook for 1 minute, shaking the pan often, until they begin to pop.

2 **Reduce the heat** to medium. Add the onion and butter and cook, stirring often, for 5 minutes, or until the onion is golden. Add the rice, cardamom, coriander, and rice and stir for 1 minute, until rice is coated.

3 **Stir in the stock** and salt, increase the heat to high, and bring to a boil. Reduce the heat to medium-low and cover. Simmer for about 17 minutes, or until the rice has absorbed all the liquid and is tender.

4 **Transfer to a warmed** serving bowl. Sprinkle with the cilantro.

VARIATION

Persian-style Rice

Cook as above, replacing the onion and spices with ½ tsp salt. Tip the rice out of the pan and keep warm. Wipe out the pan, and, while still hot, brush with 2 tsp oil and dot with 1 tbsp butter. Line with a layer of thinly sliced raw potato. Return the rice to the pan and dot the surface with another 1 tbsp butter. Place a clean kitchen towel on top of the pan, replace the lid, and cook on the lowest heat for 45 minutes, or until the potato is cooked and slightly crisp. Turn off the heat but do not remove the lid. Let stand for up to 2 hours before serving.

Kasha Pilaf

A refreshing change from rice, this makes a tasty side dish

🍴 makes 4–6 servings

🕐 prep 5 mins • cook 25 mins

2 tbsp butter

1 large onion, chopped

2 celery stalks, sliced

1⅓ cups kasha (buckwheat groats)

1 large egg

1 tsp ground sage

1 tsp ground thyme

¾ cup raisins

¾ cup coarsely chopped walnuts

salt

1 **Melt the butter** in a large frying pan over medium heat. Add the onion and celery and cook about 3 minutes, or until the vegetables begin to soften.

2 **Mix the kasha** and egg in a bowl. Add to the frying pan and cook, stirring constantly, about 1 minute, or until the grains are dry and separated. Add 2 cups water, the sage, and thyme. Increase the heat to high and bring to a boil. Cover and reduce the heat to medium-low. Simmer for about 12 minutes, or until it is almost tender.

3 **Stir in the raisins** and walnuts. Continue cooking for about 5 minutes, or until the kasha is tender and all the liquid has been absorbed. Season with salt.

Egg Fried Rice

This popular Chinese-style rice dish is an excellent way to use up leftover rice

- makes 4–6 servings
- prep 5 mins • cook 10 mins
- make sure the rice is cold, not freshly made
- wok or large frying pan

1 tbsp **vegetable oil**

2 **scallions**, sliced

1 **green** or **red bell pepper**, cored, seeded, and diced

4–6 cups **cold cooked rice**

2 **eggs**, beaten

2 tbsp **soy sauce**

1 **Heat a wok** or large frying pan over a high heat until very hot. Add the oil and swirl around. Add the scallions and pepper and stir-fry for 2 minutes, or until softened but not colored.

2 **Add the rice** to the wok and stir-fry about 5 minutes until heated through. Push the rice away from the center of the wok, pour in the eggs, and stir until scrambled and set.

3 **Once the eggs** are scrambled, toss all the ingredients together, add the soy sauce, and serve at once.

● **Good with** all stir-fried dishes, such as beef with peppers, or chicken with cashew nuts.

VARIATION

House Special Fried Rice

Add chopped celery, peas, corn, sliced napa cabbage, seeded and sliced mild jalapeño peppers, or any other leftover vegetables, along with cubes or strips of cooked meat or chicken. Add bean sprouts at the last minute or they will lose their crunchiness.

Egg Noodles with Lemongrass and Herbs

Serve these fragrant noodles with simply roasted chicken or pork

- makes 4 side-dish servings
- prep 10 mins • cook 5 mins
- low fat
- wok

12oz (350g) **fresh Asian-style egg noodles** or fresh linguine

2 tbsp plus 2 tsp **vegetable oil**

2 tbsp **soy sauce**

2 tbsp fresh **lemon** juice

pinch of **sugar**

4 **scallions**, thinly sliced

1 stalk **lemongrass**

1in (2.5cm) piece of **fresh ginger**, peeled and shredded

2 tbsp finely chopped **chives**

2 tbsp chopped **cilantro**

1 **Bring a large pot** of salted water to a boil over high heat. Add the noodles and cook according to the package directions. Drain, rinse under cold water, and drain again. Toss with 2 tsp of the oil.

2 **Mix the soy sauce**, lemon juice, and sugar together; set aside. Remove the outer layer of the lemongrass, and cut off the tough top where it meets the tender bottom bulbous end. Cut the tender bulb into very thin slices, then mince finely.

3 **Heat the** remaining 2 tbsp oil in a wok over high heat. Add the scallions, lemongrass, and ginger and stir-fry for 1 minute or until very fragrant. Add the noodles and cook, tossing often, for 2 minutes. Stir in the soy sauce mixture and continue cooking around 2 minutes or until hot. Add the chives and cilantro and toss well. Serve immediately.

LEMON AND SCALLION CURLS

Before juicing the lemon, remove the zest with a vegetable peeler; cut into very fine strips. Trim a scallion, cut into 2in (5cm) lengths and then into fine shreds. Soak the lemon zest and scallion strips in a bowl of iced water for about 1 hour or until they curl into attractive shapes. Drain just before using.

Lemon Rice

This is a wonderful side dish from south India

 makes 4 servings

prep 10 mins • cook 15 mins

3 tbsp **vegetable oil**

1 tsp **yellow mustard seeds**

6 **green cardamom pods**, split

½ tsp **ground turmeric**

2 dried hot **red chiles**, cut lengthwise

½in (2.5cm) piece fresh **ginger**, peeled and finely chopped

1 **garlic clove**, peeled and crushed

10 fresh or dried **curry leaves**

3 tbsp fresh **lemon** juice

4 cups cooked **basmati rice**

½ cup toasted and chopped **cashews**

2 tbsp chopped **cilantro**

1 Heat the oil in a large frying pan over medium heat. Add the mustard seeds, cardamom pods, turmeric, chiles, ginger, garlic, and curry leaves. Cook, stirring often, for 2 minutes, or until very aromatic.

2 Add the lemon juice and cook for 1 minute. Add the rice and cook, stirring occasionally, for about 3 minutes, until the rice is heated and coated in the spices. Transfer to a platter, sprinkle with the cashews and cilantro, and serve hot.

Porcini Polenta

Using dried mushrooms guarantees a rich, earthy flavor, which is ideal for serving alongside the subtle-tasting polenta

makes 4 servings

prep 5 mins, plus 20 mins for soaking • cook 20 mins

For the mushrooms

½oz (15g) **dried porcini mushrooms**

4 tbsp **olive oil**

1 **garlic clove**, chopped

1lb (450g) **cremini mushrooms**, sliced

salt and freshly ground **black pepper**

1 **rosemary sprig**

1 **sage sprig**

4 **thyme sprigs**

4 cups **water**

1 tsp **salt**

1⅓ cups **instant polenta**

● **Prepare ahead** The mushrooms can be cooked up to 4 hours in advance and reheated.

1 Put the dried mushrooms in a heatproof bowl and cover with boiling water. Let stand for 20 minutes. Line a fine sieve with moistened cheesecloth or paper towels. Strain the mushrooms through the sieve, reserving the liquid. Rinse the mushrooms.

2 Meanwhile, heat the oil in a large frying pan over medium heat. Add the garlic and cook, stirring, for 2–3 minutes until golden. Stir in the cremini mushrooms and thyme, and season with salt and pepper. Add the porcini mushrooms and their soaking liquid, the rosemary, and the sage, and cook, stirring occasionally, until the mushrooms are lightly browned and the liquid has almost completely evaporated.

3 Bring 4 cups water and salt to a boil in a large saucepan over a high heat. Slowly whisk in the polenta. Whisk about 3 minutes more, until the polenta is thick and tender. Season with salt and pepper.

4 Divide the polenta between 4 serving bowls. Spoon the mushrooms on top and serve at once.

● **Good with** a mixed green salad as a main course, or a hearty first course. Leftovers can be reheated.

VARIATION

Parmesan Polenta
Omit the mushrooms. When the polenta is tender, stir in 6 tbsp diced butter and ¾ cup freshly grated Parmesan cheese.

Spanish Lentils

This Spanish lentil dish gets its deep flavor from chorizo, bacon, and paprika

 makes 6 servings

🕐 prep 15 mins • cook 1 hr

1lb (450g) **brown lentils**, rinsed and drained

3oz (85g) **smoked chorizo**, thickly sliced

2 **bay leaves**

2 tbsp **olive oil**

2 **garlic cloves**, peeled

1 small slice **rustic bread**

salt

3oz (85g) slab **bacon**, thickly sliced

1 **onion**, finely chopped

1 tbsp **all-purpose flour**

1 tsp **sweet paprika**

½ cup **vegetable stock** or water

● **Prepare ahead** The dish can be refrigerated for up to 1 day and reheated.

1 **Combine the lentils**, chorizo, and bay leaves in a large saucepan with 1 quart (1 liter) water. Bring to a boil, then simmer for 35–40 minutes, or until the lentils are tender.

2 **Meanwhile**, heat 1 tbsp of the oil in a frying pan over medium-low heat. Add the garlic and cook for 2–3 minutes, stirring frequently, or until softened but not browned. Remove from the pan and reserve. Add the bread to the pan and fry over medium heat until lightly browned on both sides. Combine the bread and garlic in a food processor and process to produce coarse crumbs. Season with salt. Set the crumbs aside.

3 **Add the remaining oil** to the frying pan. Add the bacon and cook, stirring occasionally, about 5 minutes, until browned. Add the onion and cook for 3 minutes more, until the onion is tender. Sprinkle with the flour and paprika and stir well. Stir in the stock and bring to a boil. Reduce the heat to low and simmer for 2 minutes. Keep warm.

4 **Drain the lentils** and return to the saucepan. Stir in the garlic crumbs and the bacon mixture. Reheat, adding water if needed to moisten the lentils. Transfer to a serving dish and serve hot.

● **Good with** rustic bread.

Polenta

Smooth and unctuous, soft polenta is the perfect foil for northern Italian dishes with meaty sauces

🍴 makes 4 servings

🕐 prep 10 mins • cook 10 mins

6 cups **chicken** or **vegetable stock**

2 ⅓ cups **instant polenta**

2 tbsp **butter**

¾ cup freshly grated **Parmesan**, plus more to serve

salt and freshly ground **black pepper**

1 **In a large saucepan**, heat the stock over high heat until almost boiling.

2 **Gradually whisk in** the polenta, then continue to whisk about 3 minutes, until the mixture is thick and soft. Add a little more stock or water, if necessary.

3 **Stir in the butter** and Parmesan, and season with salt and pepper. Serve immediately.

● **Leftovers** can be spooned into a shallow dish, spread in an even layer, and set aside to cool and become firm. To serve, cut into slices or wedges, and fry in a little oil until golden on both sides.

Chinese Rice Porridge

Known in Asia as Rice Congee or *Jook*, it is eaten for breakfast in China when the weather is cold

- makes 4 servings
- prep 20 mins, plus standing • cook 1 hr
- low fat

6 dried **shiitake mushrooms**

2 tbsp **vegetable oil**

½in (1 cm) piece fresh **ginger**, peeled and grated

1 **garlic clove**, finely chopped

1 **carrot**, cut into julienne strips

½ tsp **crushed hot red pepper**

1 cup **long-grain rice**

3½ cups **chicken stock**

2 boneless and skinless **chicken breasts**, finely diced

2 **scallions**, white and green parts, chopped

2 tbsp **soy sauce**

freshly ground **black pepper**

2 tbsp chopped **cilantro**

● **Prepare ahead** The porridge can be made up to 2 hours ahead and reheated, adding stock or water if it has become too thick.

1 **Put the mushrooms** in a small bowl and add a cup of boiling water. Let stand about 20 minutes, until softened. Drain, reserving the soaking water. Cut the mushrooms into small pieces using kitchen scissors, discarding the stems.

2 **Heat the oil** in a wok over low heat. Add the carrot, ginger, garlic, and crushed peppers and cook gently for 5 minutes. Stir in the rice and pour in the stock. Measure two-thirds of the mushroom water and strain through a fine sieve into the rice mixture.

3 **Reduce the heat** to medium-low and simmer, stirring often, about 40 minutes. Add the chicken and cook for 10 minutes, or until the rice has broken down to a porridge-like consistency. Stir in the scallions, soy sauce, season with pepper, and sprinkle with the cilantro. Serve hot.

Thai Coconut Rice

Traditional flavorings of coconut and kaffir lime leaves enliven plain rice to create this popular Asian accompaniment

- makes 4–6 servings
- prep 25 mins • cook 40 mins

5 sprigs **cilantro**

2 tbsp **vegetable oil**

2 tbsp **butter**

2 **shallots**, finely chopped

1 fresh **hot red chile**, seeded and chopped

4 tbsp **Thai red curry paste**

2 cups **jasmine rice**

grated zest of 1 **lime**

one 14.5fl oz (411ml) can **coconut milk**

1 tsp **salt**

1 **kaffir lime leaf**, shredded

2 **scallions**, white and green parts, thinly sliced

1 **Pluck** the cilantro leaves off the stalks; finely chop the stalks and reserve the leaves.

2 **Heat the oil** and butter in a large deep frying pan over low heat. Add the shallots and chile and cook for 5 minutes, stirring often, or

until they start to turn golden. Then, stir in the curry paste and cook for another 30 seconds.

3 **Add the rice**, lime zest, and cilantro stalks. Stir for 1 minute, until the rice is well coated. Stir in the coconut milk, 1¾ cups water, and the salt. Bring to a boil, stirring occasionally. Sprinkle in the kaffir leaf and reduce the heat to medium-low. Simmer, uncovered, for 5 minutes.

4 **Stir the rice** and cover. Simmer for 15 minutes, or until the rice is tender. If the liquid has been absorbed but the rice is still not tender, add a little more water. When ready to serve, stir in the scallions and sprinkle with the reserved cilantro leaves. Serve hot.

● **Good with** a Thai red or green curry or soy-marinated roast fish or chicken.

> #### COCONUT MILK
> Coconut milk is readily available in most supermarkets. For a healthier dish, try the low-fat versions.

Rice and Peas

This dish is a staple throughout the Caribbean. Pigeon peas can be found in the Latino section of the market

🍴 makes 4 servings

🕐 prep 10 mins • cook 45 mins

15oz (420g) can **pigeon peas** (gandules) drained and rinsed

one 15fl oz (420ml) can **coconut milk**

1 large **onion**, finely chopped

1 **green bell pepper**, seeded and chopped

salt and freshly ground **black pepper**

¾ cup **basmati** or long-grain rice

cayenne pepper, for garnish

● **Prepare ahead** The dish can be prepared 1 day in advance, cooled, covered with foil, and refrigerated. Bake, covered, in a 350°F (180°C) oven until heated through.

1 Bring the peas, coconut milk, onion, and green pepper to a simmer in a saucepan over low heat and cook for 5 minutes. Season with salt and pepper.

2 Stir in the rice. Cover and simmer for 35 minutes, or until the rice is tender, stirring occasionally. Sprinkle with cayenne pepper and serve hot.

● **Good with** grilled or roasted meat and poultry, and fried fish, as a substantial side dish.

Risotto Balls

Crispy on the outside, and soft and creamy on the inside, these tasty rice balls make an unusual side dish, or can be served as a party nibble with a pesto dipping sauce

🍴 makes 4-6 servings

🕐 prep 15 mins
• cook 20-25 mins

❄ freeze the uncooked rice balls for up to 2 months

1 cup **Arborio rice**

1 **vegetable bouillon** cube

½ cup **Gruyère**

2 tbsp **pesto**

⅓ cup plain dried **bread crumbs**

vegetable oil, for deep-frying

fresh **basil** leaves, for garnish (optional)

● **Prepare ahead** The balls can be refrigerated 1 day in advance.

1 Bring the rice, bouillon, and 3¾ cups water to a boil in a large saucepan over high heat. Reduce the heat and simmer for about 15 minutes, until the rice is just tender.

2 Drain the rice well. Transfer to a bowl, stir in the Gruyère and pesto, and let cool.

3 Using moistened hands, roll the rice into walnut-sized balls. Coat in the bread crumbs.

4 Add enough oil to come halfway up the sides of a heavy frying pan and heat over high heat until the oil is simmering. In batches, fry the rice balls about 3 minutes, or until crisp and golden. Using a slotted spoon, transfer to paper towels to drain. Serve hot.

● **Good with** roast chicken, ham, or pork.

● **Leftovers** can be added to salads or eaten as a snack.

German Potato Dumplings

These light but sustaining dumplings are great for soaking up the delicious gravy from hearty casseroles and spicy goulashes

 makes 4 servings

prep 15 mins, plus cooling
• cook 35 mins

12oz (350g) **baking potatoes**, such as Burbank or russet, peeled and diced

1 large **egg**, beaten

3 tbsp **all-purpose flour**, plus more for dusting

¼ cup **semolina**

½ tsp **caraway seeds**

salt and freshly ground **black pepper**

● **Prepare ahead** You can refrigerate the uncooked dumplings for up to 2 hours .

1 Cook the potatoes in a large saucepan of lightly salted water about 20 minutes, or until tender. Drain well, and return the potatoes to the saucepan. Stir over low heat for 1 minute to evaporated the excess moisture. Mash the potatoes, then let them cool.

2 Transfer the potatoes to a large bowl. Add the egg, flour, semolina, and caraway seeds, and season with salt and pepper. Stir well. The mixture should hold its shape; if it doesn't, add a little more flour.

3 With floured hands, shape the mixture into 12 balls, then roll into sausage shapes. Place in a single layer on a plate. Refrigerate for at least 30 minutes.

4 To cook, bring a large saucepan of water a boil over high heat. Add the dumplings and reduce the heat to medium-low. Simmer for 15 minutes, until the dumplings are floating. Drain and serve hot.

● **Good with** sauerbraten with braised red cabbage.

Couscous with Pine Nuts and Almonds

A tasty alternative to rice; serve hot as a side dish or cold as a salad

 makes 4 servings

prep 15 mins, plus standing

1 cup **couscous**

1 **red bell pepper**, seeded and chopped

½ cup **raisins**

½ cup chopped **dried apricots**

½ **cucumber**, seeded and diced

¼ cup chopped pitted **Kalamata olives**

¼ cup **blanched almonds**, lightly toasted

¼ cup **pine nuts**, lightly toasted

¼ cup **olive oil**

2 tbsp fresh **lemon** juice

1 tbsp chopped **mint**

● **Prepare ahead** The couscous can be prepared several hours ahead and served at room temperature.

1 Put the couscous in a heatproof bowl. Add enough boiling water to cover the couscous by 1in (2.5cm). Let stand for 15 minutes, or until the couscous has absorbed all the water. Fluff up the grains with a fork.

2 Stir in the pepper, raisins, apricots, cucumber, olives, almonds, and pine nuts.

3 Whisk together the oil, lemon juice, and mint. Pour over the couscous and toss. Season with salt and pepper. Serve warm, or let cool and serve at room temperature.

● **Good with** grilled meats, chicken, or fish.

Potato Gnocchi

These light-as-air potato dumplings, served with a simple sage and butter sauce, make a good supper dish

- makes 4 servings
- prep 30 mins • cook 25 mins

1lb 10oz (750g) **baking potatoes**

2 large **eggs**, beaten

1⅓ cups **all-purpose flour**, as needed

For the sauce

10 tbsp **butter**

about 20 **sage** leaves

juice of ½ **lemon**

salt and freshly ground **black pepper**

● **Prepare ahead** The gnocchi can be prepared up to 2 hours before cooking, covered with plastic wrap.

1 Cook the whole, unpeeled potatoes in a pot of boiling water about 25 minutes, or until just tender. Drain and let cool. Peel the potatoes and mash with a potato ricer or rub through a wire sieve.

2 Place the warm mashed potatoes on a work surface. Make a well in the center. Add the eggs and ⅓ cup of the flour into the well. Mix the ingredients, using your hands, adding more flour as needed, to make a soft, but not sticky, dough that can be shaped. Do not add too much flour or the gnocchi will be heavy.

3 Divide the dough into 4 equal portions. Roll each portion of dough on a lightly floured work surface into a rope about ¾in (2cm) thick. Cut into pieces 1¼in (3cm) long. Press each piece lightly with the back of a fork to give the traditional concave shape. Transfer to a floured baking sheet.

4 Bring a large saucepan of lightly salted water to a gentle boil, Add the gnocchi and cook for 2 minutes, or until they float to the surface.

5 Meanwhile, make the sauce. Heat the butter and sage in a frying pan over medium heat until the butter has melted. Add the lemon juice, and salt and pepper to taste.

6 Drain the gnocchi and toss in the sauce. Serve immediately, garnished with sage leaves.

Rice Timbales

Lightly spiced rice can be pressed into ramekins to make an eye-catching side dish

- makes 6 servings
- prep 20 mins • cook 20 mins
- 6 individual ramekins

2 tbsp **olive oil**, plus more for the ramekins

½ **red bell pepper**, seeded and finely diced

2 **shallots**, finely chopped

2 tsp **ground coriander**

1 tsp **ground cumin**

1 tsp **sesame seeds**

½ tsp dried **oregano**

1½ cups **long-grain rice**

3 cups hot **chicken stock**

¼ tsp **salt**

To serve

¼ cup **olive oil**

grated zest and juice of 1 **lemon**

2 tbsp chopped **parsley**

1 Heat the oil in a medium saucepan pan over medium-low heat. Add the red pepper and shallots and cook for 5 minutes. Add the coriander, cumin, sesame seeds, and oregano and cook for 2 minutes. Add the rice and stir well. Add the stock and salt and bring to a boil. Reduce heat to medium-low, cover and cook about 17 minutes, until rice is tender.

2 Heat the olive oil, lemon zest and juice in a saucepan until boiling. Stir in the parsley.

3 Lightly oil the ramekins. Spoon equal amounts of the rice into the ramekins and press firmly with the back of a spoon. Turn out the rice out on to plates and drizzle the hot lemon oil over each. Serve hot.

VARIATION

Vegetarian Timbales

To make the timbales suitable for vegetarians, simply replace the chicken stock with vegetable stock.

Semolina Dumplings

These little dumplings are added to many a Bavarian soup, and you may want to follow suit

🍴 makes 4 servings, in a soup

🕐 prep 20 mins • cook 25 mins

⅔ cup **whole milk**

1 tbsp **butter**

pinch of grated **nutmeg**

⅓ cup plus 1 tbsp **semolina**

1 large **egg**, beaten

salt and freshly ground **black pepper**

meat or **chicken stock**, to serve

● **Prepare ahead** The dumplings can be made several hours in advance, tightly covered with plastic wrap to prevent drying.

1 Bring the milk, butter, and nutmeg to a simmer in a saucepan over medium heat. Remove the pan from the heat. Add the semolina and stir until the mixture forms a dough.

2 Gradually beat in the egg. Season with salt and pepper. If needed, adjust the consistency with a little more semolina or milk to make a soft, but malleable, dough.

3 Bring a pot of stock to a boil over high heat. Using 2 spoons, shape the semolina mixture into small dumplings, and drop them into the stock. Reduce the heat and simmer about 10 minutes, or until the dumplings are firm. Serve hot.

Spiced Orzo with Spinach

Orzo is a tiny soup pasta which looks similar to rice. It makes an ideal side dish for Mediterranean-style dishes

🍴 makes 4–6 servings

🕐 prep 5 mins • cook 25 mins

✓ low fat

8oz (220g) **orzo**

1½ tbsp **olive oil**

1 **onion**, finely chopped

2 **garlic cloves**, finely chopped

1 tsp **ground coriander**

½ tsp **ground cumin**

pinch of **cayenne** (optional)

6oz (175g) **baby spinach** leaves, washed, but not dried

4 tbsp chopped **cilantro** or parsley

salt and freshly ground **black pepper**

● **Prepare ahead** The dish can be refrigerated for up to 1 day, and served cold. If the mixture is too solid, toss with more olive oil.

1 Bring a large pan of salted water to a boil. Add the orzo and cook until tender, according to the package instructions.

2 Meanwhile, heat the olive oil in a large saucepan over medium heat. Add the onion and cook, stirring often, about 3 minutes, until softened. Stir in the garlic, coriander, cumin, and cayenne, if using, and cook for 1 minute more.

3 Stir the spinach (with the water clinging to its leaves from washing) into the saucepan. Cook, stirring often, for 3 minutes, or just until wilted.

4 Drain the orzo well, shaking off any excess water. Add the orzo to the spinach mixture and mix well. Stir in the cilantro and season with salt and pepper. Transfer to a serving bowl. Serve hot or cooled.

VARIATION

Spiced Orzo and Spinach Salad

Make the orzo with spinach, and let cool. Stir in 2 tbsp fresh lemon juice and ¼ cup extra virgin olive oil to taste. Sprinkle with ½ cup crumbled feta cheese.

Cabbage Rolls

These vegetarian cabbage rolls are lighter than the traditional version

  makes 4 servings

prep 45–50 mins
• cook 1 hr

low GI

For the filling

1 tbsp **olive oil**, plus more for the dish

1 **leek**, white part only, finely chopped

4oz (115g) **cremini mushrooms**, minced

1 **celery stalk**, finely chopped

2 cups fresh **whole wheat bread crumbs**

1 large **egg**

2 tbsp chopped **parsley**

1 tbsp fresh **lemon** juice

pinch of **ground coriander**

salt and freshly ground **black pepper**

8 **Savoy cabbage leaves**, stemmed

⅔ cup **vegetable stock**

1 tbsp **olive oil**

1 **onion**, finely chopped

2 **garlic cloves**, minced

2 cups canned **crushed tomatoes**

1 To make the filling, heat the oil in a frying pan over medium-low heat. Add the leek, mushrooms, and celery and cook, stirring often, for about 5 minutes, until softened.

2 Remove from the heat and stir in the bread crumbs, egg, parsley, lemon juice, and ground coriander. Season with salt and pepper.

3 Preheat the oven to 325°F (160°C). Oil a 13 x 9in (33 x 23cm) baking dish. Cook the cabbage leaves in boiling water for 2 minutes, until pliable. Drain and rinse under cold water. Pat dry.

4 Lay each leaf flat and divide the stuffing among the leaves. Roll up each leaf, folding in the sides to enclose the filling in a neat parcel. Place the rolls, seam side down, in the dish. Pour in the stock. Bake for 45–55 minutes, until tender.

5 Meanwhile, heat the oil in a frying pan over medium heat. Add the onion and garlic and cook, stirring occasionally, about 5 minutes, until softened. Stir in the crushed tomatoes. Reduce the heat to medium-low and simmer about 10 minutes, or until lightly thickened. Season with salt and pepper.

6 Using a slotted spoon, serve the cabbage rolls on dinner plates, with the remaining tomato sauce passed on the side.

● **Good with** crusty bread, sautéed potatoes, or brown rice.

VARIATION

German Cabbage Rolls

In place of the mushroom filling, mix together 9oz (250g) ground pork or beef, ½ cup fresh bread crumbs, and 1 egg; season with salt and pepper. Use to stuff the cabbage leaves, and tie up each roll with kitchen twine. Place in a single layer in a flameproof casserole. Add 4oz (115g) chopped bacon, lightly fried, and the tomato sauce, adding water if the sauce doesn't cover the rolls. Simmer, covered, over low heat for about 40 minutes until tender.

Celery Root Timbales

An elegant way of serving an often neglected root vegetable

makes 6 servings

prep 10 mins • cook 35 mins

six 6oz (175ml) ramekins

14oz (400g) **celery root**, pared and diced

7oz (200g) **baking potatoes**, peeled and diced

⅔ cup **heavy cream**

3 large **eggs** plus 1 large **egg yolk**

1 **garlic clove**, peeled

pinch of grated **nutmeg**

salt and freshly ground **black pepper**

1 Preheat the oven to 375°F (190°C). Place the celery root and potatoes in a large saucepan and add enough lightly salted water to cover. Cover the pot and bring to a boil. Reduce the heat to medium and simmer about 10 minutes, or until tender; drain well.

2 Purée the celery root, potato, cream, eggs, yolk, garlic, and nutmeg together in a food processor. Season with salt and pepper.

3 Butter six 6oz (175ml) ramekins. Divide the celery root mixture among the ramekins. Place in a roasting pan and add hot water halfway up the sides of the ramekins. Cover the pan with aluminum foil. Bake for about 25 minutes, or until just firm to the touch. Carefully run a knife around the inside of each ramekin and turn out onto plates.

Chile Tofu Stir-fry

This quick and easy dish takes advantage of tofu's ability to take on other flavors

- makes 4 servings
- prep 10 mins • cook 15 mins
- wok or large frying pan

2 tbsp **vegetable oil**

¾ cup **unsalted cashews**

10oz (300g) **firm tofu**, cut into 1in (2.5cm) cubes

1 **red onion**, thinly sliced

2 **carrots**, thinly sliced

1 **red bell pepper**, seeded and chopped

1 **celery stalk**, chopped

4 **cremini mushrooms**, sliced

6oz (175g) **bean sprouts**

¾ cup **vegetable or** chicken **stock**

2 tbsp **soy sauce**

2 tsp **Asian chile-garlic sauce**

1 tsp **cornstarch**

1 **Heat the oil** in a wok over high heat. Add the cashews and stir-fry for about 30 seconds or until lightly browned. Using a slotted spoon, transfer to paper towels.

2 **Add the tofu** and stir-fry about 2 minutes, or until golden. Transfer to the paper towels. Add the onion and carrots and stir-fry for 2 minutes, until crisp-tender; add the red pepper, celery, and mushrooms and stir-fry for 3 minutes more. Finally add the bean sprouts and stir-fry for 2 minutes, until hot. Always keep the heat under the wok high so that the vegetables sear quickly without overcooking.

3 **Meanwhile**, mix the stock, soy sauce, and chile sauce in a small bowl. Add the cornstarch, and stir to dissolve. Return the cashews and tofu to the wok and add the stock mixture. Stir until the sauce is bubbling and lightly thickened. Serve hot.

Roasted Beet and Feta Salad

Deep magenta with accents of white and green, serve this salad as a side dish or a first course

- makes 4 servings
- prep 10 mins • cook 1–1¼ hrs

6 small **beets**, scrubbed but unpeeled

2 tbsp **olive oil**

salt and freshly ground **black pepper**

1 **red onion**, thinly sliced

4oz (115g) **arugula**

4oz (115g) **feta cheese**, cubed

2 tbsp chopped **mint**

For the dressing

1 tbsp **balsamic vinegar**

1 tbsp **Dijon mustard**

1 tsp **honey**

3 tbsp **olive oil**

● **Prepare ahead** The roasted beets and the dressing can be refrigerated separately for up to 1 day before combining.

1 **Preheat the oven** to 400°F (200°C). Place the beets in a roasting pan. Add ½ cup water and drizzle with the oil. Season with salt and pepper. Cover the pan with aluminum foil. Roast about 1¾ hrs, or until tender.

2 **Uncover the beets** and let cool. Peel and dice the beets.

3 **Whisk the vinegar**, mustard, and honey together in a small bowl, then whisk in the oil. Combine the beets, onions, and dressing in a bowl and toss. Sprinkle the arugula, feta, and mint over the top. Toss gently, and season with salt and pepper. Serve immediately.

● **Good with** grilled lamb or steak, or on its own, as a light lunch.

VARIATION

Roasted Beet and Goat Cheese Salad

Substitute a firm, crumbly goat cheese for the feta. Scatter the salad with ¼ cup pomegranate seeds or toasted pine nuts.

Chiles en Nogada

Heart-shaped green poblano chiles are traditionally used for this recipe, but substitute ordinary green peppers if you cannot find them

 makes 4 servings

 prep 30 mins, plus cooling • cook 30 mins

 freeze the stuffed peppers, without the sauce and garnishes, for up to 3 months

9oz (250g) smoked tofu

1 tbsp fresh lime juice

salt and freshly ground black pepper

1 tbsp vegetable oil

1 onion, finely chopped

1 red bell pepper, seeded and chopped

2 jalapeño chiles, seeded and finely chopped

1 garlic clove, minced

1 cup vegetable stock

¼ cup tomato paste

8 pitted green olives, chopped

2 tbsp raisins

4 poblano or green peppers

For the sauce

½ cup ground walnuts or almonds

⅔ cup sour cream

½ cup cream cheese

To serve

¼ head iceberg lettuce, shredded

¼ cup pomegranate seeds

1 tbsp chopped cilantro

● **Prepare ahead** The peppers can be stuffed and refrigerated up to 1 day ahead.

1 **To make the filling**, mix together the smoked tofu and lime juice and season with salt and pepper. Heat the oil in a medium frying pan over medium-low heat. Add the onion, red pepper, chiles, and garlic and cook, stirring often, until softened.

2 **Stir in the tofu** and increase the heat to high. Cook, breaking up the pieces with a spoon, stirring frequently, about 6 minutes, until browned. Add the stock, tomato paste, olives, and raisins. Simmer over low heat, stirring occasionally, for about 20 minutes, or until the mixture is quite dry. Let cool.

3 **Preheat the broiler**. Line a broiler pan with aluminum foil. Broil the poblanos, turning occasionally, until the skins are blackened on all sides. Transfer to a plate and let stand until cool enough to handle. Discard the blackened skin from the peppers, but keep the stems intact. Cut a slit in the side of each pepper and remove the seeds and ribs. Fill each with equal amounts of the beef mixture.

4 **To make the sauce**, purée the ground walnuts, sour cream, and cream cheese in a blender.

5 **Line a serving platter** with the shredded lettuce and arrange the peppers on top. Top each with some of the sauce, and sprinkle with the pomegranate seeds and cilantro. Serve at room temperature.

POMEGRANATES

Pomegranate seeds can be frozen for up to 3 months. Thaw at room temperature before using.

Baked Stuffed Tomatoes

Large and meaty beefsteak tomatoes are perfect for filling

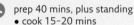 makes 4 servings

prep 40 mins, plus standing • cook 15–20 mins

4 large ripe beefsteak tomatoes

salt and freshly ground black pepper

1 tbsp olive oil

1 garlic clove, crushed

2 anchovy fillets, minced

¼ cup fresh bread crumbs

¼ cup mascarpone cheese

5oz (150g) ricotta or goat cheese

2 tbsp grated Parmesan cheese

2 tbsp finely chopped basil

1 **Cut each tomato** in half horizontally. Scoop out the insides with a spoon, sprinkle the halves with salt, and let drain.

2 **Preheat the oven** to 425°F (220°C). Heat the oil in a skillet over medium heat. Add the garlic and anchovies and stir for 30 seconds. Stir in the bread crumbs and cook until they are well coated in oil, about 2 minutes. Transfer to a plate.

3 **Mix together** the three cheeses with the basil. Season with the pepper. Fill each tomato with the cheese mixture and top with the garlic crumbs.

4 **Bake** in an oiled baking dish about 20 minutes, or until the tops are golden. Serve hot or warm.

Vegetable Kebabs

Cook these under the broiler or on a barbecue

- 🍴 makes 4 servings
- 🕐 prep 15 mins • cook 15 mins
- ❗ soak wooden skewers in cold water for 30 minutes before use to prevent burning
- 🔲 wooden or metal skewers

1 medium **zucchini**

1 red **bell pepper**, seeded

1 green **bell pepper**, seeded

1 red **onion**

8 **cherry tomatoes**

8 **button mushrooms**

⅓ cup **olive oil**

1 **garlic clove**, minced

½ tsp **dried oregano**

pinch of **crushed hot red pepper**

● **Prepare ahead** Steps 1 and 2 can be completed several hours in advance.

1 **Trim the zucchini** and cut into 8 chunks. Cut the peppers into 1in (2.5cm) pieces. Peel the onion, and cut into wedges leaving the root end intact so that the wedges do not fall apart.

2 **Thread the zucchini**, peppers, onion, tomatoes, and mushrooms in equal amounts onto 4 large or 8 small skewers. Whisk the oil, garlic, oregano, and hot pepper together in a small bowl with a fork.

3 **Position a broiler rack** 6in (15cm) from the source of heat and preheat the broiler. Place the kebabs on the broiler pan and brush generously with the garlic oil. Broil, turning often and brushing with the remaining oil, 10 to 15 minutes, until the vegetables are just tender. Serve hot or at room temperature, with any remaining oil drizzled over the kebabs.

● **Good with** a leafy salad for a light vegetarian lunch, or alongside grilled meat or fish.

VARIATION

Pesto Vegetable Kebabs

Omit the garlic and oregano. Stir 1 tbsp prepared pesto into the oil.

Parmesan Cheese and Walnut Tart

This nutty pastry works brilliantly with the creamy cheese and potato filling and makes a delicate starter or main course

- 🍴 makes 6-8 servings
- 🕐 prep 25 mins, plus chilling • cook 45 mins
- 🔲 9 x 9in (23 x 23cm) or 14 x 4½in (35 x 11cm) rectangular pan with removable bottom
- ❄ freeze for up to 3 months

1⅔ cups **all-purpose flour**, plus extra for dusting

⅓ cup **walnuts**

9 tbsp **butter**, diced and chilled

1 cup **heavy cream**

½ cup **mashed potato**

2 large **eggs**, plus 2 large **egg yolks**

1¼ cups grated **Parmesan cheese**

freshly ground **black pepper**

pinch of **nutmeg**

1 tsp chopped **rosemary**, oregano, or thyme

● **Prepare ahead** The baked tart can be refrigerated for up to 2 days.

1 **Preheat the oven** to 400°F (200°C). Pulse the flour and walnuts together in a food processor until the nuts are very finely ground. Add the butter and pulse until it resembles coarse bread crumbs. Sprinkle in 4 tbsp of cold water and pulse until it clumps together, adding more water if needed.

2 **Roll the pastry** on a floured surface into a ⅛in (3mm) thick round. Line the tart pan with the dough, trimming any excess. Prick the dough with a fork and refrigerate for 30 minutes.

3 **Line the pan** with parchment paper and baking beans. Bake for 10 minutes. Remove the paper and beans and bake for 10 minutes more until golden brown. Reduce the oven temperature to 350°F (180°C).

4 **Whisk the cream**, potato, eggs, and egg yolks together well. Add the cheese and season with the pepper and nutmeg. Pour into the pastry shell and sprinkle with the rosemary. Bake for 25 minutes, until set.

5 **Let cool** for 10 minutes, then carefully remove the sides of the pan. Slice the tart and serve warm.

● **Good with** mixed greens and tomato salad.

Vegetable Curry

In Indian cooking, cardamom, cloves, coriander, and cumin seeds are all considered "warming spices" that heat the body from within, making this an excellent winter dish

- makes 4-6 servings
- prep 20 mins • cook 35-45 mins
- ❄ freeze for up to 3 months

¼ cup vegetable oil

10oz (300g) red-skinned potatoes, diced

5 green cardamom pods, crushed

3 whole cloves

1 cinnamon stick, broken in half

2 tsp cumin seeds

1 onion, finely chopped

2 tsp peeled and grated fresh ginger

2 large garlic cloves, crushed

1½ tsp ground turmeric

1 tsp ground coriander

salt and freshly ground black pepper

one 14.5oz (411g) can chopped tomatoes

pinch of sugar

2 carrots, diced

2 fresh hot green chiles, seeded (optional) and sliced into thin rounds

1 cup sliced Savoy or green cabbage

1 cup cauliflower florets

1 cup thawed frozen peas

2 tbsp chopped cilantro

toasted sliced almonds, to garnish

● **Prepare ahead** The curry can be made 1 day ahead, covered and refrigerated. Reheat over low heat, adding water if the sauce is too thick.

1 Heat the oil in a large deep frying pan over high heat. Add the potatoes and cook, stirring often, for 5 minutes, or until golden brown. Using a slotted spoon, transfer to paper towels to drain.

2 Reduce the heat to medium. Add the cardamom pods, cloves, cinnamon, and cumin seeds and stir until the spices are very fragrant. Add the onion and cook, stirring often, for about 5 minutes, or until softened. Add the ginger, garlic, turmeric, and coriander, and season with salt and pepper. Stir for 1 minute.

3 Stir in the tomatoes with their juices and the sugar. Return the potatoes to the pan, add the carrots, chiles, and 1 cup of water, and bring to a boil, stirring often. Reduce the heat to low. Simmer, stirring occasionally, for 15 minutes, or until the carrots are just tender, adding a little water if needed.

4 Stir in the cabbage, cauliflower, and peas. Return the heat to medium and simmer for about 10 minutes, or until the vegetables are tender. Stir in the cilantro and season again. Remove and discard the cardamom pods and cloves. Transfer to a serving bowl, sprinkle with almonds, and serve hot.

● **Good with** lots of basmati rice or naan bread.

VARIATION

Paneer and Vegetable Curry

Heat a large frying pan over high heat. Add a thin layer of vegetable oil. When the oil is shimmering hot, add bite-sized cubes of paneer and fry until golden brown on all sides. Drain on paper towels. Stir into the curry just before serving, taking care not to break the paneer.

Stuffed Red Peppers

Use rice and herbs as the stuffing in place of meat

- makes 4 servings
- prep 15 mins • cook 1¼ hrs

4 red bell peppers

½ cup basmati rice

1 tbsp chopped parsley

1 tbsp chopped chives

1 tsp chopped thyme

1 tbsp fresh lemon juice

salt and freshly ground black pepper

olive oil, for drizzling

⅔ cup vegetable stock or water

freshly grated Parmesan, for serving

1 Cut the top off each pepper. Scoop out the seeds. Boil the rice in salted water for about 20 minutes, or until tender, then drain. Stir the herbs and lemon juice into the rice and season with salt and pepper.

2 Preheat the oven 325°F (160°C). Bring a large saucepan of salted water to a boil. Add the peppers, and cook for 2-3 minutes. Drain well and stand the peppers in an oiled baking dish.

3 Fill each pepper with the rice mixture. Place the tops on and drizzle with oil. Pour the stock into the dish. Cover with foil, and bake for 1 hour, or until tender. Serve hot, with the cheese on the side.

Potato and Fennel Pancakes with Mushrooms

Combine oyster mushrooms with the creminis, if you wish

makes 4 servings

prep 15 mins • cook 1 hr

3 baking potatoes

2 tbsp **butter**

4 tbsp **olive oil**

1 **onion**, chopped

1 **fennel bulb**, trimmed and finely diced

2 large **eggs**

2 tbsp **all-purpose flour**

pinch of freshly grated **nutmeg**

salt and freshly ground **black pepper**

8oz (225g) **cremini mushrooms**

1 **garlic clove**, chopped

2 tbsp chopped **thyme**

1 tsp fresh **lemon** juice

Parmesan cheese shavings, to garnish

4 tbsp **crème fraîche**, to serve

1 Place the potatoes in a large saucepan of salted water and cover. Bring to a boil, then simmer for 30 minutes, until just tender. Drain, cool, and peel. Shred the potatoes into a bowl.

2 Heat the butter in a frying pan over medium heat. Add the onion and fennel and cook until tender, about 10 minutes. Transfer to a bowl. Add the potatoes, eggs, flour, and nutmeg, and season with salt and pepper. Mix well.

3 Preheat the oven to 200°F (95°C). Heat 3 tbsp of oil in a large nonstick frying pan over medium-high heat. In batches, add about ¼ cup of the potato mixture for each pancake, and flatten with a spatula. Cook, turning once, about 7 minutes, until golden. Keep warm in the oven while making the remaining pancakes.

4 Heat the remaining oil in the frying pan over medium-high heat. Add the mushrooms and garlic and cook about 5 minutes until the mushrooms are browned. Stir in the thyme and lemon juice, and season with salt and pepper.

5 Serve the pancakes, topped with the mushrooms, Parmesan shavings, and a dollop of crème fraîche.

⬤ **Good with** a green salad.

Tofu and Mushroom Stroganoff

This recipe gives the traditional stroganoff a tasty vegetarian twist by substituting tofu chunks for the meat

makes 4 servings

prep 15 mins • cook 20 mins

2 tbsp **vegetable oil**

12oz (350g) firm **tofu**, cut into strips

1 **red onion**, thinly sliced

2 **red bell peppers**, seeded and sliced

9oz (250g) **mixed mushrooms**, quartered or sliced

2 **garlic cloves**, minced

⅔ cup **vegetable stock**

2 tbsp **smooth peanut butter**

2 tbsp **tomato paste**

2 tsp **cornstarch**

1 cup **crème fraîche** or sour cream

salt and freshly ground **black pepper**

2 tbsp finely chopped **chives**

boiled **rice**, to serve

1 Heat 1 tbsp of the oil in a large frying pan or wok over medium-high heat. Stir-fry the tofu until golden. Transfer to a plate.

2 Add the remaining 1 tbsp oil to the pan and reduce the heat to medium. Add the onions, peppers, and mushrooms and cook, stirring often, about 5 minutes, or until softened. Stir in the garlic and cook 1 minute more.

3 Stir in the stock, peanut butter, and tomato paste. Return the tofu to the pan and bring to a simmer. Cook to blend the flavors, about 3 minutes. Dissolve the cornstarch in 2 tbsp cold water and stir into the simmering liquid. Cook about 1 minute, until thickened.

4 Stir in the crème fraîche and season with salt and pepper. Sprinkle with chives and serve with hot, with boiled rice.

⌐ **USING SOUR CREAM** ¬

If using sour cream instead of crème fraîche, do not let the sauce boil.

Olive, Thyme, and Onion Tart

As the pastry shell is not prebaked, this savory tart is easier to prepare than most

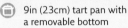

- makes 6 servings
- prep 40 mins • cook 30 mins
- 9in (23cm) tart pan with a removable bottom

For the pastry

8 tbsp butter

3 tbsp milk

1¼ cup all-purpose flour

1 tsp baking powder

¼ tsp salt

For the filling

3 tbsp olive oil

3 onions, finely sliced

2 tbsp chopped thyme

1 tsp sugar

salt and freshly ground black pepper

1 cup heavy cream

3 large eggs, beaten

¼ cup freshly grated Parmesan

2 tbsp tapenade

● **Prepare ahead** The pastry shell can be prepared up to 1 day ahead.

1 **To make the pastry**, melt the butter in the milk in a small saucepan over low heat. Stir the flour, baking powder, and salt together. Add to the saucepan and stir until the dough forms a ball. Remove from the heat and cool. Press firmly and evenly into a 9in (23cm) tart pan. Chill for 30 minutes.

2 **Preheat the oven** to 375°F (190°C). Heat the oil in a frying pan over high heat. Add the onion and cook, stirring often, for about 5 minutes. Add the thyme and sugar, and season with salt and pepper. Reduce the heat to low and cook gently, stirring occasionally, for about 30 minutes, or until onions are very soft and slightly caramelized. Meanwhile, whisk the cream, eggs, and Parmesan together.

3 **Place the tart pan** on a baking sheet. Spread the tapenade over the pastry bottom. Spread the onions on top of the tapenade and carefully pour in the cream mixture. Bake for 30 minutes, or until the filling is set and browned. Let cool on a wire cake rack. Remove the sides of the pan, slice, and serve warm or cool to room temperature.

Stuffed Eggplants

Turkish legend says these eggplants once made a holy man faint, so they are called *imanbayildi* ("the holy man swooned")

- makes 4 servings
- prep 20 mins, plus cooling • cook 1 hr 10 mins
- low GI
- freeze for up to 1 month

4 small eggplants

6 tbsp olive oil

2 large onions, finely sliced

3 garlic cloves, minced

1 tbsp ground coriander

1 tbsp ground cumin

1 tsp ground turmeric

½ tsp ground cardamom

two 14.5oz (411g) cans chopped tomatoes

½ cup golden raisins

2 tbsp chopped cilantro

1 tbsp chopped mint

1 tbsp chopped parsley

● **Prepare ahead** The stuffed eggplants should be refrigerated for at least 1 day to let the flavors develop.

1 **Preheat the oven** to 350°F (180°C). Cut the eggplants in half lengthwise and score the flesh of each in a crosshatch pattern with a sharp knife.

2 **Brush the flesh** with 4 tbsp of the oil. Place, cut sides up, in a roasting pan. Bake in the oven for 30–35 minutes, or until tender.

3 **Let the eggplants** cool. Scoop out and reserve the flesh, leaving a ¼in (6mm) shell, being careful not to split the skins. Place on a serving platter.

4 **Heat the remaining** 2 tbsp of the oil in a large, heavy-bottomed saucepan over medium heat. Add the onion and garlic and cook, stirring occasionally, about 5 minutes until softened. Add the coriander, cumin, turmeric, and cardamom and stir about 1 minute, until fragrant.

5 **Stir in the tomatoes** and their juices and bring to a boil. Reduce the heat and simmer for about 30 minutes, stirring occasionally, until reduced and thickened. Stir in the reserved eggplant flesh and raisins and cook for 10 minutes more. Let cool, then stir in the cilantro, mint, and parsley.

6 **Spoon the mixture** into the eggplant shells, and refrigerate for at least 1 day before serving.

● **Good with** an herb salad and Greek-style yogurt.

Vegetable Biryani

A satisfying dish that both vegetarians and meat-eaters will enjoy

 makes 4 servings

prep 30 mins • cook 45 mins

low fat

1 ¾ cups basmati rice

1 large carrot, sliced

2 boiling potatoes, peeled and cut into small dice

½ cauliflower, cut into small florets

3 tbsp vegetable oil

1 red onion, chopped

1 red bell pepper, seeded and chopped

1 green bell pepper, seeded and chopped

1 zucchini, chopped

⅔ cup frozen peas

2 tsp ground coriander

2 tsp curry powder

1 tsp ground turmeric

1 tsp chile powder

1 tsp cumin seeds

⅔ cup vegetable stock

½ cup cashew nuts, lightly toasted

1 **Bring a large saucepan** of water to a boil over high heat. Add the rice and cook until just tender, about 15 minutes. Drain well.

2 **Cook the carrot** and potatoes in another saucepan of salted boiling water until half-done, about 5 minutes. Add the cauliflower and cook about 5 minutes more, until all of the vegetables are tender. Drain.

3 **Heat the oil** in a large frying pan over medium heat. Add the onion and cook, stirring often, about 5 minutes, or until softened. Add the red and green peppers and the zucchini and cook, stirring often, until crisp-tender, about 5 minutes.

4 **Stir the reserved** vegetables and peas into the frying pan. Add the coriander, curry powder, turmeric, chile powder, and cumin. Cook for 1 minute, stirring often, until the spices are very fragrant.

5 **Meanwhile**, preheat the oven to 350°F (180°C). Spread half the rice into a baking dish, top with the vegetable mixture, and then the remaining rice. Cover with aluminum foil. Bake for 30 minutes, or until hot. Sprinkle with cashews and serve.

Vegetable Moussaka

Lentils replace the lamb, and yogurt is a light alternative to béchamel sauce, in this vegetarian version of a Greek favorite

 makes 4–6 servings

prep 20 mins • cook 1½ hrs

2 medium eggplants, about 1lb 8oz (70g), cut into ½in (13mm) slices

2 zucchini, cut into ½in (13mm) slices

2 onions, cut into ½in (13mm) half-moons

2 red bell peppers, seeded and cut into ½in (13mm) wide strips

4 tbsp olive oil

salt and freshly ground black pepper

2 garlic cloves, chopped

1 tbsp chopped thyme

one 14.5oz (411g) can chopped tomatoes

one 15oz (420g) can lentils, drained and rinsed

2 tbsp chopped parsley

1 ¼ cups Greek-style yogurt

2 large eggs, lightly beaten

pinch of paprika

3oz (85g) feta cheese, crumbled

2 tbsp sesame seeds

1 **Preheat the oven** to 425°F (220°C). Toss the eggplant, zucchini, onions, and red peppers in a roasting pan. Drizzle with the oil and toss. Season with salt and pepper.

2 **Roast for 10 minutes**. Stir in the garlic and thyme. Continue roasting for 30–35 minutes, or until the vegetables are tender. Reduce the temperature to 350°F (180°C).

3 **Stir the tomatoes** with their juices, the lentils, and the parsley into the roasted vegetables and season with salt and pepper as needed. Transfer the vegetables to a 9in (23cm) square baking dish.

4 **Beat the yogurt**, eggs, and paprika together and season lightly with salt and pepper (keeping in mind that the feta cheese is very salty). Spread over the vegetables and sprinkle with the feta. Place on a baking sheet and bake for 40 minutes. Sprinkle with the sesame seeds and bake for 10 minutes more, or until the top is golden brown. Let stand 5 minutes, then serve hot (or cool and serve at room temperature).

● **Good with** a mixed green salad and crusty rustic bread.

Vegetable Tempura

Making the batter with all-purpose flour and iced water helps to guarantee a delicate, light finish

- makes 4 servings
- prep 10–20 mins • cook 10 mins
- large, deep saucepan or deep-fat fryer, deep-frying thermometer

For the dipping sauce

2 tbsp sake

2 tbsp soy sauce

2 tbsp sugar

vegetable oil, for deep-frying

1⅓ cups all-purpose flour

2 cups ice-cold water

1 large egg yolk

selection of fresh vegetables, such as broccoli, carrots, and green beans, trimmed and thinly sliced, or chopped, as required

strips of scallion, to garnish

● **Prepare ahead** The dipping sauce can be made up to 2 days in advance and stored in the refrigerator, covered, until required.

1 To make the dipping sauce, put the sake, soy sauce, sugar, and 2 tbsp water in a small bowl, stir together, then set aside.

2 Pour in oil to a depth of 3in (7.5cm) in a heavy-bottomed saucepan. Heat over high heat to 375°F (190°C). Meanwhile, lightly whisk together the flour, cold water, and egg yolk in a bowl. The batter should remain lumpy, which is what makes the tempura light.

3 Preheat the oven to 200°F (100°C). Working in batches, dip the vegetable pieces into the batter, letting any excess batter drip back into the bowl. Carefully add the battered vegetables to the hot oil and deep-fry for 1–2 minutes on each side, or until golden brown. Use a slotted spoon to remove them from the pan and drain well on paper towels. Keep warm in the oven while frying the remaining vegetables.

4 Serve immediately with small bowls of the dipping sauce for each diner.

Eggplant Parmigiana

This is one of Italy's most popular dishes and a great choice for vegetarians

- makes 4 servings
- prep 40 mins • cook 30 mins
- shallow, ovenproof serving dish
- can be assembled in an ovenproof dish and frozen for up to 3 month. Bake as in step 4

½ cup all-purpose flour

2 large eggs

salt and freshly ground black pepper

2 large eggplants, cut lengthwise into ½ in slices

¼ cup olive oil, plus more as needed

2 cups tomato sauce

10oz (300g) mozzarella, drained and sliced

½ cup grated Parmesan

⅓ cup chopped basil leaves

● **Prepare ahead** Steps 1 and 2 can be done a day in advance. Or, the entire dish can be assembled a day in advance and baked just before serving.

1 Preheat the oven to 325°F (160°C). Spread the flour on a plate. Beat the eggs in a shallow bowl and season with salt and pepper. One at a time, dredge each eggplant slice in the flour, shaking off the excess, then dip it in the eggs and let the excess drip back into the bowl. Repeat with the remaining slices.

2 Heat the oil in a large skillet over a medium heat. Working in batches, if necessary, fry the eggplant slices for about 5 minutes on each side, or until golden. Drain well on paper towels.

3 Layer the tomato sauce, eggplant slices, mozzarella, Parmesan, and basil leaves in a shallow casserole dish, seasoning each layer with salt and pepper, and finishing with a layer of tomato sauce and the cheeses.

4 Place the dish on a baking sheet. Bake for 30 minutes, or until the sauce is bubbling and the cheese has melted. Serve hot.

● **Good with** a simple salad as a main meal.

VARIATION

Zucchini Parmigiana

Substitute 6–8 zucchini, thickly sliced lengthwise, for the eggplants.

Leek and Cheese Tart

Also known in France as *flamiche*, this savory puff pastry tart can be served for brunch, lunch, or supper

- makes 6 servings
- prep 30 mins • cook 45 mins
- freeze for up to 1 month

3 tbsp **butter**

2 large **leeks**, white and pale green parts only, halved lengthwise, cleaned, and thinly sliced

6oz (180g) **cream cheese**, at room temperature

¼ cup freshly grated **Parmesan**

¼ cup **heavy cream**

2 tbsp finely chopped **chives**

large pinch of freshly grated **nutmeg**

salt and freshly ground **black pepper**

one 17.3oz (484g) box thawed frozen **puff pastry**

1 **egg yolk**, beaten

● **Prepare ahead** The baked tart can be made up to 2 days in advance, covered in plastic wrap, and refrigerated.

1 Preheat the oven to 400°F (200°C). Line a large baking sheet with parchment paper.

2 Melt the butter in a medium frying pan over medium-low heat. Add the leeks, cover, and cook, stirring occasionally, for 15 minutes or until tender. Cool.

3 Mix the cream cheese, Parmesan, cream, chives, and nutmeg together in a bowl. Stir into the leeks and season with salt and pepper.

4 On a lightly floured work surface, roll 1 pastry sheet into a 12 x 9in (30 x 20cm) rectangle, then trim 1in (2.5cm) from the short side. Place on the lined baking sheet. Spread the filling over the pasty, leaving a ¾in (2cm) border. Brush the border with the beaten yolk. Roll and trim the remaining pastry to the same size. Center over the filling, and seal the edges with a fork. Refrigerate for 10 minutes. Brush the top with the egg yolk. Using the tip of a knife, pierce a few slits in the center of the tart. Score the top in a criss-cross pattern. Bake for 30 minutes, until golden brown. Let cool for 10 minutes, then slice and serve.

● **Good with** mixed greens or a tomato and onion salad.

Squash and Gorgonzola Tart

This works well with either creamy Gorgonzola *dolce*, or the firmer, sharper piccante variety

- makes 6 servings
- prep 25 mins, plus chilling • cook 1 hr 30 mins
- 8in (20cm) tart pan, parchment paper; baking beans
- freeze the unbaked pastry shell for up to 1 month

1½ cups **all-purpose flour**

8 tbsp cold **butter**, diced

salt

4 tbsp **iced water**, as needed

1lb (450g) **butternut squash**, peeled and seeds removed

olive oil, as needed

14oz (400g) **baby spinach**

2 large **eggs**, plus 1 large **egg yolk**

1¼ cups **heavy cream**

⅛ cup freshly grated **Parmesan**

½ tsp freshly grated **nutmeg**

freshly ground **black pepper**

4oz (115g) **Gorgonzola**, crumbled

1 For the dough, pulse the flour, butter, and ¼ tsp salt in a food processor until the mixture resembles coarse bread crumbs. Add the water and pulse until the dough comes together, adding more water if needed. Shape into a thick disk and wrap in plastic wrap. Refrigerate for 30 minutes. Roll out into a round about ⅛in (3mm) thick. Use the dough to line an 8in (20cm) fluted tart pan with a removable bottom. Chill for 30 minutes.

2 Preheat the oven to 400°F (200°C). Prick the bottom of the pastry shell. Line it with parchment paper and fill with baking beans. Bake about 15 minutes, until the dough looks set. Lift off the parchment paper and beans. Bake for 10 minutes more, until beginning to brown. Transfer to a wire rack.

3 Slice the squash into thick slices and spread on a baking sheet. Toss with 1 tbsp oil. Bake for 30 minutes, or until tender. Meanwhile, cook the spinach and 2 tbsp olive oil in a covered saucepan for about 4 minutes, until wilted. Drain and let cool. Whisk the eggs, egg yolk, cream, Parmesan, and nutmeg together and season to taste with salt and pepper.

4 Squeeze the spinach dry. Spread it in the pastry shell, and top with the squash and Gorgonzola. Pour in the custard. Bake for about 30 minutes, or until the custard is set. Let cool for 10 minutes. Remove the sides of the pan and serve hot.

Potatoes

Potatoes are one of the most versatile ingredients in the kitchen. They are cheap to buy, can be cooked in a variety of ways, and are always popular. The selection of main-crop and new potatoes provides plenty of variety throughout the year.

Choosing Potatoes

Potatoes come in many shapes, sizes, and colors, but most are either floury or waxy, both of which are best suited to different cooking techniques. Waxy potatoes hold their shape when cooked, making them ideal for boiling for salads or serving hot with butter and salt and pepper. Cooking potatoes become soft and fluffy, so they are great for baking, frying, and mashing. Always buy firm potatoes with smooth skins and without green patches, mold, or sprouts.

Storing

Potatoes should be stored in a cool, dark place, ideally not the refrigerator, because if they are exposed to light they develop green patches, which can be poisonous. Remove potatoes from plastic bags that can cause mold to develop.

ALL-AROUND POTATOES

Yukon Gold
With a creamy texture and buttery flavor, this potato makes excellent gratins. It is also popular with dieters because it contains less carbohydrates than most potatoes.

Sweet Potato or Yam
These come with white or orange flesh and have a rich, sweet flavor. Sweet potatoes are not a true potato, but can be cooked like any other all-around potato.

Red-skinned
Easily identified because of its skin color, this potato has a texture that falls between floury and waxy. It can be baked, boiled, fried, and mashed.

Mayan Gold
The buttery yellow flesh is as intense as the flavor of this quick-cooking potato. Especially good roasted and fried.

BAKING POTATOES

King Edward
This popular main-crop potato makes great mashed potatoes, French fries, and roast potatoes.

Maris Piper
A favorite with a soft, creamy flesh that makes great French fries and mashed potatoes.

Arran Victory
Named to celebrate the end of WW1, this potato has a distinctive purple-blue skin and a delicious white flesh. It is best mashed and roasted.

WAXY POTATOES

Fingerling
A relatively recent hybrid of new potatoes, fingerling is recognized by its long, knobby thumb shape. It has a rich flavor and smooth texture.

Charlotte
This small, oblong waxy potato is favored for its fine flavor. Best boiled or sliced and pan-fried, it also makes excellent salads.

Jersey Royal
A new potato, with a short season from April to June, this is especially valued for its flavor. Good for boiling and serving in salads.

Nicola
This small waxy potato is oval with a smooth, creamy skin and pale yellow flesh. It is best simply boiled.

Vales Emerald
A cross between Maris Piper and Charlotte, it is a flavorful, small, round potato. Serve it scrubbed and boiled with plenty of butter, or chopped in salads.

Scrub

Many recipes call for unpeeled potatoes, in which case they need to be scrubbed first. Wash them in water, lightly rubbing with a small vegetable brush to remove any dirt. Be very careful not to tear the skin.

Peel

Potatoes can be peeled before or after cooking; if cooked first, leave them until cool enough to handle before peeling. Hold the potato firmly in 1 hand and use a vegetable peeler or paring knife to cut off the skin in long strips.

Slice

Firmly hold the potato on a cutting board with one hand and hold a chef's knife in your other hand. Cut downward into slices as thick or thin as required. Cut slices to the same thickness so they cook evenly.

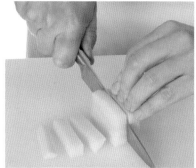

Chop

The first step to good, chunky french fries is chopping large, floury potatoes into slices ½in (1cm) thick. Stack several slices on top of each other and then cut into sticks about 3in (7.5cm) long.

Dice

Dices are equal-sized cubes. Stack slices (see above) on top of each other and cut lengthwise to the desired thickness. Turn the stack 45 degrees and cut crosswise into equal-sized cubes.

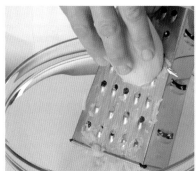

Grate

Both cooked and uncooked potatoes can be grated, most frequently for pan-frying like when making potato pancakes. Rub the potatoes downward over the coarse holes on a grater into a bowl.

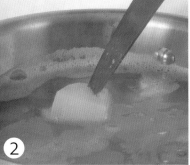

Boil

1 Potatoes can be boiled peeled or unpeeled. Cut the potatoes into equal-sized pieces and put them into a pan with lightly salted cold water to cover. Cover the pan tightly, place over high heat, and bring the water to a boil.

2 As soon as the water boils, reduce the heat slightly, uncover the pan, and leave the potatoes to gently boil until they offer no resistance when pierced with the tip of a sharp knife.

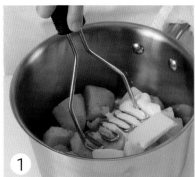

Mash

1 Boil the potatoes (see above) until they are tender. Drain them in a colander, shaking off any excess water. Return the potatoes to the pan. Add butter, milk, and salt, pepper, and nutmeg to taste. Re-cover the pan and let stand for 5 minutes.

2 Using a potato masher, mash the potatoes until they are smooth and fluffy. Adjust the seasoning and add extra butter and milk, if desired. Keep hot until ready to serve.

Potatoes

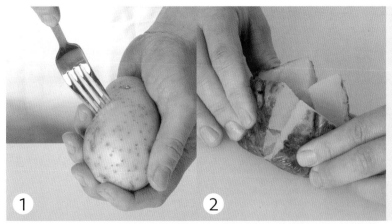

Bake

1 Preheat the oven to 425°F (220°C). Scrub unpeeled, large floury potatoes, such as King Edward, and pat dry completely. Prick all over with a fork to speed up the cooking time, then rub with olive or vegetable oil.

2 Place the potatoes directly on the oven rack and bake for 1 hour, or until they feel soft when squeezed or pierced with a knife. Remove the potatoes from the oven, cut a large, deep "X" in the top, and squeeze open. Add the topping of your choice and serve hot.

Deep-fry

1 For twice-fried golden French fries, heat enough oil for deep-frying in a deep-fat fryer to 325°F (160°C). Add the potato batons and fry for 5–6 minutes, or until lightly colored. Remove the potatoes from the oil, drain well, and let cool.

2 Reheat the oil to 350°F (180°C). Deep-fry the potatoes again for 1–2 minutes, or until crisp and golden brown all over. Remove from the oil and drain well on folded paper towels. Sprinkle with salt and serve hot.

Roast

1 Peel and cut the potatoes into equal-sized pieces. Put in a pan with lightly salted cold water to cover and boil (p231) for 10 minutes. Drain the potatoes well and set aside until cool enough to handle. Using a fork, score the potatoes all over.

2 Meanwhile, preheat the oven to 400°F (200°C), and place a roasting pan with a thin layer of vegetable oil inside. Turn the potatoes in the oil to coat, then roast for 1 hour, or until crisp. Use tongs or a large fork to remove the potatoes from the pan and drain on paper towels. Sprinkle with salt and serve hot.

Pan-fry

1 Heat a thin layer of vegetable or olive oil in a frying pan set over medium-high heat until hot. Reduce the heat to medium, add as many potato slices that will fit in a single layer, and fry for 8–10 minutes, or until the bottoms are golden.

2 Using a spatula and a knife, turn the potato slices over and fry for 5 minutes, or until both sides are golden and tender when pierced with the tip of a sharp knife. Drain the potatoes on paper towels, season to taste with salt, and serve hot.

PAN-FRIED POTATOES

Leftover potatoes are perfect sliced and pan-fried in olive oil with garlic and herbs.

Potato Skins with Cheddar and Bacon

Significantly reduce the cooking time of this filling dish by using leftover baked potatoes

🕐 1 hr   **page 38**

Potato Salad with Parma Ham

Any variety of cooked new potato can be used in this chunky Italian-style salad

🕐 25 mins   **page 117**

Potato and Parmesan Cakes

The sharp taste of Parmesan cheese enlivens the flavor of leftover mashed potatoes

🕐 40 mins   **page 245**

Shepherd's Pie

The topping is leek-flavored mashed potatoes, but any mashed potatoes can be used

🕐 50 mins   **page 344**

Carrot and Parsnip Purée with Fresh Tarragon

This rich, creamy purée can be made lighter with reduced calories by using vegetable stock instead of milk or cream

- makes 4 servings
- prep 10 mins • cook 10-15 mins
- food processor

5 large **carrots**, peeled and diced

2 large **parsnips**, peeled and diced

1 large **baking potato**, such as **Idaho** or **russet**, peeled and diced

1 tbsp **olive oil**

⅓ cup plus 1 tbsp **whole milk** or **heavy cream**, heated

2 tsp chopped **tarragon**

salt and freshly ground **white pepper**

● **Prepare ahead** The purée can be made a day in advance and gently reheated just before serving; stir in a little extra milk or cream if the consistency is too thick.

1 Bring a large saucepan of lightly salted water to a boil over high heat. Add the carrots and boil for 5 minutes. Add the parsnips and potatoes, and boil for 25 minutes longer, or until the vegetables are very tender. Drain well, shaking off any excess water.

2 Put the vegetables and olive oil in a food processor, and process to a purée. With the motor running, slowly add the milk or cream. Transfer to a bowl, stir in the tarragon and season with salt and pepper. Serve hot.

● **Good with** all roast or grilled meats, poultry, and game.

Braised Red Cabbage with Apple

Most cabbage varieties are best cooked quickly, but red cabbage is an exception, benefiting from long, slow cooking

- makes 4 servings
- prep 10 mins • cook 25 mins, plus 1-1¼ hrs for simmering

2 **bacon slices**, diced

1 **onion**, finely chopped

1 tbsp **sugar**

1 tart **apple**, such as Granny Smith, peeled, cored, and chopped

2lb (900g) shredded **red cabbage**

¼ cup **red wine vinegar**

salt and freshly ground **black pepper**

1 In a large frying pan over medium-low heat, cook the bacon until it renders its fat. Add the onion, and cook for about 5 minutes, or until softened. Add the sugar and cook for 5 minutes, until the onion is golden. Add the apple and cover. Cook, stirring occasionally, for about 3-4 minutes, until the apple is crisp-tender.

2 Add the cabbage and toss to coat thoroughly with the bacon fat. Add the vinegar, and mix well. Cover and cook over low heat for 10 minutes, or until the cabbage becomes a shade or so lighter.

3 Stir in ⅔ cup water and season with salt and pepper. Cover and simmer over medium-low heat for 1-1¼ hours, stirring occasionally, until the cabbage is very tender. Add a little more water, if necessary. Just before serving, season again with salt and pepper. Serve hot.

● **Good with** roast meats, particularly duck or game.

Deep-fried Zucchini

Crisp and delicious, you could make a double batch
of these fritters for a party platter

🍴 makes 4 servings

🕐 prep 15 mins • cook 15 mins

1 envelope (¼oz/7g) **active dry yeast**

1 cup warm **water** (about
110°F/38°C)

⅓ cup plus 1 tbsp **all-purpose flour**

vegetable oil, for deep-frying

salt and freshly ground **black pepper**

2 medium **zucchini**, cut diagonally
into ¼ in (5mm) slices

1 **Stir the yeast** into the warm
water in a small bowl and set
aside for 10 minutes, or until foamy.

2 **Put the flour** in a large bowl
and make a well in the center.
Pour the dissolved yeast into the well
and gradually incorporate the flour.

Cover with a kitchen towel and let
stand at room temperature about
1 hour, until foamy.

3 **Pour enough oil** into a large
frying pan to come about
one-third up the sides. Heat over high
heat until the oil is 350°F (180°C) on
a deep-frying thermometer. Stir down
the batter, and season with salt and
pepper. Working in batches, dip the
zucchini slices in the batter and fry
them for 5 minutes on each side, or
until golden.

4 **Drain the fried zucchini**
slices on paper towels and
sprinkle with salt. Serve immediately.

⬤ **Good with** a little dish of your
favorite dipping sauce. These fritters
are delicious as an appetizer and also
make a good accompaniment to
grilled or fried fish or chicken.

Grilled Vegetables

Perfect for summer, these vegetables are easy to
prepare and go well with any main dish

🍴 makes 4 servings

🕐 prep 20 mins, plus marinating
• cook 4–6 mins

🍽 large, nonmetallic dish, heat-
resistant pastry brush

2 **zucchini**, halved lengthwise

1 large **red bell pepper**, quartered
lengthwise and seeded

1 large **yellow bell pepper**,
quartered lengthwise and seeded

1 large **eggplant**, sliced crosswise

1 **fennel bulb**, quartered lengthwise

½ cup **olive oil**, plus extra for
brushing

3 tbsp **balsamic vinegar**

2 **garlic cloves**, chopped

¼ cup coarsely chopped **parsley**,
plus extra to garnish

salt and freshly ground **black pepper**

⬤ **Prepare ahead** The vegetables
can marinate in step 1 for several
hours. Or cook them a day in advance
and serve at room temperature.

1 **Arrange the zucchini**, red
and yellow peppers, eggplant,
and fennel, cut-sides up, in a large
nonmetallic dish. Whisk together the
oil, vinegar, garlic, parsley, and salt
and pepper to taste. Spoon over the
vegetables, and marinate at room
temperature for at least 30 minutes.

2 **Meanwhile, light** an outdoor
grill or preheat the broiler. Oil the
grill grate or the broiler pan.

3 **Lift the vegetables** out of
the marinade, and place them on
the grill or broiler rack. Cook for 3–5
minutes on each side, or until tender
and lightly charred, brushing with the
marinade. Serve warm or at room
temperature, drizzled with remaining
marinade and sprinkled with parsley.

⬤ **Good with** barbecued or grilled
steaks or chops.

Corn on the Cob

An herb and garlic butter makes a flavorful
coating for this popular vegetable

makes 8 servings

prep 10 mins • cook 15 mins

8 ears of corn

salt and freshly ground black pepper

For the herb butter

5 tbsp butter, softened

2 tsp fresh lemon juice

1 tsp Dijon mustard

1 garlic clove, finely chopped

1 shallot, finely chopped

1 tbsp finely chopped chives

1 tbsp chopped parsley

1 tbsp chopped basil

1 tbsp chopped mint

1 **To make the herb butter**, mix all of the ingredients together with a rubber spatula until combined. Transfer the butter to a sheet of waxed paper. Wrap the waxed paper around the butter and shape it into a roll, twisting the ends of the paper to seal. Refrigerate for at least 1 hour to firm the butter.

2 **Bring a large pan** of unsalted water to a boil. Discard the husks and the silky threads from the corn. Add the corn to the boiling water and cover the pan.

3 **Once the water** has returned to a boil, turn off the heat and cover the pan. Let the corn stand for 5 minutes.

4 **Carefully remove** the corn from the water with kitchen tongs and place on a serving platter. Cut the chilled butter into 8 rounds. Serve the corn with the herb butter.

Ratatouille

This popular Mediterranean dish is delicious hot or cold

makes 4 servings

prep 15 mins • cook 40 mins

¼ cup olive oil

1 onion, chopped

1 zucchini, sliced

1 small eggplant, about 8oz (225g), cut into 1in (2.5cm) cubes

1 red bell pepper, seeded, cored, and cut into 1in (2.5cm) pieces

1 garlic clove, chopped

⅔ cup vegetable stock

one 14.5oz (411g) can chopped tomatoes

2 tsp chopped oregano, plus sprigs for garnish

salt and freshly ground black pepper

1 **Heat the oil** in a large casserole over medium heat. Add the onion and cook for about 5 minutes, until soft and transparent. Stir in the zucchini, eggplant, red pepper, and garlic, and cook for 5 minutes, stirring occasionally, until the vegetables begin to soften.

2 **Add the stock**, tomatoes with their juices, and the chopped oregano and bring to a boil. Reduce the heat to low and partially cover the pan. Simmer about 25 minutes, stirring occasionally, until the vegetables are tender.

3 **Add salt and black pepper** to taste. Transfer to a serving bowl and serve immediately, garnished with oregano sprigs.

● **Good with** a bowl of grated cheese for sprinkling, over hot ratatouille, or a bottle of fruity olive oil for drizzling over cold ratatouille.

Roasted Acorn Squash

This winter squash has a sweet, slightly dry flavor

 makes 4 servings

 prep 10 mins
• cook 35 mins

2 acorn squash, halved lengthwise and seeded

2 tbsp butter, softened

4 tsp light brown sugar

● **Prepare ahead** Steps 1 and 2 can be done several hours in advance.

1 Preheat the oven to 375°F (190°C). Spread an equal amount of butter inside each squash half. Sprinkle each with 1 tsp of the brown sugar.

2 Place the halves, cut sides up, in an ovenproof dish large enough to hold them upright. Pour in enough water to come about 1 in (2.5cm) up the sides of the dish.

3 Bake for 15 minutes. Baste the melted butter and sugar mixture over the flesh, and continue baking for about 20 minutes more, until the squash are tender and glazed.

● **Good with** roast meat, especially roast loin of pork or baked ham.

● **Leftovers** can be made into a soup or reheated.

Baked Zucchini with Parmesan

This is a tasty, easy side dish

 makes 4 servings

 prep 5 mins • cook 15 mins

4 small zucchini, washed and halved lengthwise

1 tbsp olive oil

salt and freshly ground black pepper

⅓ cup freshly grated Parmesan cheese

2 garlic cloves, minced

● **Prepare ahead** Step 1 can be prepared several hours in advance.

1 Preheat the oven to 400°F (200°C). Arrange the zucchini, cut sides up, in an ovenproof dish large enough to hold them in a single layer. Lightly brush with the olive oil. Season with the salt and pepper. Mix the Parmesan and garlic together, then sprinkle over the zucchini.

2 Bake for about 15 minutes, or until the zucchini are tender and the cheese is browned.

● **Good with** roast leg of lamb, lamb chops, or baked cod.

Brussels Sprouts with Orange

Fresh orange zest, along with orange and lime juices add a burst of sunshine to this winter vegetable

 makes 4–6 servings

prep 15 mins, plus blanching the sprouts • cook 7–8 mins

1 lb (450g) Brussels sprouts

2 tbsp butter

1 shallot, finely chopped

finely grated zest of 1 orange

⅓ cup fresh orange juice

1 tbsp fresh lime juice

salt and freshly ground black pepper

● **Prepare ahead** Steps 1 and 2 can be done up to 1 day in advance. Place the hot drained sprouts in a bowl of iced water, let stand until cool, and then drain again. Pat dry with paper towels, and store in a plastic bag in the refrigerator.

1 Using a small knife, remove the outer leaves from the Brussels sprouts. To help the sprouts cook evenly and quickly, cut an "x" into the bottom of each one.

2 Bring a large saucepan of lightly salted water to a boil over high heat. Add the sprouts, return to a boil, and cook about 8 minutes, or until barely tender. Drain well. Let stand until cool enough to handle. Cut each sprout in half lengthwise.

3 Melt the butter in a large frying pan over medium-high heat. Add the shallot and cook, stirring often, about 3 minutes or until golden brown. Add the sprouts and cook, stirring often, about 2 minutes until heated through.

4 Stir in the orange zest and juice and cook for 2 minutes, or until the liquid is reduced by half. Remove from the heat and stir in the lime juice. Season with salt and pepper. Serve hot.

● **Good with** roasted turkey, ham, or pork.

Cauliflower Gratin

A great comfort food side dish that works equally well as a vegetarian main course

makes 4–6 servings

prep 15 mins • cook 15 mins

1 head of **cauliflower**, outer leaves removed, broken into large florets

1 cup fresh **bread crumbs**

For the cheese sauce

3 tbsp **butter**

3 tbsp **all-purpose flour**

1½ tsp **dry mustard**

1¾ cups **whole milk**

1 cup shredded sharp **Cheddar cheese**

salt and freshly ground **black pepper**

1 Bring a large saucepan of lightly salted water to a boil. Add the cauliflower and boil for 7 minutes, or until almost tender. Drain, rinse under cold water, and drain well. Arrange the cauliflower in an ovenproof serving dish. Position the broiler rack about 8in (20cm) from the source of heat and preheat.

2 To make the cheese sauce, melt the butter in a medium saucepan over low heat. Whisk in the flour and mustard and cook without browning for 2 minutes. Remove from the heat and whisk in the milk. Return to the heat and bring to a boil over medium heat, whisking often. Reduce the heat to low and simmer until thickened and no flour taste remains, about 2 minutes. Remove the pan from the heat, add ¾ cup of the Cheddar cheese, and whisk until melted. Season with salt and pepper. Pour over the cauliflower.

3 Toss the remaining cheese with the bread crumbs. Sprinkle over the cauliflower. Place the dish under the broiler for 3–5 minutes, or until the sauce bubbles and the crumbs are golden. Serve hot from the dish.

 Good with any roast meat or grilled sausages.

Leftovers can be refrigerated for 1 day. To reheat, cover with aluminum foil and bake in a preheated 350°F (180°C) oven for 20 minutes.

VARIATION

Herb Cauliflower Cheese
For a crisp, herbed topping, toast the bread crumbs in a little oil until golden. Add a handful of chopped herbs, such as parsley, chives, and thyme. Stir well with the reserved cheese and sprinkle over the sauce and cauliflower just before baking.

Belgian Endive with Thyme

Slow cooking reduces endive's natural bitterness

makes 4 servings

prep 5 mins • cook 30 mins

2 tbsp **olive oil**

4 heads of **Belgian endive**

1 **shallot**, chopped

2 sprigs of **thyme**

1 **bay leaf**

salt and freshly ground **pepper**

1 Heat the oil in a large deep frying pan over medium heat. Add the endives, shallot, thyme, and bay leaf. Cook, turning the endives occasionally, for about 3 minutes, until they are golden all over.

2 Add 2 tbsp water and reduce the heat to low. Cover the pan and simmer for 20–25 minutes, or until the endives are tender when pierced with a knife. Season with salt and pepper, then serve with the pan juices spooned over.

Good with grilled lamb chops. Leftovers can be sliced and tossed with orange segments and vinaigrette to make a salad.

Chickpeas with Spinach

Chickpeas are widely used in Spain as a basis for a variety of beautifully seasoned stews such as this one

 makes 4 servings

 prep 15 mins • cook 10 mins

3 tbsp **olive oil**

1 thick slice of crusty **white bread**, torn into small pieces

1lb 10oz (750g) **leaf spinach**

one 15oz (240g) can **chickpeas**, drained and rinsed

2 **garlic cloves**, finely chopped

1 tsp **sweet paprika**

1 tsp **ground cumin**

salt and freshly ground **black pepper**

1 tbsp **sherry vinegar**

1 Heat 2 tbsp of oil in a frying pan. Add the torn bread and fry, stirring occasionally, until crisp. Transfer to paper towels to drain.

2 Remove any thick stems from the spinach. Wash the spinach well and shake off any excess water. Put the spinach in a large saucepan and cook over low heat, stirring often until it has wilted. Drain in a colander and cool. A handful at a time, squeeze out as much liquid as possible. Transfer to a chopping board and chop coarsely.

3 Add the remaining oil in the frying pan over medium-high heat. Add the spinach and cook, stirring often, about 3 minutes, until warmed through. Add the chickpeas, paprika, and cumin. Season with salt and pepper. Crumble in the fried bread.

4 Add the vinegar and 2 tbsp water, and cook, stirring often, about 5 minutes, until the chickpeas are hot. Serve immediately.

Bok Choy with Oyster Sauce

Baby bok choy look more attractive but regular bok choy can be used if cut crosswise into thick slices first

 makes 4 servings

 prep 10 mins • cook 5 mins

 wok

1lb 2oz (500g) **baby bok choy**, halved lengthwise

½ cup **chicken stock**

3 tbsp **oyster sauce**

1 tbsp **soy sauce**

1 tbsp **rice wine** or dry sherry

pinch of **sugar**

2 tsp **cornstarch**

1 tbsp **vegetable oil**

one 1in (2.5cm) piece of fresh **ginger**, peeled and shredded

2 **garlic cloves**, chopped

1 Bring a large saucepan of water to a boil, add the bok choy, and blanch for 1 minute. Drain and rinse under cold water to preserve the bright green color of the leaves. Gently squeeze each bok choy to remove excess water.

2 Mix together the stock, oyster sauce, soy sauce, rice wine, and sugar in a small bowl. Sprinkle in the cornstarch and stir until dissolved. Heat the oil in a wok over medium-high heat. Add the ginger and garlic and stir-fry for 15 seconds. Add the bok choy and stir-fry for 1 minute.

3 Add the stock mixture and stir until the sauce has thickened and coats the bok choy. Transfer to a serving bowl and serve hot.

● **Prepare ahead** Step 1 can be completed several hours in advance.

● **Good with** a variety of Chinese dishes. This also makes a good side dish alongside grilled meat or fish.

Peas with Lettuce

While this dish may be best with tender fresh peas, it is a fine way to dress up frozen baby peas

🍴 makes 4–6 servings

🕐 prep 10 mins • cook 10 mins

9oz (250g) **pearl onions**

3 tbsp **butter**, at room temperature

2½ cups **shelled fresh peas** or thawed frozen baby peas

½ cup **ham** or chicken **stock**

1 tsp **sugar**

salt and freshly ground **black pepper**

1 tbsp **all-purpose flour**

2 tbsp finely chopped **mint** or parsley

1 **butter lettuce**, outer leaves reserved for another use, shredded

● **Prepare ahead** Step 1 can be completed several hours ahead. Refrigerate until ready to use.

1 Put the onions in a bowl and cover with boiling water. Let stand a few minutes. Drain, peel, and trim the onions, keeping the root end intact.

2 Melt 2 tbsp of the butter in a large saucepan over medium heat. Add the onions, cover, and cook for about 2 minutes.

3 Add the peas and stock and bring to a boil. Skim off any foam, then add the sugar and season with salt and pepper. Lower the heat and simmer for 5–8 minutes or until the peas are tender.

4 Mash the remaining butter and flour together to make a smooth paste. A little at a time, stir the butter mixture into the peas, to thicken the sauce. Stir in the shredded lettuce and mint. Adjust the seasoning and serve immediately.

● **Good with** hot or cold ham dishes. It also makes a lovely accompaniment for roast or grilled lamb.

Glazed Shallots with Red Wine

These sweet-and-sour tender shallots will perk up simply grilled meats

🍴 makes 4 servings

🕐 prep 10 mins • cook 40 mins

❄️ freeze for up to 3 months

4 tbsp **butter**

1lb (450g) small **shallots**, trimmed and peeled

1¼ cups **red wine**, such as Pinot Noir

2 tbsp **red wine vinegar**

1 tsp **sugar**

1 **thyme** sprig

1 **bay leaf**

salt

● **Prepare ahead** The shallots can be cooked a few hours in advance, and gently reheated before serving.

1 Melt 2 tbsp of the butter in a frying pan over medium heat. Add the shallots and cook, turning occasionally, about 5 minutes, until golden.

2 Add the red wine, vinegar, sugar, thyme, and bay leaf, and season with salt. Partially cover and simmer over a low heat for 30 minutes, or until tender.

3 Transfer the shallots to a serving bowl, using a slotted spoon. Increase the heat to high and boil the cooking liquid until syrupy. Remove from the heat and whisk in the remaining butter.

4 Discard the bay leaf and thyme sprig, and pour the sauce over the shallots; serve immediately.

Mixed Root Vegetable Gratin

A creamy, warming cheese-topped dish

 makes 4–6 servings

prep 10 mins • cook 1 hr

10in (25cm) oval ovenproof gratin dish

butter for the pan

2 medium parsnips, peeled and thinly sliced

1 large baking potato, peeled and thinly sliced

½ small celery root, pared and thinly sliced

1¾ cups heavy cream, plus more as needed

⅔ cup whole milk

1 garlic clove, crushed

pinch of nutmeg

salt and freshly ground black pepper

½ cup shredded Gruyère cheese

1 **Preheat the oven** to 350°F (180°C). Butter the gratin dish; Overlapping the slices, layer the parsnips, potato, and the celery root.

2 **Mix the cream**, milk, garlic, and nutmeg, season with salt and pepper. Pour over vegetables. Sprinkle with the cheese. Bake for 1 hour, or until tender and golden. Let stand 5 minutes then serve hot.

Sweet Potato and Sage Gratin

Look no further for an out-of-the-ordinary sweet potato dish for holiday entertaining

makes 6 servings

prep 20 mins • cook 1 hr

10in (25cm) oval ovenproof gratin dish

1¼ cups heavy cream

2 tbsp chopped sage

⅛ tsp freshly grated nutmeg

salt and freshly ground black pepper

4 tbsp butter, cut into small cubes plus more for the dish

2¼lb (1 kg) orange-fleshed sweet potatoes, thinly sliced

Prepare ahead Cover and refrigerate the cooked gratin for up to 2 days; reheat before serving.

1 **Preheat the oven** to 400°F (200°C). Whisk the cream, sage, and nutmeg together and season with salt and pepper. Butter an ovenproof gratin dish. Layer the sweet potatoes in the dish, pouring in the cream mixture as you go, and finishing with the cream.

2 **Cover with aluminum foil** and bake the for 1 hour, or until the gratin is completely tender when pierced in the center with the tip of a sharp knife.

Good with roast pork, ham, or turkey.

VARIATION

Gruyère Gratin

Sprinkle with ½ cup shredded Gruyère cheese before baking. Serve with a crisp green salad to make a vegetarian meal.

Potato-Herb Galette

A good accompaniment for roasted and grilled meats

 makes 6 servings

prep 20 mins • cook 25 mins

1lb (450g) baking potatoes, peeled, boiled until tender, drained, cooled

1 small onion, finely chopped

1 large egg, beaten

3 tbsp finely chopped mixed herbs, such as parsley, thyme, and chives

2 tbsp all-purpose flour

pinch of freshly grated nutmeg

salt and freshly ground black pepper

1 tbsp olive or vegetable oil

Prepare ahead The galette can be made up to 4 hours in advance.

1 **Preheat the oven** to 350°F (180°C). Grate the potatoes. Mix the potatoes, onion, egg, herbs, flour, and nutmeg together and season with salt and pepper.

2 **Heat the oil** in a 10in (25cm) nonstick frying pan over medium heat. Add the potato mixture, spreading it to make a thick potato pancake. Cook for 5 minutes, or until the underside is browned. Place a baking tray on top of the pan and flip the galette over. Slide it back into the pan to brown the other side. Bake for 15 minutes, or until cooked through.

Ultimate Mashed Potatoes

Mash with a twist

- makes 6 servings
- prep 10 mins • cook 45 mins

3lb (1.35kg) **baking potatoes**, such as Burbank, peeled and cubed

salt and freshly ground **black pepper**

2 tbsp **heavy cream**

2 tbsp **whole milk**

6 tbsp **butter**

1 cup (4oz/115g) shredded **Cheddar**

4 **scallions**, white and green parts, chopped

2 tbsp chopped **parsley**

2 tbsp finely chopped **chives**

1 tbsp prepared **horseradish**

1 **Place the potatoes** in a large saucepan and add cold water to cover. Bring to a boil and add a little salt. Cover and reduce the heat to medium. Cook at a brisk simmer for 20-30 minutes, or until tender.

2 **Drain well**. Return to low heat and stir for a minute or two to evaporate excess liquid.

3 **Add the cream**, milk, and butter and mash. Add the Cheddar, scallions, parsley, chives, and horseradish and mix well. Season with salt and pepper and serve hot.

Potato Gratin

This baked potato dish is rich with cream and fragrant with garlic and nutmeg

- makes 4-6 servings
- prep 15-20 mins • cook 1½ hrs
- mandoline or food processor fitted with fine slicing blade

2lb (900g) white- or red-skinned **boiling potatoes**

salt and freshly ground **black pepper**

2½ cups **heavy cream**

1 **garlic clove**, cut in half

pinch of freshly **ground nutmeg**

3 tbsp **butter**, at room temperature, cut up, plus more for the dish

- **Prepare ahead** The potatoes can be peeled, sliced, and stored in water to cover for several hours.

1 **Preheat the oven** to 350°F (180°C). Butter a 2qt (2 liter) shallow baking dish.

2 **Peel the potatoes**. Using a mandoline, a food processor fitted with a fine slicing blade, or a large knife, slice the potatoes into rounds

about ⅛in (3mm) thick. Rinse the slices in cold water. Drain and pat dry with paper towels or a clean kitchen towel.

3 **Place the potatoes** in layers in the baking dish, seasoning with salt and pepper as you go.

4 **Bring the cream**, garlic, and nutmeg to a boil in a saucepan. Pour the cream over the potatoes. Dot the top with the butter.

5 **Cover** with aluminum foil. Bake about 1¼ hours, or until the potatoes are just tender. Remove the foil. Increase the oven temperature to 450°F (250°C) and bake until the top is golden, about 10 minutes. Serve hot.

- **Good with** salad for supper, or as a side dish to smoked fish or broiled or roasted meats.

VARIATION

Potato and Cheese Gratin

Add 2 finely chopped anchovies to the cream at step 4. Sprinkle 1 cup shredded Gruyère cheese, between the potato layers, saving a little for sprinkling on the top.

Roast Artichokes with Tomato and Garlic

This is such a simple accompaniment but very colorful and tasty

- makes 4 servings
- prep 5 mins • cook 1 hr

one 14oz (400g) can **artichoke hearts**, drained and halved

8 small **plum tomatoes** on the vine

12 **garlic cloves**, unpeeled

2 tbsp **olive oil**

2 tsp **balsamic vinegar**

few sprigs of **thyme** (optional)

sea salt and freshly ground **black pepper**

1 **Preheat the oven** to 275°F (140°C).

2 **Place the artichoke hearts** in a shallow baking dish with the tomatoes. Scatter the garlic cloves in the dish. Drizzle with the olive oil and balsamic vinegar, add the thyme, if using, and season with salt and black pepper.

3 **Roast for 1 hour**, until the garlic is very tender.

- **Good with** roast or grilled meats, fresh breads, or savory tarts.

Roast Sweet Potato with Sesame Glaze

Roasting these vegetables brings out their natural sweetness

- 🍴 makes 6 servings
- 🕐 prep 10 mins • cook 50 mins

5 orange-fleshed sweet potatoes (yams), peeled

2 tbsp olive oil

salt and freshly ground black pepper

2 tbsp sesame seeds

1 tbsp honey

1 tbsp soy sauce

1 **Preheat the oven** to 400°F (200°C). Cut the potatoes into large chunks and place on a baking sheet. Drizzle with the oil and season with salt and pepper. Roast the potatoes for 30 minutes, turning halfway through, until almost tender.

2 **Mix together** the sesame seeds, honey, and soy sauce. Pour over the sweet potatoes, and toss. Roast 20 minutes more, or until well glazed and tender.

● **Good with** roast chicken or pork.

Carrot and Tarragon Timbales

The aromatic flavor of tarragon permeates these tender carrot and cheese custards

- 🍴 makes 4 servings
- 🕐 prep 10 mins • cook 25 mins
- 🍲 six 6oz (180ml) ramekins
- ❄️ freeze in the ramekins for up to 3 months

butter, for the ramekins

12oz (350g) carrots, coarsely grated

1½ cups (6oz/175g) shredded Gruyère cheese

2 large eggs, lightly beaten

2 tbsp crème fraîche or heavy cream

2 tbsp finely chopped tarragon

½ tsp dry mustard

freshly ground black pepper

● **Prepare ahead** The unbaked timbales can be refrigerated for up to 8 hours.

1 **Preheat the oven** to 400°F (200°C). Butter six 6oz (180ml) ramekins. Line the bottoms with rounds of wax paper, and butter the wax paper.

2 **Bring a saucepan** of water to a boil over high heat. Add the carrot and cook for 30 seconds. Drain and rinse under cold running water. A handful at a time, squeeze the carrot dry and place in a large mixing bowl.

3 **Add the Gruyère**, eggs, crème fraiche, tarragon, and dry mustard to the carrots and mix well. Season with black pepper. Divide among the ramekins. Cover each with a circle of buttered wax paper, buttered side down.

4 **Place the ramekins** in a roasting pan and add enough hot water to come halfway up the sides of the ramekins. Bake for 25 minutes or until they are just set and firm on top.

5 **Remove the ramekins** from the pan. Remove the top paper rounds. One at a time, run a dull knife around the inside of a ramekin. Place a small plate over the ramekin, and invert the ramekin and plate together to unmold the timbale. Remove the bottom paper round. Serve hot.

● **Good with** a tomato salad as a starter, or as an accompaniment to roast chicken or roast beef.

VARIATION

Sweet Potato and Herb Timbale

Replace the carrot with sweet potatoes and use a milder cheese, such as Cheddar. Instead of using tarragon, try parsley, sage, or chives.

Pan-grilled Eggplant and Zucchini Salad

Serve at room temperature to allow the flavors to merge

- 🍴 makes 6 servings
- 🕐 prep 15 mins, plus standing • cook 30 mins
- 🍱 ridged grill pan

2 **eggplants**, thinly sliced lengthwise

salt and freshly ground **black pepper**

2 tbsp **extra virgin olive oil**, plus more for brushing

1 tbsp **balsamic vinegar**

2 **garlic cloves**, peeled and chopped

4 small **zucchini**, trimmed and sliced

mint leaves, to garnish

1 **Sprinkle the eggplant** slices with 2 tsp salt and let stand in a colander for 30 minutes.

2 **Mix together** the oil, vinegar, and garlic, and season with salt and pepper.

3 **Preheat a ridged grill pan** over high heat. Brush the zucchini with a little olive oil, and season with salt and pepper. Cook the zucchini, turning once, about 3 minutes, until tender. Transfer to a large bowl.

4 **Rinse the eggplants** and pat dry with paper towels. Brush the eggplants with olive oil and cook for about 5 minutes, turning once. Transfer to the bowl, add the dressing, and mix. Stir in the mint leaves. Let stand for at least 30 minutes before serving.

● **Good with** grilled, broiled, or roast meats.

● **Leftovers** can be used to add "bite" to cold chicken, meat, or cheese sandwiches.

Glazed Carrots with Thyme

These carrots are a good accompaniment to roast beef, pork, lamb, or poultry

- 🍴 makes 4 servings
- 🕐 prep 10 mins • cook 15 mins

1 lb (450g) **carrots**, thinly sliced

grated zest of 1 **orange**

¼ cup fresh **orange** juice

1½ tbsp **butter**

1 tbsp **brown sugar**

1 **garlic clove**, crushed and peeled

salt and freshly ground **black pepper**

½ tsp chopped **thyme**

● **Prepare ahead** Complete through the end of step 2 several hours in advance, then finish cooking just before serving.

1 **Place the carrots**, orange zest and juice, butter, sugar, and garlic in a small saucepan, and season with salt and pepper. Add enough cold water to barely cover the carrots.

2 **Bring to a boil**, then cover and cook over a medium-high heat for 8–10 minutes, or until the carrots are just tender.

3 **Remove the cover** and boil until all the liquid has evaporated and the carrots are glazed and golden at the edges, shaking the pan occasionally to prevent sticking. Just before serving, sprinkle in the thyme leaves.

Potato and Parmesan Cakes

These little cakes make a nice change from mashed potatoes

 makes 4 servings

 prep 20 mins • cook 20 mins

1lb 10oz (750g) **baking potatoes**, such as Burbank or russet, peeled and cut into 1in (2.5cm) chunks

⅓ cup freshly grated **Parmesan**

1 large **egg yolk**

salt and freshly ground **black pepper**

3 tbsp **all-purpose flour**

vegetable oil for frying

1 tbsp **capers**

lemon wedges, to serve

● **Prepare ahead** The cakes can be made 2–3 days in advance, covered, and refrigerated.

1 Bring a saucepan of lightly salted water to a boil over high heat. Add the potatoes, reduce the heat to medium-low, and simmer about 15 minutes, until tender. Drain well. Pass the potatoes through a potato ricer into a bowl. (Alternatively, rub through a sieve.)

2 Add the Parmesan and egg yolk, season generously with salt and pepper, and mix. Divide into 8 equal balls and flatten into little cakes, each 2in (5cm) in diameter. Spread the flour in to a plate, and season with salt and pepper. Coat the potato cakes in the flour and refrigerate until needed.

3 Pour enough oil into a frying pan to come ⅛ in (3mm) up the sides and and heat over medium heat. In batches, add the potato cakes and fry for about 2 minutes on each side, or until golden. Transfer to paper towels to drain.

4 Increase the heat to high. Add the capers and fry for about 45 seconds, or until crisp. Drain on paper towels. Place the potato cakes on a platter, sprinkle with the capers, and serve with lemon wedges.

Grilled Eggplant with Pomegranate Vinaigrette

Fresh pomegranate seeds enliven this warm salad

 makes 6 servings

 prep 10 mins • cook 10 mins

 ridged grill pan

6 tbsp **olive oil**, plus more for brushing

3 tbsp **pomegranate molasses**

3 tbsp chopped **cilantro**

salt and freshly ground **pepper**

3 large **eggplants**, cut into ½in (1cm) slices

2 **shallots**, very finely sliced

fresh **pomegranate seeds**, to garnish

1 To make the vinaigrette, whisk together the olive oil, pomegranate molasses, and cilantro, and season with salt and pepper. Set aside until ready to serve.

2 Preheat the grill pan over high heat. Brush both sides of the eggplant with olive oil, and season with salt and pepper. Cook, turning once, about 5 minutes, until seared with grill marks and tender.

3 Layer the eggplants and shallots in a serving dish and pour the vinaigrette on top. Scatter with fresh pomegranate seeds and serve.

VARIATION

Grilled Eggplant with Feta Cheese

Substitute finely sliced red onion for the shallots. and scatter with 2oz (60g) crumbled feta cheese just before serving.

Potato Pancakes

What could be simpler than *latkes*, traditionally served with sour cream, apple sauce, or both

 makes 4 servings

 prep 20 mins, plus standing • cook 30 mins

low GI

4 large **baking potatoes**, shredded

2 **onions**, shredded

2 large **eggs**, beaten

2 tbsp **matzo meal** or flour

salt and freshly ground **black pepper**

vegetable oil, for frying

applesauce, to serve

sour cream, to serve

1 Rinse the shredded potatoes in a colander under cold running water and drain for 10 minutes. Squeeze the potatoes in a clean kitchen towel to remove as much liquid as possible. Transfer to a bowl.

2 Add the onion, egg, and matzo meal and stir well. Season generously with salt and pepper.

3 Add enough oil to come ¼in (5mm) up the sides of a large frying pan and heat over medium heat until the oil shimmers. Add heaping tablespoons of the batter to the oil and flatten slightly into pancakes. Cook, turning once, until golden brown on both sides, about 6 minutes. Using a slotted spatula, transfer to paper towels to drain.

4 Serve immediately, with the applesauce and sour cream on the side, if liked.

VARIATIONS

German Potato Pancakes
Reibeplatzchen or *Kartoffel Puffer* are made in a similar way. Squeeze the shredded potatoes over a bowl, reserving the drained liquid. Carefully pour away the liquid and add the starchy residue to the potato and onion mixture. Substitute flour or ground oats for the matzo. Serve with herb butters and smoked salmon for an appetizer, or with a generous sprinkling of sugar as a dessert.

Swedish Potato Pancakes
Raggmunk are similar pancakes but are fried in butter. Omit the matzo meal, onion, and oil. Whisk together 1½ cups whole milk and ⅔ cup all-purpose flour. Stir in 1¾lb (800g) shredded potatoes (do not rinse), with salt and pepper. Melt 4 tbsp butter in a large frying pan and fry the pancakes in batches if necessary, spreading and pressing each one flat, so they are crisp and thin. Serve with lingonberry preserves and fried salt pork.

Corn and Peppers

Colorful and popular with children, this is a good side dish for everyday meals

 makes 4 servings

prep 15 mins • cook 8 mins

4 **ears of corn**

2 tbsp **butter**

2 **scallions**, green and white parts, sliced

½ small **green bell pepper**, seeded and diced

½ small **red bell pepper**, seeded and diced

salt and freshly ground **black pepper**

1 Remove the husks and silks from the corn. Using a sharp knife, cut the corn kernels from the cobs. Break up any kernels that are stuck together.

2 Melt the butter in a large saucepan over medium heat. Add the corn, scallions, green and red peppers, and ¼ cup water. Bring the mixture to a boil and cook about 5 minutes, or until the corn is tender. Season with salt and pepper and serve.

USING CANNED OR FROZEN CORN

If you are in a hurry, this recipe also works well with 3 cups frozen corn or canned corn.

Sweet Potato Purée with Horseradish

Baking sweet potatoes makes them intensely sweet and full of flavor

- makes 4-6 servings
- prep 10 mins
  • cook 45-60 mins
- freeze for up to 3 months

2¼lb (1.1kg) orange-fleshed **sweet potatoes**, pricked with a fork

salt and freshly ground **pepper**

⅔ cup **heavy cream**, plus more for pouring (optional)

1 tbsp **horseradish**

● **Prepare ahead** The purée can be made, covered, and refrigerated 1 day ahead, and reheated gently.

1 Preheat the oven to 425°F (220°C). Place the potatoes on a aluminum foil-lined baking sheet. Bake about 50 minutes, until tender. Let cool until easy to handle.

2 Peel the potatoes. Transfer to a food processor and purée. With the machine running, pour in the cream. Add the horseradish and pulse. Season with salt and pepper. Transfer to a saucepan and stir over medium heat until piping hot. Drizzle a little cream on top, if desired, and serve hot.

Fennel Remoulade

This fresh-tasting Italian bulb works well with the creaminess of the sauce

- makes 6 servings
- prep 15 mins

3 tbsp **mayonnaise**

3 tbsp fresh **lemon** juice

2 tbsp **Dijon mustard**

2 **shallots**, thinly sliced

2 tbsp finely chopped **parsley**

2 tbsp finely chopped **tarragon**

1 tsp rinsed **capers**

½ tbsp chopped **cornichons**

1 large **fennel bulb**, finely shredded

salt and freshly ground **black pepper**

● **Prepare ahead** Refrigerate the ingredients, without the mayonnaise mixture, up to 1 day ahead. Add the mayonnaise mixture 1 hour before serving.

1 Mix the mayonnaise, lemon juice, and mustard together in a large bowl. Stir in the shallots, parsley, tarragon, capers, and cornichons.

2 Add the fennel and mix. Season with salt and pepper. Cover and refrigerate at least 1 hour, or until chilled. Serve cold.

● **Good with** crab cakes, smoked fish, or cold meats.

VARIATION

Celery Root Remoulade

Blanch a celery root in salted boiling water for 2 minutes. Drain, pat dry, and cut into fine strips. Use instead of the fennel.

Creamed Spinach with Pine Nuts

Pine nuts contrast well with the smooth texture of creamed spinach

- makes 4 servings
- prep 10 mins • cook 3-4 mins

1½ lb (675g) fresh **spinach**

3 tbsp **crème fraîche** or heavy cream

½ tsp freshly grated **nutmeg**

salt and freshly ground **black pepper**

½ cup (2oz/60g) **pine nuts**, toasted

1 Remove the tough stems from the spinach leaves. Wash well and shake dry.

2 Place the spinach with any remaining water clinging to the leaves in a large saucepan. Cover and cook over low heat for 3-4 minutes, until just wilted.

3 Stir in the crème fraîche and nutmeg and season well with salt and pepper.

4 Spoon into a serving dish and sprinkle with the pine nuts. Serve hot.

● **Good with** roast meats, poultry, and full-flavored fish, such as salmon or tuna.

Creamed Rutabaga

This delicious and versatile vegetable purée can be served in place of mashed potatoes

 makes 4–6 servings

prep 10 mins • cook 30 mins

2½lb (1.1kg) **rutabaga**, pared and cut into chunks

4 tbsp **butter**

3 tbsp **heavy cream**

pinch of grated **nutmeg**

salt and freshly ground **black pepper**

● **Prepare ahead** The purée can be refrigerated up to 2 days and reheated.

1 Place the rutabaga in a large saucepan with lightly salted water to cover. Cover and bring to a boil. Reduce the heat to medium-low and cook about 30 minutes, or until tender. Drain well.

2 Return to the saucepan over a very low heat. Add the butter. Mash the rutabaga with a potato masher, then mix in the cream and nutmeg. Season with salt and pepper. Transfer to a serving bowl and serve hot.

● **Good with** roast and grilled meats, and vegetarian dishes.

Pisto Manchego

Similar to ratatouille but with a touch of vinegar to heighten the flavors, this Spanish dish goes well with grilled chorizo

 makes 4–6 servings

prep 10 mins • cook 30 mins

2 tbsp **olive oil**

1 **garlic clove**, chopped

2 **onions**, chopped

2 **green bell peppers**, seeded and sliced

1 **red bell pepper**, seeded and sliced

3 **zucchini**, diced

1 large ripe **tomato**, skinned, quartered, and seeded

1 tbsp **red wine vinegar**

½ tsp **sugar**

salt and freshly ground **black pepper**

2 tbsp chopped **parsley**

● **Prepare ahead** The pisto manchego can be refrigerated for up to 2 days before serving. Reheat or serve at room temperature.

1 Heat the oil in a large frying pan over medium heat. Add the garlic and onions and cook, stirring often, for about 5 minutes, or until the onions are translucent.

2 Add the peppers and cook, stirring often, for 5 minutes, or until the peppers soften. Add the zucchini and cook for 5 minutes more. Add the tomatoes, vinegar, and sugar and cook, stirring occasionally, for 15 minutes.

3 Season with salt and pepper. Transfer to a warm serving bowl, and sprinkle with parsley.

● **Good with** grilled meats and fish. Or serve as a hot appetizer, topped with slices of fried chorizo and chopped hard-boiled eggs.

Onion Confit

A sweet and tangy accompaniment that complements most roasted or grilled dishes

makes 4–6 servings

prep 5 mins • cook 35–45 mins

2 tbsp **butter**

2lb (900g) **onions**, thinly sliced

½ cup packed light **brown sugar**

3 tbsp **sherry vinegar**

1½ tbsp **crème de cassis** (optional)

2 tsp **salt**

● **Prepare ahead** The confit can be refrigerated for up to 1 week.

1 Melt the butter in a large heavy saucepan over medium heat. Stir in the onions and cook for 5 minutes until beginning to soften.

2 Add the sugar, vinegar, crème de cassis, if using, and salt, and stir well, and simmer uncovered for 30–40 minutes, stirring occasionally so the confit does not scorch. Serve warm or at room temperature.

● **Good with** grilled or roasted meat and poultry.

Cajun-spiced Potato Wedges

This peppery dish was developed by the French settlers of Louisiana

 makes 6 servings

prep 10 mins
• cook 35–45 mins

4 potatoes, unpeeled

3 red onions, cut into 8 wedges

1 lemon, cut into 6 wedges

12 garlic cloves, unpeeled

4 bay leaves

⅓ cup olive oil

3 tbsp fresh lemon juice

1 tbsp tomato paste

1 tsp sweet paprika

1 tsp dried oregano

1 tsp dried thyme

½ tsp cayenne pepper

½ tsp ground cumin

salt and freshly ground black pepper

● **Prepare ahead** The potatoes can be prepared through step 2 several hours before roasting.

1 Preheat the oven to 400°F (200°C). Cut the potatoes into thick wedges. Parcook in a large pan of salted boiling water for 3 minutes. Drain well. Combine the potatoes, onions, lemon, garlic, and bay leaves in a large roasting pan.

2 Whisk together the oil, lemon juice, tomato paste, paprika, oregano, thyme, cayenne, and cumin, pour over the potatoes, and toss. Season with salt and pepper.

3 Roast for 30–40 minutes, turning frequently with a metal spatula, until the potatoes are tender and have absorbed the liquid. Serve hot.

Mushrooms in Cream Sauce

Make the most of seasonal mushrooms with this filling side dish

🍴 makes 4 servings

🕐 prep 10 mins • cook 25 mins

1lb (450g) **mixed mushrooms**, such as cremini, stemmed shiitake, white, and oyster

5oz (140g) sliced **bacon**, chopped

4 tbsp **butter**

1 **onion**, finely chopped

2 **garlic cloves**, finely chopped

½ cup **dry white wine**

pinch of freshly grated **nutmeg**

1½ cups **crème fraîche** or heavy cream

1 tbsp **cornstarch**

salt and freshly ground **black pepper**

1 tbsp chopped **tarragon**

1 **Place the mushrooms** in a colander and rinse quickly under cold running water to clean them.

Cut large mushrooms in halves or quarters.

2 **In a large frying pan**, cook the bacon over medium heat until lightly browned. Transfer to paper towels to drain.

3 **Add the butter** to the pan and melt. Add the onion and cook about 5 minutes, until browned. Add the mushrooms and garlic and cook, stirring often, for about 10 minutes until browned. Add the wine and nutmeg and bring to a boil. Cover and simmer for 5 minutes.

4 **Stir in** the crème fraîche and reserved bacon. Dissolve the cornstarch in 1 tbsp water. Stir into the sauce and cook until thickened. Season with salt and pepper. Just before serving, stir in the tarragon.

● **Good with** steak or pork chops. It can also be tossed with pasta.

Asparagus with Mustard Sauce

Tender asparagus spears are served cold with a simple dressing

🍴 makes 4 servings

🕐 prep 15 mins • cook 3–4 mins

1½ lbs (675g) **asparagus**

2 tbsp chopped **red onion**

For the mustard sauce

¼ cup **olive oil**

1 tbsp **white wine vinegar**

1 tbsp **Dijon mustard**

2 tbsp plain **Greek-style yogurt**

1 tsp finely chopped **tarragon**

salt and freshly ground **black pepper**

● **Prepare ahead** The cooked asparagus and dressing can be refrigerated several hours in advance.

1 **Snap off** the tough ends of the asparagus. Peel the lower half of each asparagus with a vegetable peeler. Fill a large frying pan with enough water to come ½in (1½cm) up the sides and bring to a simmer.

Add the asparagus. Cover, and cook 3–4 minutes, or until just tender. Drain and rinse under cold running water. Pat dry with paper towels. Refrigerate while making the sauce.

2 **For the sauce**, whisk the oil, vinegar, mustard, and tarragon together in a bowl. Whisk in the yogurt until smooth. Season with salt and pepper.

3 **Divide the asparagus** among salad plates. Top with the mustard sauce and sprinkle with the red onion. Serve immediately.

VARIATION

Asparagus with Creamy Garlic Sauce

Combine ½ cup plain yogurt, 1 tbsp chopped chives, 1 garlic clove, ½ tsp finely grated lemon zest, and a pinch of cayenne pepper in a bowl. Chill, covered, for at least 2 hours. Remove the garlic before serving.

Roast Squash with Ginger

Spicy vegetables make a punchy side dish

 makes 8 servings

 prep 20 mins • cook 40 mins

1 butternut squash, peeled and seeded

5 tbsp olive oil, plus more for the pan

2 fresh hot red chiles, seeded and minced

2in (5cm) piece fresh ginger, peeled and cut into julienne

1 tbsp honey

1 tsp salt

3 tbsp chopped mint

2 limes, cut into wedges

1 Preheat the oven to 350°F (180°C). Cut the squash in half where the bulbous part meets the "neck." Slice the squash into strips about ½in (1cm) thick. Spread in an oiled roasting pan. Whisk the oil, 2 tbsp warm water, chiles, ginger, honey, and salt. Pour over the squash and mix well.

2 Bake, shaking the pan occasionally to discourage sticking, for about 40 minutes, or until tender. If the mixture seems dry, add a little more olive oil or water.

3 Transfer the squash to a large platter and sprinkle with the mint. Serve warm, with the lime wedges for squeezing.

Tomato and Eggplant Confit

An ancient method of preserving meat, confit infuses flavor into vegetables

 makes 6 servings

prep 5 mins, plus standing • cook 10 mins

¾ cup olive oil

4 garlic cloves, peeled

1 eggplant, about 10oz (300g), cut into 3in (7.5cm) sticks

2 cups halved cherry tomatoes

salt and freshly ground black pepper

10 basil leaves, torn into pieces, plus whole leaves to garnish

1 Heat the oil in a frying pan over medium-high heat until it begins to simmer. Add the garlic and cook about 3 minutes. Discard the garlic. In batches, add the eggplant to the oil and fry, stirring often, for 3 minutes, until golden brown. Transfer to paper towels to drain.

2 Discard all but 2 tbsp of the oil from the pan. Add the tomatoes and cook for 1–2 minutes, until slightly softened. Transfer to a bowl.

3 Add the eggplant to the bowl and season well with salt and pepper. Add the basil and mix gently. Cover with plastic wrap and let stand for 1 hour to develop the flavors.

4 Check the seasoning. Garnish with the basil and serve warm.

Stir-fried Broccoli with Sesame Seeds

The added flavorings transform broccoli into something special

 makes 4–6 servings

prep 5 mins • cook 6 mins

1 large head of broccoli

1 tbsp sesame seeds

1 tbsp vegetable oil

1 tbsp soy sauce

⅛ tsp crushed hot red pepper

¼ cup vegetable stock or water

salt and freshly ground black pepper

1 Cut the broccoli into florets. Pare the stems and cut them crosswise into thin slices.

2 Heat a large frying pan or wok over medium heat. Add the sesame seeds and cook, stirring almost constantly, about 1–2 minutes. Transfer to a plate.

3 Add the oil, soy sauce, and hot pepper to the pan and stir combine. Add the broccoli and stir-fry for about 2 minutes.

4 Pour in the stock and cover. Cook for about 2 minutes longer, or until crisp-tender. Stir in the sesame seeds and season with salt and pepper. Serve hot.

● **Good with** grilled meats.

Fish and Chips

Make this British classic at home with a yeast batter that remains crisp to the very last bite

- makes 4 servings
- prep 20 mins, plus standing • cook 30 mins
- deep-frying basket, thermometer

¼oz (7g) packet of **active dried yeast**

¼ cup warm (110°F/38°C) **water**

¼ cup warm (110°F/38°C) **milk**

pinch of **sugar**

¾ cup **all-purpose flour**

2lb (900g) **baking potatoes**, such as russet or Burbank

vegetable oil, for deep-frying

1½lb (675g) skinless **cod fillet**, cut into 4 serving pieces

salt and freshly ground **black pepper**

parsley sprigs, for serving

lemon wedges, for serving

1 To make the batter, sprinkle the yeast over the warm water in a medium bowl. Let stand for 5 minutes. Stir to dissolve the yeast. Stir in the milk and sugar. Add the flour and whisk until smooth. Cover with a towel and let stand in a warm place until bubbling, about 1 hour.

2 Peel the potatoes and cut into sticks about 2½in (6cm) long and ½in (1cm) wide. Rinse, drain, and pat dry with paper towels.

3 Preheat the oven to 250°F (130°C). Fill a wide, deep saucepan halfway with oil and heat to 325°F (160°C). Place half the potatoes in a deep-frying basket and lower carefully into the hot oil. Deep-fry for 5 minutes, or until the potatoes are tender but pale-colored. Drain and transfer to a baking sheet. Repeat with the remaining potatoes.

4 Line another baking sheet with paper towels. Season the cod with salt and pepper and dust with flour. Increase the oil temperature to 375°F (190°C). In two batches, dip the cod in the batter, carefully add to the oil, and deep-fry until golden brown. Transfer to the sheet and keep warm in the oven.

5 Return all the potatoes to the frying basket and deep-fry for 3–4 minutes, shaking the basket occasionally. Drain well. Serve hot, garnished with parsley and lemon.

DEEP-FRIED PARSLEY
Tie several sprigs of parsley together with kitchen twine. Lower into the hot oil and fry for about 5 seconds, or until the sprigs darken and become crisp. Snip off the string and serve as a bunch on the side of the plate, or crumble over the fish.

Shellfish and Tomato Stew

This rustic stew is delicious served for lunch or dinner

- makes 4 servings
- prep 10 mins • cook 30 mins

2 tbsp **olive oil**

2 **shallots**, finely chopped

1 **celery stalk**, finely chopped

2 **garlic cloves**, chopped

2 **anchovies** in oil, rinsed and chopped

pinch of crushed **hot red pepper**

salt and freshly ground **black pepper**

one 14.5oz (411g) can **chopped tomatoes**

1 cup dry **white wine**

1 cup bottled **clam juice**

8oz (230g) large **shrimp**, peeled and deveined

8oz (230g) **sea scallops**

3 tbsp fresh **lemon** juice

1 tsp **capers**, drained and rinsed

1 Heat the oil over medium heat. Add the shallots, celery, garlic, anchovies, and hot pepper. Cook, stirring often, until softened. Stir in the tomatoes, wine, and clam juice, bring to a boil, then simmer for 20 minutes.

2 Add the shrimp, scallops, lemon juice, and capers. Cook about 5 minutes, or until the seafood is opaque. Season with salt and pepper.

Grilled Tuna with Tomato Salsa

These should be served straight from the pan while still sizzling hot

 makes 4 servings

 prep 10 mins, plus 1 hr marinating • cook 8 mins

 ridged grill pan, pastry brush

2 **tuna steaks**, each weighing 1–1¼lb (450–600g)

6 tbsp **olive oil**, plus more for brushing

2 **garlic cloves**, finely chopped

2 tbsp fresh **lime** juice

2 tsp chopped **rosemary**

salt and freshly ground **black pepper**

2 ripe medium **tomatoes**, halved, seeded, and chopped

4 **scallions**, finely chopped

small pinch of crushed **hot red pepper** (optional)

lime wedges, to garnish

1 cup coarsely chopped **arugula**

1 Put the tuna in a nonmetallic shallow dish. Whisk together 4 tbsp oil, 1 garlic clove, 1 tbsp lime juice, and the rosemary in a small bowl; season with pepper. Pour over the tuna, making sure both steaks are coated. Cover with plastic wrap and marinate in the refrigerator for 1 hour.

2 Meanwhile, to make the salsa, put the tomatoes, scallions, and hot pepper in a nonmetallic bowl. Stir in 2 tbsp olive oil and the remaining garlic and lime juice, then season with salt and pepper. Cover and refrigerate until ready to serve.

3 Ten minutes before grilling, remove the tuna and salsa from the refrigerator. Heat the ridged grill pan over high heat until a splash of water "dances" on the surface. Brush the ridges with a little of the marinade.

4 Remove the tuna from the marinade and reserve the marinade. Place the tuna on the grill pan and cook for 3 minutes, brushing with the marinade. Carefully turn over the tuna and grill for another 2–4 minutes, until the outside is browned but the meat is still pink in the center.

5 Transfer to a cutting board and let stand for 2 minutes. Cut each steak in half crosswise. Combine the arugula and salsa and serve with the tuna, garnished with lime wedges.

Haddock with Cheese Sauce

With a layer of freshly-cooked spinach under the poached haddock, this classic dish is a colorful one-pot meal

 makes 4 servings

 prep 25 mins • cook 25 mins

 freeze for up to 1 month

1½lb (675g) skinless **haddock** or **cod fillet**, cut into 4 serving pieces

1¼ cups **whole milk**

⅔ cup bottled **clam juice**

9oz (250g) fresh **spinach**, well washed, stemmed, and chopped

salt and freshly ground **black pepper**

pinch of grated **nutmeg**

2 tbsp **butter**, plus more for the dish

2 tbsp **all-purpose flour**

1 cup shredded **Cheddar**

1 cup fresh **whole wheat bread crumbs**

½ cup freshly grated **Parmesan**

2 tbsp chopped **parsley**

● **Prepare ahead** The entire dish, without the breadcrumb topping, can be made a few hours ahead. Bake in a preheated 350°F (180°C) oven for about 25 minutes, then add the topping and broil until browned.

1 Bring the haddock, milk, and clam juice to a boil in a frying pan over medium heat. Reduce the heat to low, cover, and simmer for 6–8 minutes, or until the fish is opaque.

2 Meanwhile, put the spinach in a medium saucepan. Cover and cook over medium-low heat for 3 minutes, or until wilted. Season with salt, pepper, and the nutmeg. Spread the spinach in a buttered shallow ovenproof dish. Arrange the fish over the spinach, leaving the cooking liquid in the pan. Cover with aluminum foil to keep the fish warm.

3 Melt the butter over low heat. Whisk in the flour and let bubble for 1 minute without browning. Whisk in the poaching liquid and bring to a boil over medium heat, whisking often. Stir in the Cheddar until melted, then season with salt and pepper. Pour the sauce over the fish and spinach. Mix the bread crumbs, Parmesan, and parsley together and sprinkle over the sauce.

4 Position a broiler rack about 6in (15cm) from the heat and preheat the broiler. Broil about 2 minutes, or until the topping is golden brown. Serve immediately.

Smoked Salmon Mornay

The dish can be made using hot smoked salmon instead, but season carefully as the fish is already salted.

Fish in Coconut Stew

This is a popular Brazilian stew, rich with creamy coconut milk. An authentic ingredient is palm oil (*dendê*), which lends a distinctive flavor and color, but you can use more olive oil instead

 makes 4 servings

 prep 15 mins • cook 35 mins

4 tbsp olive oil

1 onion, thinly sliced

3 ripe tomatoes, skinned, seeded, and chopped

1 red bell pepper, seeded and thinly sliced

1 green bell pepper, seeded and thinly sliced

1 cup canned coconut milk

1 tbsp tomato paste

salt and freshly ground black pepper

1¾lb (800g) firm white fish, such as cod and snapper, cut into large chunks or strips

3 tbsp palm oil (optional)

1 tbsp chopped cilantro

For the salsa

1 ripe tomato, skinned, seeded, and chopped

1 small red onion, finely chopped

1 garlic clove, finely chopped

1 tbsp red wine vinegar

1 tbsp fresh lime juice

1 tbsp vegetable oil

1 tbsp chopped parsley

1 tsp hot pepper sauce

● **Prepare ahead** Prepare, cool, and refrigerate the stew up through step 1 up to 1 day ahead. When ready to serve, heat and add the fish. The salsa can be made up to 1 day ahead, but stir in the chopped parsley at the last minute.

1 Heat the olive oil in a deep frying pan over medium heat. Add the onion and cook, stirring

frequently, for 5 minutes, until tender but not browned. Add the tomatoes and the peppers. Reduce the heat to medium-low and simmer, stirring occasionally, for 20 minutes, until the vegetables have softened and released their juices. Stir in the coconut milk and tomato paste and return to a boil. Season with salt and pepper.

2 Meanwhile, make the salsa. Mix all the ingredients together and spoon into a serving bowl. Set aside to allow the flavors to blend.

3 Add the fish to the coconut milk mixture and cook, stirring occasionally, for 7 minutes, until the fish is opaque throughout. Do

not overcook. Stir in the palm oil, if using.

4 Transfer the stew to a heated serving dish and sprinkle with the cilantro. Serve hot, with the salsa passed on the side.

VARIATION

Farofa de Dendê

To make this traditional side dish, heat 2 tbsp *dendê* oil in a frying pan over medium heat. Add 1 chopped onion and cook 5 minutes until tender. Add ½ cup manioc flour and 15 soaked drained, and finely chopped dried shrimp. Cook, stirring, until the flour is toasted, about 5 minutes.

Baked Trout with Almonds

Delicate trout enhanced with citrus and a nutty texture

 makes 4 servings

prep 10 mins • cook 25 mins

4 trout, cleaned and rinsed

2 lemons, halved and thinly sliced

6 tbsp butter, melted

½ cup sliced natural almonds

¾ cup dry white wine

salt and freshly ground black pepper

3 tbsp finely chopped parsley

1 Preheat the oven to 400°F (200°C). Butter a shallow baking dish. Make a few diagonal slashes about ¼in (5mm) deep on both sides of each fish. Arrange the fish side by side and tuck the lemon slices into the slashes.

2 Drizzle 2 tbsp of melted butter over the fish. Bake uncovered for 20 minutes or until the fish flakes easily with a fork.

3 Meanwhile, heat the remaining butter in a frying pan over medium heat. Add the almonds and cook, stirring, until lightly browned. Add the wine, bring to a boil, and cook until reduced by half, about 2 minutes. Mix in the parsley and season with salt and pepper. Transfer the fish to plates, spoon the almond mixture on top, and serve.

Skate Wings with Brown Butter

Keep an eye on the butter—it should be
nut brown, with no black flecks

makes 4 servings

prep 10 mins • cook 25 mins

Court bouillon

⅓ cup **dry white wine**

½ **lemon**, sliced

½ **onion**, thickly sliced

5 **black peppercorns**, crushed

1 **garlic clove**, crushed

2 sprigs **parsley**

2 sprigs **thyme**

1 **bay leaf**

1 tsp **salt**

4 skinless **skate wings**

12 tbsp **butter**, cut into pieces

4 tsp fresh **lemon** juice

3 tbsp finely chopped **parsley**

2 tbsp **nonpareil capers** in brine,
rinsed

1 **To make the court bouillon**,
bring 1 quart (1 liter) water and
all of the ingredients to a boil in a very
large frying pan over medium heat.
Reduce the heat to low and simmer
for 10 minutes. Let cool until tepid.

2 **Add the skate** to the frying
pan. Return to a bare simmer
over medium heat. Cover and poach
for 7–10 minutes, until the flesh can
easily be lifted from the bone. Using
a slotted spatula, transfer each wing
to a dinner plate.

3 **Meanwhile**, melt the butter in
a large saucepan over medium-
high heat, swirling the pan so the
butter melts evenly. Cook until the
milk solids turn a dark hazelnut
brown, using a spoon to skim the
surface if necessary to check the
color. Remove from the heat and add
the lemon juice.

4 **Scatter the parsley** and
capers over the skate wings. Pour
the brown butter over the skate. Serve
at once.

● **Good with** boiled new potatoes
and lemon wedges.

● **Leftovers** The poaching liquid
can be used in any recipe that calls
for fish stock, from soup to risotto to
paella. Cool, cover, refrigerate, and
use within 2 days.

Salmon Fishcakes

Ideal as a main course or made bite-sized as a canapé

makes 6 servings

prep 30 mins, plus cooling and
chilling • cook 30 mins

freeze well-wrapped cooked
salmon cakes up to 1 month

1lb (450g) **baking potatoes**, such as
Burbank or russet, peeled and cubed

2lb (900g) skinless **salmon fillets**

1 **onion**, halved

a few **black peppercorns**

2 **bay leaves**

4 whole **scallions**, finely chopped

3 tbsp chopped **dill**

2 tbsp **prepared horseradish**

grated zest of 1 **lemon**

2 tbsp fresh **lemon** juice

pinch of **cayenne**

salt and freshly ground **black pepper**

For the coating

1½ cups **fresh bread crumbs**

4 tbsp chopped **chives or parsley**

½ cup **all-purpose flour**

2 large **eggs**, beaten

½ cup **vegetable oil**

1 **Boil the potatoes** in salted
water over medium heat about
20 minutes or until very tender. Drain
well, return to the pan, and mash.

2 **Meanwhile**, place the salmon
in a frying pan and cover with cold
water. Add the onion, peppercorns,
and bay leaves. Bring to a boil, then
simmer for 5 minutes. Remove from
the heat, drain in a colander, and let
cool completely, about 20 minutes.

3 **Flake the salmon** into a large
bowl. Add the mashed potatoes,
scallions, dill, horseradish, lemon zest
and juice, and cayenne and mix well.
Season with salt and pepper. Shape
into 12 round cakes. If you have time,
refrigerate 1 hour before cooking.

4 **Process** the bread crumbs and
chives in a food processor until
well combined. Put the flour, eggs,
and bread crumbs in shallow dishes.
Coat the salmon cakes in flour, then
egg, then the herbed bread crumbs.

5 **Heat the oil** in a frying pan
over medium heat. In batches,
add the salmon cakes and cook for
about 3 minutes on each side, or
until crisp and golden brown. Transfer
to paper towels to drain. Serve hot,
with the lemon wedges.

Fisherman's Pie

A British favorite, with its creamy filling and mashed-potato topping. It can be as luxurious or as homely as desired, depending on the seafood used.

 makes 4 servings

 prep 25 mins • cook 50 mins–1 hr

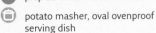 potato masher, oval ovenproof serving dish

1lb (450g) **baking potatoes**, such as Burbank or russet, peeled and cut into 1in (2.5cm) chunks

1¾ cups **whole milk**

8 tbsp **butter**

salt and freshly ground **black pepper**

1½lb **haddock** or **cod fillets**

10oz (300g) **medium shrimp**, peeled and deveined, shells reserved

4 **black peppercorns**, lightly crushed

1 **bay leaf**

¼ cup **all-purpose flour**

2 tbsp **heavy cream**

1 tbsp chopped **parsley**

½ tsp fresh **lemon** juice

pinch of **cayenne pepper**

● **Prepare ahead** Step 1 can be completed up to a day in advance. The fish can also be poached 1 day in advance; cover and chill the fish and reserve the milk until needed. The prawns can be shelled and deveined several hours in advance, and chilled until needed.

1 **Boil the potatoes** in a large saucepan of lightly salted water about 15 minutes, or until tender. Drain well. Mash until smooth, then beat in ⅓ cup milk and 3 tbsp butter. Season with salt and pepper.

2 **Meanwhile, combine** the haddock and remaining milk in a large frying pan. Simmer about 10 minutes until the fish flakes easily. Use a slotted spoon to transfer the fish to a plate. Add the shrimp shells (reserve the shrimp), peppercorns, and bay leaf to the milk and simmer over very low heat for 10 minutes.

3 **Preheat the oven** to 425°F (220°C). Melt 4 tbsp butter in a saucepan over medium heat. Whisk in the flour and cook for 1 minute. Strain the milk mixture into the saucepan and whisk well. Cook, whisking often, until the sauce comes to a boil and thickens.

4 **Stir in the cream**, parsley, and lemon juice, and seaon with the cayenne, salt, and pepper. Flake in the fish and add the reserved shrimp.

5 **Spoon the fish mixture** into a baking dish, top with the mashed potatoes, and dot with the final 1 tbsp butter. Place on a baking sheet. Bake for 20–25 minutes, or until the topping is golden and the filling is hot when you stick a knife into it.

● **Good with** a bowl of minted peas on the side.

● **Leftovers** can be pulsed in a blender or food processor, formed into patties, rolled in fresh bread crumbs, flavored with chopped herbs and fried.

CHOOSING FISH

Cod, hake, halibut, salmon, and monkfish are all suitable to substitute for or include with the haddock. A large scallop per diner adds a touch of luxury.

Tuna Carpaccio

This updated version of carpaccio uses tuna served with a lemony potato salad

 makes 4 servings

prep 10–15 mins • cook 20 mins

5 tbsp **extra virgin olive oil**, plus extra for drizzling

½ tsp chopped **thyme**

grated zest of 1 **lemon**

5 small **Yukon Gold potatoes**, scrubbed

salt

¼ cup **mayonnaise**

1 tsp **nonpareil capers**, rinsed

2 tbsp **vegetable oil**

14oz (400g) **sushi-grade tuna fillet**

1 **Mix 4 tbsp** of the olive oil, thyme, and zest together. Set aside.

2 **Boil the potatoes** about 25 minutes until tender. Drain, cool, peel, and cut into thick slices. Place in a bowl. Drizzle with the remaining 1 tbsp olive oil, mix with mayonnaise, and season with salt.

3 **Heat the vegetable oil** in a small skillet over high heat. Fry the capers about 2 minutes, until crispy. Drain on paper towels.

4 **Slice** the tuna thinly across the grain. Divide the slices among 4 plates. Scatter with capers, sprinkle with salt, and drizzle with olive oil. Add equal amounts of the potatoes to each, and serve immediately.

Baked Flounder with Bacon

This is a tasty and unusual way of cooking
delicate flounder or sole

 makes 4 servings

 prep 10 mins • cook 20 mins

low GI

2 tbsp **olive oil**

4 **bacon** slices, coarsely chopped

3 **scallions**, white and green parts,
chopped

4 **flounder** fillets, 6oz (175g) each

freshly ground **pepper**

4 tbsp **butter**

2 tbsp fresh **lemon** juice

1 tbsp chopped fresh **parsley**

1 Preheat the oven to 400°F
(200°C). Heat the oil in a
flameproof roasting pan over
medium heat. Add the bacon and
scallions, and cook for 2 minutes,
stirring frequently. Add the flounder,
skin side down, baste with the oil, and
season with pepper.

2 Bake for 15 minutes, basting
once or twice. Transfer each fillet
to a plate. Drain the bacon and
scallions in a sieve.

3 Heat the butter in a small
saucepan over medium heat
about 2 minutes, until golden brown.
Add the reserved bacon and scallions
with the lemon juice, and stir in the
parsley. Spoon over the fish and serve
immediately.

● **Good with** stir-fried or steamed
vegetables, such as spinach, green
beans, or carrots.

Baked Salmon with Cucumber Dill Sauce

Equally good with salmon steaks or fillets, this light dish
is quickly prepared

 makes 4 servings

 prep 10 mins, plus standing
• cook 10 mins

½ **cucumber**, peeled, seeded, and
finely chopped

salt

1 cup plain low-fat **yogurt**

2 tsp Dijon **mustard**

1 **scallion**, finely chopped

1 tbsp chopped **dill** or mint

freshly ground **black pepper**

4 skinless **salmon** fillets, about
6oz (175g) each

2 tsp **olive oil**

1 tbsp fresh **lemon** juice

● **Prepare ahead** The sauce
can covered and refrigerated up
to 2 days ahead.

1 To make the sauce, toss the
cucumber with ½ tsp salt in a
sieve and let stand to drain for 1 hour.
Rinse with cold water and pat dry with
paper towels. Mix the cucumber,
yogurt, mustard, scallion, and dill.
Season with salt and pepper.

2 Preheat the oven to 400°F
(200°C). Arrange the salmon in
an oiled shallow baking dish. Brush
with oil, sprinkle with lemon juice,
and season with salt and pepper.

3 Bake in the oven for 8–10
minutes, until the salmon is
opaque when pierced with the tip of a
knife. Using a slotted spatula, transfer
the salmon to dinner plates. Stir the
pan juices into the cucumber sauce.
Spoon the sauce over the salmon.
Serve hot.

● **Good with** buttered new
potatoes and steamed asparagus.

VARIATION

Salmon Pasta

To make a quick pasta salad, leftover
salmon and sauce can
be tossed with cooked pasta
and refrigerated.

Fish

There are many ways to cook fresh fish, and straightforward, uncomplicated cooking techniques produce the best results. As an added bonus, fishmongers do all the gutting, filleting, and scaling. So, when you want a healthy meal in a hurry, think fish—we've even got inspirational ideas for using the leftovers.

Choosing Fish

Freshness is the most important consideration when buying fish. If the fish smells "fishy" or there is any hint of ammonia, don't buy it. All fish come from one of three basic groups:

Oily round fish have plump, rounded bodies. The dense, rich flesh can be barbecued, grilled, or pan-fried.

White round fish have similar bodies, but the flesh is more tender and flaky, and responds well to all stuffing, frying, grilling, and steaming.

Flat fish are almost 2-dimensional with delicate flesh. They are sold whole or filleted.

OILY ROUND FISH

Mackerel
Often served with gooseberries to cut the richness. This versatile fish can be fried or grilled. Great for quick pâtés, too.

Salmon
Available farmed and wild, and smoked and plain, salmon is a very versatile oily fish.

Tuna
Whole tuna is very large, so it is usually sold cut into steaks. The meaty flesh can be barbecued, grilled, pan-fried, or roasted.

Sardine
An oily fish that is cooked whole or in fillets. It is especially good barbecued.

WHITE ROUND FISH

Haddock
With its flavorful white flesh, this fish is excellent for making fish and chips.

Seabass
Popular in Chinese cookery, this white-fleshed fish can be grilled, baked, or pan-fried.

FLAT FISH

Lemon Sole
A delicate flat fish that requires quick, gentle cooking to avoid over-cooking.

Turbot
The most expensive flat fish, this has delicate flesh that is excellent pan-fried.

WHAT TO LOOK FOR

If possible, press the flesh gently to test that it is firm and stiff, not limp or floppy

The eyes should be bright with black pupils and transparent corneas, not sunken or cloudy

The tail should look fresh and moist, not dry or curled

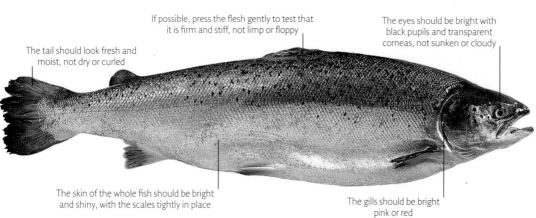

The skin of the whole fish should be bright and shiny, with the scales tightly in place

The gills should be bright pink or red

Storing

After buying, take fish home immediately, ideally in a cool bag. Loose fish should be rinsed with cold water, patted dry, and then put on a plate with a lip. Cover with plastic wrap and place in the bottom of the refrigerator to prevent any raw juices from dripping on other food. Cook within a day. Packaged fish from the supermarket should be left in the packaging and refrigerated right away. Cook according to the use-by date on the label. Keep all fish refrigerated until just before cooking—never leave at room temperature.

Bake in Foil

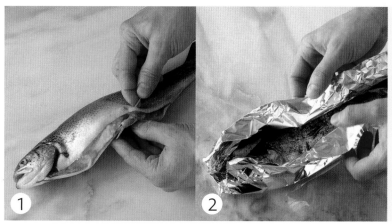

1 Use this technique for baking a whole fish. If the recipe includes a stuffing, spoon it into the cavity, then secure in place with 1 or 2 wooden toothpicks.

2 Wrap the fish in lightly greased or buttered foil to make a well-sealed parcel. Bake in a preheated oven at 350°F (180°C) for 25 minutes for small fish, or 35–40 minutes for large fish, or until the flesh along the backbone is opaque.

Steam

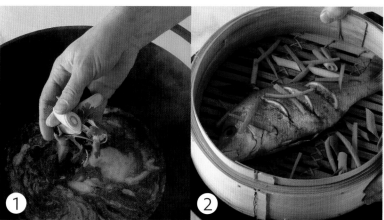

1 To use a bamboo steamer, pour water into a wok to just below where the steamer fits. Add any flavorings, such as lemons and herbs, then bring the water to a simmer. Put the basket in the wok, making sure the base does not touch the water.

2 Put the fish in the steamer and sprinkle any extra flavorings overtop. Cover tightly and steam fillets for 3–4 minutes; whole fish up to 12oz (350g) for 6–8 minutes; and whole fish up to 2lb (900g) for 12–15 minutes, or until the flesh is opaque and flakes easily.

Grill

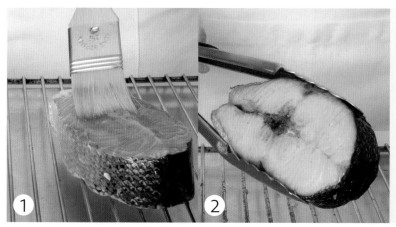

1 Brush a grill rack with vegetable oil. Add the fish, brush the surface with a little oil, and season to taste with salt and pepper. Position the grill rack 4in (10cm) from the heat and grill for half the time specified in the recipe.

2 Using tongs, carefully turn the fish over and continue grilling for the remaining time, or until the flesh flakes easily.

Pan-fry

1 Heat equal amounts of oil and butter in a heavy frying pan over medium-high heat until foaming. Season the fish, then add it to the pan, skin-side down, and fry for half the time specified in the recipe. Use a spatula to turn the pieces over.

2 Continue frying the fish for the remaining cooking time, or until it is golden brown and the flesh flakes easily when tested with a fork.

Fish

Marinades

Teriyaki Marinade
Mix all the ingredients together, then use to marinate the fish for up to 2 hours. Use any leftover marinade to baste the fish while grilling or baking.

- 3 tbsp **soy sauce**
- 1 tbsp **sesame oil**
- 1 tbsp **sweet sherry**
- 1 tbsp **vegetable oil**
- 1 tbsp chopped **scallion**
- 2 tsp grated **orange** zest
- 1 **garlic clove**, minced
- pinch of **ground ginger**

Yogurt-mint Marinade
Mix the ingredients and marinate the fish for up to 2 hours. Remove from the marinade and scrape off the excess before grilling or baking.

- 5½oz (150g) plain **yogurt**
- 2 tbsp **olive oil**
- 2 tbsp chopped **mint**
- 1 tbsp grated **lemon** zest
- ¼ tsp ground **cilantro**
- ¼ tsp ground **cumin**
- **salt** and **pepper**, to taste

Sauces

Balsamic Sauce
Bring all the ingredients to a boil. Reduce the heat and simmer, stirring, until thickened.

- 1 tbsp **brown sugar**
- 2 tbsp **balsamic vinegar**
- 1 tsp **cornstarch**
- 1 **vegetable stock cube**, crumbled
- ⅔ cup **water**

Tarragon Sauce
Combine all the ingredients, cover, and chill until required. Serve with fried fish.

- ⅔ cup **sour cream**
- 4 tbsp chopped **tarragon**
- 1 tsp **Dijon mustard**
- 1 tbsp **lemon** juice
- **salt** and **pepper**, to taste

Flavored Butters

Anchovy Butter
Beat all the ingredients together, then roll in wax paper and chill until required.

- 4 tbsp **butter**, softened
- 2 **anchovy fillets**, drained and finely chopped
- ½ tbsp grated **lemon** zest
- pinch **cayenne pepper**
- **black pepper**, to taste

Herbed Green Butter
Beat all the ingredients together, then roll in wax paper and chill until required.

- 4 tbsp **butter**, softened
- 6 **spinach leaves**, blanched, dried, and very finely chopped
- 1 **shallot**, finely chopped
- 1 tsp each finely chopped **chervil**, **parsley**, and **tarragon**
- **salt** and **pepper**, to taste

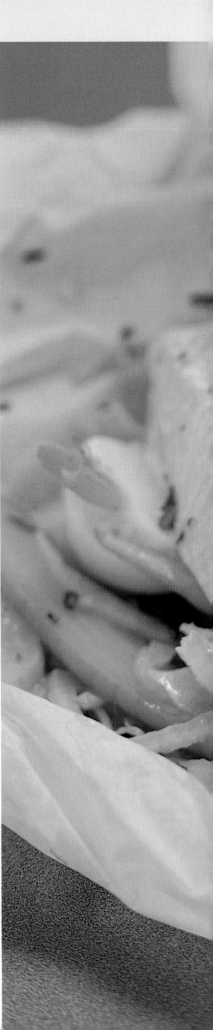

NO-FUSS FLAVORINGS

- **Add a Little Citrus** Drape fillets with thin lemon, lime, or orange slices just before baking. You can also perk up poached and fried fish with a squeeze of lemon when serving.

- **Think Asian** Add grated fresh ginger, shredded scallions, thinly sliced seeded chiles, and a splash of soy sauce when baking or poaching fish, especially oily fish like mackerel and salmon.

- **Add Mexican Flair** Serve grilled fish with a spicy tomato salsa, chopped fresh cilantro, and lime juice.

- **Go for Herbs** If you use herb leaves in a poaching recipe, add the flavor-packed stems to the liquid.

- **Add a Taste of the Med** Serve grilled or fried fish with Rouille (p114), Salsa Verde (p281), or Quick Aioli (p280) for a taste of the Mediterranean.

flavorings & leftovers

BAKING *EN PAPILLOTE*

Cooking fish en papillote, or wrapped in wax paper (p506), with herbs and vegetables, and a splash of stock, white wine, or water, guarantees tender, moist results.

Ideas for Using Leftovers

Salmon Rillettes

Leftover cooked salmon can be combined with the smoked salmon in this rich pâté-like spread.

🕐 15 mins   **page 30**

Smoked Haddock and Herb Fishcakes

Use any leftover white fish in place of haddock.

🕐 40 mins   **page 43**

Fish Stock

Most leftover fish bones and heads make good stock, but do not use those from oily fish.

🕐 30 mins   **page 103**

Pasta and Tuna Niçoise Salad

Swordfish or salmon can be used instead of tuna.

🕐 35 mins   **page 117**

Kedgeree

Flaked, cooked cod, monkfish, or trout can be incorporated into this traditional breakfast dish.

🕐 40 mins   **page 209**

Salmon Fishcakes

Leftover salmon, or any cooked oily fish, can be used in these easy-to-make fishcakes.

🕐 1 hr   **page 255**

Fisherman's Pie

Use large chunks of leftover fish to this so they don't become tough or fall apart.

🕐 80 mins   **page 256**

Seafood Salad

Add flakes of any cooked white fish to this colorful salad with its spicy dressing.

🕐 45 mins   **page 268**

Swordfish Skewers with Arugula Salad

Tender and flavorsome, these can be cooked on the grill or under a hot broiler

makes 4 servings

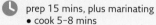
prep 15 mins, plus marinating • cook 5–8 mins

long metal skewers

6 tbsp **olive oil**

3 tbsp fresh **lemon** juice

4 tbsp finely chopped **parsley**

1 tsp **chili powder**, to taste

4 **swordfish steaks**, each weighing about 8oz (225g), deboned and skinned, if necessary, and cut into 1in (2.5cm) cubes

2 **orange**, **yellow** or **red peppers**, cored, seeded, and cut into 1in (2.5cm) pieces

For the arugula salad

½ cup **extra virgin olive oil**

4 tbsp **balsamic vinegar**

2 **garlic cloves**, finely chopped

salt and freshly ground **black pepper**

1 bunch **arugula**, well-rinsed and finely chopped

1 Whisk together the olive oil, lemon juice, parsley, and chili powder in a large glass or ceramic bowl. Add the swordfish pieces and stir gently. Cover and marinate in the refrigerator for 30 minutes to 1 hour, turning the fish cubes over once.

2 When ready to cook, preheat the broiler and position the broiler rack 4in (10cm) from the heat. Oil 8 long metal skewers. Thread the fish and peppers on to the skewers. Broil the skewers for 5–8 minutes, brushing with the marinade and turning occasionally, until the fish is cooked through and flakes easily. (Alternatively, cook the skewers on an outdoor grill.)

3 Meanwhile, to make the arugula salad, whisk the oil, vinegar, garlic, and salt and pepper to taste in a large bowl. Add the arugula and toss.

4 Put any remaining marinade in a small pan and boil rapidly for a minute. Serve the fish with the marinade spooned over it, accompanied by salad.

Salmon in Puff Pastry

Baking salmon *en croute* keeps it moist and succulent

makes 4 servings

prep 25 mins • cook 30 mins

4oz (115g) **cream cheese**, softened

½ cup chopped, lightly packed **watercress leaves**

salt and freshly ground **black pepper**

1lb 8oz (670g) skinless **salmon fillet**

1 sheet thawed frozen **puff pastry** (half 17.3oz (484g) package)

beaten **egg**, to glaze

● **Prepare ahead** The salmon in pastry can be prepared, covered with plastic wrap, and refrigerated up to 12 hours ahead.

1 Preheat the oven to 400°F (200°C). Lightly oil a large baking sheet. Mix the cream cheese and watercress together until combined; season with salt and pepper.

2 Cut the salmon fillet vertically in half. Place the pastry sheet on a lightly floured work surface and roll out into a 12 x 10in (30 x 25cm) rectangle. With a sharp knife or kitchen scissors, trim the edges straight. Pierce all over with a fork. Transfer to the baking sheet.

3 Place 1 salmon fillet in the center of the pastry. Spread with the cream cheese mixture, then top with the other salmon fillet. Brush the edges of the pastry with water. Fold the long sides up and overlap over the salmon, and press the seam closed. Fold up the shorter sides and press closed. Brush with beaten egg and decorate with the trimmings, if desired, and brush again. Pierce two or three holes in the pastry.

4 Bake for 30 minutes, until the pastry is golden brown.

5 Let stand for 3 minutes, then slice and serve hot.

● **Good with** hollandaise sauce or lemon wedges.

Herring in Oatmeal with Gooseberry Sauce

A traditional British dish that could also be made in the summer with bluefish fillets and gooseberries in season

 makes 4 servings

 prep 10 mins • cook 25 mins

 gooseberry sauce can be frozen for up to 6 months

For the gooseberry sauce

12oz (350g) **gooseberries**, fresh or frozen

2 tbsp **butter**

2 tbsp **sugar**, or more to taste

¼ tsp freshly grated **nutmeg**

salt and freshly ground **black pepper**

For the fish

4 **herring**, cleaned and fins trimmed

1 cup steel-cut **oatmeal**

● **Prepare ahead** The sauce can be made several hours in advance.

1 **To make the sauce**: Cook the gooseberries with 2 tbsp water in a saucepan over medium heat for 4–5 minutes, until tender. Purée in a food processor, then add the butter, sugar, and nutmeg, and season with salt and pepper. Keep warm.

2 **Cut the heads off** the herring and slit them open along the belly right down to the tail. Open the fish out flat and place them skin side up on a cutting board. Bone each fish into a "butterfly" by pressing firmly all along the backbone with the heel of your palm until it is completely flat, then turn it over and pull away the backbone, snipping it off at the tail end with scissors. Remove any small bones left behind in the fish with a pair of tweezers. Alternatively, fillet the herrings.

3 **Spread the oatmeal** on a large plate and season generously with salt and pepper. Coat the herrings in the oatmeal, pressing it well onto the fish.

4 **Position a broiler rack** 6in (15cm) from the source of heat and preheat the broiler. Arrange the herring in a broiler pan. Broil for 6–8 minutes, turning once, until the flesh looks opaque when flaked. Serve with the gooseberry sauce.

● **Good with** steamed or boiled new potatoes and a mixed salad.

Cod in Tomato Sauce

The tomatoes and wine add sweetness to this Spanish dish

 makes 4 servings

prep 10 mins • cook 30 mins

2 tbsp **olive oil**

2¼lb (1kg) **cod fillet**, cut into 4 portions

1 large **onion**, finely sliced

1 **garlic clove**, minced

1¼ cups **fish stock**

4 large ripe **plum tomatoes**, peeled, seeded, and chopped

½ cup **white wine**

2 tsp **tomato paste**

½ tsp **sugar**

2 tbsp chopped **parsley**

salt and freshly ground **black pepper**

1 **Preheat the oven** to 400°F (200°C). Heat the oil in a flameproof casserole over medium-high heat. Add the fish, skin side down, and cook, for 1 minute, or until the skin is crisp. Turn and cook for 1 minute longer. Using a slotted spatula, transfer to a plate.

2 **Add the onions** and garlic to the casserole and reduce the heat to medium. Cook, stirring frequently, for about 4 minutes, until softened. Add the stock, tomatoes, wine, and tomato paste and bring to a simmer. Simmer, stirring often, for 10–12 minutes.

3 **Place the fish** in the sauce and bake for 5-10 minutes, or until barely opaque. Transfer the fish to a platter and tent with aluminum foil to keep warm.

4 **Cook the sauce** over medium-high heat about 3 minutes, until reduced and thickened. Stir in half the parsley and season to taste with salt and pepper. Divide the sauce among 4 dinner plates and place a piece of fish on top. Serve at once, sprinkled with the remaining parsley.

VARIATION

Halibut in Tomato Sauce

Replace the cod with the same quantity of halibut and use basil and dried chile flakes, instead of the parsley.

Stuffed Sardines in Grape Leaves

Fresh sardines are full of flavor, and this easy rice and herb stuffing soaks up the tasty juices from the fish

makes 4 servings

prep 10 mins • cook 25 mins

For the stuffing

¼ cup **Arborio rice**

¼ cup **pine nuts**, lightly toasted

¼ cup **dried currants**

3 tbsp chopped **parsley**

1 tbsp chopped **mint**

1 tbsp chopped **dill**

juice of ½ **lemon**

salt

pinch of **cayenne pepper**

For the fish

12 whole **sardines**, cleaned

12 large **bottled grape leaves**, rinsed in cold water

2 tbsp **olive oil**

lemon wedges, to serve

1 Cook the rice in a large saucepan of lightly salted boiling water for about 20 minutes, or until just tender. Drain, rinse under cold running water, and drain again.

2 Combine the rice, pine nuts, currants, parsley, mint, dill, and lemon juice. Season with salt and a pinch of cayenne pepper.

3 Divide the stuffing among the sardines, packing firmly into each cavity. Tightly overwrap each sardine with a vine leaf. Brush lightly with the olive oil.

4 Preheat a broiler or build a hot fire in an outdoor grill. Broil or grill the sardines, turning once, for 4-5 minutes, until the sardine flesh is opaque (open one to check). Transfer the fish to a platter. Serve hot, with the lemon wedges.

● **Good with** new potatoes and a crisp salad.

Grilled Halibut with Green Sauce

A fresh-tasting dish that is easy to prepare and cooks in minutes

makes 6 servings

prep 10 mins • cook 4 mins

For the sauce

1 cup **packed mixed herbs** (parsley, chives, mint, tarragon, and chervil)

½ cup **olive oil**

1 tbsp **tarragon vinegar**

2 **garlic cloves**

salt and freshly ground **black pepper**

sugar (optional)

For the fish

6 thick **halibut fillets**, about 5oz (140g) each

1 tbsp **olive oil**

salt and freshly ground **black pepper**

lemon wedges, for serving

1 Process the herbs, oil, tarragon vinegar, and garlic in a blender until smooth. Season with salt and pepper. If it tastes slightly bitter, add sugar to taste. Transfer the sauce to a bowl, cover, and refrigerate until serving.

2 Preheat the broiler or build a fire in an outdoor grill. Lightly brush each fillet with oil and season with salt and pepper. Broil or grill, turning once, about 4 minutes, until the fish is barely opaque when pierced with the tip of a sharp knife. Transfer to plates and serve, with the green sauce and the lemon wedges.

VARIATION

Seared Salmon with Green Sauce

Substitute six salmon fillets for the halibut.

Mixed Fried Fish

Crisp strips of fried fish are served with a peppery mayonnaise sauce

 makes 4 servings

prep 20 mins • cook 10 mins

For the sauce

1 cup packed **arugula leaves**

½ cup **mayonnaise**

1 **garlic clove**, minced

1 tsp fresh **lemon** juice

salt and freshly ground **black pepper**

For the fish

½ cup **all-purpose flour**

salt and freshly ground **black pepper**

2 large **eggs**, beaten

1 cup **panko** (Japanese bread crumbs)

9oz (250g) mixed **skinless white fish fillets**, such as cod and snapper

8oz (225g) skinless **salmon fillet**

12 large **shrimp**, peeled and deveined

vegetable oil, for deep frying

1 **To make the sauce**, process the arugula, mayonnaise, garlic, and lemon juice until the arugula is puréed. Season with salt and pepper. Spoon into a serving dish and chill until it is time to serve.

2 **Place the flour** in a shallow bowl and season with salt and pepper. Beat the eggs in a second bowl. Spread the panko in a third bowl. Cut the fish fillets into 8 equal portions. Toss the fish and shrimp in flour, then dip in beaten egg, and coat in panko.

3 **Preheat the oven** to 200°F (95°C). Pour enough oil into a large deep saucepan to come halfway up the sides. Heat over high heat to 350°F (180°C). In batches, fry the seafood for 2–3 minutes, or until crisp and golden. Using a slotted spoon, transfer to paper towel-lined baking sheets and keep warm in the oven until all of the fish is fried.

4 **Divide the fish** among dinner plates and serve immediately, with the sauce served separately.

Mackerel with Cucumber Salad

Perfect for a summer lunch, the mackerel can be grilled or cooked on the barbecue

 makes 4 servings

 prep 30 mins • cook 10 mins

1 **cucumber**, peeled

1 **shallot**, finely chopped

1 tbsp chopped **dill**, plus more to garnish

½ **green bell pepper**, seeded and chopped

2 tbsp fresh **lemon** juice

½ tsp **Dijon mustard**

¼ cup **olive oil**, plus more to serve

salt and freshly ground **black pepper**

4 whole small **mackerel**, cleaned and boned

1 **To make the salad**, run a vegetable peeler down the length of the cucumber to shave it into long thin strips, discarding the seeds.

Combine the cucumber, shallot, dill, and green pepper.

2 **Whisk the lemon juice** and mustard in a small bowl, and whisk in the oil. Pour over the vegetables, season with salt and pepper, and toss.

3 **Position the broiler rack** 6in (15cm) from the source of heat and preheat the broiler. Cut two or three slashes into the skin of each side of the fish. Season with salt and pepper. Broil, turning once, for about 8 minutes, until the flesh is opaque when pierced with the tip of a knife. Serve hot with the cucumber salad.

● **Good with** boiled new potatoes tossed with olive oil and chopped dill.

● **Leftover** fish can be flaked and used as a tasty omelet filling or added to a salad.

Halibut with Chunky Romesco

A deliciously fresh but gutsy dish, and great for a midweek supper or dinner with friends

makes 6 servings

prep 10 mins • cook 30 mins

6 thick halibut fillets, about 5oz (140g) each

4 tbsp extra virgin olive oil

salt and freshly ground black pepper

2 cups fresh bread crumbs

½ cup coarsely chopped natural almonds

2 garlic cloves, finely chopped

3 tbsp chopped parsley

For the romesco

one 12oz (350g) jar roasted red peppers, drained, rinsed, and patted dry

3 tbsp extra virgin olive oil

1 tbsp sherry vinegar

¼ tsp cayenne pepper

pinch of smoked paprika

1 Preheat the oven to 450°F (230°C). Brush the bottom of a 13 x 9in (33 x 23cm) baking dish with 1 tbsp of the oil. Add the fish, skinned side down. Season with salt and pepper.

2 Heat 2 tbsp of the oil in a large, heavy frying pan over medium heat. Add the bread crumbs, almonds, and garlic and cook, stirring often, until golden. Stir in the parsley. Spoon the mixture over the fish. Cover with aluminum foil and bake for 15 minutes. Uncover and bake 5 minutes more, until the fish is opaque when pierced with a knife.

3 Meanwhile, to make the romesco sauce, pulse the red peppers, oil, vinegar, cayenne, and paprika in a food processor. Transfer the sauce to a serving bowl.

4 Remove the fish from the oven and drizzle with the remaining 1 tbsp olive oil. Serve hot, topped with the romesco sauce.

Monkfish with Mussels and Pancetta

Pieces of monkfish with mussels in a creamy tomato sauce combine to make a fabulous main course

makes 4 servings

prep 20 mins • cook 30 mins

do not use mussels that do not shut when lightly tapped

1 tbsp olive oil

1 tbsp butter

3 garlic cloves, minced

one 14.5oz (411g) can chopped tomatoes

½ cup dry white wine

4oz (115g) pancetta, sliced

1lb (450g) monkfish, cut into 1in (2.5cm) pieces

2lb (900g) mussels, cleaned

½ cup heavy cream

juice of ½ lemon

2 tbsp chopped parsley

1 Heat the oil and butter in a large flameproof casserole over medium heat. Add the garlic and cook, stirring often, until softened, about 3 minutes. Add the tomatoes and their juices along with the wine, and simmer for 5 minutes.

2 Meanwhile, cook the pancetta in a frying pan over medium heat for about 6 minutes, or until crisp. Transfer to paper towels, let cool, then chop coarsely.

3 Stir the monkfish into the tomato sauce, top with the mussels, and cover. Cook, shaking the pan occasionally, until the mussels have opened, about 5 minutes. Discard any mussels that remain shut.

4 Using a slotted spoon, transfer the monkfish and mussels to a deep serving bowl and cover to keep warm. Bring the tomato sauce to a boil over high heat. Add the cream, lemon juice, pancetta, and 1 tbsp of the parsley. Boil about 1 minute, until slightly thickened. Pour over the seafood, sprinkle with the remaining parsley, and serve hot.

● **Good with** a crisp green salad, and warm crusty bread.

Baked Porgy

This Spanish dish also works well with other whole fish, such as snapper or trout

 makes 4 servings

prep 10 mins, plus marinating • cook 1 hr

2 **porgy**, about 1lb 5oz (600g) each

2 tbsp **tapenade**, preferably homemade

1 **lemon**

3 tbsp **olive oil**

1½lb (700g) **red-skinned potatoes**, very thinly sliced

1 **onion**, thinly sliced

2 red or green **bell peppers**, seeded and sliced into thin rings

4 **garlic cloves**, chopped

2 tbsp chopped **parsley**

1 tsp **hot smoked paprika**

½ cup **dry white wine**

salt and freshly ground **black pepper**

● **Prepare ahead** The fish can be prepared to the end of step 1 up to 6 hours in advance.

1 Make 2 parallel diagonal cuts in the thickest parts on each side of each fish. Place in a nonmetallic dish and spread the tapenade over the inside and outside of the fish. Cut 2 slices of the lemon. Tuck a lemon slice into each fish and squeeze the juice from the remaining lemon over the top. Cover and refrigerate for at least 1 and up to 2 hours.

2 Preheat the oven to 375°F (190°C). Coat an ovenproof dish with 1 tbsp of the oil. Layer half the potatoes in the dish. Layer the onions and peppers on top, sprinkle with the garlic and parsley, sprinkle with the paprika, then top with the remaining potatoes. Drizzle the remaining oil over the potatoes and sprinkle with 3 tbsp water. Cover with aluminum foil. Bake for 40 minutes.

3 Increase the oven to 425°F (220°C). Place the fish on top of the potatoes, pour the wine over the fish, and season well with salt and pepper. Return the dish to the oven, uncovered, for 20 minutes, until the fish is opaque when pierced with a knife. Serve immediately.

Salt Cod Braised with Vegetables

Here, salt cod (*bacalao*) is simmered with the fragrant Spanish aromas of garlic, bay, and saffron to a lovely tenderness

 makes 4 servings

 prep 20 mins, plus soaking • cook 40 mins

 soak the fish for at least 24 hrs in enough water to cover, changing the water 2–3 times to remove salt

3 tbsp **olive oil**

1 **onion**, finely diced

2 **leeks**, white part only, finely sliced

3 ripe **tomatoes**, peeled, seeded, and chopped

3 **garlic cloves**, minced

1lb 2oz (500g) **baking potatoes**, peeled and diced

generous pinch of **saffron**

2 **bay leaves**

salt and freshly ground **black pepper**

1¾lb (800g) thick-cut **salt cod**, soaked, drained, and cut into 4 pieces

½ cup **dry white wine**

2 tbsp chopped **parsley**

1 Heat the oil in a large, shallow flameproof casserole over medium-low heat. Add the onion and leek and cook, stirring often, about 5 minutes, until tender.

2 Stir in the tomatoes and garlic and cook for 2 minutes. Add the potatoes, saffron, and bay leaves, and season well with salt and pepper.

3 Place the salt cod, skin side up, on the vegetables. Pour in the wine and 1 cup water. Bring to a simmer. Cook, shaking the casserole every 5 minutes or so to release gelatin from the fish to thicken the sauce, for about 25 minutes, or until the potatoes are tender.

4 Sprinkle with parsley and serve hot, from the casserole.

Salmon en Papillote

Cooking in a tightly sealed paper packet or *papillote* ensures that the cooking juices are retained and keeps the fish moist

🍴 makes 4 servings

🕐 prep 25 mins • cook 15 mins

olive oil, for the parchment paper

4 salmon fillets, 6oz (175g) each

4 small ripe tomatoes, sliced

1 large lemon, sliced into 8 rounds

8 tarragon sprigs

● **Prepare ahead** The salmon parcels can be refrigerated up to 6 hours before baking.

1 Cut 4 heart-shaped pieces of baking parchment large enough for the salmon to fit on one half.

2 Preheat the oven to 400°F (200°C). For each fillet, brush a parchment heart with olive oil. Place 1 sliced tomato on one half of the heart. Top with 1 salmon fillet, 2 lemon slices, 2 tarragon sprigs, and season with salt and pepper. Fold the heart over to enclose the fish and vegetables. Tightly crimp the edges to create a tight seal. Repeat with the remaining ingredients. Place the parcels on a baking sheet. Bake for about 15 minutes, until the paper browns.

3 Place the salmon parcels on dinner plates. Serve immediately, with scissors so each guest can open their packet.

● **Good with** *Beurre Blanc* (a classic butter sauce) poured over the fish or served alongside.

Seafood Salad

Suitable for lunch, a picnic, or a light supper in the back yard, this chilled salad is an ideal summer dish

🍴 makes 4 servings

🕐 prep 20 mins • cook 25 mins

For the dressing

2 tbsp olive oil

grated zest and juice of 1 lemon

juice of 1 lime

1 tbsp honey

1 fresh hot red chile, seeded and thinly sliced

2 tbsp chopped mint

salt and freshly ground black pepper

For the salad

1 tbsp olive oil

8 small scallops

8 large shrimp, peeled and deveined, with tail intact

14oz (400g) skinless salmon fillet, cut into strips

1 bunch watercress

½ cucumber, cut in half lengthwise, seeded and thinly sliced

1 To make the dressing, whisk all the ingredients together in a bowl.

2 Heat the oil in a large nonstick frying pan over medium-high heat. Add the scallops and cook, turning once, for about 2 minutes, or until opaque. Transfer to a bowl. Add the shrimp to the pan and cook about 3 minutes, or they turn pink. Transfer to the bowl. Add the salmon and cook, turning gently to avoid breaking up the fish too much, about 3 minutes, or until opaque. Add to the bowl. Cool and refrigerate at least 1 hour, until chilled.

3 Add half of the dressing to the seafood and toss gently. Spread the watercress and cucumber on a large serving platter and drizzle with the remaining dressing. Arrange the seafood on top and serve.

Mediterranean-style Grilled Sardines

Popular in coastal regions all over southern Europe, this is the way to enjoy these oily fish at their very best

 makes 4 servings

 prep 15 mins, plus marinating • cook 5 mins

8 large whole **sardines**, cleaned

8 **thyme** or lemon thyme sprigs, plus more to garnish

4 **lemons**

3 tbsp **olive oil**

1 tsp **ground cumin**

2 **garlic cloves**, crushed

● **Prepare ahead** Refrigerate the marinating fish for at least 2 and up to 12 hours before grilling.

1 Rinse the sardines inside and out and pat with paper towels. Insert a sprig of thyme inside each fish. Place them in a shallow nonmetallic dish. Grate the zest and squeeze the juice from 3 of the lemons. Whisk the lemon zest and juice, oil, cumin, and garlic together in a bowl. Pour over the sardines. Cover and refrigerate for 2 hours.

2 Preheat the broiler. Transfer the sardines to an oiled broiler rack, reserving the marinade. Broil for 2–3 minutes on each side, basting with the marinade.

3 Thinly slice the remaining lemon. Transfer the sardines to a serving platter and serve immediately, garnished with the lemon wedges and more thyme sprigs.

Fisherman's Tuna Stew

This fish stew, which Basque fisherman call *marmitako de bonito*, was originally made at sea to provide for a hungry crew

 makes 4 servings

 prep 10 mins • cook 35 mins

2lb (900g) **baking potatoes**

1lb 10oz (750g) **tuna steaks**

12oz (340g) **roasted red peppers**

3 tbsp **olive oil**

1 large **onion**, finely sliced

2 **garlic cloves**, minced

1 **bay leaf**

salt and freshly ground **black pepper**

one 14.5oz (411g) can **chopped tomatoes**

2 cups **frozen baby peas**

2 tbsp chopped **parsley**

1 Peel the potatoes and cut into thick rounds. Cut the tuna into pieces roughly the same size as the potatoes. Cut the peppers into strips.

2 Heat the oil in a flameproof casserole over medium heat. Add the onion, garlic, and bay leaf and cook, stirring often, for about 5 minutes, or until the onions are translucent. Stir in the potatoes. Add cold water to cover and season with salt and pepper. Bring to a boil and cook about 10 minutes, or until the potatoes are almost tender. Add the tomatoes and cook for 5 minutes.

3 Reduce the heat to medium-low. Add the tuna and cook for 5 minutes. Add the peas and pepper strips and and simmer for 10 minutes. Sprinkle with parsley. Ladle into soup bowls and serve hot.

VARIATION

Fisherman's Stew
Make the recipe above, but use 1lb 10oz (750g) mixed fish and shellfish, such as cod, haddock, and large peeled shrimp, instead of tuna.

Chinese-style Steamed Bass

An impressive restaurant-style dish that brings out the clean, delicate flavors of the fish and is easy to prepare

 makes 4 servings

 prep 15 mins • cook 10-12 mins

2-tier steamer or large pan with 2 bamboo steamers and stand

½ cup **soy sauce**

½ cup **Chinese rice wine** or dry sherry

4 tbsp peeled and finely shredded **fresh ginger**

4 small **sea bass**, cleaned

2 tbsp **Asian sesame oil**

1 tsp **salt**

8 **scallions**, cut into 3in (7.5cm) shreds

one 2in (5cm) piece **fresh ginger**, peeled and julienned

4 **garlic cloves**, chopped

2 small fresh **hot red chiles**, seeded and minced

grated zest of 2 **limes**

½ cup **vegetable oil**

1 **Add water** to the bottom compartment of a steamer and bring to a boil over high heat. Mix the soy sauce, rice wine, and shredded ginger together.

2 **Score the fish** with cuts about 1in (2.5cm) and ¼in (6mm) deep on both sides. Rub the fish inside and out with the sesame oil and salt.

3 **Scatter one-third** of the scallions in a heatproof serving dish and add 2 fish and half of the soy sauce mixture. Place in one tier of the steamer. Repeat with another serving dish, one-third of the scallions, and the remaining fish and soy sauce mixture. Cover the steamer and cook for 10-12 minutes, until the fish is opaque when pierced with a knife.

4 **Meanwhile**, heat the oil in a saucepan over medium-high heat until shimmering. Sprinkle the fish with remaining scallions, julienned ginger, garlic, chiles, and lime zest. Drizzle the hot oil over the fish and serve.

Tuna with Warm Cucumber and Fennel Salad

Tuna is often cooked with Asian flavors, but here the profile is Mediterranean

 makes 4 servings

prep 15 mins, plus cooling • cook 6 mins

4 **tuna steaks**, about 5½oz (150g) each

6 tbsp **olive oil**

salt and freshly ground **black pepper**

1 **fennel bulb**, cored and sliced

1 **cucumber**, peeled, seeded, and diced

2 **shallots**, finely chopped

2 **lemons** (1 juiced, 1 cut into wedges)

3 tbsp chopped **mint**, **parsley**, and/or **chervil**

8 **anchovy fillets**

1 **Brush 2 tbsp** of the oil over the tuna steaks. Season with salt and a generous amount of pepper. Refrigerate until ready to cook.

2 **Heat 2 tbsp** of the remaining oil in a frying pan over medium-high heat. Add the fennel and cook, stirring often, about 4 minutes, just until crisp-tender. Transfer to a bowl and let cool.

3 **Add the cucumber**, shallots, lemon juice, remaining 2 tbsp oil, and the herbs to the fennel and mix. Season with salt and pepper.

4 **Heat a large frying pan** over high heat until very hot. Add the tuna and cook, turning once, about 1 minute per side, until seared.

5 **Transfer** each tuna steak to a dinner plate. Using a slotted spoon, serve the salad on top, and drape 2 anchovies over each serving. Garnish each with a lemon wedge. Spoon the dressing around the tuna and serve immediately.

● **Good with** buttered new potatoes with parsley.

Spiced Fish and Shrimp

A fine example of the Nonya cuisine of Singapore

 makes 4 servings

prep 30 mins • cook 20 mins

1 small **onion**, roughly chopped

2 **garlic cloves**, crushed and peeled

1oz (30g) **dried shrimp**

2 fresh **hot red chiles**, seeded and roughly chopped

1 tsp **shrimp paste**

½ cup plus 5 tbsp **peanut oil**

1 **red onion**, peeled and thinly sliced

1 **red bell pepper**, seeded and chopped

1 **green bell pepper**, seeded and chopped

1 cup canned **baby corn**

12oz (350g) firm **white fish** fillets, such as monkfish, skinned and cut into bite-size pieces

16 large **shrimp**, peeled and deveined

hot cooked **rice noodles**, to serve

1 Purée the onion, garlic, dried shrimp, chiles, and shrimp paste in a blender. Add ½ cup of the oil and process until smooth.

2 Heat 2 tbsp oil in a wok over medium-low heat. Add the onion mixture and cook, stirring often, about 10 minutes, or until relatively dry. Transfer to a bowl.

3 Wipe out the wok. Add 2 tbsp oil and heat over high heat. Add the onion and stir-fry for 1 minute. Add the red and green peppers and stir-fry for 3 minutes. Add the baby corn and stir-fry for 1 minute more, until the vegetables are crisp-tender. Transfer to a plate.

4 Add the remaining 1 tbsp of oil to the wok and heat. Add the fish and shrimp and stir-fry for 2 minutes, or until opaque. Return the onion mixture and vegetables to the wok and stir-fry about 1 minute. Serve hot.

● **Good with** broccoli and snow peas in oyster sauce.

Finnan Haddie with Spinach and Pancetta

Some stores carry this deeply smoked fish for a quick supper

 makes 6 servings

prep 10 mins • cook 15-20 mins

1 tbsp **olive oil**

1 tbsp **butter**, plus more for the dish

1 **onion**, finely chopped

3oz (85g) sliced **pancetta** or bacon, chopped

1lb (450g) **spinach leaves**, washed

½ cup **crème fraîche** or heavy cream

½ cup freshly grated **Parmesan**

salt and freshly ground **black pepper**

1¾lb (800g) **finnan haddie**, skinned

juice of ½ **lemon**

½ cup fresh **bread crumbs**

1 Preheat the oven to 375°F (190°C). Butter an ovenproof serving dish. Melt the oil and butter together in a frying pan over medium-high heat. Add the onion and pancetta and cook until lightly browned, about 5 minutes.

2 In batches, stir in the spinach and cook until wilted. Stir in the crème fraîche and 6 tbsp of the Parmesan. Season with salt and pepper and simmer until it has thickened slightly.

3 Spoon the spinach mixture into the dish. Place the finnan haddie on top. Sprinkle with lemon juice. Mix the bread crumbs and remaining 2 tbsp Parmesan and sprinkle over the fish. Bake for 15-20 minutes, or until the fish is piping hot.

Leaf-wrapped Asian Sole

Gently steamed fish makes a healthy, tasty supper

 makes 4 servings

 prep 15 mins • cook 10 mins

low fat

4 **sole fillets**, about 6oz (175g) each

4 tsp fresh **lemon** juice

4 tsp **soy sauce**

2 tsp fresh **ginger**, peeled and grated

Asian sesame oil, to drizzle

¼ tsp **ground white pepper**

16–20 large **bok choy leaves**, tough stalks removed

1 **Drizzle each sole fillet** with 1 tsp lemon juice, 1 tsp soy sauce, ½ tsp ginger, and a light, even drizzle of sesame oil. Gently roll the fillets lengthwise and arrange them on a heatproof plate.

2 **Fill a large saucepan** fitted with a steamer with 1in (2.5cm) water; bring to the boil, then reduce the heat to a simmer.

3 **Blanch the bok choy** leaves for several seconds in the water, or until soft, then place them briefly into a bowl of iced water.

4 **Wrap each fillet** in 4–5 leaves, securing with cocktail sticks if necessary. Set the plate with the fish on the steamer rack, place the lid on the steamer, and steam for 8–10 minutes, or until the fish becomes opaque.

● **Good with** a mix of stir-fried vegetables, or with boiled white rice.

VARIATION

Spinach-wrapped Sole

Use unblanched leaf spinach instead of bok choy. Replace the soy sauce, ginger, and sesame oil with a little butter over the fillets, and sprinkle with chopped tarragon.

> **STEAMING FISH**
>
> Steaming fish ensures that none of the flavors are lost during cooking.

Herb-baked Swordfish

Rosemary is not usually used with fish, but it perfectly complements the meaty flavor of swordfish

 makes 4 servings

 prep 20 mins • cook 15–20 mins

low fat

4 **swordfish steaks** about 6oz (175g) each, skin removed

salt and freshly ground **black pepper**

2 tbsp **extra virgin olive oil**, plus more for the dish

1 **fennel bulb**, thinly sliced

4 ripe **tomatoes**, sliced

1 **lemon**, sliced

4 tbsp chopped **parsley**

1 tbsp chopped **mint**

2 tsp finely chopped **rosemary**

1 tsp chopped **thyme**

½ cup **dry white wine**

1 **Preheat the oven** to 350°F (180°C). Season the swordfish with salt and pepper. Lightly oil a large baking dish. Spread the fennel in the dish and season with salt and pepper.

2 **Place the swordfish** in the dish in a single layer. Top with the tomato and lemon. Mix the parsley, mint, rosemary, and thyme together, and sprinkle over the fish. Pour the wine and the oil over the fish. Cover with aluminum foil.

3 **Bake for 15–20 minutes**, or until the fish look opaque when flaked with a knife. Serve immediately, with the pan juices.

● **Good with** steamed new potatoes and green vegetables, such as broccoli or green beans.

VARIATION

Herb-baked Tuna

Replace the swordfish with 4 fresh tuna steaks of the same weight. Throw in a handful of Kalamata olives and complete as above.

Spicy Shrimp Gratin

The most popular seafood is cloaked with cheese sauce and broiled until golden

 makes 6 servings

 prep 10 mins, plus marinating • cook 15–16 mins

large flameproof serving dish

1½lb (675g) large **shrimp**, peeled and deveined

juice of 2 **limes**

few drops of hot **red pepper sauce**

2 tbsp **olive oil**

2 **red onions**, finely sliced

3 fresh **hot red chiles**, seeded and minced

3 **garlic cloves**, minced

salt and freshly ground **black pepper**

1 cup **heavy cream**

¾ cup shredded **Gruyère**

1 Toss the shrimp, lime juice, and hot pepper sauce in a bowl and let stand for about 15 minutes.

2 Position the broiler rack about 8 inches from the source

of heat and preheat the broiler. Heat the oil in a large frying pan over medium heat. Add the onions and cook, stirring occasionally, about 5 minutes, until softened. Add the chiles and garlic and cook about 5 minutes more, until tender.

3 Spread in a large, ovenproof serving dish. Drain the shrimp and arrange over the onions. Season with salt and pepper. Pour in the cream sprinkle with the Gruyère.

4 Broil about 5 minutes, or until the shrimp turn opaque and the cheese is golden brown. Serve immediately.

● **Good with** fresh bread and a crisp green salad.

> ### Oven Cooking
> As an alternative, you can bake the shrimp at 400°F (200°C) for 20 minutes.

Lobster Thermidor

This irresistibly indulgent seafood dish is thought to be named in honor of the play *Thermidor*, which opened in 1894 in Paris

 makes 4 servings

 prep 25 mins • cook 20 mins

2 **cooked lobsters**, 1½lb (675g) each

For the sauce

2 tbsp **butter**

2 **shallots**, finely chopped

½ cup **dry white wine**

⅔ cup **heavy cream**

½ cup **fish stock**

2 tbsp chopped **parsley**

2 tsp chopped **tarragon**

1 tbsp fresh **lemon** juice

½ tsp **dry mustard**

¾ cup shredded **Gruyère**

salt and freshly ground **black pepper**

sweet paprika, for garnish

lemon wedges, for serving

1 Cut the lobsters in half lengthwise. Remove the meat from the claws and tail, along with any coral or meat from the head.

Cut the lobster meat into bite-sized pieces. Clean out the body shells and reserve.

2 To prepare the sauce, melt the butter in a small saucepan over medium-low heat. Add the shallots and cook about 2 minutes, until softened. Add the wine and boil for 2–3 minutes to reduce the liquid by about half.

3 Add the cream and stock and boil rapidly, stirring often, about 7 minutes, until reduced and beginning to thicken. Stir in the parsley, tarragon, lemon juice, and mustard. Stir in half of the Gruyère. Season with salt and pepper.

4 Preheat the broiler. Add the lobster meat to the sauce, then divide between the lobster shells. Sprinkle the remaining cheese over the top.

5 Place on a foil-lined broiler rack. Broil for 2–3 minutes, until bubbling and golden. Sprinkle with a little paprika. Serve hot, with lemon wedges.

Calamari Salad with Mint and Dill

Fresh herbs and grilled seafood make a delicious warm salad

 makes 4–6 servings

 prep 20 mins, plus marinating • cook 5 mins

2¼lb (1kg) small **calamari**, cleaned

For the marinade

2 tbsp chopped **parsley**

1 tbsp chopped **mint**

1 **garlic** clove, minced

2 tsp ground **coriander**

1 tsp ground **cumin**

2 tsp **sweet paprika**

¼ cup **olive oil**

For the salad

2 tbsp fresh **lime** juice

¼ cup **extra virgin olive oil**

2 tbsp chopped **dill**

salt and freshly ground **black pepper**

3oz (85g) **mâche** or watercress sprigs

12 **mint sprigs**

1 small **red onion**, thinly sliced

1 **To prepare the calamari**, cut off the tentacles. Cut the body in half lengthwise and score the flesh in diagonal cuts to form a diamond pattern. Cut the tentacles into bite-sized pieces. Place in a bowl.

2 **To make the marinade**, mix together the parsley, mint, garlic, coriander, cumin, and paprika, adding the oil gradually to make a paste. Add the mixture to the calamari and stir to coat evenly. Cover and marinate in the refrigerator for at least 30 minutes.

3 **Preheat the broiler**. Line the broiler pan with foil. Arrange the calamari on the broiler pan and broil for 4–5 minutes, turning once, until just opaque. Season lightly with salt and pepper and sprinkle with 1 tbsp of the lime juice.

4 **Meanwhile**, shake the oil, dill, and remaining 1 tbsp lime juice in a small jar, season with salt and pepper, then shake again. Combine the mâche, mint, and onion on a platter and toss with the dressing. Top with the grilled calamari and serve immediately.

Seafood Curry

This quick curry is flavored with chiles, coconut, and lime

 makes 4 servings

prep 15 mins • cook 10–12 mins

1lb 5oz (600g) skinless **white fish fillets**, such as cod or haddock, cut into bite-sized pieces, rinsed and patted dry

½ tsp **salt**

½ tsp **ground turmeric**

½ **onion**, chopped

1 tbsp peeled and chopped **fresh ginger**

1 **garlic** clove, minced

2 tbsp **vegetable oil**

1 tsp **black mustard seeds**

4 **green cardamom pods**, lightly crushed

2–4 **dried red chiles**, lightly crushed

2 cups canned **coconut milk**

12 large **shrimp**, peeled and deveined

2 tbsp fresh **lime** juice

salt and freshly ground **black pepper**

cilantro leaves and **lemon** wedges, to garnish

1 **Put the fish** in a nonmetallic bowl. Sprinkle with the salt and turmeric. Set aside.

2 **Purée the onion**, ginger, and garlic in a blender or a food processor. Heat a large wok or deep frying pan over high heat until hot. Add the oil and swirl it to coat the bottom of the pan. Reduce the heat to medium. Add the mustard seeds, cardamom pods, and chile and stir until the mustard seeds sputter and "jump." Add the onion paste and cook, stirring often, for 3 minutes until it just begins to color.

3 **Stir in the coconut milk**. Boil for 2 minutes. Reduce the heat to medium-low and add the fish, with any juices in the bowl. Spoon the sauce over the fish and simmer for 2 minutes, occasionally basting the fish with the sauce, taking care not to break up fish.

4 **Add the shrimp** to the pan and simmer for a 2 minutes more, or until the shrimp turn opaque and the fish flakes easily. Add the lime juice and season to taste with salt and pepper. Serve hot, garnished with the cilantro leaves and lemon wedges.

Shrimp Diavolo

If hot as the "devil," is too hot, use less of the hot red pepper

 makes 4 servings

prep 5 mins • cook 20 mins

2 tbsp **olive oil**

1 **onion**, chopped

1 **red bell pepper**, seeded and sliced

3 **garlic cloves**, minced

½ cup **dry white wine**

1 cup canned **crushed tomatoes**

½ tsp **crushed hot red pepper**, or more to taste

1lb (450g) large **shrimp**, peeled and deveined

2 tsp **Worcestershire sauce**

● **Prepare ahead** The sauce can be prepared up to 2 hours ahead; add the shrimp just before serving.

1 Heat the oil in a large frying pan over medium heat. Add the onion and cook about 5 minutes, until beginning to turn golden.

Add the red pepper and cook for 5 minutes more, until softened.

2 Stir in the garlic and cook for 1 minute, or until fragrant. Stir in the wine and boil about 2 minutes until reduced by half.

3 Stir in the tomatoes and bring to a boil. Reduce the heat to medium-low and simmer about 5 minutes, or until slightly reduced. Season with crushed hot pepper.

4 Stir in the shrimp and cook about 3 minutes, or until they turn opaque. Stir in Worcestershire sauce and serve immediately.

● **Good with** steamed rice.

VARIATION

Shrimp à la Basquaise
Dice the red pepper and add 1 diced green pepper. Cook as above, omitting the Worcestershire sauce.

Mussels in White Wine Sauce

Cooking in wine, garlic, and herbs is one of the easiest ways to prepare mussels, and one of the best

 makes 4 servings

prep 20 mins • cook 10 mins

 discard any mussels that do not close when tapped

4 tbsp **butter**

2 **onions**, finely chopped

8lb (3.6kg) **mussels**, cleaned

2¼ cups **dry white wine**

2 **garlic cloves**, minced

4 **bay leaves**

2 sprigs **thyme**

salt and freshly ground **black pepper**

2–4 tbsp chopped **parsley**

1 Melt the butter in a soup pot over medium heat. Add the onion and cook about 6 minutes, until lightly browned. Add the mussels, wine, garlic, bay leaves, and thyme, and season with salt and pepper. Cover and bring to a boil over high heat. Cook shaking the pan often, for about 6 minutes, or until the mussels have opened.

2 Transfer the mussels to large serving bowls, discarding any mussels that do not open. Cover the bowls with a large clean kitchen towel to keep the mussels warm.

3 Strain the liquor through a fine sieve into a saucepan and bring to a boil over high heat. Add the parsley and adjust the seasoning. Pour the sauce over the mussels and serve immediately.

● **Good with** plenty of French bread for sopping up the juices.

SERVING MUSSELS

Provide diners with additional bowls for the empty shells, finger bowls of warm water, and a slice of lemon. To serve as a starter, halve the recipe.

Sweet and Sour Shrimp

This is a fresher, lighter version of the Chinese take-out standard, with a fragrant sauce spiked with chile, garlic, and ginger

- 🍴 makes 4 servings
- 🕐 prep 20 mins • cook 10 mins
- 🍲 wok

3 tbsp rice wine vinegar

2 tbsp honey

2 tbsp soy sauce

2 tbsp ketchup

1 tbsp sugar

2 tbsp vegetable oil

1 green bell pepper, seeded and cut into strips

1 small carrot, cut into matchsticks

1 celery stalk, cut into matchsticks

3 shallots, peeled and sliced

1 tbsp peeled and grated fresh ginger

1 fresh hot red chile, seeded and minced

1 garlic clove, minced

1lb (450g) medium shrimp, peeled and deveined

2 scallions, white and green parts, cut into thin strips

1 **Stir the vinegar**, honey, soy sauce, sugar, and ketchup in a small pan over a low heat until the sugar is melted.

2 **Heat the oil** in a large frying pan or wok over high heat. Add the green pepper, carrot, celery, shallots, ginger, chile, and garlic. Stir-fry until the green pepper softens, about 3 minutes.

3 **Add the shrimp** and stir-fry for about 2 minutes or until they turn pink. Pour in the vinegar mixture and stir-fry for 1 minute until the shrimp and vegetables are coated and everything is heated through.

4 **Transfer to** a platter and garnish with the scallions. Serve hot.

⬤ **Good with** hot cooked rice.

VARIATION

Sweet and Sour Fish

Substitute cubes of firm white fish, such as monkfish, for the shrimp. Strips of sole or sea bass would also work well, but take care not to overcook them, or they will disintegrate.

Clams in White Wine

This is one of the simplest ways to serve fresh clams, and one of the best

- 🍴 makes 4–6 servings
- 🕐 prep 10 mins, plus soaking time • cook 15 mins
- ❗ soak the clams in cold, salted water for 1 hr to clean them; discard any that are already open

2 tbsp olive oil

1 onion, finely chopped

2 garlic cloves, minced

2¼lb (1kg) littleneck clams, soaked for 1 hr, drained, and scrubbed well

½ cup dry white wine

1 tsp chopped thyme

2 bay leaves

1 tbsp chopped parsley

1 **Heat the oil** in a large saucepan. Add the onion and garlic and cook, stirring often, for 4–5 minutes, until tender and translucent.

2 **Add the clams**, wine, thyme, and bay leaves, and stir well. Cover and cook, shaking the pan occasionally, about 4 minutes or until the clams have opened.

3 **Uncover and cook** for another few minutes, until the sauce has lightly thickened.

4 **Sprinkle with parsley**. Transfer the clams and the sauce to soup bowls, and serve at once.

⬤ **Good with** crusty bread, to soak up the juices.

Squid in Olive Oil and Paprika

A delightfully simple way to prepare squid, this is usually made with hot paprika, but sweet paprika is delicious, too

🍴 makes 4 servings

🕐 prep 5 mins • cook 5 mins

❗ buy squid already cleaned

1 lb (450g) cleaned **squid**

2 tbsp **olive oil**

2 **garlic cloves**, finely chopped

1 tbsp fresh **lemon** juice

2 tsp hot **paprika**

salt

1 **lemon**, cut into wedges, for serving

1 **Slice the squid** "tube" into ¼in (1 cm) rings and cut each tentacle in half.

2 **Heat the oil** in a frying pan over medium heat. Add the garlic and cook, stirring, for 1 minute. Raise the heat to high and add the squid. Cook, stirring, for 3 minutes until the squid looks opaque and is hot.

3 **Stir in** the lemon juice and paprika, and season with salt.

4 **Serve immediately**, with lemon wedges for squeezing.

● **Good with** other tapas such as chorizo and olives.

Thai Crab Cakes

These make a delicious lunch or light supper dish served with a salad

🍴 makes 18 small crab cakes

🕐 prep 30 mins, plus 1 hr chilling • cook 20 mins

❄ if the crabmeat has not previously been frozen, the crab cakes can be frozen for up to 1 month

1 lb (450g) white **crabmeat**

½ cup finely chopped **green beans**

1 fresh hot **green** or **red chile**, seeded and minced

1 tbsp Thai **fish sauce**

1 tbsp finely chopped **Chinese** or garlic **chives**

2 **kaffir lime leaves**, cut into wafer-thin slices, or grated zest of 1 lime

1 large **egg white**, lightly beaten

all-purpose **flour**, for coating, plus more for the baking sheet

vegetable **oil**, for deep-frying

● **Prepare ahead** Steps 1 and 2 can be completed several hours ahead. Keep crab cakes refrigerated until ready to cook.

1 **Flake the crabmeat** into a bowl, picking it over carefully to remove any small, sharp pieces of shell. Add the green beans, chile, fish sauce, chives, and lime leaves, and mix together.

2 **Add the egg white**, stirring to bind the mixture. Dust your hands with flour and shape the mixture into 18 small balls. Flatten them slightly into cakes. Place on a floured baking sheet, spaced slightly apart so they don't stick together, and refrigerate for 1 hour or until firm.

3 **Preheat the oven** to 200°F (95°C). Pour enough oil into a large, deep frying pan to come about 1 in (2.5cm) up the sides, and heat to 325°F (160°C). In batches, dredge the crab cakes in flour, shaking off the excess. Fry for about 3 minutes, until golden. Transfer to a baking sheet lined with paper towels, and keep warm in the oven.

● **Good with** a spicy dipping sauce made from rice vinegar, fish sauce, and crushed hot red pepper flakes.

Coquilles St Jacques

This scallop dish is equally impressive as a main course or as an appetizer

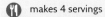

- makes 4 servings
- prep 20 mins • cook 50 mins
- 4 large scallop shells, pastry bag with ½in (1cm) plain tip
- freeze for up to 3 months

For the piped potatoes

1 lb (450g) baking potatoes, peeled and cut into chunks

2 tbsp butter

large pinch of freshly grated nutmeg

salt and freshly ground black pepper

3 large egg yolks

8 large sea scallops

¼ cup dry white wine

one 3in (7.5cm) piece of celery

small sprig of thyme

4 whole black peppercorns

1 bay leaf

8oz (225g) white mushrooms

juice of ½ lemon

3 tbsp butter

1 tbsp all-purpose flour

¼ cup heavy cream or crème fraîche

½ cup shredded Gruyère

● **Prepare ahead** The shells can be can refrigerated for up to 4 hours before baking.

1 **Boil the potatoes** in lightly salted water about 20 minutes, until tender. Drain and mash with the butter and nutmeg, and season with salt and pepper. Stir over low heat about 2 minutes. Remove from the heat and cool slightly. Beat in the egg yolks. Transfer to a pastry bag fitted with a ½in (1cm) plain tip.

2 **Preheat the oven** to 425°F (220°C). Bring the scallops, ⅔ cup water, the wine, celery, thyme, peppercorns, bay leaf, and a large pinch of salt to a boil over low heat. Cover and simmer for 1–2 minutes, just until the scallops look opaque on the outside. Strain over a bowl and reserve the cooking liquid.

3 **Simmer the mushrooms** and lemon juice in a small covered saucepan over medium-low heat about 5 minutes, or until tender. Season with salt and pepper. Uncover and boil over high heat until the liquid is evaporated. Add to the scallops.

4 **To make the sauce**, melt 1 tbsp of the butter in a saucepan over low heat. Whisk in the flour and cook for 1 minute, whisking constantly. Whisk in the reserved liquid and whisk until simmering and thickened. Simmer, whisking often, until slightly reduced. Remove from the heat and stir in the cream and ¼ cup of the Gruyère. Cut each scallop into 2 or 3 pieces and stir into the sauce with the mushrooms. Season with salt and pepper.

5 **Spoon the mixture** into each shell or ramekin and sprinkle the remaining Gruyère on top. Pipe a generous border of potato around the edges of each shell. Dot with the remaining butter. Bake for about 15 minutes, or until golden. Serve hot.

● **Good with** slices of warm crusty bread and a mixed or green salad.

Breaded Fried Shrimp

Cornmeal gives these shrimp a delectable crunchiness

- makes 4 servings
- prep 20 mins, plus chilling • cook 15 mins
- deep-frying thermometer

¾ cup plain dried bread crumbs

⅓ cup yellow cornmeal

2 tsp dried marjoram or oregano

2 tsp dried thyme

¼ tsp freshly ground black pepper

½ cup all-purpose flour

4 large eggs, beaten

24 extra-large shrimp, peeled and deveined

vegetable oil for deep-frying

1 **Mix together** the bread crumbs, cornmeal, marjoram, thyme, and pepper in a shallow dish. Spread the flour in another dish. Beat the eggs in a third dish.

2 **Pat the shrimp** dry with paper towels. Coat each shrimp in the flour, shaking off the excess. Dip in the eggs, then coat with the bread crumbs. Place on a baking sheet. Refrigerate for at least 30 minutes.

3 **Pour oil** halfway up the sides of a deep saucepan and heat over high heat to 350°F (170°C). In batches, cook the shrimp for 2–3 minutes, or until golden brown. Transfer to paper towels to drain. Serve hot.

Mussels with Spicy Tomato Sauce

The distinctly Spanish flavor of smoked paprika is a welcome addition to the classic mussels in tomato sauce

 makes 4 servings

 prep 15 mins • cook 10 mins

discard any mussels that do not close when tapped

2 tbsp **extra virgin olive oil**

2 tbsp **butter**

2 **shallots**, finely chopped

1 **celery stalk**, finely chopped

1 **garlic clove**, minced

1 fresh **hot red chile**, seeded and minced

½ tsp **smoked paprika**

4lb (1.8kg) **mussels**, cleaned

2 large **ripe tomatoes**, chopped

½ cup **dry white wine**

2 tbsp chopped **parsley**

1 Heat the oil and butter in a large soup pot with lid over low heat. Add the shallots, celery, garlic, and chile and cook until the shallots have softened. Stir in the paprika.

2 Add the mussels, tomatoes, and wine and stir well. Increase the heat to medium-high and bring to a boil. Cover and cook, shaking the pan often, for about 6 minutes, or until the mussels have opened.

3 Transfer the mussels to deep serving bowls and sprinkle with parsley. Serve hot.

Good with slices of warm crusty bread to mop up the rich juices.

COOKING MUSSELS

Scrub the mussels well under cold running water. If they have thread-like "beards," pull the beards off with pliers. Farm-raised mussels do not have beards. Soak the mussels in cold salted water for about an hour before using.

Oysters Rockefeller

A traditional appetizer from New Orleans

makes 4 servings

prep 15 mins • cook 30 mins

oyster knife, blender (optional), 4 heatproof serving dishes

3½oz (100g) **baby leaf spinach**, rinsed

¼ cup chopped **shallots**

¼ cup chopped **parsley**

1 **garlic clove**, chopped

24 **live oysters** in their shells

4 tbsp **butter**

4 tbsp **all-purpose flour**

2 **anchovy fillets**, drained and finely chopped

⅛ tsp **cayenne pepper**

salt and freshly ground black **pepper**

rock salt

3 tbsp **Pernod**

1 Cook the spinach (with any water clinging from rinsing) in a saucepan over medium heat and cook, stirring occasionally, for 5 minutes, or until wilted. Drain well, and squeeze dry to remove any excess liquid. Pulse the spinach, shallots, parsley, and garlic until combined and very finely chopped in a blender or food processor; set aside.

2 Meanwhile, to shell the oysters, cover the palm of one hand with a folded kitchen towel and grip an oyster, flat side up with the hinge toward you. Insert an oyster knife horizontally into the hinge and twist, then slide the knife left and right to loosen the shell. Very carefully lift off the top shell, then use the knife to loosen the oyster from the bottom. Reserve the liquid from the shell, then refrigerate the oyster in its shell and repeat until all the oysters are open.

3 Melt the butter in a saucepan over medium-low heat. Whisk in the flour, and let bubble for 2 minutes. Whisk in the reserved oyster liquid. Stir in the spinach mixture, anchovies, cayenne, and salt and pepper to taste. Cover the pan and simmer for 15 minutes.

4 Meanwhile, preheat the oven to 400°F (200°C). Spread a thick layer of rock salt in 4 heatproof serving dishes large enough to hold 6 oysters each. Place on baking sheets and bake 5 minutes to heat the salt.

5 Stir the Pernod into the spinach. Taste and adjust the seasoning. Remove the dishes with the salt from the oven and arrange 6 oysters in their shells in each. Spoon the sauce over the oysters and bake about 5 minutes, or until the sauce looks set. Serve immediately.

Herbed Green Mayonnaise

Use your favorite herbs in this sauce, either singly or in combination

🍴 makes 5 servings

🕐 prep 10 mins

1 large **egg**, plus 2 large **egg yolks**

2 tbsp **white wine vinegar**

1 tbsp **Dijon mustard**

1 **garlic clove**

½ tsp **salt**

¼ tsp freshly ground **black pepper**

1¼ cups **vegetable oil**

¼ cup chopped **basil, dill, tarragon, cilantro,** or **sorrel**

● **Prepare ahead** The mayonnaise can be refrigerated for up to 5 days.

1 Combine the egg, yolks, vinegar, mustard, garlic, salt, and pepper. With the motor running, slowly pour in the oil until the sauce is thick and creamy.

2 Add the chopped herbs and pulse until combined. Transfer to a covered container.

● **Good with** grilled meats or in sandwiches.

Quick Aioli

This rich, creamy, garlicky sauce is delicious with fish

🍴 makes 450ml (15fl oz)

🕐 prep 10 mins

2 tbsp **white wine vinegar**

1 large **egg**, plus 2 large **egg yolks**

1 tbsp **Dijon mustard**

¼ cup **olive oil**

3 **garlic cloves**, crushed

2 tbsp fresh **lemon** juice

salt and freshly ground **black pepper**

1 Place the vinegar, egg, egg yolks, and mustard in a food processor. Blend until combined. With the motor running, pour in the oil in a steady stream.

2 When the sauce is thick and creamy, add the crushed garlic and lemon juice, and process until well combined and smooth. Season to taste with salt and pepper.

VARIATION

Classic Aioli

To make this sauce by the traditional method, place the vinegar, egg, egg yolks (all at room temperature), and mustard in a bowl set on a folded kitchen towel. Using a balloon whisk, beat until thick. Add the oil, drop by drop, whisking constantly. Whisk in the remaining oil, 1 tbsp at a time. Whisk in the garlic and lemon juice, and season with salt and pepper.

Tartar Sauce

A classic piquant sauce to serve with fish, prepared any way you like

🍴 makes 1½ cups

🕐 prep 10 mins, plus standing

1¼ cups **mayonnaise**

2 tbsp **capers**, drained and rinsed

6 **cornichons**, finely chopped

1 **shallot**, finely chopped

2 tbsp finely chopped **parsley**

2 tbsp finely chopped **tarragon**

1 tbsp fresh **lemon** juice

salt and freshly ground **black pepper**

● **Prepare ahead** Cover and refrigerate for up to 4 days.

1 Mix the mayonnaise, capers, cornichons, shallot, parsley, tarragon, and lemon juice juice in a bowl. Season with salt and pepper.

2 Cover and let stand at least 20 minutes before serving, to allow the flavors to develop. Serve at room temperature.

● **Good with** fried or grilled fish, shellfish, and crab and fish cakes.

Beurre Blanc

This classic French sauce is simple to make

🍴 makes 275ml (9fl oz)

🕐 prep 5 mins • cook 10 mins

¾ cup **dry white wine**

1 **shallot**, finely chopped

1 tbsp chopped **parsley**

1 **bay leaf**

4 whole **black peppercorns**

12 tbsp **butter**, diced

salt and freshly ground **black pepper**

1 Boil the wine, shallot, parsley, bay leaf, and peppercorns in a small saucepan. Then simmer slowly over high heat for 4–5 minutes, or until reduced by half. Remove from the heat.

2 Strain the reduced liquid through a sieve into a heatproof bowl. Place the bowl over a pan of gently simmering water and, whisking constantly, add the cubes of butter, 1 at a time. When it becomes an emulsified sauce it is ready to use. Season with salt and pepper.

● **Good with** pan-fried fish and steamed vegetables.

CHOOSING A DRY WHITE WINE FOR COOKING

Using wine in certain dishes adds a bright flavor without overpowering the ingredients. If a dish calls for a dry white wine, an unoaked, crisp wine is the most versatile. Sauvignon Blanc or Pinot Grigio are great in this sauce for fish.

Salsa Verde

This strong-flavored green sauce is packed with herbs and very versatile

 makes 4 servings

 prep 15 mins

6 **scallions**, white and green parts, minced

3 tbsp bottled **capers**, rinsed and chopped

4 **anchovy fillets** in oil, rinsed and minced

1 **garlic clove**, minced

3 tbsp chopped **parsley**

2 tbsp chopped **basil**

2 tbsp chopped **mint**

2 tsp **Dijon mustard**

2 tbsp **sherry vinegar**

½ cup **extra virgin olive oil**

salt and freshly ground **black pepper**

● **Prepare ahead** The salsa can be covered and refrigerated for up to 24 hours; let come to room temperature before serving.

1 **Combine** the scallions, capers, anchovies, and garlic in a bowl. Stir in the parsley, basil, and mint.

2 **Using a fork**, stir in the mustard, then the vinegar. Gradually stir in the oil. Season with salt and pepper.

3 **Transfer** to a serving bowl. Let stand for an hour or so to blend the flavors. Serve at room temperature.

● **Good with** grilled oily fish, such as mackerel, trout, sea bass or tuna.

● **Leftovers** can be stirred into hot, cooked pasta for a quick midweek supper. There is no need to heat the salsa, it will be warmed through by the hot pasta.

Chimichurri Sauce

A spicy sauce from Argentina that is great with grilled salmon

 makes 6-8 servings

 prep 5 mins

2 cups chopped **parsley**

⅓ cup plus 1 tbsp **extra virgin olive oil**

6 **garlic** cloves

2 tbsp **white balsamic vinegar** or white wine vinegar

1 tbsp chopped **oregano**

¼ tsp crushed **hot red pepper**

salt and freshly ground **black pepper**

● **Prepare ahead** This sauce can be refrigerated in a covered container for up to 3 days.

1 Purée the parsley, oil, vinegar, garlic, oregano, hot pepper, and 2 tbsp water in a blender. Season to taste with salt and pepper.

2 If desired, thin the sauce with oil or water before serving.

● **Good with** steaks, but also with grilled or poached chicken or salmon, or drizzled over roasted vegetables or steamed broccoli.

Chili Butter

Use this spread anywhere a touch of spice would be welcome

 makes about 1¼ cups

prep 5 mins, plus chilling

1 cup (250g) **butter**, softened

2 tbsp **chili powder**

2 tsp **ground cumin**

2 **garlic** cloves, minced

¼ cup finely chopped **cilantro**

salt and freshly ground **black pepper**

● **Prepare ahead** The chili butter can be refrigerated for up to 1 week.

1 Place the butter, chili powder, cumin, garlic and cilantro in a mixing bowl and mash together. Season with salt and pepper and mix.

2 Transfer the butter to sheet of waxed paper and mold it into a roll. Wrap the roll with the paper and twist the ends to seal. Refrigerate for 1 hour, or until firm enough to slice.

● **Good with** rich-flavored fish, such as salmon and tuna.

● **Leftovers** can be kept, wrapped in waxed paper, in the refrigerator, then sliced and melted for a quick butter sauce for pasta. Once melted, add a generous handful of cooked shrimp. Heat through, and stir to coat everything in the sauce.

Hollandaise Sauce

A quick version of the classic sauce

makes 1 cup

prep 10 mins • cook 5 mins

1 tbsp **white wine vinegar**

1½ tbsp fresh **lemon** juice

3 large **egg yolks**

salt and freshly ground **black pepper**

12 tbsp **butter**

1 Bring the vinegar and lemon juice to a boil in a small saucepan over high heat. Remove from heat.

2 Put the egg yolks in a food processor or blender with a little salt and pepper and process for 1 minute. With the motor still running, slowly add the lemon juice and vinegar mixture.

3 Add the butter to the same saucepan and melt over low heat. When the butter begins to foam, remove it from the heat. With the food processor running, slowly pour the butter through the feed tube until the sauce is thick and smooth. Serve immediately.

● **Good with** white fish, salmon, lightly poached eggs, or steamed vegetables, such as asparagus tips.

Béchamel Sauce

This white sauce uses a classic roux base; use for shrimp, salmon, or other seafood dishes

🍴 makes about 1½ cups

🕐 prep 5 mins, plus standing • cook 5 mins

❄️ freeze for up to 6 months

1¼ cups **whole milk**

1 small **onion**, sliced

1 **bay leaf**

2–3 **parsley** sprigs

6 whole **black peppercorns**

2 tbsp **butter**

2 tbsp **all-purpose flour**

pinch freshly grated **nutmeg**

salt and freshly ground **white pepper**

⬤ **Prepare ahead** Step 1 can be made several hours in advance and chillled, until ready to use.

1 **Bring the milk**, onion, bay leaf, parsley, and peppercorns to a simmer in a medium saucepan over low heat. Remove from the heat and let stand for 20 minutes. Strain.

2 **Melt the butter** in a clean medium saucepan over low heat. Whisk in the flour and let bubble without browning for 1–2 minutes.

3 **Gradually whisk in** the warm milk. Boil over medium heat, whisking almost constantly. Reduce heat and simmer, about 5 minutes, until the sauce is smooth and thick. Add the nutmeg and season with salt and pepper.

◖ VARIATIONS ◗

Cheese Sauce
Stir ¾ cup shredded sharp Cheddar and ⅛ tsp dry mustard into the simmered sauce.

Parsley Sauce
Stir 2 tbsp finely chopped parsley into the simmered sauce.

Mustard Sauce
Stir 1 tbsp Dijon mustard into the simmered sauce.

Rouille

A rich Provençale sauce, traditionally served with fish soup

🍴 makes 6 servings

🕐 prep 10 mins, plus standing

¼ tsp **saffron threads**

1 large **egg**, plus 2 large **egg yolks**

2 tbsp **white wine vinegar**

1 tbsp **Dijon mustard**

4 **garlic cloves**, minced

pinch of **cayenne pepper**

salt and freshly ground **black pepper**

1¼ cups **olive oil** (not extra virgin)

⬤ **Prepare ahead** The rouille can be refrigerated in a covered container for up to 1 week.

1 **Combine the saffron** threads and 2 tbsp hot water in small bowl. Let stand 5 minutes.

2 **Combine the egg**, egg yolks, soaked saffron mixture, vinegar, mustard, garlic, and cayenne in a food processor. With the motor running, very slowly pour in the oil until the sauce is thick and creamy. Season with salt and pepper. Store in the refrigerator.

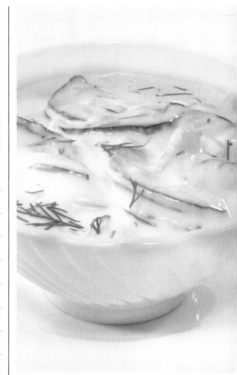

Cucumber and Dill Sauce

A fresh-tasting sauce, good with hot and cold fish dishes

🍴 makes about 1 cup

🕐 prep 5 mins

5oz (140g) **cucumber**, peeled, seeded, and finely sliced

⅔ cup **sour cream**

2 tbsp **mayonnaise**

2 tsp minced **onion**

grated zest of ½ **lemon**

1 tbsp chopped **dill**

salt and freshly ground **white pepper**

1 **Combine** all the sauce ingredients in a bowl, mixing well.

2 **Season** with with salt and pepper. Serve chilled.

Baked Poussin with Lemon and Paprika

A meltingly succulent dish that gets its subtle flavors from a blend of Egyptian and Spanish influences

 makes 4 servings

 prep 15 mins • cook 45 mins

 low fat

 freeze for up to 2 months

4 lemons

4 large ripe **tomatoes**, peeled, seeded, and chopped

1 large **onion**, finely chopped

1 tbsp sweet paprika

2 tsp **honey**

4 bay leaves

salt

cayenne pepper

4 poussins

8 garlic cloves

1 tsp balsamic vinegar

lemon wedges and bay leaves, to garnish

1 **Preheat the oven** to 400°F (200°C). Cut 2 lemons in half lengthwise, and then into thick slices. Combine the tomatoes, onion, lemon slices, paprika, honey, and bay leaves in a large ovenproof casserole with a lid. Season with the salt and cayenne.

2 **Cut the 2 remaining** lemons into quarters. Insert 2 lemon quarters and 2 garlic cloves into the cavity of each poussin. Arrange the poussins on the tomato mixture and season with salt.

3 **Cover the casserole**. Bake for 30 minutes. Uncover and reduce the oven temperature to 350°F (180°C) for 15 minutes more, or until the juices run clear when pierced in the thigh with the tip of a knife. Transfer the poussins to a platter and keep warm.

4 **Skim the fat** from the tomato mixture and discard the lemon slices and bay leaves. Purée the tomato mixture and balsamic vinegar in a food processor. Taste and adjust the seasoning. Serve the poussins hot, with the sauce.

Honey Mustard Barbecued Chicken

The sweetness of honey and the tang of whole grain mustard combine to make a delicious glaze for barbecued chicken

 makes 4 servings

prep 10 mins, plus marinating • cook 25 mins

8 chicken drumsticks or thighs

½ cup ketchup

½ cup orange juice

¼ cup balsamic vinegar

2 tbsp olive oil

1 garlic clove, minced

1 tsp dried oregano

¼ tsp ground black pepper

For the glaze

2 tbsp honey

2 tbsp whole grain mustard

grated zest of 1 lemon

● **Prepare ahead** Marinate the chicken for up to 24 hours.

1 **Make 2 or 3 deep cuts** into each drumstick. Whisk the ketchup, orange juice, vinegar, olive oil, garlic, oregano, and pepper together in a nonmetallic bowl. Add the chicken and mix to coat well.

Cover and refrigerate, occasionally turning the chicken, for at least 6 and up to 24 hours.

2 **Build a medium fire** in an outside grill. Remove the chicken from the marinade, reserving the marinade for basting. Lightly oil the grill grate. Place the chicken on the grill and cover. Grill for 20 minutes, turning and basting frequently with the marinade. Discard marinade.

3 **To make the glaze**, mix the honey, mustard, and lemon zest together. Brush the chicken with glaze and cook for 10-15 minutes more, or until the chicken juices are clear when pierced with the tip of a sharp knife.

● **Good with** a crisp green salad and grilled corn on the cob.

VARIATION

Honey Mustard Barbecued Pork

The marinade and glaze can also be used for thick-cut pork chops.

Seared Herbed Chicken with Green Herb Sauce

The crumb crust seals in the juices, keeping the meat succulent

 makes 4 servings

 prep 20 mins
• cook 20–30 mins

 freeze for up to 2 months

For the green herb sauce

1 large egg, plus 2 egg yolks

2 tbsp white wine vinegar

1 tbsp Dijon mustard

salt and freshly ground black pepper

1¼ cups vegetable oil

2 tbsp chopped basil, dill, parsley, or chives

4 boneless and skinless chicken breasts

salt and freshly ground black pepper

½ cup all-purpose flour

2½ cups fresh bread crumbs

1 cup freshly grated Parmesan cheese

2 tbsp chopped thyme

2 tbsp chopped parsley

2 large eggs, lightly beaten

¼ cup olive oil

¼ cup vegetable oil

1 For the sauce, combine the egg, yolks, vinegar, and mustard in a blender. With the machine running, gradually add the oil to make a thick and creamy mayonnaise. Season with salt and pepper. Transfer to a bowl and stir in the basil.

2 Lightly pound the chicken breasts to an even thickness and season with salt and pepper. Spread the flour in a shallow dish. Mix the bread crumbs, Parmesan cheese, thyme, and parsley in a shallow bowl. Beat the eggs in another bowl. Coat the chicken in the flour, shaking off the excess. Dip in the eggs, then coat with the breadcrumb mixture.

3 Heat the olive and vegetable oils in a large frying pan over medium-high heat until shimmering. Add the chicken and cook, turning once, until golden brown, about 10 minutes. Transfer to paper towels to drain briefly. Serve hot with the sauce passed on the side.

Pot Roast of Guinea Hen with Cabbage and Walnuts

Guinea hens gently simmered in broth are moist and flavorful, with all of the tasty juices sealed in the pot

 makes 4 servings

prep 20 mins • cook 40–45 mins

2 guinea hens, about 2¾lb (1.25kg) each

salt and freshly ground black pepper

2 tbsp butter

2 tbsp olive oil

4 strips bacon, diced

1 small onion, finely chopped

1 leek, white and pale green part only, cleaned and thinly sliced

2 celery stalks, sliced

¾ cup walnut halves

1 small Savoy cabbage, about 14oz (400g), cut into 8 wedges

½ cup hot chicken stock

1 Preheat the oven to 400°F (200°C). Season the hens inside and out with salt and pepper.

2 Heat the butter with 1 tbsp of the oil in a large, deep, flameproof casserole over medium heat. Add the hens and cook, turning occasionally, for about 10 minutes, until browned. Transfer the hens to a platter.

3 Add the remaining 1 tbsp oil to the casserole. Add the bacon, onion, leek, and celery and cook, stirring often, for about 3 minutes, until lightly colored. Add the walnuts. Return the hens to the casserole.

4 Tuck the cabbage wedges loosely into the pot and season with salt and pepper. Pour in the hot stock. Bring to a boil and cover. Bake for 40–45 minutes, or until the vegetables are tender and the guinea hen juices run clear with no sign of pink when pierced with the tip of a sharp knife.

5 Remove from the oven and let stand for 10 minutes. Transfer the hens to a carving board and cut each in half or into quarters. Place on dinner plates, top with the vegetables and pan juices, and serve hot.

Chicken Pot Pie

This is a great recipe for transforming leftover roast chicken into a satisfying family meal

- 🍴 makes 4 servings
- 🕐 prep 15 mins • cook 25 mins
- 🍲 9.5in (24cm) deep-dish pie pan
- ❄️ the pie filling can be left to cool completely, and then frozen after step 3; do not refreeze if the cooked chicken meat has previously been frozen

2½ cups **hot chicken stock**

2 **carrots**, peeled and sliced

2 **parsnips**, peeled and sliced

2 tbsp **butter**

1 **onion**, finely chopped

2 **celery stalks**, thinly sliced

2 tbsp **all-purpose flour**

10oz (280g) **frozen fava** or **lima beans**, or peas, thawed

½ tsp **dry mustard**

salt and freshly ground **black pepper**

12oz (350g) **skinless, boneless cooked chicken**, cut into bite-sized pieces

1 cup **heavy cream**

1 sheet (8½oz/240g) **frozen puff pastry**, thawed

1 large **egg**, beaten, to glaze

● **Prepare ahead** The pie can be assembled a day in advance, refrigerated, and then baked in the preheated oven.

1 **Put the stock**, carrots, and parsnips in a large saucepan over high heat and bring to a boil. Cook for 5 minutes or until the vegetables are crisp-tender. Strain in a sieve over a bowl, and reserve the stock and vegetables.

2 **Melt the butter** in another saucepan over medium heat. Add the onion and celery, and cook, stirring often, for 5 minutes or until softened. Sprinkle in the flour and stir for 1 minute.

3 **Gradually stir in** the reserved stock and bring to a boil, stirring. Reduce the heat and simmer for 2 minutes. Stir in the fava beans and mustard, and season with salt and pepper. Remove from the heat and cool until tepid. Stir in the chicken, cream, and reserved vegetables. Pour into a 9.5in (24cm) deep-dish pie pan.

4 **Preheat the oven** to 400°F (200°C). Roll out the pastry on a lightly floured surface until about ⅛in (3mm) thick. Cut out a round of dough slightly larger than the dish. Brush the dish rim with water, then position the pastry over the filling, and fold over the excess pastry so the dough is double-thick around the circumference of the pan. Crimp the pastry, glaze the top with the some beaten egg, and cut a small hole in the top.

5 **Place the pie** on a baking sheet. Bake for 25 minutes or until the pastry is puffed and golden, and the filling is hot. Let cool for a few minutes, then serve.

● **Good with** steamed broccoli and, for heartier appetites, some boiled new potatoes.

VARIATION

Chicken and Leek Pie

Replace the onion with chopped leek for a subtle flavor change and add or substitute other vegetables, such as green beans or corn.

Saffron Chicken Brochettes

Ideal for a summer barbecue

- 🍴 makes 6 servings
- 🕐 prep 10 mins, plus marinating • cook 10 mins
- ❗ to prevent burning, soak wooden skewers in water for 30 mins
- 🍲 12 wooden or metal skewers

6 **skinless, boneless chicken breasts** 6oz (175g) each, cubed

2 **red onions**, thinly sliced

3 tbsp **olive oil**

zest and juice of 3 **lemons**

¼ tsp crumbled **saffron threads**, dissolved in 1 tbsp of boiling water

salt and freshly ground **black pepper**

2 tbsp **butter**, melted

chopped **basil**, to garnish

1 **Put the chicken** and onions in a large nonmetallic bowl. Whisk together the oil, lemon zest, the juice from 2 lemons and the saffron water. Season with salt and pepper. Pour over the chicken and onions, mix gently, and cover with plastic wrap. Refrigerate for at least 2 hours.

2 **Mix the butter** and the remaining lemon juice together.

3 **Place an oiled rack** 6in (15cm) from the heat. Preheat the broiler, and thread the chicken onto the skewers. Broil, turning occasionally, brushing with the butter mixture, about 10 minutes. Garnish with the basil and serve hot.

Chicken and Apricot Tagine

The dried fruit and warm spices in this dish are the unmistakable flavors of the Middle East

- makes 4 servings
- prep 15 mins • cook 35 mins
- large flameproof casserole

2 tbsp **vegetable oil**

1 **onion**, finely chopped

1 **garlic clove**, finely chopped

1 tsp **ground ginger**

1 tsp **ground cumin**

1 tsp **ground turmeric**

pinch of **ground cinnamon**

pinch of **crushed hot red pepper**

2½ cups **chicken stock**

1 tbsp **tomato paste**

8oz (225g) **mixed dried fruit**, such as apricots and raisins, chopped if large

¼ cup fresh **orange** juice

salt and freshly ground **black pepper**

1½lb (675g) **skinless, boneless chicken breasts**, cut into bite-sized chunks

2 tbsp chopped **cilantro**, to garnish

● **Prepare ahead** The tagine can be cooked in advance, left to cool, and refrigerated for up to 2 days.

1 Heat the oil in the casserole over medium heat. Add the onion, garlic, ground spices, and hot red pepper. Cook, stirring, for 5 minutes or until the onions are softened. Stir in the stock and tomato paste, and bring to a boil, stirring.

2 Add the dried fruits and orange juice. Season with salt and pepper. Reduce the heat, partially cover, and simmer for 15 minutes or until the fruits have softened and the juices reduced slightly.

3 Add the chicken and re-cover the casserole. Simmer for 20 minutes or until the juices run clear. Adjust the seasoning, if necessary. Sprinkle with cilantro and serve hot.

● **Good with** couscous, which is the traditional accompaniment.

Chicken Paprikash

Spicy paprika adds both flavor and color to this hearty stew from Hungary

- makes 4 servings
- prep 10 mins • cook 40–45 mins
- large flameproof casserole
- can be frozen, without the parsley or sour cream, for up to 1 month; thaw before cooking

2 tbsp **vegetable oil**

8 **chicken thighs**

2 small **red onions**, sliced

1 **garlic clove**, finely chopped

1 tbsp **sweet paprika**

¼ tsp **caraway seeds**

1 cup **hot chicken stock**

1 tbsp **red wine vinegar**

1 tbsp **tomato paste**

1 tsp **sugar**

salt and freshly ground **black pepper**

9oz (250g) **cherry tomatoes**

chopped **parsley**, to garnish

sour cream, to serve

● **Prepare ahead** Steps 1–3 can be prepared up to 2 days in advance. Reheat with the tomatoes, ensuring the chicken is heated through.

1 Heat the oil in a large flameproof casserole over medium-high heat. Add the chicken thighs, skin side down. Cook about 3 minutes until the skin is golden. Turn and brown the other sides, about 2 minutes. Transfer to a plate.

2 Add the onions to the fat in the pan and cook, stirring often, for about 5 minutes, or until the onions are softened. Add the garlic and cook about 1 minute, until fragrant. Add the paprika and caraway seeds and stir for 1 minute. Return the chicken to the pan.

3 Mix together the stock, vinegar, tomato paste, sugar, and salt and pepper to taste. Pour over the chicken. Bring to a boil, then reduce the heat to low. Cover and simmer for 35 minutes, or until the chicken is tender.

4 Add the cherry tomatoes to the casserole and shake vigorously to mix them into the sauce. Cover and simmer for 5 minutes. Sprinkle with parsley and serve hot with sour cream on the side for each diner to help themselves.

Thai Green Chicken Curry

Use Thai curry paste, available at Asian markets and many supermarkets, to make this quick and flavorful dish

makes 4 servings

prep 10 mins • cook 10 mins

1 tbsp **vegetable oil**

4 skinless, boneless **chicken breasts**, about 5oz (140g) each, cut into bite-sized pieces

4 tsp **Thai green** or red curry paste (or more for a spicier sauce)

14fl oz (400ml) can **coconut milk**

2 tbsp **soy sauce**

4 large white **button mushrooms**, wiped and chopped

6 **scallions**, trimmed, green part only, cut into ¼ in (5mm) slices

salt and freshly ground **black pepper**

chopped **cilantro**, to garnish

● **Prepare ahead** This dish can be cooked in advance and reheated.

1 **Heat the oil** in a large frying pan over medium heat. Add the chicken and stir-fry for 2 minutes, or until browned. Stir in the curry paste.

2 **Add the coconut milk** and soy sauce, and bring to a boil, stirring often. Reduce the heat, and stir in the mushrooms ,and most of the scallions. Simmer for about 8 minutes, or until the chicken is tender, and the juices run clear when pierced with the point of a knife. Add salt and pepper to taste.

3 **Serve hot**, garnished with the cilantro and remaining scallions.

● **Good with a bowl** of long-grain rice or plain noodles.

Creamy Tarragon Chicken

Fresh tarragon and cream is a classic pairing in French cuisine

makes 4 servings

prep 10 mins • cook 35 mins

large flameproof casserole

the dish can be left to cool completely after step 2, then frozen for up to 1 month; thaw at room temperature, then complete the recipe

2 tbsp **butter**

1 tbsp **canola oil**

4 **chicken breasts**, with skin and bones

9oz (250g) **shallots**, sliced

1 tsp dried **herbes de Provence**

2 **garlic cloves**, finely chopped

salt and freshly ground **black pepper**

1 cup **hot chicken stock**

½ cup **dry white wine**

1 cup **crème fraîche**

2 tbsp chopped **tarragon**, plus extra sprigs to garnish

● **Prepare ahead** Steps 1 and 2 can be prepared up to 1 day in advance and kept in a covered container in the refrigerator. Reheat and make sure the chicken is completely heated through before stirring in the crème fraîche.

1 **Melt the butter** with the oil in a large flameproof casserole over medium-high heat. Add the chicken breasts, skin sides down, and cook for 3 minutes, or until golden brown. Turn them over and brown the other sides, about 2 minutes more.

2 **Turn the chicken breasts** skin sides up, then sprinkle with the shallots, *herbes de Provence*, garlic, and salt and pepper to taste. Add the stock and wine and bring to a boil. Reduce the heat to low, cover the casserole, and simmer for 25 minutes, or until the chicken is tender and the juices run clear when pierced with the tip of a a knife. Transfer the chicken to a platter and tent with aluminum foil. Boil the sauce over high heat until reduced by about half.

3 **Stir in the crème fraîche** and chopped tarragon and continue boiling until thickened. If the sauce becomes too thick, add more chicken stock; then adjust the seasoning, if necessary. Coat the chicken with the sauce, garnish with the tarragon, and serve hot.

● **Good with** boiled long-grain rice, or try mashed potatoes with olive oil, and chopped pitted black olives.

Chicken in a Pot

A one-pot meal wonderfully flavored with hard apple cider and root vegetables

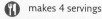 makes 4 servings

 prep 10 mins • cook 1¾ hrs

large deep flameproof casserole

freeze after step 3, once cooled completely, for up to 3 months; thaw at room temperature, then reheat

1 **chicken**, about 3¾lb (1.7kg), trussed

2 tbsp **vegetable oil**

1 tbsp **all-purpose flour**

2 cups **hard apple cider**

1 cup **chicken stock**

1 **bouquet garni** (1 celery stalk, 4 thyme sprigs, 4 parsley sprigs tied)

salt and freshly ground **black pepper**

12oz (350g) **baby carrots**, peeled

12oz (350g) **baby new potatoes**, scrubbed, but unpeeled

2 **leeks**, thickly sliced

¼ cup chopped fresh **parsley**

1 **Preheat the oven to** 325°F (160°C). Using kitchen twine, tie the chicken drumsticks together. Tie twine across the breast to secure the wings down. Heat the oil in a large flameproof casserole over medium heat. Add the chicken and brown on all sides. Transfer to a plate. Sprinkle flour into the casserole and stir for 2 minutes over low heat until barely browned. Stir in the cider and stock, and bring to a boil.

2 **Return the chicken** to the casserole, breast-side up. Add the bouquet garni and salt and pepper to taste. Cover and bake for 1¼ hours. Add the carrots, potatoes, and leeks. Return to the oven and bake for about 40 minutes more, or until the juices run clear when pierced.

3 **Transfer the chicken** to a carving board. Let stand for 10 minutes. Discard the bouquet garni. Carve the chicken, return to the pot, and sprinkle with parsley. Serve hot.

● **Good with** creamy mashed potatoes and green beans or a green leafy vegetable. Leftovers can be tossed with frisée, grated carrot, and vinaigrette dressing to make a salad.

Chicken Schnitzels

A quick dish that is suitable for a family supper or dinner party

makes 4 servings

prep 10 mins, plus at least 30 mins chilling • cook 12 mins

can be frozen up to 3 months; thaw, then reheat in a 350°F (180°C) oven

⅓ cup **all-purpose flour**

1 large **egg**

½ cup fine dry **bread crumbs**

4 skinless, boneless **chicken breasts**

salt and freshly ground **black pepper**

6 tbsp **canola oil**

4 **lemon** halves, to serve

● **Prepare ahead** The chicken can be prepared up to step 3, and then covered and refrigerated for up to 8 hours.

1 **Spread the flour** in a shallow bowl, beat egg in another bowl, and spread the bread crumbs in a third bowl.

2 **Put the chicken breasts**, and the thin, small fillets, if attached, between 2 sheets of waxed paper and pound with a rolling pin until they are about ¼in (5mm) thick. Season with salt and pepper.

3 **Coat the chicken** one piece at a time, first in the flour, then in the beaten egg, and then in the bread crumbs, pressing them on to both sides. Refrigerate, uncovered, for at least 30 minutes. Preheat the oven to 200°F (95°C).

4 **When ready to cook**, heat 3 tbsp of the oil in a very large nonstick frying pan over medium-high heat until hot. Add 2 schnitzels to the pan and fry for 3 minutes on each side, until golden brown, and the juices run clear when pierced with the tip of a knife.

5 **Drain the schnitzels** well on paper towels, and keep warm in the oven. Heat the remaining oil in the pan, then add the remaining schnitzels, and fry as above. Serve with the lemon halves.

● **Good with** sautéed potatoes and green beans. Leftovers are good eaten cold with potato salad.

VARIATION

Veal Schnitzels

Substitute 4 thinly sliced veal scallops (no need to pound) for the chicken and prepare and fry in exactly the same way.

Roast Chicken

Giving the same level of care and concentration to a simple process like roasting chicken as you do to a complex culinary *tour de force* produces surprisingly fine results. As with all cooking, the enemy is dryness, and this can be avoided by paying attention to detail: the heat of the oven and the chicken's position in it, the amount of butter or oil, and the length of time allocated to cooking. Buy the biggest bird you can afford—and be inspired by our ideas for leftovers, on the page opposite.

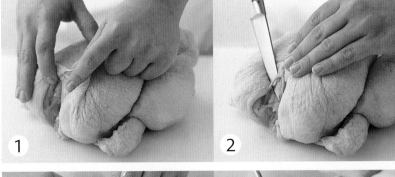

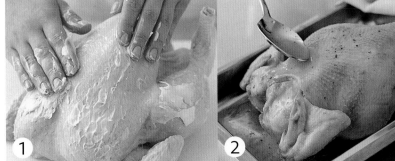

- makes 6 servings
- prep 15 mins • cook 15 mins per 1lb (450g), plus 15 mins resting
- low GI

1 oven-ready **chicken**, about 5lb (2.2kg)

2 tbsp **butter** or **olive oil**

salt and freshly ground **black pepper**

10oz (300g) **stuffing of your choice** (optional; see pp360–361)

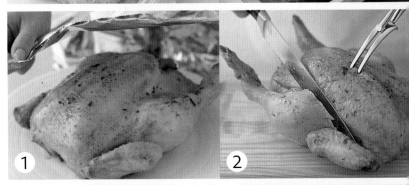

CHOOSING YOUR BIRD

Age, exercise, and a good diet all add flavor—and, it must be said, expense—to chickens. Supermarkets and butchers sell many varieties of birds that reflect all these conditions.

Supermarket birds, the most economical, are fed a special diet that puts weight on the breasts quickly. The birds will most likely have been raised indoors with little exercise, so, consequently, they have very little flavor.

Here are some common labels for chicken:

Free-range The chickens have access to daytime open-air runs for at least half their life.

Traditional Free-range The poultry houses for these chickens shouldn't contain more than 4,000 birds. These cannot be stocked more than 12 per 10 square feet, and must be one of the slow-growing breeds.

Free-range Total Freedom In addition to the traditional free-range specifications (above), these birds should have unlimited open-air runs.

Organic These birds come from a farm with organic status as recognized by a certification organization. As well as being fed a diet of organic grains and soybeans, organic chickens can not be treated with drugs or antibiotics, and must have outdoor access.

When you get your chicken home from the shop, immediately put it in the bottom of the refrigerator in its wrapping on a plate with a rim, or put it in a covered container. Do not let any raw juices drip on any cooked food. Keep the chicken refrigerated and observe the use-by date.

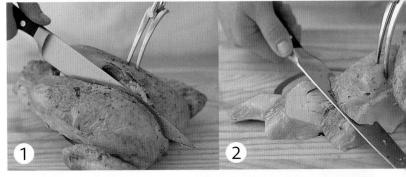

COMMON CLASSIFICATIONS

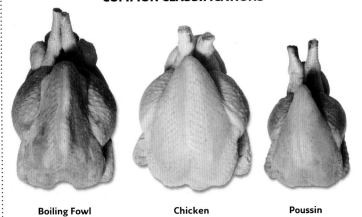

Boiling Fowl   **Chicken**   **Poussin**

Add Stuffing

Stuffing can be pushed under the skin, rather than putting it in the central cavity, to help keep the breast meat moist as the bird roasts. Blend the stuffing ingredients together (see right), then carefully ease the skin away from the breast and gently push the stuffing under the skin from the neck end (see far right). This also ensures the stuffing cooks through.

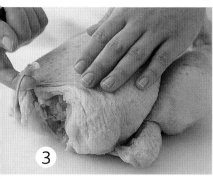

Remove the Wishbone

1 **Put the raw bird** on a large, clean cutting board and pull the skin back from around the neck cavity. Locate the wishbone with your finger and work it loose by gently moving your finger back and forth.

2 **Insert a small, sharp** knife behind the bone and gently work it down to the bottom of one of the wishbone's "arms," then cut it free from the flesh. In an older chicken, the wishbone will be quite strong.

3 **Pull the wishbone out** by hooking your finger under the center and gently tugging until it comes free. Removing the wishbone before roasting makes the bird much easier to carve when serving.

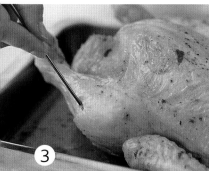

Prepare, Baste, & Roast

1 **Smear butter** or rub oil all over the outside of the bird, then season well with salt and pepper inside and out. (If you are stuffing the bird, push the stuffing under the breast skin.)

2 **Baste the chicken** at regular intervals while it roasts. Turn the bird breast-side down after the first 30 minutes of the cooking time so the juices help baste the breast meat.

3 **Turn the chicken** breast-side up for the last 20 minutes of the cooking time to crisp and brown the skin. The bird is cooked when the juices run clear when skewered in the thickest part of the leg.

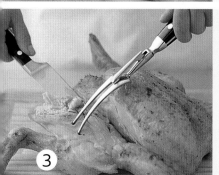

Rest & Carve

1 **Transfer the bird** to a cutting board, breast-side up, cover with foil, and let rest in a warm place for 15 minutes. This allows the juices to flow throughout the bird and keep the meat moist.

2 **To carve the bird**, remove the legs by cutting the skin between the leg and the body and pushing the blade down to where the leg bone joins the body. It is easiest if you angle the blade into the body slightly.

3 **Work the blade** from side to side a little to loosen the joint, then, with a slight sawing motion, push the blade through the joint, cutting the leg free. Transfer the leg to a warmed serving plate and repeat with the other leg.

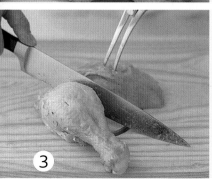

Portion

1 **Remove a breast** by cutting as if you are dividing the bird in half, just to one side of the breastbone. As the blade hits the bone, cut along it to remove all the meat; repeat on the other side.

2 **Place one breast** cut-side down on the cutting board. Using horizontal strokes, slice the breast into as many slices as possible, leaving the wing with a piece of breast meat attached.

3 **Carve each leg** by cutting it in half through the joint at the midway point. You shouldn't need to cut through any bone. As you reach the joint, work the blade into the joint to separate the pieces.

Make Gravy

Using a large spoon (see right), skim off most of the fat from the pan juices. Put the roasting pan over low heat. Mix 1 tbsp all-purpose flour with 1 tbsp of the chicken fat and whisk it into the remaining pan juices. Add 1¼ cups stock or water and bring to a boil, whisking constantly (see far right). Strain the gravy, pour into a serving dish (see p292), and serve hot.

Roast Chicken

Serve with...

Roast potatoes (p231) and a green vegetable of your choice are traditional accompaniments for roast chicken, but there are plenty of other choices. Avoid getting in a rut and try these recipes for variety:

- Lemon Rice (p213)
- Brussel Sprouts with Orange (p237)
- Peas with Lettuce (p240)
- Ultimate Mashed Potatoes (p242)
- Potato Gratin (p242)
- Corn and Peppers (p246)
- Creamed Spinach with Pine Nuts (p247)
- Grilled Vegetables (p235)
- Cauliflower Gratin (p238)
- Bread Sauce (p358)

A Flavor Booster

Cranberry and Sage Sauce

This is a quick-and-easy sauce that really perks up a roast chicken meal. You can make it while the chicken is resting before it is carved.

6 tbsp **cranberry jelly**

3 tbsp **lemon** juice

2 tbsp chopped fresh **sage**

salt and freshly ground **black pepper**

Mix all the ingredients together in a small pan over medium heat. Simmer, stirring, until the jelly dissolves. Stir in a couple of tablespoons of the roasting juices and season to taste with salt and pepper. Serve hot with the carved chicken.

ROASTING POUSSINS

Each roast poussin will serve 2 people. Calculate the cooking time at 12 minutes per 1lb (500g), plus 12 minutes extra. Since the flavor has less time to develop in these small birds, consider adding your own flavor booster (see above). The meat dries out quickly, so protect the breasts and add extra flavor by covering them with a few slices of bacon before roasting.

SERVING ROAST CHICKEN

After carving your chicken, arrange it on a hot serving plate or platter, along with any stuffing, ready for serving at the table. Pour the hot gravy into a serving dish.

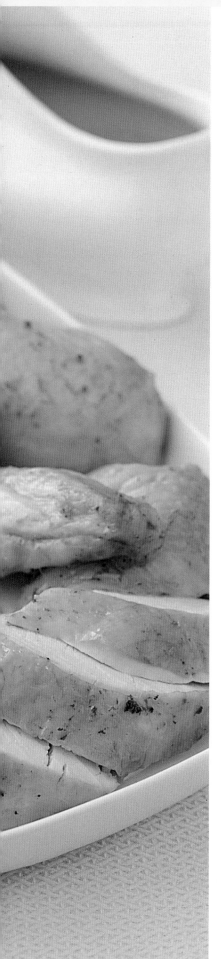

Chicken Croustades

Flavored with tarragon, chicken leftovers are transformed into a stylish party snack

🕐 prep 15 mins   **page 59**

Coronation Chicken Rolls

Perk up packed lunches and picnics with these dainty, lightly curried sandwiches

🕐 prep 15 mins • cook 5 mins   **page 89**

Club Sandwich

You can cut the cooking time to less than half when you use leftover chicken in this traditional two-handed sandwich

🕐 prep 15 mins • cook 15 mins   **page 86**

Chicken Stock

Leftover chicken bones make a flavorsome stock for using in soups, stews, and casseroles

🕐 prep 10 mins • cook 1 hour   **page 102**

Cock-a-Leekie Soup

Traditionally made with a whole chicken, this is just as hearty with pieces of cooked chicken

🕐 prep 10 mins • cook 40 mins   **page 113**

Chicken and Noodle Stir-fry

This quick one-pot meal becomes even quicker when made with cooked chicken

🕐 prep 20 mins • cook 10 mins   **page 204**

Jambalaya

Cooked chicken, spicy sausages, and shrimp are combined to make a filling one-pot dish

🕐 prep 30 mins • cook 45 mins   **page 210**

Thai Green Chicken Curry

Using a jar of green curry paste along with cooked chicken makes a speedy supper dish

🕐 prep 10 mins • cook 10 mins   **page 288**

Chicken Croquettes

These can be served as a snack with drinks or as part of a simple family meal

🕐 prep 30 mins • cook 20 mins   **page 299**

Tandoori Chicken

As tender and flavorful as the classic restaurant dish, this at-home recipe has a more natural color

 makes 4 servings

 prep 10–15 mins, plus at least 3 hrs marinating • cook 25–35 mins

For the tandoori marinade

1 **onion**, coarsely chopped

2 large **garlic cloves**, crushed and peeled

one ½in (13mm) piece **fresh ginger**, peeled and coarsely chopped

3 tbsp fresh **lemon** juice

1¼ tsp **chili powder**, to taste

1 tsp **garam masala**

¼ tsp **salt**

pinch of **ground turmeric**

pinch of **hot paprika**

pinch of **saffron** threads

4 **chicken legs**, skin removed

vegetable oil, for the broiler rack

4 tbsp **butter**, melted

1 **red onion**, thinly sliced, to serve

lemon wedges, to serve

● **Prepare ahead** The chicken can be marinated in the refrigerator for up to 24 hours.

1 To make the marinade, purée the onion, garlic, and ginger in a blender or food processor. Add the lemon juice, chili powder, garam masala, salt, turmeric, paprika, and saffron and process to combine.

2 Pierce the chicken legs all over with a fork. Place them in a nonmetallic bowl. Add the marinade and mix well. Cover with plastic wrap. Refrigerate for at least 3 hours, occasionally turning the pieces.

3 Preheat the oven to 425°F (220°C). Line a roasting pan with aluminum foil. Place a broiler rack over the pan and oil the rack. Remove the chicken from the marinade, and arrange on the rack. Brush with half of the melted butter.

4 Roast for about 25 minutes, or until the chicken is cooked through and the juices run clear when pierced with the tip of a knife.

5 Remove the pan from the oven. Preheat the broiler. Pour off the juices that have accumulated in the pan. Brush the chicken with more butter. Broil the chicken, still on the rack and pan, about 8in (20cm) from the source of heat for about 5 minutes, until the edges of the chicken are lightly charred. Serve hot, with the onions and lemon wedges.

Arroz con Pollo

This one-dish chicken and rice meal is served wherever there are Spanish-speaking cooks

 makes 4 servings

 prep 20 mins • cook 45 mins

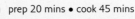 low fat by removing chicken skin

2 tbsp **olive oil**

8 **chicken thighs**

1 **onion**, finely sliced

1 **green** and 1 **red bell pepper**, both seeded and chopped

2 **garlic cloves**, finely chopped

one 14.5oz (411g) can **chopped tomatoes**, drained

1 tsp **smoked paprika**

1 tsp chopped fresh **thyme**

1 tsp dried **oregano**

1 **bay leaf**

1 cup **long-grain rice**

pinch of **saffron** threads

3¼ cups **chicken stock**

2 tbsp **tomato paste**

2 tbsp fresh **lemon** juice

salt and freshly ground **black pepper**

¾ cup **frozen peas**, rinsed

1 Preheat the oven to 350°F (180°C). Heat 1 tbsp of the oil in a large flameproof casserole dish over high heat. Add the chicken thighs and brown, turning once, about 5 minutes. Transfer chicken to a plate and set aside.

2 Pour the remaining 1 tbsp oil to the casserole and reduce the heat to medium. Add the onion and cook about 3 minutes, until softened. Stir in the green and red peppers and garlic and cook for 5 minutes, until they soften. Add the tomatoes, smoked paprika, thyme, oregano, and bay leaf, then stir in the rice. Stir for 1–2 minutes.

3 Crumble in the saffron, then stir in the stock, tomato paste, and lemon juice. Season with salt and pepper.

4 Return the chicken thighs to the casserole, nestling them in the rice. Cover and bake for 15 minutes. Add the peas and bake for 10 minutes more, or until the rice is tender and has completely absorbed the cooking liquid. Serve immediately, while still hot.

Chicken Kiev

Make sure the chicken is thoroughly coated in egg and bread crumbs to prevent the butter from leaking out

🍴 makes 4 servings

🕐 prep 25 mins, plus chilling time
• cook 8–10 mins

8 tbsp **butter**, softened

2 **garlic cloves**, crushed through a press

2 tbsp chopped **parsley**

grated zest of 1 **lemon**

salt and freshly ground **black pepper**

4 boneless, skinless **chicken breasts**

3 tbsp **all-purpose flour**

1 large **egg**, beaten

1½ cups fresh **bread crumbs**

vegetable oil, for deep-frying

● **Prepare ahead** The chicken can be prepared through step 3 and refrigerated for up to 1 day.

1 Combine the butter, garlic, parsley, and lemon zest in a bowl. Season with salt and pepper. On a piece of plastic wrap, shape into a thick rectangle, then enclose in the plastic wrap. Refrigerate at least 1 hour, until firm.

2 One at a time, pound each breast between two sheets of plastic wrap with a meat pounder to an even thickness. Season the breasts. Cut the butter into 4 equal sticks and place a stick on each chicken breast. Fold in the sides, then roll up the chicken completely around the butter.

3 Roll each chicken packet in flour, then in beaten egg, and finally into the bread crumbs to coat evenly. Take care to keep the chicken closed around the butter.

4 Add enough oil to come halfway up the sides of a large saucepan and heat over high heat to 350°F (180°C). Add the chicken and cook about 5 minutes, until deep golden brown.

5 Transfer the cooked chicken to paper towels and drain briefly. Serve hot.

Southern Fried Chicken

This is succulent comfort food from the Deep South, with the traditional accompaniment of a smooth cream gravy

🍴 makes 4 servings

🕐 prep 20 mins, plus chilling
• cook 25 mins

▣ large plastic food bag, large deep saucepan, deep-frying thermometer

1⅔ cups **all-purpose flour**

1 tsp dried **thyme**

1 tsp **Cajun seasoning**

1 tsp **sugar**

salt and freshly ground **black pepper**

4 **chicken drumsticks**

4 **chicken thighs**

2 large **eggs**

vegetable oil, for deep-frying

For the cream gravy

1½ tbsp **all-purpose flour**

1¼ cups **whole milk**

● **Prepare ahead** Steps 1 and 2 can be completed 1 hour or more before cooking.

1 Combine the flour, thyme, Cajun seasoning, and sugar in a large self-sealing plastic bag and season well with salt and pepper.

2 One at a time, add the drumsticks and thighs to the bag and shake until coated. Transfer to a wax paper-lined baking sheet.

3 Beat the eggs in a shallow dish. Dip the floured chicken in the egg, then return to the flour and coat again. Place the chicken on the baking sheet and chill for 30 minutes.

4 Fill a large deep saucepan halfway with oil and heat over high heat to 325°F (170°C). Add the chicken and deep-fry for about 20 minutes or until cooked through. Transfer to paper towels.

5 To make the cream gravy, transfer 2 tbsp of the frying oil to a saucepan. Whisk in the flour. Cook over low heat for 1 minute, then whisk in the milk. Cook, whisking often, until thickened. Season with salt and pepper.

Chicken Chow Mein

This popular one-pot Chinese dish is a colorful, tasty medley of noodles, chicken, mushrooms, and vegetables

- makes 4 servings
- prep 15 mins • cook 15 mins
- low in saturated fat

12oz (350g) fresh Asian-style **egg noodles** or linguine

4 tbsp plus 1 tsp **vegetable oil**

½ cup **chicken stock**

¼ cup **soy sauce**, plus more to serve

1 tbsp **rice wine** or dry sherry

1 tsp **cornstarch**

4 **scallions**, white and green parts, cut into 1in (2.5cm) lengths

5oz (140g) **shiitake mushrooms**, stemmed and sliced

1 small **red pepper**, seeded and chopped

one ¾in (2cm) piece of **fresh ginger**, peeled and shredded

6 skinless and boneless **chicken thighs**, cut into bite-sized pieces

4oz (115g) **green beans**, cut into 1in (2.5cm) lengths

1 **Bring a large pot** of lightly salted water to a boil over high heat. Add the noodles and cook according to the package instructions. Drain and rinse under cold running water. Drain and toss with 1 tsp of the oil. Mix the stock, soy sauce, and rice wine in a bowl, sprinkle in the cornstarch and stir to dissolve.

2 **Heat 1 tbsp of the oil** in a wok or large frying pan over high heat. Add the scallions, mushrooms, red pepper, and ginger. Stir-fry until crisp-tender, about 3 minutes. Transfer to a plate.

3 **Heat 2 tbsp of the oil** and heat. In two batches, add the chicken and stir-fry until the chicken is cooked through, about 5 minutes. Transfer to the vegetables.

4 **Add the remaining 1 tbsp** oil to the wok and heat. Add the green beans and stir-fry for 2 minutes or until crisp-tender.

5 **Add the noodles** and return the chicken and vegetables to the wok. Add the stock mixture and stir-fry about 2 minutes, or until the noodles are piping hot. Serve at once, with soy sauce for seasoning.

VARIATION

Seafood Chow Mein

Instead of chicken, use the same weight of raw shrimp, shelled and deveined, or a mixture of shrimp and other seafood such as scallops. Reduce the cooking time to 1–2 minutes. In step 3, add 4oz (115g) of bean sprouts along with the green beans.

STIR-FRY NOODLES

Always add fresh noodles towards the end of a stir-fry recipe. They will go soggy if overcooked. If using dried noodles, boil them first, then rinse and drain until ready to use.

Chicken with Pancetta

Olives and capers give this dish a Mediterranean flavor

- makes 6 servings
- prep 15 mins • cook 45 mins

8oz (225g) **pancetta**, diced

4 tbsp **olive oil**

4 **garlic cloves**, chopped

6 **chicken breasts**

salt and freshly ground **black pepper**

3 tbsp **all-purpose flour**

¼ cup **capers**, rinsed and drained

2 tbsp **white wine vinegar**

12 pitted and chopped **Kalamata olives**

1 tbsp chopped **thyme**

½ cup **heavy cream**

1 **Cook the pancetta** in the oil over medium heat until browned, about 7 minutes. Add the garlic and cook 1 minute. Transfer to a plate, leaving the fat in the pan.

2 **Dust the chicken** with flour, salt, and pepper. In batches, brown chicken in the pan fat about 5 minutes. Stir in the pancetta, capers, vinegar, olives, and thyme. Cover and simmer about 35 minutes, until cooked through. Transfer to a platter.

3 **Add the cream** to the pan and boil about 3 minutes, until thickened. Season. Pour over the chicken and serve hot.

Chinese-style Lemon Chicken

This is one of those dishes that was probably invented to appeal to Western diners, as lemons are rarely used in Chinese cooking

- makes 4 servings
- prep 20 mins, plus standing • cook 30 mins
- deep-frying thermometer

For the chicken

1¼ cups all-purpose flour

1 tsp baking powder

¼ tsp baking soda

¼ tsp salt

4 boneless chicken breasts

vegetable oil, for deep-frying

bok choy, steamed, to serve

hot cooked rice, to serve

For the lemon sauce

¼ cup fresh lemon juice

3 tbsp cornstarch

1½ cups chicken stock

2 tbsp honey

2 tbsp light brown sugar

one ½in (1cm) piece of fresh ginger, peeled and shredded

● **Prepare ahead** The batter can be made a couple hours in advance.

1 Sift the flour, baking powder, baking soda, and salt into a large bowl, add 1¼ cups cold water and whisk until smooth. Set aside for 30 minutes.

2 Preheat the oven to 200°F (100°F). Line a baking sheet with paper towels. Add enough oil to come about halfway up the sides of a heavy deep frying pan. Heat over high heat to 350°F (180°C) on a deep-frying thermometer. In batches, dip the chicken into the batter. Carefully add to the oil and deep-fry, turning once, for 5-6 minutes, or until golden. Transfer to the baking sheet and keep warm in the oven.

3 Meanwhile, make the sauce. Pour the lemon juice into a medium saucepan, sprinkle in the cornstarch, and whisk until smooth. Add the stock, honey, sugar, and ginger. Stir over low heat until the sauce comes to a boil and thickens. Simmer for 1 minute.

4 Arrange the chicken on a serving platter and spoon the hot sauce on top. Serve hot with the bok choy and rice.

Chicken Korma

A mild curry popular in Indian restaurants, this is a fragrant and aromatic dish with a creamy sauce

- makes 4 servings
- prep 20 mins • cook 45 mins
- freeze for up to 1 month

4 tbsp vegetable oil or ghee

8 boneless and skinless chicken thighs, cut into 1in (2½cm) pieces

2 large onions, thinly sliced

2 garlic cloves, crushed

1 tbsp ground coriander

1 tbsp ground cumin

1 tsp ground turmeric

1 tsp chili powder

1 tsp ground cardamom

½ tsp ground ginger

⅔ cup low-fat plain yogurt

1 tbsp cornstarch

1¼ cups chicken stock

⅔ cup heavy cream

1 tbsp fresh lemon juice

1 Heat 2 tbsp of the oil in a large frying pan over medium-high heat. In batches, add the chicken and cook, stirring occasionally, for about 5 minutes, until browned. Transfer to a plate.

2 Add the remaining 2 tbsp oil to the pan and reduce the heat to medium. Add the onions and garlic and cook, stirring often, about 5 minutes, until golden. Add the coriander, cumin, turmeric, chili powder, cardamom, and ginger and reduce the heat to low. Cook, stirring often, about 2 minutes, or until the spices are fragrant.

3 Mix the yogurt and cornstarch together, then stir into the pan. Stir in the remaining stock. Bring to a boil, stirring constantly. Return the chicken to the pan and simmer, stirring occasionally, for 15 minutes, or until the chicken is opaque.

4 Stir in the cream and lemon juice and simmer for 5 minutes more. Serve hot.

● **Good with** herb-flecked rice.

Indian Garlic Chicken

Based on a classic Indian dish called *Murg Massalam*, this recipe can be roasted, broiled, or grilled

- 🍴 makes 4 servings
- 🕐 prep 10 mins, plus marinating • cook 1 hr
- ❄️ can be frozen up to 1 month

1 chicken, about 3¾lb (1.75kg), cut into 8 pieces, skin removed

For the marinade

¼ cup plain low-fat yogurt

2 tbsp fresh lemon juice

1 tbsp honey

2 garlic cloves, finely chopped

1 tsp salt

1 tsp ground ginger

½ tsp ground cardamom

½ tsp ground coriander

¼ tsp ground cumin

¼ tsp ground turmeric

1 With a sharp knife, make a few shallow slashes in the chicken flesh and place in a nonmetallic dish.

2 To make the marinade, mix all the ingredients in a small bowl. Pour over the chicken, and toss until well coated. Cover and refrigerate for at least 1 hour and up to 1 day.

3 Preheat the oven to 400°F (200°C). Line a deep roasting pan with foil. Arrange the chicken in the pan. Pour about ⅔ cup water into the pan to form a shallow layer. Spoon any remaining marinade over the chicken. Bake for about 45 minutes, or until the chicken pieces are golden and crisp show no sign of pink when pierced at the bone. Serve hot or cold.

● **Good with** basmati rice, flavored with a cinnamon stick and a few cardamom pods, a green salad, and naan bread.

VARIATION

Grilled Garlic Chicken
Roast the chicken for 35 minutes. Build a fire on an outdoor grill. Grill, the chicken, turning occasionally, until crisp, about 5 minutes. To broil, position a broiler rack 8in (20cm) from the heat and line the rack with foil. Broil the chicken, turning often, until almost cooked through, about 35 minutes. Move the rack 2in (5cm) closer to the heat and grill until browned, about 5 minutes more.

Chicken Cacciatore

This Italian dish translates as "hunter-style chicken," and is traditionally served with polenta to soak up the delicious juices

- 🍴 makes 4 servings
- 🕐 prep 20 mins • cook 35–40 mins
- ✓ low fat
- 🍲 flameproof casserole

4 chicken legs, about 3lb 3oz (1.5kg) total weight

salt and freshly ground black pepper

2 tbsp olive oil

1 onion, chopped

2 garlic cloves, sliced

¾ cup dry white wine

one 14.5oz (411g) can chopped tomatoes

⅔ cup chicken stock

7oz (200g) white mushrooms, sliced

1 celery stalk, chopped

1 tbsp tomato paste

2 tsp chopped rosemary

2 tsp chopped sage

8 pitted Kalamata olives, halved

1 Trim any excess fat from the chicken and season them with salt and pepper. Heat 1 tbsp of the oil in a large flameproof casserole over medium-high heat. In batches, add the chicken and cook, turning once, for about 4 minutes, until browned. Transfer to a plate. Pour the fat out of the pan.

2 Add the remaining 1 tbsp oil and heat over medium-low heat. Add the onion and garlic and cook, stirring often, about 3 minutes, until softened. Stir in the wine and boil for 1 minute, scraping up the browned bits in the pan. Stir in the tomatoes, stock, mushrooms, celery, tomato paste, rosemary, and sage and bring to a simmer.

3 Return the chicken to the pan and cover. Simmer for 40 minutes, or until the chicken shows no sign of pink when pierced at the bone. During the last 10 minutes, add the olives. Serve hot.

● **Good with** soft polenta or pasta and a mixed green salad.

Chicken Croquettes

These savory nuggets, crunchy outside and meltingly soft inside, are a fine way to use leftover chicken. Here is a Spanish version

- 🍴 makes 4 servings
- 🕐 prep 30 mins • cook 20 mins
- ❄ can be frozen for up to 3 months

5 tbsp butter

⅓ cup all-purpose flour

1¾ cups whole milk

1 cup finely chopped cooked chicken

1 tsp tomato paste

salt and freshly ground black pepper

¾ cup dried bread crumbs

3 large eggs

vegetable oil, for deep-frying

1 Melt the butter in a medium saucepan over medium-low heat. Whisk in the flour. Let bubble without browning for 2 minutes. Whisk in the milk and increase the heat to medium. Bring to a boil, whisking often. Reduce the heat to low and cook, whisking often, until the sauce is very thick, about 5 minutes.

2 Stir in the chicken and tomato paste and season with salt and pepper. Transfer the mixture to a bowl. Press a piece of plastic wrap directly on the surface and pierce a few holes in the wrap. Let stand about 2 hours, until completely cooled.

3 Line a baking sheet with wax paper. Spread the bread crumbs in a shallow dish. Beat the eggs in another shallow dish. Use two soup spoons to form 12 thick ovals about 1½–2in (3-4cm) long. Roll in the bread crumbs, coat with the eggs, roll again in the bread crumbs, and place on the baking sheet.

4 Preheat the oven to 200°F (100°C). Line another baking sheet with paper towels. Add enough oil to a large, heavy frying pan to come halfway up the sides and heat until the oil is 350°F (170°C). In two batches, add the croquettes and deep-fry, turning frequently, about 3 minutes, or until deep golden brown. Transfer to the paper towels, and keep warm in the oven.

5 Serve the croquettes on a heated serving platter.

Chicken in Balsamic Vinegar

This cold chicken dish has a lovely hint of sweetness from the balsamic vinegar and raisins

- 🍴 makes 6 servings
- 🕐 prep 50 mins, plus overnight marinating • cook 20 mins

4 boneless and skinless chicken breasts

salt and freshly ground black pepper

1 cup dry white wine

1 cup extra virgin olive oil

¼ cup balsamic vinegar

¼ cup raisins, plumped up in boiling water for 10 mins and drained

1 tbsp chopped basil or tarragon

zest of 1 lemon

assorted mixed greens, such as arugula and watercress, to serve

½ cup pine nuts, toasted, to serve

lemon wedges, to serve

1 Preheat the oven to 375°F (190°C). Using a flat meat pounder, lightly pound the chicken breasts between 2 sheets of plastic wrap to an even thickness. Place the chicken in a lightly oiled shallow roasting pan. Season with salt and pepper, then pour the wine over the chicken. Cover with a piece of parchment paper cut to fit inside of the pan. Bake for about 20 minutes, or until the chicken is opaque when pierced with a knife. Uncover the chicken, reserve 2 tbp of the pan juices, and let the chicken and pan juices cool.

2 Whisk together the oil and vinegar in a small bowl, then whisk in the reserved pan juices. Add the raisins, basil, and lemon zest. Arrange the chicken in a nonmetallic dish. Pour the dressing over the chicken and cover with plastic wrap. Refrigerate, turning the chicken at least once in the dressing, for at least 12 hours and up to 24 hours.

3 Remove from the refrigerator 1 hour before serving. Arrange the mixed greens on a serving platter. Thinly slice the chicken, and place on the greens. Sprinkle with the pine nuts and garnish with the lemon wedges. Serve at once.

Chicken Pasties

A complete and filling lunch in a pastry packet

- makes 4 servings
- prep 30 mins, plus chilling • cook 35 mins

For the dough

2⅓ cups **all-purpose flour**

12 tbsp cold **butter**, diced

2 large **eggs**

For the filling

½ cup **cream cheese**

4 **scallions**, thinly sliced

2 tbsp chopped **parsley**

salt and freshly ground **black pepper**

12oz (350g) boneless and skinless **chicken breast**, cut into ¾ in (2cm) dice

1 **red-skinned potato**, peeled and cut into ½in (1cm) dice

1 small **sweet potato**, peeled and cut into ½in (1cm) dice

1 **To make the dough**, sift the flour into a bowl, then rub in the butter until the mixture resembles fine bread crumbs. Beat the eggs and 3 tbsp of cold water together. Set aside 1 tbsp of the mixture for

glazing, and pour the rest over the dry ingredients, and mix to a dough. Wrap in plastic wrap and refrigerate for 20 minutes.

2 **Meanwhile**, mix the cream cheese, scallions, and parsley in a bowl, and season to taste with salt and pepper. Stir in the chicken, potato, and sweet potato.

3 **Preheat the oven** to 400°F (200°C). Divide the dough into 4 pieces. Roll out each piece on a lightly floured surface. Using a small plate as a guide, cut into an 8in (20cm) round about ⅛in (3mm) thick.

4 **Spoon a quarter** of the filling into the center of each round. Brush the edges with water and bring together to seal, then crimp. Transfer the pasties to a baking sheet.

5 **Brush** with the reserved egg mixture. Make a slit in the tops and bake for 10 minutes, then reduce the heat to 350°F (180°C) and cook for 25–30 minutes, or until a thin knife comes out clean when inserted into the center.

6 **Remove from the oven** and serve the pasties hot or cold.

Roast Goose

Goose meat is rich in flavor, making it a perfect choice for a festive dinner party or special holiday meal

- makes 6 servings
- prep 20 mins • cook 3 hrs
- freeze, cooked, for up to 3 months

1 **goose**, thawed, 11lb (5kg)

salt and freshly ground **black pepper**

2 small **onions**, cut in half

⅔ cup hearty **red wine**

1 **Preheat the oven** to 350°F (180°C). Prick the skin all over with a meat fork, rub with salt, and sprinkle with pepper. Tuck 2 onion halves in the neck cavity and the 2 halves in the body cavity.

2 **Place the goose**, breast side up, on a rack in a roasting pan. Cover the pan tightly with aluminum foil. Roast for about 3 hours, occasionally basting the goose with the fat in the pan, until until the goose is a rich amber brown color and a meat thermometer, inserted in the thickest part of the thigh, reads 180°F (85°C). Remove the foil during the last 40 minutes.

3 **Transfer the goose** to a serving platter and tent with foil. Let stand 20 minutes before carving. Carefully pour off the pan juices and fat into a heatproof bowl. Skim off the fat and reserve the pan juices. (Save the fat for another use, if you wish.)

4 **Heat the pan** over high heat, add the red wine, and scrape up the browned bits in the pan with a wooden spoon. Pour in the skimmed juices. Boil about 2 minutes, until slightly reduced.

5 **Carve the goose** and serve with the wine sauce.

Duck Breasts with Mushroom Sauce

Special enough to serve to dinner guests, this recipe is surprisingly quick and easy

 makes 4 servings

 prep 20 mins • cook 25 mins

 ridged cast-iron grill pan

4 boneless **duck breasts**, about 7oz (200g) each

salt and freshly ground **black pepper**

2 tbsp **olive oil**

6oz (175g) **white mushrooms**, halved or quartered

4 **scallions**, chopped

1 tbsp fresh **lemon** juice

1 tbsp **sun-dried tomato paste**

1 tsp **cornstarch**

1¼ cups **chicken stock**

2 tbsp chopped **parsley**

3 tbsp **white wine**

1 Score the duck skin with a thin sharp knife. Season the breasts with salt and pepper.

2 Heat the oil in a large frying pan over medium heat. Add the mushrooms and scallions and cook, stirring often, about 5 minutes, until the mushrooms are tender. Stir in the lemon juice and tomato paste.

3 Dissolve the cornstarch in ¼ cup of the stock and return to the remaining stock. Stir into the mushroom mixture. Bring to a boil, stirring often, until simmering and thickened. Stir in the parsley and season with salt and pepper. Remove the sauce from heat and keep warm.

4 Heat a ridged grill pan over medium-high heat. Add the duck, skin side down. Cook until the skin is golden brown, pouring off the fat as needed, about 8 minutes. Turn and cook about 2 minutes more, until the duck is medium-rare.

5 Place the duck on a platter and tent with aluminum foil. Pour off any fat in the pan. Return to medium-high heat. Add the wine and stir to release any browned bits in the pan. Stir into the sauce.

6 Slice the duck and transfer to dinner plates. Top with the sauce, and serve hot.

Chicken Gumbo

This hearty soup-stew from Cajun country will have the richest flavor if you use chicken thigh meat

 makes 4 servings

prep 20 mins • cook 50 mins

1 tbsp **vegetable oil**

1 **onion**, chopped

2 **celery ribs**, chopped

1 **green bell pepper**, seeded and chopped

1 **garlic clove**, chopped

1lb (450g) boneless and skinless **chicken thighs**, cubed

2 tsp **sweet** or hot **paprika**

½ tsp dried **oregano**

½ tsp ground **cumin**

1 tbsp **all-purpose flour**

2 cups **chicken stock**

one 14.5oz (411g) can **chopped tomatoes**

4oz (115g) **andouille** or kielbasa **sausage**, sliced

8oz (225g) frozen sliced **okra**

salt and freshly ground **black pepper**

1 Heat the oil in a large saucepan over medium heat. Add the onion, celery, and green pepper and cook for 5 minutes, stirring often, until softened. Stir in the garlic.

2 Add the chicken and cook, turning frequently, about 10 minutes, or until lightly browned. Stir in the paprika, oregano, cumin, and the flour. Stir for 1 minute, then stir in the stock, tomatoes, and sausage.

3 Boil, then reduce the heat to and simmer for 20 minutes. Add the okra and simmer for 20 minutes, until the chicken is tender. Season with salt and pepper and serve hot.

VARIATION

Seafood Gumbo
Replace the chicken with 1lb (450g) large raw shrimp, shelled, and deveined, and add in step 3 with the okra.

Chicken Stew with Herb Dumplings

This hearty winter casserole is a main meal in itself, but is especially good when served with freshly steamed vegetables

 makes 4 servings

 prep 15 mins • cook 50 mins

 large, flameproof casserole

freeze, without dumplings, for up to 3 months

4 chicken thighs

4 chicken drumsticks

salt and freshly ground black pepper

⅓ cup all-purpose flour

3 tbsp olive oil

2 carrots, sliced

2 leeks, cleaned and sliced

2 celery stalks, sliced

½ rutabaga, pared and diced

2 cups chicken stock

2 tbsp Worcestershire sauce

For the dumplings

1 cup all-purpose flour

1 tsp baking powder

1 tsp dried Italian seasoning

¼ tsp salt

⅛ tsp freshly ground black pepper

4 tbsp butter, cut into small cubes

1 tbsp chopped parsley

⅓ cup milk, as needed

1 **Season the chicken** with salt and pepper. Dredge in the flour to coat. Heat 2 tbsp oil in a casserole over medium-high heat. In batches, add the chicken, turning occasionally, until golden brown. Transfer to a plate. Pour the fat from the pan.

2 **Add the remaining** oil to the pan. Add the carrots, leeks, celery, and rutabaga and cook, stirring occasionally, until beginning to brown. Stir in the stock and Worcestershire sauce. Return the chicken to the pan and simmer, covered, for 20 minutes.

3 **Meanwhile**, whisk the flour, baking powder, dried herbs, salt, and pepper in a medium bowl. Cut in the butter until the mixture resembles coarse bread crumbs. Add the parsley and stir in enough milk to make a soft dough. Divide into 12 balls.

4 **Arrange 12 spoonfuls** of the dough in the stew, cover, and simmer for 20 minutes. Serve hot.

Chicken Pinwheels with Pasta

Simply prepared, these light rolls of chicken breast have zesty Italian flavor

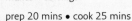 makes 4 servings

prep 20 mins • cook 25 mins

 low fat

freeze the pinwheels for up to 1 month

4 boneless and skinless chicken breast halves

salt and freshly ground black pepper

1 garlic clove, crushed through a press

16 large basil leaves, plus more to serve

12 sun-dried tomato halves in oil, drained

olive oil, for brushing

1 cup canned crushed tomatoes

¾ cup dry white wine

8oz (230g) penne, cooked

● **Prepare ahead** Prepare through step 3, then cover and refrigerate for a few hours until ready to bake.

1 **Preheat the oven** to 400°F (200°C). One at a time, lightly pound each chicken breast with a flat meat pounder between 2 sheets of plastic wrap until the breast is about ¼in (5mm) thick.

2 **Place the chicken breasts**, smooth sides down, on a work surface. Season with salt and pepper. Spread each breast with a little garlic. Arrange 4 basil leaves and 3 sun-dried tomato halves evenly over each piece of chicken.

3 **Roll up** the chicken to enclose the filling and secure with wooden toothpicks. Lightly oil a shallow baking dish. Place the breasts in the dish and brush with oil. Pour the crushed tomatoes and wine around the breasts.

4 **Bake, basting with** the sauce halfway through, about 25 minutes, until the chicken is opaque when pierced with a knife.

5 **Transfer the chicken** to a carving board. Let stand for 5 minutes. Remove the toothpicks and cut crosswise into ½in (13mm) thick slices. Arrange the slices on individual dinner plates. Add the penne and spoon the sauce on top. Garnish with basil and serve hot.

Sweet and Sour Chicken

This classic dish is one of the most popular of all Chinese-American culinary creations

 makes 4 servings

 prep 30 mins, plus standing • cook 25 mins

 wok or large frying pan, deep-frying thermometer

For the batter

¾ cup all-purpose flour

¾ tsp baking powder

⅛ tsp salt

1 cup lager beer

For the sauce

½ cup chicken stock

3 tbsp soy sauce

3 tbsp rice vinegar

2 tbsp ketchup

1 tbsp honey

one ¾in (2cm) piece fresh ginger, peeled and shredded

1 tsp cornstarch dissolved in 1 tbsp cold water

4 skinless and boneless chicken breasts, cut into 1in (2.5cm) pieces

vegetable oil, for deep-frying

½ cup all-purpose flour

2 tbsp unsalted cashew nuts or whole blanched almonds

½ red bell pepper, seeded and chopped

8 scallions, cut into 1in (2.5cm) lengths

½ cup cubed fresh or drained canned pineapple

● **Prepare ahead** Steps 1 and 2 can be completed several hours in advance.

1 To make the batter, sift the flour, baking powder, and salt into a large bowl. Make a well in the center, add ½ cup of the beer, and whisk, gradually adding the remaining beer. Let stand for 30 minutes.

2 To make the sauce, stir the stock, soy sauce, vinegar, ketchup, honey, and ginger in a small saucepan over low heat until the honey is melted. Stir in the dissolved cornstarch and bring to a simmer. Cook, stirring often, until just thickened. Set aside.

3 Preheat the oven to 200°F (95°C). Fill a wok halfway with oil. Heat to 350°F (180°C). Place the flour in a bowl. In batches, toss the chicken in the flour, then coat in the batter and add to the hot oil. Deep-fry about 3 minutes. Transfer the chicken to a baking sheet lined with paper towels and keep warm in the oven.

4 Pour all but 2 tbsp oil from the wok and return to high heat. Add the cashews and stir-fry for 30 seconds. Transfer to the baking sheet. Add the red pepper to the oil and stir-fry 2 minutes, or until crisp-tender. Add the scallions and pineapple and stir-fry for 1 minute.

5 Pour the sauce into the wok, add the chicken and stir until coated. Transfer to a serving platter, sprinkle with cashews, and serve hot.

Checking the Oil Temperature

If you don't have a deep-frying thermometer, check the oil temperature with a piece of day-old bread. Drop it in the pan; it will rise to the surface if the oil is hot enough.

Chicken with Herb Sauce

A punchy sauce for chicken

 makes 4 servings

 prep 10 mins • cook 30 mins

6 boneless and skinless chicken breasts

1 small onion, sliced

1 carrot, chopped

1 celery stalk, chopped

a few parsley sprigs

For the sauce

½ cup packed parsley leaves

½ cup packed basil leaves

1 tbsp nonpareil capers, rinsed

1 tbsp red wine vinegar

2 anchovy fillets in oil, drained

1 garlic clove, minced

½ cup olive oil

salt and freshly ground black pepper

1 Preheat the oven to 375°F (190°C). Place the chicken in a roasting pan. Add the onion, carrot, celery, and parsley and enough water to cover. Cover with aluminum foil. Bake for 30 minutes. Remove from the oven, uncover, and let cool.

2 Pulse the parsley, basil, capers, vinegar, anchovies, and garlic in a food processor until combined. With the machine running, slowly pour in the oil. Season with salt and pepper.

3 Remove the chicken from the liquid and thinly slice across the grain. Transfer to a platter, top with the sauce, and serve.

Duck with Shallot Confit

The spices and melted honey lend comforting winter flavors to the duck

 makes 6 servings

prep 10 mins • cook 30 mins

For the shallot confit

8oz (225g) **shallots**, peeled and thickly sliced

⅔ cup **honey**

2 tbsp peeled and minced **fresh ginger**

⅔ cup **red wine vinegar**

6 **duck breasts**

1 tbsp **honey**

½ tsp **Asian five-spice powder**

salt and freshly ground **black pepper**

● **Prepare ahead** The shallot confit can be covered and refrigerated for up to 3 days.

1 **To make the confit**, combine the shallots, honey, and ginger in a saucepan. Cook over medium heat, stirring often, until the shallots are pale.

2 **Stir in the vinegar** and bring to a boil. Reduce the heat to medium-low and simmer for about 8 minutes, or until the liquid is syrupy. Stir in ⅔ cup of water and simmer for about 8 minutes more, or until the mixture is golden and thickened, but not runny.

3 **Meanwhile**, preheat the oven to 400°F (200°C). Score the duck skin in a crosshatch pattern. Heat a large frying pan over medium-high heat. In batches, add the duck breasts, skin side down, and cook about 4 minutes, until the skin is browned, pouring off the fat as needed. Turn and cook the other side 2 minutes, until browned. Transfer to a roasting pan, skin side up. Brush with honey, sprinkle with the five-spice powder and salt and pepper. Bake for about 8 minutes, or until the duck breasts are medium-rare when pierced in the center.

4 **Transfer** to a carving board and let stand for 5 minutes. Carve on the diagonal into thick slices, transfer to dinner plates, and serve with the confit.

● **Good with** a sweet potato purée, sautéed bok choy, or green beans with sesame seeds.

Turkey à la King

This dish is a time-honored way of using turkey leftovers after a holiday meal

 makes 4 servings

prep 15 mins • cook 15 mins

freeze for up to 3 months

2 tbsp **vegetable oil**

4 tbsp **butter**

1 **onion**, finely sliced

1 **red bell pepper**, seeded and chopped

1 **green bell pepper**, seeded and chopped

6oz (175g) **white mushrooms**, sliced

2 tbsp **all-purpose flour**

salt and freshly ground **black pepper**

2 cups **whole milk**, heated

3-4 cups diced **cooked turkey**

sweet paprika, for garnish

● **Prepare ahead** The dish can be cooled, covered, and refrigerated up to 1 day ahead, then reheated gently before serving.

1 **Heat the oil** and butter in a large pan over medium heat. Add the onion and red and green peppers and cook, stirring occasionally, until softened, about 5 minutes. Add the mushrooms and cook until they soften, about 5 minutes more.

2 **Sprinkle** in the flour. Stir in the milk and cook, stirring constantly, until the sauce is boiling and thickened. Season with salt and pepper to taste.

3 **Stir in the turkey** and simmer for about 5 minutes, stirring occasionally, until the turkey is heated through. Sprinkle with the paprika and serve hot.

● **Good with** steamed rice, mashed potatoes, or egg noodles.

Chicken à la King

Substitute the turkey with the same quantity of chicken. Replace half the milk with chicken stock, and the mushrooms with sliced zucchini.

Chicken Jalousie

Although it looks impressive, this dish is quick to make with store-bought puff pastry and leftover chicken

makes 4 servings

prep 25 mins • cook 25 mins

2 tbsp **butter**

2 **leeks**, white and pale green part only, cleaned and thinly sliced

2 tsp **all-purpose flour**, plus more for rolling

½ cup **chicken stock**

2½ cups chopped **boneless cooked chicken**

1 tsp chopped **thyme**

1 tsp fresh **lemon** juice

salt and freshly ground **black pepper**

one 17.3oz (484g) box thawed **frozen puff pastry**

1 large **egg**, beaten

1 **Melt the butter** in a saucepan over low heat. Add the leeks and cook for 5 minutes until tender. Sprinkle in the flour and stir. Stir in the stock and bring to a boil, stirring often. Remove from the heat and stir in the chicken, thyme, and lemon juice. Season well with salt and pepper. Cover with plastic wrap and let cool.

2 **Preheat the oven** to 425°F (220°C). Dampen a large baking sheet. Roll out one sheet of the puff pastry on a lightly floured surface. Trim into a 10 x 6in (30 x 15cm) rectangle. Place the pastry on the baking sheet. Roll out and trim the remaining pastry to 10 x 7in (30 x 18cm) rectangle. Lightly dust it with flour, then fold in half lengthwise. Make cuts ½in (1cm) apart along the folded edge to within 1in (2.5cm) of the outer edge.

3 **Spoon evenly over** the puff pastry base, leaving a 1in (2.5cm) border. Dampen the edges of the pastry with water. Place the second piece of pastry on top and press the edges together to seal; trim off the excess. Brush with beaten egg. Bake for 25 minutes or until golden-brown and crisp. Cool briefly, then slice and serve hot.

Good with roasted vegetables such as zucchini, and eggplant.

Chicken Biryani

For special occasions, this subtly spiced, aromatic dish from India is often decorated with small pieces of edible silver leaf

makes 4 servings

prep 20 mins • cook 30 mins

low fat

2 tbsp **vegetable oil**

2 tbsp **butter**

1 large **onion**, thinly sliced

2 **garlic cloves**, crushed and peeled

one 3in (7.5cm) **cinnamon stick**, broken into 2 or 3 pieces

6 **cardamom pods**

6 **curry leaves** (optional)

3 tbsp **curry powder**

1 tsp **ground turmeric**

½ tsp **ground cumin**

4 boneless and skinless **chicken breasts**, cut into 1in (2.5cm) pieces

1½ cups **basmati rice**

½ cup **golden raisins**

3¾ cups **chicken stock**, as needed

2 tbsp **toasted sliced almonds**

Prepare ahead The biryani can be cooled, covered, and refrigerated for up to 1 day. Pour a few tablespoons of melted butter on top, cover, and bake in a 350°F (180°C) oven about 30 minutes.

1 **Heat the oil** and butter in a large flameproof casserole over medium heat. Add the onion and garlic and cook, stirring often, about 4 minutes, until translucent. Add the cinnamon, cardamom pods, and curry leaves, if using, and cook, stirring often, for 5 minutes, until fragrant.

2 **Add the curry powder**, turmeric, and cumin, and stir for 1 minute. Add the chicken.

3 **Add the rice** and raisins and stir well. Pour in enough stock to just cover the rice. Bring to a boil. Reduce the heat to medium-low and cover. Simmer about 15 minutes or until the rice is tender and has absorbed the stock, adding more stock if the mixture becomes dry.

4 **Transfer** to a serving dish, fluffing the rice with a fork. Sprinkle with almonds and serve hot.

Chicken Wrapped in Pancetta and Sage

This is a light but elegant main course to which you can add grilled peppers and olives

  makes 6 servings

  prep 20 mins
• cook 1 hr 15 mins

12 small plum tomatoes, halved

3 tbsp olive oil, plus more to drizzle

salt and freshly ground black pepper

3 skinless and boneless chicken breasts

12 sage leaves

12 slices of pancetta, unrolled

6oz (170g) mixed baby greens

For the dressing

⅓ cup olive oil

1½ tbsp cider vinegar

2 tsp chopped parsley

1 shallot, finely chopped

1 tsp light brown sugar

salt and freshly ground black pepper

● **Prepare ahead** The chicken can be covered with plastic wrap and refrigerated up to 1 day ahead.

1 Preheat the oven to 300°F (150°C). Put the tomatoes into a roasting pan, drizzle with olive oil, and season with salt and pepper. Roast in the oven for 1 hour, or until slightly dried and caramelized.

2 To make the dressing, place the ingredients in a small bowl and whisk together until thickened slightly. Season to taste with salt and pepper.

3 Cut each chicken breast into 4 pieces. Top each with a sage leaf, then wrap as tightly as possible with a piece of pancetta.

4 Heat the olive oil in a large frying pan and brown the chicken pieces on each side. Lower the heat and continue to cook the chicken, turning, for 10 minutes, or until cooked through.

5 Serve the chicken with the greens and the roasted tomatoes, drizzled with the dressing.

French Roast Chicken

The method of herb butter slipped under the chicken's skin makes for a very tasty chicken

  makes 4 servings

prep 15 mins
• cook 1 hr 30 mins

8 tbsp butter, softened

¼ cup chopped herbs, such as tarragon, parsley, and/or chives, plus sprigs to garnish

2 garlic cloves, finely chopped

1 chicken, about 4lb (1.8kg)

1 lemon

salt and freshly ground black pepper

2 cups chicken stock

½ cup dry white wine, as needed

● **Prepare ahead** The herb butter can be refrigerated up to 1 day ahead; bring to room temperature before using.

1 Preheat the oven to 375°F (190°C). Mash the butter, herbs, and garlic together. Beat the herbs and garlic into the butter. Ease your fingers between the breast skin and chicken flesh, being careful not to tear the skin. Tuck the butter under the skin. Pierce the lemon all over with a fork and place inside the body cavity. Truss with kitchen string, if desired. Season with salt and pepper.

2 Put the chicken on a rack in the roasting pan. Pour 1½ cups of the stock and the wine over the chicken. Roast for about 1½ hours, or until an instant-read thermometer inserted in the thickest part of the thigh, not touching a bone, reads 170°F (77°C). If the liquid evaporates from the bottom of the pan, add a little more wine.

3 Transfer the chicken to a platter. Cover with aluminum foil and let stand for 10 minutes. Spoon off the fat from the pan. Add the remaining ½ cup stock and bring to a boil over high heat. Boil, stirring often, about 3 minutes, until slightly reduced. Garnish the chicken with the herb sprigs and serve hot, with the pan juices.

Chicken Fricassée

There are many variations of this one-pot French chicken stew

 makes 4 servings

 prep 15 mins
• cook 1 hr 15 mins

 low fat

4 **boiling potatoes**, peeled and diced

2 tbsp **olive oil**

4 **chicken drumsticks**, skin removed

4 **chicken thighs**, skin removed

salt and freshly ground **black pepper**

2 tbsp **all-purpose flour**

4oz (115g) small **white mushrooms**

4 **shallots**, sliced

2 **garlic cloves**, minced

2 tsp chopped **rosemary**

⅔ cup **dry white wine**

1¼ cups **chicken stock**

1 **bay leaf**

1 Cook the potatoes in a saucepan of boiling water for 5 minutes. Drain well.

2 Heat the oil in a large frying pan over medium-high heat. Season with chicken with salt and pepper and dust with the flour. Add to the pan and cook, turning often, about 6 minutes, until browned. Transfer to a plate. Add the shallots to the pan and cook, stirring often, about 2 minutes, until softened. Add the potatoes, mushrooms, garlic, and rosemary, and cook 2 minutes more.

3 Add the wine, bring to a boil, and cook for 1 minute. Add the stock and return to the boil. Return the chicken to the pan, add the bay leaf, and cover. Reduce the heat and simmer about 50 minutes, or until the chicken is very tender. Discard the bay leaf and adjust the seasoning with salt and pepper. Serve hot.

German Chicken Fricassée

Add a squeeze of fresh lemon juice, a pinch of grated nutmeg, and a dash of Worcestershire sauce in step 4. Toward the end of cooking time, stir in 1 cup thawed frozen peas. Just before serving, mix 1 large egg yolk and ¼ cup heavy cream. Remove the pan from the heat, and stir the yolk mixture into the sauce. Serve with boiled rice.

Chicken Breasts in Garlic Sauce

Don't be put off by the large quantity of garlic, as the flavor mellows in the cooking

 makes 4 servings

 prep 10 mins • cook 40 mins

 shallow flameproof casserole

freeze, without the cream and thyme, for up to 3 months

15 **garlic cloves**, unpeeled

1 tbsp **olive oil**

1 tbsp **butter**

4 **chicken breasts**, with skin and bone

2 cups **hard dry cider**

1 cup **apple** juice

1 **bay leaf**

¾ cup **heavy cream**

salt and freshly ground **black pepper**

1 tbsp chopped **thyme**

1 Preheat the oven to 350°F (180°C). Parcook the unpeeled garlic cloves in boiling salted water for 4 minutes. Drain, rinsed under cold running water, and peel. set aside.

2 Heat the oil and butter in a shallow flameproof casserole over medium-high heat. Add the chicken, skin side down, and cook for about 4 minutes, or until the skin is deep golden brown. Turn over, add the cider, apple juice, garlic cloves, and bay leaf, and bring to a simmer. Cover and bake for 20–25 minutes, or until the chicken shows no sign of pink when pierced with a knife.

3 Using a slotted spoon, transfer the chicken and half of the garlic to a deep platter and keep warm. Skim the fat from the cooking juices, then bring to a boil over high heat. Cook, crushing the garlic into the sauce with a spoon, about 5 minutes, or until thickened.

4 Add the cream and cook for 1 minute. Season with salt and pepper. Return the chicken to the casserole and baste. Sprinkle with the thyme and serve immediately.

● **Good with** boiled new potatoes and green beans.

Devilled Turkey

Serve these spicy stir-fried turkey strips as
a healthy lunch or supper

makes 4 servings

prep 10 mins • cook 15 mins

2 tbsp **olive oil**

1lb (450g) **turkey breast cutlets**,
cut into strips

1 **onion**, finely chopped

1 **red bell pepper**, seeded and cut
into strips

1 **orange bell pepper**, seeded and
cut into strips

1 **garlic clove**, minced

3 tbsp fresh **orange** juice

2 tbsp **whole grain mustard**

2 tbsp **mango chutney**

¼ tsp **sweet paprika**

2 tbsp **Worcestershire sauce**

1 fresh **hot red chile**, seeded
and minced

1 **Heat the oil** in a nonstick
frying pan over a high heat. Add
the turkey and cook, stirring often,
about 5 minutes, until lightly
browned. Transfer to a plate.

2 **Add the onion** and stir-fry
about 2 minutes, or until it is just
beginning to color. Add the red and
orange peppers and garlic and stir-fry
about 3 minutes.

3 **Mix the orange juice**,
mustard, chutney, paprika,
Worcestershire sauce, and chile
together until well combined. Stir into
the vegetables and return the turkey
to the pan. Cook about 5 minutes or
until piping hot and the turkey is
opaque throughout. Serve hot.

● **Good with** stir-fried spinach and
rice or noodles.

VARIATION

Devilled Chicken or Pork

Substitute strips of boneless and
skinless chicken breast or pork
tenderloin for the turkey.

Guinea Hen with Spiced Lentils

Guinea hen has a somewhat more assertive flavor than chicken,
and it makes a good partner for spicy, earthy lentils

makes 4 servings

prep 20 mins
• cook 1 hr 15 mins

3lb (1.35kg) **guinea hen**

2 **carrots**, cut into chunks

2 **celery stalks**, halved

2 **shallots**, halved

1 **bay leaf**

10 whole **black peppercorns**

2 tbsp **olive oil**

5oz (140g) **pancetta**, finely diced

1 **garlic clove**, crushed

1 small fresh **hot red chile**, seeded
and minced

1½ cups **French green (Puy) lentils**,
rinsed and well drained

¼ cup chopped **parsley**

salt and freshly ground **black pepper**

1 **Put the guinea hen** in a pan
with the carrots, celery, shallots,
bay leaf, and peppercorns. Cover with
cold water, bring to the boil, then
simmer for 45 minutes, covered.

2 **Lift the guinea hen** on
to a plate; keep warm. Strain the
poaching liquid back into the pan and
boil for 10 minutes, or until reduced.

3 **Meanwhile, heat** the oil in
a pan and cook the pancetta,
stirring often, for about 6 minutes, or
until golden. Add the garlic and chile,
and cook gently for about 2 minutes,
stirring often. Remove from the heat
and add the lentils.

4 **Pour** 1¾ cups of the reduced
stock into the lentils. Bring to
a boil, then simmer, uncovered, for
30 minutes, until tender, adding
stock as needed. Add the chopped
parsley and season with salt and
pepper. Meanwhile, remove the
skin from the guinea hen and cut
into pieces.

5 **Serve the lentils**, topped with
pieces of guinea hen. Spoon over
the stock, if desired.

Lemon Honey Chicken Breasts with Mustard Mayonnaise

This simple but tasty dish can be broiled or grilled

 makes 6 servings

prep 25 mins, plus marinating
• cook 15–20 mins

3 tbsp fresh **lemon** juice

3 tbsp **balsamic vinegar**

3 tbsp **soy sauce**

3 tbsp **olive oil**

2 tbsp **honey**

2 **garlic cloves**, minced

2 fresh **hot red** or green **chiles**, seeded and minced

6 skinless and boneless **chicken breasts**, about 6oz (175g) each

For the mustard mayonnaise

2 large **egg yolks**

2 tbsp **sherry vinegar**

1 tbsp **lemon** juice

1½ tsp **Dijon mustard**

¾ cup plus 2 tbsp **vegetable oil**

12 **basil leaves**

salt and freshly ground **black pepper**

● **Prepare ahead** The marinating chicken and the mayonnaise can be refrigerated for up to 1 day.

1 Mix the lemon juice, vinegar, soy sauce, oil, honey, garlic, and chiles in a zippered plastic bag. Season with the pepper. Score a shallow criss-cross pattern on the skinned side of each chicken breast, and add to the marinade. Refrigerate for at least 2 hours.

2 To make the mayonnaise, combine the egg yolks, vinegar, lemon juice, and mustard in a food processor. With the motor running, slowly add the oil in a steady steam until the mayonnaise is smooth and creamy. Add basil and pulse until chopped. Season with salt and pepper. Transfer to a bowl, cover and refrigerate for at least 1 hour.

3 Remove the chicken from the marinade. Preheat a broiler or build a fire in an outdoor grill. Add the chicken and cook about 12 minutes, until the chicken shows no sign of pink inside. Slice the chicken breasts and serve with the mayonnaise.

Chicken with Thyme and Lemon

The combination of lemon, thyme, and a light, buttery glaze makes this chicken a special dinner dish

 makes 4 servings

prep 15 mins, plus standing
• cook 1 hr

low fat

1 **chicken**, about 4lb (1.8kg), jointed into 8 pieces

salt and freshly ground **black pepper**

1 **lemon**

1 tbsp **butter**, softened

1 tbsp **olive oil**

2 tsp chopped **thyme**

2 **garlic cloves**, minced

½ cup **dry white wine**

1 Preheat the oven to 400°F (200°C). Spread the chicken in a single layer in a roasting pan. Season with salt and pepper.

2 Grate the lemon zest into a bowl. Add the butter, oil, thyme, and garlic, and combine.

3 Dot the lemon and thyme mixture evenly over the chicken. Cut the reserved lemon into chunks and tuck around the chicken. Pour the wine over the chicken.

4 Roast the chicken for 50–60 minutes. Turn and baste the chicken occasionally, until the chicken is golden brown and and the juices run clear when the meat is pierced with a knife. Add a little more wine if the juices cook away. Serve hot.

● **Good with** a mixed salad and oven-baked potato wedges.

Chicken Jalfrezi

A spicy chicken curry made with chiles and mustard seeds

 makes 4 servings

 prep 20 mins • cook 25 mins

 low fat

 freeze for up to 3 months

2 tbsp **vegetable oil**

2 tbsp **garam masala**

2 tsp **ground cumin**

2 tsp yellow **mustard seeds**

1 tsp **ground turmeric**

1 **onion**, sliced

1in (2.5cm) piece of **fresh ginger**, peeled and finely minced

3 **garlic cloves**, minced

1 **red bell pepper**, seeded and sliced

½ **green bell pepper**, seeded and sliced

2 fresh **hot green chiles**, seeded and finely minced

1½lb (675g) skinless and boneless **chicken thighs** or breasts, cut into 1in (2.5cm) pieces

1 cup canned **chopped tomatoes**

3 tbsp chopped **cilantro**

● **Prepare ahead** The curry can be refrigerated for up to one day. Reheat, adding a little more stock, if needed.

1 Heat the oil in a large saucepan over a medium heat. Add the garam masala, cumin, mustard seeds, and turmeric, and and stir for 1 minute, until fragrant.

2 Add the onion, ginger, and garlic, and cook, stirring often, for about 2 minutes, until the onion starts to soften. Add the red and green peppers and the chiles and cook for 5 minutes, stirring often.

3 Increase the heat to medium-high. Add the chicken, and cook until it begins to brown. Add the tomatoes and cilantro, lower the heat, and simmer for 10 minutes, or until the chicken is cooked through, stirring frequently. Serve hot.

● **Good with** basmati rice.

Spicy Orange Duck

The traditional flavor combination of rich duck and tangy orange is given a modern twist in this recipe

 makes 6 servings

 prep 15–20 mins • cook 25–30 mins

For the sauce

4 large **oranges**

½ cup **sugar**

¼ cup hearty **red wine**

½ inch (1cm) piece of **fresh ginger**, peeled and shredded

1 tbsp **sweet chili dipping sauce**

1 tbsp **Thai fish sauce**

1 tbsp **rice vinegar**

2 whole **star anise**

3in (7.5cm) **cinnamon stick**

1 small fresh **hot red chile**, seeded and finely sliced into thin rounds

6 boneless **duck breast** halves, about 7oz (200g) each

salt and freshly ground **black pepper**

2 tbsp **honey**

2 **scallions**, white and green parts, cut into 2in (5cm) strips

1 Preheat the oven to 425°F (220°C). To make the sauce, peel the zest from 1 orange using a vegetable peeler. Cut the zest into short thin strips. Juice the oranges to make 1½ cups of juice. Combine the orange zest and juice with the rest of the sauce ingredients in a medium saucepan and bring to a boil, stirring. Simmer, stirring occasionally, for 12 minutes, or until lightly syrupy.

2 Trim the duck breasts of excess fat and lightly score the skin with a sharp knife. Season with salt and pepper and brush the skin with honey. Heat a large nonstick frying pan over medium-high heat. Add the duck breasts, skin side down, and cook until the skin is golden brown, about 4 minutes. Turn and cook until the flesh side is lightly browned, about 2 minutes more. Transfer the frying pan with the breast to the oven and bake for 6 minutes until the meat is still pink in the center when pierced with a sharp knife. Transfer to a carving board and let stand for 5 minutes.

3 Slice the duck and arrange the slices on dinner plates. Spoon the sauce over the duck then scatter the scallion strips on top. Serve at once.

● **Good with** mashed sweet potatoes and crisp-tender green beans tossed with sesame seeds.

Duck Breasts with Cherries

Many supermarkets now carry Pekin duck breasts, which are smaller than the Moulard variety

🍴 makes 4 servings

⏱ prep 15 mins • cook 20 mins

4 boneless **duck breasts**, about 7oz (200g) each

½ tsp **salt**, plus more to taste

½ tsp lightly crushed **black peppercorns** , plus more to taste

For the sauce

1 tbsp **butter**

1 **shallot**, finely chopped

⅓ cup **ruby port**

1 tbsp **maple syrup**

1 whole **star anise**

1 sprig of **rosemary**

½ cup **chicken stock**

2 cups pitted fresh **bing cherries**

salt and freshly ground **black pepper**

● **Prepare ahead** The sauce can be made and refrigerated up to 2 days in advance.

1 **Score the skin** of each duck breast with a sharp knife. Season with the salt and crushed pepper.

2 **Place the duck breasts**, skin-side down, in a large frying pan. Cook over medium-high heat for about 8 minutes. Turn and brown the other sides, about 3 minutes for medium-rare. Transfer to a carving board and let stand for 5 minutes.

3 **To make the sauce**, melt the butter in a saucepan over medium heat. Add the shallot and cook, stirring often, about 2 minutes, until softened.

4 **Stir in the port**, maple syrup, star anise, and rosemary, and boil for 30 seconds. Add the stock and boil for about 3 minutes, or until slightly reduced. Add the cherries, and cook for 2 minutes more, until heated. Season with salt and pepper. Slice each breast on the diagaonal into thick slices and transfer each to a plate. Top with the sauce and serve hot.

Turkey Cutlets with Artichokes

A delicious take on the classic veal dish, this features coated cutlets topped with a tomato and artichoke sauce

🍴 makes 4 servings

⏱ prep 10 mins • cook 20–25 mins

¼ cup **all-purpose flour**

½ tsp each **salt** and freshly ground **black pepper**

4 **turkey breast** cutlets, about 4oz (115g) each

3 tbsp **olive oil**

1 small **onion**, finely chopped

¼ cup **dry white wine**

one 6oz (170g) jar **marinated artichoke hearts**, drained

1 cup drained canned **chopped tomatoes**

few **basil** leaves, torn

1 **Combine the flour**, salt, and pepper on a plate. Dip the turkey in the seasoned flour until lightly well coated, shaking off any excess. Heat 1 tbsp of the oil in a large frying pan over medium heat. Add 2 of the cutlets and cook, turning once, 2-3 minutes each side, or just until golden brown and cooked through. Transfer to a platter and cover with aluminum foil to keep warm. Repeat the process with the remaining cutlets and 1 tbsp oil.

2 **Add the remaining 1 tbsp** oil to the pan and cook the onion for 4–5 minutes, or until softened. Add the wine and bring to a boil, stirring up up the brown bits from the bottom of the pan. Stir in the artichokes, tomatoes, and basil and bring to a boil. Spoon over the cutlets and serve hot.

● **Good with** buttered fettuccine or other flat pasta noodles.

VARIATION

Veal Cutlets with Artichokes

If you would like to try the classic veal version, simply replace the turkey breasts with the same weight of veal cutlets and continue with the recipe, as above.

Roast Turkey with Spiked Gravy

Everyone needs a solid recipe for the holiday turkey, and this one fits the bill

 makes about 12 servings

 prep 30 mins
• cook 3½ hrs

 rest turkey 30 mins before carving

 freeze the cooked turkey and stuffing for up to 3 months

14lb (6.3kg) turkey

cornbread stuffing

8 tbsp **butter**, softened

salt and freshly ground **black pepper**

6 tbsp **all-purpose flour**

3 cups **turkey** or **chicken stock**, as needed

¼ cup **bourbon** (optional)

1 Preheat the oven to 325°F (165°C). Remove the neck, giblets, and fat from the tail area and save for another use. Stuff the neck cavity loosely with stuffing, and pin the neck skin to the back with a skewer. Loosely fill the body cavity with stuffing and cover the exposed stuffing with foil. Using kitchen twine, tie the drumsticks together and secure the wings to the body.

2 Place the turkey on a rack in a roasting pan. Rub with the butter and season with salt and pepper. Loosely cover the breast area with foil. Add 2 cups water to the pan.

3 Roast, basting every hour or so (lifting the foil to do so), estimating about 15 minutes per pound, for about 3½ hours, until an instant-read thermometer inserted in the thickest part of the thigh, not allowing it to touch a bone, reads 175°F (79°C). During the last hour of cooking, remove the foil. Transfer the turkey to a platter. Let stand for 30 minutes.

4 Meanwhile, make the gravy. Pour the pan drippings into a glass bowl. Skim off and measure 6 tbsp fat; discard remaining fat. Add enough stock to degreased drippings to make 1 quart (1 liter).

5 Place the pan over medium heat. Add the fat, whisk in the flour, and let cook 1 minute. Whisk in the stock mixture and bourbon, if using, scraping up the browned bits, and bring to a boil. Simmer over low heat, whisking often, until thickened, about 10 minutes. Season with salt and pepper and pour into a sauceboat.

6 Carve the turkey and serve with the gravy.

● **Good with** the traditional accompaniments of sweet potatoes, cranberry sauce, mashed potatoes, and green beans or Brussels sprouts.

● **Leftovers** Spread the leftover stuffing in a buttered shallow baking dish, cover with aluminum foil, and refrigerate until 30 minutes before serving. Bake in a 350°F (180°C) oven until heated through.

> ### TURKEY GRAVY
> Don't throw away the turkey juices; use them to make a delicious gravy with a little flour and stock.

Grilled Poussins

Poussin (baby chicken) weigh barely one pound each

 makes 4 servings

prep 5 mins • cook 30–35 mins

4 **poussins**, about 1lb (450g) each

salt and freshly ground **black pepper**

4 tbsp **butter**

2 tbsp fresh **lemon** juice

2 tbsp **Worcestershire sauce**

1 tsp dried **tarragon**, crumbled

1 tsp dried **thyme**, crumbled

1 Position the rack about 6in (15cm) from the source of heat and preheat the broiler. Cut each poussin in half lengthwise. Season with salt and pepper. Place the poussins, skin side down, on an oiled broiler pan. Broil 20 minutes, or until lightly browned.

2 Meanwhile, in a small saucepan, melt the butter, and stir in the lemon juice, Worcestershire sauce, tarragon, and thyme. Brush the poussins with some of the butter mixture. Turn them skin side up, and brush again. Broil about 12 minutes more, basting occasionally with the butter mixture, or until golden brown and the juices run clear when pierced with a sharp knife.

Garlicky Turkey Burgers

A popular snack dish

 makes 4 servings

 prep 10 mins • cook 6 mins

1 lb (454g) ground turkey

⅓ cup fresh bread crumbs

2 tbsp finely chopped onion

2 tbsp chopped parsley

2 tsp Dijon mustard

2 garlic cloves, finely chopped

1 large egg white

½ tsp each salt and freshly ground black pepper

vegetable oil cooking spray

4 seeded buns, toasted

1 large ripe tomato, sliced

1 cup shredded lettuce

1 Mix the turkey, bread crumbs, onion, parsley, pepper, mustard, garlic, egg white, and salt and pepper together in a bowl until well combined. Form into 4 burgers, each about 1cm (½in) thick.

2 Spray a large nonstick frying pan with the oil and heat over medium heat. Add the burgers and cook, turning once, about 8 minutes, until they spring back in the center when pressed. Place a turkey burger in each bun, top with the tomatoes and lettuce, and serve.

Good with your favorite condiments and pickles.

Crispy Roast Duck

This Asian method of cooking duck makes the most of its sweet, succulent flesh

 makes 2–4 servings

 prep 1 hr 15 mins, plus drying and resting • cook 1 hr 35 mins

 meat hook or kitchen string

1 duck, about 1½lb (1.6kg)

3 tbsp oyster sauce

1 tsp Chinese five-spice powder

1 tsp salt

For the glaze

3 tbsp honey

2 tbsp Chinese rice wine or dry sherry

1 tbsp dark soy sauce

Prepare ahead The duck must be air-dried for several hours before roasting.

1 Rinse the duck inside and out with cold running water. Pat dry with paper towels. Mix together the oyster sauce, five-spice powder, and salt and spread it inside the duck.

2 Bring a large kettle of water to a boil. Tie some kitchen twine under the wings so the duck can be hung up. Place the duck in a colander in the sink. Pour some boiling water over the duck—the skin will tighten. Pat the duck with paper towels. Repeat the pouring and drying process five more times.

3 To make the glaze, bring the honey, rice wine, soy sauce, and ⅔ cup water to a boil over high heat. Reduce the heat to medium-low and simmer briskly about 12 minutes, or until sticky. Let cool slightly. Brush the glaze all over the duck.

4 Hang the duck over a roasting pan in a cool place. Train an electric fan on the duck. Let stand for about 4 hours, or until the skin is dry.

5 Preheat the oven to 450°F (230°C). Place the duck on a rack in a roasting pan, breast side up. Pour 2 cups water into the pan. Roast for 20 minutes. Reduce the oven temperature to 350°F (180°C) and roast for 1 hour 15 minutes, or until the duck skin is shiny, crisp, and golden brown.

6 Let stand for 10 minutes. Using a large, sharp knife, cut into quarters. Arrange the duck on a serving platter and serve hot.

Turkey Kebabs

A great dish to barbecue

 makes 6 servings

 prep 20 mins, plus marinating • cook 10–12 mins

 soak skewers for 30 mins

 6 wooden skewers

¼ cup soy sauce

2 tbsp olive oil

2 garlic cloves, finely chopped

¾ tsp ground ginger

¼ tsp crushed hot red pepper

1½lb (675g) skinless boneless turkey breasts, cut into 1in (2.5cm) cubes

1 red bell pepper, seeded and cut into 1in (2.5cm) pieces

1 green bell pepper, seeded and cut into 1in (2.5cm) pieces

1 large zucchini, cut into 1in (2.5cm) pieces

1 cup plain yogurt

½ tsp ground cumin

2 tbsp chopped mint

1 Combine the soy sauce, oil, garlic, ginger, and red pepper flakes in a zippered plastic bag. Add the turkey and refrigerate for at least 1 hour.

2 Preheat the broiler. Thread the turkey, peppers, and zucchini onto skewers. Broil for 5-6 minutes on each side, or until cooked through.

3 Mix the yogurt, mint, and cumin; serve with the kebabs.

Chicken Piri-Piri

Portugal's favorite chicken is really hot and spicy

🍴 makes 4 servings

🕐 prep 20 mins, plus cooling and marinating • cook 1 hr 15 mins

1 chicken, about 3½ lb (1.6kg)

6 fresh hot red or green chiles

½ cup olive oil

¼ cup red wine vinegar

2 tsp hot paprika

½ tsp dried oregano

3 garlic cloves

1 tsp salt

1 Preheat the oven to 375°F (190°C). Spread the chiles on a baking sheet. Roast about 15 minutes, until shriveled. Let cool, then remove the stalks from the chiles. Combine the whole chiles, oil, vinegar, paprika, oregano, garlic, and salt in a saucepan. Simmer over low heat for about 3 minutes. Let cool. Purée in a blender.

2 To butterfly the chicken, use kitchen shears to remove the backbone of the chicken. Press down on the breastbone to spread out the chicken. Transfer the chicken to a nonreactive dish. Coat the chicken with the marinade. Cover and refrigerate for least 1 hour.

3 Preheat the oven to 400°F (200°C). Remove the chicken from the marinade and place on a baking sheet, skin side up. Roast about 1 hour. Serve hot.

Chicken Tikka Masala

This creamy Indian dish gets extra flavor from its marinade

🍴 makes 4 servings

🕐 prep 20 mins, plus marinating • cook 25 mins

❄ freeze for up to 3 months

8 skinless and boneless chicken thighs

2 garlic cloves

1 in (2.5cm) piece fresh ginger, peeled and sliced

2 tbsp fresh lime juice

1 fresh hot red chile, seeded

2 tbsp chopped cilantro, plus more to garnish

2 tbsp vegetable oil

1 red onion, chopped

1 tsp ground turmeric

1 tsp ground cumin

1¼ cups heavy cream

1 tbsp tomato paste

1 tbsp fresh lemon juice

salt and freshly ground black pepper

1 Place the chicken thighs in a single layer in a shallow dish. Purée the garlic, ginger, lime juice, chile, cilantro and 1 tbsp of the oil in a food processor. Spread over the chicken. Cover and refrigerate for at least 2 and up to 8 hours.

2 Heat the remaining oil over medium-high heat. Add the onion and cook about 4 minutes, until beginning to brown. Stir in the turmeric and cumin and cook for 30 seconds. Remove from the heat.

3 Preheat the broiler. Line the broiler rack with oiled aluminum foil. Remove the chicken from the marinade, reserving the marinade. Place on the rack and broil, turning occasionally, about 5 minutes, until the chicken is singed and almost cooked through.

4 Meanwhile, add the reserved marinade to the onion mixture. Stir in the cream, tomato paste, and lemon juice. Bring to a boil over high heat, stirring often. Add the chicken to the sauce and reduce the heat to medium. Simmer for 5 minutes, until the chicken is cooked through. Season with salt and pepper. Sprinkle with cilantro and serve hot.

⚫ **Good with** pilau rice or warm naan bread.

Guinea Hen Breasts with Mustard Sauce

Guinea hen is less gamey in flavor than grouse

🍴 makes 4 servings

🕐 prep 40 mins • cook 25 mins

½ cup dry vermouth or sherry

⅔ cup chicken stock

1 cup heavy cream

1 tbsp vegetable oil

4 skinless and boneless guinea hen breasts

salt and freshly ground black pepper

2 tsp whole grain mustard

1 tbsp chopped chives

1 To make the sauce, reduce the vermouth by half in a saucepan over high heat. Add the stock, boil, and reduce by half again. Add the cream and cook until thick. Set aside.

2 Meanwhile, preheat the oven to 475°F (240°C). Heat the oil in an ovenproof frying pan over high heat. Add the breasts skin-side down and cook about 4 minutes. Flip and season with salt and pepper. Transfer to the oven and roast about 10 minutes, until the juices run clear when pierced with a fork. Transfer to a platter.

3 Pour the fat from the skillet and return to medium heat. Add the sauce and stir to loosen the browned bits in the pan. Whisk in the mustard and chives. Slice the breasts and spoon the sauce on top. Serve hot.

Chicken with Chorizo

Inspired by Spanish cuisine, this is sure to become a favorite chicken dish

 makes 4 servings

prep 10 mins
• cook 1 hr 10 mins

freeze for up to 1 month

3 tbsp olive oil

4 chicken legs

salt and freshly ground black pepper

9oz (250g) smoked chorizo, cut into bite-sized pieces

1 red onion, thinly sliced

1 tsp ground coriander

1 red bell pepper, seeded and chopped

1 yellow bell pepper, seeded and chopped

1 large zucchini, sliced

2 garlic cloves, minced

1 tsp dried thyme

one 14.5oz (411g) can chopped tomatoes

1 cup chicken stock

¼ cup dry sherry

1 Preheat the oven to 350°F (180°C). Heat the oil in a large flameproof casserole over medium-high heat. Season the chicken with salt and pepper. Add the chicken and cook, turning occasionally, about 6 minutes, until browned; remove.

2 Add the chorizo to the casserole and cook, stirring often, for about 3 minutes; remove. Reduce the heat to medium-low and add the onion. Cook, about 5 minutes, or until softened. Add the coriander and stir for 1 minute. Add the peppers, zucchini, garlic, and thyme, and cook about 5 minutes, or until the peppers begin to soften.

3 Add the tomatoes, stock, and sherry and bring to a boil. Return the chicken and chorizo to the casserole, cover, and bake 40 minutes, or until the chicken is tender.

VARIATION

Spicy Chicken Casserole

Add 9oz (250g) chopped new potatoes with the onion. In step 3, add a pinch of dried chile flakes.

Coq au Vin

A French classic that is perfect for entertaining

makes 4 servings

prep 30 mins
• cook 1 hr

large flameproof casserole

freeze for up to 3 months

1 chicken, cut into 8 pieces

2 tbsp all-purpose flour

salt and freshly ground black pepper

4 tbsp butter

4oz (115g) pancetta, diced

1 carrot, diced

1 celery stalk, chopped

2 garlic cloves, minced

one 750ml bottle Pinot Noir

¼ cup brandy or Cognac

4 sprigs thyme

1 bay leaf

1 tbsp olive oil

1lb (450g) white boiling onions, peeled

1 tsp brown sugar

1 tsp red wine vinegar

8oz (225g) small white mushrooms

1 Sprinkle the chicken with 1 tbsp of the flour and season with salt and pepper. Melt 2 tbsp of the butter in a large flameproof casserole over medium heat. In batches, add the chicken and cook about 6 minutes, turning, until golden brown on all sides. Transfer to a plate.

2 Add the pancetta, carrot, celery, and garlic and cook about 5 minutes, until softened. Sprinkle in the remaining flour, stir well, and cook for 1 minute. Add the wine and brandy and bring to a boil, stirring up the browned bits in the pan. Return the chicken to the pan and add the thyme and bay leaf. Cover, reduce the heat to medium-low, and simmer about 30 minutes.

3 Meanwhile, melt the remaining butter with the oil in a frying pan over medium heat. Add the onions and cook about 6 minutes, until lightly browned. Stir in the sugar, vinegar, and 1 tbsp water. Add the onions and mushrooms to the chicken. Cook until the chicken is cooked through, about another 15 minutes.

4 Transfer the chicken and vegetables to a deep platter and keep warm. Discard the thyme and bay leaf. Skim off the fat from the surface of the sauce. Bring to a boil over high heat and cook for about 5 minutes, until the sauce thickens. Season with salt and pepper. Pour over the chicken and serve hot.

Grilled Quail with Ginger Glaze

These quail have a sweet and sour southeast Asian style. Cook them on a barbecue, under a grill, or on a hot griddle pan

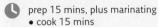

- makes 4 servings
- prep 15 mins, plus marinating • cook 15 mins
- the quail can be frozen in the marinade for up to 1 month

8 quail

limes wedges, to serve

For the marinade

3 tbsp sweet chilli dipping sauce

3 tbsp finely chopped cilantro

2 tbsp fresh lime juice

1 tbsp Asian sesame oil

1 garlic clove, crushed

one ½in (13mm) piece peeled and finely grated fresh ginger

1 garlic clove, crushed through a press

1 **Using poultry shears** or strong scissors, cut each quail down one side of the backbone. Open the quail and place on a work surface, skin side up. Press each quail firmly on the breastbone to flatten. Slash the breast skin with a knife.

2 **Mix the marinade** ingredients in a small bowl. Place the quail in a nonmetallic dish. Brush the marinade over the quail, especially in the cuts. Cover and refrigerate for at least 1 hour and up to 2 days.

3 **Position the broiler** rack 6in (15cm) from the source of heat and preheat the broiler. Line a broiler pan with oiled aluminum foil and place the quail on the pan. Broil, for 12–15 minutes, turning once, until golden brown and the juices show no trace of pink when pierced at the bone with the tip of a sharp knife.

4 **Serve hot**, with lime wedges for squeezing.

VARIATION

Grilled Quail with Hoisin

For a sweet, Chinese barbecue flavor, replace the chilli sauce with hoisin sauce and the sesame oil with 1 crushed garlic clove.

Braised Partridge with Red Cabbage

Delicate-tasting partridge are good pot-roasted as the flavors become concentrated in the pot

- makes 4 servings
- prep 15 mins • cook 1 hr
- large flameproof casserole

4 young partridge

salt and freshly ground black pepper

2 tbsp butter

1 tbsp vegetable oil

4 slices pancetta, chopped

2 onions, thinly sliced

1 garlic clove, minced

½ head red cabbage, cored and finely shredded

2 Granny Smith apples, peeled, cored, and sliced

¾ cup apple juice

2 tbsp red wine vinegar

6 juniper berries, crushed

1 strip of orange zest

3 tbsp red currant jelly

1 **Preheat the oven** to 400°F (200°C). Season the partridges all over with salt and pepper. Melt the butter in a large, flameproof casserole over medium-high heat. One at a time, add the partridges and cook, turning often, about 10 minutes, until browned. Transfer to a plate.

2 **Add the oil** to the pan and heat. Add the pancetta, onions, and garlic. Cook over medium heat for about 4 minutes, or until the bacon begins to brown. Add the cabbage, apples, apple juice, vinegar, juniper berries, and orange zest and bring to a boil. Cover and simmer for 10 minutes.

3 **Stir in the jelly**. Place the partridges in the casserole and cover. Transfer to the oven for 25–30 minutes, until the partridge juices are clear, not pink, when the meat is pierced with a fork.

4 **Let stand**, uncovered, for 10 minutes before serving.

Autumn Game Casserole

Mixed game makes a wonderfully rich-flavored dish. Use chunks of boneless and skinless turkey or pork loin as a substitute

- 🍴 makes 4 servings
- 🕐 prep 20 mins
  - cook 1 hr 30 mins
- 📦 flameproof casserole
- ❄️ freeze for up to 3 months

2 tbsp **olive oil**

1lb 2oz (500g) **mixed boneless and skinless game**, such as pheasant, partridge, venison, rabbit, and pigeon, diced

1 **onion**, sliced

1 **carrot**, sliced

1 **parsnip**, sliced

1 **fennel bulb**, sliced, fronds reserved

2 tbsp **all-purpose flour**

1 cup **chicken stock**

¾ cup **hard apple cider** or apple juice

9oz (250g) **cremini mushrooms**, thickly sliced

½ tsp **fennel seeds**

salt and freshly ground **black pepper**

● **Prepare ahead** The casserole can be cooked, cooled, and refrigerated for up to 2 days, and will improve in flavor during that time.

1 **Preheat the oven** to 325°F (160°C). Heat 1 tbsp of the oil in the casserole over medium-high heat. Add the game and cook for 3–4 minutes, stirring occasionally, until lightly browned. Transfer to a plate.

2 **Add the remaining oil** to the pot and heat. Add the onion, carrot, parsnip, and fennel and cook for 4–5 minutes, stirring occasionally, until lightly colored. Sprinkle in the flour and stir. Gradually stir in the stock and cider. Add the mushrooms and fennel seeds, then return the meat to the pan.

3 **Season with salt** and pepper and bring to a boil. Cover and bake for about 1½ hours, or until the meat is tender.

4 **Sprinkle the casserole** with the reserved fennel fronds and serve hot.

Roast Quail with Apple and Calvados

Wrap the quail in pancetta to keep the flesh moist. The apples and Calvados add a rich, sweet flavor to the dish

- 🍴 serves 4
- 🕐 prep 10 mins
  - cook 25–30 mins
- ✓ low fat
- ❄️ freeze for up to 3 months

8 **quail**

½ tsp freshly grated **nutmeg**

salt and freshly ground **black pepper**

small bunch of **sage leaves**

8 slices of **pancetta**, unrolled

2 **Granny Smith apples**, peeled, cored, and sliced

1 tbsp **butter**, melted

2 tsp **raw** or light brown **sugar**

4 tbsp **Calvados** or applejack

● **Prepare ahead** The quail can be prepared through step 1, covered and refrigerated, up to 1 day ahead.

1 **Preheat the oven** to 400°F (200°C). Season the quail inside and out with the nutmeg, salt, and pepper, then tuck a couple of sage leaves into the cavity. Wrap a strip of pancetta around each bird, tucking the ends underneath.

2 **Place the apples** in a large roasting pan, and toss with the butter and sugar. Arrange the quail on the apples. Roast for 25–30 minutes, turning occasionally, until both the quail and apples have turned golden brown.

3 **Transfer the quail** and apples to a serving platter. Stir the Calvados into the roasting pan and stir over high heat until it boils. Cook for 30 seconds, then pour over the quail and apples. Serve at once.

● **Good with** roast potatoes and green beans.

Braised Pheasant

Game birds are lean, so braising keeps pheasant nice and moist

- 🍴 makes 6 servings
- 🕐 prep 40 mins
  • cook 1 hr 30 mins
- 🍲 large flameproof casserole

2 tbsp **olive oil**

4 tbsp **butter**

2 **pheasants**, about 1lb 10oz (750g) each

salt and freshly ground **black pepper**

8oz (250g) **cremini mushrooms**

2 tbsp chopped **thyme**

1 large **onion**, finely chopped

4oz (115g) sliced **bacon**, chopped

750ml bottle hearty **red wine**

1 **Heat 1 tbsp of the oil** and 2 tbsp of the butter in a large frying pan over medium-high heat. In two batches, add the pheasants and cook, turning occasionally, about 10 minutes, until browned. Season with salt and pepper. Transfer to a large casserole large enough to hold both birds snugly.

2 **Add the mushrooms** and thyme to the frying pan and cook about 5 minutes, until browned. Add to the casserole.

3 **Preheat the oven** to 375°F (190°C). Add the remaining 1 tbsp oil to the pan. Add the onion and bacon and cook, stirring often, for 5 minutes, or until the onion starts to brown. Add to the casserole. Add the wine and bring to a simmer over medium heat. Cover and bake for 1½ hours, or until a pheasant leg pulls away from the bird easily. Transfer the pheasants to a platter. Strain the solids, reserving the liquid, and add the solids to the platter. Tent with aluminum foil to keep warm.

4 **Skim the fat** from the cooking liquid. Return to the casserole and boil about 10 minutes, until reduced by two thirds. Remove from the heat, whisk in the remaining butter, and season. Transfer to a sauceboat. Carve the pheasant and serve with the sauce.

● **Good with** mashed carrots, rutabagas, and green beans.

Roast Partridge with Grapes in Sauternes

The fruity Sauternes complements the rich flavor of the game

- 🍴 makes 6 servings
- 🕐 prep 1 hr, plus standing
  • cook 35 mins

For the sauce

1½ cups **Sauternes**, or other sweet white wine

1 cup halved **green seedless grapes**

2 **shallots**, finely chopped

1½ cups **chicken stock**

2 tbsp cold **butter**, diced

salt and freshly ground **black pepper**

6 whole **partridges**

salt and freshly ground **black pepper**

4 tbsp **butter**, cut into 12 slices

12 **sage leaves**

12 slices **bacon**

2 tbsp **olive oil**

1 **To start the sauce**, combine the wine and grapes and let stand for at least 1 hour.

2 **Cut the breasts** off the partridges. Season with salt and pepper. For each breast, place a slice of butter and a sage leaf on the under side, and wrap in 1 slice of bacon.

3 **Heat the oil** in a large frying pan over medium-high heat. Add the breasts and cook, turning once, about 3 minutes, until browned on both sides. Place in an oiled roasting pan, skin side up; set aside. Leave any fat in the pan.

4 **Preheat the oven** to 375°F (190°C). To continue the sauce, add the shallots to the frying pan and cook about 2 minutes, until softened. Strain the wine into the pan, reserving the grapes. Bring to a boil and cook to reduce to ⅓ cup. Stir in the stock and boil until reduced again to ⅓ cup. Add the grapes and cook for 1 minute; set aside.

5 **Roast the breasts** for 12 minutes, turning once. Before serving, bring the sauce back to a simmer. Remove from the heat and whisk in the butter. Season with salt and pepper. Serve with the sauce.

VARIATION

Roast Pheasant with Grapes in Sauternes

Replace the partridge breasts with 6 pheasant breasts, using 2 sage leaves and 2 slices of bacon for each. Roast the pheasant breasts for 15 minutes.

Squab Breasts on Croûtes

Cut the breasts from squab for the recipe, or use small duck breasts, cooking them for about 10 minutes total

 makes 4 servings

prep 10 mins, plus marinating • cook 4–5 mins

For the marinade

¼ cup hearty **red wine**

2 tbsp **balsamic vinegar**

finely grated zest and juice of 1 **orange**

8 **squab breasts**

salt and freshly ground **black pepper**

2 tbsp **olive oil**

1 tbsp **butter**

2 **shallots**, sliced

3oz (85g) slab **bacon**, rind discarded, cut into sticks

8 slices **rustic bread**

2 tbsp **Dijon mustard**

4oz (115g) **mâche** (lamb's lettuce)

1 **For the marinade**, combine the ingredients in a zippered plastic bag. Add the squab, and refrigerate for at least 8 hours.

2 **Remove the squab** from the marinade and reserve. Season the squab with salt and pepper. Heat 1 tbsp of the oil in a large frying pan over medium heat. Add the bacon and cook, stirring, about 5 minutes, until golden. Stir in the shallots and cook for 2 minutes more. Transfer to a plate and tent with aluminum foil.

3 **Melt the butter** over medium-high heat. Add the squab and cook, turning once, for 5 minutes, or until golden on both sides. Meanwhile, brush the bread slices with the remaining oil and toast until golden. Spread with the mustard.

4 **Transfer the squab** to the plate and tent with foil. Pour the reserved marinade into the pan, bring to a boil, and cook about 5 minutes, or until reduced by half.

5 **Cut each squab** breast in half diagonally Divide the mâche among 4 dinner plates. Top each salad with a slice of toasted bread, 4 breast portions, and the lardon and shallot mixture. Drizzle with the reduced marinade and serve at once.

Grouse with Garlic Cream Sauce

Young grouse are the best for roasting. Serve one per person

 makes 4 servings

prep 15 mins • cook 30–35 mins

freeze for up to 3 months

1 **garlic** head

1 tsp **olive oil**

4 young **grouse**

salt and freshly ground **black pepper**

4 tbsp **butter**

5 sprigs **thyme**

8 slices **bacon**

⅔ cup dry **white wine**

1 cup **heavy cream**

freshly grated **nutmeg**

● **Prepare ahead** The sauce can be cooled, covered, and refrigerated for up to 3 days. Be sure to whisk well while reheating.

1 **Preheat the oven** to 400°F (200°C). Remove the loose outer husk from the garlic. Cut the garlic crosswise about ¼in (5mm) from the top to expose the flesh. Drizzle with the olive oil and wrap in foil. Roast the garlic for about 45 minutes, until tender. Squeeze the soft flesh out of the hulls into a small bowl. Mash with a fork and set aside.

2 **Season the grouse** with salt and pepper. Top each with 1 tbsp of butter and a sprig of thyme. Wrap each grouse with 2 strips of bacon.

3 **Arrange the grouse** in a roasting pan. Roast for 25–30 minutes, basting halfway through the roasting time.

4 **Transfer the grouse** to a serving platter and cover to keep warm. Place the pan over high heat and stir in the wine. Add the remaining sprig of thyme and boil about 3 minutes, or until the liquid is reduced by half. Stir in the cream and boil, stirring often, about 5 minutes, until reduced and slightly thickened. Remove the thyme sprig.

5 **Stir the garlic** flesh into the sauce and season with nutmeg, salt, and pepper. Serve the grouse hot, with the sauce on the side.

● **Good with** roasted cherry tomatoes and mashed potatoes.

Spanish Meatballs

These little veal and pork meatballs—*albóndigas* in Spanish—are popular served as tapas

🍴 makes 48

🕐 prep 20 mins • cook 1 hr

▢ large flameproof casserole

❄ freeze for up to 3 months

1lb 10oz (750g) ground **veal**

9oz (250g) ground **pork**

½ cup minced **parsley**, plus more for garnish

2 **garlic cloves**, minced

½ tsp **ground nutmeg**

½ cup **whole milk**

⅓ cup **bread crumbs** (from day-old bread)

2 tbsp **olive oil**

3 **onions**, finely chopped

1 tbsp **all-purpose flour**, plus more for dusting

1¾ cups hearty **red wine**

2 large **eggs**, beaten

salt and freshly ground **black pepper**

1 cup **vegetable oil**

● **Prepare ahead** The meatball mixture can be refrigerated for up to 24 hours. Or, the entire dish can be cooked up to 2 days in advance and reheated.

1 **Mix the veal**, pork, parsley, and garlic together in a large bowl. Combine the bread crumbs and milk in a small bowl and set aside.

2 **Heat the olive oil** in a large flameproof casserole over medium heat. Add the onions and cook, stirring frequently, about 5 minutes, or until softened. Sprinkle in the flour and stir for 1 minute. Pour in the wine and bring to a simmer. Cook, stirring occasionally, 15 minutes, until lightly thickened. Rub through a wire sieve and return to the casserole. Season with salt and pepper. Set the sauce aside.

3 **Squeeze the excess** milk from the bread crumbs and add to the meat mixture. Add the eggs and 3 tbsp of the wine sauce, season with salt and pepper, and mix well. Roll the mixture into 48 balls, each about the size of a golf ball. Dust the balls with the flour.

4 **Heat the vegetable oil** in a large frying pan over medium-high heat. In batches, add the meatballs and cook, turning often, until browned. Using a slotted spoon, transfer to paper towels to drain.

5 **Bring the sauce** and meatballs to a simmer. Reduce the heat to low and cook until the meatballs are cooked through. Sprinkle with parsley and serve warm.

● **Good with** crusty bread or as a main course dish with mashed potatoes and green beans.

● **Leftovers** can be coarsely chopped, mixed with their sauce, then warmed and used to fill a toasted pita.

BAKING MEATBALLS

Instead of frying the meatballs, they can be baked for 30 minutes in a preheated 350°F (180°C) oven.

Steak au Poivre

This restaurant classic can easily be made at home

🍴 makes 4 servings

🕐 prep 10 mins • cook 12 mins

4 sirloin steaks or filet mignons, about 8oz (225g) each

½ tsp **dry mustard**

1–2 tsp **black peppercorns**

2 tbsp **vegetable oil**

¼ cup **sherry** or brandy

⅔ cup **crème fraîche**

1 **Trim any excess fat** from the steaks. If using filet mignons, flatten slightly with a meat mallet. Sprinkle with the mustard.

2 **Crush the peppercorns** in a mortar or under a saucepan and press on both sides of the steaks.

3 **Heat the oil** in a large frying pan over high heat. Add the steaks and cook, 2–3 minutes each side for a rare steak, 4 minutes each side for medium, and 5–6 minutes each side for well done. Transfer to a platter and tent with aluminum foil.

4 **Add the sherry** to the pan and stir up the browned bits. Add the crème fraîche and cook for 3 minutes, until slightly thickened. Place the steaks on individual plates and top with the sauce. Serve hot.

Veal Scaloppine

This popular Italian dish uses a classic method to prepare veal

 makes 4 servings

prep 10 mins • cook 8 mins

½ cup **all-purpose flour**

salt and freshly ground **black pepper**

4 **veal scallops**, about 6oz (180g) each, patted dry

4 tbsp **butter**

2 tbsp **olive oil**

¼ cup **dry white wine**

1 cup **veal** or chicken **stock**

2 tbsp chopped **parsley**

lemon wedges, to serve

● **Prepare ahead** The veal can be pounded in advance and refrigerated until required.

1 **Preheat the oven** to 200°F (100°C). Season the flour with salt and pepper to taste. One at a time, put a veal scallop between 2 sheets of wax paper and pound with a rolling pin until very thin. Coat the veal on both sides with the flour, then shake off the excess; set aside.

2 **Melt** 1½ tbsp of the butter with the oil in a large frying pan over medium heat until sizzling. Add 2 scallops and cook for 1–2 minutes on each side, pressing down firmly with a spatula to keep the meat as flat as possible, until golden. Transfer the veal to a plate and keep warm in the oven. Repeat with the remaining veal, adding 1½ tbsp butter to the frying pan.

3 **Add the wine** to the pan, increase the heat, and let boil for about 1 minute. Add the stock and any juices from the plate of veal and continue boiling until the liquid is reduced by half. Stir in the parsley, remaining butter, and salt and pepper to taste.

4 **Place the veal** on dinner plates and top with the pan juices. Serve at once with lemon wedges for squeezing over the veal.

● **Good with** sautéed spinach or a green salad. Leftovers are delicious served cold: try slicing into strips and mixing with dressed salad leaves.

Swedish Meatballs

Although these are regarded as a Swedish national dish, they are popular in all the Scandinavian countries

 makes 4 servings

prep 30 mins, plus chilling • cook 20 mins

freeze meatballs (without sauce) for up to 3 months, cooked or uncooked

½ cup fresh **bread crumbs**

½ cup **heavy cream**

4 tbsp **butter**

1 small **onion**, finely chopped

8oz (230g) **ground sirloin**

8oz (230g) **ground lamb**

1 large **egg**, beaten

¼ tsp freshly grated **nutmeg**

salt and freshly ground **black pepper**

For the sauce

¾ cup **heavy cream**

½ cup **beef** or lamb **stock**

1 **Combine the bread** crumbs and cream in a large bowl; set aside. Meanwhile, heat 1 tbsp butter in a frying pan over medium-low heat. Add the onion and cook about 4 minutes, until translucent. Let cool.

2 **Add the beef**, lamb, cooled onions, egg, and nutmeg to the soaked bread crumbs and season with salt and pepper. Cover with plastic wrap and refrigerate for 1 hour.

3 **With damp hands**, shape the meat mixture firmly into balls about the size of ping pong balls, and place on a baking sheet. Cover and refrigerate again for about 1 hour.

4 **Melt the remaining** 3 tbsp butter in a large frying pan over medium heat. In batches, add the meatballs and cook, turning occasionally, for 10 minutes, until evenly browned and cooked through. Using a slotted spoon, transfer to paper towels to drain. Transfer to a bowl and tent with aluminum foil to keep warm.

5 **Pour off the fat** from the pan. Add the cream and stock, bring to a boil over medium heat, and cook about 2 minutes, until lightly thickened. Drizzle with meatballs with the sauce, and serve hot.

● **Good with** new potatoes and steamed broccoli for a main course.

VARIATION

Chicken and Veal Meatballs
Replace the ground beef and lamb with ground chicken or turkey and veal for a lighter version of these Swedish meatballs.

Meat Loaf

This recipe is great served hot for a weekday family meal,
or cold in a packed lunch or sandwich

- makes 4 servings
- prep 20 mins • cook 30 mins
- 8 x 4in (20 x 10cm) loaf pan

vegetable oil, for the pan

12oz (340g) ground beef round

8oz (225g) ground pork

1 onion, finely chopped

⅓ cup packed fresh bread crumbs

2 tbsp chopped parsley

2 tsp spicy brown mustard

1 tsp paprika

salt and freshly ground black pepper

1 large egg, beaten

3 hard-boiled eggs, peeled

For the sauce

½ cup sour cream

3 small sour pickles (cornichons), chopped

1 tbsp capers, chopped

1 tbsp finely chopped parsley

● **Prepare ahead** The loaf can be prepared through step 4 and refrigerated for up to 8 hours. The sauce can be covered and refrigerated for up to 3 days.

1 Preheat the oven to 400°F (200°C). Lightly oil an 8 x 4in (20 x 10cm) loaf pan.

2 Mix together the ground beef, pork, onion, bread crumbs, parsley, mustard, and paprika and season with salt and pepper. Stir in the beaten egg and mix thoroughly.

3 Evenly spread half of the mixture in the pan. Arrange the hard-boiled eggs down the center, then top with the remaining meat mixture and smooth the top.

4 Cover the loaf pan with aluminum foil. Bake for about 50 minutes, until firm. Let stand for 10 minutes before turning out on to a warmed platter.

5 To make the sauce, mix the sour cream, pickles, capers, and parsley.

6 Serve the meat loaf cut into slices, with the sauce spooned over and extra on the side.

● **Good with** a salad of arugula and halved cherry tomatoes.

Hamburgers

These burgers are enriched
with onions and egg yolk

- makes 4 servings
- prep 15 mins • cook 10 mins
- freeze uncooked hamburgers for up to 3 months

1lb (450g) ground chuck or sirloin

½ onion, minced

1 large egg yolk

salt and freshly ground black pepper

olive oil

4 sesame seed buns, cut in half and lightly toasted

1 Combine the ground beef, onion, and egg yolk in a mixing bowl. Season generously with salt and pepper, and mix well with wet hands.

2 Shape into 4 burgers about 4in (10cm) in diameter.

3 Position a broiler rack about 6in (15cm) from the source of heat. Preheat the broiler and lightly oil the broiler pan. Add the burgers and broil for 3 minutes on each side for medium-rare, or longer if you prefer.

4 Serve burgers warm in toasted sesame seed buns.

● **Good with** your favorite condiments (ketchup, mustard, and mayonnaise) and toppings (sliced onions, sliced tomatoes, shredded lettuce, and dill pickles).

Chinese Chile Beef Stir-fry

This hot stir-fry is a good choice for lovers of Chinese food who like their dishes spicy rather than sweet and sour

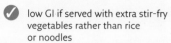

 makes 4 servings

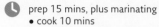 prep 15 mins, plus marinating • cook 10 mins

low GI if served with extra stir-fry vegetables rather than rice or noodles

wok or large deep frying pan

3 tbsp **soy sauce**, preferably dark sauce

2 tbsp **rice vinegar**

1 tsp **Chinese five spice powder**

1lb (450g) **beef round steak**, cut into thin strips

freshly ground **black pepper**

4 tbsp **vegetable oil**

½ **red bell pepper**, seeded and thinly sliced

1 fresh **hot red chile**, seeded and finely chopped

1 **garlic clove**, crushed and chopped

1 tsp peeled and grated **fresh ginger**

1 cup **broccoli florets**

1 cup **snow peas**

1 tsp **cornstarch**

½ cup **beef stock**

few drops of **Asian sesame oil**

1 Mix the soy sauce, vinegar, and five spice powder together in a bowl. Add the beef and toss well. Season well with black pepper. Cover and refrigerate for at least 2 and up to 12 hours.

2 Heat 2 tbsp oil in a wok over high heat. Add the bell pepper and stir-fry until crisp-tender, about 3 minutes. Add the chile, garlic, and ginger and stir-fry for 1 minute. Add the broccoli and snow peas and stir-fry for 2 minutes. Transfer to a platter.

3 Add the remaining oil to the wok and heat over high heat. Drain the beef from the marinade, reserving the marinade. Add the beef to the wok and stir-fry for 1 minute. Return the vegetables to the wok and pour in the marinade. Dissolve the cornstarch in the stock, and stir into the wok. Stir-fry the steak and vegetables until the sauce is boiling.

4 Transfer to a plate, drizzle with the sesame oil, and serve at once.

VARIATION

Chicken Chile Stir-fry

Substitute skinless and boneless chicken breast for the beef.

Beef Strogonoff

This classic Russian dish was named after the Strogonov family

makes 4 servings

prep 15 mins • cook 25 mins

2 tbsp **butter**

1 **onion**, thinly sliced

8oz (225g) **cremini mushrooms**, sliced

1½lb (700g) **filet mignon**, cut across the grain into 2 x ½in (5 x 13mm) strips

salt and freshly ground **black pepper**

3 tbsp **all-purpose flour**

1 tbsp **sweet paprika**, plus extra for sprinkling

2 tbsp **olive oil**

1¼ cups **sour cream** or crème fraîche

1 tbsp **Dijon mustard**

2 tbsp fresh **lemon** juice

1 Heat the butter in a large frying pan over medium heat. Add the onion and cook about 8 minutes, until golden. Add the mushrooms and cook about 5 minutes, until they begin to brown. Transfer to a plate.

2 Meanwhile, season the beef with salt and pepper. Mix the flour and paprika together in a large bowl, add the beef and toss well. Add the oil to the pan and increase the heat to high. In batches, add the beef and cook, stirring occasionally, for about 3 minutes, until the meat is seared. Transfer to a plate.

3 Return the beef, onions, and mushrooms to the pan. Stir over high heat for 1 minute. Reduce the heat to medium-low. Stir in the sour cream and mustard and heat, but do not boil.

4 Stir in the lemon juice and season with salt and pepper. Sprinkle with paprika and serve hot.

● **Good with** rice or egg noodles.

VARIATION

Veal Strogonoff

Substitute 16 whole peeled small shallots for the onions. Use 1½lb (700g) veal filet instead of the beef. At the end of step 3, pour in 3 tbsp Cognac and immediately set it alight, shaking the pan until the flame is extinguished.

Balsamic Beef Salad

Colorful and filling, this makes a substantial summer salad

- makes 6 servings
- prep 20 mins
  - cook 1 hr 5 mins

For the dressing

½ cup **extra virgin olive oil**

2 tbsp **balsamic vinegar**

1 **garlic clove**, pressed

2 tbsp chopped **basil**

2 tsp chopped **oregano** or marjoram

1½ tsp **brown sugar**

1 tsp **whole grain mustard**

salt and freshly ground **black pepper**

2 small **red bell peppers**

4 tbsp **olive oil**

2 small **red onions**, cut into wedges

6oz (175g) **cherry tomatoes**

1 tbsp **balsamic vinegar**

1lb 5oz (600g) **beef tenderloin**, trimmed and tied

6oz (165g) **mesclun**

1 **To prepare the dressing**, process the ingredients in a blender. Season with salt and pepper.

2 **Preheat the broiler**. Broil the peppers, turning from time to time, until blackened on all sides. Let cool until handleable. Remove the blackened skin, seeds, and ribs. Cut the peppers into thick strips.

3 **Preheat the oven** to 375°F (190°C). Place the onions on a rimmed baking sheet, toss with 1 tbsp of the oil, and season with salt and pepper. Roast for 20 minutes. Add the cherry tomatoes, drizzle with 1 tbsp more oil, and the vinegar. Roast for 10 minutes more, until the onions are tender. Let cool.

4 **Increase the oven** temperature to 425°F (220°C). Heat remaining 4 tbsp oil in a large frying pan over high heat. Add the beef and cook, turning occasionally, about 10 minutes, until browned on all sides. Transfer to a roasting pan. Roast about 20 minutes until a meat thermometer reads 130°F (55°C) for medium-rare meat. Transfer to a carving board. Let cool, and thinly slice the beef.

5 **Toss the mesclun** with ¼ cup of dressing. Add the beef, red pepper, onions, and cherry tomatoes. Serve with extra dressing on the side.

Thai Red Beef Curry

Thai curry paste is sold at Asian markets and some supermarkets

- makes 4 servings
- prep 20 mins • cook 15 mins

450g (1lb) **sirloin steak**, thinly sliced along the grain

3 tbsp **vegetable oil**

1 large **garlic clove**, minced

½ **onion**, thinly sliced

1 **red bell pepper**, seeded and thinly sliced

7oz (200g) **white mushrooms**, sliced

1½ tbsp **Thai red curry paste**

2 cups canned **coconut milk**

1½ tbsp **Asian fish sauce**

1 tbsp **light brown sugar**

4oz (115g) **baby spinach leaves**

3 tbsp shredded **Thai basil leaves**

1 **Toss the beef**, 1 tbsp of the oil, and the garlic together. Heat a large wok over high heat. In batches, add the beef and stir-fry for 30 seconds to 1 minute, until the beef starts to change color. Using a slotted spoon, transfer to a plate.

2 **When all the beef** has been stir-fried, add the remaining oil to the wok and heat until shimmering. Add the onion and pepper and stir-fry for 2 minutes. Add the mushrooms and stir for 2 minutes more, or until all the vegetables are tender.

3 **Stir in the curry paste**. Add the coconut milk, fish sauce, and sugar and bring to a boil, stirring. Reduce the heat to medium and return the beef to the pan, along with the spinach and basil. Cook, stirring often, for 3 minutes, or until the beef is heated through and the spinach has wilted.

THAI RED CURRY PASTE

To make your own curry paste, put 2½oz (75g) chopped shallots, 2 garlic cloves, 8 fresh bird's-eye chiles, a 6in (15cm) piece of lemongrass, a ½in (1cm) piece of galangal, 1 kaffir lime leaf, ½ tsp ground coriander, ¼ tsp fish sauce, ¼ tsp ground cumin, and ½ tsp salt in a blender and process to form a paste. Refrigerate in an airtight container, for up to 1 month. For a less fiery paste, seed the chiles.

Beef Wellington

Always impressive for a dinner-party main course

makes 6 servings

prep 45 mins • cook 30–45 mins

2¼lb (1kg) **beef tenderloin**, cut from the thick end, well trimmed

salt and freshly ground **black pepper**

2 tbsp **vegetable oil**

3 tbsp **butter**

2 **shallots**, finely chopped

1 **garlic clove**, minced

9oz (250g) **cremini mushrooms**, finely chopped

1 tbsp **brandy** or Madeira

one 17.3oz (484g) box thawed **frozen puff pastry**

1 large **egg**, beaten, for glazing

1 Preheat the oven to 425°F (220°C). Season the meat with salt and pepper. Heat the oil in a frying pan over high heat. Add the beef and cook, turning often, about 5 minutes. Place the beef on a rack in a roasting pan. Roast for 10 minutes. Let cool.

2 Meanwhile, melt the butter in a frying pan over medium heat. Add the shallots and garlic and cook, stirring, for 2-3 minutes, until just softened. Add the mushrooms and cook 4-5 minutes more, stirring occasionally, until the juices have evaporated. Add the brandy and boil for 30 seconds. Let cool.

3 Roll one pastry sheet and trim into a rectangle 2in (5cm) larger than the beef fillet. Place on a baking sheet and prick well with a fork. Bake 12-15 minutes, or until crisp and golden. Let cool, then trim any uneven edges with a serrated knife.

4 Place the pastry rectangle on a baking sheet. Spread ⅓ of the mushroom mixture down the center. Place the beef on top and spread the remaining mushroom mixture on top. Roll out the remaining pastry sheet large enough to cover the beef. Brush the exposed edge of the pastry with beaten egg. Place the rolled dough over the beef, tucking and pressing the dough to the baked pastry base to adhere.

5 Brush with beaten egg. Decorate with pastry trimmings, and brush again. Make a slit in the center. Bake about 30 minutes, until 130°F for rare. Let stand for 10 minutes before serving.

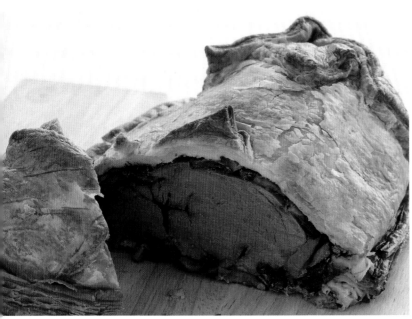

Blanquette de Veau

A simple, delicately flavored French veal stew in white sauce

makes 4 servings

prep 15 mins • cook 1½ hrs

large flameproof casserole

1½lb (675g) **boneless veal shoulder**, cut into 2in (5cm) pieces

2 **onions**, chopped

2 **carrots**, chopped

2 tbsp fresh **lemon** juice

1 **bouquet garni** (6 parsley stalks, 1 celery rib, 1 bay leaf, 5 black peppercorns, 3 fresh thyme sprigs, tied in cheesecloth)

salt and freshly ground **black pepper**

6 tbsp **butter**

16 **white pearl onions**, peeled

8oz (225g) **cremini mushrooms**, quartered

2 tbsp **all-purpose flour**

3 tbsp **heavy cream**

1 large **egg yolk**

chopped **parsley**, to garnish

1 Combine the veal, onions, carrots, lemon juice, and bouquet garni in a flameproof casserole and season with salt and pepper. Add enough water to cover. Bring to a boil over medium heat. Reduce the heat to low and simmer about 1 hour, or until the meat is tender.

2 Meanwhile, melt 2 tbsp of the butter in a frying pan over medium heat. Add the pearl onions and cook, stirring occasionally, about 5 minutes, until lightly browned. Add 2 tbsp of the remaining butter and the mushrooms. Cook, stirring occasionally, for 5 minutes, or until the mushrooms are tender.

3 Strain the stew, reserving 2¼ cups of the cooking liquid. Add the meat and vegetables to the mushroom mixture and cover.

4 Melt the remaining butter in a saucepan over medium-low heat. Whisk in the flour and cook for 1 minute. Whisk in the cooking liquid. Bring to a boil, whisking often.

5 Whisk the cream and egg yolks in a bowl, and gradually whisk in 1 cup of the sauce. Return to the saucepan. Pour the sauce over the meat and heat without boiling, stirring gently. Sprinkle with the parsley and serve hot.

Hungarian Goulash

This warming winter stew makes a great main course for entertaining, since it can be made well in advance

- 🍴 makes 4–6 servings
- 🕐 prep 25 mins • cook 2½ hrs
- ✓ low GI
- ❄ freeze without the sour cream for up to 3 months

4 tbsp vegetable oil

2lb (900g) beef chuck, cut into 1in (2.5cm) cubes

2 large onions, thinly sliced

2 red bell peppers, seeded and chopped

2 garlic cloves, finely chopped

1 tbsp paprika, plus more to garnish

one 14.5oz (411g) can chopped tomatoes, drained

2 tbsp tomato paste

1 tbsp all-purpose flour

1¼ cups beef stock

1 tsp chopped thyme

salt and freshly ground black pepper

⅔ cup sour cream

1 Preheat the oven to 325°F (160°C). Heat 2 tbsp of the oil in a large flameproof casserole over medium-high heat. Add the beef in batches, and cook for about 5 minutes, turning occasionally, until browned.

2 Add the remaining oil to the casserole and reduce the heat to medium. Add the onions, peppers, and garlic, and cook, scraping up the bits in the casserole, about 5 minutes, until the onions are transparent. Add the paprika and stir for 1 minute.

3 Stir in the tomatoes and tomato paste. Dissolve the flour in ¼ cup of the stock, then stir into the casserole with the remaining stock and thyme, and season to taste. Bring to a boil, stirring often.

4 Cover tightly. Bake for 2 hours, or until the beef is tender.

5 To serve, spoon the goulash into individual bowls. Top each with a generous dollop of sour cream and sprinkle with a little paprika.

● **Good with** buttered tagliatelle.

VARIATION

With Potato Dumplings

Combine 2 cups of mashed potatoes with 1 beaten egg, 3 tbsp all-purpose flour, 3 tbsp semolina (pasta) flour, and ½ tsp caraway seeds. The mixture should hold its shape; if not, add flour. Shape into 12 balls and refrigerate for 20 minutes. Cook for 15 minutes in a pot of simmering water, until fluffy.

Boeuf Bourguignon

Long, slow braising allows the beef to absorb the rich flavors of the wine and herbs and tenderizes it in the process

- 🍴 makes 4–6 servings
- 🕐 prep 25 mins • cook 2½ hrs
- ✓ low GI
- ❄ freeze for up to 3 months

6oz (175g) sliced bacon, chopped

2 tbsp vegetable oil

2lb (900g) beef chuck, cut into 1½in (4cm) cubes

salt and freshly ground black pepper

12 small shallots, peeled

1 tbsp all-purpose flour

1¼ cups red wine, preferably Pinot Noir

1¼ cups beef stock

4oz (115g) white mushrooms, quartered

1 tsp dried herbes de Provence

1 bay leaf

3 tbsp chopped parsley

● **Prepare ahead** This stew (as well as the Goulash and Daube) can made up to 2 days ahead, cooled, covered, and refrigerated. Reheat in a 350°F (180°C) oven for 30 minutes.

1 Preheat the oven to 325°F (160°C). Cook the bacon in a flameproof casserole over medium heat until lightly browned. Transfer to paper towels to drain.

2 Add 1 tbsp oil to the casserole and increase the heat to medium-high. Season the beef with salt and pepper. In batches, add the beef and cook, turning occasionally, about 5 minutes, or until browned. Transfer to a plate.

3 Meanwhile, heat the remaining 1 tbsp oil in a frying pan over medium heat. Add the shallots and cook, stirring, until lightly browned, about 5 minutes.

4 Return the beef to the casserole. Sprinkle with flour and stir well. Stir in the wine and stock and bring to a boil over high heat. Add the shallots, mushrooms, bacon, herbs, and bay leaf, and cover. Bake for about 2 hours until the meat is very tender.

5 Sprinkle with chopped parsley, and serve.

● **Good with** mashed potatoes, buttered baby carrots, and broccoli or green beans.

Beef Daube with Wild Mushrooms

This stew is redolent with red wine and earthy mushrooms

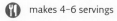 makes 4–6 servings

prep 30 mins • cook 2½ hrs

large flameproof casserole with a tight-fitting lid

can be frozen up to 3 months

2 tbsp olive oil

2 tbsp butter

2lb (900g) beef chuck, cut into 3in (7.5cm) pieces

salt and freshly ground pepper

2 tbsp all-purpose flour

4oz (115g) pancetta, chopped

1 large onion, finely chopped

1 celery stalk, finely chopped

3 garlic cloves, minced

3 carrots, diced

1 tbsp chopped thyme

one 750ml bottle hearty red wine

zest and juice of 1 orange

2 tbsp brandy (optional)

1 tbsp tomato paste

1oz (30g) dried porcini mushrooms

6oz (175g) cremini mushrooms, sliced

1 Heat the olive oil and butter in a large, flameproof casserole over medium-high heat. Season the beef with salt and pepper. Toss the beef in the flour. In batches, add to the casserole. Cook, turning occasionally, about 5 minutes, until browned. Transfer to a plate.

2 Add the pancetta, onion, celery, bacon, and garlic to the casserole and cook about 7 minutes, until lightly colored. Return the beef to the casserole and add the carrots and thyme. Pour in the wine, the orange zest and juice, brandy, if using, and the tomato paste. Bring to a boil. Reduce the heat to low and cover. Simmer for 1 hour.

3 Soak the dried mushrooms in hot tap water to cover about 30 minutes, until softened. Drain well and chop the mushrooms. Add the soaked and fresh mushrooms to the casserole and continue cooking until the beef is very tender, about 1 hour longer. Serve hot.

● **Good with** buttered egg noodles or parslied boiled potatoes.

● **Leftovers can be** reheated with crushed tomatoes for a pasta sauce.

Osso Bucco

Veal shanks have a richness unlike any other cut of meat and turn this stew into an extraordinary meal

makes 4 servings

prep 15 mins • cook 1¾ hrs

hind shanks make the best, meatiest osso bucco

large flameproof casserole

complete steps 1–3, then leave to cool completely and freeze for up to 1 month. Thaw completely, then reheat and complete step 4

four 1½in (4cm) thick veal shanks

salt and freshly ground black pepper

¼ cup all-purpose flour

2 tbsp butter

2 tbsp olive oil

1 small onion, chopped

4 garlic cloves, chopped

½ cup beef stock or water, as needed

¼ cup tomato paste

3 tbsp chopped parsley

2 anchovy fillets in oil, minced

grated zest of 1 lemon

● **Prepare ahead** The stew can be cooked, then chilled for up to 2 days. Reheat gently, then complete step 4.

1 Season the veal with salt and pepper. Dredge in the flour and shake off any excess.

2 Melt the butter with the oil in a large flameproof casserole over medium-high heat. Add the veal and cook, turning occasionally, about 5 minutes, or until browned all over. Transfer to a plate. Add the onion and garlic to the casserole and reduce the heat to medium-low. Cook, stirring occasionally, for 5 minutes or until softened but not colored.

3 Stir in the stock and tomato paste, season with salt and pepper, and bring to a boil. Return the veal to the casserole. Reduce the heat to low and cover. Simmer for 1½ hours or until the veal is tender. Check the stew occasionally, and if the cooking liquid has reduced too much, add more stock. The finished cooking liquid should be quite thick.

4 Stir the parsley, anchovies, and lemon zest into the casserole, Adjust the seasoning and serve immediately.

● **Good with** a saffron-flavored risotto or cooked long-grain rice.

● **With the addition** of some chopped canned tomatoes and herbs, leftovers can be made into a ragú to spoon over pasta.

Steak

A well-cooked steak is delicious, quick, and easy to cook. Tender, juicy steaks are perfectly suited to the quick-cooking techniques of grilling, chargrilling, broiling, barbecuing, and pan-frying, so with a little practice, a satisfying meal can be on the table no time.

Choosing Steak

Supermarkets and butchers sell many types of steak, varying in price and quality. Only buy steaks that look fresh, with a slightly moist appearance. Any fat around the edge should be white or creamy white.

In hot weather, transport steaks home in an insulated bag, and at all times of the year, immediately refrigerate them. Steaks from the supermarket can be left in their tray, but those from the butcher should be taken out of plastic, put on a plate with a lip to avoid dripping, and covered with wax paper. Never buy packaged steaks with torn packaging.

Like all raw meat, steaks should be stored at the bottom of the refrigerator so the raw juices do not cross-contaminate other foods. Cook steaks within 3 days of purchasing, or according to the use-by date.

Chilled steaks should be removed from the refrigerator 15 minutes before cooking to return to room temperature, but no longer than that.

What Steak, What Dish?

There are many ways to cook steak, other than for simply serving on its own. Steaks are the main ingredients in recipes as diverse as simple sandwiches to impressive main courses, such as Beef Wellington (p325), but not all steak cuts are suitable for all dishes. Be sure to buy the correct cut for every dish to avoid over- or under-cooking and get the best results.

T-bone Steak Thick and meaty, this is best grilled, pan-fried, or broiled.

Rump Steak Can be substituted for sirloin steak in most dishes.

Sirloin Steak A less expensive alternative to fillet steak for stir-fries and salads, it can be cut into chunks for steak pies and casseroles. Also very good for grilling.

Minute Steak Great in sandwiches, pan-fried with eggs for breakfast, and often used in the classic French dish *steak frites*.

Fillet Steak Good for quick-cooking dishes, such as Beef Stroganoff (p323) and stir-fries, as well as beef cooked in pastry and beef salads.

MARBLING

The best-quality steaks have thin lines of white fat running through them. This is called marbling.

Marbling adds flavor and helps keep the meat tender. If you are concerned about this small amount of fat, broiling, chargrilling, and grilling are the best cooking techniques to use, as the fat melts away during cooking.

Avoid buying meat with yellow marbling, as this can be an indication the meat is old and might be tough.

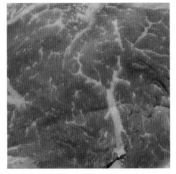

Look for thin lines of white intermuscular fat when buying steaks. These are an indication of tenderness.

Types of Steak

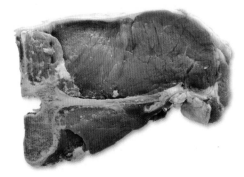

T-bone Steak
Thicker than most steaks, this has a bone left in, which adds extra flavor. Suitable for high-heat quick cooking techniques, and especially good for grilling. Porterhouse is a similar, but thicker, steak.

Rump Steak
Similar to a sirloin (see below), but slightly less tender, so less expensive. The texture can be variable, and the meat is often lean, so it will often require marinating or tenderizing.

Sirloin Steak
A moderately expensive, boneless steak with a good flavor and tender texture. This steak is suitable for all cooking techniques.

Minute Steak
Quick pan-frying is the best cooking technique for this very thin, boneless steak. It must be cooked quickly to prevent it from becoming tough, hence its name.

Filet Steak
The most tender and expensive steak, good for celebratory meals. This thick, boneless steak can be chargrilled, grilled, or pan-fried. It also can be broiled, but other less expensive steaks are more suitable.

cooking steak

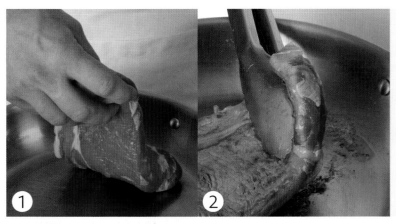

Pan-fry

1 **Heat a heavy** frying pan over high heat until very hot, but not smoking. Brush the pan with a very thin layer of vegetable oil, put the steak in the pan, and fry for half the time specified below, or in a specific recipe.

2 **Using tongs**, turn the steak over and fry for the remaining time. Use the finger test (below) to determine when the steak is cooked as desired. Remove the steak from the pan, cover with foil, and let rest for 5 minutes before serving.

Grill

Light the grill well in advance so the coals are glowing and ash gray. When ready to cook, brush the steak with vegetable oil, and place it on the rack. Follow the timings below, or in a specific recipe, and use tongs to turn the steak over halfway through the cooking time.

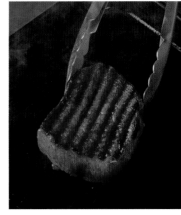

Pan-grill

Heat a ridged cast-iron grill pan until it is very hot, but not smoking. Brush the steak with oil before putting it in the pan. Follow the timings below, or in a specific recipe, and use tongs to turn the steak over halfway through the cooking time.

Cooking Steaks to Perfection

The timings below are for barbecuing, grilling, or broiling sirloin, rump, and T-bone steaks 1½in (4cm) thick. Timings will vary depending on the type of pan, the exact degree of heat, and the quality and thickness of the meat. Turn the meat after half the specified cooking time.

VERY RARE

Cook until just seared on both sides. The steak feels very soft when pressed, and the interior is reddish purple.
• Cook for 2–3 minutes

RARE

When drops of blood come to the surface, turn the steak over. It feels soft and spongy, and the interior is red.
• Cook for 6–8 minutes

MEDIUM

Turn the steak when drops of juice are first visible. The steak offers resistance when pressed and is pink in the center.
• Cook for 10–12 minutes

WELL DONE

Turn the steak when drops of juice are clearly visible. The steak feels firm and is uniformly brown throughout.
• Cook for 12–14 minutes

TESTING FOR DONENESS

Take a tip from chefs and use this simple touch test to determine how a steak is cooked. Press the steak to determine how much resistance it has. A very rare steak will feel like the heel of your thumb on a relaxed hand. As you press the tip of your thumb to the tips of your fingers, the heel of your thumb becomes firmer. A rare steak feels like the heel of your thumb when you press your thumb and index finger together; for medium (below), press your thumb and middle finger together; for well done, press your thumb and little finger together.

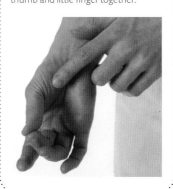

Steak   329

Steak

Flavor Boosters for Steak

Good-quality steaks have plenty of flavor, but you can add extra flavor by marinating them before cooking or serving them with flavored butters or a simple sauce.

Keep a selection of flavored butters in the refrigerator or freezer for adding instant impact. Simply place a slice of flavored butter on top of the just-cooked steak, and as it melts, the butter and its flavorings mingle with the steak juices.

When a marinade contains an acidic ingredient, use a nonmetallic bowl and don't marinate the steak for longer than 2 hours.

Anchovy Butter
Beat the ingredients together, then roll in wax paper and chill.

4 tbsp **butter**, softened

2 **anchovy fillets**, finely chopped

½ tbsp grated **lemon** zest

pinch **cayenne pepper**

black pepper

Chile-orange Marinade
Combine all the ingredients in a nonmetallic bowl, stirring to dissolve the sugar. Marinate up to 8 hours.

juice of 2 large **oranges**

juice of 1 **lime**

3 **garlic cloves**, crushed

a few drops of **Tabasco sauce**

salt and **black pepper**

Red Wine Marinade
Combine all the ingredients in a nonmetallic bowl. Use any leftover marinade to baste cooking steaks.

16fl oz (500ml) **dry red wine**

3 tbsp **red wine vinegar**

2 **garlic cloves**, crushed

1 strip **lemon** zest

chopped fresh **herbs**, to taste

Mustard Cream Sauce
Combine ingredients, mix, season to taste, and serve alongside steak.

⅔ cup **sour cream**

4 tbsp **mayonnaise**

1½ tbsp **mustard**

½ tsp **horseradish sauce**

¼ tsp **sugar**

salt

Red Wine Sauce
Boil the wine in the pan's cooking juices until reduced by half. Stir in the crème fraîche. Add the parsley, season, and serve alongside steak.

1 cup **dry red wine**

⅔ cup **crème fraîche**

2 tbsp chopped **parsley**

salt and **black pepper**

MELTING FLAVOR

As a slice of fresh herb butter (p236) melts, it creates an instant sauce, adding extra flavor to the perfectly grilled steak.

Carrot and Parsnip Purée with Tarragon

This is a flavorsome winter accompaniment

🕐 25 mins   **page 234**

Grilled Vegetables

Serve this Mediterranean-style dish hot or at room temperature with grilled steaks

🕐 35 mins   **page 235**

Potato-Herb Galette

Like a large potato pancake, this grated potato dish can be cut into wedges to serve with steak

🕐 45 mins   **page 241**

Mushrooms in Cream Sauce

Omit the toast and serve these tasty mushrooms alongside steaks

🕐 35 mins   **page 250**

Roast Sweet Potatoes with Sesame Glaze

These make a colorful change from french fries

🕐 1 hr   **page 243**

Chimichurri

In Argentina, this piquant sauce is always served with broiled and grilled steaks

🕐 5 mins   **page 282**

Béarnaise Sauce

This traditional French sauce is a classic accompaniment to grilled steaks

🕐 15 mins   **page 359**

Horseradish Sauce

Beef and horseradish is a culinary match that is difficult to top

🕐 10 mins   **page 360**

Steak and Ale Pie

Beer helps to tenderize the beef and imparts a delicious flavor

- 🍴 makes 4 servings
- 🕐 prep 20 mins, plus cooling • cook 2¼ hrs
- ▭ 9in (23cm) pie dish

1½lb (675g) **beef chuck**, trimmed and cut into ¾in (2cm) pieces

salt and freshly ground **black pepper**

3 tbsp **all-purpose flour**

3 tbsp **vegetable oil**

1 large **onion**, chopped

4oz (115g) **white mushrooms**, halved

1 **garlic clove**, minced

¾ cup **beef stock**

¾ cup **dark ale**

1 tbsp **Worcestershire sauce**

1 tbsp **tomato paste**

½ tsp dried **thyme**

1 **bay leaf**

1 sheet thawed frozen **puff pastry**

1 large **egg**, beaten, to glaze

● **Prepare ahead** The filling can be cooked, cooled, and covered 1 day ahead.

1 Season the beef with salt and pepper. Toss in the flour and shake off the excess.

2 Heat 2 tbsp of the oil in a large nonstick frying pan over medium-high heat. In batches, add the beef and cook, turning, for 5 minutes until browned. Transfer to a large saucepan.

3 Add the remaining 1 tbsp oil to the frying pan. Add the onion and cook over medium heat, stirring, until softened. Add the mushrooms and garlic and cook, stirring, about 5 minutes, until the mushrooms begin to brown. Transfer to the saucepan. Stir in the stock, ale, Worcestershire sauce, tomato paste, thyme, and bay leaf into the saucepan and bring to a boil. Reduce the heat to medium-low, cover, and simmer about 1½ hours, or until the meat is tender.

4 Transfer the meat and vegetables to the pie dish. Reserve ⅔ cup of the sauce, and pour the rest over the meat mixture. Let cool.

5 Preheat the oven to 400°F (200°C). Roll out the puff pastry on a floured surface to a thickness of ⅛in (3mm). Cut an 11in (28cm) round. Cut ¾in (2cm) strips from the trimmings. Brush the rim of the pie dish with water, and place the strips around it. Brush with water. Place the pastry round over the dish and press the pastry edges together to seal. Trim off the excess with a knife.

6 Crimp the pastry edge and use the pastry trimmings to make decorations, if desired. Brush the pastry with beaten egg, make a hole in the middle, and affix the decorations on the pastry, if using. Place the dish on a baking sheet. Bake for 25 minutes, or until the pastry is puffed and dark golden. Serve immediately, with the reheated reserved gravy passed on the side.

Chile con Carne

A Tex-Mex classic

- 🍴 makes 4–6 servings
- 🕐 prep 5 mins • cook 50 mins
- ❄ freeze for up to 3 months

1 tbsp **olive oil**

1 **onion**, thinly sliced

1 **garlic clove**, crushed

2 tbsp **chile powder**

1 tsp **ground cumin**

1½lb (675g) **ground round**

one 15oz (420g) can **red kidney beans**, drained and rinsed

one 14.5oz (411g) can **chopped tomatoes**

2 tbsp **tomato paste**

salt and freshly ground **black pepper**

chopped **cilantro** and **sour cream**

1 Heat the oil in a large saucepan over medium heat. Add the onions and cook for 5 minutes, or until softened. Add the garlic and cook 1 minute. Stir in the chile powder and cumin, then the beef. Cook, breaking up the beef with a spoon, until it browns all over, about 5 minutes.

2 Stir in the beans, tomatoes, and tomato paste and bring to a boil. Reduce the heat, cover, and simmer for 40 minutes, stirring occasionally, until thickened. Season with salt and pepper. Serve hot, sprinkled with cilantro and topped with sour cream.

Roast Rib of Beef

Be sure to let this magnificent roast stand at least 15 minutes

 makes 4–6 servings

🕐 prep 20 mins, plus standing ● cook 1½–2 hrs

3lb 3oz (1.5kg) **beef rib roast with bones**

2 tbsp **butter**, softened

salt and freshly ground **black pepper**

For the gravy

2 tbsp **all-purpose flour**

2 cups **beef stock**

1 Preheat the oven to 425°F (220°C). Spread the beef with the butter and season with salt and pepper. Place the beef, bone-side down, in a roasting pan.

2 Roast for 15 minutes. Reduce the oven temperature to 375°F (190°C) and roast to the desired doneness, allowing 15 minutes per 1lb (450g) plus 15 minutes for medium-rare beef.

A meat thermometer inserted in the thickest part of the roast will read 130°F (55°C).

3 Transfer the beef to a platter and tent with aluminum foil. Let stand for 15–20 minutes before carving.

4 To make the gravy, discard all but 2 tbsp of fat from the roasting pan. Place the pan over medium heat. Whisk in the flour, scraping up the browned bits in the pan. Whisk in the stock and bring to a boil, whisking constantly, until thickened and smooth. Reduce the heat to low and simmer for 2 minutes. Season with salt and pepper. Strain into a gravy boat. Carve the beef and serve with the gravy.

● **Good with** Yorkshire puddings, roast potatoes, and vegetables of your choice.

Beef Salad with Caramelized Walnuts

This works well for a crowd and can be served warm or cold

 makes 6 servings

🕐 prep 20 mins ● cook 45 mins

4 medium **beets**

4 tbsp **olive oil**

salt and freshly ground **black pepper**

2¼lb (1kg) **beef tenderloin**, trimmed and tied

3½ cups **walnut halves**

1 tbsp **honey**

1 tbsp **sugar**

6oz (175g) **arugula**

1 tbsp **balsamic vinegar**

finely chopped **chives** for garnish

For the horseradish cream

½ cup **crème fraîche** or sour cream

1 tbsp freshly grated or prepared **horseradish**

1 tbsp **lemon** juice

salt and freshly ground **black pepper**

1 Preheat the oven to 425°F (220°C). Toss the beets with 1 tbsp of the oil and season. Wrap each in aluminum foil. Place on a

baking sheet and roast 45 minutes, or until tender. Unwrap and let cool. Peel and cut each beet into eighths.

2 Heat a large frying pan over medium-high heat. Rub the beef with 1 tbsp of the olive oil and season. Cook the beef, turning, until browned on all sides, about 8 minutes. Transfer to a roasting pan and roast until a meat thermometer reads 125°F (52°C) for medium-rare. Leave for 15 minutes before carving.

3 Reduce the temperature to 400°F (200°C). Toss the walnuts with the honey and sugar and season with salt. Spread on a baking sheet. Bake 3 minutes, until glazed. Transfer to a plate and cool.

4 Meanwhile, to make the horseradish cream, stir the crème fraîche, horseradish, and lemon juice and season with salt and pepper.

5 Toss the arugula with the vinegar and remaining oil. Season, and spread on a serving platter. Add the beets and walnuts, and sprinkle with chives. Slice the beef thinly and arrange on the salad. Serve with horseradish cream on the side.

Filet Mignons with Walnut Pesto

A great dish for autumn, when walnuts are at their peak

 makes 6 servings

🕐 prep 15 mins • cook 4–12 mins

For the walnut pesto

1 cup walnut halves

½ cup freshly grated Parmesan

2 garlic cloves, minced

2 tbsp chopped tarragon

2 tbsp chopped parsley

1½ tsp red wine vinegar

½ cup extra-virgin olive oil

salt and freshly ground black pepper

6 filet mignons, about 6oz (175g) each

olive oil, for brushing

1 **To make the walnut pesto,** toast the walnuts in a 350°F (170°C) oven for 10 minutes. Let cool. Transfer to a food processor and add the Parmesan, garlic, tarragon, parsley, and vinegar. With the machine running, add the oil to make a coarse paste. Season with salt and pepper.

2 **Heat a ridged frying pan** over high heat. Lightly brush the steaks with oil and season with salt and pepper. Cook the steaks in the pan for about 3 minutes on each side for medium-rare. Transfer to dinner plates and serve hot, with a dollop of the walnut pesto.

Sauerbraten

This pot roast, with its richly spiced sauce, is especially tender thanks to a combination of long marinating and slow cooking

🍴 makes 4–6 servings

🕐 prep 30 mins, plus marinating • cook 2–2¼ hrs

❄ freeze for up to 2 months

For the marinade

2 cups hearty red wine

⅔ cup red wine vinegar

2 onions, thinly sliced

1 tbsp light brown sugar

½ tsp freshly grated nutmeg

4 whole allspice berries, lightly crushed

4 black peppercorns, lightly crushed

2 bay leaves, crumbled

½ tsp salt

2¼lb (1 kg) beef chuck or round roast

2 tbsp vegetable oil

1 onion, sliced

1 celery stalk, chopped

1 tbsp all-purpose flour

⅓ cup crushed gingersnap cookies

● **Prepare ahead** The beef should be marinated for at least 2 days before cooking.

1 **Bring the wine,** vinegar, ⅔ cup water, onions, sugar, nutmeg, allspice, peppercorns, bay leaves, and salt to a boil in a saucepan. Let cool completely.

2 **Place the beef** in a bowl and pour in the cooled marinade. Cover with plastic wrap and refrigerate, turning the meat over every 8 hours or so, for 2–3 days.

3 **Preheat the oven** to 350°F (180°C). Lift the beef from the marinade, drain well, then pat dry with paper towels. Strain the marinade into a bowl, discarding the spices.

4 **Heat the oil** in a large flameproof casserole over medium-high heat. Add the beef and cook about 10 minutes, until browned on all sides. Transfer to a plate. Add the onion and celery to the casserole and cook, stirring constantly, for about 5 minutes, until beginning to brown. Sprinkle in the flour and stir for 1 minute. Stir in 2 cups of the reserved marinade and bring to a boil, stirring often.

5 **Return the beef** to the casserole and baste with the liquid. Cover tightly. Bake for about 2¼ hours, or until very tender.

6 **Transfer the beef** to a serving platter and tent with aluminum foil. Strain the cooking liquid into another saucepan, bring to a boil, and cook until reduced to about 1¼ cups. Whisk in the gingersnaps and cook, whisking often, until the sauce is smooth and lightly thickened. Season with salt and pepper. Slice the beef crosswise, spread the slices on the platter, and spoon some of the sauce over. Serve hot, with the rest of the sauce passed on the side.

● **Good with** potato dumplings and green vegetables.

● **Leftovers** can be thinly sliced and piled into rustic bread with braised red cabbage and a little spicy mustard.

Beef Kebabs with Lime, Ginger, and Honey

Sweet, tart, and spicy meet in this delicious marinade

🍴 makes 4 servings

🕐 prep 20 mins, plus marinating • cook 4–8 mins

❗ soak wooden skewers in cold water for 30 minutes to prevent burning

🗄 wooden skewers

3 **scallions**, white and green parts, chopped

one 2in (5cm) piece of **fresh ginger**, peeled and sliced

2 tbsp fresh **lime** juice

1 tbsp **soy sauce**

1 tbsp **honey**

1 tbsp **olive oil**

1lb (450g) **beef sirloin**, cut into 1in (2.5cm) cubes

16 **cherry tomatoes**

salt and freshly ground **black pepper**

For the avocado cream

1 ripe **avocado**, peeled, pitted, and chopped

2oz (55g) **cream cheese**, softened

2 **scallions**, chopped

1 fresh **hot green chile**, seeded and chopped

1¾oz (50g) **cream cheese**

1 **For the marinade**, purée the scallions, ginger, lime juice, soy sauce, honey, and oil. Place the beef pieces in a nonreactive bowl and add the marinade. Cover with plastic wrap and refrigerate for 1–2 hours.

2 **For the avocado cream**, process the avocado, cream cheese, scallions, and chile. Season with salt and pepper.

3 **Preheat the broiler**. Thread the beef cubes and cherry tomatoes onto wooden skewers.

4 **Cook the beef kebabs** for about 3 minutes on each side, or until medium-rare. Season with salt and pepper and serve hot, with the avocado cream.

Roast Beef Tenderloin with Red Currant Jus

A sweet-tart sauce adds character to tender but mildly flavored beef

🍴 makes 6 servings

🕐 prep 30 mins, plus resting • cook 40 mins–1 hr 10 mins

4oz (115g) **sliced bacon**, finely chopped

2 cups **tawny** or ruby **port**

⅔ cup **beef stock**

2 tbsp **red currant jelly**

1 tsp **cornstarch**, dissolved with 1 tbsp cold water

2¼lb (1kg) **beef tenderloin**, tied

salt and freshly ground **black pepper**

2 tsp **olive oil**

⬤ **Prepare ahead** The sauce can be made up to 2 days in advance.

1 **To make the sauce**, cook the bacon in a nonstick frying pan over medium heat for about 6 minutes, or until crisp. Transfer to paper towels to drain. Wipe the pan clean. Combine the port, stock, and jelly in the pan, bring to a boil, and cook about 5 minutes, or until reduced by ¼. Whisk in the dissolved cornstarch and cook until lightly thickened. Stir in the reserved bacon.

2 **Preheat the oven** to 400°F (200°C). Season the beef with salt and pepper. Heat the oil in a large frying pan over high heat. Add the beef and cook, turning occasionally, until browned on all sides, about 10 minutes. Transfer to rack in a roasting pan. Roast about 20 minutes, or until a meat thermometer reads 130°F (55°C) for medium-rare.

3 **Transfer to a** carving board and let rest for 15 minutes before carving. Slice the beef and serve with the sauce.

VARIATION

Duck Breasts with Red Currant Jus

Substitute 4 sautéed duck breasts for the filet. Substitute pancetta for the bacon, and a hearty red wine for the port.

Pork and Bean Stew

Otherwise known as *feijoada*, this is the national dish of Brazil and is made with a variety of porks

 makes 8 servings

🕐 prep 15 mins, plus overnight soaking • cook 1 hr 35 mins

❗ the beans need to be cooked the day before

1lb (250g) **dried black-eyed beans**

2 **pigs' feet**

9oz (250g) **smoked pork spareribs**, smoked pork chops, or cubed ham

6oz (175g) **slab bacon**, in one piece

1 cup canned **chopped tomatoes**

1 tbsp **tomato paste**

1 **bay leaf**

salt and freshly ground **black pepper**

2 tbsps **vegetable oil**

1lb (450g) boneless **center-cut pork loin**, cut into thick slices

1 **onion**, finely chopped

2 **garlic cloves**, finely chopped

6oz (175g) **chorizo sausage**, diced

1 fresh **hot green chile**, seeded and minced (optional)

1 **orange**, cut into wedges, to garnish

3 **spring onions**, white and green parts, chopped, to garnish

● **Prepare ahead** The stew can be made a day in advance and reheated.

1 **Rinse and drain** the beans. Place in a bowl and add enough cold water to cover by 1in (2.5cm). Let stand at room temperature for 8–12 hours.

2 **Drain the beans** and place in a soup pot. Cover with fresh water and bring to the boil over high heat. Boil for 10 minutes, skimming off any foam. Lower the heat and cover. Simmer for 1 hour.

3 **Meanwhile**, place the pigs' feet, ribs and bacon in a large saucepan with the tomatoes, tomato paste, and bay leaf. Add enough cold water to cover and bring to a boil over high heat. Reduce the heat to low and cover the pot. Simmer for 50 minutes. Season with salt and pepper.

4 **Drain the beans** in a colander, reserving the cooking liquid. Return the beans to the pot and add the meats with their cooking liquid. Add enough of the reserved bean liquid to barely cover. Return to a boil. Reduce the heat to medium-low, cover, and simmer for 20 minutes.

5 **Meanwhile**, heat 1 tbsp of the oil in a large frying pan over medium-high heat. In batches, add the pork tenderloin and brown on both sides, about 4 minutes. Add the pork tenderloin to the simmering bean mixture and cook for 10 minutes more, or until the meats are tender and the beans are very soft.

6 **Wipe out** the frying pan. Add the remaining oil and heat over medium heat. Add the onion and garlic and cook, stirring frequently, about 4 minutes, until soft and translucent. Add the chorizo and chile, if using, and cook for 2 minutes more, stirring often. Add 3 tbsp of the cooked beans and mash well with the back of a spoon. Stir the mashed beans and sausage to the pot of beans, and cook for 10 minutes.

7 **To serve**, remove the larger pieces of meat and cut them up. Spread the beans in a wide serving bowl, and top with the meats. Garnish with the orange wedges and scallions and serve hot.

● **Good with** cooked white rice, steamed or fried shredded kale, and a tomato salsa.

VARIATION

Quick Pork and Bean Stew

Delete the dried beans. Substitute 3 cans of black-eyed peas (or other canned beans, such as red kidney or pinto), drained and rinsed, and add to the simmered meats in step 3.

Danish Meatballs

Use any meat variety

🍴 makes 4 servings

🕐 prep 15 mins • cook 10 mins

❄ raw or cooked meatballs can be frozen for up to 3 months

1 cup loosely packed fresh **bread crumbs**

⅓ cup **whole milk**

1 large **egg**, beaten

½ tsp dried **thyme**

1 tsp **salt**

¼ tsp freshly ground **black pepper**

9oz (250g) **ground pork**

9oz (250g) **ground turkey** or chicken

1 **onion**, grated

all-purpose flour, for shaping

2 tbsp **vegetable oil**

lemon wedges, to serve

1 **Mix the bread crumbs**, and milk in a medium bowl and let stand 5 minutes. Mix in the egg, thyme, salt, and pepper.

2 **Add the pork**, turkey, and onion and mix with your hands until combined. With lightly floured hands, shape into about 16 balls.

3 **Heat the oil** in a large frying pan over medium heat. Add the meatballs and cook, turning often, for 8–10 minutes, until golden brown.

4 **Drain on paper towels**. Serve hot, with lemon wedges.

Pork Chops with Green Peppercorn Sauce

These soft, mild peppercorns add a gentle spice to the creamy sauce

 makes 4 servings

 prep 10 mins • cook 15 mins

4 center-cut pork loin chops

salt and freshly ground black pepper

1 tbsp vegetable oil

2 tbsp butter

1 large shallot, finely chopped

¼ cup dry sherry

⅔ cup chicken stock

1½ tbsp green peppercorns in brine, rinsed, drained, and lightly crushed

¼ cup crème fraîche or heavy cream

● **Prepare ahead** The sauce can be made up to 2 days in advance, cooled, covered, and refrigerated.

1 Trim the chops of excess fat and season with salt and pepper. Heat the oil in a large, heavy frying pan on medium heat. Add the pork chops and cook for 6–8 minutes on each side, depending on thickness, until golden brown and the juices run clear. Transfer to a warm plate and cover with foil.

2 To make the sauce, melt the butter in the pan. Add the shallot and cook, stirring often, for about 2 minutes, or until tender. Add the sherry, and cook for 1 minute, stirring up the browned bits in the pan. Add the stock and peppercorns and cook about 2 minutes, or until slightly reduced.

3 Stir in the crème fraîche. Spoon the sauce over the chops and serve immediately.

● **Good with** hashed brown potatoes and freshly steamed green vegetables.

Pork Chops with Blue Cheese Stuffing

This filling is both savory and sweet and the pecans add a delightful crunchy texture

 makes 4 servings

 prep 10 mins • cook 12–16 mins

 wooden toothpicks

For the stuffing

1 sweet apple such as Golden Delicious, peeled and finely diced

3oz (85g) Roquefort or Stilton, crumbled

⅓ cup chopped pecans

2 scallions, chopped

4 center-cut pork loin chops

1 tbsp olive oil

salt and freshly ground black pepper

1 Combine the stuffing ingredients and set aside.

2 Trim the excess fat from the pork chops. With a small sharp knife, make a horizontal slit through the fat side of each chop, cutting through the meat almost to the bone to make a pocket.

3 Divide the stuffing evenly among the chops, tucking it firmly into the pockets. Secure with wooden toothpicks.

4 Preheat the broiler. Place the pork chops on a baking sheet, brush with oil, and season with salt and pepper. Broil for 6–8 minutes on each side, depending on thickness, or until golden brown and the juices run clear. Remove the toothpicks and serve.

● **Good with** trimmed green beans and new potatoes.

Cassoulet

A hearty bean and meat dish from southwest France

 makes 4 servings

 prep 30 mins, plus soaking
• cook 3 hrs 45 mins

 large flameproof casserole

2 cups **dried Great Northern beans**

1 tbsp **olive oil**

8 **Italian pork sausages**

9oz (250g) **pancetta**, diced

2 **onions**, finely chopped

1 **carrot**, chopped

3 **garlic cloves**, minced

4 **duck legs**

1 sprig of **thyme**

1 **bay leaf**

salt and freshly ground **black pepper**

2 tbsp **tomato paste**

3½ cups hot **water**

one 14.5oz (411g) can **chopped tomatoes**

1 cup **white wine**

2 cups **bread crumbs**

1 **garlic clove**, minced

1 tbsp chopped **parsley**

1 Place the beans in a large saucepan and add enough cold water to cover by 1in (2.5cm). Bring to a boil over high heat. Cook for 10 minutes. Remove from the heat, cover, and let stand 2–3 hours. Drain.

2 Heat the olive oil in a large frying pan over medium-high heat. Add the sausages and cook for 7–8 minutes, until browned. Transfer to a plate. Add the pancetta and cook for 5 minutes, until browned. Transfer to the sausages. Add the onions and carrot and reduce the heat to medium. Cook, stirring occasionally, for 10 minutes, or until tender. Add the garlic and cook for another minute. Set aside for 1 minute.

3 Preheat the oven 425°F (220°C). Prick the duck skin all over with a fork and put on a rack in a roasting pan. Roast for 30 minutes, until lightly browned. Transfer the duck to the sausages and reserve 2 tbsp of the fat in the pan. Reduce the oven temp to 275°F (140°C).

4 In a large flameproof casserole, layer half the beans, the onions and carrot, sausages, pancetta, duck legs, thyme, and bay leaves, followed by the remaining beans.

5 Dissolve the tomato paste in the hot water, then stir in the tomatoes and their juices and the wine. Pour over the beans. Cover and bake for 2 hours. Remove from the oven and uncover. The cassoulet should be thick, but moist. Taste and season with salt and pepper and add a little hot water, if needed. Return to the oven and bake, uncovered, for 1 hour more.

6 To make the topping, mix the bread crumbs and garlic. Heat the reserved duck fat in a large skillet over medium heat. Add the crumbs and cook, stirring often, about 7 minutes, until golden brown. Drain on paper towels. Stir in the parsley. Remove the cassoulet from the oven and stir. Sprinkle the bread crumb topping over in a thick, even layer, and serve hot.

Pork and Leek Pie

A chunky pie with a crisp crust

 makes 4 servings

 prep 25 mins, plus cooling
• cook 1 hr 10 mins

2 tbsp **vegetable oil**

1lb (450g) **boneless pork loin**, cut into 1in (2.5cm) cubes

2 **leeks**, white and pale green parts, thickly sliced

6oz (175g) **white mushrooms**, halved

1 tsp chopped **thyme**

1 cup **apple** juice

⅔ cup **chicken stock**

2 tbsp **tomato paste**

salt and freshly ground **black pepper**

1 tbsp **cornstarch**

Shortcrust Pastry (pp436–437)

1 large **egg**, beaten, to glaze

1 Heat the oil in a frying pan. Brown the pork, remove, and set aside. Add the vegetables and thyme, and cook for 5 minutes. Add the apple juice, stock, tomato paste, and cornstarch and bring to a boil, stirring until thickened. Return the pork, season with salt and pepper, and simmer for 25 minutes; cool.

2 Transfer the pork and vegetables to a pie dish. Roll out the pastry and use to cover the dish, decorating the top with the trimmings. Make a hole in the pastry, glaze with the egg, and chill for 30 minutes. Preheat the oven to 400°F (200°C). Bake 35 minutes, until the pastry is browned.

Barbecued Spare Ribs

Marinate the ribs overnight before baking, if you wish

 makes 4 servings

 prep 5 mins, plus marinating
• cook 1 hr 30 mins

⅓ cup mango chutney

one 14.5oz (411g) can chopped tomatoes, drained

⅓ cup tomato ketchup

⅓ cup white wine vinegar

¼ cup packed light brown sugar

2 tbsp Thai sweet chile sauce

2 tbsp soy sauce

2 tsp smoked paprika

3 garlic cloves, finely minced

4½lb (2kg) pork spare ribs

salt and freshly ground black pepper

1 **Rub the chutney** through a sieve into a large bowl. Add the tomatoes, ketchup, vinegar, brown sugar, chile sauce, soy sauce, paprika, and garlic and mix well.

2 **Preheat the oven** to 375°F (190°C). Season the ribs with salt and pepper. Combine the ribs and chutney mixture into a large roasting pan, overlapping the ribs. Cover tightly with aluminum foil. Bake for 1 hour.

3 **Baste the ribs** and continue baking, uncovered, for about 30 minutes, until tender. Let cool for 5 minutes. Cut into individual ribs, then pile onto a serving platter.

Spanish Stew

A filling one-pot meal known as *Cocido* in Spain

 makes 4 servings

prep 25 mins
• cook 2 hrs 45 mins

4 tbsp olive oil

4 small onions, quartered

2 garlic cloves, sliced

9oz (250g) beef chuck, cut into 4 thick slices

6oz (175g) slab bacon, cut into 4 thick pieces

4 pork spare ribs, cut into ribs

4 thick slices pork belly, about 1lb 2oz (500g) in total

4 chicken thighs

1½ cups white wine

6oz (175g) smoked chorizo, cut into 4 pieces

6oz (175g) morcilla

1 smoked ham hock

1 bay leaf

salt and freshly ground black pepper

8 small boiling potatoes

4 carrots, halved lengthwise

1 head Savoy cabbage, quartered

one 15oz (420g) can chickpeas

3 tbsp chopped parsley, to garnish

1 **Heat 1 tbsp oil** in a saucepan over medium-low heat. Add the onions and garlic and cook, stirring, for 10 minutes, until softened.

2 **Heat the remaining** 3 tbsp oil in a frying pan over medium-high heat. In batches, brown the meats and chicken. Add to the saucepan with the onions and garlic.

3 **Pour the wine** into the frying pan and boil over high heat, scraping up the bits, for 3 minutes, or until reduced by half. Pour into the saucepan. Add the chorizo, morcilla, ham hock, and bay leaf. Add cold water to cover and season. Bring to a boil. Cover, reduce the heat, and simmer for 1½ hours.

4 **Add the potatoes** and carrots and simmer for 30 minutes. Add the cabbage and garbanzo beans and cook until the meats are very tender, about 15 minutes more. Discard the bay leaf and ham hock. Divide the meat and vegetables among 4 bowls. Ladle in some of the broth, sprinkle with the parsley, and serve hot.

Honey-glazed Ham

Boiling the ham first makes it nice and moist

 makes 10–12 servings

prep 15 mins • cook 2 hrs

7lb (1.35kg) boneless ham butt

1 large onion, quartered

3 bay leaves

12 peppercorns

½ cup honey

grated zest and juice of 1 orange

about 20 whole cloves

orange slices, to garnish

1 **Place the ham** in a pot and add cold water to cover. Add the onion, bay leaves, and peppercorns and bring a boil over medium heat. Lower the heat to medium-low and simmer for 1½ hours. Drain the ham and cool slightly.

2 **Preheat the oven** to 400°F (200°C). Combine the honey, orange zest, and juice.

3 **Trim off the ham skin,** leaving a layer of fat. Cut crisscrosses in the fat and push in the cloves. Line a roasting pan with foil. Place the ham on a rack in the pan and pour in 1 cup water. Brush the ham with half of the honey mixture.

4 **Bake the ham** for 10 minutes. Baste with the remaining honey mixture. Bake another 10 minutes or until glazed. Let stand for 20 minutes. Garnish with orange slices.

Lamb Tagine with Couscous

Dried apricots and orange juice, along with cumin, coriander, ginger, and thyme, give this the distinct flavor and aroma of Moroccan cuisine

- makes 4 servings
- prep 10 mins, plus at least 3 hrs marinating • cook 1½ hrs
- large flameproof casserole
- can be frozen for up to 1 month; thaw over low heat, then bring to a boil before serving

1 onion, thinly sliced

1 tsp ground cumin

1 tsp ground coriander

1 tsp ground ginger

1 tsp dried thyme

2 tbsp vegetable oil

2lb (900g) boneless lamb, such as shoulder, cut into 1in (2.5cm) cubes

2 tbsp all-purpose flour

1½ cups fresh orange juice

2 cups chicken stock

salt and freshly ground black pepper

4oz (120g) dried apricots

mint leaves, to garnish

For the couscous

1 cup plus 2 tbsp quick-cooking couscous

salt

● **Prepare ahead** The tagine can be cooked up to 2 days in advance.

1 Put the onion, cumin, coriander, ginger, thyme, and 1 tbsp of the oil in a large, non-metallic bowl. Add the lamb and stir well. Cover and refrigerate for at least 3 hours or overnight.

2 When ready to cook, preheat the oven to 325°F (160°C). Put the flour in a small bowl and slowly whisk in the orange juice until smooth, then set aside.

3 Heat the remaining oil in a large, flameproof casserole over a high heat. Add the spiced lamb and cook, stirring frequently, for about 5 minutes, or until browned.

4 Stir the orange juice mixture into the casserole with the stock. Season with salt and pepper. Bring to a boil, stirring often. Cover and bake for 1 hour.

5 Remove the casserole from the oven. Stir in the apricots. Return to the oven and bake for 20 minutes more, or until the lamb is tender.

6 Meanwhile, prepare the couscous. Mix the couscous with salt to taste in a large heatproof bowl and add boiling water to cover by 1in (2.5cm). Cover with a folded kitchen towel and let stand for 10 minutes, or until the couscous is tender. Fluff with a fork and keep warm. When the lamb is tender, taste and adjust the seasoning. Sprinkle with mint leaves and serve with the hot couscous.

> **TAGINE**
>
> This north-African earthenware cooking pot, traditionally used as a portable oven, is perfect for cooking stews like this. The conical lid acts as a heat retainer and the top is a cool handle. Alternatively, use a casserole with a tight-fitting lid.

Lamb with Blueberries

Tender lamb noisettes (filet mignons) are a special treat

- makes 4 servings
- prep 10 mins • cook 8–12 mins

12 lamb noisettes, cut 1½in (13cm) thick

salt and freshly ground black pepper

2 tbsp olive oil

3 scallions, chopped

⅔ cup lamb or chicken stock

1½ tbsp red currant jelly

1 cup blueberries

2 tbsp finely chopped mint plus sprigs, to garnish

1 Season the lamb with salt and pepper. Heat 1 tbsp oil in a large, heavy-bottomed frying pan over high heat. Cook the lamb in batches for 3–4 minutes on each side, until browned and medium-rare. Transfer to a plate and tent with foil to keep warm.

2 Add 1 tbsp of the oil to the pan. Add the scallions and cook for 2–3 minutes. Stir in the stock and jelly and cook until the jelly is dissolved and the liquid boils.

3 Add the blueberries and simmer, uncovered, for 2 minutes, then add the mint.

4 Transfer the lamb to dinner plates and spoon the sauce on top. Serve immediately.

Lamb Koftas

Middle Eastern spices flavor these tender, ground lamb kebabs. A raita of cucumber and yogurt is the ideal accompaniment

- 🍴 makes 4 servings
- 🕐 prep 15 mins, plus chilling • cook 8–10 mins
- ❗ soak the wooden sticks in water to prevent them from burning
- 🗇 16 wooden sticks

1 slice of **white bread**, crusts discarded, torn into small pieces

3 tbsp **whole milk**

1lb (450g) **ground lamb**

1 tbsp chopped **cilantro**

1 tbsp chopped **parsley**

1 tbsp **ground cumin**

1 **garlic clove**, minced to a purée

½ tsp **salt**

½ tsp freshly ground **black pepper**

vegetable oil, for brushing

For the raita

1½ cups **plain yogurt**

4oz (120g) **cucumber**, peeled, seeded, and diced

1 Soak 16 wooden sticks in hot water for at least 30 minutes. Soak the bread in the milk for 5 minutes.

2 Combine the ground lamb, cilantro, parsley, cumin, garlic, salt, and pepper in a large bowl. Squeeze the milk from the bread, add the bread to the bowl and mix thoroughly with your hands. Discard any remaining milk.

3 Using wet hands, roll the mixture into 16 balls. Carefully slide each ball onto a wooden skewer.

4 Meanwhile, preheat the broiler and position the rack about 4in (10cm) from the source of heat. Line the broiler pan with aluminum foil and lightly oil.

5 Put the koftas on the pan and broil, turning frequently, for about 8 minutes for medium-rare, or 10 minutes for well done. Transfer to a platter. Mix the yogurt and cucumber with a little salt to taste and serve on the side.

● **Prepare ahead** The shaped koftas can be refrigerated up to 1 day before cooking. The sauce can be made an hour or two in advance.

Braised Lamb

This dish packs plenty of flavor with its tomato, olive, and herb sauce

- 🍴 makes 6 servings
- 🕐 prep 20 mins • cook 1½ hrs
- 🗇 flameproof casserole with a lid
- ❄ can be frozen for up to 1 month

2lbs (900g) **lamb leg steaks**

salt and freshly ground **black pepper**

¼ cup **olive oil**

1 large **onion**, peeled

2 **garlic cloves**, peeled

1 fresh **hot red chile** or ½ tsp hot red pepper flakes

¼ cup hearty **red wine**

one 14.5oz (411g) can **chopped tomatoes**

⅔ cup pitted **Kalamata olives**

1½ tsp chopped **thyme** or 1 tsp dried thyme

thyme and **parsley** leaves to garnish

1 Season the lamb steaks with salt and pepper. Heat the olive oil in a large casserole over medium-high heat. In batches, brown the meat on both sides. Transfer to a plate.

2 Meanwhile, pulse the onion, garlic, and chile in a food processor until it forms a coarse paste. Add to the casserole and reduce the heat to medium-low. Cook, stirring often, for 5 minutes. Stir in the wine, then the tomatoes and thyme. Bring to a simmer over high heat.

3 Return the lamb to the casserole. Reduce the heat to low and cover. Simmer until the lamb is very tender, about 45 minutes. During the last few minutes, stir in the olives. Season with salt and pepper.

4 Serve hot, sprinkled with thyme and parsley.

● **Prepare ahead** The braise will be even better if refrigerated for at least 1 day and up to 3 days. To serve, let stand at room temperature for 1 hour, then reheat over low heat for 30 minutes, until hot.

● **Good with** couscous cooked in vegetable stock.

Irish Stew

There are many versions of this dish, all of which are based on lamb and potatoes. This one is a hearty casserole

- makes 4–6 servings
- prep 20 mins
  - cook 1 hr 30–40 mins

3 large **baking potatoes**, peeled and thickly sliced

2lb (900g) boneless **lamb shoulder**, cut into 1½in (3.5cm) pieces

3 large **onions**, sliced

3 **carrots**, thickly sliced

salt and freshly ground **black pepper**

large sprig of **thyme**

1 **bay leaf**

2½ cups **lamb stock** or beef stock

● **Prepare ahead** The stew can be made up to 2 days ahead, cooled, covered, and refrigerated. Reheat thoroughly in the oven before serving.

1 Preheat the oven to 325°F (160°C). Beginning and ending with potatoes, layer the lamb, onions, and carrots in a large, heavy casserole, seasoning each layer with salt and pepper. Tuck in the thyme and bay leaf. Add the stock and cover.

2 Bake for 1 hour. Uncover and bake 30–40 minutes more, until the potatoes are browned and the meat is very tender. Serve hot.

● **Good with** a fresh green vegetable, such as kale or broccoli.

VARIATION

Beef and Potato Stew
Substitute boneless beef chuck for the lamb.

Navarin of Lamb

Lighter than many stews, navarin contains lamb with young spring vegetables

- makes 4 servings
- prep 30 mins • cook 1½ hrs
- freeze for up to 3 months

1 tbsp **butter**

1 tbsp **olive oil**

2lb (900g) **boneless shoulder of lamb**, cut into 1½in (3.5cm) pieces

2 small **onions**, quartered

1 tbsp **all-purpose flour**

1½ cups **lamb stock** or beef stock

2 tbsp **tomato paste**

1 **bouquet garni** of 1 celery stalk, 2 bay leaves, and 1 sprig of thyme

salt and freshly ground **black pepper**

10oz (300g) small **new potatoes**

10oz (300g) **baby carrots**

10oz (300g) **baby turnips**

6oz (175g) **green beans**

● **Prepare ahead** Cook through step 2, then cool, cover, and refrigerate for up to 1 day. Bring to a boil and finish the recipe.

1 Melt the butter with the oil in a large flameproof casserole over medium-high heat. In batches, add the lamb and cook, turning occasionally, about 5 minutes, or until browned. Set aside. Cook the onions in the casserole until they begin to soften.

2 Return the lamb to the casserole. Sprinkle with the flour and stir well for 1 minute. Stir in the stock, then add the tomato paste and bouquet garni. Season with salt and pepper. Bring to a boil and cover. Simmer for 1 hour, 15 minutes.

3 Stir in the potatoes, carrots, and turnips and cook, covered, for 15 minutes. Stir in the beans, cover, and cook for another 15 minutes, until the lamb and vegetables are tender.

● **Good with** lots of crusty French bread for soaking up the stew.

● **Leftovers** can be refrigerated for up to 2 days.

Roast Lamb with White Beans

French cooks prefer delicate flageolet beans for this rustic dish, but any small white bean will do

- makes 4 servings
- prep 15 mins
  - cook 1hr 30 mins

3lb (1.35kg) **leg of lamb**, or shanks

2–3 sprigs **rosemary**

1 tbsp **olive oil**

salt and freshly ground **black pepper**

two 15oz (440g) cans **flageolet** or white Northern **beans**, drained

4 **plum tomatoes**, cut in halves lengthwise

4 **garlic cloves**, coarsely chopped

⅔ cup **dry white wine**

1 tbsp **tomato paste**

● **Prepare ahead** The lamb can be prepared through step 1 and refrigerated up to 1 day ahead.

1 Preheat the oven to 350°F (180°C). With a small, sharp knife, make several deep cuts into the flesh of the lamb. Strip the leaves from 1 rosemary sprig, and push a few rosemary leaves into each cut. Place the lamb in a roasting pan, with the oil, and season with salt and pepper.

2 Bake for 1 hour. Combine the beans, tomatoes, garlic, and remaining rosemary. Remove the lamb from the oven and spoon the bean mixture around it. Mix the wine and tomato paste together and pour over the beans.

3 Cover the pan with aluminum foil, then continue baking, stirring the beans after 15 minutes, for about 30 minutes, until a thermometer inserted in the thickest part of the lamb reads 130°F. Let stand for 15 minutes before serving.

Lamb Kebabs

Middle Eastern spices flavor these tender, minced-lamb kebabs. A raita of cucumber and yogurt is the ideal accompaniment

- makes 4 servings
- prep 15 mins, plus 2 hrs marinating • cook 10 mins
- low fat, low GI
- 16 wooden skewers

1lb (450g) boned **leg of lamb**, cut into 1in (2.5cm) cubes

½ cup **olive oil**

3 tbsp fresh **lemon** juice

1 small **red onion**, finely chopped

1 tbsp chopped **lemon thyme**

salt and freshly ground **black pepper**

16 **shallots**, blanched

16 **cherry tomatoes**

16 **button mushrooms**

1 **red pepper**, seeded and cut into squares

pita bread, to serve

lettuce leaves and cucumber slices, to serve

1 Place the lamb into a large nonmetallic dish. Mix the oil, lemon juice, onion, and thyme and pour over the lamb. Season with salt and pepper, cover, and refrigerate for 2 hours, stirring occasionally. Soak 16 wooden skewers in cold water.

2 Drain the lamb, reserving the marinade.

3 Preheat the broiler. Thread the lamb, shallots, tomatoes, mushrooms, and red peppers onto the skewers. Grill for about 10 minutes, turning frequently and basting with the marinade.

4 Serve hot, with warmed pita bread and the lettuce and cucumber slices.

VARIATION

Curried Lamb Kebabs

Add crushed garlic, chopped cilantro, and 1 tsp each of ground cumin and curry powder.

Shepherd's Pie

Traditionally a recipe to use meat and potatoes from a roast lamb, this version is topped with a potato and leek mash

 makes 4–6 servings

 prep 30 mins • cook 30 mins

For the topping

2lb (900g) **baking potatoes**, peeled and chunked

2 **large leeks**, white and pale green parts only, split lengthwise, sliced

⅓ cup **whole milk**, warmed

4 tbsp **butter**

salt and freshly ground **black pepper**

For the filling

1½lb (750g) **ground lamb**

2 tbsp **vegetable oil**

1 **large onion**, chopped

1 **garlic clove**, minced

2 **carrots**, sliced

⅓ cup hearty **red wine**

2 tbsp **all-purpose flour**

1 cup **lamb** or beef **stock**

2 tbsp chopped **parsley**

1 tbsp **Worcestershire sauce**

1 tbsp chopped **rosemary**

● **Prepare ahead** The pie can be prepared, covered, and refrigerated, up to 1 day in advance. Increase the baking time to 40 minutes.

1 To make the topping, boil the potatoes in a large saucepan of lightly salted water until almost tender, about 15 minutes. Add the leeks and cook until the potatoes are tender, about 5 minutes longer. Drain well and return to the saucepan.

2 Mash the potatoes and leeks together. Return to low heat and stir in the milk and butter. Season with salt and pepper. Remove from the heat.

3 Meanwhile, make the filling. Preheat the oven to 400°F

(200°C). Cook the lamb in a large frying pan for 5 minutes, stirring to break up the meat, until lightly browned. Pour off the fat. Transfer the lamb to a bowl.

4 Heat the oil in the frying pan over medium heat. Add the onion and garlic and cook, stirring often, for about 4 minutes, or until softened. Add the carrots. Return the lamb to the frying pan.

5 Add the wine, increase the heat to high, and cook for 3 minutes, or until the wine has evaporated. Stir in the flour, then the stock, parsley, Worcestershire sauce, and rosemary. Bring to a boil, then reduce the heat to low and simmer for 5 minutes. Season with salt and pepper.

6 Spread the filling in a baking dish and cover with the potato topping. Place on a baking sheet and bake for 30 minutes, or until the topping is golden. Let stand 5 minutes, then serve straight from the dish.

● **Good with** a simple green vegetable, such as steamed broccoli or minted peas.

● **VARIATION**

Cottage Pie

Virtually the same dish made with beef, rather than lamb. For a cottage pie, follow the recipe above, but substitute ground round for the lamb, 1 cup fresh or frozen peas for the carrots, and thyme for the rosemary. If you wish, omit the leeks from the topping and stir 2 tbsp prepared horseradish into the potatoes instead.

Lamb Steaks with Herbs and Mustard

A quick summer supper dish

 makes 4 servings

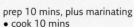 prep 10 mins, plus marinating • cook 10 mins

6 tbsp chopped **parsley, thyme, mint**, and/or **marjoram**

2 **garlic cloves**, chopped

1 tbsp **green peppercorns**, drained and crushed

4 **lamb steaks** or 12 lamb rib chops

½ cup **olive oil**

3 tbsp fresh **lemon** juice

grated zest of 1 **lemon**

2 tsp **Dijon mustard**

salt

1 Mix the herbs, garlic, and peppercorns together. Rub all over the lamb, pressing to help the herbs adhere. Place in a shallow dish. Drizzle with 2 tbsp of the oil and 1 tbsp of the lemon juice. Cover and let marinate for at least 2 hours.

2 Position a broiler rack 6in (15cm) from the broiler and preheat. Oil the broiler pan. Place the lamb on the pan. Broil, turning once, about 8 minutes, until well browned.

3 Meanwhile, whisk the remaining 2 tbsp lemon juice with the lemon zest, mustard, and salt, then whisk in the remaining 6 tbsp oil. Serve the lamb topped with the lemon mixture.

Marinated Lamb Roast with Carrot Salsa

You can also use this marinade for grilled boneless leg of lamb

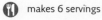 makes 6 servings

prep 20 mins, plus marinating • cook 15 mins

For the marinade

2 tbsp **soy sauce**

1 tbsp chopped **fresh rosemary**

1 tbsp **honey**

juice of 2 **limes**

salt and freshly ground **black pepper**

¼ cup **olive oil**

juice of ½ **lemon**

1 tbsp **pomegranate molasses**

1 tbsp chopped **mint**

5 large **carrots**, thinly sliced

1 **red onion**, thinly sliced

1 **garlic clove**, minced

⅓ cup **toasted sunflower seeds**

2lb (900g) **boneless loin of lamb**

1 tbsp **vegetable oil**

● **Prepare ahead** The carrot salsa can be made 1 day in advance and kept in the refrigerator.

1 Combine the marinade ingredients in a zippered plastic bag. Add the lamb and turn to coat. Chill for at least 4 and up to 24 hours.

2 Whisk the olive oil, lemon juice, pomegranate molasses, and mint in a bowl. Add the carrots, red onion, and garlic and mix. Season with salt and pepper. Cover and marinate for at least 1 hour.

3 Preheat the oven to 400°F (200°C). Heat the oil in a skillet over high heat. Remove the lamb from the marinade and add to the pan. Cook, turning, until browned on all sides, about 10 minutes. Transfer to a roasting pan and roast about 10 minutes, or until an instant-read thermometer inserted in the center of the roast reads 130°F (55°C). Transfer to a carving board and let stand 10 minutes. Carve the lamb. Mix the sunflower seeds into the salsa and serve with the lamb.

Quick Lamb Curry

Use leftover lamb for this dish and adjust the spiciness of the sauce with the amount of curry powder

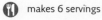 makes 4 servings

prep 15 mins • cook 25 mins

freeze for up to 3 months

2 **green bell peppers**, seeded and quartered

1 **onion**, quartered

3 **garlic cloves**, sliced

one 1in (2.5cm) piece fresh **ginger**, peeled and chopped

2 tbsp **vegetable oil**

1 tbsp **black mustard seeds**

1 tbsp **curry powder**

one 14.5oz (411g) can **chopped tomatoes**

½ cup canned **coconut milk**

4 cups (bite-sized pieces) **cooked lamb**

1 cup **frozen peas**

salt and freshly ground **black pepper**

chopped **cilantro**, to garnish

1 Purée the green peppers, onion, garlic, and ginger with 1 tbsp water in a blender.

2 Heat 1 tbsp of the oil in a large saucepan over medium-high heat. Add the mustard seeds and cook, stirring frequently, for about 30 seconds, or until they begin to pop. Pour in the onion purée and cook, stirring often, for about 3 minutes, until the purée is thick and fairly dry.

3 Add the remaining 1 tbsp oil and the curry powder and stir for 30 seconds. Stir in the tomatoes with their juice and cook for 1 minute, stirring often, then stir in the coconut milk and mix well.

4 Add the lamb and peas and return to a boil. Reduce the heat to low and cover. Simmer for about 6 minutes, until the peas are tender. Season with salt and pepper. Garnish with the cilantro and serve hot.

● **Good with** rice or naan bread, or as part of a feast with other curries.

● **Leftovers** are delicious cut into smaller pieces and served warm as a baked potato topping.

Moussaka

Greece's most famous dish, moussaka is usually baked in a large dish. This version makes individual servings, which are easier to freeze

- makes 6 servings
- prep 30 mins, plus standing • cook 1½ hrs
- 6 x 16oz (445ml) individual freezer-to-oven casseroles
- freeze for up to 3 months

2 large eggplants, cut into ¼in (5mm) rounds

salt and freshly ground black pepper

8 tbsp olive oil

1 large onion, chopped

1lb (450g) ground lamb

½ cup hearty red wine

2 cups canned crushed tomatoes

½ cup lamb or beef stock

2 tsp dried oregano

1 tsp sugar

1lb (450g) baking potatoes, such as Burbank, cut into ¼in (5mm) slices

¼ cup freshly grated Parmesan

¼ cup plain dried bread crumbs

For the topping

1 cup plain Greek-style yogurt

3 large eggs

1 tbsp cornstarch

½ cup cottage cheese

½ cup crumbled feta cheese

● **Prepare ahead** The moussaka can be baked, cooled, covered, and refrigerated up to 1 day ahead. Reheat in a 350°F (180°C) oven for 30-40 minutes.

1 **Toss the eggplant** with 2 tbsp salt in a colander. Let stand in the sink to drain for 30 minutes. Rinse well under cold running water. Drain and pat dry.

2 **Meanwhile**, heat 2 tbsp of the oil in a large saucepan over medium heat. Add the onion and cook, stirring occasionally, until softened, about 5 minutes. Add the lamb and increase the heat. Cook, breaking up the meat with a spoon, about 5 minutes, until it loses its raw look. Pour off excess fat.

3 **Add the wine** and boil for 2 minutes. Stir in the tomatoes, stock, 1 tsp of the oregano, and sugar. Season with salt and pepper. Simmer, uncovered, over medium heat, stirring occasionally, for 30 minutes, or until the meat sauce is quite thick.

4 **Preheat the broiler.** Brush the eggplant on both sides with the remaining 6 tbsp oil. In batches, broil the eggplant, turning once, about 5 minutes, until golden brown on both sides. Boil the potato slices in a large saucepan of lightly salted water for about 8 minutes, until just tender. Drain.

5 **To make the topping**, whisk the yogurt, eggs, and cornstarch together until smooth, then whisk in the cottage cheese and feta.

6 **Preheat the oven** to 350°F (180°C). Lightly oil 6 individual freezer-to-oven casseroles. In each casserole, starting with the eggplant, alternate 2 layers each of eggplant and meat sauce. Top with the potato slices, then the yogurt sauce. Mix the Parmesan, bread crumbs, and the remaining 1 tsp oregano and sprinkle over the potatoes.

7 **Bake for 45 minutes**, or until golden brown and bubbling. Serve while moussaka is hot.

VARIATION

Moussaka with Cheese Sauce

Substitute 2 cups White Sauce (page 280), mixed with ½ cup shredded Cheddar, for the yogurt. Sprinkle with a little extra cheese before baking.

Roast Lamb with Root Vegetables

A flavorsome dish that is quick and easy to prepare

- makes 4-6 servings
- prep 10 mins, plus resting • cook 45 mins

1 large red onion, peeled and quartered

18 baby carrots, trimmed and peeled

2 parsnips, peeled, each cut into 4-6 pieces

8oz (225g) small new potatoes, scrubbed

1 garlic head, separated into cloves, unpeeled

2 tbsp plus 2 tsp olive oil

2 tbsp balsamic vinegar

salt and freshly ground black pepper

1½lb (675g) lamb loin, trimmed

1 **Preheat the oven** to 400°F (200°C). Combine the vegetables and garlic in a roasting pan. Toss with 2 tbsp oil and the vinegar. Season with salt and pepper. Roast for 25 minutes.

2 **After about 20 minutes**, heat the remaining oil over high heat. Season the lamb with salt and pepper. Add to the pan and cook, until browned on all sides. Transfer to the roasting pan with the vegetables. Roast about 10 minutes, until the center of the lamb is 130°F (55°C). Allow the lamb to rest for 10 minutes.

3 **Slice the lamb** and serve alongside the roasted vegetables.

Lamb Chops with Chermoula

Chermoula is a Moroccan herb and spice sauce that works well as a marinade

🍴 makes 6 servings

🕐 prep 15 mins, plus marinating • cook 15 mins

1 red onion, finely chopped

½ cup plus 2 tbsp olive oil

¼ cup chopped mint

¼ cup chopped cilantro

grated zest and juice of 1 lemon

2 cloves of garlic, minced

1 tsp ground cumin

1 tsp ground coriander

¼ tsp smoked sweet paprika

salt and freshly ground black pepper

12 lamb rib chops

4 ripe plum tomatoes, chopped

1 tbsp balsamic vinegar

1 To make the chermoula, combine the red onion, ½ cup of the oil, 3 tbsp each of the mint and cilantro, the lemon zest and juice, the garlic, cumin, coriander, and paprika in a bowl. Season with salt and pepper. Add the lamb chops and mix well to coat in the chermoula. Let stand 30 minutes.

2 Mix the tomatoes, vinegar, remaining 2 tbsp oil, and 1 tbsp each mint and cilantro in a bowl and season with salt and pepper.

3 Preheat a broiler or build a hot fire in an outdoor grill. Remove the chops from the marinade. Broil or grill for about 5 minutes per side, until browned.

4 Serve the lamb hot, with the tomato salad.

● **Good with** spiced tabbouleh or hot, buttered couscous.

● **Prepare ahead** The meat can marinated in the refrigerator for up to 24 hours.

Warm Lamb Salad with Pomegranate and Walnuts

Pomegrante molasses (evaporated pomegranate juice) is available at Mediterranean grocers

🍴 makes 6 servings

🕐 prep 20 mins, plus marinating • cook 15–20 mins

For the marinade

2 tbsp pomegranate molasses

1 tbsp olive oil

3 garlic cloves, minced

pinch of cayenne

4 sprigs of thyme

For the vinaigrette

1 shallot, finely chopped

1 tbsp sherry vinegar

1 tbsp pomegranate molasses

2 tbsp walnut oil

2 tbsp olive oil

1½lb (675g) boneless loin of lamb

6oz (175g) mesclun

1 head of Belgian endive leaves

½ cup chopped walnuts, toasted

1 pomegranate, seeded

salt and freshly ground black pepper

1 For the marinade, mix the pomegranate molasses, oil, garlic, cayenne, and thyme in a zippered plastic bag. Add the lamb and season with salt and pepper. Refrigerate for at least 4 hours, occasionally turning the bag over.

2 To make the vinaigrette, combine the shallot, vinegar, and pomegranate molasses in a bowl and let stand for 15 minutes. Whisk in the walnut and olive oils. Season with salt and pepper.

3 Preheat the oven to 375°F (190°C). Heat an ovenproof frying pan over high heat. Remove the lamb from the marinade. Add to the pan and cook, turning occasionally, about 10 minutes, until browned. Roast for about 10 minutes, until an instant-read thermometer inserted in the center of the lamb reads 130°F (55°C) for medium-rare. Transfer the lamb to a carving board and let stand for 10 minutes.

4 Carve the lamb. Divide the mesclun and endive among dinner plates and top with the sliced lamb. Sprinkle with the walnuts and pomegranate seeds. Drizzle with the vinaigrette and serve immediately.

Lamb Braised with Green Peas and Preserved Lemons

This Moroccan dish reaches its peak flavor when refrigerated a day or so before serving and reheated

 makes 6 servings

 prep 15 mins, plus marinating • cook 1½ hrs

 large flameproof casserole

 freeze for up to 3 months

2 onions, finely chopped

3 tbsp chopped **parsley**, plus more for garnish

3 tbsp chopped **cilantro**, plus more for garnish

3 **garlic cloves**, chopped

1 tsp peeled and grated **fresh ginger**

½ cup **olive oil**

2¼lb (1kg) **boneless leg of lamb**, cut into thick slices

2¼ cups **lamb** or beef **stock**

2 **preserved lemons** (available at specialty grocers)

salt and freshly ground **black pepper**

1lb (450g) **frozen peas**

fresh **lemon** wedges, to garnish

1 **Combine the onions**, parsley, cilantro, garlic, ginger, and olive oil in a large dish. Add the lamb. Cover and refrigerate for at least 8 hours.

2 **Remove the lamb**, reserving the marinade. Heat a frying pan over medium-high heat. In batches, add the lamb and cook, turning occasionally, about 5 minutes, until browned. Transfer the lamb to a flameproof casserole.

3 **Add the marinade** and stock to the casserole and bring to a boil over high heat. Reduce the heat to medium-low and cover. Simmer for 1 hour.

4 **Cut the preserved lemons** into quarters, discard the flesh, then thinly slice the rinds. Add to the pan and continue simmering for another 30 minutes, or until the lamb is very tender.

5 **Season with salt** and pepper. Stir in the peas and simmer about 5 minutes, until they are cooked. Sprinkle with lots of chopped parsley and cilantro and serve hot, with lemon wedges.

● **Prepare ahead** The dish can be made up to 3 days in advance.

Lamb Kebabs

Skewered pieces of lamb served with a tomato vinaigrette

 makes 6 servings

 prep 10 mins, plus marinating • cook 10 mins

 soak the skewers in water for one hour before using to prevent burning

 wooden skewers

2 tbsp **coriander seeds**, toasted

2¼lb (1kg) boneless **leg of lamb**, cut into 1½in (3.5cm) chunks

¾ cup **olive oil**

2 tsp **honey**

4 **garlic cloves**, minced

grated zest of 1 **lemon**

salt and freshly ground **black pepper**

2 tbsp **red wine vinegar**

5 ripe **tomatoes**, skinned, seeded, and chopped

6 tbsp coarsely chopped **cilantro**

1 **Crush the coriander seeds** in a mortar and pestle. Place with the lamb, ¼ cup oil, 1 tsp honey, 2 garlic cloves, and the lemon zest in a bowl. Season with pepper and mix. Cover and chill for 2 hours.

2 **Whisk together** the vinegar with the remaining ½ cup oil, 1 tsp honey, and 2 garlic cloves. Add the tomatoes and cilantro and mix.

3 **Preheat the broiler**. Thread the meat onto the skewers. Season with salt. Broil, turning, about 7 minutes for medium-rare meat. Serve with the tomato vinaigrette.

Slow-roasted Greek Lamb

This lamb will be well-done, but spoon-tender

 makes 4–6 servings

 prep 10 mins • cook 4½–5 hrs

3lb (1.35kg) **leg of lamb roast**, on the bone

2 tbsp **olive oil**

3 **garlic cloves**, minced

1 tsp **ground cinnamon**

1 tsp **dried thyme**

1 tsp **dried oregano**

juice of 1 **lemon**

salt and freshly ground **black pepper**

1 **onion**, sliced into rings

2 **carrots**, halved lengthwise

2 tbsp chopped **parsley**

1 **Preheat the oven** to 300°F (150°C). Place the lamb in a roasting pan. Mix together the oil, garlic, cinnamon, thyme, and oregano. Brush over the lamb. Sprinkle with lemon juice and season with salt and pepper. Add the onion and carrots.

2 **Fill the roasting pan** halfway with water. Bake for 3 hours, basting every 30 minutes; add more water to keep the vegetables moist.

3 **Cover with foil**. Bake another 1½ hours, until very tender.

4 **Remove** from the oven and let stand for 20 minutes. Carve, sprinkle with the parsley, and serve.

Harissa Lamb with Eggplant

Harissa, the fiery Moroccan spice paste, is available at specialty food shops. Use lamb chops, if you prefer

 makes 6 servings

prep 15 mins, plus marinating • cook 50 mins

5 tbsp fresh **lemon** juice

3 tbsp **olive oil**

2 tbsp chopped **mint**, plus more for garnish

1 tbsp **harissa**

2lb (900g) boneless **loin of lamb**

2 **eggplants**

½ cup plain **Greek-style yogurt**

2 tbsp **tahini**

2 **garlic cloves**, minced

salt and freshly ground **black pepper**

● **Prepare ahead** Store the eggplant sauce and marinate the lamb in the refrigerator for up to 1 day. Bring the sauce to room temperature before serving.

1 Preheat the oven to 425°F (220°C). Combine 2 tbsp lemon juice, 1 tbsp oil, the mint, and harissa in a zippered plastic bag. Add the lamb and turn to coat.

Refrigerate for at least 1 hour and up to 24 hours.

2 Meanwhile, place the eggplants on a baking sheet and prick with a fork several times. Bake for 30 minutes or until the skins have blackened. Let cool until easy to handle. Remove and discard the skins. Drain the eggplant flesh in a colander for 15 minutes. Purée the eggplant, yogurt, remaining 3 tbsp lemon juice, tahini, and garlic in a blender. Season with salt and pepper.

3 Remove the lamb from the marinade. Season with salt. Heat the remaining 2 tbsp olive oil in a large ovenproof frying pan over high heat. Add the lamb and cook, turning occasionally, about 10 minutes, until browned. Transfer to the oven and roast about 10 minutes, until an instant-read thermometer inserted in the center reads 130°F (55°C) for medium-rare. Transfer to a platter and let stand 10 minutes.

4 Carve the lamb and serve on warmed plates with the purée. Pour the pan juices over, and sprinkle with chopped mint.

Butterflied Leg of Lamb

For even cooking, make large cuts in the thickest part of the lamb and open them up so the lamb lies as flat as possible

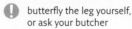 makes 8 servings

prep 15 mins, plus marinating and resting • cook 30 mins

butterfly the leg yourself, or ask your butcher

4lb (1.8kg) **butterflied leg of lamb**, trimmed

For the marinade

1 cup hearty **red wine**

½ cup **soy sauce**

3 **garlic cloves**, minced

3 tbsp chopped **mint**

For the salsa

2 tbsp **olive oil**

1 **garlic clove**, minced

1 fresh **hot red chile**, seeded and minced

4 ripe **fresh tomatoes**, peeled, seeded, and chopped

1 tbsp chopped **marjoram**

2 **red bell peppers**, roasted, peeled and chopped

salt and freshly ground **black pepper**

1 To prepare the lamb, place it on a work surface, skin side down. Make 3 deep cuts in the thickest parts of the lamb, being sure not to cut all the way through. Place a piece of plastic wrap over the lamb and pound heavily with a flat meat pounder to give the meat a fairly even surface.

2 For the marinade, combine the wine, soy sauce, garlic, and mint in a large zippered plastic bag. Add the lamb, close the bag, and refrigerate at least 2 hours.

3 For the salsa, heat the oil in a saucepan over low heat. Add the garlic and chile and cook 3 minutes, until the garlic starts to color. Add the tomatoes and marjoram and simmer for 30 minutes, until the tomatoes are softened. Add the peppers and cook for 10 minutes more. Season with salt and pepper. Keep warm.

4 Build a medium-hot fire in an outdoor grill. Remove the lamb from the marinade and pat dry. Grill, turning occasionally, about 30 minutes, until an instant-read thermometer inserted in the thickest part of the lamb reads 130°F (55°C). Let stand 10 minutes. Slice and serve with the sauce passed on the side.

Steak and Kidney Pudding

A classic old English recipe that is just the dish for hearty appetites

- makes 6-8 servings
- prep 30 mins • cook 4 hrs
- 6-cup ovenproof bowl, steamer or deep pan with a lid
- freeze for up to 3 months

For the pastry

1⅔ cups **self-rising flour**

½ tsp **salt**

5½ oz (150g) **suet** or lard, shredded

¼ cup **ice water**, as needed

For the filling

1½lb (675g) **round steak**

7oz (200g) **beef kidney**, trimmed

3 tbsp **all-purpose flour**

salt and freshly ground **pepper**

1 **onion**, chopped

6oz (175g) **button mushrooms**, quartered

2 tbsp **Worcestershire sauce**

¾ cup plus 2 tbsp **beef stock**, cold, as needed

● **Prepare ahead** The pastry can be made up to 1 day in advance, wrapped and refrigerated until needed.

1 To make the pastry, sift the flour and salt into a bowl. Stir in the suet. Make a well in the center. Stir in just enough ice water to mix to a soft, but not sticky, dough. Shape into a thick disk, wrap in plastic wrap, and refrigerate.

2 To make the filling, trim the excess fat from the steak. Cut the meat and kidney into bite-sized pieces. Season the flour with salt and pepper then toss the steak and kidney pieces in the flour to coat evenly. Mix with the onion and mushrooms.

3 Roll out two-thirds of the pastry. Line a 6-cup ovenproof

bowl with the pastry, letting the excess hang over the side. Add the meat mixture, packing it snugly in the bowl, taking care not to tear the pastry. Sprinkle in the Worcestershire sauce, and add just enough stock to cover three-quarters of the filling.

4 Roll out the remaining pastry to make a lid. Brush the overhanging edge of the pastry with cold water. Place the lid on top, and press the two layers of pastry together to seal. Flute the edges.

5 Cut a circle of parchment paper larger than the top of the bowl. Pleat the top, to create surplus

paper that will allow the pudding to expand. Secure on top of the bowl. Cover this with a double layer of pleated aluminum foil. Firmly crimp the foil around the rim of the bowl to secure it, or tie with kitchen string.

6 Place the bowl on a steamer rack in a large stockpot. Add boiling water to almost reach the bottom of the bowl. Cook at a brisk simmer, adding more boiling water as needed as the water evaporates, for 4 hours, or until the crust is firm. To serve, remove the foil and paper. Run a knife around the edge of the pudding to loosen, then turn out on to a serving plate.

Kidneys with Mustard Sauce

This makes a tasty lunch, first course, or supper dish

- makes 4 servings
- prep 10 mins, plus soaking • cook 11–15 mins

4 **lamb kidneys**

2 tbsp **butter**

1 tbsp **olive oil**

1 large **onion**, finely chopped

2 **garlic cloves**, minced

8 **cremini mushrooms**, sliced

3 tbsp dry **vermouth** or red wine

4 tbsp **lamb** or beef **stock**

2 tsp **Dijon mustard**

salt and freshly ground **black pepper**

1 Peel away any skin from the kidneys and cut out the core and membranes. Soak in water to cover for 5–10 minutes. Drain and pat dry with paper towels.

2 Heat the butter and oil in a frying pan over medium heat. Cook the onion, stirring often, for 2–3 minutes. Increase the heat, add the kidneys and garlic, and cook for 3 minutes, stirring.

3 Add the mushrooms, and cook for 2–3 minutes more. Add the vermouth and stock and boil about 1 minute, until slightly reduced.

4 Reduce the heat and cover. Cook for 4 minutes, or until the kidneys are tender and cooked through. Stir in the mustard and season with salt and pepper.

Sauté of Liver, Bacon, and Shallots

Quick to cook, tender calves' liver is the perfect partner to salty bacon and is served here in a rich sauce

 makes 4 servings

prep 10 mins • cook 10 mins

12oz (350g) calves' liver

8 thick bacon slices, preferably maple cured

1 tbsp olive oil

2 tbsp butter

4 shallots, thinly sliced

⅔ cup dry vermouth

1 tsp Dijon mustard

dash of Worcestershire sauce (optional)

salt and freshly ground black pepper

1 Cut the liver and the bacon into strips about 2in (6cm) long and ½in (1.5cm) wide.

2 Heat 1 tbsp each oil and butter in a large frying pan over medium heat. Add the shallots and cook, stirring frequently, for 5 minutes, or until golden. Transfer to a plate.

3 Add the remaining oil and butter to the pan and increase the heat to high. Add the liver and bacon and cook for 3-4 minutes, until the liver is seared and slightly pink inside.

4 Return the shallots to the pan. Pour in the vermouth, and boil, scraping up any browned bits in the pan with a wooden spoon, for 1-2 minutes.

5 Reduce the heat to medium-low and stir in the mustard and the Worcestershire sauce (if using). Season with salt and pepper and serve at once.

● **Good with** mashed potatoes and green beans for a tasty supper dish.

VARIATION

Lamb's Liver and Bacon
Use the same quantity of lamb's liver. Add a dash of Tabasco sauce for an extra touch of spice.

Braised Oxtail with Wine and Herbs

Oxtail is high in gelatin, and it gives extraordinary texture to the sauce in this robust dish

 makes 6 servings

prep 20 mins • cook 2-3 hrs

freeze for up to 3 months

6½lb (3kg) oxtail, cut into 1½in (3.5cm) lengths

½ cup all-purpose flour

4 tbsp olive oil

1 tbsp honey

2 tbsp chopped thyme

2 tbsp chopped rosemary

salt and freshly ground black pepper

2 onions, chopped

2 carrots, cut into large chunks

1 fennel, diced

2 garlic cloves, sliced

2 fresh hot red chiles, chopped

one 750ml bottle hearty red wine

chopped parsley, to garnish

● **Prepare ahead** The stew can be cooled, covered, and refrigerated for up to 2 days, and gets better as it rests.

1 Preheat the oven to 300°F (150°C). Toss the oxtail in flour to coat lightly. Heat 2 tbsp of the oil ina large frying panover medium-high heat. In batches, add the oxtail and cook, turning occasionally, about 5 minutes, until browned. Transfer to a large flameproof casserole.

2 Drizzle the honey over the oxtail. Sprinkle with the thyme and rosemary, and season with salt and pepper.

3 Heat the remaining oil in the frying pan. Add the vegetables, garlic, and chiles and cook for 6 minutes, until softened. Stir into casserole and add the wine. Cover and bake for 2-3 hours, until the oxtail is very tender. Skim the fat from the surface of the sauce. Garnish with chopped parsley and serve hot.

Sausages with Lima Beans

A fresher version of pork and beans, this satisfying supper dish is especially good on a cold winter evening

- makes 4 servings
- prep 10 mins • cook 30 mins
- can be frozen for up to 3 months

12 sweet Italian pork sausages

1 tbsp olive oil

1 onion, sliced

1 celery rib, chopped

2 garlic cloves, crushed

⅓ cup white wine

one 14.5oz (411g) can chopped tomatoes

3 tbsp ketchup

1 tsp sweet paprika

salt and freshly ground black pepper

1½ cups thawed frozen lima beans

1 tbsp chopped basil or parsley

1 **Position a** broiler rack 6in (15cm) from the source of heat and preheat the broiler. Prick the sausages with a fork. Arrange on the broiler rack and broill about 10 minutes, turning occasionally, until cooked through. Transfer to a plate.

2 **Meanwhile, heat the oil** in a saucepan over medium-low heat. Add the onion, celery, and garlic, and cook, stirring frequently, about 5 minutes, or until softened. Increase the heat to medium-high and add the wine. Bring to a boil, then stir in the canned tomatoes with their juices. Stir in the ketchup and paprika, season with salt and pepper, and bring to a boil. Reduce the heat to medium-low and simmer, uncovered, for about 20 minutes, or until lightly thickened.

3 **Stir in the** lima beans and sausages. Simmer for 10 minutes. Sprinkle with basil and serve hot.

● **Leftovers** can be reheated and eaten with crusty bread to mop up the juices.

Boudin Noir and Sautéed Apples

Boudin noir (literally "black sausage") and apples is a classic combination. In Latino markets, it is called *morcilla* or *morcela*

- makes 4 servings
- prep 10 mins • cook 20 mins

3 Golden Delicious apples, peeled, cored, and thickly sliced

2 tbsp butter

2 tsp light brown sugar

2 tsp vegetable oil

8 large slices of boudin noir

4 slices bacon, cut lengthwise into thin strips

½ cup hard cider

1 **Cut each apple slice** in half crosswise. Melt the butter in a frying pan over medium heat. Add the apples and brown sugar. Cook, stirring often, for 8–10 minutes, until the apples are softened and slightly caramelized. Transfer to a plate and tent with aluminum foil to keep warm.

2 **Wipe out the pan**. Add the oil and heat over medium-high heat. In batches, add the boudin noir and cook, turning once, for about 6 minutes, until slightly crisp. Transfer to the plate. Add the bacon to the frying pan and cook, stirring frequently, for about 3 minutes, or until cooked through and slightly crisp. Transfer to the plate. Add the cider to the pan and increase the heat to high. Boil until reduced and syrupy, stirring up the browned bits in the pan wth a wooden spoon.

3 **To serve, place** a slice of boudin noir on each of 4 plates. Add a layer of apples, then repeat with the remaining boudin noir and apples. Top with the bacon strips and drizzle with the pan juices.

● **Good with** chutney and whole wheat toast.

VARIATION

Boudin Blanc with Apple

Substitute boudin blanc (white sausage with chicken and veal) for the boudin noir, and add a squeeze of fresh lemon juice to the cooked apples.

Spanish Bean and Pork Stew

Known in Spain as *fabada*, this rib-sticking stew is quickly made with canned beans. Use your favorite sausages as you prefer

 makes 4 servings

prep 5 mins • cook 40 mins

9oz (250g) **chorizo** or andouille

9oz (250g) **morcilla** (Spanish blood sausage) or garlic sausage

9oz (250g) **slab bacon** or pancetta, rind removed

1 tbsp **olive oil**

¼ cup hearty **red wine**

two 15oz (420g) cans **white kidney (cannellini) beans**, drained and rinsed

pinch of **saffron threads**

1 **bay leaf**

2 cups **chicken stock**

1 Cut the sausages and bacon into 2in (5cm) chunks. Heat the oil in a large casserole over medium-low heat. Add the sausages and bacon, and cook, stirring occasionally, for about 3 minutes. Increase the heat and pour in the wine. Boil about 2 minutes, until reduced by half.

2 Stir in the beans, saffron, and bay leaf, then enough chicken stock to barely cover. Bring to a boil, reduce the heat, cover, and simmer for 30 minutes. Serve hot.

VARIATION

Dried Bean Stew

Soak 8oz (230g) dried white kidney beans in cold water to cover overnight in a medium saucepan. Drain, add fresh water to cover, and bring to a boil. Cook for 10 minutes. Skim off any foam, lower the heat, cover, and simmer for 2–3 hours, or until the beans are tender; add hot water to keep the beans barely covered. Drain.

Sausage, Bacon, and Egg Pie

This pie transports well (so it's good for picnics) and can be eaten from your hand just as well as off a plate

makes 6-8 servings

prep 15 mins, plus chilling • cook 50 mins

8in (20cm) springform pan or tart pan with removable bottom

For the pastry

1¾ cups **all-purpose flour**

12 tbsp **butter**

¼ tsp each **salt** and **pepper**

¼ cup **iced water**

1½ tbsp **ketchup**

For the filling

1lb (450g) **bulk pork sausage**

1 small **onion**, finely chopped

1 tbsp **whole grain mustard**

pinch of freshly ground **nutmeg**

salt and freshly ground **black pepper**

6 strips **bacon**

4 large **eggs**

milk, to glaze

● **Prepare ahead** The pastry dough can be wrapped in plastic wrap and refrigerated up to 1 day ahead.

1 To make the pastry pulse the flour, butter, salt, and pepper in a food processor until the mixture resembles coarse bread crumbs. Mix the water and ketchup, add to the flour, and pulse until the dough clumps (add more water, if needed). Gather into a disk, wrap in plastic wrap, and refrigerate for 30 minutes.

2 Preheat the oven to 400°F (200°C). Roll out a bit more than half of the dough on a lightly floured surface into a round about ⅛in (3mm) thick. Line an 8in (20cm) springform pan with the dough.

3 Mix the sausage, onion, mustard, and nutmeg, then season with salt and pepper. Spread in the pie crust, and top with the bacon. Make 4 indentations in the sausage with the back of a soup spoon. Crack each egg into an indentation. Roll out the remaining dough. Center over the filling, trim the excess dough, and pinch the edges to seal. Score a crosshatch pattern on top and brush with a little milk. Refrigerate for 15 minutes.

4 Bake the pie for 20 minutes. Reduce the oven to 350°F (180°C), and bake for 30 minutes, until golden brown. Cool the pie before serving.

Sausage and Mustard Casserole

This is pure winter bliss. Serve it with creamy mashed potatoes and it will remain a favorite

- makes 6 servings
- prep 15 mins • cook 45 mins
- large flameproof casserole

1 tbsp olive oil

12 Italian sweet pork sausages

1 large onion, thinly sliced

8oz (225g) cremini mushrooms

1¼ cups chicken stock

1 Granny Smith apple, peeled, cored, and cut into chunks

1 tbsp chopped sage

1 bay leaf

⅔ cup heavy cream

salt and freshly ground black pepper

2 tsp Dijon mustard

1 tsp whole grain mustard

1 tsp dry mustard

1 Heat the oil over medium heat. Add the sausages, cook until golden, and remove.

2 Add the onion and cook until softened. Add the mushrooms and cook for 5 minutes, then stir in the stock, apple, sage, and bay leaf.

3 Bring to a boil, then return the sausages. Reduce the heat, cover, and cook gently for 20 minutes, stirring often. The apple pieces should break down and thicken the sauce slightly. If they are still holding their shape, mash them with the back of a wooden spoon and stir in.

4 Mix the cream and mustards together in a bowl and season with salt and pepper. Pour into the casserole, increase the heat, and boil gently for 5 minutes, or until the sauce has thickened slightly.

● **Good with** cabbage and creamy mashed potatoes.

Choucroute Garni

This is a simpler, quicker version of a classic dish from Alsace

- makes 6-8 servings
- prep 30 mins • cook 3 hrs
- large flameproof casserole

3 tbsp rendered duck fat or vegetable oil

9oz (250g) ham steak, diced, bone discarded

1½lb (674g) pork spare ribs, cut into ribs

2 onions, chopped

2 Granny Smith apples, peeled, cored, and sliced

1 garlic clove, minced

6 whole black peppercorns, lightly crushed

6 juniper berries, lightly crushed

large sprig of thyme

2 bay leaves

2lb (900g) fresh sauerkraut, thoroughly rinsed and drained

2 cups chicken stock

1¼ cups lager beer or Riesling wine

12 small new potatoes, scrubbed

1lb (450g) smoked sausage, such as bratwurst, cut into 6 portions

salt and freshly ground black pepper

chopped parsley, to garnish

1 Heat 2 tbsp of the fat in a large flameproof casserole over medium heat. In batches, add the ham and spare ribs and cook, turning occasionally, about 5 minutes, until browned. Transfer to a plate. Add the onion to the casserole and cook until softened, about 3 minutes.

2 Add the apples, garlic, peppercorns, juniper berries, thyme, and bay leaves. Stir in the sauerkraut. Return the ham and spare ribs to the casserole and stir in the stock and beer. Bring to a simmer. Cover tightly and reduce the heat to low. Simmer for 2 hours.

3 Add the potatoes, pushing them into the sauerkraut, then cover and continue cooking for about 50 minutes, or until the potatoes are tender. Season with salt and pepper.

4 Meanwhile, heat the remaining 1 tbsp fat in a frying pan over medium heat. Add the sausage and cook, turning, about 5 minutes, until browned.

5 Spoon onto a platter and arrange the sausages on top. Sprinkle with parsley and serve hot.

● **Good with** hot mustard or horseradish on the side, and a glass of cold beer or Riesling to drink.

Toad in the Hole

Sausages baked in popover batter make a quick brunch

 makes 4 servings

 prep 20 mins, plus standing
• cook 40 mins

¾ cup all-purpose flour

pinch of salt

2 large eggs

1 ¼ cups whole milk

2 tbsp vegetable oil

8 Italian sausage links

● **Prepare ahead** The batter can be refrigerated for up to 24 hours. Whisk briefly just before using.

1 To make the batter, combine the flour and salt in a bowl and make a well in the center. Add the eggs to the well with ½ cup of the milk. Whisk, gradually beating in the remaining milk, until smooth. Let stand for 30 minutes.

2 Preheat the oven to 425°F (220°C). Pour the oil into a 13 x 9in (33 x 23cm) baking dish. Add the sausages and turn to coat in the oil. Bake for 5-10 minutes, until they are just colored and the fat is very hot.

3 Reduce the temperature to 400°F (200°C). Carefully pour the batter around the sausages. Continue baking for 30 minutes more, or until the batter is golden and crisp. Serve hot.

● **Good with** a green salad and spicy mustard.

Rabbit Provençale

Rabbit is quite lean, and benefits from braising in an herbed tomato sauce to keep it moist

🍴 makes 4 servings

🕐 prep 15 mins, plus resting
• cook 1 hr 15 mins

🍲 large flameproof casserole

2 tbsp **olive oil**

1 **rabbit**, 2¾lb (1.25kg), cut into 10 pieces

4oz (120g) **pancetta**, diced

1 **onion**, chopped

4 **garlic cloves**, finely chopped

2lb (900g) **ripe plum tomatoes**, peeled, seeded, and coarsely chopped

sprig of **fresh rosemary**, plus more to garnish

3 **sage leaves**

salt and freshly ground **black pepper**

⅔ cup **dry white wine**

¾ cup **boiling water**

1 Heat the oil in a large, flameproof casserole over medium-high heat. In batches, add the rabbit and cook, turning often, about 5 minutes, or until golden. Transfer to a plate. Pour off all but 1 tbsp of the fat in the casserole.

2 Add the pancetta and onion to the pan and cook for about 5 minutes, stirring, until the pancetta is browned and the onion softened. Add the garlic and stir for about 30 seconds. Add the tomatoes, rosemary, and sage, and season with salt and pepper. Cook for about 10 minutes, stirring often, until the tomatoes give off their juices and they thicken.

3 Stir in the wine, then return the rabbit to the casserole. Cook over medium heat for 20 minutes, or until the liquid has reduced slightly and the sauce is quite thick. Stir in the boiling water. Reduce the heat to low and partially cover. Simmer, stirring occasionally, for about 15 minutes, until the sauce is thick and the rabbit very tender.

4 Remove the pan from the heat and let stand about 10 minutes. Garnish with the rosemary sprigs and serve.

Roast Venison with Marmalade Gravy

The robust citrus flavors of the sauce complement the rich, gamey flavor of the meat

🍴 makes 4 servings

🕐 prep 20 mins, plus marinating and resting • cook 40 mins

For the marinade

1¼ cups hearty **red wine**

2 tbsp fresh **orange** juice

1 tbsp fresh **lemon** juice

1 tbsp **olive oil**

1 tbsp **dark brown sugar**

1 **garlic clove**, minced

½ tsp coarsely crushed **black peppercorns**

2¾lb (1.25kg) **boneless saddle of venison**

1 tbsp **vegetable oil**

3 tbsp **bitter orange marmalade**

● **Prepare ahead** The venison can be marinated in the refrigerator for up to 3 days.

1 Mix the marinade ingredients in a large, nonmetallic bowl. Add the venison and turn to coat. Cover and refrigerate for 24–72 hours.

2 Preheat the oven to 425°F (220°C). Remove the venison from the marinade and pat dry. Brush with the vegetable oil. Place in a roasting pan and let stand at room temperature for about 20 minutes. Strain and reserve the marinade.

3 Roast for 20 minutes. Reduce the oven temperature to 375°F (190°C). Mix the ½ cup reserved marinade and the marmalade and spoon some over the venison. Continue roasting, basting occasionally with the marmalade mixture, about 20–30 minutes, until an instant-read thermometer inserted in the center of the roast reads 130°F (55°C) for medium-rare.

4 Transfer the venison to a carving board and tent with aluminum foil. Let stand for 10–15 minutes before carving.

5 Meanwhile, skim any excess fat from the pan juices. Stir in the reserved marinade. Bring to a boil and cook about 5 minutes, until slightly reduced. Pour into a sauceboat. Carve the venison and serve with the sauce.

Rabbit with Honey and Thyme

One of the leanest meats available, rabbit is delicious when braised in a flavorful liquid

 makes 4 servings

 prep 15 mins
• cook 35–40 mins

1 tbsp **vegetable oil**

1 tbsp **butter**

1 ¾lb (800g) **rabbit**, chopped on the bone into 12–14 pieces

1 large **onion**, sliced

2 **garlic cloves**, minced

1 cup **hard apple cider**

⅔ cup **chicken stock**

1 tsp **chopped thyme**

salt and freshly ground **black pepper**

4oz (115g) **sliced bacon**, cut into strips

3 tbsp **whole grain mustard**

3 tbsp **crème fraîche**

2 tbsp **honey**

1 Heat the oil and butter in a large flameproof casserole over medium-high heat. In batches, add the rabbit and cook, turning occasionally, about 5 minutes, until browned. Transfer to a plate.

Add the onion and cook about 3 minutes, until softened. Stir in the garlic and cook 30 seconds.

2 Stir in the cider and bring to a boil, then stir in the stock. Return the rabbit to the casserole, sprinkle with the thyme, and season with salt and pepper.

3 Return to a boil, then reduce the heat to medium-low. Cover and simmer about 20 minutes, until the rabbit is tender.

4 Meanwhile, cook the bacon in a small frying pan over medium heat, stirring occasionally, about 5 minutes, until brown and crisp. Transfer to paper towels to drain.

5 Stir the mustard, crème fraîche, and honey into the casserole and bring to a boil. Serve hot, topped with the bacon.

VARIATION

Rabbit with Prunes

Add 1 cup pitted dried plums (prunes) to the pan with the cider. Increase the stock to 1 cup. Add a squeeze of fresh lemon juice at the end of cooking.

Ragout of Venison with Wild Mushrooms

This slowly simmered stew concentrates all the rich flavors of the venison and mushrooms

 makes 4 servings

 prep 15 mins • cook 1¼–2 hrs

 flameproof casserole

 freeze for up to 3 months; thaw completely before reheating

1 tbsp **olive oil**

1 tbsp **butter**

4 **shallots**, sliced

4oz (115g) **sliced bacon**, diced

1 ½lb (565g) **venison**, cut into 1½in (3.5cm) cubes

1 tbsp **all-purpose flour**

3 tbsp **brandy**

1 ¼ cups **beef stock**

9oz (250g) **wild mushrooms**, sliced

1 tbsp **tomato paste**

1 tbsp **Worcestershire sauce**

1 tsp **dried oregano**

salt and freshly ground **black pepper**

● **Prepare ahead** The ragout can be prepared through step 2, omitting the mushrooms, and simmered for 30 minutes. Cool, refrigerate until the next day, then reheat to boiling.

Add the mushrooms, reduce the heat, cover, and simmer until tender.

1 Heat the oil and butter in a large flameproof casserole over medium-high heat. Add the shallots and bacon and cook, stirring often, until the shallots begin to brown.

2 Add the venison and cook, stirring, for about 4 minutes, or until evenly colored. Stir in the flour and cook for 2 minutes, until beginning to brown. Add the brandy and stir for 30 seconds, then add the stock and mushrooms. Bring to a boil, stirring. Stir in the tomato paste, Worcestershire sauce, and oregano, and season with salt and pepper.

3 Reduce the heat to low, cover, and simmer the ragout for 45 minutes–1 ½ hours, or until the venison is tender (the cooking time will depend on the cut of meat—loin takes less time than shoulder). Serve hot.

● **Good with** pasta, plain boiled rice, or potatoes.

● **Leftovers** reheated the next day will have an even better flavor.

Bread Sauce

This British sauce is traditionally served with roast poultry

🍴 makes about 2 cups

⏱ prep 15 mins, plus 20 mins standing • cook 20 mins

2 tbsp butter

1 onion, sliced

⅔ cup heavy cream

½ tsp salt

1 bay leaf

6 whole cloves

1¼ cups fresh bread crumbs

1¼ cups whole milk, as needed

salt and freshly ground black pepper

pinch of grated nutmeg

● **Prepare ahead** Step 1 can be prepared ahead and left to infuse, or the complete sauce can be made in advance. Cover the surface of the sauce with plastic wrap to prevent a skin from forming. Refrigerate for up to 2 days. When ready to use, remove plastic wrap and gently reheat.

1 Melt the butter in a small saucepan over low heat. Add the onion and cook, stirring occasionally, until translucent, about 5 minutes. Add the cream, salt, bay leaf, and cloves. Heat for 5 minutes more. Remove from the heat, cover, and let stand for 20 minutes.

2 Discard the bay leaf and cloves. Pour onion mixture into a blender and purée.

3 Bring the bread crumbs and milk to a boil in a saucepan over medium heat. Reduce the heat to low and simmer, stirring occasionally, until the mixture is smooth and thickened.

4 Stir in the onion purée and season with salt, pepper, and nutmeg. If the sauce seems too thick, thin with additional milk. Serve hot.

● **Leftovers** Stir in 1 large egg, beaten, and some grated cheese. Pour into a buttered baking dish and bake in a 350°F (180°C) oven for 15–20 minutes, until cooked through and lightly golden on top. This savory snack can be served warm or cold.

Cumberland Sauce

This sauce, which is great with pork, offers just the right combination of sweetness and citrus flavors

🍴 makes about 1¼ cups

⏱ prep 10 mins • cook 10–15 mins

1 lemon

1 orange

1 tsp dry mustard

good pinch of cayenne pepper

pinch of salt

½ cup ruby or tawny port

⅓ cup red currant jelly

● **Prepare ahead** The sauce can be refrigerated up to 2 days ahead.

1 Remove the zest from half the lemon with a vegetable peeler. Repeat with half of the orange. Cut the zest into very thin slivers. Bring a small pan of water to a boil. Add the zest strips and cook for 5 minutes. Drain in a wire sieve and rinse under cold running water.

2 Squeeze the juice from the lemon and orange. Stir the lemon juice, orange juice, mustard, cayenne, and salt in a small saucepan until the salt dissolves. Add the port and jelly and bring to a boil over medium heat. Simmer over low heat for 5 minutes.

3 Strain the sauce through a wire sieve into a serving bowl and stir in the citrus zests. Serve hot, warm, or at room temperature.

● **Good with** ham or sausages.

VARIATION

Spicy Cumberland Sauce

For a slightly spicier version, add an extra pinch of cayenne pepper and a pinch each of ground cloves and ground ginger.

Béarnaise Sauce

Fragrant and tangy, this French sauce is great with steak

- 🍴 makes about 1 cup
- 🕐 prep 10 mins • cook 5 mins

2 small **shallots**, finely chopped

3 tbsp chopped **tarragon**

2 tbsp **white wine vinegar**

2 tbsp **dry white wine**

1 tsp **peppercorns**, crushed

3 large **egg yolks**

14 tbsp **butter**, at room temperature

salt and freshly ground **black pepper**

1 tbsp fresh **lemon** juice

1 Bring the shallots, 1 tbsp of the tarragon, vinegar, wine, and peppercorns to a boil in a heavy nonreactive saucepan over high heat. Boil for about 2 minutes, or until the mixture has reduced by half. Strain the liquid through a sieve and let cool.

2 Whisk the egg yolks and 1 tbsp water in a heatproof bowl. Place over a saucepan of barely simmering water. Whisk in the cooled liquid. Whisk in the butter, 1 tbsp at a time, until the first addition softens into a creamy sauce before adding more. Whisk in the lemon juice and remaining tarragon. Season with salt and pepper. Serve immediately.

Applesauce

Sweet-tart applesauce contrasts well with rich meats. This classic sauce is traditionally served with roast pork

- 🍴 makes 4 servings
- 🕐 prep 10 mins • cook 15 mins
- ❄️ freeze for up to 3 months

1lb 2oz (500g) **sweet dessert apples**, such as Golden Delicious or McIntosh

2 tbsp **sugar**

1 tbsp fresh **lemon** juice

½ **cinnamon stick**

pinch of **salt**

2 tbsp **butter**

● **Prepare ahead** The applesauce can be refrigerated for up to 3 days.

1 Peel, core, and roughly chop the apples. Combine the apples, ½ cup water, sugar, lemon juice, cinnamon, and salt to a simmer in a heavy-bottomed, medium saucepan. Cover and cook over medium heat for 12-15 minutes, shaking the pan occasionally, until the apples are tender but juicy. Remove the cinnamon stick.

2 Remove from the heat, Using a fork, beat in the butter. Serve hot or at room temperature.

● **Good with** roast pork, sausages, or potato pancakes.

Cranberry Sauce

A tangy sauce traditionally served with turkey

- 🍴 makes about 2 cups
- 🕐 prep 5 mins • cook 15 mins
- ❄️ freeze for up to 2 months

12oz (336g) fresh or frozen **cranberries**

1 **shallot**, finely chopped

¾ cup packed **light brown sugar**

½ cup hearty **red wine** or port

grated zest of 1 **orange**

⅓ cup fresh **orange** juice

● **Prepare ahead** Can be covered and refrigerated for up to 2 weeks.

1 Bring the cranberries, shallot, brown sugar, wine, and orange zest and juice and to a boil in a medium saucepan over medium heat, stirring often to dissolve the sugar.

2 Reduce the heat to medium-low and simmer, stirring, for 10-12 minutes, or until all of the cranberries skins have burst. Let cool.

3 Transfer to a bowl and serve chilled or at room temperature.

● **Good with** grilled poultry and pork.

Sausage and Apple Dressing

Fragrant with sage, this is a tasty side dish for any poultry

🍴 makes 4 servings

🕐 prep 10 mins • cook 40 mins

❄️ freeze for up to 2 months

2 slices day-old **white** or whole wheat **bread**, crusts removed

¼ cup **chicken stock** or milk

1 large **egg**, lightly beaten

2 **shallots**, finely chopped

1 tbsp chopped **sage**, plus whole leaves to garnish

1lb (450g) bulk **pork sausage**

1 Granny Smith **apple**, peeled and shredded

salt and freshly ground **black pepper**

a few whole **cranberries**, to garnish

● **Prepare ahead** The stuffing can be covered and refrigerated up to 1 day before baking.

1 Preheat the oven to 350°F (180°C). Cut the bread into ½in (13mm) pieces. Place in a mixing bowl, sprinkle with the stock, and let stand 5 minutes, until softened. Mash the soaked bread with a fork, then stir in the beaten egg.

2 Stir in the shallots and sage. Add the sausage and apple and season with salt and pepper. Mix until well combined.

3 Oil an 11 x 8in (28 x 20cm) baking dish. Spoon the stuffing mixture into the dish. Bake 30 minutes, or until the top is browned.

4 Garnish with the sage leaves and cranberries. Serve hot, from the dish.

● **Good with** any poultry.

● **Leftovers** make great sandwich fillings, with cranberry sauce, tomato chutney, or mustard.

> ### STUFFING TIP
>
> To make traditional American-style poultry stuffing, cook the pork in a large frying pan over medium heat about 10 minutes, until no sign of pink shows; add the shallots during the last 2 minutes. Increase the bread to 10 slices (4 cups diced bread). Mix the bread, sausage mixture, 2 tbsp sage, 2 apples, and 2 eggs, moisten with about 1 cup turkey or chicken stock, and season with salt and pepper. Makes about 6 cups, enough for a 12lb (5.5kg) turkey.

Horseradish Sauce

Serve this bracing horseradish sauce with roast beef or smoked fish

🍴 makes about 1 cup

🕐 prep 10 mins

⅔ cup **heavy cream**

1 tsp **dry mustard**

1 tsp **superfine sugar**

½ cup peeled and grated fresh **horseradish**

1 tbsp **white wine vinegar**

1 tbsp fresh **lemon** juice

salt and freshly ground **black pepper**

1 Whip the cream, mustard, and sugar in a chilled medium bowl with an electric mixer on high speed until stiff peaks form.

2 Fold in the horseradish, vinegar, and lemon juice. Season with salt and pepper. Transfer to a serving bowl, cover, and refrigerate until ready to serve.

Chestnut and Pancetta Stuffing

Chestnuts give this traditional poultry stuffing
a sweet, nutty flavor

- makes 4–6 servings
- prep 10 mins • cook 30 mins
- freeze for up to 2 months

2 tbsp **butter**

1 tbsp **olive oil**

1 **onion**, chopped

3oz (85g) **pancetta**, diced

2 cups day-old **bread crumbs**

1 cup coarsely chopped
vacuum-packed **chestnuts**

¼ cup chopped **parsley**

1 cup **turkey** or chicken **stock**,
as needed

salt and freshly ground **black pepper**

1 Preheat the oven to 350°F
(180°C). Heat the butter and oil
in a pan over medium heat. Add the
onion and pancetta and cook for
5 minutes, until the onion is soft and
the pancetta is beginning to crisp.

2 Transfer to a bowl. Add the
bread crumbs, chestnuts, and
parsley. Stir in enough broth to
moisten the crumb mixture. Season
with salt and pepper.

3 Spread in a buttered shallow
baking dish. Cover with aluminum
foil and bake for 30 minutes, until
hot. For crispy stuffing, remove the
foil after 15 minutes.

Good with poultry, or stuffed
and cooked inside the bird. (Weigh
the bird and calculate the cooking
time accordingly.)

VARIATION

Chestnut Stuffing Balls
Add 1 egg, lightly beaten, to the
mixture. Form into 8–12 balls, place
on an oiled baking sheet, and bake
for 30 minutes. Or use the stuffing
mixture, with or without added egg,
to stuff a turkey. Allow 20 minutes
roasting per pound of turkey.

Corn Bread Stuffing

Corn bread gives this easy-to-make recipe its
colorful appearance

- makes 8 servings
- prep 15 mins • cook 45 mins
- freeze for up to 2 months

6 cups crumbled **corn bread**

8 tbsp **butter**

1 large **onion**, chopped

4 **celery stalks**, chopped

1 **red pepper**, seeded and chopped

2 **garlic cloves**, crushed

2 tbsp chopped **sage**

1 **egg**, lightly beaten (optional)

1 cup **turkey** or chicken **stock**, as
needed

salt and freshly ground **black pepper**

Prepare ahead Without the
egg, the stuffing can be refrigerated
for up to 1 day before using.

1 Preheat the oven to 350°F
(180°C). Place the corn bread
on a baking sheet. Bake for about

15 minutes, until toasted and golden.
Transfer to a bowl and let cool.

2 Melt the butter in a large
frying pan over medium heat.
Add the onion, celery, and red
pepper. Cook, stirring often, for about
10 minutes, until tender. Stir in the
garlic and cook for 1 minute.

3 Stir into the cornbread. Add
the sage and season with salt and
pepper. Mix in the egg, if using. Add
enough of the stock to moisten the
cornbread without making it soggy.

4 Spread in a buttered baking
dish. Cover with aluminum foil
and bake about 30 minutes, until
heated through. If you like crispy
stuffing, remove the foil after
cooking for 15 minutes. Serve hot.

STUFFING A TURKEY

If you wish, loosely fill the neck and body
cavities of a turkey with stuffing. Cover
the exposed stuffing with foil. Stuffed
turkeys take about 20 minutes a pound
to roast to 180° (82°C) in the thickest
part of the thigh.

Warm Desserts

Sticky Rice
A popular Thai dessert made with short-grain, "glutinous" rice
🕐 35–40 mins　　　　　**page 377**

Cherry Clafoutis
This dish of fruit baked in a batter is a favorite of the French
🕐 45 mins –1 hr　　　　**page 377**

Steamed Ginger Pudding
Easy to make and very satisfying to eat, this is a traditional British dessert
🕐 1 hr 50 mins　　　　**page 379**

Hot Chocolate Cakes
These rich, very easy desserts have a creamy chocolate center—a treat for all chocoholics
🕐 30 mins　　　　**page 380**

Tapioca and Fruit Pudding
Fruit segments add color to this dessert
🕐 40 min – 1 hr　　　　**page381**

Bread and Butter Pudding
Slow baking produces a smooth, velvety texture
🕐 55 mins　　　　**page 382**

Viennese Apple Strudel
Delicate flaky pastry filled with a delicious mixture of apples and raisins
🕐 1 hr 10 mins　　　　**page 452**

Baked Jam Roll
Think of this as a biscuit with jam baked inside
🕐 40 mins　　　　**page 382**

Quick Sticky Toffee and Banana Pudding
Gooey and delicious, this is quick to prepare
🕐 15 mins　　　　**page 383**

Torrijas
A Spanish version of French toast served with maple syrup, honey, or fresh fruit compote
🕐 25 mins　　　　**page 384**

Cinnamon Pancakes with Apricots
Small, light-as-air pancakes topped with fruit
🕐 1 hr　　　　**page 384**

Peach Gratin with Muscat Sabayon
Hot peaches topped with a delicate sauce
🕐 45 mins　　　　**page 451**

Pineapple Fritters
Crisp and juicy, these must be eaten immediately
🕐 30 mins　　　　**page 451**

Baked Peaches with Marzipan and Almonds

Fragrant peaches oozing sweet juices

🕐 35–40 mins   **page 452**

Pears Poached in Wine

Wine gives a great depth of flavor to cooked fruit

🕐 35 mins   **page 453**

French Apple Tart

This two-apple tart uses apples that cook down to a purée, and ones that hold their shapes

🕐 1 hr 20 mins   **page 454**

Tarte Tatin

This caramelized upside-down apple tart is a French classic

🕐 1 hr 5 mins   **page 456**

Caramelized Autumn Fruits

This is a great way to turn autumn fruits like pears and plums into a delicious dessert

🕐 30 mins   **page 458**

Baked Pears in Marsala

An easy Italian dessert of poached fruit

🕐 1 hr   **page 457**

Blueberry Cobbler

An old-fashioned summer dessert

🕐 45 mins   **page 458**

Strawberry and Orange Crêpes

Light, melt-in-the-mouth pancakes with a creamy filling make an irresistible dessert

🕐 1 hr   ❄ 3 months   **page 460**

Apple Charlotte

This British hot fruit dessert was created for Queen Charlotte

🕐 1 hr 30 mins   **page 459**

Baked Persimmons with Biscotti Crumbs

Persimmons with a crunchy coating

🕐 40 mins   **page 460**

Quick Desserts

Semolina
A warm and comforting milk pudding

🕐 20 mins   **page 379**

Hot Chocolate Cakes
A deliciously light cake with a rich, creamy chocolate center

🕐 30 mins   **page 380**

Zabaglione
This classic Italian dessert can be served warm or cool

🕐 15 mins   **page 380**

Quick Sticky Toffee and Banana Pudding
A scrumptious mix of wintertime flavors

🕐 15 mins   **page 383**

Marzipan Oranges
Perfect little sugary fruits; serve in petits fours cases for an after dinner treat with coffee

🕐 5 mins   **page 416**

Sweet Lassi
A cooling dessert drink of sweetly spiced yogurt

🕐 5 mins   **page 391**

Chocolate Milk Shake "Float"
Rich and creamy, these will delight children of all ages

🕐 10 mins   **page 402**

Pear Gratin
Sophisticated, simple, and foolproof

🕐 15 mins   **page 454**

Bananas Flambéed with Calvados
A fabulous intense dessert

🕐 20 mins   **page 455**

Spiced Plum Compote
At their best in late summer to early autumn, plums are quick to cook

🕐 35 mins   **page 455**

Warm Fruit Compote
An ideal winter dish when supplies of fresh fruit are limited

🕐 15–20 mins   **page 456**

Citrus Zabaglione
A perfect palette cleanser to finish a meal

🕐 20 mins   **page 461**

Baked Figs with Cinnamon and Honey
A simple yet stylish dessert

🕐 25 mins   **page 461**

Pear and Grape Salad
Cucumber isn't often added to sweet dishes, but it works perfectly in this exotic fruit salad

🕐 15 mins   **page 477**

Pineapple Flambé
Rings of fresh fruit flamed with rum make a smart restaurant-style dessert

🕐 25–30 mins   **page 463**

Honey-baked Apricots with Mascarpone
Canned fruit guarantees an all-year dessert

🕐 20 mins   **page 463**

Melon Cocktail
Your choice of melon balls with honey and finished with fresh mint

🕐 15 mins   **page 480**

Strawberry Yogurt Mousse
A speedy treat that is bound to be a favorite with the kids

🕐 15 mins ❄ 3 months   **page 474**

Eton Mess
A quick indulgent mix of strawberries, cream, and meringue

🕐 10 mins   **page 472**

Mango and Papaya Salad
Light and refreshing fruit flavors in an exotic after dinner salad

🕐 25 mins   **page 481**

Berries with Citrus Syrup
Juicy seasonal berries are made even more luscious with a sweet lemon-orange syrup

🕐 15 mins   **page 478**

Citrus Fruit Salad
Refreshing, colorful, and full of vitamins, this pretty dessert is sunshine on a plate

🕐 20 mins   **page 484**

Pineapple Milk Shake
A fun drink for children, with no need for added sugar

🕐 5 mins   **page 485**

Desserts for a Crowd

Chocolate Truffle Cake
This chocolate truffle cake is rich, dark, and indulgent
🕐 20–25 mins   **page 386**

Vanilla Cheesecake
This rich yet light cheesecake is guaranteed to be a crowd pleaser
🕐 1 hr 10 mins   **page 399**

Black Forest Gâteau
The German cherry and chocolate-flavored cake—one of the most popular chocolate cakes
🕐 1 hr 35 mins ❄ 1 month   **page 414**

Lemon Meringue Tart
The contrast between the smooth, tart lemon filling and the fluffy meringue topping is a hit
🕐 1 hr   **page 432**

Panforte
The famous dried fruit and nut cake from Siena, Italy
🕐 1 hr   **page 415**

Angel Food Cake
A light-as-air cake made with your favorite summer berries
🕐 1 hr 5 mins–1 hr 15 mins   **page 417**

Prune and Almond Tart
A fabulous combination of fruit and nuts
🕐 1 hr 10 mins   **page 427**

Bienenstich
Known as Bee Sting Cake in Germany
🕐 40–45 mins   **page 418**

Chocolate Almond Cake
A dense, moist cake with a rich ganache topping
🕐 55 mins ❄ 1 month   **page 415**

Blueberry Cream Cheese Tart
Juicy blueberries perfectly complement the creamy filling
🕐 55 mins–1 hr 10 mins   **page 425**

Silesian Poppy Tart
Tarts made with poppy seeds are popular in Eastern Europe
🕐 2 hrs 5 mins   **page 431**

Victoria Sponge Cake
This light sponge cake is perfect with tea
🕐 45 mins ❄ 1 month   **page 413**

Almond and Quince Tart
A tasty almond tart topped with quince paste
🕐 1 hr 5 mins–1 hr 15 mins   **page 426**

Lemon Cheesecake
A light alternative to cheesecake, especially good for a lunchtime dessert

🕐 1 hr 50 mins ❄ 3 months   **page 400**

Whole Wheat Carrot Cake
This delicious, fiber-rich cake is a healthy choice

🕐 40 mins ❄ 1 month   **page 410**

Chocolate Chiffon Pie
A satisfying contrast between a light, smooth mousse-like filling and a crunchy crumb crust

🕐 30 mins   **page 428**

Key Lime Pie
A creamy but tart lime filling in a crumb base

🕐 40–45 mins   **page 429**

Almond and Orange Cake
This cake does not need flour or butter, so is great for people on restricted diets

🕐 1 hr 10 mins   **page 411**

Strawberry Semifreddo
This is Italian ice cream with a twist; texture and sweetness are added with crushed meringues

🕐 20 mins ❄ 3 months   **page 403**

Cannoli
Crisp pastries from Sicily filled with candied fruits and ricotta cheese

🕐 50 mins ❄ 3 months   **page 438**

Marble Cake
The marbled effect is a clever swirl of plain and chocolate batters

🕐 1 hr 30 mins   **page 411**

Profiteroles
These little cream puffs, drizzled with chocolate sauce, are a deliciously decadent dessert

🕐 1 hr ❄ 3 months   **page 439**

Lemon Tart
Variations of this ever-popular tart always appear on restaurant menus

🕐 1 hr 20 mins   **page 431**

Easy Bakes

Madeleines
These little cakes were made famous by writer Marcel Proust

🕐 15–20 mins   ❄ 1 month   **page 414**

Rice Pudding
A rich dish that is all the better for slow cooking

🕐 2 hrs 15 mins–2 hrs 45 mins   **page 378**

Steamed Ginger Pudding
A melt-in-the-mouth traditional winter dessert

🕐 1 hr 50 mins   **page 379**

Cherry Clafoutis
This French favorite can be enjoyed warm or at room temperature

🕐 1 hr 20 mins–1 hr 30 mins   **page 377**

Baked Jam Roll
A delicious raspberry filling in a biscuit

🕐 40 mins   **page 382**

Quick Sticky Toffee and Banana Pudding
A lovely winter pudding that is quick to make

🕐 15 mins   **page 383**

Quindim
This sweet, creamy and very rich dessert is a popular party dish in Brazil

🕐 40–45 mins   **page 389**

Vanilla Cheesecake
This rich yet light cheesecake is guaranteed to be a crowd pleaser

🕐 1 hr 15 mins   **page 399**

Chocolate Rice Pudding
A Portuguese version that adds chocolate to the classic dish

🕐 50 mins   **page 400**

Victoria Sponge Cake
Simple cake layers spread with jam and cream

🕐 40–45 mins   ❄ 1 month   **page 413**

Lemon Poppy Seed Muffins
Quick and easy to make, these muffins are delightful served with brunch

🕐 30 mins — **page 422**

French Almond Financiers
So-called because these cakes are said to resemble gold bars

🕐 25–30 mins ❄ 3 months — **page 412**

Vanilla Cupcakes
Colored buttercream icing topped cupcakes are irresistible

🕐 35 mins — **page 419**

Raspberry Cupcakes
Elegant cupcakes that are perfect with after-dinner coffee

🕐 30–35 mins . — **page 419**

Chelsea Buns
These sweet and spicy old-fashioned buns are a traditional tea-time treat

🕐 1 hr — **page 421**

Plum Crumble
Fresh fruit with a crunchy topping and some warm custard

🕐 40–50 mins ❄ 2 months — **page 453**

Oatmeal Cookies
Great tasting and good for you, too

🕐 30 mins — **page 442**

Oatmeal Bars
Sweet and chewy bars made from just a few pantry ingredients

🕐 1 hr — **page 444**

Chocolate Brownies
Walnut and chocolate treats are great for eating anytime

🕐 40 mins — **page 445**

Gingerbread Cookies
These delicious, spicy cookies are Christmas time favorites

🕐 40 mins — **page 445**

Apple Pie
Granny Smith apples in a flaky pastry crust can be served hot or cold

🕐 1 hr 15 mins — **page 450**

Chocolate Muffins
Buttermilk lends a delicious lightness to these chocolate muffins

🕐 30 mins — **page 423**

Apple-Ginger Crisp
Sweet dessert apples are perfect for autumn baking

🕐 1 hr 5 mins — **page 462**

Desserts to Impress

Crêpes Flambée
An anise- and maple-flavored twist on a classic

🕐 50 mins–55 mins ❄ 3 months **page 376**

Hot Orange Soufflés
Individual basic sweet soufflés, flavored with orange zest

🕐 30–35 mins ❄ 1 month **page 383**

Coeur à la Crème
These delicious little puddings are traditionally made in heart-shaped china molds

🕐 20 mins **page 385**

Raspberry Charlotte
Tart raspberry mousse is surrounded by lady fingers and topped with fresh berries

🕐 1 hr **page 387**

Almond and Orange Cake
A carrot purée and almond base makes this a great-tasting, low-calorie treat

🕐 1 hr 10 mins **page 411**

Classic Pavlova
This is named after the famous Russian ballerina, Anna Pavlova

🕐 1 hr 30 mins **page 388**

Lemon Meringue Roulade
The traditional filling is given a new twist in this impressive dessert

🕐 45 mins ❄ 3 months **page 389**

Floating Islands
Delicious meringues floating on top of vanilla-flavored custard

🕐 45 mins **page 390**

Chocolate Marquise
This rich chocolate mousse has a velvety texture and is delicious served with berries

🕐 15 mins ❄ 3 months **page 393**

Lemon and Praline Meringue
Impressive to serve, and easy to make

🕐 2 hrs 5 mins **page 393**

Paskha
A Russian Easter dish of cheese, candied fruits, and nuts baked in a flowerpot

🕐 40 mins **page 392**

Rum Babas
Little rum-soaked cakes can be made a day ahead and finished just before serving

🕐 40 mins ❄ 3 months **page 420**

Pecan and Maple Tart
This sweet, crunchy pie is a true all-American dessert—this one uses maple syrup

🕐 1 hr **page 425**

Sachertorte
A famous Viennese classic, this rich chocolate cake is glazed with a thin layer of apricot preserves and a finishing coat of shiny chocolate

🕐 1 hr 25 mins-1 hr 40 mins ❄ 3 months **page 416**

White Chocolate and Mascarpone Tarts
Mini berry-topped tarts are festive summer fare

🕐 25 mins **page 430**

Red Fruit Medley
This German-style dish makes a delicious, not-too-sweet dessert

🕐 15 mins **page 471**

Berry Medley
A cocktail of fresh berries coated in a sugar syrup and topped with cream

🕐 15-20 mins **page 468**

Apple Yogurt Compote
Served hot, warm, or cold, this is a simple yet elegant dessert

🕐 50-55 mins **page 459**

Layered Fruit Platter
Fresh summer fruits served with a rose-petal cream

🕐 15 mins **page 472**

Pear and Grape Salad
An unusual combination of fruit with the surprise addition of cucumber

🕐 15-20 mins **page 477**

Summer Berry Terrine
All the flavors of summer wrapped up in this stunning terrine

🕐 50 mins **page 474**

Lychees in Scented Syrup
A refreshing ginger-, lime-, and star anise-scented fruit dessert

🕐 20 mins ❄ 2 months **page 475**

Summer Pudding
This classic summer fruit dessert is a lucious mix of seasonal berries and juicy bread slices

🕐 20-25 mins **page 476**

Cold Desserts

Chocolate Mousse

A favorite with all the family, this creamy, rich, chocolate dessert should be served often

🕐 40 mins **page 385**

Coeur à la Crème

Delicious little puddings traditionally made in heart-shaped china molds

🕐 20 mins **page 385**

Classic Crème Brûlée

French for "burnt cream," this is a sophisticated caramel cream

🕐 1hr **page 392**

Chocolate Marquise

A rich, velvety chocolate mousse with a topping of summer berries

🕐 15 mins ❄ 3 months **page 393**

Panna Cotta with Strawberry Purée

Creamy individual desserts with seasonal fruits

🕐 5 mins **page 399**

Vanilla Custards

Chilled baked honey-flavored vanilla cream topped with saucy cherries

🕐 50 mins **page 401**

Buttermilk Panna Cotta

A traditional Italian dessert of "cooked cream"

🕐 35 mins **page 401**

Fruit Mousse

Fresh raspberries and blackberries blended with cream and set with gelatin

🕐 40 mins **page 402**

Chocolate Chip Ice Cream

White chocolate chips in a rich, dark chocolate ice cream

🕐 25 mins ❄ 1 week **page 405**

Tiramisu

One of Italy's favorite desserts, this luscious dessert gets its name, which means "pick-me-up," from the espresso coffee used to flavor the sponge base

🕐 20 mins **page 398**

Espresso Granita
A refreshing granular coffee-flavored ice

🕐 10 mins **page 404**

Vanilla Ice Cream
Creamy homemade ice cream is delicious with fresh berries

🕐 40 mins ❄ 1 week **page 405**

Orange Sorbet
A lovely, light summer dessert

🕐 25 mins ❄ 3 months **page 406**

Saffron Kulfi
An Indian ice cream made from condensed milk

🕐 10 mins ❄ 1 month **page 406**

Strawberry Ice Cream
Plump strawberries, coconut, rum, and lime flavor this summer favorite

🕐 15 mins ❄ 3 months **page 407**

Cassata Gelato
This Sicilian frozen dessert is utterly irresistible

🕐 35 mins ❄ 4 months **page 407**

Pistachio Ice Cream
A deliciously nutty ice cream

🕐 40–45 mins ❄ 3 months **page 409**

Mango Sorbet
Scoops of juicy, fragrant mangoes blended with sugar and frozen

🕐 25 mins ❄ 3 months **page 409**

Passion Fruit Puddings
A sweet milk pudding with an exotic passion fruit topping

🕐 25 mins **page 468**

Sparkling Wine Jellies with Passion Fruit
A simple but impressive dessert

🕐 30 mins **page 471**

Cold Raspberry Soufflé
This fragrant dessert just melts in the mouth

🕐 35 mins ❄ 1 month **page 470**

Mango and Orange Mousse
Two great fruit flavors blended with cream make for a refreshing dessert

🕐 40 mins **page 469**

Peach Melba
Peaches, ice cream, and a raspberry sauce make a diva-like dessert

🕐 45 mins ❄ 6 months **page 476**

Crêpes Flambée

This anise and maple-flavored twist on a classic French dessert makes a spectacular end to any dinner party

- makes 4 servings
- prep about 30 mins • cook 12–15 mins
- 8in (20cm) crêpe pan
- the crêpes can be made ahead and frozen, separated by waxed paper, for up to 3 months

For the crepes

1 cup whole milk

⅔ cup all-purpose flour

2 large eggs

1 tsp vegetable oil

pinch of salt

vegetable oil for cooking crêpes

For the flambée sauce

4 tbsp unsalted butter

½ cup maple syrup

juice and grated zest of 2 oranges

4 tbsp brandy or orange liqueur

● **Prepare ahead** Make the crêpes in advance, and layer with wax paper, then wrap in plastic wrap and refrigerate for up to 2 days.

1 **To make the crêpe** batter, process all of the ingredients in a blender or food processor until smooth. Let stand for 30 minutes.

2 **Heat an 8in (20cm)** crêpe pan over high heat until a splash of water "dances" on the surface. Pour in vegetable oil to cover the bottom, swirl the pan to coat, then pour off the excess oil. Ladle 3 tbsp of the batter into the center of the pan and immediately swirl so the batter covers the base thinly. Cook for 1 minute, or until small bubbles appear on top. Slide a metal spatula underneath and flip the crêpe over, then cook for 30 seconds, or until cooked through.

3 **To prepare the** flambée sauce, melt the butter in a separate frying pan over medium heat. Add the maple syrup, and orange juice and zest, and boil for 5 minutes, stirring often, until well combined, and slightly reduced.

4 **Add the crêpes** to the sauce. Pour in brandy and warm for a few seconds. Bring the pan and lid to the table. Carefully light brandy with a long match. Let burn 30 seconds, then cover the pan if the fire hasn't burned out. Serve at once.

Lemon and Sugar Crêpes

In Paris, these wafer-thin crêpes with the simplest of flavorings are sold by street vendors

- makes 4 servings
- prep 15 mins, plus standing • cook 10 mins
- 8in (20cm) crêpe pan
- the crêpes can be made ahead and frozen, separated by waxed paper, for up to 3 months

1 cup whole milk

⅔ cup all-purpose flour

2 large eggs

1 tsp vegetable oil, plus more for cooking crêpes

pinch of salt

lemon wedges and slices and superfine sugar, to serve

● **Prepare ahead** Make the crêpes in advance, and layer with wax paper, then wrap in plastic wrap. Reheat in the oven before topping with lemon juice and sugar.

1 **Process the milk**, flour, eggs, oil, and salt in a blender or food processor until smooth. Let stand for 30 minutes.

2 **Preheat the oven** to 200°F (95°C). Heat an 8in (20cm) crêpe or nonstick frying pan, over high heat until a splash of water "dances" on the surface. Pour in enough vegetable oil to cover the bottom, swirl the pan to coat, then pour off the excess oil.

3 **Ladle about 3 tbsp** of the batter into the center of the pan and immediately tilt and swirl the pan so the batter covers the base thinly. Cook the crêpe for about 1 minute until small bubbles appear on the top. Slide a metal spatula underneath and flip the crêpe over, then continue cooking for 30 seconds more, or until golden and cooked through.

4 **Transfer to a plate**, roll up and keep warm in the oven. Repeat, oiling the pan as needed, until all of the batter has been used. Serve the crêpes hot, sprinkled with sugar, drizzled with lemon juice and served with lemon slices.

● **Good with** a drizzle of maple syrup, or fruit purée in addition to the lemon and sugar.

Sticky Rice

Also known as "glutinous rice," this gets its name from its high proportion of starch. It is used to make a popular Thai dessert

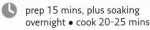 makes 4-6 servings

 prep 15 mins, plus soaking overnight • cook 20-25 mins

 steamer

1 cup **glutinous rice** (available from Asian grocers)

¾ cup well-shaken, canned **coconut milk**

2 tbsp crushed **palm sugar** or light brown sugar

2 ripe **mangoes**, peeled, pitted, and diced or sliced

1 ripe **papaya**, peeled, seeded and sliced

banana leaves, to serve

juice of 2 **limes**

1 Put the rice in a bowl and add enough cold water to cover by 2in (5cm). Let soak for 8 hours.

2 Drain the rice in a colander. Line the top part of a steamer with soaked, drained banana leaves, or moistened, squeezed-dry cheesecloth. Add the rice and spread in a thin layer. Add water to the bottom part of the steamer, and bring to a boil over high heat. Reduce the heat to medium.

3 Steam over steadily boiling water for 20–25 minutes, until the rice is tender. Heat the coconut milk and sugar in a saucepan until the sugar dissolves, then mix into the rice. Cover and leave for 15 minutes.

4 Place a scoop of rice on a banana leaf, with the fruit on the side. Drizzle with the lime juice and serve warm.

> **BANANA LEAVES**
> These can be bought in Asian stores and should be softened before use by soaking briefly in warm water.

Cherry Clafoutis

This French favorite can be enjoyed warm or at room temperature

 makes 6 servings

 prep 12 mins, plus 30 mins standing • cook 35-45 mins

 10in (25cm) quiche or flan dish

1lb 10oz (750g) **cherries**, pitted

3 tbsp **kirsch**

6 tbsp **sugar**

unsalted butter, for the dish

4 large **eggs**

1 **vanilla bean**, split

⅔ cup **all-purpose flour**, sifted

1¼ cups **milk**

pinch of **salt**

1 Toss the cherries with the kirsch and 2 tbsp of the sugar in a bowl and let stand for 30 minutes. Preheat the oven to 400°F (200°C) and butter a ceramic or glass 10in (25cm) one-piece quiche or flan dish and set aside.

2 Strain the liquid from the cherries. Whisk the eggs, drained cherry liquid, seeds from the vanilla bean, and the remaining 4 tbsp sugar in a bowl until combined. Gradually whisk in the flour, then add the milk and salt, and whisk until smooth.

3 Spread the cherries in the dish, then pour in the batter.

4 Bake for 35-45 minutes, until the top is browned and the center is firm to the touch. Serve warm or at room temperature.

● **Good with** plenty of lightly whipped heavy cream, or crème fraîche for spooning over.

VARIATION

Plum Clafoutis

Substitute small pitted plums for the cherries and add more sugar to compensate for the tartness of the plums.

Plum Pudding

Fragrant and rich with a variety of dried fruits, this is the ultimate British Christmas dessert

makes 10-12 servings

prep 45 mins, plus overnight soaking • cook 8-10 hrs

1½ quart (1½ liter) heatproof bowl

freeze for up to 1 year, after cooking, in its bowl; thaw and steam in bowl for 1½-2 hours

1 cup chopped **dried fruit**, such as figs, dates, and/or cherries

⅔ cup **raisins**

⅓ cup **dried currants**

⅓ cup mixed chopped **candied fruit peel**

⅔ cup **beer**

1 tbsp **whisky** or brandy

finely grated zest and juice of 1 **orange**

finely grated zest and juice of 1 **lemon**

½ cup **pitted dried plums**, chopped

⅓ cup **cold brewed black tea**

1 **Golden Delicious apple**, grated

8 tbsp **butter**, melted, plus more for greasing

¾ cup packed **light brown sugar**

2 large **eggs**, beaten

1 tbsp **molasses**

½ cup **all-purpose flour**

1 tsp **pumpkin pie spice**

½ tsp **baking powder**

2 cups fresh **bread crumbs**

½ cup chopped **slivered almonds**

● **Prepare ahead** The pudding is best cooked 1-2 months before eating. Wrap the pudding well in aluminum foil and refrigerate. To reheat, steam for 1½-2 hours.

1 **Put the first** 8 ingredients into a large bowl and mix well. Combine the dried plums and tea in a small bowl. Cover both bowls and let stand at least 12 hours.

2 **Drain the dried plums** and discard the tea. Add the dried plums and grated apple to the soaked fruit, followed by the melted butter, brown sugar, eggs, and molasses, stirring well.

3 **Sift in the flour**, spices, and baking powder. Add the bread crumbs and almonds. Mix well.

4 **Butter a 1½ quart** heatproof bowl. Pour in the pudding batter. Cover with a double layer of parchment paper and 1 layer of aluminum foil, crimping the foil. Place on a steamer rack in a large pot of simmering water, with the water barely touching the bottom of the bowl. Cover and steam until dark and firm, for 8-10 hours, adding more boiling water to the pot as needed.

● **Good with** whipped cream or custard sauce.

> **STEAMING TIP**
>
> The steaming can be done over 2 or 3 days. Steam it for at least 3 hours on the first day and then continue with the remaining hours on following days.

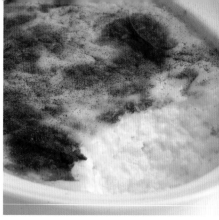

Rice Pudding

Starchy Italian rice gives this dish extra creaminess

makes 4 servings

prep 15 mins • cook 2-2½ hours

1 quart (1 liter) baking dish

¼ cup **short-grain rice** for risotto, such as Arborio

2½ cups **whole milk**

3 tbsp **sugar**

1 tbsp **butter**, plus more for the dish

pinch of **ground cinnamon** or freshly grated nutmeg

1 **Lightly butter the dish**. Rinse the rice under cold running water, then drain well. Combine the rice and the milk in a bowl and let stand for 30 minutes.

2 **Preheat the oven** to 300°F (150°C). Stir the sugar into the rice. Pour into the dish, dot with butter, and sprinkle with cinnamon. Bake for 2-2½ hours, or until the top is golden.

● **Good with** a spoonful of berry jam or fruit purée or a scoop of vanilla ice cream.

VARIATION

Turkish Rice Pudding

Cook the rice in 3 cups boiling water for 5 minutes, drain. Simmer with the milk for 15 minutes. Stir in the sugar and ¼ tsp pure vanilla extract. Cool and serve with ground cinnamon sprinkled on top.

Semolina

This milk pudding is
warm and comforting

- makes 4 servings
- prep 5 mins • cook 15 mins

2 cups whole milk

½ cup heavy cream

⅔ cup semolina (pasta flour)

⅓ cup plus 1 tbsp sugar

3 tbsp rose water

4 tsp raspberry jam, to serve

1 tbsp boiling water

1 Bring the milk and cream to
a boil over medium heat in a
medium saucepan. Whisk in the
semolina in a steady stream, then the
sugar. Bring to a boil then reduce the
heat. Simmer, whisking often, for
3–4 minutes, until very thick.

2 Remove from the heat.
Whisk in the rosewater. If desired,
thin the pudding with more milk.

3 Divide among 4 dessert cups.
Mix the jam with the boiling
water and drizzle over each pudding.
Serve warm.

VARIATION

Baked Semolina
At the end of step 2, transfer the
mixture to a buttered baking dish.
Bake in a 350°F (175°C) oven for
30 minutes, or until lightly browned.

Steamed Ginger Pudding

Easy to make and very satisfying to eat, this is
a traditional British dessert

- makes 4–6 servings
- prep 20 mins • cook 1½ hrs
- 6-cup heatproof bowl

2 tbsp golden syrup, plus more
for serving

1 tbsp fresh bread crumbs

¾ cup all-purpose flour

1 tsp ground ginger

¾ tsp baking powder

¼ tsp salt

8 tbsp butter at room temperature,
plus more for the bowl

⅔ cup sugar

finely grated zest of 1 lemon

2 large eggs, beaten

¼ cup whole milk

1 Butter a 6-cup heatproof bowl.
Pour in the golden syrup and
sprinkle with bread crumbs. Add
enough cold water to come about
1 in (2.5cm) up the sides of a large
saucepan, and bring to a boil.

2 Sift the flour, ginger, baking
powder, and salt together. Cream
the butter and sugar in a mixing bowl
until light and fluffy. Beat in the zest,
then add the eggs, one at a time,
beating well after each addition. Stir
in half the flour mixture, then the
milk, then the remaining flour.

3 Transfer the batter to the
prepared bowl. Cover with a
double layer of parchment paper
then a piece of aluminum foil,
crimping the foil securely.

4 Lower the bowl into the
saucepan of water. Cover and
reduce the heat to medium-low.
Simmer for 1½ hours, or until a
toothpick inserted in the pudding
comes out clean, adding more boiling
water to the pot if needed.

5 Remove the bowl from the
water. Let stand 5 minutes, then
remove the foil and paper. Invert and
unmold the pudding onto a serving
plate. Serve hot, with additional
warmed syrup passed on the side to
drizzle over each serving.

● **Good with** vanilla sauce, heavy
cream, or vanilla ice cream.

Hot Chocolate Cakes

A treat for all chocoholics! As if like magic, these very rich, very easy desserts bake until a light cake surrounds a rich, creamy chocolate center.

 makes 6 servings

prep 10 mins • cook 20 mins

six 6oz (175ml) custard cups or ramekins

9oz (250g) **bittersweet chocolate**, chopped

3 tbsp **butter**, softened, plus more for the custard cups

⅔ cup **sugar**

4 large **eggs**

½ tsp **pure vanilla extract**

⅓ cup **all-purpose flour**

pinch of **salt**

● **Prepare ahead** The cakes can be prepared through step 3 and stored at room temperature for up to 2 hours.

1 Preheat the oven to 400°F (200°C). Generously butter the inside of six 6oz (175g) custard cups, and line each with a round of wax paper. Butter the paper.

2 Melt the chocolate in a heatproof bowl set over, but not in, a saucepan of simmering water. Remove from the heat.

3 Beat the butter and sugar in a bowl with an electric mixer on high speed for about 3 minutes, until light and fluffy. Beat in the eggs one at a time, beating well after each addition, then add the vanilla. Sift the flour and salt together and stir into the batter, then stir in the chocolate. Divide the batter among the cups. Place the cups on a baking sheet.

4 Bake for 12–15 minutes, or until the sides are set but the centers are still soft. Top each cup with a serving plate. Protecting your hands with a kitchen towel, invert both to unmold the cake. Remove the wax paper. Serve hot.

● **Good with** a dollop of softly whipped cream or hot custard sauce flavored with grated orange zest.

● **Leftovers** can be coarsely chopped and spooned over vanilla ice cream with hot fudge sauce to make a special sundae.

CHOOSING CHOCOLATE

Substitute an exotically flavored chocolate, such as fruit, spice, coffee, or tea, for the bittersweet chocolate.

Zabaglione

This warm Italian dessert was invented by mistake in the 1600s when fortified wine was poured into egg custard

 makes 4 servings

prep 5 mins • cook 10 mins

4 large **egg yolks**

¼ cup **sugar**

8 tbsp **Marsala**

grated zest of 1 **orange**

8 **Italian ladyfingers** (savoiardi) or biscotti, to serve

1 Bring a large saucepan of water to a boil, then lower the heat to simmer.

2 Whisk the yolks, sugar, and Marsala with half the orange zest in a large heatproof bowl. Place over (but not in) the simmering water. Using a balloon whisk, whisk constantly for 5–10 minutes, or until the zabaglione is pale, thick, fluffy, and warm.

3 Immediately divide the zabaglione among 4 glasses. Garnish with the remaining orange zest; serve immediately with ladyfingers or biscotti.

Steamed Currant Pudding

Top this warm dessert with crème Anglaise

🍴 makes 4–6 servings

🕐 prep 15 mins • cook 1½–2 hrs

1⅔ cups **all-purpose flour**, plus more for shaping

1½ tsp **baking powder**

4oz (115g) shredded cold **suet**, shortening, or butter

1 cup **dried currants**

½ cup fresh **bread crumbs**

½ cup **sugar**

finely grated zest of 1 **lemon**

½ cup **whole milk**, plus more as needed

hot **crème Anglaise**

⬤ **Prepare ahead** The cooked pudding can be refrigerated for up to 2 days; reheat before serving.

1 Sift the flour and baking powder together into a bowl. Stir in the suet, then the currants, bread crumbs, sugar, and lemon zest. Stir in the milk, adding more, if needed, to make a soft dough similar to biscuit dough.

2 Turn the dough onto a lightly floured surface, and shape into a log about 6in (18cm) long. Lightly butter a 12in (30cm) sheet of aluminum foil. Place the log at one end of the foil, and roll it up. Twist the ends closed to make a packet that resembles a party favor.

3 Place a steamer rack in a large saucepan and add enough water to clear the rack. Bring to a boil. Place the foil packet in the steamer. Cover and steam over medium-low heat for about 1½ hours, until the pudding is cooked through.

4 Transfer to a platter, remove the foil, and slice. Serve hot, with crème Anglaise.

Tapioca and Fruit Pudding

Fruit segments and orange juice turn this subtle-flavored dish into something far more lively

🍴 makes 4–6 servings

🕐 prep 10 mins • cook 30–50 mins

one 11oz (308g) can **mandarin oranges** in natural juice

one 8oz (224g) can **pineapple chunks** in natural juice

2¼ cups **orange juice**, as needed

½ cup **pearl tapioca**

¼ cup **sugar**, or more as needed

½ cup thick **Greek-style yogurt** or lightly whipped cream

freshly grated **nutmeg** or ground cinnamon (optional)

1 Drain the juice from the oranges and pineapple over a measuring cup, and add enough orange juice to make 2½ cups.

2 Bring the tapioca and juice to a boil in a medium saucepan over high heat, stirring constantly.

The liquid will be very cloudy at first, then become clear. Reduce the heat to medium-low. Simmer, stirring often for about 40 minutes, or until the pearls become translucent and the mixture is thick and glossy. Brush down the side of the pan with a wet pastry brush occasionally.

3 Remove the pan from the heat and stir in the sugar, adding more to taste. Stir the fruit into the pudding. Spoon into bowls and serve hot. Top with yogurt, and sprinkle with nutmeg, if desired.

VARIATION

Fruity Tapioca

Cook the tapioca in the juice, allow to cool then stir in the yogurt or cream, followed by the fruit, and chill to make a mousse-like dessert.

Baked Jam Roll

Think of this as a biscuit with jam baked inside—it is equally wonderful with a custard sauce or whipped cream

makes 4–6 servings

prep 10 mins • cook 30 mins

1⅔ cups **all-purpose flour**

1½ tsp **baking powder**

¼ tsp **salt**

8 tbsp **cold butter**, shredded on a box grater

½ cup **whole milk**

⅓ cup **jam**, any flavor

1 large **egg**, beaten

sugar, for sprinkling

warm **crème anglaise** or whipped cream, to serve

1 Preheat the oven to 400°F (200°C). Line a baking sheet with wax paper.

2 Sift the flour, baking powder, and salt into a bowl. Mix in the butter. Stir in the milk to make a stiff dough. Roll on a lightly floured work surface into a 10 x 7in (25 x 18cm) rectangle.

3 Spread the dough with the jam. Starting from a long side, roll into a log. Lift and transfer the roll to the baking sheet, seam side down. Lightly brush with the beaten egg and sprinkle with the sugar.

4 Bake for about 25 minutes, or until golden brown and crisp. Serve with the custard sauce.

VARIATIONS

Baked Syrup Roll

Make the recipe as above, but use light corn or maple syrup instead of the jam.

Baked Marmalade Roll

Make the recipe as above, adding the grated zest of 1 orange to the dough in step 2. Use 4–6 tbsp marmalade, in place of the jam.

Bread and Butter Pudding

Slow baking will produce a pudding with a smooth, velvety texture

makes 4 servings

prep 15 mins, plus soaking • cook 40 mins

2 tbsp **butter**, plus more for the pan

5 slices day-old **white sandwich bread**

⅓ cup **raisins**

3 large **eggs**

1¼ cups **whole milk**

¾ cup **half-and-half**

⅓ cup **sugar**

1 tsp **pure vanilla extract**

¼ cup **apricot preserves**

2 tsp fresh **lemon** juice

● **Prepare ahead** The pudding can be refrigerated for up to 2 days and served cold, or reheated in a microwave oven.

1 Lightly butter an 8in (20cm) square baking dish. Butter one side of each bread slice. Cut each slice in half diagonally, and then again.

2 Sprinkle the raisins on the bottom of the baking dish. Top with overlapping bread slices, buttered sides down. Beat together the eggs, milk, half-and-half, sugar, and vanilla. Pour over the bread and let stand for at least 30 minutes.

3 Preheat the oven to 350°F (180°C). Place the dish in a roasting pan and add enough water to reach 1in (2.5cm) up the sides of the baking dish. Bake 30–40 minutes, until the center is barely set.

4 Meanwhile, bring the preserves, lemon juice, and 1 tbsp water to a boil in a small saucepan over medium heat. Strain. Brush the mixture over the top of the pudding. Let stand 5 minutes, then serve hot.

VARIATION

Fruity Bread Pudding

Substitute pitted and chopped fresh apricots, peaches, or mangoes, or dried blueberries, cherries, or cranberries for the raisins. Different breads can also be used, such as brioche or pannetone.

Hot Orange Soufflés

Hot soufflés are not difficult to make, but they do need a little care. This is a basic sweet soufflé, flavored with orange zest

 makes 4 servings

🕐 prep 20 mins • cook 12–15 mins

🍲 6 x 7oz (200ml) ramekins

❄ freeze, uncooked, in the ramekins for up to 1 month

4 tbsp **butter**

⅓ cup **sugar**, plus more for the ramekins

⅓ cup **all-purpose flour**

1¼ cup **whole milk**

grated zest of 2 **oranges**

2 tbsp fresh **orange** juice

3 large **eggs**, separated, plus 1 large **egg white**

1 Preheat the oven to 400°F (200°C). Place a baking sheet in the oven to preheat.

2 Melt the butter in a medium saucepan over medium heat. Brush six 7oz (200ml) ramekins with some of the butter. Dust the insides of the ramekins with sugar, making sure there are no gaps.

3 Whisk the flour into the remaining butter and let bubble over medium heat without browning for about 1 minute. Whisk in the milk and bring to a boil, whisking constantly. Reduce the heat to low and simmer for 2 minutes. Whisk in the orange zest and juice and all but 1 tsp of the sugar.

4 Remove from the heat and beat in the egg yolks one at a time. Whisk the whites to soft peaks, then beat in the remaining sugar. Stir a dollop of the whites into the saucepan, then fold in the remainder.

5 Divide among the ramekins. Using a knife, make a shallow circle around the ramekins about ¼in (6mm) in from the edge. Place on the hot baking sheet and bake for 15 minutes, or until the soufflés have risen but look slightly unset in the center. Serve immediately.

Quick Sticky Toffee and Banana Pudding

Gooey and delicious, this couldn't be faster to make; use ripe bananas for the best flavor

 makes 6 servings

🕐 prep 5 mins • cook 10 mins

1 cup **heavy cream**

8 tbsp **butter**

⅔ cup packed **light brown sugar**

⅓ cup **maple syrup**

6 slices store-bought **gingerbread cake**

2 large **bananas**, sliced

½ cup chopped **pecans**

● **Prepare ahead** You can assemble the pudding several hours in advance. Toss the bananas in lemon juice first and tuck them under the cake—this will keep them from going brown.

1 Preheat the oven to 375°F (190°C). Combine the cream, butter, sugar, and maple syrup in a small pan and heat gently, stirring constantly until smooth and melted.

2 Layer the cake and bananas in a 9in (33cm) square baking dish. Pour the sauce on top and sprinkle with the pecans.

3 Bake for 10 minutes, or until the sauce is bubbling. Serve hot.

● **Good with** whipped cream or vanilla ice cream.

● **Leftovers** can be reheated and used to top vanilla ice cream, chopped fresh fruit, or slices of cake.

VARIATION

Pound Cake and Banana Pudding

For a slightly less rich version, replace the gingerbread with 8oz (225g) pound cake. Pound cake is a slightly drier cake than gingerbread, so after you pour the sauce over, let the mixture soak for 10 minutes, then bake as directed.

Torrijas

This Spanish version of French toast can be served with maple syrup, honey, or fresh fruit compote

- makes 4 servings
- prep 5 mins, plus standing • cook 20 mins

8 slices **stale baguette**, crusts removed

3¼ cups **whole milk**

3 tbsp granulated **sugar**

1 **cinnamon stick**

1 cup **olive oil**, for frying

3 large **eggs**, beaten

confectioner's sugar, for sifting

maple syrup, for drizzling

1 Arrange the bread in a shallow dish. Bring the milk, sugar, and cinnamon to a boil in a saucepan, stirring often, over medium heat. Pour over the bread. Let stand for 15 minutes, until the bread has soaked up all the milk. Remove the cinnamon stick and discard.

2 Preheat the oven to 200°F (95°C) Line a baking sheet with paper towels. Heat the oil in a large frying pan over medium heat until the oil shimmers. Beat the eggs in a shallow dish. In batches, dip a slice of the bread in beaten egg to coat, then add to the frying pan. Fry, turning once, until golden. Transfer to the paper towels and keep warm in the oven.

3 Transfer to a serving platter, sift the confectioner's sugar on top, and drizzle with syrup. Serve warm.

Cinnamon Pancakes with Apricots

These small, light-as-air pancakes make a delicious brunch

- makes 16–20 pancakes
- prep 30 mins • cook 30 mins

For the apricots

9oz (250g) **ripe apricots**, pitted and sliced

¼ cup **honey**

2 tbsp fresh **lemon** juice

For the pancakes

1⅓ cups **all-purpose flour**

2 tbsp **sugar**

1¼ tsp **baking powder**

½ tsp **ground cinnamon**

2 large **eggs**

scant 1 cup **buttermilk**

4 tbsp **butter**, melted, plus more for the griddle

8oz (230g) **farmer's cheese**, for serving

● **Prepare ahead** The apricot sauce can be refrigerated for up to 2 days and reheated.

1 Simmer the apricots, honey, and lemon juice in a small saucepan over low heat for about 5 minutes, or until the apricots have softened but still hold their shape. Keep warm.

2 To make the pancakes, sift the flour, sugar, baking powder, and cinnamon together into a bowl. Make a well in the center. Beat the eggs, buttermilk, and melted butter and pour into the well. Stir until just combined.

3 Heat a nonstick frying pan over medium heat. Grease with the melted butter. Using a heaping tablespoon for each, spoon the batter into the pan. Cook until bubbles appear on the surface.

4 Flip the pancakes over and brown the other side. Transfer to a clean kitchen towel and cover to keep warm while cooking the remaining pancakes.

5 Immediately serve the pancakes on plates, topped with the hot apricot sauce and a scoop of the farmer's cheese.

Chocolate Mousse

Bittersweet chocolate mousse may be the standard, but try it with milk or white chocolate for delicious variations

🍴 makes 6 servings

🕐 prep 20 mins, plus chilling • cook 20 mins

3½oz (100g) **bittersweet chocolate**, chopped

1 tbsp **whole milk**

2 large **eggs**, separated

2 tbsp **sugar**

⅓ cup **heavy cream**

grated **chocolate** or chocolate curls, to decorate

1 **Combine the chocolate** and milk in a heatproof bowl and place over a saucepan of simmering water. Heat, stirring often, until the chocolate melts. Remove from the heat and let cool slightly.

2 **Whisk the egg yolks** and sugar in a large bowl until thick and creamy. Whisk in the chocolate mixture.

3 **Whip the cream** in a bowl until stiff peaks form. Add the chocolate mixture and fold together just until combine. Using clean beaters, whip the egg whites until stiff peaks form. Stir some of the whites into the chocolate mixture, then fold in the rest.

4 **Spoon into** individual dishes. Cover and refrigerate at least 2 hours, until chilled. Garnish with grated chocolate and serve chilled.

⬤ **Good with** biscotti, shortbread, or a little whipped cream.

VARIATION

Light Chocolate Mousse

For a sweeter and lighter taste, make the mousse with 50 percent dark chocolate or milk chocolate. Top with shavings or curls of white chocolate.

Coeur à la Crème

These delicious little puddings are made in individual heart-shaped china molds

🍴 makes 4 servings

🕐 prep 20 mins, plus draining

🗄 4 small coeur à la crème molds

8oz (225g) **cottage cheese**, drained and sieved

1¼ cups **heavy cream**, plus more to serve

3 tbsp **confectioner's sugar**

1 tsp **pure vanilla extract**

2 large **egg whites**

fresh **berries**, for serving

⬤ **Prepare ahead** These must drain in the refrigerator for at least 2 days before serving. They can be refrigerated for another 3 days after they have been drained.

1 **Mix the cottage cheese**, cream, confectioner's sugar, and vanilla extract together in a bowl. Whisk the egg whites until they form soft peaks. Fold into the cheese mixture.

2 **Fill 4 individual** coeur à la crème molds with the mixture and cover with plastic wrap. Place the molds on a wire rack over a baking sheet. Place the molds and tray in the refrigerator and allow to drain for 2–3 days.

3 **To serve**, carefully unmold the crèmes onto plates. Drizzle with more cream, garnish with the berries and serve chilled.

⬤ **Good with** a sharp, fruity sauce, such as raspberry coulis, or a chilled mixed fruit compote.

⬤ **Leftovers** can be lightly mashed with a fork and served on top of a fresh fruit salad.

> ### USING RAMEKINS
> Coeur à la crème molds are available in specialist kitchen stores. You can use ramekins to make this recipe. Line each one with a disc of greaseproof paper cut to fit. Fill the dishes with the mixture and secure a piece of muslin over the top with an elastic band. Turn over on to a wire rack over a plate or tray, and leave for 2–3 days to drain, as above.

Sherry Trifle

Made with raspberries here, this versatile dessert works well with other fruits. Try strawberries, blueberries, or even canned peaches

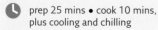
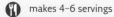
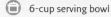

- makes 4–6 servings
- prep 25 mins • cook 10 mins, plus cooling and chilling
- 6-cup serving bowl

For the custard

2½ cups **whole milk**

2 tbsp **sugar**, plus 1 tsp for sprinkling

1 **vanilla bean**, split lengthwise

4 **egg yolks**

⅔ of a 1lb (450g) **pound cake**, sliced

½ cup **raspberry jam**

6oz (175g) **raspberries**

4 **almond cookies**, such as amaretti, crumbled

½ cup **sherry**, such as Amontillado

1¼ cups **heavy cream**

2 tbsp **sliced natural almonds** or grated chocolate, to garnish

● **Special information** When raspberries are not in season, use frozen berries, thawed and drained. The juice can be used in another recipe or to replace the sherry for making a nonalcoholic trifle.

● **Prepare ahead** The trifle can be made up to 24 hours in advance, but add the whipped cream topping and garnish just before serving.

1 **To make the custard**, bring the milk, sugar, and the vanilla bean to a simmer in a medium saucepan over low heat. Remove the vanilla bean, and use the tip of a knife to scrape the beans back into the milk. Rinse the bean and save for another use or discard.

2 **Whisk the egg yolks** in a heatproof bowl. Gradually whisk in the hot milk. Rinse out the saucepan and pour the milk mixture back into the pan. Stirring constantly with a wooden spoon, cook over low heat until the custard is thick enough to coat the back of the spoon (an instant-read thermometer will read 185°F/85°C). Strain through a wire sieve into a bowl. Sprinkle the surface with 1 tsp sugar, to help prevent a skin from forming. Let cool.

3 **Meanwhile**, spread the sliced cake with raspberry jam and sandwich together in pairs. Cut into strips about 1¼in (3cm) wide and arrange in the bottom of a 6-cup serving bowl.

4 **Add the raspberries**, pushing them down into the spaces between the cake strips. Sprinkle with the cookie crumbs, then drizzle with the sherry. Spoon the cooled custard the top. Cover and refrigerate at least 1 hour and up to 1 day.

5 **Whip the cream** until thickened but not stiff. Spread over the trifle and sprinkle with almonds. Serve chilled.

● **Leftovers** can be served on fruit jelly, ice cream, or as an accompaniment to fruit salad.

VARIATION

Chocolate Banana Trifle
Substitute chocolate-nut spread for the raspberry jam, and spread on the cake slices. Substitute 1 or 2 sliced bananas for the raspberries. Add 7oz (200g) chopped bittersweet chocolate into the hot, strained custard, let stand until melted, then whisk until smooth.

Chocolate Truffle Cake

A worthwhile indulgence

- makes 8 servings
- prep 20–25 mins, plus chilling
- 8in (20cm) springform pan

9oz (250g) **bittersweet chocolate**, chopped

2 large **egg whites**

½ cup **granulated sugar**

1½ cups **heavy cream**, whipped

2 tbsp **brandy**

6 **amaretti cookies**, crushed

confectioner's sugar, to garnish

1 **Line the pan** with plastic wrap. Melt the chocolate in a heatproof bowl set over a saucepan of simmering water and set aside.

2 **Combine** the egg whites and granulated sugar in a heatproof bowl and place over a saucepan pan of simmering water. Beat for 5 minutes, until it stands in stiff, shiny peaks.

3 **Fold the melted** chocolate into the egg whites, then the whipped cream and brandy. Pour into the pan. Cover and refrigerate for at least 4 hours, until set.

4 **Remove the sides** of the pan. Invert onto a plate. Sprinkle with the cookies and confectioner's sugar. Serve chilled.

Raspberry Charlotte

This is a show-stopper dessert with tart raspberry mousse surrounded by tender lady fingers

 makes 6 servings

 prep 50 mins, plus chilling
• cook 10 mins

8 x 2in (20 x 5cm) round cake pan

18-20 **lady fingers**, halved crosswise

2 cups **whole milk**

1 **vanilla bean**, split lengthwise

5 large **egg yolks**

⅓ cup **sugar**

2 envelopes unflavored **gelatin** powder

1 cup **heavy cream**

three 6oz (168g) baskets fresh **raspberries**

confectioner's sugar, to garnish

1 Line the bottom of the cake pan with wax paper. Arrange the lady fingers, sugar side out, around the sides of the pan.

2 Bring the milk and vanilla to a simmer in a medium saucepan over low heat. Whisk the egg yolks and sugar together in a bowl until pale. Remove the vanilla bean and whisk the milk mixture into the bowl. Rinse out the saucepan. Return the custard to the saucepan and stir over medium-low heat until the mixture is thick enough to coat the spoon (185°F/85°C). Pour through a wire sieve into a clean bowl.

3 Sprinkle the gelatin over ⅛ cup water in a small heatproof dish. Let stand for 5 minutes, until spongy. Place the dish in a frying pan of very hot water and stir until the gelatin dissolves. Stir into the custard and mix well. Place the bowl in a larger bowl of ice water and let stand, stirring often, until the custard is almost set.

4 Beat the cream just until soft peaks form. Fold the cream into the custard. Stir in half the raspberries. Carefully spoon into the lady finger-lined pan. Cover and refrigerate for at least 3 hours to set completely.

5 Invert the pan onto a platter to unmold. Arrange the remaining raspberries on top. Sprinkle with confectioner's sugar and serve chilled.

VARIATION

Chocolate Charlotte

Omit the vanilla and raspberries. Add 6oz (175g) bittersweet chocolate to the hot custard; whisk until smooth. Decorate with grated chocolate.

Rum and Chocolate Dacquoise

A dacquoise is made of crisp meringue disks layered with a filling. Serve it at a special meal

makes 4-6 servings

prep 1 hr, plus chilling
• cook 1 hr 30 mins

For the meringue

scant ½ cup **granulated sugar**

scant ½ cup **packed dark brown sugar**

3 large **egg whites**

For the filling

4oz (115g) **semisweet chocolate**, chopped

1 cup **mascarpone cheese**

2 tbsp **granulated sugar**

⅔ cup **heavy cream**

¾ cup toasted, skinned, and chopped **hazelnuts**

½ cup drained canned pitted **black cherries**

3 tbsp **dark rum**

confectioner's sugar, to garnish

1 Preheat the oven to 250°F (130°C). Draw three 7in (18cm) diameter circles on 2 pieces of parchment paper. Turn the papers upside down onto 2 baking sheets.

2 To make the meringue, mix the granulated and brown sugars together. Beat the egg whites in a bowl with an electric mixer until soft peaks form. Gradually beat in the sugars until the meringue is stiff and shiny. Using a metal icing spatula, spread the meringue evenly within the circles. Bake about 1½ hours, or until crisp and dry. Cool completely.

3 To make the filling, melt the chocolate in a heatproof bowl over a saucepan of simmering water. Beat the mascarpone and sugar together, then mix in the chocolate.

4 Whip the cream just until it holds its shape and fold into the mascarpone mixture. Fold in the hazelnuts, cherries, and rum.

5 Place a meringue round on a serving platter and spread with half of the filling. Repeat with another meringue and the filling, then the final meringue. Refrigerate for at least 30 minutes. Sift confectioner's sugar over the dacquoise and serve.

Classic Pavlova

Both Australia and New Zealand claims to have invented this meringue and fruit dessert, named after the Russian ballerina Anna Pavlova, who traveled the world in the early twentieth century

 makes 6–8 servings

 prep 15 mins plus cooling • cook 1¼ hrs

6 large **egg whites**, at room temperature

1 tsp **cider vinegar**

pinch of **salt**

1⅔ cups **sugar**

2 tsp **cornstarch**

1¼ cups **heavy cream**

6oz (170g) **strawberries**, hulled and sliced

2 **kiwi fruit**, peeled and sliced

4 **passion fruit**, cut in half

● **Prepare ahead** The meringue shell can be stored in an airtight container for up to 5 days.

1 **Preheat the oven** to 350°F (180°C). Line a baking sheet with wax paper. Beat the eggs and salt in a large bowl with an electric mixer until soft peaks form. One tablespoon at a time, beat in the sugar and beat until the whites are stiff and shiny. Towards the end, beat in the cornstarch.

2 **Spoon the meringue** onto the baking tray and spread into an 8in (20cm) round. Bake for 5 minutes. Reduce the oven temperature to 275°F (140°C) and bake about 1¼ hours, until crisp. Let cool on the baking sheet.

3 **Transfer the meringue** to a serving platter. Whip the cream until it forms stiff peaks. Spread over the meringue. Top with the strawberries, kiwi fruit, and the passion fruit pulp. Serve immediately.

VARIATIONS

Cinnamon Pavlova
Add 2 tbsp ground cinnamon with the cornstarch. Garnish with whipped cream and strawberries, or blackberries and sautéed apples.

Nutty Pavlova
Omit the vinegar and cornstarch. Fold ½ cup (2oz/55g) coarsely ground pistachio nuts or toasted, skinned hazelnuts into the stiffly beaten whites.

Brown Sugar Pavlova
Omit the vinegar and cornstarch. Substitute 1⅔ cups packed light brown sugar for the sugar.

Mocha Coffee Pavlova
Beat 3 tbsp cooled brewed espresso into the stiffly beaten whites. Drizzle with ¼ cup chocolate syrup and garnish with chocolate curls.

Brown Sugar Meringues

Brown sugar adds a lovely caramel flavour to the meringues

 makes 36 small meringues

prep 20 mins • cook 1 hr

4 large **egg whites**

1 cup packed **light brown sugar**

1 **Preheat the oven** to 250°F (130°C). Beat the egg whites in a bowl with an electric mixer until soft peaks form. Beat in the brown sugar, 2 tbsp at a time.

2 **Line 2 baking sheets** with wax paper. Using a heaping teaspoon for each, spoon the meringues, spaced about 1in (2.5cm) apart, on the baking sheet. Bake for 1 hour, or until they are crisp on the outside and slightly chewy inside.

● **Good with** whipped cream, as a filling sandwiched between the meringues, and drizzled with melted bittersweet chocolate.

> **CRISP MERINGUES**
> To make the meringues crisp, turn the oven off and leave them inside until completely cool.

Quindim

This sweet, creamy and very rich dessert is a popular party dish in Brazil

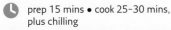

- makes 4 servings
- prep 15 mins • cook 25–30 mins, plus chilling
- four 4oz (120ml) ramekins

melted **butter**, for the ramekins

½ cup **sugar**, plus more for the molds

4 large **egg yolks**

¼ cup canned **coconut milk**

2 tbsp **desiccated coconut**

grated **fresh coconut**, toasted, to serve

● **Prepare ahead** The quindim can be refrigerated for up to 1 day before serving.

1 Preheat the oven to 350°F (180°C). Butter the insides of four 4oz (120ml) ramekins and coat with sugar, tapping out the excess.

2 Whisk the sugar and egg yolks until light and creamy. Add the coconut milk and desiccated coconut; mix well. Divide among the ramekins. Place the ramekins in a roasting pan and add enough hot water to come halfway up the sides.

3 Bake for about 25 minutes, until set. Remove from the pan and cool briefly. Run a knife around the inside of each ramekin to loosen the custard. Invert onto individual dessert plates. Refrigerate until chilled, about 3 hours. Serve chilled.

Lemon Meringue Roulade

This traditional filling is given a new twist in this impressive dessert

- makes 6–8 servings
- prep 30 mins • cook 15 mins
- 10½ x 15½in (27 x 39cm) jelly roll pan
- freeze for up to 2 months

2 tsp **cornstarch**

5 large **egg whites**

½ tsp **white wine vinegar**

1 cup plus 2 tbsp **sugar**

½ tsp **white wine vinegar**

½ tsp **pure vanilla extract**

1 cup **heavy cream**

1 cup store-bought **lemon curd**

confectioner's sugar, for sifting

1 Preheat the oven to 350°F (180°C). Line a 10½ x 15½in (27 x 39cm) pan with wax paper.

2 Dissolve the cornstarch in 2 tbsp water in a small bowl. Cook in microwave oven on High about 20 seconds, until boiling; set aside. Beat the egg whites and vinegar with an electric mixer until soft peaks form. Gradually beat in the sugar until the whites are stiff and shiny. Beat in the cornstarch mixture and vanilla.

3 Spread the mixture in the jelly roll pan. Bake about 15 minutes, until lightly browned. Let cool on a wire rack.

4 Meanwhile, whip the cream until stiff. Fold in the lemon curd.

5 Unmold the meringue on a another sheet of wax paper. Spread with the lemon cream. Starting at a long side, roll up the meringue. Transfer to a serving platter. Cover and refrigerate until serving. Sift confectioner's sugar over the roulade and serve.

Quarkspeise

Easy to make, this simple dessert has a soft texture and can be served with your favorite seasonal fruits

🍴 makes 4 servings

🕐 prep 15 mins, plus chilling

1¼ cups **heavy cream**

8oz (225g) **farmer's cheese**

2 tbsp **sugar**

2 large **egg whites**

6oz (168g) **raspberries**

3 tbsp **confectioner's sugar**

fresh **berries**, to serve

● **Prepare ahead** The dessert must be made at least 1 day before serving. Once made, it can be refrigerated for up to 3 days.

1 Whisk the heavy cream and farmer's cheese together in a bowl. Add the confectioner's sugar and whisk until smooth.

2 Beat the egg whites until stiff peaks form. Fold into the cheese mixture.

3 Line a sieve with cheesecloth and place over a bowl. Spoon the cheese mixture into the sieve and spread evenly with the back of a spoon, making sure there are no air pockets. Fold the cheesecloth over the top. Refrigerate and drain overnight.

4 Purée the raspberries and confectioner's sugar together in a blender. Rub through a fine sieve to remove the seeds. Turn the cheese mixture out onto a serving platter and remove the cheesecloth. Serve with the raspberry sauce and berries.

> **CHEESECLOTH**
>
> The tiny holes in the cheesecloth allow juices to drain slowly. It is readily available in packages at supermarkets, kitchen shops, and hardware stores.

Floating Islands

In this delicious French dessert, *Iles Flottantes*, meringues poached in milk float on top of vanilla-flavored custard

🍴 makes 4 servings

🕐 prep 15 mins, plus standing
• cook 30 mins

For the custard

2 tsp **cornstarch**

1¼ cups **whole milk**

1 cup **heavy cream**

½ **sugar**

4 large **egg yolks**

1 tsp **pure vanilla extract**

For the meringue

1 cup **whole milk**

3 large **egg whites**

¾ cup **sugar**

1oz (30g) **bittersweet chocolate**, for serving

1 To make the custard, dissolve the cornstarch in ¼ cup milk in a large saucepan. Add the remaining milk, the cream, and sugar and bring to a simmer over medium heat, stirring often.

2 Whisk the egg yolks in a bowl and whisk in the hot milk mixture. Return to the saucepan and stir over medium heat, cooking just until the custard coats the back of a wooden spoon. Do not boil. Remove from the heat and stir in the vanilla.

3 Strain the custard into a bowl. Top with a piece of plastic wrap pressed directly on the surface of the custard and pierce a few slits in the wrap. Let cool, then refrigerate at least 2 hours, until chilled.

4 To make the meringues, bring the milk and 1¼ cups water to a boil in a large frying pan over high heat. Reduce the heat to very low so it is below a simmer.

5 Beat the egg whites until they form soft peaks. Gradually beat in the sugar until the peaks are stiff and glossy. Using two large soup spoons, shape ovals of the meringue and carefully transfer them to the hot milk mixture. Do not add more than 4 meringues at once, as they will expand. Cook for 1 minute, then turn and cook for 30 seconds more, just until set. Using a slotted spoon, transfer to a clean kitchen towel to drain. Repeat with the remaining meringue. Let cool.

6 Divide the custard among shallow bowls and top with the meringues. Grate the chocolate over each and serve immediately.

Chocolate Bavarian Creams

These rich chocolate puddings get their light texture from whipped cream

- makes 4 servings
- prep 30 mins, plus cooling • cook 20 mins
- 4 x 6oz (180ml) ramekins

1 cup **whole milk**

½ cup **sugar**

3 large **egg yolks**

5oz (140g) **bittersweet chocolate**, finely chopped

1½ tsp unflavored **gelatin powder**

⅔ cup **heavy cream**

whipped cream or crème anglaise, to serve

grated **bittersweet chocolate**, to serve

1 Lightly oil four 6oz (180ml) ramekins. Heat the milk in a small saucepan over low heat until it simmers. Whisk the sugar and egg yolks together, and add a little of the hot milk. Stir the egg mixture into the saucepan. Stir constantly with a wooden spoon until the custard is thick enough to coat the spoon (185°F /85°C on an instant-read thermometer). Do not boil.

2 Strain through a wire sieve into a bowl. Add the chocolate, let stand a few minutes, then stir until melted.

3 Sprinkle the gelatin over 3 tbsp cold water in a small heatproof bowl. Let stand 5 minutes, until spongy. Place the bowl in a small frying pan of very hot water and stir until the gelatin is dissolved. Stir into the chocolate mixture.

4 Refrigerate, stirring occasionally, until cool and on the verge of setting. Lightly whip the cream just until soft peaks form. Do not overbeat. Fold the cream into the chocolate mixture and pour into the ramekins. Cover each with plastic wrap and refrigerate until set, at least 2 hours.

5 Dip each ramekin very briefly in very hot water and invert creams onto plates. Garnish with whipped cream and grated chocolate and serve chilled.

● **Good with** whipped cream or crème anglaise flavoured with grated orange zest.

Sweet Lassi

There is no better way of cooling down a fiery curry than with a tall glass of chilled lassi

- makes 4 servings
- prep 5 mins

2 cups **plain yogurt**

1¼ cups **whole milk**

1 tbsp **superfine sugar**

few drops of **rose water**

1 cup **crushed ice**

a pinch of **ground cardamom**, to serve

1 Whisk the yogurt, milk, sugar, and rose water together until evenly combined and foamy. (Or, process the ingredients in a blender until foamy.)

2 Divide the crushed ice among 4 tall glasses, and pour in equal amounts of the lassi. Sprinkle each with a little ground cardamom and serve at once.

VARIATIONS

Salted Lassi
Omit the rose water and sugar. Rub the rim of each glass with a wedge of lemon or lime and dip in coarse salt until coated. Pour in the drink and serve without straws.

Fruit Lassi
Part or all of the milk can be replaced with a tropical fruit juice such as mango or pineapple. Instead of rose water, use a few drops of vanilla or almond essence.

Classic Crème Brûlée

A classic dessert; its name is French for "burnt cream"

 makes 6 servings

 prep 20 mins, plus standing • cook 40 mins

 six 6oz (175g) ramekins

2 cups **heavy cream**

1 **vanilla pod**, split in half lengthwise

5 large **egg yolks**

¼ cup **granulated sugar**

¼ cup **demerara sugar**, or use more granulated sugar

● **Prepare ahead** The custards, without the topping, can be covered and refrigerated for up to 2 days.

1 Preheat the oven to 275°F (140°C). Heat the cream and vanilla bean in a saucepan over low heat until simmering. Remove from the heat and let stand for 1 hour.

2 Using the tip of a knife, scrape the seeds from the vanilla bean into the cream. Discard the bean or save for another use. Whisk the egg yolks and granulated sugar together in a bowl. Whisk in the cream mixture. Strain through a wire sieve into a glass measuring cup. Pour equal amounts into six 6oz (175ml) ramekins. Place the ramekins in a roasting pan and add enough hot water to come halfway up the sides.

3 Bake until the custards are barely set, about 40 minutes. Remove the ramekins from the pan and cool. Cover with plastic wrap and chill in the refrigerator at least 2 hours.

4 To serve, position a broiler rack 6in (15cm) from the source of heat and preheat the broiler. Sprinkle 2 tsp demerara sugar evenly over the top of each custard. Broil until the sugar caramelizes. Serve immediately.

VARIATIONS

Fruit Brûlée

Put a spoonful of soft berries or cooked fruit (apricots, rhubarb) in the bottom of each ramekin before adding the custard.

Chocolate Brûlée

Omit the vanilla. Add 3½oz (100g) grated white or dark chocolate to the hot milk and stir until melted.

Ginger Brûlée

Replace the vanilla pod with 3 tbsp minced stem ginger in syrup.

Paskha

This Easter dish from Russia is traditionally made in a tall wooden container, but a new flowerpot is used here

 makes 4 servings

 prep 40 mins, plus draining

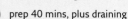 clean new 4in (10cm) diameter flowerpot, cheesecloth

⅓ cup **heavy cream**

1 **vanilla pod**, split lengthwise

1 large **egg yolk**

2 tbsp **superfine sugar**

12oz (350g) **farmer's cheese** or ricotta

4 tbsp **butter**, softened

⅓ cup chopped **blanched almonds**

¼ cup chopped **mixed candied peel**

1½oz (45g) **bittersweet chocolate**, chopped

slivered almonds, for garnish

strips of **candied orange** or lemon **peel**, for garnish

1 Place the cream in a small saucepan. Scrape the seeds from the vanilla bean into the cream and cook over low heat until hot. Whisk the egg yolk and sugar together in a bowl, then whisk in the hot cream. Let cool.

2 Beat the cheese and butter together, then beat in the cream mixture. Stir in the almonds, candied peel, and chocolate.

3 Line the flowerpot with a double thickness of rinsed and squeezed dry cheesecloth. Put the mixture into the lined mold. Place the pot on a wire rack set over a dish. Refrigerate to drain the whey for at least 1 and up to 3 days.

4 When ready to serve, turn the pashka out on to a serving dish and remove the cheesecloth. Decorate with the almonds and candied peel and serve chilled.

Lemon and Praline Meringues

These individual cakes should be assembled at the last minute

 makes 6 servings

prep 35 mins • cook 1½ hrs

For the meringues

3 large egg whites

pinch of salt

¾ cup sugar

For the praline

vegetable oil, for the baking sheet

⅓ cup sugar

½ cup whole blanched almonds

pinch of cream of tartar

For the filling

⅔ cup heavy cream

3 tbsp store-bought lemon curd

3oz (85g) bittersweet chocolate, chopped

● **Prepare ahead** Make the meringues and praline a day in advance, stored at room temperature.

1 Preheat the oven to 250°F (130°C). Line a large baking sheet with parchment paper.

2 To make the meringues, beat the egg whites and salt with an electric mixer until soft peaks form. Gradually beat in the sugar until the meringue is stiff and glossy. Transfer to a pastry bag fitted with a ¼in (6mm) star tip. Pipe the meringue on the baking sheet into six 4in (10cm) rounds. Bake for 1½ hours, or until hard and crisp.

3 Meanwhile, to make the praline, oil another baking sheet. Combine the sugar, almonds, and cream of tartar in a heavy-bottomed saucepan. Cook over low heat, stirring constantly, until the sugar dissolves. Boil until the syrup is golden. Pour onto the baking sheet. Let stand until cool, and chop the praline.

4 When ready to serve, whip the cream until soft peaks form. Fold in the lemon curd. Melt the chocolate in a heatproof bowl set over a saucepan pan of gently simmering water. Spread each meringue with melted chocolate, and let set. Top with the lemon cream and sprinkle with praline. Serve immediately with a little chocolate. Allow to set, then pile the lemon curd cream on top, sprinkle with praline and serve.

Chocolate Marquise

This very rich chocolate mousse has a velvety texture and is delicious served with tart summer berries

 makes 10-12 servings

prep 15 mins

9 x 5in (23 x 13cm) loaf pan

freeze for up to 3 months

14oz (400g) bittersweet chocolate, chopped

¾ cup plus 2 tbsp sugar

12 tbsp butter

¼ cup cocoa powder

6 large egg yolks

2 cups heavy cream

raspberries, sliced strawberries, and/or stemmed red currants, to serve

1 Line a 9 x 5in (23 x 13cm) loaf pan with plastic wrap. Melt the chocolate, sugar, butter, and cocoa in a medium saucepan over very low heat, stirring often.

2 Whisk the egg yolks in a bowl. Whisk in the chocolate mixture. Let cool. Beat the cream in a chilled bowl until soft peaks form. Fold into the chocolate mixture.

3 Pour into the loaf pan and smooth the top. Cover with plastic wrap and refrigerate at least 2 hours, until chilled and set. Invert onto a serving platter and remove the plastic wrap. Using a knife dipped into hot water, cut into slices. Serve, with the raspberries.

● **Good with** a big bowl of mixed berries and a glass of dessert wine.

● **VARIATION**

Individual Chocolate Marquises

You can make pretty individual desserts by spooning the mixture into individual ramekins, and chilling to set. Then pipe whipped cream on top, decorate with a few raspberries, dust with cocoa powder, and serve.

Chocolate

Dark and decadent, luscious, and rich, chocolate is universally adored, and makes undeniably tempting desserts. The impressive-looking ultimate chocolate cake (p397)—with its delicious combination of dark and milk chocolate ganache for filling and icing, and the easy-to-make milk and plain chocolate curls on top—is surprisingly easy to make.

Choosing Chocolate

There is a staggering selection of chocolate available today, including familiar supermarket brands, organically grown, and those made from Fair Trade sources.

Choosing chocolate first depends on whether it is for eating or for cooking. If it is for eating, the solution is simple: buy what you're in the mood for. Bear in mind, however, that dark chocolate will have fewer, if any, additional sweeteners, flavors, or dairy elements that often add the allure to fancy boxes of chocolate. For cooking, bittersweet chocolate is preferred because of its purity, making

it predictable, and not susceptible to uncontrolled variables (such as dairy or cocoa butter replacements) when cooked.

Chocolate is made in countless flavors, styles, and qualities. The bitterness of chocolate is determined by the quantity of cacao solids (including cocoa butter) against the additives, such as sugar, milk, and vanilla. A high-quality baking chocolate could contain at least 70 percent cacao solids. High-quality chocolate will not shatter, but makes a distinctive, clean snap when broken, and will melt quickly in warmth of your hand. The faster

it melts, the higher the cocoa butter content, and the smoother the texture.

CHOCOLATE FACTS

- All chocolate starts with the cocoa bean *Thobroma cacao*, which translates as "food of the gods."

- Spanish conquistadors introduced chocolate to Europe from Mexico in the 15th century. In fact, the word "chocolate" comes from the *xocolatl*, Aztec for "bitter water," which was an unsweetened chocolate drink spiced with chile.

- The first chocolate bars were produced in England in the 19th century.

- Couverture chocolate, available with cocoa solids ranging from 32–85 percent, is the type of chocolate favored by professional bakers, because of the smooth way it melts and its rich flavor. You can find it in supermarkets and gourmet food shops.

- Cocoa powder is available unsweetened and sweetened, and it is the unsweetened variety that adds an intense chocolate hit to baked goods. Sweetened cocoa powder is best used to flavor milk.

- Never let water come into contact with melted chocolate. The merest drip of water will cause the chocolate to separate and become firm, grainy, and unusable. When melting chocolate, use a bowl that fits snugly over the pan to prevent any water or steam from coming into contact with the chocolate.

- Always use paper piping bags when piping melted chocolate. They are much better to use because they are small and easy to handle, and there is no piping nozzle to clog (which happens in a normal piping bag since the chocolate sets so quickly).

Plus 70 percent Chocolate
Dark and bitter-tasting, any chocolate with more than 70 percent cacao solids listed on the label is best to use for cooking, rather than eating.

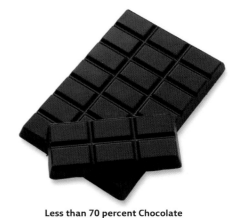

Less than 70 percent Chocolate
This category contains both bittersweet and semisweet choices. Many bakers prefer cooking with chocolate averaging 60 percent cacao.

Milk Chocolate
Milk chocolate tastes milder than dark chocolate because it contains extra sugar and milk powder, so is usually saved for eating straight from the foil, but it also makes a great mousse.

White Chocolate
Although not a true chocolate, this is still popular. It is usually made with cocoa butter, as well as sugar, milk, and vanilla. Excellent for fondues, and for flavoring tarts and cookies.

Chop

Put the chocolate on a cutting board. Work the blade of a chef's knife backward and forward over the chocolate until it is as fine or coarse as desired.

Grate

Hold a piece of chocolate firmly against a grater, press down, and rub it down against the holes. Take the piece of chocolate to the top of the grater and repeat until you have as much grated chocolate as required.

Melt

Chop the chocolate into even-sized pieces. Place them in a dry, heatproof bowl over a pan of hot water: the bottom of the bowl must not touch the water. When the chocolate starts to melt, stir until it is smooth.

Shave

Using a vegetable peeler, slowly shave the side of a chocolate bar. The curls, or shavings, will fall from the block. Refrigerate until required.

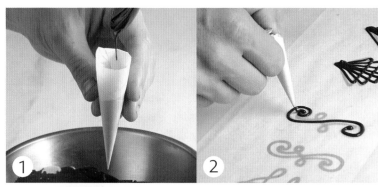

Pipe Decorations

1 Draw simple designs on a piece of paper, then tape a piece of wax paper on top. Make a couple of small paper piping bags. Spoon the melted chocolate into a paper piping bag, then fold over the top to seal. Keep the rest of the chocolate warm.

2 Using light pressure, pipe the melted chocolate on to the paper, following the design, letting the chocolate fall evenly from the tip without forcing it. Let cool at room temperature, or refrigerate. Once set, use a metal spatula to carefully lift from the paper.

Make Ganache

1 Melt the chocolate in a bowl over a pan of simmering water. Remove the pan from the heat and pour in warm cream, stirring together. The cream should not be too hot or it might cause the chocolate to seize and become grainy in texture.

2 Continue beating until the 2 ingredients are thoroughly blended. Thorough beating will cause the mixture to cool to a smooth glossy finish.

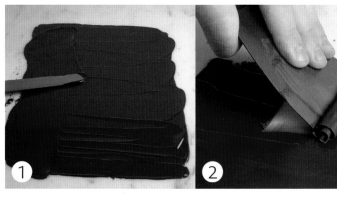

Make Curls

1 Pour cooled, melted chocolate on to a cold work surface. Using a flexible metal spatula, spread the chocolate as thinly as possible, ideally only 1⁄16in (1.5mm) thick, without leaving any holes. If the chocolate is too thick, it will not roll.

2 When the chocolate has cooled to the point of setting, mark it in parallel lines the width of a metal scraper. Holding the scraper at 45 degrees, with the blade firmly against the surface, gently push the scraper away from you to produce the curl.

Chocolate

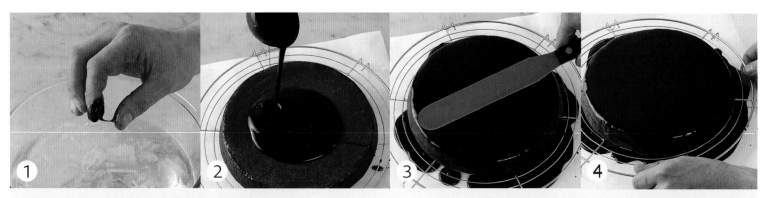

Make Professional Glossy Icing

1 **Make a light, colorless** sugar syrup with 5fl oz (150ml) water with 5oz (150g) sugar. Stir in 10oz (300g) finely chopped dark chocolate until smooth. Heat the mixture to 225°F (120°C). To test, dip your fingers in iced water, then the chocolate, and pull apart—the mixture should form a "thread."

2 **Meanwhile, brush** the cake with 3½oz (100g) apricot jam melted with 4 tbsp water. When the chocolate has reached the correct temperature, remove the pan from the heat and put it on a towel; tap the pan to knock out any air bubbles. Ladle warm icing on to the center of the cake.

3 **Use a warmed metal** spatula to smooth out the icing, using a minimum of strokes, and allowing the excess to flow off the cake onto a sheet of wax paper underneath.

4 **Without disturbing** the cake, tap the rack gently to ensure the icing is even and free of air bubbles. Let stand for 5–10 minutes before moving.

Decadent Chocolate Desserts

Chocolate Mousse
This ultimate chocolate sensation is best when made with dark chocolate
🕒 40 mins   **page 385**

White Chocolate and Mascarpone Tarts
White chocolate makes a smooth filling
🕒 45 mins   **page 430**

Chocolate Bavarian Creams
These individual puddings are custards, enriched with cream and set with gelatin
🕒 50 mins   **page 391**

Chocolate-dipped Fruits
Whatever the season, this decadent treat is perfect to serve with after-dinner drinks
🕒 30 mins   **page 470**

Black Forest Gâteau
This rich chocolate and cherry cake is a real crowd pleaser
🕒 1 hr 35 mins   **page 414**

Chocolate Chiffon Pie
The smooth, mousse-like chocolate filling contrasts with the crunchy crumb crust
🕒 45 mins   **page 428**

Double-chocolate Ice Cream
For chocolate lovers, this dark chocolate ice cream contains white chocolate chips
🕒 35–40 mins   **page 405**

Chocolate Marquise
This very rich chocolate pudding has a velvety texture and is delicious served with berries
🕒 15 mins   **page 393**

VERSATILE CHOCOLATE

Easy-to-make chocolate ganache and chocolate curls transform a basic chocolate cake into an extra-special treat.

Milk Chocolate Curls (p395)

Plain Chocolate Curls (p395)

Plain Chocolate Ganache Icing (p395)

Rich Chocolate Sponge Cake (see Black Forest Gâteau sponge recipe on p414)

Milk Chocolate Ganache Filling (p395)

Crème Caramel

Be sure to make this a few hours before serving to chill the custards and make them easier to remove from the ramekins

- makes 4 servings
- prep 20 mins, plus chilling • cook 35–40 mins
- four 7fl oz (200ml) ramekins

1¼ cups sugar

2¼ cups whole milk

1 vanilla bean, split lengthwise

4 large eggs plus 4 large egg yolks

1 Preheat the oven to 325°F (160°C). Pour boiling water into four 7oz (200ml) ramekins and set aside. Heat 1 cup of the sugar and 3 tbsp cold water in a heavy saucepan over a medium heat, stirring until the sugar dissolves. Boil without stirring, brushing down the crystals that form on the side of the pan with a pastry brush dipped in cold water, and swirling the pan by its handle, for about 5 minutes, or until the syrup has turned into a deep amber caramel.

2 Just before the caramel is done, empty the ramekins. Divide the caramel among the warmed ramekins, swirling each so that the caramel comes halfway up the sides.

3 Heat the milk and vanilla bean halves over medium heat together until simmering. Using the tip of a knife, scrape the vanilla seeds from the bean halves into the milk and discard the halves.

4 Whisk the eggs, egg yolks, and remaining ¼ cup sugar together in a large bowl. Gradually whisk in the hot milk. Pour into the ramekins. Place the ramekins in a roasting pan and add enough hot water to come halfway up the sides of the ramekins. Bake for 25–30 minutes, or until the custards are just set in the center. Remove from the pan. Cool to room temperature. Cover and refrigerate until chilled, at least 3 hours.

5 One at a time, gently pull the edges of the custard away from the sides of the ramekin using a fingertip. Place a serving plate over the top of the ramekin and invert on to the plate. Serve chilled.

VARIATION

Ginger Crème Caramel

Add 2 tbsp chopped drained stem ginger in syrup to the custard when heating the milk. Substitute ¼ cup stem ginger syrup for the sugar.

Tiramisu

One of Italy's favorite desserts, this luscious dessert gets its name, which means "pick-me-up," from the espresso

- makes 6 servings
- prep 20 mins, plus cooling and at least 4 hrs chilling

½ cup cold brewed espresso or French roast coffee

⅓ cup coffee-flavored liqueur

12oz (350g) mascarpone cheese

3 tbsp superfine sugar

1½ cups heavy cream

about 14 Italian ladyfingers (savoiardi)

cocoa powder and coarsely grated semisweet chocolate, to decorate

● **Prepare ahead** The dish can be assembled early on the day of serving.

1 Mix the coffee and liqueur together in a shallow, wide bowl and set aside.

2 Mix the mascarpone and sugar in a bowl until the sugar dissolves. Whip the cream in another bowl until it holds its shape, then fold it into the mascarpone mixture. Put a few spoonfuls of the mascarpone mixture in the bottom of a serving dish.

3 Dip and turn one ladyfinger in the coffee mixture until just moistened, then place it on top of the mascarpone in the dish; repeat with 6 more ladyfingers, placing them side by side. Cover with half the remaining mascarpone mixture. Dip and layer the remaining ladyfingers. Top with the remaining mascarpone and smooth the surface. Cover the bowl with plastic wrap and refrigerate for at least 4 hours.

4 Just before serving sprinkle the top with cocoa powder and grated chocolate.

Vanilla Cheesecake

This rich yet light cheesecake is guaranteed to be a crowd pleaser

- makes 10–12 servings
- prep 20 mins, plus standing and 6 hrs chilling • cook 50 mins
- 9in (23cm) springform pan

4 tbsp **butter**, plus more for the pan

1½ cups crushed **graham crackers**

1 cup plus 1 tbsp **sugar**

1½lb (675g) **cream cheese** (not reduced fat) at room temperature

4 large **eggs**, separated

1 tsp pure **vanilla extract**

one 16oz container **sour cream**

kiwi fruit, thinly sliced, to garnish

● **Prepare ahead** The crust can be assembled a day in advance and refrigerated until required.

1 Preheat the oven to 350°F (180°C). Lightly butter the bottom and side of a 9in (23cm) springform pan.

2 To make the crust, melt the butter in a medium saucepan over medium heat. Add the graham cracker crumbs and 1 tbsp sugar and mix well. Press the crumbs into the bottom and 1in (2.5cm) up the sides of the springform pan.

3 Combine the cream cheese, egg yolks, ¾ cup of the sugar, and the vanilla in a bowl and mix with an electric mixer on medium speed until smooth. In a separate bowl, using clean beaters, beat the egg whites until stiff. Fold the egg whites into the cream cheese mixture. Pour into the pan and smooth the top.

4 Bake for 45 minutes, or until the sides have risen and are beginning to brown. Transfer to a wire rack and let cool for 10 minutes.

5 Meanwhile, increase the oven temperature to 400°F (200°C). Whisk the sour cream and remaining ¼ cup sugar in a bowl. Pour over the cheesecake and smooth the top. Return the cheesecake to the oven and bake for 10 minutes more, until the topping looks set around the edges. Cool completely on a wire rack. Cover and refrigerate for at least 6 hours. Remove the sides of the pan, garnish with the kiwi fruit, and serve chilled, cutting the cheesecake with a wet knife.

● **Good with** sliced strawberries or other seasonal berries, sprinkled with a little confectioner's sugar.

Panna Cotta with Strawberry Purée

Seasonal fruits complement this creamy Italian dessert

- makes 4 servings
- prep 5 mins, plus at least 3 hrs chilling
- 4 individual ramekins or custard cups

2 tbsp **water**

1½ tsp **unflavored gelatin powder**

1¼ cups **heavy cream**

3–4 tbsp **superfine sugar**

1 tsp **vanilla essence**

8oz (250g) **strawberries**, hulled, plus 4 whole **strawberries** for garnish

● **Prepare ahead** The panna cottas can be made a day in advance and refrigerated.

1 Pour the water into a small heatproof bowl and sprinkle in the gelatin. Let stand for 3–5 minutes until the gelatin softens and looks spongy. Bring 1in (2.5cm) water to a boil in a medium saucepan, then remove from heat. Set the bowl of gelatin in the pan, and let stand, stirring often until dissolved.

2 Combine the cream and 2 tbsp sugar in another saucepan and slowly bring to a simmer over medium heat, stirring to dissolve the sugar. Turn off the heat and stir in the vanilla. Add the gelatin mixture and stir well. Carefully ladle the cream into the ramekins. Cool completely. Cover each with plastic wrap and chill at least 3 hours until set.

3 Meanwhile, purée the berries with 1–2 tbsp of the remaining sugar to taste in a blender or food processor, then cover and set aside until ready to serve.

4 To serve, quickly dip the base of each ramekin in hot water, and dry the ramekin. Working with one ramekin at a time, place a serving plate on top and invert, giving a gentle shake. Lift and remove the ramekin. Spoon the purée around each panna cotta and decorate with whole strawberries.

● **Good with** fresh fruit salad instead of the berry purée, or purée mango pulp in place of berries.

Lemon Poppy Seed Cheesecake with Berry Purée

A light alternative to cheesecake, especially good for a lunchtime dessert

- makes 8-10 servings
- prep 20 mins • cook 1½ hrs, plus cooling
- 9in (23cm) springform pan
- cake needs to chill for at least 5 hours before serving
- freeze the cheesecake and sauce for up to 3 months

2 lemons

10oz (300g) cottage cheese

10oz (300g) cream cheese, softened

1 cup sour cream

1 cup granulated sugar

3 tbsp cornstarch

4 large eggs, at room temperature

1½ tbsp poppy seeds

confectioner's sugar, for dusting

strawberries and raspberries, for garnish

For the berry purée

8oz (250g) hulled and sliced strawberries

⅓ cup granulated sugar

1 Preheat the oven to 300°F (150°C). Butter a 9in (23cm) springform pan. Grate the zest from the lemons and squeeze 4 tbsp lemon juice. Process the cottage cheese, cream cheese, sour cream, sugar, cornstarch, and 3 tbsp lemon juice in a food processor until smooth. Add the eggs and process to combine. Stir in the poppy seeds and transfer to the pan.

2 Bake for 1½ hours, or until the sides of the cheesecake are beginning to brown.

3 To make the berry sauce, purée the berries, sugar, and remaining 1 tbsp lemon juice in a food processor. Cover and refrigerate.

4 Transfer the cheesecake to a wire cake pan. Run a knife around the inside of the pan. Cool completely in the pan. Cover and refrigerate at least 5 hours, until chilled. Remove the sides of the pan, slice, and serve, with the berry purée.

Chocolate Rice Pudding

Based on the Portuguese rice pudding known as *arroz doce*, this version gets extra flair from chocolate

- makes 6-8 servings
- prep 10 mins • cook 40 mins

2½ cups **Arborio** or other short-grain rice

1 tsp **salt**

3¾ cups **whole milk**

1 tbsp **cocoa powder**

1½ cups **sugar**

6 large **egg yolks**

4 tbsp grated **bittersweet chocolate**

1 Bring 2 quarts (2 liters) water to a boil in a large saucepan. Add the rice and salt and cover. Simmer over low heat for 10 minutes. Drain.

2 Place the milk in a medium saucepan and whisk in the cocoa.

Bring to a boil over medium heat. Stir in the rice and reduce the heat. Simmer, uncovered, for 30 minutes, or until the rice is soft. Stir in the sugar. Quickly beat in the egg yolks. Return to low heat and stir constantly until the pudding is very hot but not boiling.

3 Divide the pudding among custard cups. Cover with plastic wrap and refrigerate at least 2 hours. Grate chocolate over each pudding.

VARIATION

Arroz Doce with Lemon and Cinnamon

Omit the cocoa and chocolate. In step 2, add 1 cinnamon stick and the zest of 1 lemon, removed with a vegetable peeler, to the milk. When the rice is soft, discard the cinnamon and lemon zest. Sprinkle each serving with ground cinnamon.

Vanilla Custards

Cherries give a filip to creamy, vanilla-scented custards

- makes 4 servings
- prep 10 mins, plus standing • cook 40 mins
- four 6oz (165ml) ramekins

1¼ cups **heavy cream**

½ cup **whole milk**

1 **vanilla bean**, split lengthwise

4 large **egg yolks**

3 tbsp **honey**

For the compote

½ cup **cherry preserves**

2 tbsp **kirsch** or brandy

1 **Preheat the oven** to 325°F (160°F). Bring the cream, milk, and vanilla bean to a simmer over low heat. Remove from the heat and let stand for 30 minutes. Discard the vanilla bean.

2 **Whisk the egg yolks** and honey together until pale and creamy. Whisk in the hot cream mixture. Pour into the ramekins.

3 **Place the ramekins** in a roasting pan and add hot water to come halfway up the sides. Cover the pan loosely with aluminum foil. Bake for 25 minutes, or until barely set. Remove from the pan and cool. Cover and refrigerate for 4 hours.

4 **For the compote**, warm the cherry preserves and the kirsch. Serve the chilled custards topped with a some of the cherry mixture.

Buttermilk Panna Cotta

This custardy dessert from Piedmonte in Italy translates as "cooked cream" although the cream is barely heated

- makes 4 servings
- prep 30 mins, plus setting • cook 5 mins
- low GI
- four 7oz (196ml) ramekins

For the panna cotta

2½ tsp **unflavored powdered gelatin**

1 cup **heavy cream**

½ cup **sugar**

1 tsp **pure vanilla extract**

2 cups **buttermilk**

2 tbsp chopped **pistachios**

For the sauce

8oz (225g) **strawberries**, halved

3 tbsp **maple syrup**

3 tbsp fresh **orange** juice

● **Prepare ahead** The panna cotta and sauce can be refrigerated up to 1 day before serving.

1 **To make the panna cotta**, sprinkle the gelatin over ½ cup of the heavy cream in a small bowl. Let stand for 5 minutes, or until spongy. Place the bowl in a small frying pan of simmering water. Stir until the gelatin is completely dissolved.

2 **Meanwhile**, heat the rest of the cream and the sugar in a small saucepan over low heat until the sugar is dissolved. Remove from the heat. Stir in the gelatin and vanilla. Cool slightly, then stir in the buttermilk.

3 **Rinse the** insides of 4 ramekins with cold water. Divide the cream mixture among the ramekins. Cover with plastic wrap and refrigerate at least 3 hours, until set.

4 **To make the sauce**, simmer the strawberries, maple syrup, and orange juice for 5 minutes. Transfer to a blender and purée. Let cool. Refrigerate at least 1 hour. Turn the panna cottas out onto plates, and top with the sauce and pistachios.

> **MELTING GELATIN**
> Stir the gelatin constantly while it is being heated to be sure that it is completely melted.

Strawberry Cheesecake

This no-bake cheesecake takes very little time to make

- makes 8 servings
- prep 15 mins, plus chilling
- 8in (20cm) springform pan

3½oz (100g) **bittersweet chocolate**, chopped

3 tbsp **butter**

1¼ cups **graham cracker crumbs**

9oz (250g) **mascarpone**

grated zest and juice of 2 **limes**

8oz (225g) **strawberries**

3 tbsp **confectioner's sugar**, plus more for sifting

● **Prepare ahead** The cheesecake can be refrigerated for up to 24 hours.

1 **Melt the chocolate** and butter in a small saucepan over low heat. Stir in the cracker crumbs. Press firmly and evenly into the springform pan.

2 **Mash the mascarpone** in a bowl with the lime zest and juice. Mix in the confectioner's sugar. Spread in the pan. Refrigerate for at least 1 hour to chill and set.

3 **Arrange the** strawberries over the cheesecake. Sift confectioner's sugar over the top. Remove the sides of the pan, slice into wedges, and serve chilled.

Chocolate Milk Shake "Float"

For the best flavor, use your favorite chocolate to make your milk shake

- 🍴 makes 2 servings
- 🕐 prep 8–10 mins

2oz (55g) **semisweet chocolate**, finely chopped

⅓ cup **boiling water**

4 scoops **chocolate ice cream**

1 cup **whole milk**, as needed

2 scoops **vanilla ice cream**

shaved **chocolate**, for garnish

1 Combine the chopped chocolate and boiling water in a blender, and process until the chocolate is melted.

2 Add the chocolate ice cream and about three-quarters of the milk. Process until smooth, adding enough milk to give the milk shake the desired consistency.

3 Pour into 2 glasses. Top each with a scoop of vanilla ice cream. Sprinkle with chocolate and serve.

Fruit Mousse

Make this delicious and versatile dessert with your favorite summer berries

- 🍴 makes 6 servings
- 🕐 prep 40 mins, plus chilling
- 🍲 6 dessert glasses

2 large **eggs**, separated

⅓ cup **sugar**

¼ cup **whole milk**

8oz (225g) **raspberries** and/or **blackberries**

3 tsp **unflavored gelatin**

1¼ cups **heavy cream**

● **Prepare ahead** The mousse can be refrigerated for up to 3 days before serving.

1 Whisk the egg yolks, sugar, and milk in a saucepan. Stir with a wooden spoon over low heat until slightly thickened, but do not boil. Remove from the heat.

2 Purée the berries in a blender. Strain through a wire sieve into a large bowl to remove the seeds. Stir into the yolk mixture.

3 Sprinkle the gelatin over 2 tbsp of cold water in a small bowl. Let stand 5 minutes, or until spongy. Place in a shallow pan of barely simmering water and stir until the gelatin has dissolved. Remove from the heat and let cool until tepid.

4 Slowly stir the gelatin into the berry mixture. Beat the egg whites until soft peaks form. Whip the cream in a chilled bowl until soft peaks form. Fold the whipped cream, then the egg whites, into the fruit mixture. Divide among the dessert glasses and cover with plastic wrap.

5 Refrigerate for at least 4 hours or until set. Serve chilled.

● **Good with** a garnish of fresh berries and perhaps a dollop of whipped cream.

Strawberry Semifreddo

This is Italian ice cream with a twist; texture and sweetness are added with crushed meringues

- makes 6–8 servings
- prep 20 mins, plus freezing
- 8in (20cm) springform pan, parchment paper
- freeze for up to 3 months

8 **strawberries**, hulled, plus more whole strawberries to decorate

1 cup **heavy cream**

½ cup **confectioner's sugar**

4oz (115g) **plain meringue cookies**, coarsely crushed

3 tbsp **raspberry-flavored liqueur**

For the coulis

8oz (225g) **strawberries**, hulled

1–2 tsp fresh **lemon** juice, brandy, balsamic vinegar

⅓ cup **confectioner's sugar**, as needed

● **Prepare ahead** Freeze the semifreddo for at least 6 hours. The coulis can be refrigerated for up to 3 days.

1 **Lightly brush the** springform pan with vegetable oil. Line the bottom with with parchment paper.

2 **Purée the strawberries** in a blender or food processor. Whip the cream with the confectioner's sugar just until soft peaks form. Fold into the strawberry purée, then fold in the crushed meringues and liqueur. Spread the mixture evenly in the pan. Cover and freeze for at least 6 hours or overnight.

3 **Meanwhile, make the** strawberry coulis. Purée the strawberries, then strain through a fine wire sieve to remove the seeds. Stir in the lemon juice, then the sugar, adding more sugar if needed.

4 **Just before serving**, remove the sides of the springform. Invert onto a platter and peel off the paper. Cut into slices, dipping a sharp knife into hot water between slices. Transfer each slice to a plate. Spoon the coulis around each serving and garnish each with a whole strawberry. Serve chilled.

● **Leftovers** can be refrozen for up to 3 months.

Chocolate and Hazelnut Parfaits

The metal rings needed for these smooth, creamy frozen desserts are now available at most kitchenware stores

- makes 4 servings
- prep 40 mins, plus chilling
- four 3¼in (8cm) metal rings

5½oz (150g) **bittersweet chocolate**, chopped

½ cup **sugar**

3 large **egg yolks**

2 cups **hazelnuts**, toasted, skinned, and finely ground; plus extra whole nuts, for garnish

2 cups **heavy cream**

● **Prepare ahead** The parfaits can be frozen for up to 12 hours ahead.

1 **Bring the sugar** and ¼ cup water to a boil over high heat, stirring until the sugar dissolves. Boil, brushing down any sugar crystals that form on the inside of the pan with a pastry brush dipped in cold water, until the syrup reaches soft-ball stage (235°F/118°C).

2 **Using a hand-held** electric mixer, beat the egg yolks and chocolate. With the mixer running, slowly pour the hot syrup into the chocolate mixture. Beat until melted and completely cooled. Fold in 1 cup of the hazelnuts.

3 **Whip the cream** until it forms soft peaks. Fold the cream into the chocolate mixture.

4 **Line a baking sheet** with parchment paper. Place the rings on the sheet. Tape a strip of parchment paper around each ring, rising 1in (2.5cm) above the rim. Divide the chocolate mixture among the rings.

5 **Level the surfaces** of the parfaits with a metal spatula. Freeze until firm, about 2 hours.

6 **Remove the** parchment collars. Working quickly, briefly wrap a hot, wet kitchen towel around each ring, and slide the rings off. Press the remaining hazelnuts on to the sides of the parfaits, and sprinkle the tops with more and some whole nuts. Serve frozen.

● **Good with** whipped cream and orange slices.

Zesty Lemon Granita

Refreshing and not too sweet, this is a delicious dessert after a rich main course, or a cooling treat on a hot day

- 🍴 makes 4 servings
- 🕐 prep 5-10 mins, plus cooling and at least 4 hrs freezing • cook 5 mins
- ▦ shallow, freezerproof nonreactive dish
- ❄ can be frozen for up to 1 month

6 large **lemons**

⅔ cup **sugar**

twists of **lemon peel**, to decorate

● **Prepare ahead** The granita, covered, can be frozen for up to 3 days. Crush in a food processor before serving.

1 **Using a vegetable peeler**, remove the zest from 4 of the lemons in strips. Scrape away any white pith.

2 **Bring the sugar** and 1 cup water to a boil in a small saucepan over medium heat, stirring until the sugar dissolves. Increase the heat to high and boil for 5 minutes.

3 **Pour the syrup** into a shallow, freezerproof nonreactive bowl. Stir in the lemon zest strips and let cool completely.

4 **Meanwhile, grate** the zest from the remaining 2 lemons. Squeeze the juice from all of the lemons and strain. You should have 1 cup of lemon juice. Remove and discard the lemon zest strips from the syrup. Stir in the lemon juice and grated lemon zest.

5 **Transfer the dish** to the freezer. Every 30 minutes or so, use a fork to stir and break up the frozen chunks. Continue to do this for about 4 hours or until the mixture has the texture of shaved ice. During the last 30 minutes or so, freeze serving dishes for the granita. Scoop the granita into the frozen dishes and serve immediately.

● **Good with** a small sweet cookie served alongside.

● **Leftovers** can be served in sugar cones or mixed with fresh fruit drinks.

Espresso Granita

The texture of granitas should be finely granular, like snow

- 🍴 makes 4 servings
- 🕐 prep 5 mins, plus cooling and freezing • cook 5 mins
- ▦ shallow, freezerproof dish

½ cup **sugar**

1¼ cups very strong **espresso** or French roast coffee, chilled

½ tsp **pure vanilla extract**

● **Prepare ahead** The granita, covered, can be frozen for up to 3 days. Crush in a food processor before serving.

1 **Dissolve the sugar** in 1¼ cups water in a small saucepan, stirring over medium heat until it boils. Increase the heat to high and boil, without stirring, for 5 minutes, to make a light syrup.

2 **Pour the syrup** into a shallow, freezerproof dish. Stir in the coffee and vanilla and let cool completely.

3 **Transfer to the freezer**. Every 30 minutes or so, use a fork to break up the frozen chunks. Continue to do this for about 4 hours or until the mixture has the texture of shaved ice. During the last 30 minutes or so, place the serving dishes for the granita in the freeze. Scoop the granita into the dishes and serve immediately.

Vanilla Ice Cream

Nothing beats creamy homemade vanilla ice cream; you'll keep coming back for more

- 🍴 makes about 3 cups
- 🕐 prep 25 mins, plus chilling and freezing • cook 12 mins
- 📟 ice cream machine
- ❄ freeze for up to 1 week

1¼ cups **whole milk**

1 **vanilla bean**, split lengthwise

½ cup **sugar**

3 large **egg yolks**

1¼ cups **heavy cream**

1 Bring the milk and vanilla bean to a simmer in a heavy-bottomed medium saucepan over medium-low heat. Cover and let stand 30 minutes. Remove the vanilla bean and, using the tip of a small knife, scrape the beans from the pod back into the milk. Rinse the vanilla bean and reserve for another use, if desired.

2 Whisk together the sugar and egg yolks in a large bowl until the mixture is thick and pale. Gradually whisk in the warm milk then pour into the saucepan. Cook over low heat, stirring constantly with a wooden spoon, until the mixture coats the spoon (an instant-read thermometer will read 185°F/85°C). Do not boil. Strain through a wire sieve into a bowl. Cool completely, stirring often. Cover and refrigerate at least 2 hours, until thoroughly chilled. Whisk the cream into the cooled custard.

3 Pour into the container of an ice cream machine. Freeze according to the manufacturer's instructions. Transfer to an airtight, freezerproof container and freeze for at least 2 hours.

4 Scoop the frozen ice cream into bowls and serve.

⬤ **Good with** fresh berries, or biscotti crumbled into the base of the serving glass.

VARIATION

Coffee Ice Cream

Omit the vanilla pod. Stir 2 tsp of instant coffee powder into the warm milk. Do not infuse.

White Chocolate Chip Ice Cream

With white chocolate chips in a rich, dark chocolate ice cream, this is double-chocolate heaven

- 🍴 makes 4-6 servings
- 🕐 prep 25 mins, plus freezing • cook 12 mins
- 📟 ice cream machine
- ❄ freeze for up to 1 week

1¼ cups **whole milk**

1 **vanilla bean**, split lengthwise

5oz (140g) **bittersweet chocolate**, coarsely chopped

½ cup **sugar**

3 large **egg yolks**

1¼ cups **heavy cream**

1 cup **white chocolate chips**

1 Bring the milk and vanilla bean to a simmer in a heavy-bottomed medium saucepan over medium-low heat. Add the chocolate, let stand for a few minutes, then stir until the chocolate is melted. Cover and let stand 15 minutes. Remove the vanilla bean and, using the tip of a small knife, scrape the seeds from the pod back into the milk. Rinse the vanilla bean and reserve for another use, if desired.

2 Whisk together the egg yolks and sugar in a large bowl until the mixture becomes thick and pale. Gradually whisk in the warm milk mixture, the pour into the saucepan. Cook over low heat, stirring constantly with a wooden spoon, until the mixture coats the spoon (an instant-read thermometer will read 185°F/85°C). Do not boil. Strain through a wire sieve into a bowl. Cool completely, stirring often. Cover and refrigerate at least 2 hours, until thoroughly chilled. Stir the cream into the chilled custard.

3 Pour into the container of an ice cream machine. Freeze according to the manufacturer's instructions. Stir in the white chocolate chips. Transfer into an airtight freezerproof container and freeze for at least 2 hours. Scoop into bowls and serve.

Orange Sorbet

Brightly colored and vibrantly flavored, a citrus sorbet
is a satisfying summer dessert

- makes 4 servings
- prep 10 mins, plus freezing • cook 15 mins
- ice cream machine
- freeze for up to 3 months

2 large **oranges**

¾ cup **sugar**

1 tbsp **orange blossom water**

1 large **egg white**

1 Using a vegetable peeler, remove the zest from the oranges. Bring the sugar and 1¼ cups water to a simmer in a small saucepan over medium heat, stirring to dissolve the sugar. Add the orange zest and simmer over low heat for 10 minutes. Let cool slightly. Squeeze the juice from the oranges and stir into the syrup, along with the orange blossom water.

2 Strain the orange mixture into a bowl. Beat the egg white until soft peaks form. Gradually stir the orange mixture into the white.

3 To freeze the sorbet without an ice cream machine, pour the mixture into a metal baking dish. Freeze for at least 4 hours, until almost frozen solid. Mash with a fork to break up any ice crystals, then freeze until solid. If using an ice cream machine, follow the manufacturer's directions. Transfer to an airtight container and freeze until ready to use.

VARIATIONS

Lemon Sorbet

Substitute 3 lemons for the oranges. Omit the orange blossom water.

Lime Sorbet

Substitute 5 limes for the oranges. Omit the orange blossom water

Campari

Make Lemon Sorbet with the zest and juice of 1 lemon. Stir ⅓ cup Campari into the strained syrup. Serve within 1 month, as the alcohol will increase in flavor.

Saffron Kulfi

Kulfi is a kind of ice cream that is eaten all over India. This recipe uses condensed milk for convenience

- makes 6–8 servings
- prep 10 mins, plus freezing
- 2 silicone ice cube trays
- freeze for up to 1 month

pinch **saffron threads**

½ cup **pistachios**

one 14oz (393g) can **condensed milk**

1½ cups **heavy cream**

1 In a small bowl, soak the saffron threads in 1 tbsp boiling water for 2 minutes. Chop the pistachios roughly, and reserve a few to scatter on the top. Finely chop the remaining pistachios.

2 Mix the condensed milk and finely chopped pistachios together in a bowl. Stir in the saffron and its liquid.

3 Whip the cream until it holds soft peaks. Fold it into the saffron mixture until well combined. Fill the ice cube trays with the mixture. Freeze at least 4 hours, until completely set. When frozen, place the ice cube trays into zippered freezer bags and freeze until ready to serve.

4 To serve, unmold the kulfi out of the ice cube trays onto chilled plates. Sprinkle with the reserved pistachios and serve immediately.

Tropical Strawberry Ice Cream

Creamy and delicious, this strawberry ice cream is enhanced with the tropical flavors of coconut, rum, and lime

- makes 4 servings
- prep 15 mins, plus freezing time
- freeze for up to 3 months; transfer to the fridge for 30 minutes to soften slightly before serving

one 13.5oz (378g) can **coconut milk**

7oz (200g) **white chocolate,** chopped

6oz (165g) **strawberries,** hulled

¼ cup **confectioner's sugar**

1¼ cups **heavy cream**

grated rind and juice of 1 **lime**

2 tbsp **white rum**

lime wedges and **strawberry** halves, to serve

1 Bring the coconut milk to a bare simmer in a small saucepan over low heat. Remove from the heat and add the white chocolate. Let stand a few minutes, then stir until the chocolate melts. Pour into a bowl and let cool.

2 Purée the strawberries and confectioner's sugar in a food processor. Whip the heavy cream until soft peaks form. Add the strawberry purée, whipped cream, lime zest and juice, and rum to the coconut mixture and fold together.

3 Pour into a freezerproof container and cover. Freeze at least 6 hours, or until firm. Scoop into dessert glasses, garnish with lime wedges and fresh strawberries, and serve immediately.

Cassata Gelato

This version of the Sicilian frozen dessert is loaded with fruit and utterly irresistible

- makes 6-8 servings
- prep 25 mins, plus freezing time • cook 10 mins
- 7 cup capacity metal bowl, electric mixer, blender
- freeze for up to 4 months

1 cup **sugar**

4 large **egg yolks**

1 tsp **pure vanilla extract**

1¼ cups **heavy cream,** lightly whipped

¼ cup **glacé cherries**

¼ cup **dried apricots**

¼ cup **dried pineapple**

¼ cup chopped **pistachios**

6oz (168g) fresh **raspberries**

additional **dried fruits** and **pistachio nuts,** for garnish (optional)

1 Bring the sugar and ¼ cup water to a boil in a small saucepan over high heat, stirring to dissolve the sugar. Boil for 5 minutes, until thick and syrupy.

2 Beat the egg yolks with a hand-held electric mixer, slowly adding the hot syrup, until the mixture is cooled, thick, and pale. Fold in the whipped cream and vanilla. Transfer one third of the mixture to another bowl and stir in the cherries, apricots, pineapple, and pistachios. Cover and refrigerate.

3 Purée the raspberries in a blender. Rub through a fine sieve to remove the seeds and stir into the plain cream mixture. Pour into shallow metal baking dish and freeze, stirring occasionally, with a large metal spoon, about 4 hours, until partially set. Freeze a metal bowl with about 3½ cups capacity until very cold. Spread the raspberry cream in the bottom and up the sides of the bowl, leaving a cavity in the center. Fill with the chilled fruit mixture. Cover and freeze at least 8 hours, until firm.

4 Dip the bowl into warm water for a few seconds and then invert onto a serving plate and remove the bowl. Decorate with dried fruits and pistachio nuts, if desired. Cut into wedges and serve immediately.

Coffee and Pistachio Semifreddo

You can make this luxuriously smooth Italian ice cream without an ice cream maker

- makes 8 servings
- prep 20 mins, plus freezing • cook 5–8 mins
- 8in (20cm) square metal cake pan
- freeze for up to 3 months

1 vanilla bean, split lengthwise

1 cup plus 2 tbsp sugar

1 tbsp instant coffee

1 tbsp boiling water

6 large egg yolks

¼ cup Marsala

1¼ cups heavy cream

⅔ cup plain low-fat yogurt

1 cup chopped pistachios, plus more for garnish

rose petals, for garnish (optional)

1 **Lightly oil** an 8in (20cm) square metal cake pan and line it with a sheet of plastic wrap. Scrape the seeds from the vanilla bean into a saucepan. Add the sugar and ½ cup water. Stir over medium heat until the sugar dissolves. Boil without stirring about 3 minutes, until syrupy. Dissolve the coffee granules in the boiling water, and stir into the syrup.

2 **Beat the egg yolks** and Marsala in a large bowl with an electric mixer. Beat in the coffee syrup in a steady stream, and beat about 6 minutes, until thick and tripled in volume.

3 **Whip the cream** in a chilled bowl until soft peaks form. Fold into the egg mixture with the yogurt and ¾ cup of the pistachios. Spread the cake pan and sprinkle with the remaining pistachios. Cover with plastic wrap and freeze for 4–5 hours, until firm.

4 **Invert the pan** to unmold the semifreddo onto a chilled platter, remove the plastic wrap, and turn right side up. Cut into squares with a knife dipped in hot water. Serve immediately on chilled dessert plates, sprinkled with more pistachio nuts and rose petals, if using.

● **Good with** chocolate mints, or truffles, and a cup of strong, after-dinner coffee.

Knickerbocker Glory

A truly glorious sundae with chocolate and strawberry ice cream, peaches, and strawberry topping

- makes 4 servings
- prep 15 mins

2 peaches

8 small scoops strawberry ice cream

8 tbsp strawberry ice cream topping

4 small scoops chocolate ice cream

5oz (150ml) heavy cream, whipped

colored decorating sprinkles, for garnish

4 maraschino cherries, for serving

8 rolled wafer cookies, for serving

1 **Place the peaches** in a saucepan of boiling water for about 30 seconds, or until the skins loosen. Drain and rinse under cold running water. Peel, pit, and slice the peaches. Divide half of the peach slices among 4 tall ice cream glasses. Top each with a scoop of strawberry ice cream and 1 tbsp of strawberry ice cream topping.

2 **Repeat with** the remaining strawberry ice cream, then the remaining peaches, and remaining topping. Top each with a scoop of chocolate ice cream.

3 **Top each** with whipped cream, a scattering of sprinkles, and a maraschino cherry. Serve immediately, with the cookies.

Mango Sorbet

The recipe outlined here, with ripe mangoes, is just a template for making refreshing sorbet with other seasonal fruits

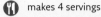 makes 4 servings

 prep 15 mins, plus freezing
• cook 10 mins

food processor

freeze for up to 3 months

2 large **mangoes**, peeled, pitted, and chopped

1 cup **sugar**

2 tbsp fresh **lemon** juice

1 large **egg white**

1 Purée the mangoes in a food processor. Strain through a wire sieve to remove any fibers. Refrigerate.

2 Bring 1¼ cups water and the sugar to a boil in a small saucepan over high heat, stirring until the sugar dissolves. Boil for 1 minute. Remove from the heat and let cool completely.

3 Stir the syrup and lemon juice into the mango purée. Beat the egg white until soft peaks form and fold into the mango mixture. Pour the mixture into a covered container and freeze for at least 4 hours, or

until slushy. Mash with a fork to break up any ice crystals. Freeze until solid. (Or, pour into an ice cream machine and freeze according to the manufacturer's instructions. Transfer to an airtight container and freeze until ready to use.)

4 Scoop into serving dishes and serve immediately.

VARIATIONS

Melon Sorbet

Substitute 1 seeded and chopped cantaloupe for the mangoes. Increase the sugar to 1¼ cups.

Papaya Sorbet

Substitute 2 very ripe papayas, seeded, peeled, and chopped, for the mangoes, and lime juice for the lemon juice. Increase the sugar to 1¼ cups.

Blueberry Sorbet

Omit the mangoes. Add 3 cups fresh blueberries and the lemon juice to the syrup and simmer for about 4 minutes, until the berries have all burst. Let cool, then purée.

Pistachio Ice Cream

Pistachio is rightfully one of the most popular ice cream flavors

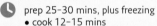 makes 4 servings

prep 25–30 mins, plus freezing
• cook 12–15 mins

ice cream machine

freeze for up to 3 months

1¼ cups **whole milk**

3 large **egg yolks**

½ cup **sugar**

½ tsp **pistachio** or almond **extract**

few drops of **green food coloring** (optional)

1½ cups coarsely chopped **pistachios**, plus more for garnish

1¼ cups **heavy cream**, lightly whipped

1 Bring the milk to a simmer in a heavy-bottomed saucepan over low heat. Beat the egg yolks and sugar in a large bowl until thick and pale. Whisk in the hot milk and then return to the saucepan. Cook the mixture over low heat, stirring constantly, until the custard thickens slightly and coats the back of a spoon.

(An instant-read thermometer will read 185°F/85°C.) Do not boil.

2 Strain through a wire sieve back into the bowl and stir in the extract and a few drops green food coloring, if using. Add the pistachios and let cool. Lightly whip the cream and fold into pistachio custard.

3 To freeze the ice cream by hand, pour the mixture into a freezer-proof container and freeze for at least 3-4 hours, until icy. Whisk well. Freeze for 2 hours more and whisk again. Cover and freeze until ready to use. To freeze ice cream in an ice cream machine, pour the mixture into the freezing compartment and churn according to the manufacturer's instructions. Transfer to a freezer proof-container, cover, and freeze until ready to use.

4 Scoop the ice cream into dessert glasses, sprinkle with chopped pistachios, and serve immediately.

Sticky Lemon Cake

The combination of fresh lemon juice and yogurt gives this cake a wonderfully fresh taste and moist texture

- makes 8 servings
- prep 15 mins, plus cooling • cook 40 mins
- 8in (20cm) round cake pan

2 lemons

12 tbsp **unsalted butter**

1¼ cups **sugar**

2 large **eggs**, plus one egg yolk

1⅓ cups **almond flour** (almond meal)

½ cup **all-purpose flour**

2 tsp **baking powder**

1⅓ cups **plain yogurt**

1 **Preheat the oven** to 325°F (175°C). Butter an 8in (20cm) cake pan, and line the bottom with a round of parchment paper.

2 **Grate the zest** and squeeze the juice from the lemons; you should have 6 tbsp juice. Cream together the butter and ¾ cup sugar, and the zest in a large bowl until light and fluffy. Beat in the eggs, one at a time.

3 **Whisk the flours** and the baking powder together to eliminate any lumps. Stir into the butter mixture, followed by the yogurt and 2 tbsp of the lemon juice.

4 **Spread in the pan.** Bake for 30 minutes, or until the center springs back when pressed.

5 **Meanwhile,** stir the remaining ½ cup sugar and 4 tbsp lemon juice in a saucepan over low heat to dissolve the sugar. Cool.

6 **Transfer the cake** to a wire rack. Pierce the cake all over with a skewer and drizzle the syrup on top. Cool for 30 minutes. Invert onto the rack, remove the pan, peel off the paper, and cool completely.

Whole Wheat Carrot Cake

This delicious, fiber-rich cake has a healthful profile

- makes 8 slices
- prep 15 mins, plus cooling • cook 20–25 mins
- two 8in (20cm) round cake pans

2 cups **whole wheat pastry flour**

2 tsp **baking powder**

2 tsp **ground allspice**

1 tsp **ground ginger**

½ tsp **salt**

1 cup **packed light brown sugar**

1 cup **butter**, at room temperature

6 large **eggs**, beaten

grated zest of 2 **oranges**

1 tsp **pure vanilla extract**

6 small **carrots**, peeled and coarsely grated (2 cups)

1 cup **raisins** or golden raisins

8oz (225g) **cream cheese**

1 cup **confectioner's sugar**

¼ cup fresh **orange** juice

1 **Preheat the oven** to 350°F (175°C). Butter two 8in (20cm) round cake pans, and line the bottoms with parchment paper. Whisk the flour, baking powder, allspice, ginger, and salt in a large bowl, then stir in the sugar. Add the butter, eggs, vanilla, and half the zest. Beat with an electric mixer set on high speed about 2 minutes or until the mixture is smooth. Stir in the carrots and raisins.

2 **Spread the batter** in the pans. Bake for about 25 minutes or until a toothpick inserted in the center comes out clean. Transfer to a wire rack and cool for 10 minutes. Invert, peel off the paper, turn right-side up, and cool completely.

3 **Meanwhile,** make the frosting. Beat the cream cheese, remaining orange zest, and confectioner's sugar. Add enough orange juice to make a spreadable frosting. Spread ½ cup of the frosting over 1 cake layer, top with the other layer, and frost with the remainder.

Almond and Orange Cake

This cake does not need flour or butter, so it's great for people on restricted diets

- 🍴 makes 8 servings
- 🕐 prep 10 mins, plus cooling • cook 1 hr
- 🍰 8in (20cm) round cake pan

7oz (200g) **carrots**, peeled and sliced

1 tbsp fresh **orange** juice, or orange- or almond-flavored liqueur

4 large **eggs**, separated

½ tsp **pure vanilla extract**

grated zest of 1 **orange**

¾ cup **sugar**

1¼ cup **almond flour** (almond meal)

confectioner's sugar, for sifting (optional)

1 Preheat the oven to 325°F (160°C). Butter an 8in (20cm) round cake pan and line the bottom with a round of parchment paper.

2 Cook the carrots in a little water about 15 minutes, or until very tender. Drain and purée with the orange juice; you should have ½ cup of purée.

3 Beat the egg yolks, vanilla, and orange zest in a large bowl with an electric mixer on high speed. Gradually add the sugar, mixing until it becomes very thick. Stir in the carrot purée and almond flour.

4 In a clean, dry bowl, with clean beaters, beat the egg whites until stiff, then fold into the batter. Spread in the pan. Bake for 30 minutes or until a toothpick inserted into the center comes out clean.

5 Transfer to a wire rack and cool for 10 minutes. Invert onto the rack, peel off the paper, and cool completely. Sift confectioner's sugar over the top before serving, if desired.

● **Good with** fresh fruit such as raspberries, blackberries, or blueberries and a spoonful of thick yogurt or whipped cream.

Marble Cake

The marbled effect is a clever swirl of plain and chocolate batters

- 🍴 makes 12 slices
- 🕐 prep 30 mins, plus cooling • cook 1 hr
- 🍰 10in (25cm) Bundt pan (12 cup capacity) or 14 x 4½ in (35 x 11cm) rectangular tin

1½ cups **butter**, softened

1¾ cups **granulated sugar**

6 large **eggs**, at room temperature

1 tsp **pure vanilla extract**

2⅔ cups **all-purpose flour**

4 tsp **baking powder**

½ tsp **salt**

½ cup **milk**

3 tbsp natural or Dutch process **cocoa powder**

confectioner's sugar, for dusting

1 Preheat the oven to 350°F (180°C). Butter and flour the pan, tapping out the excess flour.

2 Beat the butter and sugar with an electric mixer on high speed until fluffy, about 3 minutes. One at a time, beat in the eggs, beating well after each, then beat in the vanilla.

3 Sift together the flour, baking powder, and salt. On low speed, beat in half the flour mix. Beat in the milk, then the remaining flour mix.

4 Spoon one-third of the batter into the pan. Transfer half the batter into another bowl. Sift in the cocoa powder and stir. Spoon dollops of the cocoa batter into the pan, then top with the plain batter. Swirl a knife through the two batters to create a pattern, taking care not to over-mix. Bake for about 45 minutes.

5 Cool in the pan for 10 minutes, then remove. Dust with confectioner's sugar and serve.

BUNDT PAN

Inspired by the European turban pan mold, with a pattern that resembles the folds of a turban, this cake pan comes in many other intricate shapes. Inspired by the European Kuglehopf cake pan, the Bundt pan takes its name from Bund, German for a gathering of people.

Stollen

This rich, fruity, yeast bread, originally from Germany,
is a great addition to your holiday baking

- makes 1 loaf, about 16 slices
- prep 35 mins, plus overnight soaking, resting, and rising • bake 50 mins
- wrap the stollen in freezer paper and store in the freezer for up to 6 months

½ cup raisins

¼ cup dried currants

¼ cup dark rum

⅓ cup plus 1 tbsp whole milk

⅓ cup granulated sugar

1¼ oz (7g) envelope active dry yeast

3 cups unbleached flour, as needed

12 tbsp butter, at room temperature

2 large eggs

½ tsp pumpkin pie spice

1 tsp pure vanilla extract

¾ tsp salt

½ cup mixed candied fruit peel

¾ cup chopped slivered almonds

confectioner's sugar, for dusting

1 **Combine the raisins**, currants, and rum in a bowl. Let stand at least 2 hours to plump.

2 **Mix the milk** and 1 tsp of the granulated sugar in a small bowl. Sprinkle in the yeast and let stand 5 minutes, until softened. Stir to dissolve the yeast. Add ⅓ cup of flour and stir well. Cover with plastic wrap and let stand until doubled in volume, about 30 minutes.

3 **Scrape the yeast** mixture into the bowl of a heavy-duty mixer. Add the butter, eggs, remaining sugar, pumpkin-pie spice, vanilla, and salt. Mix on low speed with the paddle attachment. Gradually add the remaining flour to make a soft dough that pulls away from the sides of the bowl. Switch to the kneading hook and knead on medium speed until the dough is supple, about 8 minutes. Shape the dough into a ball.

4 **Butter a large bowl**. Add the dough and turn to coat with butter. Cover with plastic wrap. Let stand in a warm place until doubled in volume, about 1¼ hours.

5 **Punch the dough**. Transfer to a work surface and stretch into a 12 x 10in (30 x 25cm) rectangle. Drain the raisins and currants. Sprinkle the drained fruit, candied fruit peel, and almonds over the dough. Roll and knead to distribute the fruit and almonds, kneading in a bit more flour if needed. Cover and let stand for 10 minutes.

6 **Line a baking sheet** with wax paper. Roll out the dough on a lightly floured surface into a 12 x 10in (30 x 25cm) rectangle. Fold one long side over just beyond the middle, then fold over the other long side to overlap the first, curling it over slightly on top to create the traditional "swaddling" shape. Transfer to the baking sheet, cover with plastic wrap, and let stand a warm place about 45 minutes, or until doubled in volume.

7 **Preheat the oven** to 325°F (160°C). Bake the stollen for about 50 minutes, or until pale golden brown. Sift a generous amount of confectioner's sugar over it. Transfer to a wire cake rack and cool completely. Serve in thick slices.

French Almond Financiers

So-called because these cakes are said to resemble gold bars

- makes 12
- prep 15 mins • cook 10–12 mins
- 12 financier or barquette molds, or a 12-hole cake pan
- freeze for up to 3 months

½ cup ground almonds

¾ cup confectioner's sugar, sifted

3 tbsp all-purpose flour, plus more for the molds

pinch of salt

6 tbsp butter, softened plus more for the molds

3 large egg whites

½ tsp pure vanilla extract

1 **Preheat the oven** to 400°F (200°C). Butter and flour 12 financier or barquette molds (available at specialty kitchenware stores). Place on a baking sheet, if necessary.

2 **Mix** the almonds, sugar, and salt together. Heat the butter over low heat, just until melted. Whisk the egg whites until they are frothy but barely thickened. Add the butter, egg whites, and vanilla extract to the dry ingredients and fold together.

3 **Divide the batter** among the molds, filling halfway. Bake for about 12 minutes, or until they spring back when pressed lightly. Cool briefly, remove from the molds onto a wire rack, and cool completely.

Chocolate Roulade

Serve during the holidays as the French classic *bûche de Noël*

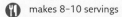

- makes 8–10 servings
- prep 30 mins • cook 15 mins, plus cooling
- 15½ x 10½ x 1in (39 x 27 x 2.5cm) jelly roll pan
- freeze for up to 6 months

For the cake

5 large **eggs**, at room temperature

¾ cup granulated **sugar**

¾ cup **all-purpose flour**

⅓ cup Dutch-process **cocoa powder**

½ tsp **baking powder**

confectioner's sugar, for sifting

For the filling and icing

⅔ cup **heavy cream**

5oz (150g) **bittersweet chocolate**, chopped

½ cup seedless **raspberry preserves**

1 Preheat the oven to 350°F (180°C). Line a 15½ x 10½ x 1in (39 x 27 x 2.5cm) jelly roll pan with wax paper.

2 Beat the eggs and sugar in a large bowl with an electric mixer at high speed about 5 minutes, until the mixture has tripled in volume.

Sift the flour, cocoa, and baking powder together. Sift over the egg mixture and carefully fold together.

3 Spread in the pan. Bake about 15 minutes, until the top springs back when pressed lightly with a finger. Sift confectioner's sugar over the cake. Place a clean kitchen towel and a cutting board over the jelly roll pan. Invert them together to unmold the cake. Remove the wax paper and place on the cake. Roll up the cake, with the paper inside. Let cool.

4 Meanwhile, to make the icing, bring the cream to a boil in a small saucepan. Add the chocolate and stir until melted. Remove from the heat and let cool for 10 minutes.

5 Unroll the cake and discard the paper. Spread the preserves over the cake. Roll up the cake again. Place the roll on a wire rack, seam side down. Spread the icing all over the top, sides, and ends of the cake. Use a fork to create ridges down the length of the cake. Transfer to a platter. Just before serving, dust with confectioner's sugar.

Victoria Sponge Cake

This light sponge cake is perfect with tea

- makes 8 servings
- prep 20 mins • cook 25 mins
- for the best results, have all your ingredients at room temperature
- two 8in (20cm) round cake pans
- freeze for up to 1 month

12 tbsp **butter**, at room temperature, plus more for the pans

1 cup granulated **sugar**

3 large **eggs**, at room temperature

1 cup plus 2 tbsp **all-purpose flour**

1 tsp **baking powder**

¼ tsp **salt**

½ cup **raspberry preserves**

⅔ cup **heavy cream**

confectioner's sugar, for sifting

1 Preheat the oven to 375°F (190°C). Lightly butter two 8in (20cm) round cake pans and line the bottoms with wax paper.

2 Beat the butter and sugar together with an electric mixer on high speed for 3 minutes, or until very pale and fluffy. One at a time, beat in the eggs, beating well after each addition. Sift the flour, baking powder, and salt together. Add to the butter mixture and beat on low speed until smooth.

3 Divide the mixture equally between the cake pans and smooth the tops. Bake for 20–25 minutes, until the cakes spring back when pressed in the centers. Let cool on a wire rack for 5 minutes. Invert and unmold onto the rack, and peel off the wax paper. Cool completely.

4 Place one cake layer upside down on a serving plate. Spread with the raspberry preserves. Lightly whip the cream until soft peaks form. Spread over the preserves. Top with the remaining layer, rounded side up. Sift confectioner's sugar over the top and serve immediately.

VARIATIONS

Banana and Dulce de Leche Cake

Omit the whipped cream and preserves. Spread the cake bottom layer with ¼ cup dulce de leche and top with 1 large banana, thinly sliced. Top with the second layer, and substitute cocoa power for the confectioner's sugar garnish.

Lemon Cheesecake

Omit the whipped cream and preserves. Beat together 6oz (175g) softened cream cheese, the grated zest of 1 lemon, 2 tbsp fresh lemon juice, and ⅓ cup confectioner's sugar. Spread over the bottom cake layer. Top with the second layer.

Black Forest Gâteau

The German Black Forest region is not just the home of the cuckoo clock, but the namesake of one of the most popular of all chocolate cakes

- makes 8 servings
- prep 55 mins • cook 40 mins
- 9in (23cm) springform pan, pastry bag, star pastry tip
- freeze for up to 1 month; defrost for 5-6 hours in the fridge

6 large eggs

scant 1 cup sugar

1 cup all-purpose flour

½ cup cocoa powder

1 tsp pure vanilla extract

two 15oz (420g) cans pitted black cherries

¼ cup Kirsch

2¼ cups heavy cream

5oz (150g) bittersweet chocolate, grated on a box grater

● **Prepare ahead** The cake can be refrigerated for up to 3 days.

1 Preheat the oven to 350°F (180°C). Lightly butter a 9in (23cm) springform pan and line the bottom with wax paper. Combine the eggs and sugar in a large heatproof bowl. Place over a saucepan of simmering water. Whisk just until the mixture is hot and the sugar is melted. Beat with an electric mixer on high speed, about 5 minutes, or until pale and tripled in volume.

2 Sift the flour and cocoa together. In two additions, sift over the egg mixture and fold in. Mix together the melted butter and vanilla. Stir about 1 cup of the batter into the butter mixture, then fold back into the batter. Spread in the pan. Bake about 40 minutes, or until the top springs back when pressed in the center. Let cool 5 minutes on a wire rack. Remove the sides of the pan, invert, and remove the bottom of the pan and wax paper. Let cool.

3 Using a long serrated knife, carefully cut the cake into three layers. Drain one can of cherries and mix 6 tbsp of the juice with the Kirsch. Roughly chop the drained cherries. Whip the cream until soft peaks form.

4 Place one cake layer onto a serving platter. Drizzle with one third of the Kirsch syrup. Spread with a thin layer of whipped cream and half the chopped cherries. Repeat with another cake layer. Top with the final layer and remaining syrup. Using a metal spatula, spread the whipped cream over the top and sides of the cake. Transfer the remaining cream to a pastry bag fitted with a star-shaped tip.

5 Using a large spoon, press the grated chocolate on the sides of the cake. Pipe swirls of cream around the top edge of the cake. Drain the second can of cherries and fill the center of the cake with the cherries. Serve chilled.

Madeleines

These little treats were made famous by writer Marcel Proust

- makes 12
- prep 15-20 mins • cook 10 mins
- madeleine pan with 12 molds
- store and freeze for 1 month

⅓ cup plus 1 tbsp sugar

2 large eggs, at room temperature

1 tsp pure vanilla extract

⅓ cup plus 2 tbsp all-purpose flour

¼ tsp baking powder

⅛ tsp salt

4 tbsp butter, melted, and cooled until tepid, plus more for the pan

confectioner's sugar, to garnish

1 Preheat the oven to 350°F (180°C). Carefully brush the indentations of the madeleine pan with melted butter. Dust with flour and tap to remove the excess.

2 Beat the sugar, eggs, and vanilla with an electric mixer on high speed for 4 minutes, until the mixture triples in volume and forms a ribbon when the beaters are lifted.

3 Sift the flour, baking powder, and salt together twice. Sift the flour mixture over the egg mixture. Pour the butter down the inside of the bowl. Using a spatula, fold gently together, keeping the batter light and airy. Spoon the batter into the molds.

4 Bake for 12 minutes, or until golden. Unmold and cool completely. Sift confectioner's sugar over the tops just before serving.

Chocolate Almond Cake

A dense, moist cake with a rich ganache topping

- 🍴 makes 8 servings
- 🕐 prep 30 mins • cook 25 mins
- 🔲 8in (20cm) springform cake pan
- ❄️ freeze for up to 1 month

5oz (125g) **bittersweet chocolate**, chopped

10 tbsp **butter**, at room temperature, plus more for the pan

¾ cup **sugar**

3 large **eggs**, separated

½ cup **almond flour** (almond meal)

½ cup fresh **bread crumbs**

½ tsp **baking powder**

1 tbsp **brandy** or rum

¼ tsp **almond extract**

For the ganache

5oz (150g) **bittersweet chocolate**, chopped

6 tbsp **butter**

1 **Preheat the oven** to 350°F (180°C). Butter an 8in (20cm) springform cake pan. Line with wax paper and dust with flour.

2 **Melt the chocolate** in a heatproof bowl over a saucepan of simmering water. Remove from the heat and cool until tepid.

3 **Beat the butter** and sugar in a bowl with an electric mixer for 3 minutes, until pale and creamy. One at a time, beat in the egg yolks, then the chocolate. Stir in the almonds, bread crumbs, baking powder, brandy, and almond extract.

4 **Beat the egg whites** in another bowl until they form soft peaks. Fold into the batter. Spread in the pan.

5 **Bake for 25 minutes**, or until a wooden toothpick inserted in the center comes out clean. Let cool for 15 minutes on a wire rack. Invert and release the cake onto the rack set over a baking sheet. Remove the paper. Let cool completely.

6 **To make the ganache**, melt the butter in a heatproof bowl set over a saucepan of simmering water. Add the chocolate and stir until melted. Pour the ganache over the cake and spread over the top and sides with a metal spatula. Let the ganache set. Cut into slices and serve.

Panforte

This famous cake from Siena, Italy, dates from the 13th century

- 🍴 makes 12–16 servings
- 🕐 prep 30 mins • cook 30 mins
- 🔲 8in (20cm) springform pan, rice paper

edible **rice** (wafer) **paper** (available online at cake suppliers), for lining, or well-oiled parchment paper

1 cup whole **blanched almonds**, toasted and roughly chopped

1 cup **hazelnuts**, toasted, skinned, and roughly chopped

⅔ cup chopped **candied orange peel**

⅔ cup chopped **candied lemon peel**

1 cup coarsely chopped **dried figs**

½ cup **rice** or all-purpose **flour**

finely grated zest of 1 **lemon**

½ tsp ground **cinnamon**

½ tsp freshly grated **nutmeg**

¼ tsp ground **cloves**

¼ tsp ground **allspice**

⅔ cup **sugar**

¼ cup **honey**

2 tbsp **butter**, plus more for the pan

confectioner's sugar, for sifting

● **Prepare ahead** The panforte will keep, wrapped in aluminum foil, for up to 3 weeks.

1 **Preheat the oven** to 350°F (180°C). Butter an 8in (20cm) springform pan. Line the bottom and sides of the pan with parchment paper. Place a round of rice paper in the bottom of the pan.

2 **Stir the almonds**, hazelnuts, candied peel, figs, rice flour, lemon zest, cinnamon, nutmeg, cloves, and allspice together in a bowl.

3 **Stir the sugar**, honey, and butter in a small saucepan over low heat until melted. Pour into the nut mixture and stir well. Spoon into the pan, and with moistened hands, press until smooth and even.

4 **Bake for 30 minutes**, until set. Transfer to a wire rack and let cool completely in the pan. Remove the sides of the pan and invert onto the rack. Peel off the parchment but leave the rice paper in place. Turn right side up.

5 **Sift confectioner's sugar** over the panforte. Slice into thin wedges and serve.

Sachertorte

Sachertorte is the epitome of fine Viennese baking, a rich chocolate cake glazed with a thin layer of apricot preseves and a finishing coat of shiny chocolate

 makes 8–12 servings

 prep 40 mins, plus cooling • cook 45–60 mins

9 x 2in (23 x 5cm) round cake pan

❄ freeze unglazed for up to 3 months

1 cup plus 2 tbsp **butter**, at room temperature

1¼ cups **sugar**

9oz (250g) **bittersweet chocolate**, melted and tepid

½ tsp **pure vanilla extract**

5 large **eggs**, separated, at room temperature

1¾ cups **all-purpose flour**

½ cup **apricot preserves**

For the chocolate glaze

1¼ cups **heavy cream**

7oz (200g) **dark chocolate**, chopped

¼ tsp **pure vanilla extract**

1 Preheat the oven to 350°F (180°C). Line a 9in (23cm) round cake pan with wax paper.

2 Beat the butter and sugar together with an electric mixer until light and fluffy. Beat in the chocolate and vanilla. One at a time, beat in the egg yolks. Fold in the flour.

3 Beat the egg whites until stiff peaks form. Stir one-fourth of the whites into the batter, then fold in the remainder. Spread evenly in the pan.

4 Bake for 45–60 minutes, or until a wooden toothpick inserted in the center comes out clean. Transfer to a wire rack and let cool for 10 minutes. Invert and unmold the cake. Remove the wax paper. Let cool completely.

5 To make the glaze, bring the cream to a simmer in a small saucepan over medium heat. Remove from the heat and add the chocolate and vanilla. Let stand until the chocolate softens, then stir until smooth. Let cool, stirring occasionally, until it thickens slightly.

6 Melt the apricot preserves in a small saucepan over low heat. Strain through a sieve. Slice the cake in half horizontally. Spread the

lower layer with some of the apricot mixture. Return the top layer. Spread the remaining apricot mixture over the top of the cake, then use a metal spatula to smooth it evenly over the top and sides. Let cool until set.

7 Place the cake on a wire rack over a baking sheet. Transfer ¼ cup of the glaze to a small bowl. Pour the remaining chocolate glaze over the cake. Use a metal spatula to smooth the glaze over the top and sides of the cake. Patch any unglazed spots with the glaze that runs onto the baking sheet. Refrigerate about 10 minutes, until the glaze sets.

8 If necessary, warm the reserved glaze until fluid. Transfer to a small plastic food storage bag and force into a corner of the bag. Snip off the corner of the bag with kitchen scissors. Squeeze the glaze out of the bag to write "Sacher" over the top of the cake in flowing script. Let cool, and serve with whipped cream.

Marzipan Oranges

Serve in petits fours cases after dinner with coffee

🍴 makes 12

🕐 prep 5 mins each

12oz (335g) **marzipan**

orange **food coloring paste**

whole **cloves**, to decorate

1 Mix the marzipan and food coloring in a bowl until combined. For each orange, roll 1oz (25g) of the mixture into a ball. Roll the ball over the coarse, star-shaped side of a box grater. Push a clove into the top. Use the blunt edge of a knife to make crease marks around the clove.

Pear Marzipan Fruits

Color the marzipan pale green. Form into pear shapes. Push cloves into the bottoms and stand on end. Color a small amount of marzipan brown and use to create stalks.

Banana Marzipan Fruits

Color the marzipan yellow. Form into sausage shapes with tapered ends. Bend toward you, then flatten the sides slightly with the back of a knife. Use thinned down brown food coloring to paint in a few streaks.

Angel Food Cake

Serve this light-as-air cake with your favorite summer berries

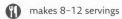makes 8–12 servings

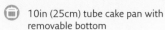prep 30 mins,
• cook 35–45 mins, plus cooling

10in (25cm) tube cake pan with removable bottom

1 cup cake flour

½ cup confectioner's sugar

12 large egg whites

½ tsp cream of tartar

1 cup superfine sugar

1 tsp pure vanilla or almond extract

For the topping

¾ cup heavy cream

3 tbsp confectioner's sugar

blueberries, raspberries, and strawberries, for serving

1 **Preheat the oven** to 350°F (180°C). Sift the flour and confectioner's sugar together.

2 **Beat the egg whites** and cream of tartar in a large bowl with an electric mixer on high speed until soft peaks form. One tablespoon at a time, beat in the superfine sugar until shiny, stiff peaks form. In three additions, sift in the flour mixture, gently folding in each addition with a large rubber spatula. Fold in the vanilla. Spoon into a 10in (25cm) tube cake pan with a removable bottom and gently smooth the top.

3 **Bake about 40 minutes,** until the top is golden brown and springs back when pressed.

4 **Invert the cake pan** on a work surface. (The cake should clear the work surface—if not, perch the cake pan on custard cups.) Cool completely. Run a long, dull knife around the inside of the pan. Remove the sides of the pan. Pull the bottom of the cake away from tube section and transfer, upside down, to a serving platter.

5 **To make the topping,** whip the cream and confectioner's sugar until soft peaks form. Spoon over the cake. Cut into slices and serve with the berries. The cake is best served the day it is baked, and is good with any combination of fresh fruit.

Apple Fruit Cake

In Britain, this dense fruit cake is a popular choice for celebrations. This may just be the best fruit cake you ever had

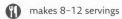makes 15 servings

prep 25 mins, plus soaking
• cook 2 hrs 10 mins

9in (23cm) square x 3in (7.5cm) deep cake pan

2½ cups raisins

2 cups pitted chopped prunes

2 cups candied cherries

2 cups peeled, cored, and finely chopped Golden Delicious apples

1⅓ cups golden raisins

2½ cups hard apple or pear cider

4 tsp pumpkin pie spice

2 cups all-purpose flour

2 tsp baking powder

½ teaspoon salt

12 tbsp butter, at room temperature

¾ cup packed dark brown sugar

3 large eggs, beaten

1¼ cups almond flour (almond meal)

For the decoration

8oz (240g) ready-to-roll fondant

confectioner's sugar, for rolling

3 tbsp apricot preserves, warmed and strained

● **Prepare ahead** The fruit must soak for 12 hours.

1 **The day before baking,** bring all the fruit, cider, and spice to a simmer. Cover and simmer for 20 minutes, or until most of the liquid has been absorbed. Remove from the heat, cover, and let stand at least 12 hours at room temperature.

2 **Preheat the oven** to 325°F (160°C) Lightly butter the cake pan and line the bottom and sides with parchment paper.

3 **Sift the flour,** baking powder, and salt together. Cream the butter and sugar with an electric mixer about 3 minutes. Gradually beat in the eggs. Stir in the flour mixture and ground almonds, then the soaked fruit and its liquid. Spread the batter evenly in the pan.

4 **Bake for about** 2½ hours, or until a wooden skewer inserted into the center of the cake comes out clean. Transfer to a rack and cool for 15 mins. Invert and unmold the cake and remove the paper and let cool.

5 **Knead the fondant** and roll into a 9in (23cm) square about ⅛in (3mm) thick. Brush the cake with the preserves. Place the fondant on the cake. Cut into pieces and serve.

Honey Cake

A sweet cake with the delicate taste of honey

- 🍴 makes 10–12 servings
- 🕐 prep 20 mins, plus cooling • cook 1 hr
- 🍰 9 x 5in (23 x 13cm) loaf pan

For the cake

1 cup **butter**, room temperature

⅔ cup packed **light brown sugar**

⅓ cup plus 1 tbsp **honey**, warmed until fluid

4 large **eggs**, lightly beaten

3¼ cup **all-purpose flour**

1½ tsp **baking powder**

1 tsp ground **cinnamon**

For the icing

⅔ cup **confectioner's sugar**

1 tbsp **honey**

1–2 tbsp hot **water**

1 Preheat the oven to 350°F (180°C). Butter a 9 x 5in (23 x 13cm) loaf pan and line the bottom with wax paper.

2 To make the cake, beat the butter and brown sugar with an electric mixer until pale and creamy. Beat in the honey. One at a time, beat in the eggs, beating well after each addition. Add a little flour if the mixture begins to curdle.

3 Sift together the flour, baking powder, and cinnamon. Stir into the butter mixture. Spread in the pan and smooth the top. Bake for 50–60 minutes, or until a wooden toothpick inserted in the center comes out clean. If the loaf is browning too quickly, tent with foil. Cool in the pan on a wire rack for 10 minutes. Invert and unmold onto the rack, peel off the paper, and let cool.

4 To make the icing, mix the confectioner's sugar and honey, then stir in enough hot water to make a fluid icing. Drizzle the icing over the cake, letting it drip down the sides.

Bienenstich

This German recipe is also known as Bee Sting Cake

- 🍴 makes 8–10 servings
- 🕐 prep 20 mins, plus 1hr 45 mins rising • cook 20–25 mins
- 🍰 8in (20cm) round cake pan

1 cup **all-purpose flour**

1 tbsp **butter**, softened, plus more for the bowl

2 tsp **sugar**

1 tsp **instant yeast**

pinch of **salt**

1 large **egg**, beaten

crème pâtissière (p524)

For the glaze

2 tbsp **butter**

¾oz (20g) **caster sugar**

1 tbsp **honey**

1 tbsp **heavy cream**

2 tbsp **slivered almonds**

1 tsp fresh **lemon** juice

1 Sift the flour into a bowl. Add the butter and rub it in with your fingertips until crumbly. Stir in the sugar, yeast, and salt. Add the egg and stir, adding enough water (about 3 tbsp) to make a soft dough.

2 Knead on a lightly floured surface for about 8 minutes, until smooth and elastic. Put in a buttered bowl, turn to coat, and cover with plastic wrap. Let stand in a warm place about 1 hour, or until doubled.

3 Preheat the oven to 375°F (190°C). Butter the cake pan and line with a round of wax paper. Punch down the dough and roll into an 8in (20cm) circle. Transfer to the pan, cover with plastic wrap, and let stand for 20 minutes, until slightly puffy.

4 Meanwhile, to make the glaze, melt the butter in a saucepan over low heat. Add the sugar, honey, and cream and stir until the sugar dissolves. Increase the heat to medium and simmer for 3 minutes until reduced by about half. Stir in the almonds and lemon juice. Let cool.

5 Carefully spread the cooled glaze over the dough, cover with the wrap, and let rise for 10 minutes more. Bake for 20–25 minutes, tenting the cake with foil if it browns too quickly. Let cool in the pan for 30 minutes, then unmold and cool.

6 Slice the cake in half crosswise. Spread the crème pâtissière on the bottom half, place the almond layer on top, and transfer to a serving plate.

Chocolate Chip Cupcakes

Children will enjoy decorating these with favorite toppings

 makes 15 cupcakes

prep 15 mins • cook 20 mins

2 muffin pans; paper liners

1 cup all-purpose flour

1 cup sugar

½ tsp baking soda

¼ tsp baking powder

¼ tsp salt

¾ cup buttermilk

2oz (55g) unsweetened chocolate, melted and tepid

4 tbsp butter, softened

1 large egg, at room temperature

½ tsp pure vanilla extract

1 cup semisweet chocolate chips

⅔ cup heavy cream

5oz (140g) semisweet chocolate, chopped

1 Preheat the oven to 350°F (180°C). Line 2 muffin pans with 15 paper muffin liners. Combine all the ingredients through the vanilla in a bowl. Beat for 3 minutes, until light and fluffy. Stir in the chocolate chips. Divide among the muffin cups. Bake about 20 minutes. Cool completely.

2 Boil the cream. Remove from the heat, add the chocolate, and stir and cool. Dip each cupcake top in the chocolate mixture to top.

Raspberry Cupcakes

Elegant cakes that are perfect with after-dinner coffee

 makes 12 cupcakes

 prep 15 mins • cook 25 mins

muffin pan, paper liners

1⅔ cups all-purpose flour

1 cup butter, softened

1 cup sugar

1 tsp baking powder

4 large eggs

2½ tsp baking powder

1 tsp pure vanilla extract

½ tsp almond extract

6oz (165g) raspberries, plus 12

3 tbsp finely chopped almonds

6oz (175g) white chocolate, chopped, plus grated, for garnish

1 Preheat the oven to 350°F (180°C). Line 12 muffin cups with paper liners.

2 Beat the flour, butter, sugar, eggs, baking powder, vanilla and almond extracts, in a bowl for 3 minutes, until pale and fluffy. Stir in the raspberries and almonds. Divide among the muffin cups. Bake for 25–30 minutes, until golden. Cool for 10 minutes; transfer the cupcakes to a wire rack to cool completely.

3 Melt the white chocolate in a heatproof bowl set over a saucepan of simmering water. Drizzle over the cupcakes. Top with grated white chocolate and a raspberry.

Vanilla Cupcakes

Colored buttercream icing and simple decorations transform these humble cupcakes into treats fit for a celebration

 makes 16 cupcakes

prep 15 mins • cook 20 mins

muffin pan, paper baking liners, pastry bag fitted with-star tip

2 cups all-purpose flour

2 tsp baking powder

1¼ cups butter, softened

1½ cups sugar

6 large eggs

⅓ cup milk

vanilla buttercream frosting (p446), colored pale pink and yellow

metallic or colored dragées, for garnish (optional)

1 Preheat the oven to 350°F (180°C). Line a 12-cup muffin pan with paper liners.

2 Sift the flour and baking powder into a bowl. Add the butter, sugar, eggs, vanilla, and milk. Beat with an electric mixer for 3 minutes, until pale and fluffy. Divide among the muffin cups. Bake 25–30 minutes, until golden brown. Let cool in the pan, then transfer to a wire rack to cool completely.

3 Pipe a swirl of frosting on top of each cupcake and decorate with the dragées, if using.

Rum Babas

These desserts are perfect to serve at a dinner party—just make these little rum-soaked cakes a day ahead and finish just before serving

 makes 4 babas

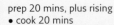 prep 20 mins, plus rising • cook 20 mins

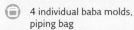 4 individual baba molds, piping bag

❄ freeze unsoaked babas for up to 3 months

For the babas

1 cup all-purpose flour

2 tbsp sugar

1 ½ tsp instant yeast

pinch salt

1 ¼ cup tepid whole milk

2 large eggs, lightly beaten

4 tbsp butter, melted and cooled, plus more for the molds

⅓ cup raisins

For the syrup

⅔ cup sugar

3 tbsp dark rum

To serve

¾ cup heavy cream

1 tbsp confectioner's sugar

1oz (30g) bittersweet chocolate, for garnish

● **Prepare ahead** You can bake the babas and make the syrup a day in advance.

1 To make the babas, combine the flour, sugar, yeast, and salt in a large bowl. Make a well in the center. Beat the milk, eggs, and butter together and pour into the well. Mix 3-4 minutes to make a smooth, thick batter. Stir in the raisins. Cover with plastic wrap and let stand in a warm place until doubled, about 45 minutes.

2 Generously butter 4 baba molds. Divide the batter among the molds. Cover with oiled plastic wrap and let rise in a warm place about 30 minutes, until doubled.

3 Preheat the oven to 400°F (200°C). Bake for about 15 minutes, or until the tops are light gold and spring back when pressed. Transfer to a wire rack and cool for 5 minutes. Unmold onto the rack and cool completely.

4 To make the syrup, bring the sugar and ½ cup water to a boil in a small saucepan over high heat, stirring to dissolve the sugar. Boil for 2 minutes. Transfer to a bowl and cool completely. Stir in the rum.

5 Use a wooden skewer to pierce holes over the surfaces of the babas. Transfer the babas to the syrup and let stand, turning often, until soaked. Stand each baba on a dessert plate.

6 Just before serving, whip the cream and confectioner's sugar just until soft peaks form. Transfer the cream to a pastry bag fitted with an open star tip, and pipe a rosette on each baba. Grate a little chocolate on each baba and serve with the remaining whipped cream.

VARIATIONS

Summer Fruit Babas

As a lighter summer variation, top the babas with summer berries rather than whipped cream.

Prune and Armagnac Babas

Substitute finely chopped prunes for the raisins, and Armagnac for the rum. Scatter a few chopped dried plums over the whipped cream instead of the chocolate.

Banana Bread

A moist cake that keeps well

 makes 8 servings

 prep 15 mins • cook 1 hr–1 hr 15 mins

▢ 8 x 4in (20 x 10cm) loaf pan

1 ¾ cups all-purpose flour

1 ½ tsp baking powder

6 tbsp butter, plus more for the pan

⅔ cup packed light brown sugar

3 ripe bananas

½ cup plain low-fat yogurt

2 large eggs

¾ cup walnuts, chopped

● **Prepare ahead** Will keep for up to 1 week in an airtight container.

1 Preheat the oven to 350°F (180°C). Butter the loaf pan and line the bottom with wax paper. Sift the flour and baking powder together into a bowl. Add the butter and use your fingertips to rub it in until the mixture resembles bread crumbs. Stir in the sugar.

2 Mash the bananas with a fork—you should have 1 cup. Add the bananas, yogurt, and eggs to the flour mixture and stir until combined. Stir in the walnuts. Spread in the pan.

3 Bake for 1 ¼ hours, or until a wooden toothpick inserted in the center comes out clean. Transfer to a wire cake rack and let cool 5 minutes. Invert onto the rack, remove the paper, and cool completely.

Chelsea Buns

These are British sticky buns, with a bit of spice in the fruit filling

🍴 makes 9 buns

🕐 prep 30 mins, plus rising
• cook 30 mins

▣ 9in (23cm) square cake pan

❄ freeze baked buns up to 1 month

2 cups **bread flour**

2 tbsp **granulated sugar**

1 tsp **instant yeast**

½ tsp **salt**

1 tbsp cold **butter**, diced

½ cup tepid **milk**

1 large **egg**, lightly beaten

For the filling

2 tbsp **butter**, melted and cooled

¾ cup **raisins, golden raisins, and/or dried currants**

⅓ cup packed **light brown sugar**

1 tsp **pumpkin pie spice**

¼ cup **honey**, to glaze

● **Prepare ahead** The buns can be stored in an airtight container for up to 2 days. Reheat before serving.

1 Mix the flour, sugar, yeast, and salt together in a large bowl. Add the butter and rub it in with your fingertips. Make a well in the center. Pour in the milk and egg and mix to form a soft dough. Knead on a lightly floured work surface for 8 minutes, or until smooth and elastic. Shape into a ball. Place in a lightly oiled bowl and turn to coat the dough. Cover tightly with plastic wrap. Let stand in a warm place about 1 hour, until doubled.

2 Lightly butter the cake pan. Knead the dough on a lightly floured surface and roll into a rectangle about 12 x 9in (30 x 23cm).

3 To make the filling, brush the surface of the dough with the melted butter, leaving a 1in (2.5cm) border along the long sides. Mix the raisins, brown sugar, and spice together and sprinkle over the butter. Starting at a long side, roll up the dough and pinch the seam closed. Slice the dough into 9 equal pieces. Arrange the slices in the pan. Cover loosely with plastic wrap and let stand about 30 minutes, until doubled.

4 Preheat the oven to 375°F (190°C). Bake for 30 minutes, until golden brown. Transfer to a wire rack. Brush the buns with the honey. Let cool for about 10 minutes, then remove from the pan and serve warm.

Cornish Saffron Buns

Saffron gives these fruit buns a light golden color and a subtle spicy flavor

🍴 makes 12 buns

🕐 prep 25 mins, plus rising
• cook 15–20 mins

❄ freeze for up to 3 months

large pinch of **saffron threads**

1 tbsp **boiling water**

4 cups **bread flour**

1 tsp **salt**

9 tbsp cold **butter**, diced

½ cup **sugar**

1¼oz (7g) envelope **instant (fast-rising) yeast**

⅔ cup **whole milk**

1 large **egg**

1⅓ cups **currants, raisins, or golden raisins**

1 Preheat the oven to 275°F (140°C). Place the saffron in a small baking dish. Bake for 10–15 minutes to toast the saffron. Let cool, then crumble to a fine powder. Stir into the boiling water and let stand about 1 hour, or overnight.

2 Sift the flour and salt into a large bowl. Add the butter and rub it in with your fingertips until the mixture resembles coarse bread crumbs. Stir in the sugar and yeast. Beat together the milk, ½ cup water, egg, and dissolved saffron. Add to the flour mixture and stir to make a soft dough.

3 Turn the dough out onto a lightly floured surface and knead for 8–10 minutes, or until smooth and elastic. Knead in the currants.

4 Divide the dough into 12 pieces. Shape each piece into a ball and flatten slightly. Place the balls on an oiled baking sheet. Cover loosely with lightly oiled plastic wrap. Let stand in a warm place for 30–40 minutes, or until they have doubled in size.

5 Preheat the oven to 425°F (220°C). Bake in the upper third of the oven for 15–20 minutes, or until the buns are light gold and sound hollow when tapped on the bottom. Transfer to a wire rack and let cool. Serve warm or cold.

● **Good with** butter.

● **Leftovers** can be allowed to go a little stale, then be used as a base for a trifle or in place of bread in a stuffing.

Apple Muffins

These are best served straight from the oven for breakfast, but are also good in lunch boxes or with afternoon tea

- makes 12 muffins
- prep 10 mins • cook 20–25 mins
- 12-cup muffin pan, paper liners

1 Golden Delicious apple, peeled, cored, and diced

½ cup packed light brown sugar

2 tsp lemon juice

1⅓ cups all-purpose flour

⅓ cup whole wheat flour

4 tsp baking powder

1 tbsp pumpkin-pie spice

½ tsp salt

¼ cup pecans, coarsely chopped

1 cup whole milk

¼ cup vegetable oil

1 large egg, beaten

turninado sugar, for sprinkling

1 Preheat the oven to 400°F (200°C). Line a 12-cup muffin pan with paper liners. Combine the apple, ¼ cup brown sugar, and the lemon juice in a bowl, and mix until the apple pieces are evenly coated. Set aside for 5 minutes.

2 Meanwhile, whisk together the flours, baking powder, pumpkin-pie spice, and salt in a large bowl. Mix in the remaining brown sugar and pecans.

3 Whisk together the milk, oil, and egg, then add the apple mixture. Pour into the dry ingredients and stir until just mixed.

4 Divide the batter among the muffin cups, filling them about two-thirds full. Sprinkle with the turninado sugar. Bake for 20–25 minutes, until the tops are rounded and light brown. Immediately unmold the muffins onto a wire rack. Serve hot, warm, or at room temperature.

● **Good with** butter when they are still hot.

Lemon Poppy Seed Muffins

Best eaten freshly made, this quick-to-make treat is perfect for brunch

- makes 12 muffins
- prep 10 mins • cook 20 mins
- 12-cup muffin pan, paper liners

2⅔ cups all-purpose flour

1½ tsp baking powder

½ tsp baking soda

¼ tsp salt

½ cup granulated sugar

2½ tbsp poppy seeds

2 large eggs

1 cup plus 2 tbsp sour cream

4 tbsp butter, melted and cooled

¼ cup vegetable oil

zest of 2 large lemons, finely grated

confectioner's sugar, for dusting

1 Preheat the oven to 400°F (200°C). Line a 12-cup muffin pan with paper liners. Sift the flour, baking powder, baking soda, and salt into a large bowl. Stir in the sugar and poppy seeds, making a well in the center.

2 In a separate bowl, beat the eggs. Stir in the sour cream, butter, oil, and lemon zest. Add to the flour mixture and stir until just mixed. Divide the batter among the muffin cups, filling each one three-quarters full.

3 Bake the muffins for 20 minutes, or until golden brown and a toothpick inserted in the center comes out clean. Remove the muffins from the pan, and transfer to a wire rack to cool. Sift confectioner's sugar over the tops while still warm.

Chocolate Muffins

These are sure to fix any chocolate cravings, and the buttermilk lends a delicious lightness to these muffins

 makes 12

 prep 10 mins • cook 20 mins

 12-cup muffin pan, paper liners

1⅔ cups **all-purpose flour**

⅔ cup Dutch-process **cocoa powder**

2 tsp **baking powder**

½ tsp **baking soda**

¼ tsp **salt**

¾ cup packed **light brown sugar**

1 cup plus 2 tbsp **buttermilk**

⅓ cup plus 2 tbsp **vegetable oil**

2 large **eggs**

½ tsp **pure vanilla extract**

1 cup **semisweet chocolate chips**

1 **Preheat the oven** to 400°F (200°C). Line a 12-cup muffin pan with paper liners.

2 **Sift the flour**, cocoa powder, baking powder, baking soda, and salt into a large bowl. Stir in the brown sugar, then make a well in the center.

3 **Whisk together the** buttermilk, oil, eggs, and vanilla. Pour into the well in the flour mixture and stir until the batter is just combined. Fold in the chocolate chips. Divide the batter among the muffin cups, filling each one three-quarters full.

4 **Bake for 20 minutes**, or until a toothpick inserted in the center comes out clean. Remove the muffins from the pan, transfer to a wire rack, and cool completely.

Barm Brack

This Irish fruit bread is sometimes served for Halloween with little charms baked inside, which are supposed to forecast your luck for the following year

- 🍴 makes serves 6-8 servings
- 🕐 prep 15 mins, plus soaking and rising • cook 50 mins
- 🍳 8in (20cm) round cake pan
- ❄ freeze for up to 3 months

3½ cups mixed **raisins, golden raisins,** and/or **currants**

⅔ cup hot brewed strong **black tea**

3½ cups **bread flour**

4 tbsp **butter**, at room temperature, plus more for the bowl

⅔ cup **sugar**

¼oz (7g) envelope **instant yeast**

1 tsp **ground pumpkin pie spice**

½ tsp **salt**

⅔ cup **milk**, lukewarm

2 large **eggs**

1 Mix the dried fruit and tea in a medium bowl. Cover and let stand overnight.

2 Put the flour in a large bowl. Mix in the butter until the mixture resembles fine breadcrumbs. Stir in the sugar, yeast, spice, and salt. Lightly beat the milk and one egg together, add to the flour mixture, and stir to make a stiff dough.

3 Drain the dried fruit and pat dry. Turn the dough out onto a lightly floured surface and knead for 8-10 minutes, until smooth and elastic. Pat out the dough into a rectangle, sprinkle with the drained fruit, roll up, and knead just until the fruit is distributed. (Do not knead too much, or the soft fruit will start break up.) If the dough becomes too sticky, knead in a little more flour.

4 Lightly butter an 8in (20cm) round cake pan. Shape the dough into a ball and press it into the pan. Cover the pan with a piece of oiled plastic wrap. Let stand a warm place for 40-60 minutes, or until the dough has doubled in size.

5 Preheat the oven to 400°F (200°C). Beat the remaining egg and lightly brush the top of the bread with the egg. Bake for 20 minutes. Reduce the oven temperature to 350°F (180°C) and bake for another 20-30 minutes, or until it sounds hollow when removed from the pan and tapped on the bottom. If the bread starts to brown too quickly, cover it with aluminum foil.

6 Transfer to a wire rack and let cool. Serve the bread warm or at room temperature.

● **Good with** lots of butter.

Pecan and Maple Tart

This sweet, crunchy pie is a true all-American dessert.
This version uses maple syrup

- makes 6–8 servings
- prep 15 mins, plus chilling • cook 45 mins
- 9in (23cm) fluted tart pan with a removable bottom, baking beans

1 refrigerated **pie dough round** for a 9in (23cm) pie

¾ cup packed **light brown sugar**

⅔ cup **maple syrup**

4 tbsp **butter**

pinch **salt**

3 large **eggs**

½ tsp **pure vanilla extract**

1 ¾ cups coarsely chopped **pecans**

1 Preheat the oven to 400°F (200°C). Line a 9in (23cm) pie dish with the pie dough. Prick the dough all over with a fork. Refrigerate for 15 minutes.

2 Line the dough with wax paper, then fill with baking beans. Place the pie dish on a baking sheet. Bake for 10 minutes or until the pastry looks set. Remove the paper and beans and prick the dough again.

Bake for about 10 minutes more, until the pastry is beginning to brown. Transfer to a wire rack and let cool. Reduce the oven temperature to 350°F (180°C).

3 Meanwhile, cook the brown sugar, maple syrup, butter, and salt in a medium saucepan over low heat, stirring until the sugar dissolves. Remove from the heat and cool until tepid. Whisk in the eggs, one at a time, then the vanilla. Stir in the pecans, then pour into the tart shell.

4 Bake 40–50 minutes, or until the filling is barely set. Tent the tart with aluminum foil if it is browning too quickly. Transfer to a wire rack and let cool for 20 minutes. Remove the sides of the pan. Serve warm, or cool completely.

● **Good with** crème fraîche, whipped cream, or ice cream.

Blueberry Cream Cheese Tart

Serve this in the summer when blueberries are at their peak

- makes 8 servings
- prep 25 mins, plus chilling • cook 30–45 mins
- 9in (23cm) tart pan with a removable bottom

For the pastry

1 ¼ cups **all-purpose flour**

2 tbsp **sugar**

6 tbsp cold **butter**, diced

1 large **egg yolk**

For the filling

4oz (115g) **cream cheese**, softened

⅓ cup **superfine sugar**

¼ cup **sour cream**

3 large **eggs**, beaten

grated zest of 1 **lemon**

pinch grated **nutmeg**

12oz (350g) fresh **blueberries**

confectioner's sugar, for garnish

● **Prepare ahead** The tart can be refrigerated for up to 2 days.

1 Preheat the oven to 400°F (200°C). To make the dough, stir the flour and sugar together in a bowl. Add the butter and rub it with your fingertips until the mixture resembles coarse bread crumbs. Mix the egg yolk with 3 tbsp cold water, add the flour mixture, and stir.

2 On a lightly floured surface, roll the dough into a ⅛in (3mm) round circle and use to line a 9in (23cm) tart pan with a removable bottom. Prick it lightly all over with a fork. Chill for 30 minutes. Line the dough with wax paper and fill with baking beans. Bake for 10 minutes. Remove the paper and baking beans and bake for 10 minutes more, until the crust is golden and crisp. Remove from the oven. Reduce the oven temperature to 350°F (180°C).

3 Beat the cream cheese, sugar, sour cream, eggs, lemon zest, and nutmeg with an electric mixer until well combined. Spread in the tart shell and top with the blueberries. Bake for 25–30 minutes, or until the filling is just set. Transfer to a wire rack and let cool. Remove the sides of the pan. Sift confectioner's sugar over the top, slice, and serve.

VARIATION

Raspberry Cream Cheese Tart

Use the same quantity of fresh raspberries in place of the blueberries.

Almond and Quince Tart

Sweet-tart quince paste is available at specialty markets and in the Latino section of many supermarkets

 makes 6–8 servings

 prep 20 mins, plus chilling • cook 45–55 mins

9in (23cm) tart pan with removable bottom, baking beans

For the almond pastry

1 cup **all-purpose flour**, plus more for dusting

3 tbsp **almond flour** (almond meal)

1 tbsp **confectioner's sugar**

5 tbsp **butter**, at room temperature

1 large **egg yolk** beaten with 1½ tbsp **water**

grated zest of ½ **lemon**

For the filling

1 cup blanched slivered **almonds**

grated zest and juice of ½ **orange**

grated zest and juice of ½ **lemon**

2 tbsp **almond liqueur**

10 tbsp **butter**, at room temperature

⅓ cup **confectioner's sugar**

3 large **eggs**

To complete

6oz (175g) **quince paste** (*membrillo*) or quince preserves

squeeze of **lemon** juice

confectioner's sugar, for dusting

1 **To make the pastry**, pulse the flour, almond flour, and confectioner's sugar in a food processor to combine. Add the butter and pulse until the mixture resembles coarse bread crumbs. Add yolk mixture and lemon zest and pulse until the dough clumps together. Gather into a thick disk, wrap in plastic wrap, and refrigerate for 30 minutes.

2 **To make the filling**, process the almonds in the food processor until coarsely ground. Add the orange and lemon zests and juices with the liqueur, and process to combine. With the machine running, one tablespoon at a time, add the butter. Stop the machine, add the confectioner's sugar, and process until smooth. With the machine runnning, one at a time, add the eggs, stopping to scrape the bowl as needed.

3 **Roll the dough** on a lightly floured work surface into a ⅛in (3mm) thick round. Line the round tart pan with a removable bottom with the dough and prick well with a fork. Refrigerate for 30 minutes.

4 **Preheat the oven** to 400°F (200°C). Line the dough with aluminum foil and baking beans. Bake about 15 minutes, until the crust looks set. Remove the foil and beans and bake for 10 minutes longer. Let cool. Reduce the oven temperature to 350°F (180°C).

5 **Melt the quince paste** with 1 tbsp water and the lemon juice over low heat until melted. Spread evenly in the tart shell. Spread the almond mixture on top. Bake for about 35 minutes until the filling is golden. Let cool 15 minutes. Remove the sides of the pan and transfer to a platter. Dust with confectioner's sugar and serve warm.

Treacle Tart

A traditional British favorite

 makes 8 servings

 prep 30 mins • cook 30 mins

9in (23cm) tart pan with removable bottom

1½ cups **all-purpose flour**

1 tbsp **sugar**

8 tbsp cold **butter**, cubed

1 large **egg yolk**

1½ cups **golden syrup**

zest of 1 large **lemon**, finely grated

1 tbsp **lemon** juice

½ tsp **ground ginger**

1 cup fresh **bread crumbs**

1 **Preheat the oven** to 400°F (200°C). Mix the flour and sugar in a bowl. Add the butter and mix until the dough resembles coarse bread crumbs. Mix the egg yolk with 3 tbsp cold water. Add to the dough and stir until it comes together.

2 **On a lightly floured** surface, roll the dough into a ⅛in (3mm) circle to line the tart pan. Trim the excess and prick with a fork. Chill for 30 minutes. Line with wax paper, fill with baking beans, and bake for 10 minutes. Remove the paper and beans and bake for 5 minutes. Remove and reduce the oven temperature to 375°F (190°C).

3 **Warm the syrup** in a saucepan with the lemon. Add the ginger. Sprinkle the bread crumbs in the tart shell, pour in the syrup, and let stand for 5 minutes. Use the dough trimmings to make a lattice top. Bake for 20–30 minutes.

Prune and Almond Tart

A fabulous combination of fruit and nuts

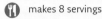

- makes 8 servings
- prep 20 mins, plus chilling • cook 50 mins
- 9in (23cm) tart pan with a removable bottom, baking beans

1 ¼ cups all-purpose flour

1 tbsp sugar

¼ tsp salt

6 tbsp butter, chilled, cut into cubes

1 large egg yolk beaten with 1 ½ tbsp cold water

For the filling

1 cup pitted dried plums (prunes)

2 tbsp brandy

1 cup toasted blanched almonds

⅔ cup sugar

½ cup heavy cream

2 large eggs plus 1 large egg yolk

2 tbsp butter, at room temperature

grated zest of ½ orange

¼ tsp almond extract

1 **Pulse the flour** and sugar in a food processor to combine; add the butter and pulse until the mixture resembles bread crumbs. Add the yolk, then pulse just until the pastry begins to clump together. Roll out on a floured surface into a ⅛in (3mm) thick round. Line the tart pan with the dough. Cover with plastic wrap and refrigerate for 30 minutes.

2 **Meanwhile**, place the plums in a saucepan with water to barely cover, and add the brandy. Simmer over low heat for 5 minutes, or until the plums are plumped. Let cool.

3 **Preheat the oven** to 400°F (200°C). Line the tart pan with wax paper and fill with baking beans. Bake for 10 minutes, or until the pastry looks set. Remove the paper and beans, then bake for 10 minutes more, or until the pastry is browned. Transfer the pan to a rack and cool.

4 **Process** ½ cup of the almonds and the sugar until finely ground. Add the remaining ingredients and process until smooth.

5 **Drain the prunes**. Pour the almond cream into the cooled pastry and arrange the prunes on top. Sprinkle with the remaining almonds.

6 **Bake 30 mins** in a 350°F (180°C) oven, or until the filling is set and golden brown. Cool, remove the sides of the pan, slice, and serve.

Mince Pies

Mince pies are a must for many bakers at the holidays. These individual pies are perfect for gift-giving

- makes 9 small pies
- prep 20 mins, plus resting • cook 10–12 mins
- 3½in (9cm) and smaller, decorative cookie cutters

1 Granny Smith apple

2 tbsp butter, melted, plus more for the pan

½ cup golden raisins

½ cup raisins

¼ cup dried currants

¼ cup mixed candied peel

¼ cup chopped almonds or hazelnuts

3 tbsp dark brown sugar

1 tbsp brandy or whisky

1 tsp pumpkin pie spice

grated zest of 1 lemon

½ banana

one 17.3 oz (484g) box thawed frozen puff pastry sheets

1 **Preheat the oven** to 375°F (190°C). Lightly butter 9 cups in a muffin pan.

2 **Grate the apple** (including the skin) into a bowl. Add the butter, golden raisins, raisins, currants, mixed peel, almonds, brown sugar, brandy, pumpkin pie spice, and lemon zest and mix well. Dice the banana, add to the bowl, and mix again.

3 **Roll out the puff pastry** into a 14in (35cm) square. Prick the dough well with a fork. Cut out 9 rounds of dough with a 3½in (9cm) diameter cookie cutter. Fit the rounds into the muffin cups. Divide the apple mixture among the cups. Using 3in (7.5cm) diameter decorative cookie cutters, cut out 9 shapes or rounds. Place on top of the filling. Refrigerate for 10 minutes.

4 **Bake for about 25 minutes**, or until the pastry is golden brown. Carefully remove from the cups and cool on a wire cake rack.

- **Prepare ahead** The pies can be prepared and stored for up to 3 days.

Chocolate Chiffon Pie

Rich and indulgent, this pie offers a satisfying contrast between a light, smooth mousse-like filling and a crunchy crumb crust

- makes 8-10 servings
- prep 20 mins, plus chilling • cook 8-10 mins
- 9in (23cm) tart pan with a removable bottom

For the crust

1½ cups graham cracker crumbs

2 tbsp sugar

5 tbsp butter, melted

For the filling

1 envelope unflavored gelatin powder

⅔ cup heavy cream

2oz (55g) unsweetened chocolate, chopped

¼ tsp pure vanilla extract

2 large eggs, separated, plus 1 large egg yolk

¾ cup sugar

pinch salt

¼ tsp cream of tartar

To decorate

¾ cup heavy cream

2 tbsp confectioner's sugar

grated bittersweet chocolate

1 **To make the crust**, preheat the oven to 375°F (190°C). Mix the graham cracker crumbs, butter, and sugar until combined. Press firmly and evenly in a 9in (23cm) tart pan with a removable bottom. Bake for about 10 minutes, or until the crust looks set. Let cool completely on a wire rack.

2 **To make the filling**, sprinkle the gelatin over ¼ cup water and let stand about 5 minutes, until spongy. Meanwhile, heat the cream in a medium saucepan over medium heat until simmering. Remove from the heat, add the chocolate and vanilla, and stir until the chocolate melts. Add the softened gelatin and whisk well until dissolved.

3 **Meanwhile**, using an electric mixer, beat the 3 egg yolks with ½ cup of the sugar and the salt for about 2 minutes, until the mixture is thick and creamy. Slowly beat in the chocolate mixture, mixing until well blended. Cover the bowl with plastic wrap and refrigerate about 15 minutes, or until cool and on the verge of setting.

4 **Beat the egg whites** and cream of tartar in a large bowl until soft peaks form. Beat in the remaining ¼ cup sugar, one tablespoon at a time, until stiff peaks form. Remove the chocolate mixture from the refrigerator and beat with the mixer for 2 minutes. Stir in about one-fourth of the whites, then fold in the remainder. Spoon the chocolate mixture into the crumb crust and smooth the top.

5 **In a separate bowl**, beat the cream with the confectioner's sugar until stiff peaks form. Swirl the whipped cream over the filling. Grate additional chocolate over the cream. Refrigerate for at least 2 hours. Remove the sides of the pan and serve chilled.

Apple and Pear Galette

Sugar-coated fruit in pastry

- makes 8 servings
- prep 40 mins, plus chilling • cook 45 mins

6 tbsp cold butter, diced

2 tbsp cold vegetable shortening

1¼ cups all-purpose flour

3-5 tbsp iced water

1lb (450g) Golden Delicious apples

1lb (450g) ripe Bosc pears

¼ cup sugar

2 tbsp apricot preserves, melted

1 **Rub in** 4 tbsp butter and all the shortening into the flour until the mixture resembles coarse bread crumbs. Stir in enough water to make a dough that holds together. Gather into a disk. Wrap in plastic wrap and refrigerate for 30 minutes.

2 **Preheat the oven** to 425°F (220°C). On a floured surface, roll out the pastry to a 15in (38cm) round. Transfer to a baking tray, hanging the excess over the sides.

3 **Peel, core, and cut** the apples and pears into ¼in (5mm) thick slices. Arrange the fruit in concentric circles on the pastry, leaving a 1½in (4cm) border. Sprinkle with the sugar and dot with 2 tbsp butter. Fold up and pleat the pastry around the fruit.

4 **Bake 45 minutes**, or until the fruit is tender and the crust is golden brown. Brush with the preserves. Serve warm.

Banana Cream Pie

This traditional American pie makes a rich and creamy end to any meal

- makes 8–10 servings
- prep 20 mins, plus chilling • cook 25 mins
- 9in (23cm) pie dish, baking beans

1 refrigerated **pie dough round** for a 9in (23cm) pie

4 large **egg yolks**

½ cup **sugar**

¼ cup **cornstarch**

¼ tsp **salt**

2 cups **whole milk**, heated

1 tsp **pure vanilla extract**

3 ripe **bananas**

½ tbsp fresh **lemon** juice

1½ cups **heavy cream**

3 tbsp **confectioner's sugar**

● **Prepare ahead** The filling can be refrigerated, with wax paper pressed on its surface, up to 1 day ahead. The baked piecrust can be wrapped in aluminum foil and stored up to 1 day at room temperature.

1 **Preheat the oven** to 400°F (200°C). Line a 9in (23cm) pie dish with the pie dough. Prick the dough all over with a fork.

2 **Line the dough** with wax paper, then fill with baking beans. Place the pie dish on a baking sheet. Bake for 10 minutes or until the pastry looks set. Remove the paper and beans and prick the dough again. Bake for about 10 minutes more, until the pastry is golden brown. Transfer to a wire rack and let cool.

3 **Meanwhile**, beat the egg yolks, sugar, cornstarch, and salt together well in a medium saucepan until the mixture is pale yellow. Whisk in the hot milk and vanilla. Cook over medium heat, stirring constantly, just until thickened and beginning to boil. Reduce the heat to low and let cook and bubble gently, stirring, for 2 minutes more. Strain through a wire sieve into a bowl, press a piece of plastic wrap on the surface, and let cool.

4 **Thinly slice** the bananas and toss with the lemon juice. Spread them in the pie shell, then top with the custard. Cover with plastic wrap and refrigerate until chilled, at least 2 hours.

5 **Beat the cream** and confectioner's sugar until stiff peaks form. Spread over the filling and serve chilled.

Key Lime Pie

Key limes can now purchased at well-stocked markets during their winter and early spring season, but regular limes work, too

- makes 8 servings
- prep 20–25 mins • cook 20 mins
- 9in (23cm) tart pan with a removable bottom

1½ cups **graham cracker crumbs**

2 tbsp **sugar**

5 tbsp **butter**, melted

For the filling

15 **key limes** or 6 limes

one 14oz (400g) can **condensed milk**

4 large **egg yolks**

¾ cup **heavy cream**

2 tbsp **confectioner's sugar**

½ tsp **pure vanilla extract**

1 **Preheat the oven** to 350°F (180°C). To make the crust, mix the graham cracker crumbs, sugar, and butter in a bowl until combined. Press firmly and evenly into the bottom and sides of a 9in (23cm) tart pan with a removable bottom. Place on a baking sheet and bake until the crust looks set, about 12 minutes.

2 **Meanwhile, grate the zest** of 6 key limes (or 2 limes) in a bowl. Juice 14 key limes (or 5 limes). You should have ½ cup lime juice.

3 **Add the condensed milk**, yolks, and lime juice to the bowl and whisk well. Pour the filling into the crust. Return to the oven and continue baking 15–20 minutes, or until the filling is set.

4 **Transfer to a wire rack** and let cool completely. Whip the cream, confectioner's sugar, and vanilla until soft peaks form Spread over the cooled pie. Thinly slice the reserved lime and use to garnish the pie. Remove the sides of the pan, slice, and serve.

● **Good with** pouring cream.

White Chocolate and Mascarpone Tarts

These pretty little tarts are ideal to serve, topped with fresh summer berries, at dinner parties

- makes 6-8 servings
- prep 10 mins, plus 20 mins chilling • cook 15 mins, plus 3 hrs setting
- 6 x 4in (10cm) tart pans with removable bottoms

For the pastry

1¼ cups all-purpose flour, plus more for rolling the dough

6 tbsp chilled butter

3 tbsp sugar

1 large egg, beaten

For the filling

7oz (200g) white chocolate, chopped

1lb (450g) mascarpone

⅔ cup heavy cream

For the topping

about 4 cups raspberries, blueberries, and small strawberries

mint leaves and confectioner's sugar for garnish

1 **To make the pastry**, stir the flour and sugar together in a bowl. Add the butter and rub it with your fingertips until the mixture resembles coarse bread crumbs. Mix the egg yolk with 3 tbsp cold water. Add the egg and process until the pastry draws together into a ball. Wrap and chill for 30 minutes.

2 **On a floured surface**, roll the dough into a ⅛in (3mm) round circle and use to line six 4in (10cm) tart pans with removable bottoms. Prick all over. Chill for 30 minutes.

3 **Preheat the oven** to 400°F (200°C). Line the dough with wax paper and fill with baking beans. Bake for 10 minutes. Remove the paper and beans and bake for 10 minutes more, until the crust is golden and crisp.

4 **Combine the** white chocolate and ½ cup of the mascarpone in a heatproof bowl. Place over a saucepan of barely simmering water and stir until melted. Remove from the heat. Add the remaining mascarpone and whisk briskly until smooth, then whisk in the cream.

5 **Spread in the tart** shells. Refrigerate for 3 hours, until softly set. Mound the berries on the tart. Garnish with mint leaves, sift with confectioner's sugar, and serve chilled.

Silesian Poppy Tart

Tarts made with poppy seeds are popular in Eastern Europe

🍴 makes 16 slices

🕐 prep 35 mins, plus cooling
• cook 1½ hrs

⬜ 11in (28cm) springform pan

1¾ cups **all-purpose flour**

2 tsp **baking powder**

1½ cups **sugar**

1¼ cups **butter**, softened

3 large **eggs**

1 tsp **pure vanilla extract**

pinch of **salt**

1 quart (1 liter) **milk**

5½oz (150g) **butter**

½ cup **semolina**

scant 1 cup **poppy seeds**, ground in a coffee grinder

4oz (115g) **farmer's cheese**

1 ripe **pear**, peeled, cored, and grated

⅓ cup **almond flour** (almond meal)

½ cup **raisins**

confectioner's sugar, for sifting

1 Sift the flour and baking powder together into a bowl. Add ⅔ cup of the sugar, 9 tbsp of the butter, 1 beaten egg, ½ tsp of the vanilla, the salt, and 4 tsp water.

Work with a wooden spoon until the dough comes together.

2 Bring the milk and remaining 1 tbsp butter to a simmer in a saucepan over medium heat. Whisk in the semolina and poppy seeds. Reduce the heat to medium-low and simmer, stirring occasionally, about 20 minutes, until the mixture is thick. Let cool for 10 minutes.

3 Preheat the oven to 350°F (180°C). Lightly butter an 11in (28cm) springform pan. Roll out half of the dough into an 11in (28cm) round and fit into the bottom of the pan. Roll out the remaining dough into a long strip about 1¼in (3cm) wide and line the sides of the pan.

4 Stir ⅔ cup plus 2 tbsp sugar, 2 eggs, and ½ tsp vanilla with the farmer's cheese, pear, almond flour, and raisins into the cooled poppy seed mixture. Spread evenly in the pan. Bake for about 1 hour, until the pastry edge is golden brown and the filling looks set.

5 Let cool for 30 minutes on a wire cake rack. Loosen the tart from the sides of the pan with a knife, then remove the sides. Sift confectioner's sugar over the tart and serve warm or cool completely.

Lemon Tart

With its creamy lemon filling, this tart is perfect with seasonal fruit

🍴 makes 6–8 servings

🕐 35 mins, plus 1 hr chilling
• cook 45 mins

⬜ 9in (23cm) tart pan with removable bottom, baking beans

For the filling

1 cup **sugar**

5 large **eggs**

grated zest and juice of 4 **lemons**

1 cup **heavy cream**

For the pastry

1¼ cups **all-purpose flour**, plus more for rolling the dough

3 tbsp **sugar**

6 tbsp chilled **butter**, diced

1 large **egg**

⬤ **Prepare ahead** The tart can be refrigerated for up to 2 days; serve at room temperature.

1 To make the filling, whisk the sugar and eggs, then whisk in the lemon zest and juice. Whisk in the cream. Cover and refrigerate while making the pastry shell.

2 To make the dough, stir the flour and sugar together in a bowl. Add the butter and rub it with your fingertips until the mixture resembles coarse bread crumbs. Mix the egg yolk with 3 tbsp cold water. Add to the flour mixture and stir until the dough comes together.

3 On a lightly floured surface, roll the dough into a ⅛in (3mm) round circle and use to line a 9in (23cm) tart pan with a removable bottom. Prick it lightly all over with a fork. Chill for 30 minutes.

4 Preheat the oven to 400°F (200°C). Line the dough with wax paper and fill with baking beans. Bake for 10 minutes. Remove the paper and beans and bake for 10 minutes more, until the crust is golden and crisp. Remove from the oven. Reduce the oven temperature to 275°F (140°C).

5 Place the tart pan on a baking sheet. Pour the chilled lemon mixture into the pastry shell, taking care that the filling doesn't spill over the edges. Bake for 30 minutes, or until just set. Let cool, remove the sides of the pan and serve.

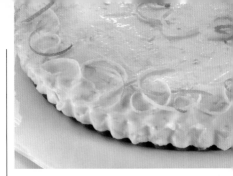

Lemon Meringue Tart

With the contrast between the smooth, tart lemon filling and the fluffy meringue topping, this pie is certain to be a hit

 makes 8–10 servings

 prep 20 mins, plus cooling • cook 40 mins

 9in (23cm) tart pan with removable bottom, baking beans

14oz (400g) **shortcrust pastry** (pp436–437)

4 large **lemons**

1¼ cups **sugar**

4 large **eggs**, separated

3 tbsp **cornstarch**

2 tbsp **butter**, diced

½ tsp **cream of tartar**

½ tsp **pure vanilla extract**

1 Preheat the oven to 400°F (200°C). Fit the pastry into a 9in (23cm) tart pan with a removable bottom, fitting it tightly into the corners, and trim the excess dough. Prick the dough with a fork. Line with wax paper and fill with baking beans. Chill for 30 minutes.

2 Place on a baking sheet and bake for 10 minutes, until the dough looks set. Remove the paper and the beans and bake until the dough is crisp and golden brown, about 10 minutes more. Transfer to a wire rack. Reduce the oven temperature to 350°F (180°C).

3 Meanwhile, to make the filling, grate the zest from 2 of the lemons. Juice the lemons: you should have ¾ cup of juice.

4 Whisk ¾ cup of the sugar, the egg yolks, and cornstarch together in a bowl until the mixture is pale yellow. Gradually whisk in 1 cup water and the lemon juice. Add the butter. Pour into a saucepan. Bring to a simmer over medium heat, stirring constantly, until simmering and thickened. Reduce the heat to low and let bubble for 30 seconds. Strain through a wire sieve. Stir in the zest. Spread evenly in the tart shell.

5 Beat the egg whites in a large bowl with an electric mixer until foamy. Add the cream of tartar and beat until soft peaks form. Beat in the remaining ½ cup sugar, a tablespoon at a time, until the meringue is thick and glossy. Spread the meringue over the hot filling, being sure that it touches the pie crust on all sides.

6 Place the tart on a baking sheet. Bake for 12–15 minutes until the meringue is tinged light brown. Transfer to a wire rack and let cool completely. To slice, dip a thin, sharp knife into a tall glass of hot water before each slice.

Citrus Cream Tart

A refreshing variation on key lime pie, this is quick to make

 makes 6–8 servings

 prep 20 mins, plus chilling

 9in (23cm) tart pan with removable bottom

1 cup crushed **gingersnap cookie crumbs**

4 tbsp **butter**, melted

1¼ cups **heavy cream**

two 14oz (400g) cans **condensed milk**

grated zest and juice of 4 **lemons**, plus 1 extra lemon for garnish

grated zest and juice of 4 **limes**, plus 1 extra lime for garnish

● **Prepare ahead** The tart can be refrigerated for 1 day before serving.

1 Mix the cookie crumbs and melted butter together. Press evenly in the bottom of a 9in (23cm) tart pan with a removable bottom. Refrigerate about 1 hour, until firm.

2 Process the cream and condensed milk together in a food processor. With the machine running, add the zest and juice of the lemons and limes. Spread in the cookie crust and refrigerate until set, at least 1 hour or overnight.

3 When ready to serve, remove the zest from ½ lemon and ½ lime with a vegetable peeler and cut into thin strips. Sprinkle over the tart and serve chilled.

Lenguas de Gato Cookies

Long and flat, these crisp cookies translate as "cat's tongues" in Spanish

- 🍴 makes about 20 cookies
- 🕐 prep 20 mins • cook 15 mins
- 📷 pastry bag

4 large **egg whites**, at room temperature

¾ cup **heavy cream**

3 tbsp **sugar**

1 tsp **pure vanilla extract**

1 cup **all-purpose flour**

● **Prepare ahead** These cookies can be made several days in advance and stored in an airtight container.

1 **Preheat the oven** to 375°F (190°C). Line 2 large baking sheets with parchment paper.

2 **Beat the egg whites** with an electric mixer until soft peaks form. Beat the cream, sugar, and vanilla until about as thick as sour cream. Fold in the whites. In three additions, sift the flour over the mixture, folding it in after each addition.

3 **Transfer the meringue** to a pastry bag with a ½in (13mm) plain tip. Pipe 3in (7.5cm) long strips of batter on the baking sheet, spacing them at least 2in (5cm) apart. Bake about 15 minutes, until the edges are golden brown in color. Let cool briefly, then transfer to a wire rack to cool completely.

● **Good with** hot chocolate, chocolate mousse, or ice cream.

Kaiserschmarrn

Legend says that this Austrian pancake was created for Emperor Franz Josef. Roughly translated as "Emperor's Mishmash," it is warming and delicious

- 🍴 makes 4 servings
- 🕐 prep 10 mins • cook 10 mins

⅔ cup **all-purpose flour**

4 large **eggs**, separated, at room temperature

¼ cup plus 4 tsp **sugar**

⅔ cup **whole milk**

2 tbsp **butter**

¼ cup **raisins**

confectioner's sugar, for serving

plum preserves, or apple sauce, for serving

1 **Whisk the flour** egg yolks, ¼ cup granulated sugar, and milk together in a bowl with a clean whisk until smooth. Beat the egg whites in a separate bowl until stiff peaks form. Fold into the batter.

2 **Melt 1½ tsp** of the butter in an 8in (20cm) nonstick frying pan over medium heat. Pour in one-fourth of the batter and sprinkle with 1 tbsp raisins. Cook 1 minute, until the underside is browned. Turn the pancake and brown the other side. Transfer to a plate. Repeat with the remaining butter, batter, and raisins.

3 **Tear the pancakes** into pieces using 2 forks. Return the pancake pieces to the frying pan (or a larger one, if you have it) and sprinkle with the remaining 4 tsp sugar. Cook over medium heat about 1 minute, until piping hot.

4 **Sift confectioner's sugar** on top and serve immediately, with the plum preserves on the side.

VARIATION

Kaiserschmarrn with Rum

For a more luxurious dish, soak the raisins in rum for an hour or so.

Pastry

There is nothing wrong with using ready-made pastry when you want to make a quick tart or pie, but making your own melt-in-your-mouth pastry is very satisfying. Once you master making and using these basic pastries, you'll have great scope for expanding your sweet and savory baking repertoire.

Shortcrust Pastry

For anyone new to pastry-making, this is the recipe to start with. This rich, crisp pastry is easy to make and used for both sweet and savory dishes, such as these Empanadas (p47). Use shortcrust pastry for:

- Sweet and savory tarts and tartlets
- Sweet and savory pies
- Quiches and flans
- Cornish pasties

Baked shortcrust pastry *has a crisp and firm, but light texture.*

Rough Puff Pastry

This flaky, butter-rich pastry is quicker and easier to make than traditional puff pastry, and can be used in any recipe calling for puff pastry, such as this Leek and Cheese Flamiche (p229). Use rough puff pastry in any of the following dishes:

- Meat, fish, and fruit pies
- Fish or meat cooked in pastry
- Vol-au-vents
- Fruit turnovers

Rough puff pastry *dough produces delicate layers of butter-rich pastry.*

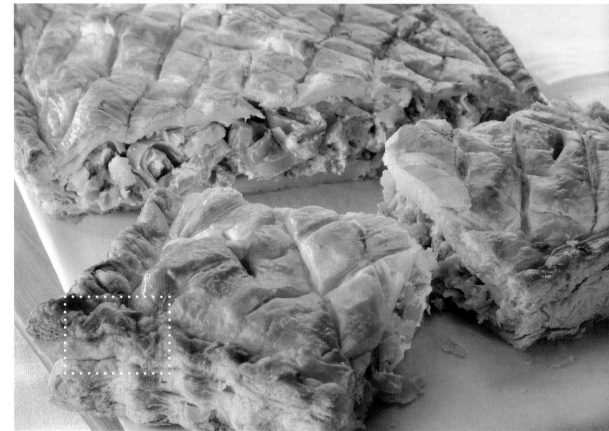

Sweet Shortcrust Pastry

Called *pâte sucrée* in French, this is a basic shortcrust pastry that includes sugar, and is the pastry used for this classic French Apple Tart (p454). Other uses include:

- Sweet tarts and tartlets
- French galettes
- Petits fours

Sweet shortcrust pastry *makes a crisp case for fruit and creamy fillings.*

Choux Pastry

Very easy to make, this pastry bakes into thin, hollow balls that can contain sweet or savory fillings. Unlike other pastries, choux pastry is too soft to roll out, so it is piped or simply dropped from the spoon on to a baking sheet, which is how these savory Cheese Puffs (p153) are formed. You also can use it for:

- Profiteroles
- Eclairs
- Gougères
- Croquembouches

Choux pastry *dough bakes to form crisp, hollow balls for filling.*

Pastry

Shortcrust Pastry

1 **Sift 6oz (175g)** all-purpose flour and a pinch of salt into a large bowl. Add 3oz (85g) chilled, diced butter or margarine. Lightly stir the butter to coat it in the flour.

Rough Puff Pastry

1 **Sift 9oz (250g)** all-purpose flour into a bowl. Add 3oz (85g) chilled diced butter and 3oz (85g) chilled diced white vegetable fat, then stir in the flour to coat. Add 5fl oz (150ml) iced water and a squeeze of lemon juice, and stir with a knife to bind.

Sweet Shortcrust Pastry

1 **Sift 7oz (200g)** all-purpose flour and a pinch of salt on to a work surface. Make a well in the center and add 3oz (85g) soft butter, 4 tbsp sugar, and 3 beaten egg yolks. Blend the ingredients in the well together with your fingertips.

Choux Pastry

1 **Bring 8fl oz (240ml) water** and ½ cup diced butter to a boil over high heat. Remove the pan from the heat and tip in 5oz (140g) all-purpose flour sifted with 1 tsp salt and 1 tsp sugar all at once and beat until the pastry is smooth.

Tips for Perfect Pastry

- Add chilled water, eggs, and fat straight from the refrigerator.
- Add liquid to the flour and fat mixture gradually. Flours have different absorption rates, so you might not need all of it.

- Work quickly. The less you handle the dough, the lighter and more delicate the baked pastry will be.
- Refrigerate your pastry dough for at least 30 minutes before rolling out. This makes it easier to roll and

helps prevent dough from "shrinking" while baking.
- If at any time the pastry becomes sticky, immediately return it to the refrigerator for 15 minutes before continuing with the recipe.

- Dust the work surface and rolling pin very lightly with flour when rolling out pastry. If too much extra flour is incorporated at this stage, the baked pastry will be tough.

how to make & use pastry

2 Quickly and lightly rub the butter into the flour with your fingertips until the mixture resembles coarse bread crumbs. Sprinkle in 2 tbsp iced water. Stir gently to mix.

3 Use your fingers to gather the pastry and roll it around to form a ball, handling it as little as possible. Wrap the pastry ball in plastic wrap and chill for at least 30 minutes before using.

2 Roll out the dough on a lightly floured surface into a rectangle 3 times as long as it is wide. Fold the top third of the pastry down, then bottom third up, as if folding a letter. Seal the open edges closed with the rolling pin. Wrap in plastic wrap and chill for 15 minutes.

3 With the unfolded edges at the top and bottom, roll and fold the pastry as in step 2. Turn the pastry 90 dgrees and repeat the rolling, folding, and turning twice more. Wrap and chill again for at least 30 minutes before using.

2 Using your fingertips, gradually work the sifted flour into the butter mixture until it resembles coarse bread crumbs. If the butter mixture is too sticky and crumbs don't form, work in a little extra flour.

3 Gather the dough into a ball, then knead it very quickly and lightly until it is smooth and pliable. Shape it back into a ball, wrap in plastic wrap, and chill for at least 30 minutes before using.

2 Return the pan to the heat and stir until the dough forms a ball and comes away from the sides of the pan. Quickly remove the pan from the heat.

3 Gradually beat in 4 eggs, one at a time, beating well after each addition. Continue beating until the mixture becomes shiny and drops off the spoon when shaken. It is now ready to use.

Tips for Better Baking

- Preheat the oven to the specified temperature before baking.
- For nonsoggy double-crust pies, such as Apple Pie (p450), cut slits in the top of the crust to let steam escape during baking.
- Very lightly splash the baking sheet with water before baking rough puff or puff pastry. The water creates steam in the hot oven, which helps form the many delicate layers.

Savory Uses

Cheese Straws
Use rough puff or ready-made puff pastry to make these party favorites
🕐 35 mins   page 55

Gruyère Tart
A combination of wholemeal and plain flours adds flavor to this shortcrust pastry crust
🕐 1 hr 10 mins   page 165

Chicken Pot Pie
Use rough puff pastry in this recipe to give a delightful contrast to the pie's creamy filling
🕐 35 mins   page 286

Sweet Uses

Pecan and Maple Tart
This American favorite with shortcrust pastry is very rich and filling
🕐 1 hr 45 mins   page 425

Lemon Meringue Pie
A creamy lemon filling and light meringue are encased in a shortcrust pastry case
🕐 1 hr 10 mins   page 432

Profiteroles
A French classic, these cream-filled choux buns are always a popular dessert
🕐 1 hr   page 439

WHAT CAN I DO WITH LEFTOVER PASTRY?

- Leftover shortcrust and sweet shortcrust pastry trimmings can be gathered together, shaped into a ball, wrapped in plastic wrap, and refrigerated for up to 3 days, or frozen for up to 6 months to be used in other recipes.

- Unbaked choux-pastry shapes can be refrigerated for up to 12 hours before filling and baking.

- Unbaked rough puff pastry can be refrigerated for up to 3 days and used in other recipes, but it is difficult to re-use trimmings because re-rolling will knock out all the air that forms the layers.

- Rolled and shaped rough puff pastry, such as vol-au-vents, can be frozen for up to 6 months and then baked straight from the freezer, adding 5 minutes to the baking time.

Cannoli

These crisp pastries filled with candied fruits and ricotta cheese are a Sicilian speciality

- makes 16
- prep 30 mins, plus cooling • cook 20 mins
- 8 cannoli molds, large saucepan, deep-frying thermometer
- ❄ the uncooked pastry will freeze for up to 3 months

For the pastry

1½ cups **all-purpose flour**, plus more for rolling

pinch of **salt**

4 tbsp **butter**

3 tbsp granulated **sugar**

1 large **egg**, plus 1 large **egg white**

3 tbsp **dry white wine** or Marsala, as needed

vegetable oil, for deep-frying

For the filling

12oz (350g) **ricotta cheese**

½ cup **confectioner's sugar**, plus more for sifting

2oz (60g) **bittersweet chocolate**, grated or very finely chopped

finely grated zest of 1 **orange**

⅓ cup finely chopped **candied orange** and/or lemon peel

● **Prepare ahead** The fried shells can be stored at room temperature and the filling chilled for up to 8 hours before filling and serving.

1 **To make the pastry**, sift the flour and salt into a bowl. Add the butter and rub it in until the mixture looks like bread crumbs. Stir in the sugar. Beat the egg and add to the flour mixture. Stir, adding enough wine to make a soft dough. Knead on a floured work surface until smooth.

2 **Roll out the pastry** on a lightly floured work surface until less than ⅛in (3mm) thick. Cut into

16 x 3in (7.5cm) squares. Beat the egg white until foamy. Dust 4 cannoli tubes with flour. Wrap a pastry square loosely around each tube, with the points facing east-west. Dampen the overlapping pastry with egg white and press together to seal.

3 **Pour enough oil** into a large saucepan to come halfway up the sides and heat over to 350°F (180°C) on a deep-frying thermometer. Add the cannoli and fry for 3 minutes, or until golden and crisp. Drain on paper towels. While the first batch cools, repeat with 4 more tubes and pastry squares. When cool enough to handle, carefully twist and pull the metal tubes out of the cannoli shells. Repeat to make 16 cannoli shells.

4 **To make the filling**, mix together ricotta, confectioner's sugar, candied peel, chocolate, and orange zest. Spoon the filling into the shells. Dust with confectioner's sugar and serve immediately.

Mini Chocolate Nut Pastries

Tasty bite-sized chocolate pastries—the perfect treat

- makes 24
- prep 25 mins, plus resting • cook 10–12 mins

1 cup **ground hazelnuts**

3 tbsp **hazelnut-** or almond-flavored liqueur

2½oz (75g) **bittersweet chocolate**, grated

2 tbsp **confectioner's sugar**, plus more for serving

2 thawed frozen **filo sheets**

3 tbsp **honey**, warmed

1 **Preheat the oven** to 375°F (190°C). Lightly butter a baking sheet. Mix the hazelnuts, liqueur, chocolate, and confectioner's sugar.

2 **Cut out** twenty-four 3½in (9cm) squares from the filo. Place a teaspoon of the chocolate mixture in the middle of each square. Brush a little water around the edge, gather the sides around the filling, and pinch in to form a purse-like shape.

3 **Place the pastries** on the baking sheet. Bake for 10–12 minutes, or until golden in color. Brush with honey, and let cool for 5 minutes. Sift confectioner's sugar over the top of the pastries. Serve warm or cooled.

Profiteroles

These little cream puffs, drizzled with chocolate sauce, are a deliciously decadent dessert

🍴 makes 4 servings

🕐 prep 30 mins, plus cooling • cook 30 mins

▣ piping bag with a ½in (1cm) plain tip and a ¼in (5mm) plain tip

❄ unfilled cream puffs can be cooled and packed into freezer bags or an airtight container and frozen for up to 3 months; thaw at room temperature for 30 mins before filling and serving

For the cream puffs

½ cup **water**

½ cup **all-purpose flour**

⅛ tsp **salt**

4 tbsp **butter**, cut into 4 slices

2 large **eggs**, beaten

For the sauce and filling

1½ cups **heavy cream**

4oz (115g) **bittersweet chocolate**, chopped

2 tbsp **butter**

2 tbsp **light corn syrup**

2 tbsp **confectioner's sugar**

½ tsp **pure vanilla extract**

1 Preheat the oven to 425°F (220°C). Line 2 large baking trays with wax paper. Sift the flour on to a separate piece of wax paper.

2 To make the cream puffs, combine the water, butter, and salt in a small saucepan and bring to a boil over medium-low heat; make sure the butter melts. Add the flour and cook, stirring, for 1 minute until the mixture forms a very thick paste that lightly covers the bottom of the pan. Remove and cool for 5 minutes.

3 Gradually stir the eggs into the paste (it will be loose at first,

but will come together with stirring) to make a stiff, smooth, and shiny dough. Spoon the dough into a pastry bag fitted with a ½in (1cm) plain tip.

4 Pipe 16 walnut-sized rounds on the prepared baking sheets. Bake for 15–18 minutes, until well puffed and golden. Remove from the oven and make a small slit in the side of each puff to allow the steam to escape. Return to the oven for 3–5 minutes more, until crisp. Cool completely on the sheet.

5 To make the sauce, bring ½ cup of the cream to a simmer in a small saucepan over medium

heat. Remove from the heat and add the chocolate, butter, and syrup. Let stand until the chocolate is softened, then whisk until smooth. Keep warm.

6 To make the filling, clean the pastry bag and tip. Whip the remaining 1 cup cream with the confectioner's sugar and vanilla in a chilled bowl until stiff. Transfer to the pastry bag fitted with the tip. Cut each puff in half crosswise. Fill the bottom half of each with whipped cream and replace the top.

7 To serve, pour the sauce over the puffs and serve at once.

Chocolate Eclairs

Instead of piping mounds on to the prepared baking sheets, pipe 2in (5cm) lengths and bake as for the puffs. You should be able to make 10 eclairs. Let them cool, then fill as for the puffs, and spread with 5½oz (150g) melted bittersweet chocolate that has been allowed to cool. Let set for a few minutes in the refrigerator before serving.

Cantucci

From Tuscany, these crisp, twice-baked almond cookies are ideal for dipping in glasses of coffee or vin santo after a meal

 makes 32 cookies

 prep 10 mins, plus cooling • bake 40 mins

 can be frozen up to 3 months; thaw at room temperature

butter for baking sheet

3 large eggs, plus 2 large egg yolks

2½ cups all-purpose flour

1⅓ cups toasted and chopped natural almonds

¾ cup sugar

2 tsp baking powder

finely grated zest of 1 orange

● **Prepare ahead** The dough can be shaped as in step 3, and refrigerated for up to 2 days.

1 Preheat the oven to 375°F (190°C) and butter one large baking sheet. Whisk the eggs and yolks together in a bowl. Transfer 2 tbsp of the mixture to a small bowl and set aside.

2 Combine the flour, almonds, sugar, baking powder, and orange zest in a large bowl and stir together. Make a well in the center, add the beaten egg mixture, and stir to form a stiff dough.

3 Gather the dough into a ball, then cut in half. On a lightly floured surface, shape each portion into a log about 2in (5cm) wide and 1in (2.5cm) tall. Place the logs well apart on the baking sheet. Flatten them slightly and brush the tops with some of the reserved egg mixture.

4 Bake for 20 minutes or until logs are lightly browned and feel set when pressed in the center. Remove from the oven and increase the temperature to 400°F (200°C).

5 Cool the logs for 10 minutes. Transfer to a cutting board. With a serrated knife held on a slight diagonal, cut into ½in (1cm) pieces. Return the slices to the baking sheet, flat sides down, and continue baking for 8 minutes more, or until crisp and golden. Cool on the baking sheet for 5 minutes, then transfer to wire racks to cool completely.

● **Good with** a glass of vin santo for dunking, or with coffee or tea.

Chocolate Chip Cookies

These cookies are soft, chewy, and cakey, and perfect to fill up the cookie jar

 makes 2 dozen cookies

prep 15 mins • bake 15–20 mins

½ cup plus 1 tbsp unsalted butter, softened

⅔ cup packed light brown sugar

1 large egg

3 tbsp light corn syrup

½ tsp pure vanilla extract

1¼ cups all-purpose flour

1¼ tsp baking powder

¼ tsp salt

1 cup semisweet chocolate chips

1 Preheat the oven to 350°F (180°C) and line 2 large baking sheets with parchment.

2 Mix together the butter and sugar with an electric mixer set on high speed for 2 minutes, until light and fluffy. Beat in the egg, corn syrup, and vanilla. Whisk the flour, baking powder, and salt to combine. On low speed, mix into the butter mixture. Stir in the chocolate chips, or reserve for sprinkling.

3 Drop tablespoons of the dough on the baking sheets, spacing them 1in (2.5cm) apart. Sprinkle the chocolate chips on the cookies, if reserved. Bake about 15 minutes, until the edges start to brown. Cool on the baking sheets for 3 minutes, then transfer the cookies to wire racks to cool.

VARIATION

Multi-chip Cookies

Choose milk, dark, or white chocolate chips or use bars of chocolate broken into small pieces.

Shortbread

This popular Scottish classic has become
an essential for afternoon tea

- 🍴 makes 10 cookies
- 🕐 prep 15 mins • bake 20 mins
- 📋 3in (7.5cm) fluted cookie cutter
- ❄️ the dough can be wrapped in plastic wrap and refrigerated for up to 1 week, or frozen for up to 3 months; thaw at room temperature for 30 mins before baking

12 tbsp **unsalted butter**, softened

⅓ cup plus 1 tbsp **superfine sugar**, plus extra for sprinkling

1⅔ cups **all-purpose flour**, plus extra for rolling out the dough

½ tsp **salt**

● **Prepare ahead** Make the shortbread dough, wrap in plastic wrap, and refrigerate up to 24 hours in advance of baking.

1 **Preheat the oven** to 350°F (180°C). Beat the butter and sugar together in a medium bowl with an electric mixer set on high speed, about 2 minutes, or until light in color. Add the flour and salt and stir together with a wooden spoon to make a firm dough.

2 **Turn onto** a lightly floured surface and knead gently until smooth. Roll the dough out to ¼in (5mm) thickness. Using a 3in (7.5cm) fluted cookie cutter, cut out 10 rounds, re-rolling as necessary.

3 **Arrange the cookies** spaced about ½in (1cm) apart on a large baking sheet. Prick the tops with a fork. Bake about 20 minutes, or until lightly golden. Sprinkle the hot cookies with sugar and cool on the baking sheet.

● **Good with** a freshly brewed pot of tea.

VARIATION

Chocolate Chip Shortbread

Mix ½ cup semisweet or milk chocolate chips into the dough in Step 1 and proceed as above.

Almond Spritz Cookies

These delicate, buttery, piped cookies are usually made at Christmas time

- 🍴 makes about 5½ dozen cookies
- 🕐 prep 45 mins • bake 12–15 mins
- 📋 cookie press or pastry bag

2 cups **unsalted butter**, softened

1⅓ cups **sugar**

1 tsp **pure vanilla extract**

½ tsp **almond extract**

3⅔ cups **all-purpose flour**

½ tsp **salt**

1 cup **almond flour (almond meal)**

9oz (250g) **semisweet** or milk **chocolate**, coarsely chopped

1 **Preheat the oven** to 350°F (180°C). Line 3 large baking sheets with parchment paper.

2 **Beat the butter** in a large bowl with an electric mixer set on high speed until smooth. Gradually beat in the sugar, and beat 2 minutes, until light and fluffy. Beat in the vanilla and almond extracts. On low speed, beat in about two-thirds of the flour and the salt. Stir in the almond flour and the remaining flour. Knead in the bowl until smooth.

3 **Fit a pastry bag** with a ¾in (2cm) wide star tip. In batches, transfer the dough to the bag. Pipe out 3in (7.5cm) lengths of the dough, spacing them 1in (2.5cm) apart onto the baking sheets. Bake 12–15 minutes until golden. Transfer to a wire rack to cool, but reserve the parchment-lined baking sheets.

4 **Melt the chocolate** in a small bowl placed in a pan of barely simmering water, taking care not to splash any water into the chocolate. Dip one end of the cookies into the melted chocolate, and return to the baking sheets to cool and set the chocolate. Store in an airtight container for 2–3 days.

VARIATION

Marbled Cookies

Sift 2 tbsp cocoa powder with 1 tbsp sugar. Mix into a third of the dough. Combine two-thirds plain dough and one-third cocoa dough in the pastry bag. Pipe out and proceed as above.

Raspberry Sables

Originating from Normandy, the name of these rich cookies comes from the French for "sand," as they have a light, crumbly texture

- makes 12–16
- prep 15 mins, plus chilling • cook 8–10 mins
- 3in (7.5cm) round cookie cutter
- freeze the unbaked dough for up to 1 month

1 cup **all-purpose flour**

¾ cup **confectioner's sugar**

10 tbsp **butter**, softened, plus more for the baking sheet

¼ cup **almond flour**

1 large **egg yolk**

½ tsp **almond extract**

raspberry preserves

● **Prepare ahead** The dough can be refrigerated for up to 1 week. The unfilled cookies will keep for several days in an airtight container.

1 Combine the flour, confectioner's sugar, butter, almond flour, egg yolk, and almond extract in a food processor and process to form a soft dough. Remove from the machine, wrap in plastic wrap, and refrigerate for 30 minutes. (Or, beat together the sugar, butter, and egg yolk, then stir in the flour, almond flour, and almond extract.)

2 Preheat the oven to 375°F (190°C). Lightly butter two baking sheets. Roll out the dough on a lightly floured work surface to a thickness of ⅛in (3mm). Using a 3in (7.5cm) round cookie cutter, cut out rounds and transfer to the baking sheet. Gather up the scraps and re-roll as needed, but do not overhandle the dough.

3 Bake for 8–10 minutes, or until pale gold. Let cool slightly on the baking sheets, then transfer to a wire rack to cool completely. Sandwich the cookies together, using about 1 tsp raspberry preserves for each pair.

● **Good with** fresh raspberries replacing the preserves and whipped cream for a delicious dessert.

Oatmeal Cookies

If you're watching your saturated fats, try these cookies, made with oil instead of butter

- makes 30 cookies
- prep 10 mins • cook 20 mins

1 ¾ cups **rolled (old-fashioned) oats**

⅔ cup packed **light brown sugar**

½ cup **sunflower oil**, plus more for the baking sheets

1 large **egg**, beaten

½ tsp **pure vanilla extract**

● **Prepare ahead** The cookies can be stored in an airtight container for up to 1 week.

1 Preheat the oven to 325°F (160°C). Lightly oil two baking sheets.

2 Stir the oats, brown sugar, and oil in a bowl until well combined. Add the egg and vanilla extract and mix again.

3 Drop heaping teaspoons of the batter on the baking sheets, spacing them 1in (2.5cm) apart. Flatten them slightly with the back of a fork. Bake for 15–18 minutes, or until golden.

4 Let the cookies cool on the baking sheets for 1–2 minutes. Transfer the cookies to a wire rack and let cool completely.

● **Good with** a glass of milk as an after-school snack, or as part of a packed lunch or picnic.

Peanut Butter Cookies

Substitute 1 tbsp of rolled oats with 1 tbsp crunchy peanut butter. Finish and bake as above.

Florentines

These crisp Italian cookies are loaded with fruits and nuts and coated with thin layers of luxurious dark chocolate

🍴 makes about 18 cookies

🕐 prep 40 mins • cook 10 mins

⅓ cup sugar

4 tbsp butter

1 tbsp honey

½ cup all-purpose flour

¼ cup chopped mixed candied peel

¼ cup finely chopped candied cherries

¼ cup finely chopped sliced blanched almonds

1 tbsp heavy cream

1 tsp lemon juice

6oz (175g) bittersweet chocolate, coarsely chopped

1 Preheat the oven to 350°F (180°C). Line two baking sheets with parchment paper.

2 Melt the sugar, butter, and honey together in a medium saucepan over low heat. Remove from the heat and let cool until just warm. Stir in the flour, candied peel, cherries, almonds, cream, and lemon juice. Drop teaspoons of the dough, spaced 1½in (3.5cm) apart on the baking sheets.

3 Bake for 10 minutes, or until pale brown. Do not let them get too dark. Let cool on the baking sheets for about 3 minutes to set, then transfer to a wire cake rack and cool completely.

4 Melt the chocolate in a small heatproof bowl set over a saucepan of hot, not simmering, water. Remove from the heat. Spread a thin layer of chocolate on the flat side of each cookie, and return to the wire rack, upside down, to set. Repeat with a second layer of chocolate. Just before they set, make a wavy line in the chocolate with the tines of a fork.

> ### BAKE TEST
> Test-bake a few cookies to gauge how the mixture is working: if they are a bit thick add more honey, if they are too thin with too many holes, add more flour.

Macaroons

These cookies are crisp outside and slightly chewy inside. When storing, they tend to dry out—so just give in to temptation

🍴 makes 24 cookies

🕐 prep 10 mins • cook 15 mins

2 medium egg whites

1¼ cups sugar

1 cup almond flour (almond meal)

3 tbsp white rice flour

¼ tsp almond extract

24 blanched almonds

● **Prepare ahead** The macaroons will keep for a few days stored in an airtight container.

1 Preheat the oven to 350°F (180°C). Beat the egg whites with an electric mixer until stiff peaks form. One tablespoon at a time, beat in the sugar, and beat until the mixture is stiff and glossy. Fold in the almond flour, rice flour, and almond extract.

2 Line a large baking sheet with wax paper. Using a rounded teaspoon for each cookie, drop 24 mounds of the batter, spaced well apart, on the baking sheet. Top each mound with a blanched almond.

3 Bake for 12-15 minutes, or until the cookies are pale gold.

4 Cool the macaroons on the baking sheet. Carefully peel the cookies from the paper. Store in an airtight container.

● **Good with** coffee, tea, or other treats, such as oatmeal cookies or chocolate-covered florentines.

Hazelnut Macaroons
Substitute hazelnut flour (hazelnut meal), hazelnut or vanilla extract, and peeled hazelnuts for the almond flour, almond extract, and blanched almonds.

Spitzbuben

Buttery rings sandwiched together with preserves, these are also called *Ischl* tartlets

 makes 9 large cookies

 prep 30 mins • cook 10 mins

 3in (7.5cm) fluted cookie cutter, 1in (2.5cm) plain cookie cutter

 freeze the raw cookie dough for up to 1 month

8 tbsp **butter**, at room temperature

⅔ cup **sugar**

1 large **egg**, beaten

¼ tsp **pure vanilla extract**

2¼ cups **all-purpose flour**

¼ tsp **salt**

⅔ cup **raspberry** or **strawberry** preserves

confectioner's sugar, for sifting

1 Beat the butter in a mixing bowl with an electric mixer until smooth. Add the sugar and beat again until pale and fluffy. Gradually beat in the egg and vanilla. Sift in the flour and salt and stir until combined. The dough must be firm enough to roll out; add more flour, if needed.

2 Preheat the oven to 375°F (190°C). Line 2 baking sheets with wax paper. Roll out the dough on a lightly floured work surface to ¼in (5mm) thickness on a lightly floured surface. Using a fluted 3in (7.5cm) cookie cutter, gathering and rerolling the trimmings as needed, cut out 18 rounds. Using a plain 1in (2.5cm) cookie cutter, cut the centers out of 9 of the rounds.

3 Place the rounds on the baking sheets. Bake 10 minutes, until the cookies are pale golden. Transfer to a wire rack and let cool.

4 Spread each of the solid cookies with about 1 tbsp of the preserves. Top each with a cut-out cookie. Sift confectioner's sugar over the cookies and serve.

Tuile Cookies

These light, crisp cookies curl up gently as they cool

 makes 15 cookies

 prep 10 mins • cook 30 mins

3 tbsp **butter**, softened

½ cup **confectioner's sugar**

1 large **egg**

⅓ cup **all-purpose flour**

1 Preheat the oven to 400°F (200°C). Beat the butter and confectioner's sugar in a bowl with an electric mixer until light and fluffy. Beat in the egg. Gently fold in the flour.

2 Line a baking sheet with baking parchment or a silicone baking liner. Place about 1½ tsp of the batter on the lined baking sheet and spread it out thinly to about a 3in (7.5cm) diameter. Make another 1 or 2 rounds on the same baking sheet. Bake for 5–8 minutes, or until they are just beginning to turn pale gold.

3 Remove the baking sheet from the oven. Working quickly, one at a time, slide a metal icing spatula under a cookie and drape over a rolling pin so that they cool in a curved shape. Repeat with the remaining batter.

> #### TIGHTER CURLS
> For more tightly curled cookies, wrap the tuiles around the oiled handle of a wooden spoon instead of draping them over a rolling pin.

Oatmeal Bars

These chewy bars, known as flapjacks in Britain, use only a few pantry ingredients

 makes 16–20

prep 15 mins, plus cooling • cook 40 mins

9in (23cm) square baking pan

1 cup **butter**, plus more for the pan

1 cup packed **light brown sugar**

2 tbsp **light corn syrup**

3½ cups **rolled (old-fashioned) oats**

● **Prepare ahead** The bars can be stored in an airtight container for up to 5 days.

1 Preheat the oven to 300°F (150°C). Lightly butter a 9in (23cm) square baking pan.

2 Heat the butter, brown sugar, and syrup in a large saucepan and stir over medium-low heat until the butter has melted. Remove from the heat and stir in the oats.

3 Spread evenly in the pan. Bake for 40 minutes, or until evenly golden and just beginning to brown at the edges.

4 Transfer to a wire rack and let cool 10 minutes. Cut into bars and let cool completely.

Chocolate Brownies

These chewy, but cakey brownies make a tempting snack

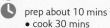 makes 12 brownies

prep about 10 mins
• cook 30 mins

8in (20cm) square cake pan, wire rack

2oz (60g) **unsweetened chocolate**, chopped

2 tbsp **butter**

1¼ cups packed **light brown sugar**

3 large **eggs**

1 tbsp **honey**

1 tsp **pure vanilla extract**

⅔ cup **all-purpose flour**

¾ tsp **baking powder**

¼ tsp **salt**

1¼ cups coarsely chopped **walnuts**

½ cup **white chocolate chips**

⬤ **Prepare ahead** The brownies will stay fresh tightly wrapped in foil or stored in an airtight container for up to 5 days.

1 **Preheat the oven** to 350°F (175°C). Lightly butter an 8in (20cm) square cake pan and line the bottom with wax paper.

2 **Combine the chocolate** and butter in a small heatproof bowl. Place in a frying pan of barely simmering water and stir occasionally until melted. Remove the bowl from the water and cool slightly.

3 **Whisk** the brown sugar, eggs, honey, and vanilla together until combined, then gradually whisk in the melted chocolate. Sift the flour, baking powder, and salt. Stir into the chocolate mixture. Add the walnuts and white chocolate chips and stir just until mixed. Spread in the pan.

4 **Bake for 30 minutes**, until a wooden toothpick inserted in the center comes out with a moist crumb. Cool completely in the pan on a wire rack.

5 **When cooled**, invert the brownies onto a board, remove the pan and wax paper, and cut into 12 pieces.

Gingerbread Cookies

Without the egg white glaze and nuts, you can use this dough to roll out and cut into shapes for holiday cookies

makes about 45 cookies

prep 30 mins, plus cooling
• cook 8–10 mins

cookie cutters of your choice, parchment paper

1¾ cups **all-purpose flour**, plus more for rolling

2 tsp **ground ginger**

2 tsp **baking powder**

½ tsp **pumpkin-pie spice**

1 cup **almond flour**

¾ cup plus 2 tbsp **sugar**

9 tbsp **butter**, at room temperature

⅓ cup **honey**

1 large **egg**, separated

4 tsp **milk**

½ tsp **pure vanilla extract**

chopped skinned **hazelnuts** or almonds, to decorate

1 **Preheat the oven** to 350°F (180°C). Line 2 baking sheets with parchment paper.

2 **Sift the flour**, ginger, baking powder, and pumpkin-pie spice together. Stir in the almond flour. Beat the sugar and butter together in another bowl with an electric mixer until pale. Beat in the honey, egg yolk, milk, and vanilla. Stir in the flour mixture to make a stiff dough. Gather into a thick disk, wrap in plastic wrap, and refrigerate for 1 hour.

3 **Roll out the dough** on a lightly floured work surface to a thickness of about ¼in (5mm). Cut out the cookies. Place on baking sheets 1in (2.5cm) apart. Gather up and re-roll the scraps as needed. Beat the egg white. Brush the cookies with the egg white and sprinkle with the hazelnuts. Bake for about 10 minutes, or until lightly browned.

4 **Let cool** on the baking sheets for 5 minutes. Transfer to wire racks and cool completely.

Dulce de Leche

This caramelized dessert sauce originated in Argentina but is now beloved all over the world

🍴 makes 8 servings

🕐 prep 5 mins • cook 3¼ hrs

3 qts (3 liters) whole milk

3 cups sugar

3 tbsp white wine vinegar

1 Bring the milk and sugar to a boil in a large, heavy-bottomed saucepan, stirring to dissolve the sugar. Stir in the vinegar—the milk will curdle.

2 Reduce the heat to medium-low. Simmer 3 hours, or until the liquid has evaporated entirely and the sauce is toffee-brown. Let cool completely.

● **Good with** vanilla ice cream or fresh fruit such as sliced bananas or fruit compotes.

● **Leftovers** can be stirred into slightly softened vanilla ice cream and refrozen.

Rich Vanilla Buttercream Icing

This simple recipe can be used to ice cupcakes and to sandwich cake layers together

🍴 makes almost 2 cups

🕐 prep 10 mins

8 tbsp butter, at room temperature

3 tbsp whole milk, as needed

1 tsp pure vanilla extract

3½ cups confectioner's sugar

● **Prepare ahead** The icing can be refrigerated in a covered container for 2 days. Bring to room temperature before using. If too stiff to spread, stir in a little extra milk.

1 Beat the butter, 2 tbsp milk, and the vanilla in a large bowl with an electric mixer until smooth.

2 With the mixer on low speed, gradually add the confectioner's sugar, beating until the frosting is spreadable. If the frosting is too stiff, add the remaining milk.

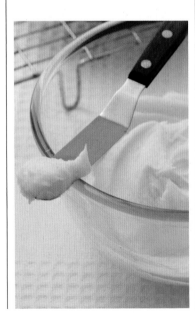

Chocolate Dessert Sauce

Serve this sauce warm or cold over a variety of desserts. For best results, use a 70 percent dark chocolate

🍴 makes 1–2 cups

🕐 prep 5 mins • cook 6–7 mins

8oz (225g) bittersweet chocolate, chopped

2 tbsp butter

¼ cup golden syrup

3 drops pure vanilla extract

● **Prepare ahead** Store the sauce, covered, in the refrigerator for up to 1 week; reheat gently.

1 Place all the ingredients along with 2 tbsp water into a small saucepan and heat gently, stirring, for 6–7 minutes, or until smooth and glossy.

● **Good with** ice cream, profiteroles, and poached fruit.

━━ **VARIATION** ━━

Chocolate and Coffee Dessert Sauce

For a more sophisticated chocolate sauce, add 5–6 tbsp strong black coffee, 2 tbsp brandy, and 1–3 tbsp confectioner's sugar, to taste.

Butterscotch Dessert Sauce

Rich and buttery, this sauce is a hit with young and old

🍴 makes just over 1 cup

🕐 prep 5 mins • cook 5 mins

6 tbsp butter

⅔ cup packed light brown sugar

scant 1 cup heavy cream

● **Prepare ahead** The sauce can be refrigerated up to 1 week. To keep the sauce from separating, warm it in a few batches, letting the first portion heat before adding another.

1 Melt the butter in a small saucepan over low heat. Stir in the sugar and cook, stirring often, until the sugar dissolves.

2 Pour in the cream and stir until well combined and glossy. Increase the heat and boil gently, whisking, for 2 minutes, until thickened slightly. Remove from the heat and allow the sauce to cool. Serve warm or cold.

● **Good with** ice cream or for a treat, with pancakes stacked with whipped cream, sliced bananas, and toasted pecan nuts.

Raspberry Coulis

This quick and easy fruit sauce is an excellent way to add a fresh flavor to many desserts

🍴 makes just over 1 cup

🕐 prep 10 mins

❄️ freeze for up to 6 months

12oz (350g) fresh **raspberries**

¼ cup **water**

3 tbsp **superfine sugar**, as needed

2 tsp fresh **orange** or lemon juice

● **Prepare ahead** The sauce can be refrigerated for up to 2 days before serving.

1 **Purée the raspberries**, water, sugar, and juice.

2 **Using a wooden spoon**, push the purée through a fine sieve into a bowl, discarding the seeds. Taste and adjust the flavor with sugar or juice if needed.

3 **Cover and refrigerate** at least 1 hour, until chilled.

● **Good with** poached pears, chocolate cake, mixed berries, or drizzled over vanilla ice cream.

Ginger Cream Sauce

This spiced custard sauce is great for dipping fruits, cookies, or even cubes of cake

🍴 makes 8 servings

🕐 prep 10 mins, plus infusing • cook 45 mins

3¾ cups **heavy cream**

⅔ cup **sugar**

8oz (225g) fresh **ginger**, peeled and sliced

4 **star anise**

6 large **egg yolks**, beaten

five-spice powder, for sifting (optional)

1 **Bring the cream** and sugar to a simmer over medium heat. Remove from the heat and stir in the ginger and star anise. Cover and let stand for 1 hour. Reheat the milk until piping hot. Strain the milk into a bowl.

2 **Whisk the yolks** in another bowl until thickened. Whisk in the hot cream. Strain the cream mixture back into the saucepan.

3 **Cook over** low heat, stirring constantly, until the custard coats the back of a spoon. Do not boil. Pour into eight dessert dishes and sift five-spice powder on top, if desired. Serve warm.

● **Good with** fruit slices and berries, for dipping.

Crème Anglaise

This classic vanilla sauce is wonderful warm as a dessert sauce or chilled and poured over berries

🍴 makes about 1½ cups

⏱ prep 5 mins • cook 10 mins

1 ¼ cups **whole milk**

1 **vanilla bean**, split lengthwise, or
1 tsp **vanilla extract**

3 large **egg yolks**

3 tbsp **sugar**

● **Prepare ahead** The sauce can be made up to 3 days in advance and refrigerated until required.

1 Heat the milk and vanilla bean, if using, in a medium saucepan until it bubbles form around the edges. Remove from the heat and let stand for 10 minutes. Using the tip of a knife, scrape half of the seeds from the bean into the milk. Rinse the vanilla bean and save for another use.

2 Beat the yolks and sugar in a heatproof bowl. Gradually whisk in the hot milk. Rinse and dry the saucepan, and return the milk mixture to the pan.

3 Cook over medium-low heat, stirring constantly with a wooden spoon, until the custard is thick enough to coat the spoon (an instant-read thermometer will read 185°F (85°C)). Do not boil.

4 Strain through a sieve into a bowl. If not using the vanilla bean, stir in the vanilla extract. To serve warm, use immediately. Or place plastic wrap directly on the surface, pierce a few holes in the wrap, and let cool.

VARIATION

Citrus Crème Anglaise
Add the grated zest of 1 lemon or orange to the strained custard.

Crème Pâtissière

This sweet pastry cream is a rich and creamy filling for fruit tarts and cream puffs

🍴 makes about 1¼ cups

⏱ prep 10 mins • cook 5 mins

1 ¼ cups **whole milk**

2 large **egg yolks**

¼ cup **sugar**

2 tbsp **all-purpose flour**

2 tbsp **cornstarch**

¼ tsp **pure vanilla extract**

● **Prepare ahead** The pastry cream can be refrigerated, with wax paper pressed on its surface, for up to 2 days.

1 Bring the milk to a simmer in a saucepan over medium heat.

2 Whisk the yolks and sugar together in a bowl. Whisk in the flour and cornstarch. Gradually whisk in the hot milk.

3 Return the mixture to the saucepan. Cook over medium-low heat, whisking constantly, until it comes to a full boil and is smooth.

4 Let cool slightly, then stir in the vanilla. If not using immediately, cover with a piece of buttered wax paper pressed directly onto the surface of the pastry cream.

Chocolate Custard

This is a rich sauce, that can be served hot or cold

 makes about 1½ cups

🕐 prep 5 mins, plus cooling • cook 10 mins

1¼ cups **whole milk**

3 large **egg yolks**

⅓ cup **sugar**

4oz (120g) **bittersweet chocolate**, finely chopped

½ tsp **pure vanilla extract**

● **Prepare ahead** The sauce can be cooled, covered, and refrigerated for up to 1 day before serving.

1 Bring the milk just to a simmer in a saucepan over medium heat. Do not boil.

2 Whisk the yolks and sugar together in a heatproof bowl until pale yellow and thick. Slowly whisk in the warm milk.

3 Return the mixture to the saucepan. Cook over low heat, stirring constantly with a wooden

spoon, until the custard coats the spoon (an instant-read thermometer will read 185°F (85°C)). Remove from the heat. Add the chocolate and vanilla. Let stand until the chocolate softens, then melts.

4 Strain through a sieve into a bowl. Serve warm, or let cool, cover, and refrigerate at least 1 hour, until chilled.

● **Good with** fresh fruit or poured over sponge cake.

VARIATION

Chocolate-orange Custard

Stir the grated zest of 1 orange to the strained sauce.

Rich Custard

Served warm or cold, this custard sauce is a great embellishment for many desserts

 makes about 1¼ cups

🕐 prep 10 mins • cook 15 mins

3 large **egg yolks**

2 tbsp **sugar**

½ tsp **cornstarch**

⅔ cup **whole milk**

⅔ cup **heavy cream**

2–3 strips of **lemon** zest

● **Prepare ahead** Can be made up to 2 days in advance, covered, and refrigerated until required.

1 Whisk together the egg yolks, sugar, cornstarch, and 3 tbsp of the milk together in a heatproof bowl until well blended.

2 Bring the remaining milk, cream, and lemon zest to a simmer in a saucepan over medium heat. Remove from the heat, cover,

and let stand for 10 minutes. Whisk the cream mixture into the yolks. Return to the saucepan. Cook over low heat, stirring constantly with a wooden spoon, for about 5 minutes, or until the mixture coats the back of a spoon. Strain into a bowl. Serve hot or chilled.

● **Good with** hot pudding and fresh pies.

VARIATION

Vanilla Custard

Omit the lemon zest and replace with 1 split vanilla bean. After the mixture has stood, remove the vanilla and scrape the seeds from the bean into the milk mixture with the tip of a small knife. Complete the recipe as above. The cleaned bean can be stored in a jar of sugar, for at least 2 weeks to make vanilla sugar.

Apple Pie

When you are short on time, use pre-made pie crusts. Including some Granny Smith apples will make a tangier pie

🍴 makes 8-10 servings

🕐 25 mins, plus chilling • cook 50 mins

🍽 9in (23cm) pie pan, wire cake rack

one 15oz (420g) package **refrigerated pie crusts**

grated zest of 1 **lemon**

2 tbsp fresh **lemon** juice

6 **Golden Delicious apples**, peeled, cored, and thinly sliced

⅓ cup **sugar**

3 tbsp **all-purpose flour**

1 tsp **pumpkin-pie spice**

2 tbsp **milk**, to glaze the dough

1 **Place a baking sheet** in the oven and preheat to 400°F (200°C). Mix the lemon zest and juice in a large bowl. Peel, core, and thinly slice the apples, and toss them with the lemon mixture as they are sliced. Add the sugar, flour, and pumpkin pie spice and mix well.

2 **Line** a 9in (23cm) pie pan with a pie crust and brush the edge with water. Spread the apple filling in the pan. Center the second pie crust over the filling. Press the edges of the crusts together to seal them, then flute them. Brush the top of the pie crust with milk and cut a few slits in the crust.

3 **Place the pie** on the hot baking sheet. Immediately reduce the oven temperature to 375°F (190°C). Bake the pie for 50-55 minutes or until the pastry is golden brown.

4 **Transfer the pie** to a wire cake rack and cool for at least 1 hour. Cut into wedges and serve warm, or cool completely and serve at room temperature.

● **Good with** a scoop of vanilla ice cream or crème anglaise.

Portuguese Apple Fritters

These light, batter-coated rings enclose tender apple, with the aromatic flavors of anise and cinnamon

🍴 makes 4 servings

🕐 prep 20 mins • cook 15-20 mins, plus 1 hr resting

🍲 deep-frying thermometer

3 large **Golden Delicious apples**

¾ cup **sugar**

¼ cup **anise liqueur**, such as Anisette or ouzo

2 tbsp fresh **lemon** juice

⅔ cup **milk**

⅓ cup plus 1 tbsp **olive oil**

2 large **eggs**

1¾ cups **all-purpose flour**

1½ tsp **baking powder**

¼ tsp **ground cinnamon**

vegetable oil, for deep-frying

confectioner's sugar, for dusting

1 **Peel, core, and thinly slice** the apples into rounds about ⅛in (4mm) thick. Toss the apples, ¼ cup of the sugar, the liqueur, and lemon juice in a bowl. Let stand for 30 minutes.

2 **Meanwhile**, whisk the remaining ½ cup sugar, milk, oil, and eggs together in a bowl. Sift in the flour, baking powder, and cinnamon and stir until smooth. Set aside for 30 minutes.

3 **Pour enough oil** to come halfway up the sides of a large skillet and heat over high heat to 350°F (180°C). In batches, dip the drained apple slices in the batter. Deep-fry about 3 minutes, until golden brown. Using a slotted spoon, transfer to paper towels to drain. Serve warm, dusted with confectioner's sugar.

● **Good with** vanilla ice cream, or plain, with a cup of coffee.

Peach Gratin with Muscat Sabayon

Sabayon is really the French version of zabaglione—a warm dessert sauce that is as versatile as it is delicious

🍴 makes 4 servings

🕐 prep 20 mins • cook 25 mins

4 ripe **peaches**, peeled

2 **figs**, quartered (optional)

6 tbsp **sugar**

pinch of **ground cardamom**

grated zest of 1 **lemon**

2 tbsp fresh **lemon** juice

4 large **egg yolks**

¼ cup **Muscat wine**

1 **Preheat the oven** to 400°F (200°F).

2 **Halve each peach** and remove the pit, then cut each half into 3 wedges. Place the peaches, with the figs (if using) in a gratin dish and sprinkle with 2 tbsp of the sugar, the cardamom, and lemon zest and juice. Bake for 20–25 minutes, until the peaches are juicy and glazed. Remove the peaches from the oven. Position a broiler rack 6in (15cm) from the source of heat and preheat the broiler.

3 **Combine the yolks**, remaining 4 tbsp sugar, and wine in a heatproof bowl. Place the bowl over a saucepan of simmering water. Beat with an electric mixer for about 4 minutes, or until the mixture has tripled in volume.

4 **Pour the sabayon** over the peaches. Broil until the topping is glazed, about 30 seconds. Serve hot.

VARIATION

Red Fruits with Marsala Sabayon

Substitute 12oz (350g) strawberries, hulled and halved, and 6oz (175g) each raspberries and stemmed red currants (or blueberries) for the peaches. Toss with 2 tbsp sugar, ¼ tsp ground cinnamon, and the finely grated zest and juice of 1 lime. Let stand for at least 2 or up to 8 hours at room temperature. Make the sabayon as above, substituting sweet Marsala wine for the Muscat.

Pineapple Fritters

Crisp and juicy, these must be served immediately

🍴 makes 4 servings

🕐 prep 20 mins, plus resting • cook 10 mins

For the batter

¾ cup plus 2 tbsp **all-purpose flour**

3 tbsp **sugar**

pinch of **salt**

⅔ cup **whole milk**

2 large **eggs**, 1 separated

1 **pineapple**, peeled, cored, and sliced into ½in (1.5cm) rings, then cut in half crosswise

vegetable oil, for deep-frying

confectioner's sugar, to serve

1 **To make the batter** combine the flour, sugar, and salt in a large bowl. Add the milk, 1 egg, and 1 egg yolk. Whisk quickly until smooth and lump-free.

2 **Beat the egg white** until stiff peaks form, and fold gently into the batter.

3 **Add enough oil** to come halfway up the sides of a large frying pan, and heat to 350°F (180°C) over high heat. Dip the pineapple into the batter, then carefully add to the oil. Deep-fry for about 3 minutes, or until golden brown on both sides.

4 **Using a slotted spoon**, transfer to paper towels to drain. Sift confectioner's sugar on top and serve hot.

VARIATION

Banana Fritters

Use 4 bananas, each cut in half lengthwise then in half crosswise, instead of pineapple.

Viennese Apple Strudel

It doesn't matter if served warm or cold,
apple strudel is always appreciated by lovers of fine desserts

 makes 10–12 servings

prep 30 mins, plus resting
• cook 40 mins

2¼lb (1kg) **Golden Delicious apples**

½ cup **raisins**

½ cup **granulated sugar**

½ cup chopped **blanched almonds**

3 tbsp **dark rum**

½ tsp **pure vanilla extract**

grated zest of ½ **lemon**

4 sheets thawed frozen **filo dough**

4 tbsp **butter**, melted, plus more for
the baking sheet

⅔ cup fresh **bread crumbs**

confectioner's sugar, for garnish

1 Preheat the oven to 350°F
(180°C). Butter a large baking
sheet. Peel, core, and cut the apples
into ½in (13mm) dice. Combine in a
bowl with the raisins, sugar, almonds,
rum, vanilla, and lemon zest.

2 Place a filo sheet on a work
surface and brush with melted
butter. Repeat with the remaining
pastry sheets.

3 Sprinkle the bread crumbs
over the pastry, leaving a 1in
(2cm) border. Spoon the filling over
the bread crumbs. Fold in the short
sides to cover about 1in (2.5cm) of
the filling. Starting from a long side,
roll up the pastry, tucking in the filling
if it escapes. Transfer to the baking
sheet and brush with melted butter.

4 Bake for 30–40 minutes,
brushing with the remaining
melted butter after 20 minutes, until
golden brown.

5 Let cool on the baking sheet.
Sift liberally with confectioner's
sugar. Serve warm, or at room
temperature.

● **Good with** whipped cream.

PREPARING THE APPLES

To ensure that your strudel does not turn
soggy, choose crisp apples and avoid
ones that are too ripe. Also, avoid cutting
the apples too small, since they will
soften while baking.

Baked Peaches with Marzipan and Almonds

You cannot beat the fresh
fragrant flavor of ripe baked
peaches oozing sweet juices

 makes 4 servings

prep 15 mins
• cook 20–25 mins

shallow ovenproof dish

4 ripe **peaches**, halved lengthwise
and pitted

2oz (60g) **marzipan**

1½ tbsp **heavy cream**

¼ cup **slivered almonds**

1 tbsp **honey**

2 tbsp **light brown sugar**

½ cup **sweet wine** or Marsala

1 Preheat the oven to 400°F
(200°C). Place the peaches in
a baking dish, cut sides up. Mash the
marzipan with the cream. Spoon
into the peaches. Sprinkle with the
almonds and drizzle with the honey.
Sprinkle with the sugar, then with
the wine.

2 Bake for about 20 minutes, or
until just tender. Cover and let
stand 5 minutes.

● **Good with** crème fraîche.

Plum Crumble

This late-summer dessert is suitable for both family suppers and dinner parties for friends

 makes 4 servings

prep 10 mins
• cook 30–40 mins

freeze for up to 2 months

For the topping

1 cup all-purpose flour

7 tbsp cold butter, cubed

⅓ cup packed light brown sugar

⅔ cup rolled (old-fashioned) oats

1lb 5oz (600g) plums, halved and pitted

maple syrup or honey, to drizzle

● **Prepare ahead** The topping can be frozen for up to 1 month.

1 Preheat the oven to 400°F (200°C). To make the topping, combine the flour and butter in a large mixing bowl and rub in the butter with your fingertips until the mixture is combined. Work in the sugar and oats. The mixture should remain lumpy.

2 Spread the plums in an ovenproof dish and drizzle with the maple syrup. Crumble the topping over the plums. Bake for 30–40 minutes, or until the top is golden brown and the juices are bubbling.

● **Good with** ice cream or warm custard.

VARIATION

Rhubarb Crumble

Use 1lb 10oz (750g) rhubarb, cut into 1in (2.5cm) lengths. Generously drizzle the rhubarb with honey and a squeeze of orange juice, then crumble the topping over the fruit and bake.

Pears Poached in Wine

Wine gives a great depth of flavor to cooked fruit

makes 4 servings

prep 5 mins • cook 30 mins

4 firm ripe pears

1 cup hearty red wine

¼ cup packed light brown sugar

1 tbsp fresh lemon juice

one 3in (7.5cm) cinnamon stick

¼ tsp freshly grated nutmeg

4 whole cloves

● **Prepare ahead** The pears can be refrigerated for up to 3 days.

1 Peel the pears, leaving the stems attached. Cut a small slice from the bottom of each so that the pears will stand up.

2 Stir the wine, sugar, lemon juice, cinnamon, nutmeg, and cloves in a large saucepan over low heat until the sugar dissolves. Add the pears to the saucepan and cover.

3 Simmer, frequently turning and basting the pears, for 20 minutes, or until the pears are tender.

4 Using a slotted spoon, transfer the pears to a deep serving dish. Discard the cinnamon stick and cloves. Boil until the wine mixture is syrupy and reduced by about one-third. Pour the syrup over the pears.

5 Serve warm or let cool in the syrup and refrigerate until chilled.

● **Good with** low-fat yogurt for a low-fat dessert, or with whipped cream or ice cream if you want something more indulgent.

VARIATION

Pears in White Wine

Substitute white wine or cider for the red wine, and the result will be paler and more golden in color. Choose a sweet white wine or cider.

French Apple Tart

Use two different apple varieties—one to cook into a purée, and the other to create a sliced apple topping that holds its shape

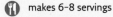

- makes 6-8 servings
- prep 20 mins, plus chilling • cook 1 hr
- 9in (23cm) tart pan with removable bottom, baking beans
- freeze for up to 1 month

1 refrigerated **pie dough round** for 9in (23cm) pie

3 tbsp **butter**

1lb 10oz (750g) **McIntosh apples**, peeled, cored, and chopped

⅔ cup **sugar**

2 tbsp **Calvados** or brandy

grated zest and juice of ½ **lemon**

2 **Granny Smith apples**, peeled, cored, and thinly sliced

3 tbsp **apricot preserves**, warmed and strained

1 **Preheat the oven** to 400°F (200°C). Fit the pie dough into a 9in (23cm) tart pan with a removable bottom, fitting it tightly into the corners, and trim the excess dough. Prick the dough with a fork. Line with wax paper and fill with baking beans. Place on a baking sheet and bake for 15 minutes, until the dough looks set. Remove the paper and beans and bake until lightly browned, about 5 minutes more. Transfer to a wire rack and let cool. Reduce the oven temperature to 350°F (180°C).

2 **Melt the butter** in a medium saucepan over low heat. Add the McIntosh apples and cover tightly with a lid. Cook, stirring occasionally, for 15 minutes, or until broken down into a chunky sauce.

3 **Strain through** a coarse sieve into a bowl, then return to the saucepan. Stir in all but 1 tbsp of the

sugar, the Calvados, and lemon zest. Cook and stir over medium heat about 5 minutes, until quite thick.

4 **Spoon the applesauce** into the tart shell. Arrange the Granny Smith apple slices in concentric circles over the applesauce. Brush with the lemon juice and sprinkle with the reserved sugar.

5 **Bake for 30-35 minutes**, or until the apple slices are golden and tender. Brush the top with the warm apricot preserves. Let cool on a wire rack for 15 minutes. Remove the sides of the pan. Serve warm or cold.

● **Good with** vanilla ice cream or crème fraîche.

Pear Gratin

A sophisticated, simple, and foolproof dessert

- makes 4 servings
- prep 10 mins • cook 3-5 mins

4 ripe **Comice pears**

6oz (155g) **blackberries**

½ cup coarsely chopped **walnuts**

8oz (225g) **mascarpone cheese**

2 tbsp **dark brown sugar**

1 **Position a broiler rack** 6in (15cm) from the source of heat and preheat the broiler. Quarter the pears and remove the cores. Place skin side down in a flameproof serving dish. Sprinkle with the blackberries and walnuts. Drop spoonfuls of mascarpone cheese over the pears and sprinkle with the brown sugar.

2 **Broil for 3-5 minutes**, or until the mascarpone is bubbly and sugar begins to caramelize.

3 **Serve warm**, with crisp buttery cookies.

VARIATION

Pear and Raspberry Gratin
Substitute raspberries for the blackberries and granola for the brown sugar.

Bananas Flambéed with Calvados

Alcohol can boost and blend flavors, as shown in this simple dessert of bananas, citrus, and apple brandy

🍴 makes 4 servings

🕐 prep 10 mins • cook 10 mins

2 oranges

4 ripe bananas

4 tbsp unsalted butter

½ cup packed light brown sugar

2 tbsp lime juice

3 tbsp Calvados, applejack, or brandy

1 Remove the zest from half an orange with a potato peeler and mince the zest. Squeeze the juice from both oranges—you should have about ½ cup.

2 Peel the bananas and halve lengthwise. Melt 3 tbsp of the butter in a large nonstick frying pan over medium-high heat. Add the banana and cook until lightly browned on both sides. Transfer to a plate, cover, and keep warm.

3 Add the remaining 1 tbsp butter to the pan and melt. Sprinkle in the sugar and cook, stirring occasionally. Add the orange juice and zest and lime juice, bring to a boil, and cook until thickened, about 2–3 minutes.

4 Add the Calvados. Light with a long-handled match and cook until the flames burn out. Return the bananas to the pan and turn gently in the sauce to reheat.

● **Good with** vanilla or coconut ice cream, perhaps garnished with toasted coconut shavings and wedges of lime for a more elaborate dessert.

Spiced Plum Compote

During their late summer to early autumn season, cook with plums often to make simple desserts like this one

🍴 makes 4 servings

🕐 prep 15 mins • cook 15–20 mins

1 lb (450g) ripe red plums

1 orange

⅓ cup sugar

1 star anise

½ cinnamon stick

● **Prepare ahead** Can be made up to 2 days before serving. Keep chilled.

1 Cut the plums in half and remove the pits. Remove the zest from the orange with a vegetable peeler. Squeeze the juice.

2 Combine the sugar, 1¼ cups water, orange zest and juice, star anise, and cinnamon stick in a medium saucepan. Bring to a simmer over medium heat, stirring to dissolve the sugar.

3 Add the plums and stir gently. Reduce the heat to low and simmer for 8–15 minutes until the plums are tender, but still hold their shape. Discard the star anise, cinnamon stick, and orange zest. Serve, warm or chilled, in dessert cups, topped with Greek yogurt and honey, if you like.

VARIATION

Creamy Apricot Compote

Bring ⅔ cup water, ⅓ cup sugar, and ½ tsp ground cinnamon to a simmer in a medium saucepan. Add 1 lb (450g) halved and pitted ripe apricots. Cover and simmer over low heat for 10–15 minutes, until tender but still holding their shape. Stir in ¼ cup heavy cream. Top each serving with toasted sliced almonds.

Tarte Tatin

This French classic is an upside-down apple tart

makes 6-8 servings

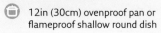
prep 30 mins, plus setting • cook 35 mins

12in (30cm) ovenproof pan or flameproof shallow round dish

For the pastry

10 tbsp **butter**, at room temperature

¼ cup **sugar**

2 cups **all-purpose flour**, plus more for rolling out the dough

1 large **egg**, beaten

For the apple topping

10 tbsp **butter**, softened

1 cup **sugar**

6 **Granny Smith apples**, peeled, cored and quartered

● **Prepare ahead** You can make the pastry up to 1 day in advance, wrapped and refrigerated.

1 To make the pastry, cream together the butter and sugar until light and creamy. Gradually mix in the flour. Stir in the beaten egg and mix just until the dough comes together. Turn the mixture on to a lightly floured surface and knead a few times until smooth. Wrap in plastic wrap, and refrigerate for at least one hour and up to 24 hours.

2 Preheat the oven to 425°F (220°C). For the topping, melt the butter in a 12in (30cm) ovenproof frying pan or flameproof shallow round baking dish over medium heat. Stir in the sugar. Increase the heat to medium-high and cook, stirring often, for 5 minutes, or until the mixture is bubbling and light brown. Remove from the heat.

3 Arrange the apples, rounded sides down, tightly packed together, in the pan. The pan will be full.

4 Roll out the pastry into a round just large enough to fit over the top of the apples. Arrange the pastry on top of the fruit and tuck the edges into the pan. Bake for 30 minutes, or until the pastry is lightly browned. Let cool for 10 minutes. Heat the pan briefly over medium heat, shaking it gently to be sure that the apples aren't sticking to the skillet. Hold a round platter over the pan. Using pot holders, holding the pan and platter together, invert them to unmold the tart. Serve warm.

> **VARIATION**

Tarte aux Poires

Substitute 6–8 small ripe pears, such as Bosc, for the apples. Small pears give the best results.

Warm Fruit Compote

A good winter dessert when fresh fruit supplies are limited

makes 4 servings

prep 10 mins • cook 5-10 mins

2 tbsp **butter**

6 **pitted dried plums**, chopped

6 **dried apricots**, chopped

2 large **apples**, peeled, cored, and chopped

1 firm ripe **pear**, peeled, cored, and chopped

1 **cinnamon stick**

2 tsp **sugar**

2 tsp **lemon** juice

yogurt or honey, to serve

● **Prepare ahead** The compote can be made several days in advance, cooled, covered, and refrigerated.

1 Melt the butter in a heavy saucepan over medium heat. Add the fruit and cinnamon stick. Cook gently, stirring often, until the fruit has completely softened.

2 Stir in the sugar and heat for a couple of minutes, or until the sugar has dissolved.

3 Remove the pan from the heat, and stir in the lemon juice. Serve warm with a spoonful of yogurt or a drizzle of honey.

Poached Apples with Ginger

This delightfully simple dessert can be served hot or cold

makes 4-6 servings

prep 15 mins • cook 30 mins, plus cooling and chilling

✔ low fat

3 pieces **stem ginger** in syrup

3lb (1.35kg) **Golden Delicious** or Braeburn **apples**, peeled, cored, and thinly sliced

⅔ cup **apple** juice

1 tbsp **ginger syrup** (from the jar)

● **Prepare ahead** The poached apples can be refrigerated in an airtight container for up to 5 days.

1 Finely chop the stem ginger. Combine the apples and juice in a saucepan. Bring to a boil. Reduce the heat to medium-low, cover, and simmer about 15 minutes, until the apples are barely tender.

2 Remove from the heat and stir in the ginger and syrup. Cool slightly, to serve warm. (Or cool completely and refrigerate, to serve chilled.)

● **Good with** a drizzle of fresh cream or a scoop of vanilla ice cream.

Spiced Baked Apple with Walnuts

This great winter warmer is easy to prepare

 serves 4

🕐 prep 10-15 mins • cook 30 mins

✓ low fat

4 large Golden Delicious apples

1 lemon, cut in half crosswise

¾ cup walnut halves

2 tbsp butter

1 tbsp raisins

1 tbsp light brown sugar

¼ tsp ground cinnamon

1 **Preheat the oven** to 350°F (145°C). Carefully cut a 1in (2.5cm) slice from the top of each apple. Rub cut surfaces of the apples with the lemon as you work. Using an apple corer or a small, sharp knife, remove the core from each apple, leaving the bottom ¼in (3mm) intact.

2 **Put the walnuts**, butter, raisins, brown sugar, and cinnamon into a food processor and pulse several times. The mixture should be coarse, not puréed.

3 **Fill each apple** cavity with the walnut mixture and replace the tops. Arrange the apples upright in a shallow, ovenproof dish, then pour in about ½in (1cm) water.

4 **Bake for 30 minutes** or until the flesh is tender when pierced with the point of a knife. When slightly cooled, carefully remove the apples from the baking dish, transfer them to serving plates, and serve hot.

⬤ **Good with** large spoonfuls of crème fraîche or vanilla ice cream, or with crème anglaise. Leftovers can be reheated and served with heavy cream, or enjoyed cold.

Baked Pears in Marsala

Serve this easy Italian dessert comfortingly warm from the oven or bracingly chilled

 makes 4-6 servings

🕐 prep 10 mins, plus chilling • cook 30 mins-1 hr

6 ripe but firm **pears**, such as Bosc, peeled, halved, and cored

1 cup dry Marsala

½ cup granulated sugar

1 tsp vanilla extract

one 3in (7.5cm) cinnamon stick

1 cup heavy cream

2 tbsp confectioner's sugar

⬤ **Prepare ahead** The dish can be completed a day in advance and gently reheated. The cream can be whipped several hours in advance.

1 **Preheat the oven** to 300°F (150°C). Place the pears in an ovenproof dish, cut side up, and sprinkle with the Marsala, sugar, and vanilla, then pour in 1 cup of water. Tuck in the cinnamon stick.

2 **Bake uncovered** for about 30 minutes, basting occasionally, until tender.

3 **Meanwhile**, in a chilled bowl whip the cream, gradually adding the confectioner's sugar until firm peaks form. Serve the pears warm (or cool to room temperature and refrigerate until chilled), in their syrup, with the whipped cream.

⬤ **Good with** ladyfingers or Amaretti cookies.

VARIATION

Baked Peaches, Apricots, or Plums in Marsala

Substitute peeled, halved, and pitted peaches, apricots, or plums for the pears. Bake for about 25 minutes, until tender. If you don't have Marsala, or if you want a sweeter dessert, substitute medium-dry sherry or port.

Blueberry Cobbler
An old-fashioned summer dessert

🍴 makes 4 servings

🕐 prep 15 mins • cook 30 mins

4 ripe **peaches**, peeled, pitted, and sliced

1lb (450g) **blueberries**

¼ cup **sugar**

grated zest of ½ **lemon**

For the topping

1⅔ cup **all-purpose flour**

⅓ cup plus 1 tbsp **sugar**

2 tsp **baking powder**

5 tbsp cold **butter**, diced, plus more for greasing the baking dish

pinch of **salt**

½ cup **buttermilk**

1 large **egg**

3 tbsp **sliced almonds**

1 Preheat the oven to 375°F (190°C). Butter an 11½ x 8in (29 x 20cm) baking dish. Combine the peaches, blueberries, sugar, and lemon zest in the dish.

2 Sift the flour, ⅓ cup of the sugar, baking powder, and salt into a bowl. Add the butter and rub it in with your fingertips until the mixture resembles coarse bread crumbs.

3 Beat the buttermilk and egg together. Stir into the flour mixture to make a soft, sticky dough. Drop walnut-sized spoonfuls of the dough over the fruit, leaving a little space between each one. Sprinkle with the almonds and the remaining 1 tbsp of sugar.

4 Bake for 30 minutes, or until the topping is golden brown and the juices are bubbling and a wooden toothpick inserted into the topping comes out clean. Let cool briefly and serve hot or cooled until warm.

● **Good with** whipped cream or ice cream.

Caramelized Autumn Fruits
This is a great way to turn autumn fruits into a delicious dessert

🍴 makes 6 servings

🕐 prep 10 mins • cook 20 mins

3 Granny Smith **apples**

3 firm ripe **Bosc pears**

4 firm ripe **red plums**

4 tbsp **butter**

⅓ cup **sugar**

2 tbsp **orange** juice or water

1 Peel and core the apples and pears and cut into quarters. Keep separate. Halve the plums and remove the pits.

2 Melt the butter in a large nonstick frying pan over medium heat. Add the sugar and the orange juice and stir until the sugar dissolves. Increase the heat and boil until the mixture starts to turn golden brown.

3 Add the apples, reduce the heat to medium-low, and cook, stirring occasionally, for 3 minutes, until they start to soften. Add the pears and cook 2 minutes more.

4 Next, add the plums and cook, stirring occasionally, about 2 minutes, until all the fruit is just tender but not falling apart. Serve warm.

● **Good with** crème fraîche or ice cream; poured over individual baked meringues with whipped cream; or with a crème brûlée.

VARIATION

Caramelized Summer Fruits

Substitute apricots, peaches, and blackberries for the autumn fruits, cooking the apricots and peaches first, then adding the blackberries at the end.

Apple Charlotte

This British hot fruit dessert was created for Queen Charlotte

- makes 6-8 servings
- prep 50 mins
  - cook 40 mins
- 9in (23cm) springform pan

3lb (1.35kg) **Golden Delicious apples**, peeled, cored and sliced

½ cup plus 3 tbsp **sugar**

½ cup **golden raisins**

grated zest and juice of 1 **lemon**

10 tbsp **butter**, melted

one 1lb (450g) loaf **white sandwich bread**, unsliced

½ tsp **ground cinnamon**

confectioner's sugar, for garnish

1 Combine the apples, ½ cup of the sugar, raisins, and lemon zest and juice in a heavy saucepan. Cover and cook over low heat for 8-10 minutes, shaking the pan occasionally, until the apples are very tender and beginning to fall apart.

2 Preheat the oven to 375°F (190°C). Brush the inside of the pan with some of the butter. Remove the crusts from the bread, then cut the bread into 14 slices. Brush both sides of each bread slice with butter. Mix together the remaining 3 tbsp sugar and the cinnamon and sprinkle over one side of the bread.

3 Place 3 slices of bread, sugared side down, in the bottom of the pan, trimming to fit. Cut 8 slices in half, and slightly overlap them, sugared side out, to line the sides of the pan.

4 Spoon the apple mixture into the bread shell. Cover with the remaining bread slices, sugared side up, trimming to fit as necessary. Fold over the bread slices on the side of the pan to slightly overlap the top of the charlotte. Bake 30-35 minutes, or until crisp and golden. Let stand for 5 minutes, then remove the sides of the pan. Sprinkle with confectioner's sugar and serve warm.

Apple Yogurt Compote

Served hot, warm, or cold, this is the simplest of desserts

- makes 4 servings
- prep 15 mins
  - cook 35-40 mins
- low fat

2½lb (1.2kg) **Cortland** or Jonathan **apples**

1 tbsp fresh **lemon** juice

⅓ cup **apple** juice

⅓ cup **sugar**

⅓ cup **heavy cream**

● **Prepare ahead** The compote can be refrigerated for up to 3 days.

1 Reserve half an apple for garnish. Peel, core, and thinly slice the remaining apples. Place the slices in a saucepan and sprinkle with the lemon juice as they are cut.

2 Add the apple juice and sugar. Cook over medium heat, stirring until the liquid comes to a boil. Reduce the heat to medium-low and cover. Simmer, stirring occasionally with a wooden spoon, about 35 minutes, or until the apples are reduced to a sauce.

3 Let cool slightly. Rub through a sieve to make a smooth purée.

4 Divide the purée among four glasses. Top with the cream. Thinly slice the remaining apple and garnish the compotes with the apple slices. Serve warm or chilled.

● **Good with** ice cream, cream, or evaporated milk instead of the whipped cream.

● **Leftovers** can be served alongside pork chops, or eaten as a snack.

Strawberry and Orange Crêpes

Light, melt-in-the-mouth pancakes with a creamy filling make an irresistible dessert

- 🍴 makes 4 servings
- 🕐 prep 30 mins, plus standing • cook 30 mins
- ❄️ freeze the pancakes for up to 3 months

For the crêpes

1 cup all-purpose flour

1 cup whole milk

2 large eggs

2 tbsp butter, melted, plus more for the pan

1½ tsp sugar

pinch of salt

For the filling

12oz (350g) strawberries, hulled and sliced

2 oranges, peeled and segmented

1lb (450g) ricotta cheese

1–2 tbsp clear honey

finely grated zest of ½ lemon

1 To make the crêpes, process the flour, milk, eggs, butter, sugar, and salt in a blender until smooth. Let stand for 30 minutes.

2 Lightly grease a frying pan with melted butter. Add about 3 tbsp of the batter to the pan, and tilt and swirl the pan so the batter covers the bottom. Cook until the underside is golden brown. Turn the crêpe and cook until the other side is golden. Transfer to a plate.

3 Repeat with the remaining batter, buttering the pan as

needed. You should have 8 crêpes. Separate the crêpes with pieces of wax paper.

4 To make the filling, place half of the strawberries and orange segments in a serving bowl and reserve. Mix the ricotta, honey, and lemon zest together. Divide the ricotta filling and remaining strawberries and oranges evenly over the crêpes. Fold each crêpe into a triangle.

5 Serve at once with the reserved strawberries and oranges on the side.

Baked Persimmons with Biscotti Crumbs

If using Hachiya persimmons, be sure they are quite soft. Fuyu persimmons can be firm

- 🍴 makes 4 servings
- 🕐 prep 20 mins • cook 20 mins

4 small persimmons

2 tbsp butter, diced

1 tbsp honey

½ cup crushed biscotti

finely grated zest and juice of 1 large orange

1 cup mascarpone

¼ cup superfine sugar

1 Preheat the oven to 350°F (180°C). Remove and discard the stems from the persimmons and cut each fruit in half lengthwise. Place in a shallow baking dish, cut sides up.

2 Dot the fruit with the butter and drizzle with the honey. Sprinkle the biscotti over the fruit and pour the orange juice over all. Bake for 20 minutes, or until the topping is beginning to brown.

3 Meanwhile, mix the mascarpone, superfine sugar, and orange zest together. Serve the persimmons hot or warm, with the mascarpone mixture on the side.

Apple Brown Betty

This fruit dessert with a crumb topping dates back to Colonial times

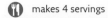 makes 4 servings

prep 30 mins
• cook 35-45 mins

9in (23cm) square baking dish

6 tbsp butter

3 cups fresh bread crumbs

2lb (900g) cooking apples, such as Granny Smith or Golden Delicious

½ cup packed light brown sugar

1 tsp ground cinnamon

½ tsp pumpkin pie spice

grated zest of 1 lemon

2 tbsp fresh lemon juice

1 tsp pure vanilla extract

1¼ cups heavy cream

1 tbsp confectioner's sugar

1 Preheat the oven to 350°F (180°C). Melt the butter in a frying pan. Add the bread crumbs and mix well.

2 Peel, quarter, and core the apples. Slice them and put in a bowl. Add the brown sugar, cinnamon, pumpkin pie spice, lemon zest and juice, and vanilla. Mix well.

3 Spread half of the apples in a 9in (23cm) square baking dish. Cover with half of the bread crumbs. Repeat with the remaining apples and bread crumbs.

4 Bake for 35-45 minutes, until the topping is golden brown and the apples are tender. If the topping is browning too quickly, reduce the heat to 325°F (170°C), and tent with foil. Whip the cream with the confectioner's sugar. Serve the betty warm, with the cream.

Citrus Zabaglione

This hot dessert is a refreshing way to end a meal

 makes 4 servings

prep 15 mins • cook 5 mins

4 flameproof serving dishes

2 pink grapefruit

2 grapefruit

2 oranges

1 large egg, plus 2 egg yolks

scant ½ cup Marsala

⅓ cup plus 1 tbsp sugar

1 Position a broiler rack 6in (15cm) from the source of heat and preheat the broiler. Segment the grapefruit and oranges. Divide the citrus segments among 4 individual flameproof serving dishes.

2 Beat the egg and egg yolks together in a heatproof bowl until just beginning to foam. Beat in the Marsala and sugar.

3 Place the bowl over a saucepan of simmering water. Beat with an electric mixer for about 4 minutes, or until the zabaglione is very thick, fluffy, and warm. Spoon over the fruit. Grill for about 1 minute, or until the topping is golden. Serve immediately.

VARIATION

Add 6oz (168g) fresh raspberries or blueberries to the citrus.

Baked Figs with Cinnamon and Honey

A simple-to-prepare, but stylish end to a meal

makes 4 servings

prep 2-3 mins • cook 20 mins

6 firm figs

2 tbsp honey

2 tbsp brandy or rum

pinch of ground cinnamon

1 Preheat the oven to 350°F (180°C). Cut the figs in half and place closely together in a shallow baking dish.

2 Drizzle with the honey and brandy, and sprinkle each fig with a generous pinch of cinnamon.

3 Bake for 20 minutes, or until softened. Check the figs after 10 minutes, as they may differ in ripeness slightly and require different cooking times. Serve warm, or at room temperature.

● **Good with** mascarpone, vanilla ice cream, or crème fraîche.

● **Leftovers** can be refrigerated for up to 2 days.

German Apple Cake

This moist apple cake is made special with a delicious crumbly streusel topping

- makes 6–8 servings
- prep 30 mins, plus chilling • cook 45–50 mins
- 8in (20cm) springform pan, wire rack
- freeze, wrapped, for up to 6 months

For the streusel topping

¾ cup all-purpose flour

⅓ cup packed light brown sugar

2 tsp ground cinnamon

6 tbsp butter, cut into pieces

2 Granny Smith apples

12 tbsp butter, at room temperature

¾ cup packed light brown sugar

grated zest of 1 lemon

3 large eggs

1¼ cups all-purpose flour

1¼ tsp salt

3 tbsp whole milk

1 To make the topping, mix the flour, sugar, and cinnamon in a bowl. Add the butter and rub it in. Shape into a thick disk, wrap in plastic wrap, and refrigerate for 30 minutes.

2 Preheat the oven to 375°F (190°C). Butter an 8in (20cm) springform pan and line the bottom with wax paper. Peel and core the apples, and cut them into wedges.

3 Beat the butter, sugar, and lemon zest together until pale and creamy. Beat the eggs, one at a time, into the butter mixture. Sift the flour, baking powder, and salt together. Add to the bowl, along with the milk, and mix until smooth.

4 Spread half of the batter into the pan. Top with half of the apples. Repeat. Grate the streusel over the apples.

5 Bake for 45–50 minutes, or until a toothpick inserted into the center comes out clean. Let stand on a wire rack for 10 minutes. Remove the sides of the pan and cool. Serve warm or cold.

Apple-Ginger Crisp

Few desserts say "autumn baking" more than an apple crisp

- makes 4 servings
- prep 20 mins • cook 45 mins

1lb 2oz (500g) Golden Delicious apples, peeled, cored, and thinly sliced

3 tbsp chopped crystallized ginger

1 tbsp fresh lemon juice

for the topping

¾ cup all-purpose flour

6 tbsp butter, at room temperature

½ cup packed light brown sugar

½ cup rolled (old-fashioned) oats

1 Preheat the oven to 375°F (190°C). Combine the apples, ginger, and lemon juice in a 6 cup square baking dish and toss.

2 To make the topping, combine the flour and butter in a large mixing bowl and rub in the butter with your fingertips until the mixture is combined. Work in the sugar and oats. The mixture should remain lumpy.

3 Crumble the topping over the apples. Press the topping down gently to level it. Bake for 45 minutes, until golden and crisp. Serve hot, warm, or cold.

● **Good with** crème anglaise or ice cream.

Apple and Blackberry Crumble

Replace 1 of the apples with 7oz (200g) blackberries.

Pineapple Flambé

Fresh pineapple is flamed with rum to produce a delicious, show-stopping dessert

- makes 4 servings
- prep 15–20 mins
  - cook 10 mins

1 ripe **pineapple**

¼ cup **dark rum** or brandy

2 tbsp fresh **lime** juice

¼ cup **butter**

¼ cup **light brown sugar**

ground **cinnamon**, for dusting

1 Peel the pineapple and remove the "eyes." Slice into rounds about ½in (⅓mm) thick, reserving any pineapple juice. Cut out the core using a small round cookie cutter or the tip of a sharp knife.

2 Place the pineapple and its juices, rum, and lime juice in a large frying pan and cook over medium-low heat about 1 minute, just until the liquid is warm. Carefully ignite the pan juices with a long-handled match. Cook until the flames die down.

3 Dot the pineapple with the butter and sprinkle with the brown sugar. Cook while gently shaking the pan until the butter and sugar combine into a glaze. Spoon into dessert dishes and serve hot, dusted with the cinnamon.

● **Good with** ice cream or whipped cream.

VARIATION

Apricot Flambé

Cook 10 apricots, halved and pits removed, in ¼ cup butter for 3–4 minutes, or until softened. Stir in ¼ cup light brown sugar and the juice of ½ lemon. Heat 4 tbsp apricot brandy in a ladle and ignite; pour over the apricots, and allow the flames to die out before serving.

> ### CHOOSING PINEAPPLE
> A fresh pineapple should be an even brown color. Avoid any with dark patches. It should have a fresh, fragrant aroma; if it does not smell, it is not fresh enough. Should you buy one that is not completely ripened, leave it on a windowsill to ripen further in the sun.

Honey-baked Apricots with Mascarpone

This Italian dessert, with just a hint of spice, makes the most of the short apricot season

- makes 4 servings
- prep 10 mins • cook 10 mins

4 ripe, juicy **apricots**, halved and pitted

3 tbsp **honey**

3 tbsp **sliced almonds**

pinch of **ground ginger** or cinnamon

⅔ cup **mascarpone cheese**, for serving

● **Prepare ahead** The dish can be assembled, ready for baking, several hours in advance.

1 Preheat the oven to 400°F (200°C). Lightly butter a shallow baking dish just large enough to hold the apricots.

2 Arrange the apricots in the dish, cut sides up. Brush with the honey, then sprinkle with the almonds and a dusting of the ginger.

3 Bake for 15 minutes, or until the apricots are tender when pierced with the tip of a knife and the almonds are toasted. Serve hot or cooled in dessert glasses, with a dollop of the mascarpone.

● **Good with** vanilla ice cream or thick whipped cream, instead of the mascarpone.

Jam

It might seem old-fashioned to spend time making jam when shops have such a wide choice, but the best way to make breakfast extra special is to have a jar of homemade jam in the cupboard. These simple steps show you how easy it is to get started.

Apples
Apples should feel heavy and have a tight, smooth, shiny skin. Apples make excellent jam because of their high pectin levels.

Plums
Tart red plums make excellent jam. Choose plump, round fruits with smooth skins that yield slightly to gentle pressure.

Choosing Fruit

Making jam is a time-honored way of preserving seasonal produce. Ideally buy fruit from a loose display so you can select the best. Fruits that feel heavy for their size are likely to contain the most juice. Do not buy any bruised or moldy fruits, or those that look damp and smell musty.

Storing

Ripe fruit spoils quickly, so handle it as little as possible. Remove fruit from any packaging and put it in the refrigerator to slow the ripening process. Or, take advantage of seasonal gluts and freeze fruit for jam-making later in the year. As many fruits collapse when thawed, be sure to label the container with the weight before freezing, so the balance of fruit, sugar, pectin, and acid won't be upset.

Cranberries
The best cranberries for jam have a bright red color and look full and round.

Strawberries
The best strawberries are well shaped, glossy, and red throughout. The hull should be green and fresh looking.

Equipment and Preparation

Assembling your Equipment

If you don't have a preserving pan, use a very large, stainless-steel saucepan deep enough to prevent you from being scorched by the boiling jam, with a solid base to distribute heat evenly. A sugar thermometer (see left) clips to the inside of the pan for easy reading to see when jam reaches the setting temperature of 220°F (104°C). If you don't have one, however, follow the recipe and test for a set using the cold plate or flake tests (see p465).

Long-handled spoons prevent you being burned while stirring and skimming, and using plastic funnels reduces the risk of burning yourself when pouring the hot jam into jars.

Choosing and Sterilizing your Jars

The best jars to use are those with self-sealing lids that form airtight seals, which prevents bacteria from destroying the jam during storage. This is an important consideration for any jams you intend to keep for a long time.

All jars and their closures must be crack-free, clean, and sterilized before being filled with hot jam. Wash all the jars and lids in hot, soapy water and rinse in hot water, or wash in a dishwasher. Put the jars and lids on a wire rack in a large pan, making sure they do not touch each other or the pan's side. Pour in enough boiling water to cover, then boil rapidly for 10 minutes. Using tongs, remove the jars from the water and drain upside-down on clean kitchen towels. Place the jars on a baking sheet in a preheated 210°F (100°C) oven for 15 minutes to dry.

THE SCIENCE BEHIND THE SET

Pectin and acid are two natural substances found in fruits in varying amounts. For a jam to set properly, it must contain specific proportions of acid, pectin, and sugar. Pectin is concentrated in fruit skins and cores, and slightly underripe fruits contain the most. Slightly underripe fruits also contain the most acid, so buy fruits for jam-making just when they are coming into season. Recipes using fruits low in either acid or pectin will include commercial pectin or acid in the form of lemon juice or vinegar.

YIELDS

When making any jam recipe, always treat the quantity it makes as a guideline and be prepared to have a little more or a little less. The actual yield will vary because of several factors, including the size of the fruit, their degree of ripeness, and the size of the pan and the jars.

Gooseberries
Choose gooseberries that are large with a slight tawny blush.

Raspberries
These should look plump and uniformly colored without any leaves or stems.

Blackberries
Pick or buy blackberries with a deep, dark black-blue hue and that smell fragrant.

Nectarines
The reddish-yellow skin should be smooth and the fruit should feel only slightly firm.

Blueberries
Look for berries that are plump with a blue-gray "bloom." They should feel firm, not soft.

Figs
Choose fruit that feel heavy for their weight and yield slightly when gently pressed. Do not buy any that are soft or smell sour.

Red Currants
The currants should be uniformly colored and not bruised or crushed.

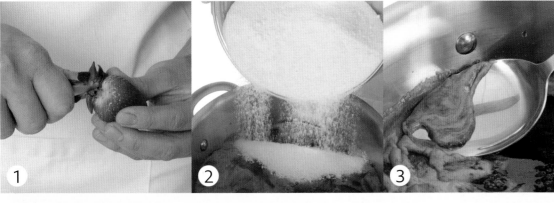

How to Make Jam

1 Prepare fruit The first step to making any homemade jam is preparing the fruit. To make the Strawberry Jam (p466) begin by hulling the strawberries. Other fruits, such as apricots, plums, cherries, and nectarines should be pitted first.

2 Add sugar Put your fruit in the pan, then add all the sugar at once and stir with a wooden spoon over a low heat until it completely dissolves. Bring to a rolling boil. When you think the sugar has dissolved, swirl the spoon in the mixture and check on the back of the spoon that no crystals are visible. If the sugar isn't completely dissolved at this point, the jam will be grainy.

3 Skim the surface After testing for a set (see right), keep the pan off the heat and use a large metal spoon to remove any scum from the surface. The jam is now ready to be poured into dry, warm sterilized jars. Leave the jars to cool, then label and date. Jams with an air-tight seal will keep for up to a year in a cool, dark place. They should then be refrigerated after opening.

TESTING FOR A SET

Cold Plate Test Put a little of the jam on a chilled plate and let cool, then push it gently. If the surface wrinkles, the jam is set. If not, boil a minute longer and retest.

Flake Test Hold some jam on a wooden spoon above a bowl for a few seconds, then tilt the spoon. The jam should fall off in flakes. If not, boil a minute longer and retest.

Jam

Strawberry Jam

4½lb (2kg) strawberries

6 tbsp lemon juice

4lb (1.8kg) sugar

1 Put a small plate in the refrigerator to chill before you begin. Hull the strawberries, weighing them occasionally to determine when you have 4lb (1.8kg) hulled berries. Halve the berries, put them in the nonmetallic bowl, and lightly crush with a large fork.

2 Put the crushed berries, accumulated juices, and the lemon juice in a large pan and bring to a boil. Reduce the heat to low and simmer for 5–10 minutes, stirring, or until the berries are soft.

3 Add the sugar and stir over a low heat until it completely dissolves. Increase the heat and boil rapidly for 15 minutes, without stirring, or until the jam reaches the setting point. Remove the pan from the heat and test for a set.

4 With the pan still off the heat, use a large metal spoon to skim the surface. Let the jam cool slightly so that a thin skin forms and the berries are evenly distributed throughout. Pour the jam into the prepared jars to within ⅛in (3mm) of the tops and seal. Let the jam cool, then label and date the jars. Store in a cool, dark place until ready to use, then refrigerate after opening.

Apricot Jam

3lb (1.35kg) apricots

2 tbsp lemon juice

3lb (1.35kg) sugar

1 Put a small plate in the refrigerator to chill before you begin. Halve and pit the apricots. Crack a few of the pits with a hammer and take out the kernels; discard the rest. Put the kernels into a heatproof bowl and pour in enough boiling water to cover. Leave for 1 minute, then transfer to a bowl of cold water. Drain again and rub off the skins with your fingers.

2 Put the apricots, kernels, lemon juice, and 10fl oz (300ml) water into a large stainless-steel pan and bring to a boil. Lower the heat and simmer, stirring occasionally, for 25 minutes, or until the apricot skins are soft, the fruit is tender, and the mixture reduces by one-third.

3 Add the sugar to the pan and stir until it completely dissolves. Increase the heat and bring the mixture to a boil, without stirring, for 10 minutes, or until it reaches the setting point. Remove the pan from the heat and test for a set.

4 With the pan still off the heat, use a large metal spoon to skim the surface and remove the kernels. Immediately pour the jam into the prepared jars to within ⅛in (3mm) of the tops and seal. Let the jam cool, then label and date the jars. Store in a cool, dark place until ready to use, then refrigerate after opening.

Blueberry Jam

4lb (1.8kg) blueberries

3lb (1.35kg) sugar

juice of 2 lemons

pinch of salt

1 Put the blueberries in a large nonmetallic bowl with half the sugar, the lemon juice, and the salt. Stir to mix, then cover and let stand at room temperature, without stirring, for 5 hours. Meanwhile, put a small plate in the refrigerator to chill.

2 Pour the contents of the bowl into a large stainless-steel pan over a low heat. Add the remaining sugar and stir until the sugar completely dissolves.

3 Increase the heat and bring the mixture rapidly to a boil, without stirring, then boil for 10–12 minutes, or until it reaches the setting point. Remove the pan from the heat and test for a set.

4 With the pan still off the heat, use a large metal spoon to skim the surface. Let the jam cool slightly, then pour it into the prepared jars to within ⅛in (3mm) of the tops and seal. Let the jam cool, then label and date the jars. Store in a cool, dark place until ready to use, then refrigerate after opening.

SAFE STORAGE

Once you've made and potted your jam, be sure to label the jars clearly with the date. Keep in a cool, dark place, and store in the refrigerator after opening.

Delicious Ways to Use Fruit Jam

Baked Jam Roll
This warm, comforting family favorite tastes great with strawberry or any other fruit jam
🕐 40 mins   **page 382**

Sherry Trifle
Vary this traditional dessert by using a different flavored fruit jam each time you make it
🕐 35 mins   **page 386**

Victoria Sponge Cake
Always popular for tea, homemade fruit jam and whipped cream make a luscious filling
🕐 40–45 mins   **page 413**

Raspberry Sablés
With a thin layer of jam between butter-rich cookies, these are irresistible with tea or coffee
🕐 20–25 mins   **page 442**

Passion Fruit Puddings

This sweet, fruit-flavored milk pudding is perfect for family lunches or dinner parties with friends

- makes 4 servings
- prep 15 mins, plus chilling • cook 10 mins
- 1¼ cup custard cups or ramekins

⅔ cup plus 1 tbsp **cornstarch**

1 quart (1 liter) **whole milk**

⅓ cup **sugar**

8 ripe **passion fruit**

1 Sprinkle the cornstarch over 1 cup milk in a bowl and stir to dissolve. Bring the remaining 3 cups milk just to a boil over medium heat. Whisk the hot milk into the cornstarch mixture then return to the saucepan and stir over medium-low heat until the mixture simmers. Reduce the heat to very low and simmer gently for 5 minutes. Stir in the sugar.

2 Rinse the molds with cold water. Cut 3 of the passion fruit in half, scoop out the seeds, and rub through a sieve over a bowl, discarding the seeds. Sir into the cornstarch mixture, then divide among the molds. Press a piece of plastic wrap directly on the surface of each pudding. Refrigerate for at least 2 hours or until set.

3 Briefly dip the bottom of each mold in a bowl of hot water. Unmold each onto a dessert plate. Cut the remaining 5 passion fruit in half, and spoon equal amounts of the fruit over the puddings. Serve chilled.

● **Good with** crisp, buttery cookies.

Berry Medley

Your favorite fresh berries in a light lemon syrup makes a refreshing summer dessert

- makes 4 servings
- prep 15 mins, plus cooling • cook 2 mins

½ cup **sugar**

grated zest of 1 **lemon**

3 tbsp fresh **lemon** juice

1¾lb (800g) fresh **strawberries**, **raspberries**, and/or **blueberries**

● **Prepare ahead** Chill the fruit and syrup for at least 1 hour before serving.

1 Bring 1¾ cups water and the sugar to a boil in a small saucepan over medium heat, stirring to dissolve the sugar. Stop stirring, increase the heat to high, and boil for 2 minutes.

2 Remove from the heat. Stir in the lemon zest and juice and let cool completely.

3 Hull the strawberries and cut large ones in half. Combine the berries in a bowl and add the syrup. Stir gently to coat evenly. Cover and refrigerate until chilled. Spoon into bowls and serve.

● **Good with** a large dollop of whipped cream.

VARIATION

Winter Salad
Use sliced apples and segmented oranges, instead of berries. For an exotic version, try papaya and mango, and use lime in the syrup.

Mango and Orange Mousse

A light and refreshing dessert

 makes 4 servings

 prep 40 mins, plus chilling

2 large ripe **mangoes**

¼ cup fresh **orange** juice

finely grated zest of 1 **orange**

¼ cup **superfine sugar**

2 tsp **unflavored gelatin powder**

pinch of **salt**

1 large **egg white**

⅔ cup **heavy cream**

1 Cut the flesh off both sides of the mango stone. Scoop out the flesh and discard the skin. Set aside 1 piece of mango. Cut the remaining mango, including the flesh clinging to the stone, into chunks. Purée with the orange juice in a food processor. Transfer to a bowl and stir in the orange zest and superfine sugar.

2 Sprinkle the gelatin over 3 tbsp water in a small heatproof bowl and let stand for 5 minutes until softened. Place the bowl in a saucepan of gently simmering water and stir until the gelatin has completely dissolved. Cool slightly, then stir into the mango purée.

3 Whip the egg white and salt in a large, clean bowl until stiff peaks form. Fold the egg white mixture into the mango mixture.

4 Whip the cream to soft peaks. Fold half into the mango mixture. Divide the mixture among 4 dessert glasses. Refrigerate until the mousses are set, at least 1 hour or up to 2 days.

5 Slice the reserved mango. Top each serving with a dollop of whipped cream and a mango slice. Serve chilled.

Cold Raspberry Soufflé

This light, fragrant dessert just melts in the mouth

- makes 6 servings
- prep 30 mins, plus chilling
- six 6oz (175g) ramekins
- open-freeze, undecorated; when frozen, place in a freezer bag, seal, and return to the freezer for up to 1 month

1 tbsp **vegetable oil**

4 tbsp **rose water**

1 tbsp **powdered gelatin**

12oz (350g) fresh **raspberries**

¾ cup **confectioner's sugar**, sifted

1 tbsp fresh **lemon** juice

2 cups **heavy cream**

4 large **egg whites**

mint leaves, for garnish

1 Make a double-thick strip of wax paper large enough to tape around the outside of six 6oz (175g) ramekins, and wide enough to stand 2in (5cm) above the rim. Lightly brush the exposed inside of the wax paper with vegetable oil.

2 Place the rose water in a small bowl, sprinkle with the gelatin, and let stand for about 2 minutes, or until spongy. Place the bowl in a larger bowl of boiling water and stir until the gelatin dissolves. Remove from water and let cool slightly.

3 Reserve 12 raspberries. Purée the remaining raspberries in a food processor. Rub through a very fine sieve over a bowl to discard the seeds. Stir in the confectioner's sugar and lemon juice, then gradually stir in the gelatin. Refrigerate until just beginning to set.

4 Whip the cream until soft peaks form. Fold the cream into the raspberry mixture. In another bowl, beat the egg whites until stiff peaks form, and gently fold into the raspberry mixture. Pour into the ramekins. Refrigerate for at least 2 hours, until set.

5 Carefully peel off the wax paper from around the ramekins. Decorate each soufflé with raspberries and a few mint leaves.

● **Leftovers** are delicious spooned between meringues as a filling.

VARIATION

Blackberry Soufflé
Use fresh blackberries in place of the raspberries, taking extra care to remove all of the seeds from the purée before adding to the whipped cream.

Chocolate-dipped Fruits

This decadent treat is perfect with after-dinner drinks

- makes 4–6 servings
- prep 20 mins • cook 10 mins

12 Cape gooseberries

12 strawberries

3½oz (100g) high-quality bittersweet chocolate

● **Prepare ahead** The dipped fruits can be refrigerated for up to 24 hours.

1 Pull back the papery leaves of each gooseberry to expose the round orange fruit. Leave the stems and hulls on the strawberries. Line a baking sheet with wax paper.

2 Chop the chocolate. Transfer to a heatproof bowl. Place over a saucepan of barely simmering water and melt, stirring occasionally. Remove the chocolate from the saucepan.

3 Holding the fruit by the stalks, dip each fruit into the chocolate and place on the tray. Work quickly, as the chocolate does not take long to set.

4 Refrigerate until the chocolate is set. Serve chilled.

Red Fruit Medley

When summer berries are in season, make this German-style compote, *Rote Grütze*

🍴 makes 4 servings

🕐 prep 10 mins • cook 5 mins

8oz (240g) **bing cherries**, pitted

6oz (175g) **raspberries**

6oz (175g) **red currants**, stemmed

6oz (175g) **blackberries**

6oz (175g) **strawberries**, quartered if large

3 tbsp **light brown sugar**

2 tbsp **cornstarch**

extra sugar to prevent a skin from forming. Let cool, then refrigerate, covered with plastic wrap.

1 **Place all the fruit** in a saucepan with ⅔ cup water and bring slowly to the boil.

2 **Combine the sugar** and cornflour with 3 tbsp cold water to form a smooth paste. Gradually stir into the fruit. Cook gently, stirring, until the juices begins to thicken.

3 **Transfer to a bowl**. Spoon the mixture into individual dishes.

⬤ **Prepare ahead** This dish can be refrigerated 1 day before serving. Before storing, sprinkle with a little

⬤ **Good with** crème anglaise.

Sparkling Wine Jellies with Passion Fruit

For a special occasion, you may want to use champagne, but any good sparkling wine will do

🍴 makes 6 servings

🕐 prep 20 mins, plus soaking and 4 hrs setting • cook 10 mins

🍱 six 7oz (200ml) champagne or dessert glasses, or bowls

2 envelopes **powdered gelatin**

one 750ml bottle **sparkling wine**

½ cup **sugar**

2 tbsp **fresh lemon juice**

2 or 3 **passion fruits**

unsprayed **rose petals**, to decorate

1 **Sprinkle the gelatin** over ½ cup of the wine. Let stand until the gelatin softens, about 5 minutes.

2 **Combine** another ½ cup wine, with the sugar and lemon juice in a nonreactive medium saucepan. Stir

over low heat until the sugar dissolves. Add the softened gelatin and stir until the gelatin dissolves; do not boil. Cool slightly. Stir in the remaining wine. Let stand until cooled.

3 **Meanwhile**, cut each passion fruit in half and scoop out the contents. Divide the pulp among 6 champagne glasses. Add ¼ cup gelatin to each glass. Leave the remaining gelatin mixture at room temperature. Refrigerate the glasses about 30 minutes, until the gelatin sets.

4 **Divide** the remaining gelatin mixture among the glasses and return to the refrigerator. Chill for at least 4 hours, or until completely set.

5 **Garnish** each gelatin with rose petals and serve chilled.

Layered Fruit Platter with Rose Cream

Fresh summer fruits served with a rose-petal cream make this
easy-to-prepare summer dessert rather special

- 🍴 makes 4 servings
- 🕐 prep 15 mins
- ❗ ensure that the roses have been grown without pesticides or other chemical sprays

1 small **pineapple**

crushed ice

1 ripe **mango**, peeled, pitted, and cut into thick wedges

6oz (175g) **strawberries**, washed, hulled, and halved

1 ripe **fig**, quartered

1 **kiwi**, peeled and cut into chunks

2 **passion fruits**, halved

pale pink **rose petals**, to serve

For the rose petal cream

1 dark red **rose**

⅔ cup **half-and-half**

1 tbsp **sugar**

2 tsp fresh **lemon** juice

⅔ cup **heavy cream**

● **Prepare ahead** The rose petal cream can be made in advance and refrigerated for up to 1 day.

1 **Quarter the pineapple** lengthwise through the leaves. Run a sharp knife between the flesh and the skin, being careful to keep the shape of the pineapple intact. Keeping the pineapple flesh in position, cut it vertically into slices, being sure not to cut through the skin.

2 **Place the crushed ice** on a platter. Arrange the pineapple on the ice, and surround with the mango, strawberries, fig, kiwi, and passion fruit.

3 **To make the rose cream**, remove the red rose petals from the rose, and set aside 3 petals for a garnish. Purée the remaining petals, half-and-half, and sugar in a blender. Add the lemon juice. Beat the heavy cream with an electric hand mixer or whisk until soft peaks form. Add the rose petal mixture and beat again until soft peaks form again. Transfer to a serving bowl. Add the reserved red petals.

4 **Scatter the pale pink** rose petals over the fruit and serve with the rose petal cream.

Eton Mess

A favorite British dessert, named for the famous school, Eton

- 🍴 makes 4 servings
- 🕐 prep 10 mins

12oz (350g) **strawberries**, hulled and sliced

2 tbsp **sugar**

2 tbsp **orange** juice or orange-flavored liqueur

1¼ cups **heavy cream**

5oz (130g) store-bought **meringue** cookies

● **Prepare ahead** The berries and whipped cream can be prepared several hours in advance. Assemble just before serving.

1 **Combine the strawberries**, sugar, and orange juice in a bowl, and crush them with a fork.

2 **Whip the cream** just until stiff peaks form. Coarsely crush the meringues into small bite size pieces—you should have about 2 cups crushed meringues.

3 **Stir the crushed meringue** into the whipped cream. Add the berries and their juices, and fold together. Spoon into dessert cups and serve immediately.

Toffee Apples

You know fall has arrived when you have a craving for these chewy treats

🍴 makes 4

🕐 prep 15 mins • cook 10 mins

⬜ wooden lollypop sticks, candy thermometer

4 small apples, stems removed

generous 1 cup demerara sugar

2 tbsp butter

1½ tsp light corn syrup

1 tsp cider vinegar

vegetable oil, for greasing

⬤ **Prepare ahead** The toffee apples can be stored in a cool dry place for up to 2 days.

1 **Push a wooden stick** firmly into the stalk end of each apple.

2 **Bring the demerara sugar**, ⅓ cup water, butter, syrup, and vinegar to a boil in a heavy-bottomed, medium saucepan, stirring just until the sugar is dissolved. Attach a candy thermometer to the saucepan. Cook,

without stirring, brushing down the crystals that form inside the pan with a pastry brush dipped in cold water, until the syrup reaches the soft-crack stage, 270-290°F (135-145°C).

3 **Meanwhile**, line a baking tray with wax paper and lightly grease the paper. Remove the pan from the heat. Dip an apple into the caramel to coat, tilting the pan if necessary, and stand the apple on the lined baking sheet. Working quickly, repeat with the remaining apples.

4 **Let stand until** the apples are completely cold and the toffee has hardened.

> **DEMERARA SUGAR**
> This flavorful sugar has large golden brown crystals, and is available at specialty and natural food stores.

Caramel Oranges

This sweet caramel sauce is a perfect match for the sliced fruit

🍴 makes 4 servings

🕐 prep 10 mins, plus standing • cook 15 mins

4 oranges

1 cup superfine sugar

crème fraîche, to serve

⬤ **Prepare ahead** The dessert can be refrigerated for up to 2 days.

1 **Remove the zest** from 1 of the oranges using a vegetable peeler. Cut the zest into very thin slivers and set aside.

2 **With a sharp knife**, cut the zest and pith away from all of the oranges. Slice each orange into rounds, then stack the rounds back into their original shapes. Place the sliced oranges in a bowl.

3 **Bring the sugar** and ⅓ cup water to a boil in a saucepan over medium heat, stirring until the sugar dissolves. Increase the heat to high and boil, brushing down the crystals

that appear on the side of the pan with a wet pastry brush, without stirring, until it forms a dark amber caramel. Carefully add ⅓ cup hot water (the caramel will sputter), and stir until the caramel dissolves. Add the orange zest and simmer for 4 minutes.

4 **Pour the caramel sauce** over the oranges. Cool, cover, and refrigerate for at least 4 hours.

5 **On each plate**, fan out the orange slices and drizzle with the caramel. Top with a dollop of crème fraîche and serve chilled.

⬤ **Leftovers** can be chopped and used to top a fresh fruit salad or orange or lemon jello.

Strawberry Yogurt Mousse

This speedy dessert is bound to be a favorite with the kids

 makes 4 servings

prep 15 mins, plus chilling

refrigerate the evaporated milk overnight or freeze for 30 minutes

1lb (450g) ripe **strawberries**

¾ cup **evaporated milk**, well chilled

2 tbsp **superfine sugar**

1 cup thick, **Greek-style yogurt**, plus more to serve

● **Prepare ahead** The mousse can be made several hours in advance.

1 **Slice the strawberries** and set a few aside. Divide half the strawberries among 4 dessert glasses. Purée the remaining strawberries in a food processor or blender. Strain through a sieve to remove the seeds.

2 **Beat the chilled** evaporated milk with an electric mixer on high speed about 7 minutes, or until doubled in volume. Beat in the sugar. Stir in the strawberry purée and yogurt until well combined. Spoon into the glasses and refrigerate for 15–20 minutes, until lightly set.

3 **Garnish** with a dollop of yogurt and the reserved strawberries.

Summer Berry Terrine

All the flavors of summer wrapped up in this stunning terrine

 makes 4-6 servings

 prep 45 mins, plus chilling • cook 5 mins

9 x 5in nonstick loaf pan

⅓ cup **sugar**

½ cup **orange-flavored liqueur**

2 tbsp fresh **lemon** juice

2 tbsp unflavored **gelatin powder**

8oz (225g) **raspberries**

4oz (115g) **red currants**, stemmed

5oz (140g) **blueberries**

8oz (225g) **strawberries**, quartered

● **Prepare ahead** The terrine must be refrigerated for at least 3 hours before serving.

1 **Bring 2 cups water** and the sugar to a simmer in a saucepan over low heat, stirring to dissolve the sugar. Increase the heat to high and boil 1–2 minutes to reduce slightly. Let cool 5 minutes, then stir in the liqueur and lemon juice.

2 **Sprinkle the gelatin** over ½ cup cold water in a small heatproof bowl. Let stand about 5 minutes, until spongy. Place the bowl in a frying pan of simmering water and stir until the gelatin dissolves. Stir into the syrup.

3 **Place a 9 x 5in** (22 x 13cm) nonstick loaf pan in a roasting pan. Add enough ice water to come halfway up the sides of the loaf pan. Scatter the raspberries in the bottom of the loaf pan. Add enough of the gelatin mixture to cover. Let set.

4 **Sprinkle the red currants** and blueberries over the raspberry layer, and add enough of the gelatin mixture to cover. Let this layer set. Finally, add a layer of strawberries and pour in the remaining gelatin mixture. Remove the loaf pan from the water. Cover and refrigerate until completely set, at least 3 hours (preferably 8 hours).

5 **Dip the loaf pan** in a bowl of hot water for a few seconds. Invert and unmold the terrine onto a platter. Serve chilled.

● **Good with** additional berries and whipped cream or crème fraîche.

● **Leftovers** can be used in trifles or sliced and served cold alongside poultry dishes.

Berry Mascarpone Fool

This pretty dessert can be made with any berries of your choice

🍴 makes 4 servings

🕐 prep 15 mins, plus chilling

12oz (350g) **raspberries**, or blackberries or sliced strawberries

⅔ cup **sugar**

juice of 1 **lemon**

⅔ cup **heavy cream**

½ cup **mascarpone**, at room temperature

mint leaves for garnish

blueberries, for garnish

● **Prepare ahead** The fools can be refrigerated overnight.

1 **Reserve a few berries** for garnish. Purée the remaining berries and sugar in a food processor or blender. Strain through a sieve to remove any seeds. The purée should be quite thick. Add the lemon juice.

2 **Whisk the cream** in a chilled bowl until soft peaks form. Whisk the mascarpone in another bowl to soften it. Fold the mascarpone into the cream. Stir half of the berry purée into the cream mixture.

3 **Divide the berry** purée among 4 glasses and top with the cream mixture. Garnish each with the reserved berries and a mint leaf. Refrigerate for at least 2 hours, until chilled. Serve cold.

Fruit Purées

If you do not have a food processor or blender, you can use a hand mixer or purée fruits by hand, although it will take a little more effort. Mash the fruits with a fork, then push through a sieve, for a smooth texture.

Lychees in Scented Syrup

Look for fresh lychees in Asian markets during their spring season, although you may find imported lychees in late winter

🍴 makes 4 servings

🕐 prep 10 mins • cook 10 mins

✓ low fat

❄ freeze for up to 2 months; thaw at room temperature for 2–3 hours

⅓ cup **demerara** or **turbinado sugar**

grated zest and juice of 1 **lime**

1 whole **star anise**

1lb 5oz (600g) **lychees**

2 pieces of **stem ginger** in syrup, chopped

● **Prepare ahead** Can be refrigerated for up to 2 days.

1 **Bring ⅔ cup water**, the sugar, lime juice, and star anise to a boil in a saucepan over medium heat, stirring until the sugar has dissolved.

Increase the heat to high and boil for 7 minutes, until syrupy. Let cool.

2 **Meanwhile**, peel the lychees and remove the pits, if desired. Place in a serving bowl. Add the ginger and its syrup.

3 **Pour the syrup** over the lychees. Cover and refrigerate for at least 1 hour, until well chilled. The star anise can be served with the lychees as a decoration, but it cannot be eaten.

● **Good with** vanilla ice cream or a drizzle of heavy cream.

VARIATION

Strawberries in Scented Syrup

Substitute quartered or halved strawberries for the lychees.

Summer Pudding

This classic summer fruit dessert is traditionally made with currants, but blackberries and raspberries work well, too

- makes 6 servings
- prep 20–25 mins, plus chilling
- 1 quart (1 liter) bowl

1 cup stemmed **black currants** or blackberries

1 cup stemmed **red currants** or raspberries

⅔ cup **sugar**

2 cups sliced **strawberries**

1 cup **blueberries**

12 slices **white sandwich bread**, crust removed

● **Prepare ahead** This dessert benefits from being refrigerated overnight before serving. It will keep, refrigerated, for up to 3 days.

1 **Cook** the black and red currants and sugar in a saucepan over medium heat, stirring often, until the fruit gives off its juices. Stir in the strawberries and blueberries and cook just until they begin to soften.

2 **Cover the bottom** of the bowl with a round of bread trimmed to fit. Line the sides of the bowl with bread slices as needed, trimmed and overlapping to fit.

3 **Spoon** some of the fruit juices over the bread. Fill the bowl with the fruit, packing it well. Cover with the remaining bread, trimmed to fit.

4 **Place the bowl** on a plate. Cover with plastic wrap. Place a small plate inside the bowl and weigh with a heavy can of food. Refrigerate at least 8 hours or overnight.

5 **Uncover the bowl** and turn the pudding out onto a serving platter. Serve chilled.

● **Good with** ice cream or whipped cream.

Peach Melba

Auguste Escoffier created this dish for opera singer Dame Nellie Melba when he was head chef of the Savoy Hotel, London

- makes 4 servings
- prep 20 mins • cook 25 mins
- freeze the raspberry sauce for up to 6 months

1½ cups **granulated sugar**

4 **peaches**

9oz (250g) **raspberries**

1 tbsp **confectioner's sugar**

1 tbsp fresh **lemon** juice

1 tsp **arrowroot** or cornstarch

4 scoops **vanilla ice cream**

1 **Put the sugar** in a saucepan and add 2½ cups water. Bring slowly to the boil, ensuring all the sugar has dissolved before it boils. Lower the heat and simmer for 5 minutes.

2 **Meanwhile, dip** the peaches in boiling water for 15–30 seconds and peel off the skins. Put the peaches in the syrup and cook over a low heat, turning occasionally, for 15 minutes, or until tender.

3 **Put the raspberries,** confectioner's sugar, and lemon juice in a saucepan. Mix the arrowroot with 2 tbsp water and add to the pan. Bring to a boil, then strain through a sieve. Taste and add more sugar or lemon juice, if required. Let the peaches and raspberry sauce cool. Cut each peach in half and remove the pit.

4 **To serve**, place a scoop of ice cream in each dish, put 2 peach halves on top, and pour over some of the cold raspberry sauce.

VARIATION

Pear Melba

Although this is not authentic, you can use 4 pears instead of the peaches. Peel the pears, cut each in half and remove the cores and stalks. Poach, as for the peaches, and serve in the same way.

THICKENING THE SAUCE

Depending on the juiciness of the raspberries, the sauce may be thinner than you'd like. To thicken, mix 1 tsp arrowroot with a little water and add to the sauce.

Pear and Grape Salad

You don't often think of adding cucumber to sweet dishes, but it works perfectly in this exotic fruit salad

makes 4 servings

prep 10 mins • cook 5–6 mins

1 cucumber

2 lemongrass stalks

⅓ cup granulated or raw sugar

2 ripe red-skinned pears

1 cup green seedless grapes

1 cup red seedless grapes

¼ cup packed small mint leaves

● **Prepare ahead** The salad can be refrigerated up to 2 days in advance.

1 Trim the ends from the cucumber. Cut in half lengthwise. Using a teaspoon, scoop out and discard the seeds, and thinly slice. Cut the bottom 4in (10cm) from each lemongrass stalk, and discard the tops. Discard the tough outer leaves from the lemongrass. Halve the lemongrass lengthwise and smash with a rolling pin.

2 Bring the lemongrass, sugar, and a scant 1 cup of water to a boil in a saucepan over medium heat, stirring to dissolve the sugar. Boil for 1 minute. Remove from the heat and stir in the cucumber. Let cool.

3 Discard the lemongrass. Quarter and core the pears, and slice into thin wedges. Transfer to a serving bowl and add the green and red grapes, cucumber, and syrup. Refrigerate for at least 2 hours to chill. Sprinkle with the mint leaves and serve chilled.

Pears Hélène

This classic dessert combines poached pears with a decadent chocolate sauce

makes 4 servings

prep 10 mins • cook 20 mins

½ cup sugar

1 vanilla bean, split lengthwise

4 ripe Bosc pears

5oz (130g) bittersweet chocolate, finely chopped

½ cup heavy cream

● **Prepare ahead** The pears and sauce can be refrigerated in separate containers for up to 3 days.

1 Bring the sugar and 1¼ cups water to a simmer in a saucepan over medium heat, stirring to dissolve the sugar. Add the vanilla bean.

2 Peel the pears, leaving the stems attached, and place in the saucepan. Cover and reduce the heat to medium-low. Simmer the pears, turning them occasionally, about 20 minutes, until tender. Using a slotted spoon, transfer to a dish and let cool. Remove the vanilla bean (which can be rinsed, dried and used again) and reserve the poaching syrup.

3 To make the chocolate sauce, melt the chocolate in a bowl set over a saucepan of very hot water. Heat the cream and ¼ cup of the poaching syrup in a saucepan over medium heat until almost boiling. Remove from the heat, add the chocolate, and stir until smooth.

4 Serve each pear in a shallow bowl, topped a drizzle of the sauce. Serve immediately, with the rest of the sauce on the side.

● **Good with** ice cream or a dollop of whipped cream.

● **Leftovers** The leftover syrup, which will keep, covered and refrigerated, for up to 5 days, can be tossed with fresh fruit for a salad.

Berries with Citrus Syrup

Juicy seasonal berries are made even more luscious with a sweet lemon-orange syrup

- makes 4 servings
- prep 5 mins, plus macerating • cook 10 mins
- low fat

1 lb (450g) **mixed red berries**, such as raspberries, strawberries, and red currants

⅔ cup **sugar**

zest of 1 **lemon**, cut into thin strips

1 tbsp fresh **orange** juice

4 sprigs **mint**, leaves only

● **Prepare ahead** The berries can be macerated for up to 1 hour.

1 Place the mixed berries in a serving dish.

2 Bring the sugar and ½ cup water to a boil in a saucepan over medium heat, stirring until the sugar dissolves. Increase the heat to high and boil for 5 minutes, until slightly reduced. Let cool. Stir in the lemon zest and orange juice.

3 Pour the syrup over the berries, and sprinkle with the mint leaves. Let stand for at least 10 minutes. Transfer to dessert glasses and serve.

● **Good with** whipped cream or ice cream.

● **Leftovers** can be blended with yogurt, apple juice, or ice to make a delicious fruit smoothie.

Pineapple with Mint

This fruit platter makes a refreshing end to any meal

- serves 4–6
- prep 20 mins, plus chilling
- low fat

1 large ripe **pineapple**

1 **pomegranate**

finely grated zest and juice of 1 **lime**

3 tbsp chopped **mint**

2 tbsp **light brown sugar**

2 tbsp **dark rum** (optional)

● **Prepare ahead** The fruit can be chilled up to 3 hours before serving.

1 Using a sharp knife, cut the peel from the pineapple. Quarter lengthwise. Cut out and discard the woody core from each quarter then thinly slice the pineapple crosswise. Arrange on a large platter.

2 Cut the pomegranate in half and remove the seeds, discarding the membranes. Scatter the seeds over the pineapple. Sprinkle the lime juice over the fruit.

3 Combine the lime zest, mint, and brown sugar in a small bowl. Sprinkle over the fruit, with the rum, if using. Refrigerate for at least 30 minutes, until chilled.

● **Good with** thick Greek yogurt.

VARIATION

Pineapple with Chile
Dissolve ¼ cup sugar in ½ cup water. Add 1 finely diced chile and boil for 10 minutes, or until syrupy. Serve poured over the pineapple slices.

Orange and Rosemary Tart

Similar to the classic lemon tart, the rosemary adds a delicate scented flavor to the orange

🍴 makes 6–8 servings

🕐 prep 30 mins, plus chilling
• cook 1 hr

🍱 8in (20cm) tart pan with removable bottom, baking beans

For the pastry

1⅓ cup all-purpose flour

6 tbsp cold butter, diced

1 tbsp confectioner's sugar

1 tbsp chopped rosemary

1 large egg

For the filling

2 cups fresh orange juice

2 sprigs rosemary

scant 1 cup sugar

4 large eggs

½ cup heavy cream

grated zest of 2 oranges

1 **Preheat the oven** to 350°F (180°C). Pulse the flour, butter, confectioner's sugar, and rosemary in a food processor until it resembles coarse bread crumbs. Mix the egg and 2 tbsp water. Add to the bowl and pulse until the dough comes together, adding more water if needed. Gather into a thick disk. Wrap in plastic wrap and refrigerate for 30 minutes.

2 **Roll out the dough** on a lightly floured work surface into a round about ⅛in (3mm) thick. Line an 8in (20cm) tart pan with the dough. Refrigerate for 30 minutes.

3 **Line the dough** with wax paper and fill with beans. Bake at 400°F (200°C) for 10 minutes. Remove the paper and beans and bake for 10 minutes more, until the crust is golden. Remove from the oven. Reduce the oven temperature to 325°F (160°C).

4 **Meanwhile**, make the filling. Bring the orange juice and rosemary to a boil in a saucepan. Reduce the heat to medium and simmer about 20 minutes, until reduced to 1 cup. Strain into a bowl, discarding the rosemary, and let cool.

5 **Add the sugar**, eggs, cream, and orange zest and whisk until combined. Pour into the pastry shell. Bake for 35 minutes, or just until the filling is set. Let cool, remove the sides of the pan, and serve.

Grape and Elderflower Gelatins

Look out for delicate and fragrant elderflower liqueur or syrup

🍴 makes 4 servings

🕐 prep 15 mins, plus setting
• cook 5 mins

3 tsp unflavored gelatin powder

½ cup elderflower liqueur

whipped cream, for serving

seedless green grapes, for serving

● **Prepare ahead** The gelatins can be refrigerated for up to 2 days.

1 **Sprinkle the gelatin** over ½ cup water in a small bowl. Let stand about 5 minutes, or until the mixture is spongy. Place the bowl in a small frying pan of simmering water. Stir the gelatin mixture constantly until melted. Remove from the frying pan.

2 **Stir 2 cups** tepid water, the liqueur, and the dissolved gelatin together in a large measuring cup until combined. Divide among four 8oz (240ml) dessert glasses. Refrigerate at least 3 hours, until set. Top each with a dollop of whipped cream and some grapes, and serve chilled.

Melon Cocktail

This colorful dish can be made with any melon, cut with a melon baller for a formal event or into cubes for a casual snack

- 🍴 makes 4 servings
- 🕐 prep 15 mins, plus chilling
- ✓ low fat
- 🗄 melon baller

about 1⅓lb (600g) **watermelon**

about 1⅓lb (600g) **cantaloupe**

about 1⅓lb (600g) **honeydew**

3 tbsp finely chopped **mint**, plus sprigs for garnish

2 tbsp **honey**

● **Prepare ahead** The fruit can be prepared up to 4 hours in advance and refrigerated until ready to serve.

1 **Using a melon baller**, scoop balls of each melon, or cut the fruit into 1in (2cm) cubes. Place the fruit in a large bowl. Add the chopped mint and honey and toss gently.

2 **Cover and refrigerate** for at least 30 minutes, stirring occasionally to allow the melon to absorb the honey and mint flavors.

3 **When ready to serve**, spoon the melon and any juices into individual serving dishes. Garnish each serving with mint.

● **Good with** a rich meal as a light palate-cleansing dessert, or as a refreshing starter.

VARIATION

Exotic Fruit Cocktail

Use one kind of melon and add any variation of cut fruit, such as star fruit, pineapple, kiwi, mango, blueberries, and strawberries.

Apple-berry Tart

Apples are always the beginning of a good tart

- 🍴 makes 6–8 servings
- 🕐 prep 20 mins, plus chilling ● cook 1 hr
- 🗄 8in (20cm) tart pan with removable bottom, baking beans

For the pastry

1⅓ cups **all-purpose flour**, plus more for rolling

1 tbsp **granulated sugar**

6 tbsp cold **butter**, diced

1 large **egg**

For the filling

4 **Golden Delicious apples** or Bosc pears

1 cup **heavy cream**

⅓ cup packed **light brown sugar**

3 large **egg yolks**

1 tsp **pure vanilla extract**

½ cup **blackberries**, raspberries, or blueberries

2 tbsp **granulated sugar**

1 tsp **ground cinnamon**

1 **To make the pastry**, pulse the flour, butter, and sugar in a food processor until it resembles coarse bread crumbs. Add the egg and pulse until the dough comes together, adding more water if needed. Gather into a thick disk. Wrap in plastic wrap and refrigerate for 30 minutes.

2 **Roll out the dough** into a round about ⅛in (3mm) thick. Line the tart pan with the dough. Refrigerate for 30 minutes. Preheat the oven to 400°F (200°C). Line the dough with wax paper and fill with baking beans. Bake for 10 minutes. Remove the paper and beans and bake for 10 minutes, until golden. Remove from the oven. Reduce the temperature to 375°F (190°C).

3 **Meanwhile**, peel, core, and thinly slice the apples. Whisk together the cream, brown sugar, egg yolks, and vanilla. Arrange the apples and berries in the pastry shell. Pour in the cream mixture. Sprinkle with granulated sugar and cinnamon. Bake for 40–45 minutes, or until set. Serve warm or cold.

Mango and Papaya Salad

Tropical fruit flavors combine
in this refreshing dessert

 makes 4 servings

🕐 prep 15 mins • cook 10 mins

✓ low fat

one 1in (2.5cm) piece **ginger in syrup**, cut into thin strips

2 tbsp **syrup from ginger**

2 tbsp **sugar**

grated zest of 1 **lime**

2 tbsp fresh **lime** juice

1 **pomegranate**, seeds only

1 large ripe **mango**

1 large ripe **papaya**

1 small **melon** such as Ogen or Charentais

lime wedges, to serve

● **Prepare ahead** The ginger dressing can be refrigerated up to 2 days. The fruit can be refrigerated in an airtight container up to 1 day.

1 Combine the ginger, ginger syrup, sugar, and ½ cup of water in a saucepan. Bring to a boil over medium heat, stirring to dissolve the sugar. Simmer for 5–6 minutes until slightly reduced. Remove from the heat, stir in the lime zest and juice and the pomegranate seeds. Let cool.

2 Peel the mangoes. Use a sharp knife to cut the flesh away from the stones. Slice the mango and arrange the slices on a plate. Halve, seed, and peel the papaya. Cut into wedges and arrange on the mango. Halve and seed the melon. Cut the melon flesh into bite-sized chunks. Add to the mango and papaya.

3 Spoon the ginger dressing over the fruit. Serve with lime wedges.

● **Good with** Greek yogurt or whipped cream.

Apricot and Yogurt Parfait

Enjoy this dish for breakfast or a light dessert

🍴 makes 4 parfaits

🕐 prep 5 mins, plus cooling • cook 25–30 mins

✓ low fat

❄ freeze for up to 3 months

12oz (350g) **dried apricots**

1¼ cups **orange** juice

½ cup thick **Greek yogurt**

1 cup **muesli** or granola

2 tbsp **pistachio nuts**, slivered

● **Prepare ahead** The purée can be refrigerated for up to 5 days.

1 Combine the apricots and orange juice in a small saucepan and bring to a simmer over medium heat. Lower the heat and cover. Simmer for 25–30 minutes, or until very tender.

2 Cool slightly. Transfer the apricot mixture to a food processor and purée. If the mixture is too thick, add a little more orange juice.

3 Serve warm or cold, in individual serving dishes with layered Greek yogurt, muesli, and pistachio slivers.

VARIATION

Peach Parfait
Instead of apricots, use 12oz (350g) dried peaches. The parfait also makes a delicious sauce for ice cream, thinned with a little juice or a liqueur, such as apricot brandy or Amaretto.

Pear, Mascarpone, and Hazelnut Tart

This fruity, rich tart with its deliciously nutty topping is a sensation for dinner parties

 makes 8 servings

 prep 20 mins, plus chilling • cook 50 mins

9in (23cm) tart pan with removable bottom, baking beans

For the pastry dough

1¼ cups **all-purpose flour**, plus more for rolling out

3 tbsp **sugar**

grated zest of ½ **lemon**

6 tbsp **butter**, chilled and diced

1 large **egg**, beaten

For the filling

⅔ cup **mascarpone**

½ cup **sugar**, plus more for sprinkling

1 large **egg** plus 1 large **egg yolk**

3 tbsp **whole milk**, as needed

1 tsp **pure vanilla extract**

4 canned and drained **pears**, sliced

⅓ cup **toasted, skinned, hazelnuts**, roughly chopped

2 tbsp **apricot preserves**, strained

1 **For the pastry**, pulse the flour, sugar, and zest in a food processor. Add the butter and pulse until the mixture resembles bread crumbs. Add the egg and pulse until the dough begins to clump together. Chill for 30 minutes. Roll out on a floured work surface into a round about ⅛in (3mm) thick. Line a 9in (23cm) tart pan with a removable bottom, and trim the excess. Refrigerate for 30 minutes.

2 **Preheat the oven** to 375°F (190°C). Line the pan with a round of wax paper and fill with baking beans. Bake about 12 minutes until the pastry looks set and begins to brown. Remove the paper and beans and bake 10 more minutes, until the pastry is lightly browned. Cool on a wire rack.

3 **Reduce the temperature** to 325°F (170°C). Mix the mascarpone, sugar, egg and yolk, milk, and vanilla together until smooth and pour into the tart shell. Arrange the sliced pears in the filling, sprinkle with the hazelnuts, and then the sugar. Bake for 30 minutes or until the filling is just set.

4 **Cool on a wire** rack. Brush with the preserves, slice, and serve.

Raspberry-banana Smoothie

The delicious drink contains no added sugar, so is ideal for anyone who is looking for a healthy choice

makes 4 servings

prep 5 mins

1½ cups **frozen raspberries** or strawberries, or a combination

1 **banana**, broken into pieces

3 tbsp **plain low-fat yogurt**

2½ cups **pineapple** or apple **juice**

1 **Combine the raspberries**, banana, and yogurt in a blender. Add the juice, cover, and process until the mixture is smooth.

2 **Pour into** 4 tall glasses and serve chilled.

● **Good with** breakfast or brunch—a great way to ensure you start the day with vitamin-rich fruits.

VARIATION

Thicker Smoothie
Add another banana. If you prefer to use fresh fruits, add your own choice of raspberries, blackberries, strawberries, or blueberries plus 2 or 3 ice cubes.

Fresh Orange Gelatins

This jelly is wonderful served after a rich main course, as it is light, refreshing, and not too sweet

- 🍴 makes 6 servings
- 🕐 prep 20 mins, plus soaking and chilling • cook 10 mins
- 🍽 6 x 1 cup dessert glasses, ramekins, or gelatin molds

vegetable oil, for the dessert glasses

4 oranges, peeled

3⅔ cups fresh or bottled orange juice, as needed

2 envelopes plain powdered gelatin

½ cup plain low-fat yogurt, preferably Greek

● **Prepare ahead** The gelatins can be made and chilled for up to 2 days before serving.

1 **Over a glass measuring** cup, cut the oranges into segments, catching the juice in the cup. Lightly oil six 1-cup dessert glasses, ramekins, or gelatin molds. Divide three-fourths of the orange segments among the glasses, reserving the rest for garnish. Add enough orange juice to the measuring cup to reach 3¾ cups. Cover and refrigerate the reserved orange segments.

2 **Pour ½ cup** of the orange juice in a small heatproof bowl. Sprinkle in the gelatin. Let stand for 5 minutes, until the juice has absorbed the gelatin. Place the bowl in a small frying pan of simmering water. Stir constantly until the gelatin is completely dissolved. Stir about ½ cup of the orange juice into the softened gelatin, then mix this back into the measuring cup of juice.

3 **Divide the gelatin** mixture among the dessert cups. Refrigerate for at least 2 hours, or until set.

4 **Top each serving** with yogurt and a few reserved orange segments, and serve chilled.

VARIATION

Grapefruit Gelatins

Substitute 1 or 2 grapefruits, depending on size, for the oranges. Use grapefruit juice or a mixture of grapefruit and orange juice.

┌─ **JELLY MOLDS**
│ If you used individual molds, dip each one
│ briefly into a bowl of hot water. Press gently
│ around the inside of each mold to loosen
│ the gelatin. Unmold onto a dessert plate.
└─

Sour Cream, Apple, and Almond Tartlets

Almonds and apples are the perfect combination for this sweet pastry dessert

- 🍴 makes 6 servings
- 🕐 prep 20 mins, plus chilling and cooling • cook 45 mins
- 🍽 6 x 4in (10cm) tartlet pans with removable bottoms, baking beans
- ❄ freeze for up to 3 months

For the pastry dough

1¼ cups all-purpose flour, plus more for rolling out

6 tbsp butter, chilled and diced

3 tbsp sugar

1 large egg yolk

For the filling

1¼ cups sour cream or crème fraîche

1 cup almond flour (almond meal)

4 large eggs

½ cup packed light brown sugar

2 tbsp maple syrup

2 tbsp almond-flavored liqueur

1 tsp pure vanilla extract

3 Granny Smith apples, peeled, cored, and sliced

1 tbsp granulated sugar

1 **Pulse the flour**, butter, and sugar, until the mixture resembles bread crumbs. Add the yolk and pulse until the dough begins to clump together. Chill for 30 minutes. Divide the dough into 6 portions, and roll each on a floured work surface into an ⅛in (3mm) thick round to fit a 4in (10cm) tartlet pan. Prick the dough. Refrigerate for 30 minutes.

2 **Preheat the oven** to 400°F (200°C). Line each tart pan with wax paper and fill with baking beans. Bake for 10 minutes. Remove the paper and beans and bake for another 10 minutes, until golden. Remove the pans and reduce the temperature to 375°F (190°C).

3 **To make the filling**, whisk the sour cream, almond flour, eggs, brown sugar, maple syrup, liqueur, and vanilla extract. Divide among the pans. Top with the apples and sprinkle with sugar. Bake 20 minutes, until set. Cool for 10 minutes. Remove the sides of the pans and cool completely. Serve at room temperature.

Rhubarb and Ginger Meringue Cake

Tart rhubarb and spicy ginger combine to make a tasty filling for this delicious meringue cake

 makes 6–8 servings

prep 30 mins, plus cooling
• cook 1 hr

For the meringues

4 large **egg whites**, at room temperature

pinch of **salt**

1 cup **sugar**

For the filling

1 lb 5 oz (700g) **rhubarb**, trimmed and sliced 1 in (2.5cm) thick

½ cup **sugar**

3 tbsp chopped **crystallized ginger**

½ tsp **ground ginger**

1 cup **heavy cream**

confectioner's sugar, for sifting

● **Prepare ahead** The meringues can be stored in an airtight container for up to 1 week. The filling can be refrigerated 1 day in advance.

1 Preheat the oven to 350°F (180°C). Line 2 baking sheets with parchment paper.

2 Beat the egg whites with an electric mixer until soft peaks form. One tablespoon at a time, beat in the sugar until the whites are stiff.

3 Spread the meringue on the baking sheets into two 7in (18cm) circles. Bake for 5 minutes. Reduce the oven temperature to 250°F (130°C) and bake for 1 hour, until crisp. Cool completely.

4 Meanwhile, cook the rhubarb, sugar, chopped ginger, ground ginger, and 2 tbsp water in a large covered saucepan over medium-low heat for 20 minutes, or until tender. Let cool. If too liquid, drain off some of the juices. Refrigerate for 2 hours.

5 Whip the cream until stiff peaks form and fold in the rhubarb. Spread 1 meringue with the rhubarb cream and top with the remaining meringue. Dust with confectioner's sugar and serve.

Citrus Fruit Salad

Refreshing, colorful and full of vitamins, this is sunshine in a bowl

 makes 4 servings

prep 20 mins

✔ low fat

3 oranges

1 grapefruit

1 ruby grapefruit

2 **clementines** or mandarins

juice of 1 **lime**

1–2 tbsp **sugar** (optional)

lime zest, to decorate (optional)

● **Prepare ahead** The salad can be covered and refrigerated for up to 24 hours.

1 With a sharp knife, cut away the skin and pith from the oranges and grapefruit. Cutting toward the core of the fruit and working over a bowl, cut away each segment, sliding the knife blade close to the membrane that separates them.

2 Place all the segments in a bowl. Squeeze any remaining juice from the membranes, then discard the membranes.

3 Peel the clementines and divide into segments. Add to the bowl, then add the lime juice. Sprinkle with the sugar, if using. Cover and refrigerate at least 2 hours, until chilled.

4 Using a slotted spoon, spoon the salad into dessert cups and garnish with the lime zest, if using. Serve chilled.

VARIATION

Sweet Citrus Salad
Make as above, but replace the 2 grapefruits with 1 pomelo or ugli fruit. These fruits have naturally sweeter flavors, so you can omit the sugar entirely.

Pear and Star Anise Tart with Ginger Crust

Firm-ripe Bosc pears are best; they won't thin the creamy filling

- makes 6-8 servings
- 30 mins, plus infusing • cook 45 mins
- 9in (23cm) tart pan with a removable bottom, baking beans
- freeze for up to 3 months

For the pastry

1 ¼ cups **all-purpose flour**, plus more for rolling

½ tsp **ground ginger**

6 tbsp cold **butter**, diced

1 large **egg yolk**

For the filling

1 ¼ cups **heavy cream**

5 whole **star anise**

3 large **egg yolks**

3 tbsp **granulated sugar**

2 tbsp **butter**

3 tbsp **light brown sugar**

4 ripe **Bosc pears**, peeled, cored, and sliced

1 Combine the flour and ginger. Add the butter and rub it with your fingertips until the mixture resembles coarse bread crumbs. Mix the egg yolk with 3 tbsp cold water. Add to the flour mixture and stir until the dough comes together, adding water if needed. Gather into a thick disk. Wrap in plastic wrap and refrigerate for 30 minutes.

2 On a lightly floured surface, roll the dough into a ⅛in (3mm) round circle and use to line the tart pan. Chill for at least 30 minutes.

3 Meanwhile, bring the cream and star anise to a boil over low heat. Remove from the heat and let stand for 1 hour. Whisk the egg yolks and granulated sugar. Remove the star anise from the cream, and whisk the cream into the yolks.

4 Melt the butter in a frying pan over medium heat. Add the brown sugar and stir until melted. Add the pears and cook, stirring occasionally, about 5 minutes, until tender and coated in caramel. Cool slightly.

5 Preheat the oven to 375°F (190°C), with a baking sheet in the oven. Arrange the pears in concentric circles in the tart shell, then pour in the cream. Place the tart pan on the baking sheet. Bake for 25-30 minutes, or until the filling is set. Let cool on a wire rack. Remove the sides of the pan and serve.

Mango and Lime Smoothie

This drink makes a refreshing start to the day, and the lime gives a little hidden "kick"

- makes 4 servings
- prep 5 mins

2 ripe **mangoes**, peeled, stoned, and chopped

2 ripe **bananas**, peeled and chopped

1 cup chilled **orange** juice

¼ cup **plain yogurt**

2 tbsp fresh **lime** juice

1 Combine the mangoes, bananas, orange juice, yogurt, and lime juice with 6 ice cubes in a blender. Process until smooth. Serve at once.

- **Good with** low fat muffins for a nutritious breakfast.

VARIATION

Tropical Fruit Smoothie

Substitute pineapple juice for the orange juice, and the pulp of 2 or 3 passion fruits for the lime juice.

Pineapple Milk Shake

A fun drink for children, with no need for added sugar

- makes 2 servings
- prep 5 mins

2 ripe **bananas**, peeled and chopped

⅔ cup **whole milk**

2 **pineapple rings** from a can, chopped

2-3 tbsp **pineapple juice**, from the can

1 scoop **vanilla ice cream**

1 Process all of the ingredients in a blender until smooth. Pour milk shakes into 2 chilled glasses. Serve immediately, with straws.

Techniques Eggs

Separate

Many recipes call for either yolks or whites. Smell cracked eggs before using to be sure that they are fresh

1 In a nonreactive bowl, break the shell of an egg by tapping it against the rim of the bowl. Insert your fingers into the break, and gently pry the two halves apart. Some of the white will escape into the bowl.

2 Gently shift the yolk back and forth between the shell halves, allowing the white to fall into the bowl. Take care to keep the yolk intact. Place the yolk into another bowl, and set aside. Remove any shells that may have fallen into the bowl.

Beat Egg Whites

For the best results, use room temperature egg whites, a copper bowl, and a balloon whisk

1 Place the egg whites in a perfectly clean bowl and begin beating slowly, using a small range of motion to break up their viscosity.

2 Continue beating steadily, using larger strokes, until the whites have lost their translucency, and begin to foam.

3 Incorporating as much air as possible, increase your speed and range of motion, until the whites have "mounted" to the desired volume, and are stiff, but not dry.

4 Test by lifting the whisk; the peaks should be firm but glossy, and the tips should droop gently.

Poach

Use fresh eggs, as they have thicker whites, and are less likely to disperse when cooking

1 Crack an egg onto a small plate, being careful not to break the yolk, then slide it into a pan of gently boiling water with vinegar (see "Poaching Water.")

2 Using a slotted spoon, gently lift the white over the yolk just until set. Repeat with remaining eggs. Adjust the heat to a gentle boil, and poach for 3–5 minutes, or until the whites are completely set.

3 Place the eggs in another pan of gently simmering salted water for 30 seconds to remove the taste of the vinegar. Then, using a slotted spoon, place the eggs on a clean dish towel to drain briefly.

POACHING WATER

In the boiling water, add 1 tsp of white vinegar to every quart (1 liter) of water. This will help the egg white to coagulate, rather than form streamers in the water. Do not add salt, as it will discourage coagulation.

Boil

Despite the name, eggs must be simmered, never boiled. If a green ring appears, it is the result of overcooking (or an old egg)

For Soft-boiled

The whites will be set, and the yolks runny. Use a pot large enough to hold the eggs in a single layer. Cover them with at least 2in (5cm) of cold water. Bring the water to a boil over high heat, then immediately lower to a simmer for 2–3 minutes.

For Hard-boiled

Both the whites and the yolks will be set. Once the water comes to a boil, lower the heat and simmer for 10 minutes. When the eggs have cooked, place the pot under cold running water to stop the cooking process. Peel away, and discard the shells when cool enough to handle.

Scramble

Scramble as you like, whether you prefer your curds large, small, or completely scrambled in traditional French-style

1 **Crack the eggs** into a bowl, making sure to remove any fallen shell. With a fork, break the yolks and beat the eggs. Season with salt and freshly ground black pepper.

2 **Heat a nonstick frying pan** over medium heat, then melt enough butter to lightly coat the base of the pan. When the butter has melted, pour in the beaten eggs.

3 **Using a wooden spoon**, pull the setting egg from the edges into the center of the pan to cook the raw egg. For larger curds, let the egg set longer before scrambling.

For creamier eggs, add a little milk when beating the eggs in step 1, or add a little cream just before the eggs are finished.

Make a Classic Folded Omelet

A 3-egg omelet is easiest to cook; any more than 6 eggs will be difficult to handle

1 **Beat and season** the eggs with salt and freshly ground black pepper. Heat a nonstick frying pan over medium heat, and melt 1 tbsp of butter. Add the eggs, shaking the pan, so the eggs can spread evenly.

2 **Stir the eggs** gently with a fork while continuing to shake the pan. Stop stirring the eggs just as soon as they are set. Fold the side of the omelet nearest to you halfway over itself.

3 **Sharply tap the handle** of the pan to encourage the other side of the omelet to curl over the folded portion, and slide to the edge of the pan.

4 **Tilt the pan** over a serving plate, so that the omelet falls onto the plate, seam side down. Serve immediately.

Techniques Fruit and Nuts

Make Lemon Zest Julienne

These strips are used in a large variety of recipes as flavorings and garnishes. Choose unwaxed lemons, if possible

1 **Using a peeler**, remove strips of the zest with as little of the bitter pith as possible.

2 **If any pith remains**, use a sharp knife to slice it off by running your knife along the peel away from you. Using a rocking motion with your knife, slice the peel into thin strips.

Peel and Prepare Apples

Choose apples that are sweet-smelling, firm, and unbruised. The skin should be taut and unbroken

Core and Peel

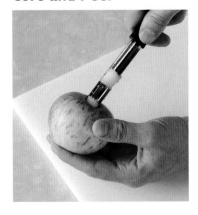

1 **Core an apple** by pushing a corer straight into the stalk of the apple, through to the bottom. Twist and loosen the core, then pull it out with the corer.

2 **Using a peeler** or small paring knife, gently remove the skin of the apple by cutting a circular path around the body from top to bottom.

Make Rings

Place the cored apple onto its side, and hold it steady on a clean cutting board. Using a sharp knife, slice down through the apple. Repeat, making slices of even thickness.

Chop

After slicing, stack the rings, a few at a time. Slice down through the pile, then repeat crosswise in the opposite direction, making pieces of about the same size.

Section Citrus Fruit

Sectioning citrus fruit ensures clean and precise wedges for a more attractive garnish

1 **With a sharp knife**, cut a small piece of peel from the top and base of the fruit so it can stand upright. Holding it firmly, slice down and around the flesh, following the contour of the skin. Try to remove as much of the white pith as possible. Use a small knife to cut away any pith left clinging to the fruit.

2 **The fruit will now** reveal the contours of each section, which is separated from the next by a membrane. Cut into and along the edge of a section. Cut back along its outer edge, which will free the membrane. Repeat this process with all the sections, discarding the membranes. This technique works with all citrus fruit.

Prepare a Mango

Cutting "halves" on each side of the fibrous pit and turning the mango "inside out" is the cleanest way to remove the flesh

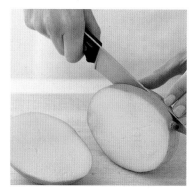

1 Standing the mango on its side, cut the fruit by running your knife just to one side of the pit; repeat the cut on the other side, so that a single slice remains with the pit attached.

2 With the halves flesh-side up, score the flesh lengthwise into strips, then cut crosswise, cutting to, but not through, the skin. Press the skin side of the mango "inside out," so that the flesh is exposed, and can be easily removed. Run your knife along the skin to remove the cubes.

Cut Pineapple

Preparing fresh pineapple is simple. Be careful when handling the prickly outer skin

Make Rings

1 With a sharp knife, cut the top and base off the pineapple. Stand the fruit upright and follow the contour of the flesh, removing the skin in long strips from top to bottom. Dig out any "eyes."

2 To make the rings, turn the pineapple on its side, and cut into slices. Use a small, round cookie cutter to remove the center of each ring.

Make Slices

1 Quarter the fruit, then cut lengthwise to remove the core at the center of each piece. Beginning at the leaf end, cut between the flesh and the skin.

2 Cut the flesh crosswise against the skin, making slices of even width. Repeat, cutting the other quarters into slices.

Peel Peaches and Nectarines

Removing the skin is necessary for many desserts, sauces, and purées

1 With a small, sharp knife, cut a small cross in the skin at the base of the fruit. This will make it easier to remove the skin.

2 Immerse the fruit in boiling water for 30 seconds. With a slotted spoon, remove the fruit from the water, and transfer it to another bowl filled with cold water. When the fruit is cool enough to handle, remove it from the water, and carefully pull the skin from the flesh with your fingers.

Poach Fruit

Choose firm, slightly unripe fruits, as they will hold their shape better, and the poaching will complete the ripening

Poach Fruit in Sugar Syrup

1 **Apples, apricots, pears,** peaches, plums, and quinces are all suited to poaching. Pit or core, then halve the fruit. Add to simmering sugar syrup, making sure that the fruit is completely submerged. Sweeter syrups ensure that the fruit will retain its shape.

2 **Poach the fruit** for 10–15 minutes, or until tender, and remove with a slotted spoon. Boil the syrup until it is slightly reduced, strain, then pour over the fruit to serve.

Poach Pears in Wine

1 **Heat red wine** with spices or flavoring—fresh citrus zest, whole cinnamon sticks, fresh ginger, or vanilla beans—and sugar and stir until the sugar dissolves. Peel the pears and add to the pan. Poach at a simmer for 15–25 minutes, or until tender.

2 **Remove the pan** from the heat, and let the pears cool in the liquid. When cool, remove the pears with a slotted spoon and set aside. Bring the liquid to a boil. When the syrup is slightly reduced, pour over the pears and serve.

Make a Sauce for Crêpes

Crêpes are a simple dish; this sauce makes them elegant. For a flambé sauce, see p376

1 **In a large frying pan**, heat 2 tbsp orange or lemon juice with 1 tbsp sugar and 1 pat butter over low heat. Simmer the sauce for 5 minutes, or until slightly thickened.

2 **Place the crêpes** into the pan one at a time, coating evenly with the sauce.

3 **Fold a crêpe in half**, then in half again, and transfer immediately to a plate. Repeat with the remaining crêpes.

FOR FLAMBÉING

For impressive presentation, setting the crêpes aflame is always exciting. Place the crêpes back into the pan with the sauce, plus brandy or liqueur. Cook for a few seconds to warm. Remove from the heat, and carefully light the brandy with a long match. Let burn 30 seconds, then cover the pan if the fire hasn't burned out. Serve immediately.

Peel Chestnuts

Choose chestnuts that are heavy, with smooth, shiny shells

> ### BLANCHING CHESTNUTS
> Instead of roasting the chestnuts to split their shells, they can also be blanched. Place the chestnuts in a saucepan with plenty of cold water to cover, and bring to a boil. When the shells split, drain the chestnuts on paper towels, and peel when cool enough to handle.

1 Using a small, sharp knife, score the flat side of the chestnut, making an "x" to keep it from exploding when hot.

2 Roast the chestnuts until the shells split, about 30 minutes. When they are cool enough to handle, peel off the shells and the inner skins.

3 Coarsely chop the chestnuts with a sharp knife if you wish to use them for stuffing.

Prepare Almonds

If you wish, you can peel, blanch, slice, and chop almonds yourself

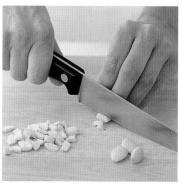

1 To blanch, place the almonds in a bowl and cover with boiling water. Let stand for 2–3 minutes, then drain in a colander.

2 To peel, pinch each almond between your thumbs and index fingers to slip the nut out of its skin. Alternatively, rub the nuts in a dish towel to remove the skin.

3 To slice, hold each nut flat on a cutting board. Using a large, sharp knife, cut the almonds into slices. To make thin slivers, carefully slice the almonds lengthwise.

4 To chop, use a large, sharp knife to cut the nuts to the required size – coarse or fine. Other nuts can be chopped in the same way.

Shell Walnuts and Pecans

Walnuts and pecans are used in both savory and sweet dishes

Use a nutcracker. The inner skin is difficult to peel away, but perfectly fine to eat. Be very careful to keep your fingers out of the way of the nutcracker.

Skin Pistachios

Inside the hard tan-colored shell is a delicious green nut

Place the shelled pistachios in a bowl, and blanch as for almonds, above. Rub the skins off between sheets of paper towel or a dish towel.

Cook Rice by Absorption

In the West, packaged rice is thoroughly cleaned, so soaking it before cooking will only wash away the nutrients

1 Put the rice and water or stock into a large saucepan. Bring to a boil over medium heat, stir once, and lower the heat to simmer uncovered for 10–12 minutes, or until all or almost all the liquid is absorbed.

2 Remove the saucepan from the heat and cover with a clean, folded towel and a tight-fitting lid. Return to the lowest heat and leave the rice to steam, without removing the lid, for 10 minutes.

3 Remove the folded towel and replace the lid. Leave the rice to sit for 5 minutes, covered with the lid. Uncover, fluff the rice with a fork, and serve.

PERFECT RICE

For perfect rice, always buy good-quality rice and use a heavy-bottomed pan with a tight-fitting lid. There should be 1½–2 times as much water as there is rice. (Follow the package directions if there are any.) Do not salt the cooking water, as it will cause the rice grains to rupture. Instead, try flavoring the rice using stock instead of water.

Make Basic Risotto

The best risotto is made from a combination of rich, well-flavored stock, and constant stirring

1 Heat the stock in a saucepan and keep at a gentle simmer. In a separate, large saucepan, heat the oil and butter. When the butter is melted, add the onion, and cook until it is softened, but not brown. Stir in the risotto rice, coating the grains in the butter and oil.

2 Add the wine, bring to a gentle boil, and stir until absorbed. Add a ladleful of simmering stock, and stir until it is absorbed. Continue adding stock by the ladleful, stirring, until the rice is tender, but *al dente*. This will take 20–25 minutes.

3 Stir in a little more butter, and some Parmesan. Season to taste with salt and pepper, cover the saucepan, and remove from the heat. Let the risotto stand for 2 minutes before serving.

Risotto should be creamy, but never mushy, with distinguishably separate grains of rice. Only use risotto rice. The medium-short stubby grains will swell, but still maintain their individual shape. Use any well-flavored fish, chicken, or vegetable stock.

Make Soft and Set Polenta

A staple of Italian cooking, polenta, made from cornmeal, is one of the most versatile grains

For Soft Polenta

1 Bring a large pan of salted water to a boil. Gradually pour in the polenta, whisking quickly and continuously to ensure that no lumps form, and the mixture is smooth.

2 Reduce the heat to very low, and continue cooking for 40–45 minutes, until creamy and coming away from the edge of the pan. Whisk occasionally to prevent a skin. Stir in butter and Parmesan, and season.

For Set Polenta

1 Make soft polenta, but omit the butter and cheese. Pour onto an oiled baking sheet, spread with a wet spatula to a thickness of ¾in (2cm), then cool and set. (Keep up to 4 days, covered, in the refrigerator.)

2 When ready to use, place the polenta onto a cutting board. Cut into the desired shapes. Brush with olive oil, then cook on a hot, ridged grill pan for about 3–5 minutes on each side.

Cook Dried Pasta

Keep dried pasta on hand, as it is the start of many quick dishes

1 Bring a large pan of salted water to a rapid boil, and gently pour in the pasta. Stir well.

2 Boil uncovered, using the recommended cooking time on the package as a guide, until *al dente*.

3 Drain the pasta by pouring it into a large colander, shaking it gently to remove any excess water.

> ### HOW TO TELL WHEN PASTA IS *AL DENTE*
>
> *Al dente* is Italian for "to the tooth," which refers to the slightly chewy texture of perfectly cooked pasta. It is best to refer to your taste, rather than the package instructions. Test often. Use tongs or a slotted spoon to remove a piece of pasta from the cooking water, and rinse it under cold water to cool. Take a bite–it should retain some texture. Don't believe you can test it by tossing it against the wall to see if it sticks–that would surely indicate overcooked pasta. If you will be cooking the pasta further as part of a recipe, it is especially important not to overcook it.

Boil Noodles

Most Asian noodles are boiled for a few minutes before using; rice noodles only need to be soaked in boiling water

1 To boil Asian-style noodles, bring a large saucepan of water to a rolling boil. Add the noodles, allow the water to return to a boil, then cook until the noodles are softened and pliable, about 2 minutes.

2 Drain the noodles in a strainer. Refresh under cold running water to prevent them from cooking further, then drain. Toss the noodles with a little oil to prevent them from sticking. Use immediately, or proceed with a recipe.

Techniques Vegetables

Steam

This is a healthy way to prepare vegetables, but if over-steamed, the vegetables will lose their vibrant color and flavor

1 Bring about 1in (2.5cm) water to a boil in the bottom pan of a steamer. Place the vegetables in the upper basket, and position it above the bottom pan. Bring the water to a boil over medium heat.

2 When the steam rises, cover the pan with a tight-fitting lid and cook until the vegetables are just tender. Test by pricking with the tip of a paring knife. Remove from the heat, and serve.

Stir-fry

This cooking method uses very little oil, so the vegetables retain their natural flavors, and take hardly any time to cook

STIR-FRYING TIPS

For best results, have all the vegetables prepared, measured, at hand, and cut to approximately the same size. Vegetables or meats that take longest to cook should be added first. Season to taste with salt, pepper, soy sauce, Chinese hot sauce, or chile flakes.

1 Heat the wok or pan and add the oil (sunflower, canola, or peanut), tilting the pan to spread the oil around the base. When very hot, add flavorings, such as garlic, ginger, chile, or scallions, and quickly toss.

2 Add the desired vegetables and toss, moving them from the center to the sides. If using meat, add it before the vegetables, allowing the meat to sit and cook for a few seconds before continuing to stir.

3 Some vegetables, such as broccoli, benefit from steaming for just a few minutes after the initial frying. Add a little water and cover the wok. Cook until the vegetables are just tender, and still crisp.

Cut Carrot Batonnets

This method of cutting vegetable sticks is also suitable for any long straight vegetable such as parsnips and zucchini

1 Peel each carrot and cut in half crosswise. Set the mandoline blade to ¼in (5mm) thickness. Hold the mandoline steady with one hand and press the carrot firmly with the palm of the other, being careful to keep your fingers clear of the blade. Slide each carrot up and down a few times, until the slices are the right thickness and uniform in size. Alternatively, use a chef's knife.

2 Stack the slices of carrot in the order in which they fell from the mandoline into flat piles on a board. Hold firmly and cut into neat rectangles, all the same size, with a chef's knife, then cut lengthwise into thin sticks or batonnets about ¼in (5mm) wide.

Peel and Dice an Onion

Once an onion is halved, it can be sliced or diced. This technique is for quick dicing, which helps prevent your eyes from watering

1 **Using a sharp chef's knife**, cut the onion lengthwise in half. Peel off the skin, leaving the root in place to hold the layers together.

2 **Lay one half** flat-side down. Make a few slices into the onion horizontally, cutting up to, but not through the root.

3 **Cut the onion** in half vertically, slicing down through the layers, again, cutting up to, but not through the root end.

4 **Cut across** the vertical slices to produce even dice. Use the root to hold the onion steady, then discard when the onion is diced.

Wash and Cut Leeks Julienne

The mildest member of the onion family, leeks are wonderful in soups and sauces, but need to be thoroughly washed

1 **With a chef's knife**, trim off the root end and some of the dark, green leafy top. Cut the leek in half lengthwise and fan it open, holding the white end. Rinse the leek under cold running water to remove the grit. Gently shake off any excess water, and dry with paper towels.

2 **For julienne**, cut off the dark green part of the leek and discard, then cut the leek crosswise into sections of the required length. Lay each section flat-side down, and slice into fine strips about ⅛in (3mm) wide.

Peel and Chop Garlic

Garlic is used in many recipes and peeling it is easy once you know how

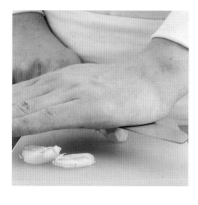

Choosing Garlic

Pre-peeled garlic is convenient if you plan to use it within a few days, but buying it fresh, and preparing it yourself is preferred. Choose fresh bulbs that are firm and compact. The skin should be smoothly attached to the base of the bulb, not tattered, or frayed. Although garlic keeps for up to 2 months in a cool, dark, and dry place, be sure to check that the cloves are still firm, and free of sprouts. Never store garlic in the fridge.

1 **Lay each garlic clove** flat on a cutting board. Place the side of a chef's knife blade on it. Lightly strike the blade to break the skin.

2 **Peel and discard** the skin and cut the ends off from each clove.

3 **Chop the garlic** roughly, then sprinkle with a little salt to prevent it from sticking to the knife. Continue chopping as necessary.

Peel and Seed Tomatoes

When tomatoes are used in sauces and soups that will not be strained, they are often peeled and seeded

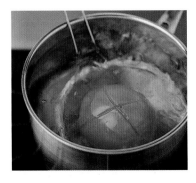   

1 **Remove the green stem,** score an "x" in the skin of each tomato at the base, then immerse in a pan of boiling water for 20 seconds, or until the skin loosens.

2 **With a slotted spoon,** remove the tomato from the boiling water, and submerge it in a bowl of ice water to cool.

3 **When cool enough** to handle, use a paring knife to peel away the loosened skin.

4 **Cut each tomato** in half and gently squeeze out the seeds over a bowl and discard.

Prepare Broccoli

How to separate broccoli florets from the head

1 **Lay the broccoli** head flat on a clean cutting board. With a chef's knife, cut off, and discard the thick stalk just below the florets.

2 **Remove the florets** by sliding the knife between their stems to separate them. Rinse the florets in cold water and drain in a colander.

Prepare Cauliflower

How to separate cauliflower florets from the main stalk

1 **Lay the head** of cauliflower on its side on a cutting board. With a chef's knife, cut off the large stalk and remove any leaves.

2 **Using a small paring knife,** carefully cut the florets from the central stem. Rinse the florets in cold water, and drain in a colander.

Trim Leafy Greens

Before cutting and cooking hearty greens such as Swiss chard, kale, and collard greens, you must wash and trim them

1 **Discard all limp** and discolored leaves. Using a chef's knife, slice each leaf along both sides of the central rib, then remove the rib and discard. Wash the leaves well in a sink filled with cold water; repeat. Shake the leaves to remove excess water. Pat dry in a clean dish towel, or with paper towels.

2 **Grab a handful** of leaves and roll them loosely into a bunch. Cut across the roll into strips of the desired width.

Halve and Pit an Avocado

The flesh of an avocado is a rich, buttery, and luxurious addition to salads, soups, and dips

1 **With a chef's knife**, slice into the avocado, cutting all the way around the pit.

2 **Gently twist** the halves in opposite directions to separate.

3 **Strike the pit** with your knife blade to pierce it firmly and lift the knife to remove the pit.

4 **Use a wooden spoon** to carefully release the stone from your knife and discard.

5 **Quarter the avocado** and use a paring knife to peel away, and discard the skin.

6 **To dice an avocado**, cut it into neat slices lengthwise, then repeat crosswise to the desired size.

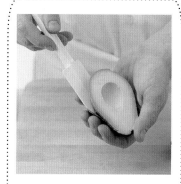

Alternatively, you can slice an avocado. Halve and remove the pit, then scoop out the flesh with a rubber spatula, keeping it whole if possible. Place on a cutting board, and cut into slices, or wedges. Rub the flesh with lemon to prevent browning.

Trim Asparagus

To ensure tender asparagus, especially when you have thicker spears, trim and peel them

1 **With a chef's knife**, cut the tough ends from the spears. Alternatively, snap the bottom of the asparagus spears at their natural breaking point.

2 **Holding the tip** of an asparagus spear gently, use a vegetable peeler to remove a thin layer of skin from the stalk, rotating the spear to peel all sides.

Prepare Artichokes

Artichokes can be served whole with the leaves trimmed, or cut back entirely to just use the "hearts"

To Serve Whole

1 Holding the stalk to steady the artichoke, cut the tough tips off with sturdy kitchen scissors.

2 Use a chef's knife to cut the stem flush with the base, so the artichoke will sit upright.

3 Cut off the pointed top, and pull away any dark outer leaves. The artichoke is now ready to cook.

To Serve the Hearts

1 Cut or pull away all of the large leaves from the artichoke, then cut the stem flush with the base.

2 Cut off the remaining soft "cone" of leaves in the middle just above the hairy choke.

3 Cut away the bottom leaves with a paring knife, trimming the base so it is slightly flattened.

4 Scoop out the choke with small spoon, removing all the hairy fibers. Rub the exposed surface generously with lemon juice.

Roast Beets

Roasting brings out the natural sweetness in beets and other tubers

1 Preheat the oven to 400°F (200°C). Trim all but 1in (2.5cm) from the stem, wash, dry, drizzle with olive oil, then salt and wrap in foil.

2 Place the beets in a shallow roasting pan, and bake in the middle of the oven until tender, about 45 minutes. Set aside until cool.

3 When cool enough to handle, peel the skins with a paring knife. You can wear disposable gloves to prevent staining your hands.

4 Slice the beets, and season with salt and pepper to taste. Serve either warm or cool.

Prepare Bell Peppers

Red, green, orange, and yellow peppers add their brilliant color and sweetness to stir-frys and distinctive flavor to many dishes

1 Place the pepper on its side and cut off the top and bottom. Stand the pepper on one of the cut ends, and slice it in half lengthwise. Remove the core and seeds.

2 Open each section and lay flat on the cutting board. Sliding the knife sideways, remove the remaining pale, fleshy ribs.

3 Cut the peppers into smaller sections, following the divisions of the pepper. Slice or chop, according to the recipe you are using.

For stuffing and roasting, cut around the stalk, and remove with the core attached. Rinse away the stray seeds and dry.

Roast and Peel Peppers

Pepper skins can be indigestible. Roasting makes removing their skins easy and enhances their flavor and sweetness

1 Using long-handled tongs, hold the pepper over an open flame to char the skin on all sides.

2 Put peppers into a plastic bag and seal tightly. Set the bag aside to allow steam to loosen the skins.

3 When the peppers have cooled completely, use your fingers to peel away the charred skin.

4 Pull off the stalk, keeping the core attached if possible. Discard seeds, and slice the flesh into strips.

Seed and Cut Chiles

Chiles contain capsaicin, a pungent compound that is a strong irritant to skin, and mucus membranes

1 Cut the chile lengthwise in half. Using the tip of your knife or a small spoon, scrape out and discard the seeds, ribs, and stem.

2 Flatten each chile half with the palm of your hand, and slice lengthwise into strips.

3 For dice, hold the strips firmly together, and slice crosswise to make equal-size pieces.

SAFETY TIP

Once you have touched the seeds and inner membranes of hot chiles, never touch your eyes or nose, as it will burn painfully. Wash your hands immediately after preparing the hot chiles, or better yet, wear disposable gloves, which should be thrown away afterward.

Halve, Seed, and Peel Winter Squash

The skin of winter squash is hard and thick, and must be peeled either before, or after cooking

1 Holding the squash firmly on a cutting board, use a chef's knife to cut the squash lengthwise in half, working from the stalk end to the core end.

2 Using a spoon, remove the seeds and fibers from each squash half and discard.

3 If planning to cut the squash into chunks for a recipe, use a vegetable peeler or knife to remove the skin.

Rehydrate Dried Mushrooms

Mushrooms preserved by drying, which intensifies their flavor, must be soaked before use

1 To rehydrate dried mushrooms, place the mushrooms—either wild or cultivated—into a bowl of hot water. Allow them to soak for at least 15 minutes.

2 Use a slotted spoon to remove the mushrooms from the soaking liquid. If you plan to use the soaking liquid as well as the mushrooms, strain the liquid through a coffee filter, or fine cheesecloth, to remove any sand or grit.

Make Deep-fried Potatoes

Any vegetable with a high starch content, such as potatoes, sweet potatoes, or parsnips, can be sliced thinly and deep-fried

1 Preheat the oil or fryer to 325°F (160°C). Meanwhile, using a mandoline or knife, thinly slice the peeled potatoes.

2 When the oil is hot, add a batch of potatoes, using a frying basket to lower them into the oil.

3 Fry until crisp and golden brown on both sides, about 2 minutes. Lift the potatoes out of the oil and drain briefly on paper towels.

4 Keep hot, uncovered in a warm oven, until all the potatoes are fried. Sprinkle with salt to taste, and serve immediately.

Core and Shred Cabbage

Shredded cabbage is used in many recipes, but the vibrant purple variety makes an attractive side dish

1 **Hold the head of cabbage** firmly on the cutting board, and use a chef's knife to cut it in half, straight through the stem end.

2 **Cut each half again** lengthwise through the stem, and cut out the hard central core from each quarter.

3 **Working with one quarter** at a time, place the cabbage cut-side down on the board. Cut across the cabbage, creating shreds.

Shuck Corn and Cut Off Kernels

One of the sweetest vegetables, nothing is better than fresh corn

1 **Remove the husks** and the silk from the ear of corn. Rinse the shucked corn under cold running water. Pat dry with paper towels.

2 **Hold the ear upright** on a cutting board. Using a chef's knife, slice straight down the sides to cut the kernels off the cob.

3 **To extract the "milk,"** hold the cob upright in a bowl, and use your knife to scrape down the length of the cob.

Chop Herbs

Chop fresh herbs just before using to release their flavor and aroma

1 **To chop leaves** (a mixture or a single variety as the basil leaves above), gather them together, and roll them up tightly.

2 **Using a large, sharp knife**, slice through the herbs, holding them together with your other hand.

3 **Gather the herbs** into a pile and chop, using a steady rocking motion, turning the pile 90° until you have the size you want.

Techniques Fish and Shellfish

Clean a Round Fish

While most fish you buy have already been gutted, there may be occasions when you need to know how to do this yourself

Through the Stomach

1 On a clean work surface, place the fish on its side. Holding it firmly with a fish knife, small chef's knife, or kitchen scissors, make a shallow incision in the underside of the fish, cutting from just below the fin to the head.

2 Pull out the viscera (everything in the stomach cavity), using your hands. Using kitchen scissors, cut off the gills, being careful not to cut yourself, since they can be very sharp.

3 Rinse the cavity with cold, running water to remove any remaining blood or viscera. Pat dry with paper towels. The fish can now be scaled and trimmed (see below).

Through the Gills

1 First use kitchen scissors to snip off the gills at the base of the head. They are very sharp, so hook your index finger around them to pull them out.

2 Put your fingers into the hole left by the removed gills, and pull out the viscera.

3 Using kitchen scissors, make a small slit in the stomach at the ventral (anal) opening. Use your fingers to pull out any remaining viscera. Rinse with cold, running water, and pat dry. The fish can now be scaled and trimmed (see below).

Scale and Trim Fish

Use either a fish scaler, or the blunt side of a chef's knife to scrape off the scales if you plan to eat the skin

1 Lay the fish on top of a clean work surface, covered with a plastic bag or newspaper. Holding the fish by the tail, scrape off the scales from the tail toward the head. Turn the fish over, and scrape off the scales on the other side.

2 Using kitchen scissors, cut off and remove the dorsal (back) fin, the belly fins, and the two fins on either side of the head. If desired, trim the tail with the scissors, cutting it into a neat "v" shape.

Fillet and Skin a Fish

There is no need to scale a fish beforehand if you plan to skin the fish fillets

1 Gut the fish through the stomach. Then, using a large chef's knife, cut into the head end, just behind the gills, cutting at an angle, until you reach the backbone. Cut the fish down the length of the back and ribcage. Turn the fish over and repeat.

2 Place the fillet, skin-side down, on a clean work surface. Insert a fish knife into the flesh near the tail end. Turn the blade at a slight angle, and cut through the flesh just to the skin. Turn the blade of the knife almost flat, and grab hold of the end of the skin. Holding the knife firmly, close to the skin, pull the skin away, cutting it off the fillet.

Bone a Flatfish

Popular flatfish varieties include flounder, sole, and halibut

1 Skin the fish (see box, right). Lay it, skinned-side up, on a board, and using a filleting knife, cut down the center, through the flesh just to the backbone. Free the fillet on one side by cutting horizontally to the outer edge of the fish. Turn, and repeat to free the other fillet.

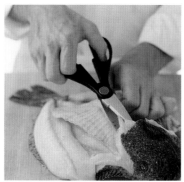

2 Slide the knife blade under the backbone to loosen the bone from the flesh. Use kitchen scissors to snip the backbone from the head and tail ends, as well as the center, to cut the backbone into pieces.

3 Lift the backbone pieces from the fish, cutting them from the flesh with the knife where necessary, and discard. Before stuffing, be sure to check for, and remove any remaining bones.

SKINNING A FLATFISH

To hold the shape of the fish, the white-skinned side is left attached to the flesh. The dark skin is usually removed because it is tough. Using kitchen scissors, trim the fins from the belly and back, leaving about ¼in (5mm) still attached to the fish. Place the fish white-side up, and make a small cut at the tail end to separate the dark skin from the flesh. Insert the knife between the flesh and the dark skin. Keeping the knife blade flat against the skin, grab the skin at the tail end firmly with your other hand, and pull to separate the flesh neatly away from the skin. Discard the dark skin.

Bone a Round Fish

Once gutted, scaled, and trimmed, a round fish can be boned through the stomach and stuffed for cooking

1 Open up the fish by making an incision from the tail to the head. Using the blade of your knife, loosen the ribcage (transverse bones) from the flesh on the top side, then turn the fish over to loosen the transverse bones from the flesh on the other side.

2 Using kitchen scissors, snip the backbone from the head and tail ends. Starting at the tail, peel the backbone away from the flesh and discard. The transverse bones will come away with the backbone. Before stuffing, be sure to check for, and remove any remaining bones left in the flesh.

Bake *en Papillote*

The term *en papillote* is French for "cooked in paper," which keeps the fish nice and moist by steaming it in its own juices

1 Cut a heart shape 2in (5cm) longer than twice the size of the fish out of parchment paper. Brush the paper with oil and place a piece of fish on one half of the heart with herbs and vegetables. Drizzle with white wine.

2 Fold over the other half of the paper and twist the edges to seal the package. Repeat for the other pieces of fish. Preheat the oven to 450°F (230°C). Place the packages on a preheated baking sheet and bake for 12–15 minutes, until the packages are puffed up and browned.

Remove the Meat from a Crab

Shown below is a common European crab, but the Dungeness crab is prepared in much the same way

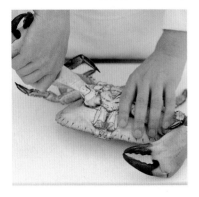

1 Place the cooked crab on its back on a chopping board, and firmly twist the claws and legs to break them from the body.

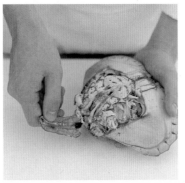

2 Lift the triangular tail flap on the underside of the body (the apron), twist it off, and discard.

3 Crack and separate the central section from the shell. Lift off the shell and remove any white meat from it using a teaspoon or fork.

4 Use your fingers to remove the gills ("dead man's fingers") from the central body section and discard. Also discard the intestines on each side of the shell, or clinging to the body.

5 Crack or cut the central body section into several large pieces. Using a lobster pick or skewer, dig out all the white meat and reserve in a bowl. Remove and discard any remaining pieces of membrane.

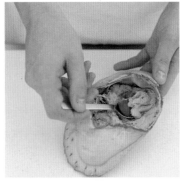

6 Remove the soft brown meat from the shell using a teaspoon, and reserve with the white meat. (There is no brown meat in Dungeness crab.) Remove and discard the head sac. If there is any roe in the shell, it too can be reserved.

7 To crack the shell on each leg, use poultry shears or the blunt side of a heavy knife. Remove the meat in one piece, using a lobster pick. Add to the white meat.

8 With lobster crackers or a nutcracker, crack the shell of the claws. Remove and reserve the white meat, and discard any bits of remaining membrane.

Prepare Mussels

Mussels must be scrubbed and debearded before use

1 In the sink, scrub the mussels under cold, running water. Rinse away grit or sand, and remove any barnacles with a small, sharp knife. Discard any mussels that are open.

2 To remove the "beard," pinch the dark stringy piece between your fingers, pull it away from the mussel shell, and discard. (Farmed mussels do not have beards.)

Open Scallops

Scallops can sometimes be bought in the shell

1 Hold the scallop firmly, flat-side up and using a thin, flexible knife, keep the blade close to the top shell of the scallop, and slide the knife around to sever the muscle.

2 Run the knife along the bottom shell to detach the scallop. Cut off and discard the viscera and fringe-like membrane. Rinse scallop and coral before use.

Shuck Oysters

When shucking oysters, practice makes perfect. Use a towel to protect your hands from the oysters' sharp shells

1 Holding the oyster flat in a towel will help prevent the knife from accidentally slipping. Insert the tip of an oyster knife into the hinge to open the shell. Keep the blade close to the top of the shell so the oyster is not damaged. Cut the muscle and lift off the top shell.

2 Detach the oyster from the bottom shell by carefully sliding the blade of your knife beneath the oyster. Take care not to cut the oyster or to spill out the delicious brine. The oysters can be served raw on the half shell (but be sure to scrub the shells thoroughly before opening), or removed and cooked.

Open Clams

Clams must be cleaned well, as they tend to be very sandy

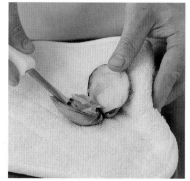

1 Discard any open clams. Place the clam in a towel to protect fingers, insert the knife tip and twist to force the shells apart.

2 Sever the muscle and release clam. If serving raw on the half shell, snap off the top shell. For soft shell clams, remove dark membrane.

Peel and Devein Shrimp

The gritty intestinal veins of large shrimp are usually removed

1 Remove the head and legs by pulling them off with your fingers, then peel away the shells, saving them for stock, if you like.

2 Using the tip of a paring knife or toothpick, hook the vein where the head was and gently pull it away from the body. Rinse and pat dry.

Cut Up a Chicken

Poultry is often left whole for roasting, poaching, and slow-cooking in a pot. For other cooking methods, cut into 4 or 8 pieces

Remove the Wishbone
Using a small, sharp knife, scrape the flesh away from the wishbone, then use your fingers to twist and lift it free.

1 Place the bird breast-side up on a cutting board. Using a chef's knife, cut down and through the skin between one of the legs and the carcass to separate the leg from the rest of the body.

2 Bend the leg back as far as you can to break the leg joint. When the ball is free from the socket, you will hear a pop.

3 Cut the leg away from the backbone, then repeat with the other leg. You can divide the leg into thigh and drumstick if you like.

4 Fully extend one wing, then use sharp poultry shears to cut off the wing tip at the second joint. Repeat to remove the other wing tip.

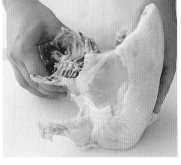

5 Using your hands, firmly grasp the backbone, and break it away from the breast section.

6 Using poultry shears, remove the lower end of the backbone (which has no flesh attached to it) from the remaining breast section.

7 Use poultry shears to cut along the breastbone from top to bottom. Trim unwanted sections of breastbone.

8 The chicken is now cut into 4 pieces: 2 breasts and 2 legs. Any leftover bones (such as the backbone) can be used to flavor chicken stock.

9 Use poultry shears to cut through the ribs two-thirds of the way along each breast diagonally, producing two breast pieces, one with a wing. Repeat with the other whole breast.

10 Cut each leg through the joint above the drumstick that connects it to the thigh, and cut through to separate. Repeat with the other leg.

11 The chicken is now cut into 8 pieces ready for cooking: 2 breast pieces with wings attached, 2 breast pieces, 2 thighs, and 2 drumsticks.

Bone Poultry

For quickly cooked dishes, there is an advantage to boning poultry

Detach the Breast

1 **Using poultry shears**, cut away the ribs and backbone. Work from the thickest wing end of the breast toward the narrowest end.

2 **Using a boning knife**, separate the flesh from the bone by following the contours of the breastbone to cut the fillet off. Use the breastbone in stock, if you wish.

POULTRY TOOLS

A boning knife is essential for removing the flesh from the bones. The blade is thin and short, which gives most of its control to the tip as it works all angles, and cuts through flesh and ligaments. Choose one with a slightly flexible blade. Never cut onto the bone or you will blunt the tip. Poultry shears are also an invaluable tool when cutting and boning poultry pieces. The curved blades and long handles give the shears more power to cut through ribcages and backbones. Use poultry shears to cut through, rather than around, bones. Choose a pair that are comfortable to hold and easy to clean.

Bone a Leg

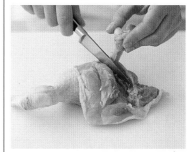

1 **Place the leg skin-side** down on a cutting board. Using a sharp knife, cut halfway through the flesh at the beginning of the thigh bone. Cut along the bone to the knuckle. Scrape to expose the bone, then ease it from the flesh.

2 **With the same technique**, start from the knuckle, and cut down the length of the drumstick. The bones will be exposed, but will be joined at the central knuckle joint.

3 **Lift the bones up** and away from the central knuckle joint. Using short strokes with the tip of your knife, remove the 2 bones from the flesh. Use in stock or discard.

Bone a Thigh

1 **Place the thigh skin-side** down on a cutting board. Use a small, sharp boning or paring knife to locate the bone at one end.

2 **Cut an incision** through the flesh, following the contour of the exposed bone. Cut around the bone to cut it completely free from the flesh, and discard or use for stock.

Bone a Drumstick

1 **Starting in the middle** of the drumstick, insert the tip of your knife until you locate the bone. Slice along the bone in both directions to expose it fully.

2 **Open the flesh** and neatly cut around the bone to free it completely from the flesh, and discard, or use to flavor stock.

Butterfly a Bird

Ideal for grilling or broiling, this preparation for small poultry such as Cornish hens, flattens the bird to ensure even cooking

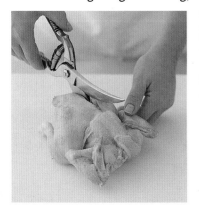

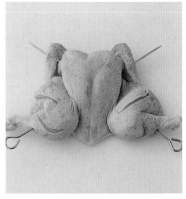

1 **Place the bird breast-side** down on a sturdy cutting board. Using poultry shears, cut along both sides of the backbone, remove it completely, and discard or use for stock. Open the bird and turn it over.

2 **Using the heel of one hand** and the other hand to stabilize, press down firmly to crush the breastbone. Once flattened, use a sharp knife to cut slits into the legs and thighs to ensure even cooking.

3 **Carefully push** a metal skewer diagonally through the left leg to the right wing, then a second skewer through the right leg to the left wing. The skewers are optional.

4 **The bird can now** be brushed with a marinade if desired, then grilled, broiled, or roasted in the oven.

Marinate Chicken

Using a marinade will produce tender and flavorful chicken

Mix the ingredients of your marinade in a bowl. In a separate bowl, large enough to hold the chicken in a single layer, coat the chicken with the marinade, turning the pieces to coat it all over. Cover the bowl with plastic wrap, and chill in the refrigerator for an hour or more, depending on the marinade, and the time available.

NOTE

Marinating poultry can serve two purposes. If using an **acid-based marinade** (such as red wine or vinegar), it will break down tough proteins, and tenderize the meat. Leave poultry to marinate in an acid-based marinade for no longer than 1 hour.

Oil-based marinades, mixed with aromatics (such as garlic, chile, or ginger), are used for the sole purpose of flavoring the meat. Marinating time for an oil-based mixture can be 4 hours or more.

Stuff a Boneless Chicken Breast

Avoid the temptation to overstuff the chicken breasts. The more stuffing, the more likelihood of leakage during cooking

1 **Using a sharp knife**, cut a pocket about 1½in (4cm) deep into the side of the breast fillet. Make your cut so that both sides of the pocket are the same thickness, which will ensure even cooking.

2 **Gently press the stuffing** into the pocket, and roll back the flesh to enclose it. Secure with a toothpick. Rolling the stuffed fillet in a crumb coating before cooking will help seal the pocket, and keep the stuffing inside.

Breading Chicken or Meat

This technique is used most commonly for frying chicken, but also works nicely for pork or veal

1 **Place each fillet** between 2 pieces of plastic wrap, then pound with a rolling pin until the fillets have spread out, and flattened to the size of a cutlet.

2 **Remove the plastic wrap** and season the fillets to taste with salt, pepper, and freshly chopped herbs. Dip the seasoned fillets into beaten egg, coating each side evenly.

3 **Roll the fillets** in bread crumbs, pressing an even coat to both sides. Repeat the process with the remaining fillets.

Frying Heat ½in (1cm) of oil in a frying pan until hot, and fry the fillets for 4–5 minutes on each side until cooked through and golden. Drain on paper towels.

Carve Poultry

All white-fleshed poultry, including turkey and chicken, can be carved using this technique

1 **Let the roasted bird rest** on a platter for 10–20 minutes. Collect the juices and add to the sauce or gravy. Place the bird breast side up on a cutting board. Staying close to the body of the bird, cut down through each leg at the joint, then cut to separate the drumstick from the thigh. Repeat with the other leg.

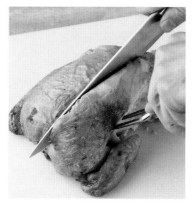

2 **Using a carving fork**, hold the bird steady against the surface of the cutting board. Keeping the carving knife as close to the breastbone as possible, slice downward and lengthwise along one side of the bone to release the breast. Repeat on the other side.

3 **Cut the breast pieces** in half on a slight diagonal, leaving a good portion of breast meat attached to the wing. Repeat, separating the breast and wing of the other side.

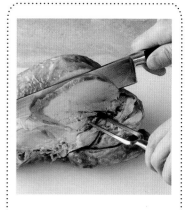

Carve the Breast Meat
To slice the breast meat from the body, hold the bird steady with a fork and make a horizontal cut under the breast meat above the wing. Cut all the way to the breastbone. Carve neat, even slices from the breast, keeping your knife parallel to the rib cage. Repeat, slicing on the other side.

Butterfly a Leg of Lamb

The leg consists of 3 bones: the pelvic, which is the broadest, then the thigh, and shank

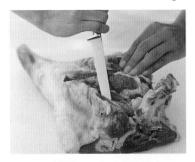

1 Place the lamb on a cutting board, fleshiest-side down. Locate the pelvis at the widest end of the leg, and hold it firmly while using a sharp, long-bladed knife to cut around and expose the leg bone.

4 When you reach the bottom of the leg, cut through the sinew and tendons to release the bone completely from the flesh. All 3 bones (the pelvis, thigh, and shank) should come away in one piece.

2 Make an incision from the pelvis to the bottom of the leg, cutting through the flesh just to the bone. Using short strokes (to prevent tearing the meat), work your knife closely around the leg bone, releasing it from the flesh.

5 Open out the leg so that the meat lies flat on the cutting board. With short strokes, make cuts downward through the thick meaty pieces on either side.

3 Keeping close to the bone, continue using short strokes down the length of the leg. Cut away the flesh from around the ball and socket joint, and down the length of the shank bone.

6 Open out the flesh of the butterflied leg. If there are areas that are thicker than others, cut thin fillets from the thick piece and fold it over a thin area. This is helpful for even cooking.

Bone a Saddle of Lamb

Once the bones are removed, the whole saddle of meat is perfect for stuffing

1 Using a sharp knife, cut away the membrane covering the fatty side of the saddle, then turn it over onto a clean cutting board. Working from the center, use short strokes to cut off the 2 fillets from either side of the backbone, and reserve, to cook alongside the saddle.

2 Loosen the outside edge of one side of the backbone using short, slicing strokes. Working from the side edge toward the center, release the side of the backbone. Repeat with the other side.

3 Starting at one end, use short, slicing strokes to cut under and around the backbone so that it comes free, taking care not to pierce through the skin. As the bone is released from the flesh, lift it away and cut beneath it.

4 Work from the center outwards, to cut away the meat and fat from the outer flaps. When the flaps are clean, square off the edges. Turn the saddle over, lightly score through the fat on the other side, and stuff and cook as desired.

Roast a Rib of Beef

This classic takes little effort to prepare, but leaves a lasting impression when cooked to perfection

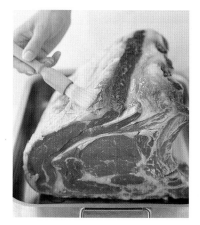

1 Remove the meat from the refrigerator about 1 hour in advance to allow it to come to room temperature. Preheat the oven to 450°F (230°C). Brush with oil and scatter with fresh herbs, such as thyme or rosemary. Alternatively, make multiple cuts into the fat and stick slivers of garlic and herbs inside. Position the meat rib-side down, in a roasting pan and place in the oven.

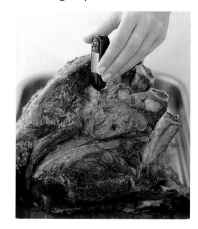

2 After 15 minutes, reduce the oven temperature to 350°F (180°C), then continue roasting for the calculated amount of time (approximately 75-90 minutes or more, depending on the size), basting occasionally. The most accurate way to test for doneness is to insert a meat thermometer (120°F /50°C for rare.) Before carving, leave the roast to stand for 15–30 minutes, covered with aluminum foil.

Carve Roast Beef

It is important to let your roast rest for 15–30 minutes so the meat relaxes, and retains its flavorful juices

1 Place the roast on a cutting board with the ends of the ribs facing up. Holding the meat steady with a carving fork, use a sawing action to cut downwards between the bones and the meat to separate them. Discard the bones.

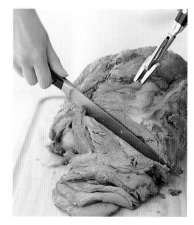

2 Turn the boneless roast fat-side up on the cutting board. Holding it steady with the fork, cut downward, across the grain of the meat into thin slices, again using a sawing action with the knife. Reserve the pan juices to make gravy.

Grill Steaks

Tender, prime cuts of meat are suitable for cooking under the broiler, on a barbecue, or on a ridged cast-iron grill pan

1 Preheat the grill pan over high heat for 4–5 minutes. (Alternatively, preheat the broiler or build a fire on an outside grill.) Use steaks about 1 in (2.5cm) thick. Brush both sides of the steaks with oil, and season with salt and freshly ground black pepper.

2 When the grill pan is very hot, place the steaks diagonally across the ridges. Cook for 1 minute, then rotate the steaks 45 degrees and cook for another 1–2 minutes. Flip the steaks over and repeat on the other side, for a total of about 6 minutes for rare meat. Remove the steaks from the grill pan, and let rest before serving.

Make Hamburgers

Ground round makes the juiciest burgers, but use leaner sirloin, if you prefer

1 **Place the ground meat** in a bowl, with chopped shallots, breadcrumbs, and herbs if you wish. Season with salt and freshly ground black pepper, and mix together with your hands.

2 **Divide the meat** into patties about 4in (10cm) thick. If you have the time, chill for at least 30 minutes before grilling. Chilling firms the meat and helps it stay together while cooking.

3 **Heat the grill pan** over medium-high heat. Place the burgers on the pan and cook for about 6 minutes, turning once, for medium-rare burgers.

BETTER BURGERS

Make ordinary burgers into something exquisite by adding veal, pork, lamb, sausage meat, or even foie gras to your ground beef. Also try adding chopped onions, chopped fresh parsley, basil, chervil, or other herbs, or your favorite spice mix. Always season with salt and freshly ground black pepper. Remember, if you are adding other meats to the beef, that the burgers should be cooked through, rather than served rare.

Boil a Ham Hock and Glaze a Ham

Boiling a ham hock or ham roast will remove any extra saltiness left from the brine it was cured in

To Boil

1 **Place the ham hock** in a large bowl, cover with cold water, and leave it to soak in the refrigerator for at least 24 hours to dilute the salty brine.

2 **Remove the ham** and rinse it under cold running water. Place it in a large saucepan, cover with cold water, and bring to a boil. Allow to boil for 5 minutes, or until the scum rises to the surface. Drain, rinse again, and return to a clean pan. Add the stock and other flavoring ingredients, pouring in enough stock to cover the meat. Bring to a boil, cover, then simmer over very low heat for 2½ hours. After cooking, the meat will be very tender.

To Glaze

1 **Boil or roast the ham** following your recipe. Using a sharp knife, score the fat into a diamond-shaped pattern, which will allow the glaze to penetrate, and flavor the meat.

2 **Warm a glaze** of brown sugar and mustard (or another glaze of your choice), until it is melted, then spread it evenly over the fat so that the glaze falls into the cuts. Bake the ham following your recipe, covered loosely with aluminum foil. Open out the foil for the last 30 minutes of roasting, to brown the top of the ham. Do not allow the glaze to burn.

Make Crisp Pork Roast
Perfectly browned pork skin is a real treat; here's how to do it

1 Using a very sharp knife, score the rind of a pork shoulder widthwise, working from the center outward. Repeat for the other end.

2 Massage the rind liberally with salt, then rub the entire shoulder with a little oil. Roast the meat, but do not baste.

3 When finished resting, hold the meat with a carving fork and cut just beneath the crisp skin. Lift away the skin in one piece.

4 Using kitchen scissors or a sharp knife, cut the skin crosswise in half. Serve it to accompany the roast pork.

Prepare Kidneys
One whole veal kidney weighing approximately 1lb 2oz (500g) will serve 4 people

1 Using your hands, gently pull away and discard the fat (suet) that surrounds the whole kidney.

2 Lay the kidney upside down, with the fatty core facing up. With the point of a sharp knife, cut around the core, remove, and discard.

3 Now that the membrane is released, use your fingers to peel it from the kidney and discard.

4 Using a sharp knife, cut the kidney into pieces, following the natural curves of the lobes. Prepare the kidneys as desired.

Deglaze a Roasting Pan
The drippings and meat juices that remain on the bottom of your roasting pan provide rich flavor for making gravy

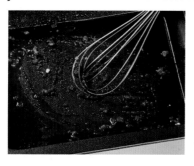

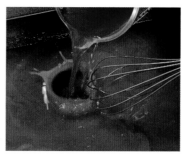

1 Pour all but about 2 tbsp of the fat from the roasting pan, leaving the juices and sediment. Bring the juices to a low simmer, then whisk in 2 tbsp of flour.

2 Using a dish towel, hold the pan at an angle so all the juices collect in one corner. Briskly whisk, being sure to scrape the bottom and the sides of the pan.

3 Gradually add 1½ cups stock, whisking until smooth, and bring the gravy to a simmer. Season to taste.

THE PERFECT GRAVY
To ensure smooth, lump-free gravy, it is important to whisk constantly. For thicker gravy, add less stock, and for a thinner one, add more. Add a splash of red wine before adding the stock, or flavor with a little Worcestershire sauce. Season to taste, although it probably will not need much salt, if any.

Techniques Sauces

Make Hollandaise

A well-made hollandaise sauce should have a rich yellow color, and be somewhat tart, and fluffy

1 In a small, heavy-bottomed saucepan, bring 2 tbsp white wine vinegar, 2 tbsp water, and 1 tbsp of lightly crushed, white peppercorns to a boil. Lower the heat and simmer for 1 minute, or until the mixture has reduced by one-third.

2 Remove from the heat, and let stand until cool, then strain the liquid into a heatproof bowl. Add 4 egg yolks to the liquid, and whisk.

3 Place the bowl over a saucepan of simmering water. (The water should be filled to just below the bottom of the bowl.) Whisk the mixture until the sauce thickens, and is ribbonlike, creamy, and smooth in texture, 5–6 minutes.

4 Place the bowl on a dampened dish towel to prevent it from slipping. In a thin stream, slowly pour in 9oz (250g) clarified butter, and whisk until the sauce is thick and glossy.

5 Gently whisk in the juice of half a lemon, then season to taste with salt, freshly ground white pepper, and cayenne pepper. Serve immediately. This recipe will make 2½ cups.

Make a Classic Vinaigrette

Vinaigrette is about balance of ingredients: it should flavor and complement a salad or other dish, but never dominate it

1 In a clean bowl, combine 2 tsp Dijon mustard, 2 tbsp good-quality white wine vinegar, and freshly ground black pepper.

2 Gradually whisk in ½ cup extra-virgin olive oil in a thin stream until completely emulsified. Adjust the seasoning if necessary.

3 Serve as a salad dressing, or in place of a heavier sauce for fish, poultry, or pasta. This recipe will make ⅔ cup of dressing.

> ### VINAIGRETTE VARIATIONS
> A simple variation to this classic recipe is to use the juice of 1 lemon, or a good-quality balsamic, champagne, or rice wine vinegar. Or, add fresh herbs or fruit. Other great flavor additions are shallots, garlic, and truffles. Transform vinaigrette into other dressings by adding additional ingredients to classic vinaigrette: orange and rosemary–orange zest and juice, and chopped rosemary; honey and ginger–mild honey and grated fresh ginger.

Make Mayonnaise

Emulsified sauces turn out better when all ingredients are brought to room temperature before using

1 Place 2 egg yolks, 1 tsp Dijon mustard and 1 tsp white wine vinegar in a mixing bowl. Add a pinch of salt and freshly ground white (preferably) or black pepper.

2 Steady the bowl on a dampened dish towel and gradually add 1 cup vegetable or canola oil–drop by drop to begin with, then a drizzle, and then a thin stream, as the sauce begins to thicken, whisking continuously.

3 As the sauce begins to thicken, add the oil in a slow, steady stream, and continue whisking to keep the emulsion stable.

4 When all the oil has been incorporated, and the mayonnaise is smooth and thick, stir in 2 tsp of fresh lemon juice and adjust the seasoning to taste. This recipe makes 1¼ cups.

Rescue Curdled Mayonnaise

1 When mayonnaise separates into coagulated flecks of egg and oil, it has curdled. This can happen for many reasons. The most likely causes are: the egg yolks or the oil were too cold; the mixing bowl was not clean; the oil was added too quickly; or too much oil was added.

2 The mayonnaise can easily be rescued. Simply place 1 egg yolk into a clean mixing bowl, and very slowly, trickle in the curdled mayonnaise, whisking continuously.

3 Continue whisking in the curdled mixture until it is all incorporated, and very smooth.

Mayonnaise-based Sauces

Classic mayonnaise is the basis of many emulsified sauces.

To make **aioli**, add 4 crushed garlic cloves to the egg yolks, then continue following the recipe. Serve with hot or cold fish, or as a dip for vegetables.

To make **rouille**, add a pinch of saffron and ¼ tsp of cayenne pepper to the finished aioli (above). This is traditionally served with the Mediterranean fish soup, bouillabaisse.

To make **tartare sauce**, add 1 tsp Dijon mustard, 2½ tbsp finely chopped gherkins, 2 tbsp rinsed and chopped capers, 2 tbsp chopped chervil, and 2 finely chopped shallots to the finished mayonnaise. Serve with deep-fried, or pan-fried fish.

Make Béchamel Sauce

Endlessly versatile, béchamel (the king of white sauces), has been used for many years in classic cooking

1 **Stick 4 whole cloves** into a small onion, cut in half. Place in a saucepan with 2½ cups whole milk and 1 bay leaf. Bring to a simmer, then allow the milk to cool for 20 minutes.

2 **Melt 4 tbsp unsalted** butter over low heat in a separate pan. Whisk in 4 tbsp flour and cook gently about 1 minute until it becomes a pale yellow roux.

3 **Remove the pan** from the heat. Strain the milk into the roux, and whisk vigorously until the sauce is smooth. Return the pan to medium heat, still whisking, until the sauce thickens, and comes to a boil, about 4–5 minutes.

4 **Reduce the heat,** and simmer gently for 5 minutes until smooth, thick, and glossy. Season to taste with salt, white pepper, and nutmeg. This recipe makes 2½ cups.

Clarify Butter

The clear liquid fat separates from the milk solids when gently heated, and can be used for sauces and higher-temperature cooking

1 **Cut unsalted butter** into cubes and place in a saucepan. Heat gently over low heat just until the milk solids have separated from the fat. Do not let the butter get too dark, as that will destroy its fresh taste. Skim off any froth.

2 **Remove from the heat,** and carefully pour the clear butter into a bowl. Discard the milk solids. Skim off any impurities from the surface of the clarified butter, and use as desired.

Make Fresh Tomato Sauce

This simple, yet versatile sauce, is perfect with fish, poultry, meat, and vegetables

> **SAUCE VARIATIONS**
>
> For a heartier, rustic sauce, remove the bay leaf, but do not strain. Add fresh thyme before serving. Also try adding freshly chopped basil or oregano. If you would like to add a spicy kick to your sauce, add a chopped fresh hot chile, or hot pepper flakes.

1 **In a saucepan** over low heat, place 2 tbsp unsalted butter, 2 chopped shallots, 1 tbsp olive oil, 1 bay leaf, and 3 crushed garlic cloves. Cover and sweat for 5–6 minutes until shallots are soft, but not brown.

2 **Seed and chop** 2¼lb (1 kg) of ripe plum tomatoes, and add them to the pan with 2 tbsp tomato paste and 1 tbsp sugar. Cook, uncovered for 5 minutes, then add 1 cup water and bring to a boil.

3 **Reduce the heat,** and simmer for 30 minutes, then season to taste with salt and pepper. Using a ladle, press the sauce through a sieve. Reheat the sauce before serving. This recipe makes 2½ cups.

Make Stock
A homemade stock is one of the most valuable ingredients you can have in your kitchen

Chicken or Meat Stock

1 Add either raw chicken bones or roasted meat bones into a large stockpot with carrots, celery, onions, and a bouquet garni of fresh herbs of your choice.

2 Cover with water, and bring to a boil. Reduce the heat and simmer for 1–3 hours, skimming frequently. Ladle the stock through a fine sieve and season to taste. Let cool and refrigerate for up to 2 days.

3 After the stock has been refrigerated, the congealed fat can easily be lifted from the surface with a slotted spoon.

Quick Skimming Fold a double-thick paper towel and pass it through the surface of the hot stock; the paper towel will absorb the fat.

Fish Stock

1 Using a sharp knife, cut the bones and trimmings of non-oily, mild fish into equal pieces. Rinse in plenty of cold water to remove the blood. Drain, and place the bones and trimmings into a large stockpot.

2 Cut carrots, celery, and onion into equal-size pieces, and add them (and any other flavorings you wish to add), into the pan with the fish. Cover with water, increase the heat, and bring to a boil.

3 Once the stock reaches a boil, lower the heat, and simmer for 20 minutes (any longer and the stock will start to become bitter). Skim off the scum that rises to the surface with a slotted spoon.

4 Ladle the stock through a fine sieve, pressing the solids against the sieve with the ladle to extract any extra liquid. Season to taste with salt and freshly ground black pepper, let cool, and refrigerate for up to 3 days.

Vegetable Stock

1 Place chopped carrots, celery, onion, and a leeks into a large stockpot. Add peppercorns, parsley, and bay leaves. Cover with water and bring to a boil. Reduce the heat and simmer for up to 1 hour.

2 Ladle the stock through a fine sieve, pressing the vegetables against the sieve to extract any extra liquid. Season to taste with salt and freshly ground black pepper, let cool, and refrigerate for up to 2 days.

Techniques Baking

Prepare and Line a Cake Pan

Greasing, flouring, or lining your pan ensures that baked layers turn out cleanly and easily

1 Melt unsalted butter (unless your recipe states otherwise), and use a pastry brush to apply a thin, even layer over the bottom and sides of the pan, making sure to brush butter into the corners, if applicable.

2 Sprinkle a small amount of flour into the pan. Shake the pan so the flour coats the bottom, and rotate the pan to coat the sides. Turn the pan upside down and tap the center to remove the excess flour.

3 If using a paper liner, instead of flouring, place a fitted piece of parchment paper directly on the bottom of the greased pan.

Parchment Lining To create the liner, stand the pan on the parchment and draw around the base with a pencil. Cut out just inside the pencil line.

Make Pastry

Pastry dough can be used directly after resting, stored for up to two days in a refrigerator, wrapped tightly in plastic wrap, or frozen

By Hand

1 Mix 1 ⅔ cups of unsalted, room temperature butter with 1 egg yolk and 1½ tsp salt in a bowl. In another bowl, mix 2 tsp sugar with 7 tbsp whole milk, also at room temperature, then gradually stir it into the butter mixture.

2 Sift 4 cups pastry flour into a bowl, then gradually stir it into the butter. When all the flour is added, continue mixing with a wooden spoon, or gently combine the ingredients with your hands.

3 Dust a work surface with flour and turn out the dough. Using the palm of your hand, lightly knead the pastry until it forms a soft, moist dough. (This recipe will make enough pastry for 4 tarts.)

4 Shape the dough into a ball (or balls), wrap it in plastic wrap, and refrigerate for at least 2 hours. Allowing the gluten and flour to relax during chilling will prevent the dough from shrinking when in the hot oven.

In a Food Processor

1 Fit the metal blade into the food processor. Put the butter, salt, egg yolk, sugar, and milk into the processor bowl, and process until smooth. Sift the flour into a separate bowl, then add it to the food processor.

2 Using the pulse button, process the mixture until it just starts to come together and stop when the pastry has formed a ball. Wrap in plastic wrap, and refrigerate for at least 2 hours.

Blind Bake a Tart Shell

Tart shells should be prebaked unfilled if they will contain moist fillings, such as custard, to prevent them from becoming soggy

1 **Once the pastry** is fitted in the pan, prick the bottom with a fork. This will allow trapped air to escape during baking. Chill in the refrigerator for at least 30 minutes.

2 **Cut out a circle** of parchment paper slightly larger than the pan. Fold the parchment in half 3 times to make a triangular shape, and clip the edges at regular intervals with scissors to ensure a close fit against the rim.

3 **Place the parchment** circle into the pan, and fill it with an even layer of dried beans or ceramic baking beans. Bake the shell in a preheated 400°F (200°C) oven for 10 minutes.

4 **Remove the beans** and parchment when cool enough to handle. Return the shell to the oven for another 5 minutes for partially baked, or 10–15 minutes for fully baked pastry. Cool on a wire rack.

Decorate Pie Crust

Before baking pies and tarts, remove excess pastry, and decorate the edges for a finished look

Trim
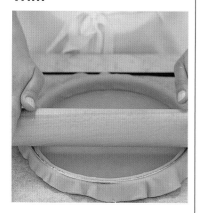

Roll the pastry out, then press it gently into the bottom of the tart pan and against the sides. Firmly roll a rolling pin over the top of the pan to trim off the excess pastry.

Forked Edge

Using a fork, press the dough to the rim of the pie plate. Repeat around the edge at even intervals.

Rope Edge

Pinch the dough between the thumb and the knuckle of your index finger, then place your thumb in the groove left by the index finger, and pinch as before. Repeat around the edge.

Fluted Edge

Push one index finger against the outside edge of the rim and pinch the pastry with the other index finger and thumb to form a ruffle. Repeat around the edge, leaving an even gap between each ruffle.

Make a Pizza Base

Rotating the dough when rolling it out is important in order to achieve a thin, even crust. For a basic pizza dough recipe, see p98

 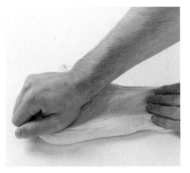  

1 Make a well in the center of the flour and add the liquid ingredients, gradually incorporating the flour to make a dough.

2 Knead the dough for 10 minutes, or until smooth. Set the dough aside in an oiled bowl, cover with plastic wrap, and allow to rise until doubled in size, about 1 hour.

3 When the dough has risen, turn it out onto a floured surface. Working from the center outward, roll the dough into a circle, rotating it by one-quarter turn each time.

4 Carefully transfer the dough to a lightly oiled baking sheet. Pinch the edges with your thumb and index finger to make a shallow rim.

Mix and Knead Yeast Dough

Dough should be well combined and kneaded to a silken and elastic finish

1 Place the flour, yeast, and salt into a large bowl. Make a well in the center, and gradually add the liquid ingredients.

2 Using your fingers, mix the wet and dry ingredients together, digging into the bottom of the bowl, and pressing the dough between your fingers to make sure all the liquid has been incorporated into the flour. (Or use a spoon if you wish.) The dough should be soft, but not sticky. Leave to rest according to the recipe used.

3 Before starting to knead, wash and dry the bowl and oil the insides. Turn the dough onto a floured surface, and fold it in half towards you.

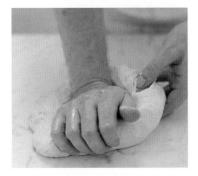

4 Using the heel of your hand, gently, but firmly press down, and away through the center to stretch and knead the dough.

5 Lift and rotate the dough a quarter turn. Repeat the folding, pressing, and rotating until the dough is smooth and elastic, about 8 minutes. Place the dough in the oiled bowl, cover with plastic wrap, and let stand until dough has doubled in size, about an hour.

6 Return the dough to the floured surface and knead briefly to invigorate the dough. Shape the dough as directed.

Glaze Pastry

Melted jelly, diluted egg, or chocolate can be brushed over pastry to produce a shiny finish

Fruit Tarts	**Turnovers**	**Pie Edges**	**Baked Tart**

For fruit tarts, apply melted jelly or light caramel over the fruit in a baked tart to give it a lustrous appearance.	**For turnovers**, brush with an egg wash (1 egg yolk, 1 tbsp water, and a pinch of salt) before baking to give the turnovers a rich, golden color, and a glossy glaze.	**Pie edges can be sealed** and tops made glossy by being brushed before baking with an egg wash.	**For a baked tart**, thinly glaze the base of a baked tart shell with melted dark or white chocolate, and allow to set to stop the crust from softening once filled.

Make Brioche Dough

Since the dough is very sticky, use a standing electric mixer. See p70 for ingredient quantities

1 Pour the flour into the bowl of an electric mixer fitted with a dough hook. Add instant dry yeast and superfine sugar. Mix on medium speed and gradually add half the eggs. Mix until smooth, then add the remaining eggs, one at a time, until fully incorporated.

2 Once the dough is mixed and begins to come away from the edges of the bowl, add the salt and diced, unsalted butter (at room temperature). Continue mixing until the dough comes cleanly away from the sides of the bowl again, and is silky in texture.

3 Transfer the dough to another large bowl. Cover with plastic wrap and leave it to rise at warm room temperature for 2–3 hours, or until doubled in size. The risen dough will be very sticky.

4 On a lightly floured work surface, punch down the dough. Return the dough to the bowl, and cover it with plastic wrap. Place it in a refrigerator and let it rise for 2 hours or overnight. Deflate once more, then shape into balls and bake.

Make Blinis

For serving with caviar or smoked fish, these yeasted pancakes are perfect little appetizers. For blini quantities and recipe, see p44

1 Sift the flour, baking powder, and salt into a bowl. Whisk in the milk and egg yolk. In a separate bowl, whisk the egg white until soft peaks form. Fold the egg white gently into the batter.

2 Heat a heavy-bottomed nonstick pan. Spoon small disks of batter into the pan and cook, undisturbed, until the edges brown, and bubbles appear on the surface. Flip over, and cook for 2–3 minutes longer, or until golden. Remove from the pan, transfer to a plate, and cover. Repeat with remaining batter.

Techniques Cakes and Desserts

Whip Cream

Depending on your recipe, you can whip to soft or stiff peaks. Chill the whisk, bowl, and cream beforehand.

1 Put the chilled cream in a bowl set in a large bowl of ice. Start beating with a broad circular motion at a leisurely pace, about 2 strokes per second (or the lowest speed on an electric hand mixer), until the cream begins to thicken. Increase to a moderate speed for soft peaks. It will barely hold its shape when lifted with the whisk.

2 For stiffly whipped cream, (firm peaks), continue beating the cream. At this point you can add other ingredients, such as superfine sugar, or vanilla. Test by lifting the whisk to see if the cream retains its shape. Be careful not to overwhip, because it will become granular and unusable as whipped cream.

Pipe

A pastry bag can be used not only to pipe whipped cream, but also buttercream, meringue, profiteroles, and éclairs

1 Choose a decorating tip, and put it in a pastry bag, then twist it to seal, and prevent leakage.

2 Holding the bag just above the nozzle with one hand, fold the top of the bag over with your other hand, creating a "collar," and begin spooning in the cream.

3 Continue filling, until the bag is three-quarters full. Twist the top of the bag to clear any air pockets. The cream should be just visible in the tip of the nozzle.

4 Holding the twisted end of the bag taut in one hand, use your other hand to gently press the cream to start a steady flow, and direct the nozzle as desired.

Make Crème Pâtissière

This pastry cream is the classic, custard-style filling for profiteroles and éclairs

1 In a heavy-bottomed saucepan over low heat, bring 1¼ cups whole milk and 1 vanilla bean, split lengthwise, to a boil.

2 Meanwhile, in a bowl, whisk 2 egg yolks with ¼ cup sugar, 2 tbsp each flour and cornstarch. Continue whisking, and slowly pour in the hot milk in a thin stream. Transfer to the pan, and whisk to boil, then remove from the heat.

3 Remove the vanilla and discard. Cut 2 tbsp room temperature butter into small cubes.

4 When the custard has cooled a little, add the butter, and briskly whisk into the sauce until it is smooth and glossy. This is best made just before serving. This recipe will make about 1¼ cups.

Test Setting Point for Jam

The chilled plate method is more reliable than a candy thermometer

Using a wooden spoon, scoop up some of the jam. Hold the jam above the bowl for a few seconds, allowing it to cool. Tilt the spoon at an angle—the jam should fall in a flake, rather than a stream.

Place a little of the jam onto a chilled plate. Allow it to cool, then push it to the side, using your finger. If the surface wrinkles, the jam is set. Alternatively, take a spoonful of hot jam, bring it to room temperature by quick chilling in the refrigerator for a minute, and if it stays in a mound when the plate is tilted, it is set.

Make Fruit Crisp

Adding a crumble topping to fresh fruit makes a quick and easy dessert. For fruit crumble recipes, see p453 and p462

SUCCESSFUL CRISP TOPPING

A perfect crisp topping should be made of coarse crumbs. Anything finer will mean the topping will have a cake-like texture rather than a rough crumble. Make sure the butter is chilled, and your hands are as cool as possible. Run your hands under cold water if they start getting too hot, or put the whole bowl in a refrigerator for a few minutes to allow the mixture to chill.

Once made, the topping can be poured into a freezer bag, and frozen until ready to use. There is no need to defrost before using. This also stops the crumble mixture clumping together when baking.

1 Rub chilled unsalted butter into all-purpose flour until it resembles coarse bread crumbs. Add sugar and rolled oats and mix together well.

2 Cut up fresh fruit and put into a buttered ovenproof dish; sweeten to taste. Spoon on the crisp mixture, and bake until golden and crisp.

Steamed Puddings

Steamed puddings are similar to baked puddings, but steaming is a slower process, and the water needs to be kept topped up

1 For ingredient quantities and pudding recipe, see p379. Mix a good-quality fruit preserve with dry sherry and some chopped, dried fruit. Stir them together in the bottom of the pudding bowl.

2 Spoon the pudding mixture over the preserves. Pleat the waxed paper and place it over the top of the bowl. Secure it firmly around the bowl with kitchen twine.

3 To keep out the steam, cover the waxed paper with pleated aluminum foil. Secure the foil to the outside of the bowl, and place the pudding in a steamer over boiling water. Make sure it doesn't boil dry.

4 Remove the pudding from the steamer. When cool enough to handle, remove the foil and waxed paper. Cover the top with a plate, invert, then lift the bowl off the pudding. Serve with Crème Anglaise.

Make Ice Cream

A rich, vanilla Crème Anglaise ice cream can be flavored in endless variations. For ice cream recipes, see pp403–409

> ### Variations on Vanilla
> The greatness of vanilla is that it goes well with almost everything. Add fresh or frozen fruit when processing the mixture to make strawberry or peach ice cream. Chop your favorite kind of chocolate, and add it with 2 tbsp of cocoa powder. Or try adding some instant coffee, a little sugar, and some almonds.

1 Prepare a batch of Crème Anglaise, and cool in a bowl set in a large bowl of ice. Stir the mixture continuously to prevent a skin from forming on the surface.

2 Continue to stir the mixture to ensure a smooth texture. When cold, fold in 1 cup heavy cream, whipped, and stir gently until the two mixtures are combined.

3 Pour the custard mixture into the canister of an ice cream maker, and process according to the manufacturer's directions. Transfer to a container, and freeze until firm.

Make Wine Granita

A frozen combination of a full-flavored syrup and water (or red or white wine), is light and refreshing after any meal

1 Make a syrup of sugar, fruit juice, water, and/or wine over low heat. Bring slowly to a boil, reduce the heat, and simmer for 2–3 minutes, stirring. Remove from the heat, let cool, then pour the liquid into a shallow baking pan and freeze. When half-frozen, use a fork to break up the frozen chunks. Repeat, once or twice, breaking up the ice crystals, until evenly frozen.

2 Remove the granita from the freezer 5–10 minutes before serving, to thaw slightly. Use a spoon to scrape up the frozen granita and serve in pre-chilled glasses.

Make a Soufflé Omelet

This airy dessert omelet is made by folding stiffly beaten egg whites with the yolks, and finishing under the broiler

1 Separate 2 large eggs. Beat the yolks with 1 tbsp superfine sugar, 1 tbsp water, and ¼ tsp vanilla extract. Whisk the whites until stiff, then stir a small amount of the yolk mixture into the whites. When incorporated, carefully fold the remaining yolks into the mixture.

2 Heat a flat frying pan over medium heat, then melt enough butter to lightly cover the bottom of the pan. Pour in the eggs, and cook until set, and the bottom is just beginning to brown. Place under a hot broiler until the top is golden. Quickly add a sweet filling, fold over, and serve immediately.

Make Crêpes

Making these crêpes involves two essential elements: the right temperature and the perfect batter. See p376 for ingredient quantities

1 Heat a little clarified butter in a nonstick crêpe pan and pour off any excess. Holding the pan at an angle, pour in a little of the batter.

2 Tilt and swirl the pan as you pour in more batter to thinly and evenly coat the bottom of the pan.

3 When the bottom of the crêpe has cooked to a pale golden color, use a spatula to loosen and flip the crêpe back into the pan. Cook until the other side is golden.

4 Put the cooked crêpe on parchment paper on a plate in a warm oven. Continue cooking the remaining crêpes, interleaving with parchment paper.

Fold Crêpes

Traditionally, crêpes are folded into fans, but other folded variations are just as attractive

Fill crêpes with about 1 tsp of sweet fruit preserves, cooked fruit, or chocolate sauce. Fold as desired and eat immediately.

Fans

To fold fans, fold one half of the filled crêpe over the other to make a semicircle, then fold in half again.

Pannequets

To fold pannequets, or squares, fold opposite sides inward to meet in the center. Then bring the top and bottom together at the center. Serve with the folded side down.

Cigarettes

To fold cigarettes, or rolls, fold opposite sides inward to meet in the center. Starting from one end, roll the crêpe, taking care not to roll too tightly, or the filling will ooze out.

Making Choux Paste

Choux paste is used for filling profiteroles, éclairs, and tarts. For ingredient quantities, see p439

1 In a saucepan, heat the water and butter until the butter melts. Increase the heat, bring to a boil, and add the flour and salt all at once.

2 Continue cooking for about 2 minutes or less, until the dough is very stiff and begins to pull away from the sides of the pan.

3 Remove from the heat and cool for 5 minutes. Whisk the eggs. Beat into the dough gradually, one egg at a time, beating hard after each addition.

4 Continue beating until the paste is very smooth and glossy. The paste is now ready to be shaped.

Shaping Choux Paste

Choux in any shape is perfect for filling with crème pâtissière, custard, or chocolate

Cream Puffs (Profiteroles)

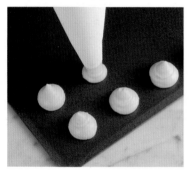

1 Pipe neat and uniform walnut-sized balls on to a lined baking sheet, pressing the nozzle gently into the paste at the end of each ball to avoid forming a peak. Allow plenty of space between each.

2 If peaks should form, dip a fork in a little beaten egg to gently flatten them. Lightly brush with beaten egg, using a pastry brush, being careful not to let the glaze drip, then bake.

3 When the cream puffs are baked, they should be puffy and golden. Make a small slit in each of the puffs to allow the steam to escape, then cool on a wire rack.

4 When cool, cut a small slit in the base of each puff. Fill the puffs by piping cream, custard, or chocolate through the slit in the base using a large, plain nozzle.

Choux Fingers

Using a plain nozzle, pipe the choux paste in strips, making each "finger" identical in length. Bake, pierce, and cool on a wire rack. Split in half, and pipe flavored mousse onto the base. Replace the top, and repeat for the other fingers.

Choux Rings

Mark out circles of your chosen size on a baking sheet, using a circular cutter dusted with flour. These templates will ensure uniform ring sizes. Following the circles, pipe choux rings using an appropriately sized ring nozzle. Bake the rings, pierce, and cool on a wire rack. Split the rings in half, fill with cream, and replace the tops.

Make Sponge Cakes

A light génoise sponge is perfect with simple cream or preserves. Add butter for a firmer sponge that will support the weight of fruit

1 **Preheat the oven** to 375°F (190°C) and line the bottom of a springform cake pan with parchment paper. Sift 1½ cups (200g) cake flour and set aside. Place 6 eggs, 1 cup sugar, 1 tbsp clear honey, and a pinch of salt in a heatproof bowl, and set over barely simmering water, making sure the water does not touch the bottom of the bowl. Using an electric mixer, beat until the mixture is creamy, pale yellow, and doubled in volume.

2 **Remove the bowl** from the heat and beat at high speed until the mixture is cool and thick. Add zest of ½ lemon, set the speed to low, and continue beating for 15 minutes to stabilize the eggs. Using a spatula, gently fold the sifted flour into the mixture until well blended. Stir a few tbsp of the mixture into 4 tbsp melted unsalted butter, then quickly fold the two mixtures together, taking care not to lose any volume.

3 **Pour the batter** into the prepared cake pan, smooth the top, and place it into the oven. Reduce the heat to 350°F (180°C) and bake for 30–40 minutes, or until golden brown and springy to the touch. Remove from the oven and leave to cool in the pan for 10 minutes. Slide a knife around the edges of the cake pan, then release the springform. Peel off the paper lining, and cool on a wire rack.

4 **To cut layers**, place the cake on a firm, level surface. Place one hand on top to steady the cake and using a sharp, long-bladed, serrated edge knife, score an even guideline around the cake. Following your guideline, cut through the layer completely. Using a spatula, carefully lift the layer, set aside, and fill the cake. You can also slice the cake into 3 or 4 layers depending on its depth.

Jelly Roll

A jelly roll is less likely to tear if filled and rolled up while it is still warm and flexible

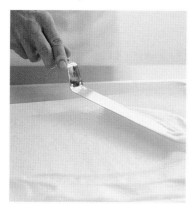

1 **Make the mixture** for the sponge cake (above), following the instructions for the génoise above, and taking care to fold the egg white and yolk mixtures together very gently, so that none of the volume is lost. Then gently fold in the flour.

2 **Transfer the batter** to the lined jelly roll pan, and spread evenly to the edge using a spatula. Bake until golden and springy to the touch. Sprinkle with a little sugar, and cover with a clean piece of parchment paper. Carefully turn the cake out onto a work surface.

3 **Slowly peel away** the lining paper, pressing down onto it with a ruler to avoid tearing the cake. Spread with your desired filling to within ¾in (2cm) of the edge. Lifting the cake with the help of a new piece of parchment paper underneath, roll up with gentle pressure.

4 **Lay the roll** on another sheet of paper, draping one end of the paper over it. Hold the other end of the paper with one hand, and push a ruler against the roll with your free hand. This will tighten and shape the roll evenly. Remove the paper, cover the cake, and refrigerate for 2 hours. Trim the ends before serving.

Make French Meringue

This lighter-than-air meringue is crisp on the outside, and soft and yielding inside. For ingredient quantities, see p388

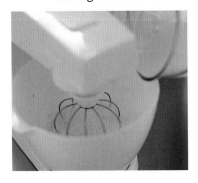

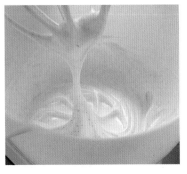

1 **In the bowl** of an electric mixer, beat the egg whites on medium speed, gradually adding half the sugar, and the vanilla seeds.

2 **Continue beating** until the mixture is shiny and smooth, and will hold a peak when the beaters are lifted from it.

3 **Using a rubber spatula**, gradually fold in the rest of the sugar, lifting the egg whites up and over from the bottom, being careful not to lose any volume.

4 **Shape then bake** in a preheated 225°F (120°C) oven according to recipe directions. Turn off the oven, prop the door open, and leave to dry for 8 hours or overnight.

Piped Meringue

Using a pastry bag with different nozzles, meringue can be piped into many shapes and sizes, or applied as a topping to a tart or pie

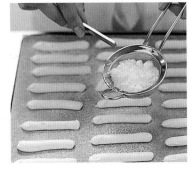

For discs or layers, on a lined baking sheet using a pastry bag with a star tip, pipe meringue in a spiral beginning at the center. Bake in a preheated 225°F (120°C) oven for 1 hour 20 minutes, then let dry.

For shells, using a pastry bag with a round tip, pipe the meringue in equal-sized dollops about 3in (7.5cm) in diameter. Bake for 1 hour 10 minutes (the center will be slightly golden if broken open), then let dry.

For fingers, using a pastry bag with a round tip, pipe the meringue into sticks about 3in (7.5cm) long. Dust lightly with confectioner's sugar. Bake for 30–35 minutes, then let dry.

To cover a tart, using a pastry bag with a star tip, pipe the meringue over the tart in attractive peaks. Dust with confectioner's sugar and place under a preheated broiler for a few minutes, until golden brown.

Use Sheet or Powdered Gelatin

Whether you are using unflavored gelatin in sheet or powdered form, it must first be soaked in a little cold water

1 **Soak 4 sheets** (equal to about one ¼ oz/7g envelope of powdered gelatin) in a bowl in cold water to cover for at least 10 minutes. After soaking, squeeze out as much water from the sheets as possible before using. If using powdered gelatin, sprinkle 1 envelope over ¼ cup cold liquid and let soften for 3–5 minutes.

2 **Warm water** or flavored liquid over low heat in a small saucepan. Remove the pan from the heat, and add the gelatin sheets and stir until completely dissolved. For powdered gelatin, place the bowl in simmering water and stir until dissolved.

Make Caramel

To help prevent the sugar from crystallizing, add some glucose syrup (available at candy supply stores)

Make Syrup

1 **Bring 1½ cups sugar**, ½ cup water, and 6 tbsp liquid glucose to a boil in a saucepan over high heat, stirring to dissolve the sugar. Boil, using a wet pastry brush to brush down any sugar crystals that form on the sides of the pan.

2 **Cook the syrup** without stirring until it is dark golden brown. Stop the cooking by plunging the saucepan in a bowl of iced water.

Make Sauce

Carefully whisk warmed heavy cream into the caramel (it will bubble up). Cook over low heat until the sauce is smooth and glossy.

Use a candy thermometer when making candy to ensure accurate temperatures.

Prepare Chocolate

Chill the chocolate before cutting and grating, since the warmth of your hands will quickly melt it

Chop

For chopping, use your hands to break the chocolate into small pieces, then chill the pieces in the freezer for a few minutes. Place the chilled chocolate on a cutting board. Using a sharp knife, hold the tip down with your other hand, and chop, using a rocking motion.

Grate

For grating, rub chilled chocolate against the face of the grater, using the widest holes. Once the chocolate begins to melt, stick it back in the freezer. Once re-hardened, continue grating until you have enough.

Melt

To melt chocolate, bring a pan of water to a boil, and reduce the heat to low. Place the chopped chocolate in a heatproof bowl, and set it over the gently simmering water. Allow the chocolate to melt, then stir with a wooden spoon until it is smooth. Alternatively, melt in a microwave.

Make Curls

For curls, spread soft or melted chocolate onto a cool marble surface. When it solidifies, use the blade of a chef's knife to scrape the chocolate into curls.

Index

Acknowledgments

For Carroll & Brown Limited

Project Manager Chrissie Lloyd
Project Editor Chrissa Yee
Managing Art Editor John Casey

Commissioning Editor Susie Johns
Senior Editor Helen Barker-Benfield
Recipe Editor Jacqueline Bellefontaine
Editors Louise Coe, Beverly LeBlanc, Kate Pollard, Wanda Allardice,
Rhona Kyle, Lucy Jessop, Ian Wood, Michele Clarke

Art Directors Anne Fisher, Denise Brown, Luis Peral-Aranda,
Tracy Stewart-Murray, Ruth Hope
Designers Emily Cook, Richard Walsh, Paul Stradling, Oliver Keen
Technical Advisor George Taylor

Food Stylists Teresa Goldfinch, Wendy Strang, Sarah Lee, Liz Cambio, Lizzie Harris,
Marie-Ange Lapierre, Jane Oliver, Brian Brooke, Sam Squire, Madeleine Cameron,
Katie Giovanni, Liz Franklin, Patricia Dunbar, Viv Gill, Lorna Brash, Tonia George

Photographers Carole Tuff, Tony Cambio, William Shaw, Stuart West, David Munns,
David Murray, Adrian Heapy, Nigel Gibson, Kieran Watson, Roddy Paine,
Gavin Sawyer, Ian O'Leary

Recipe Developers Christine France, Caroline Marson, Lorna Brash, Clare Lewis,
Catherine Atkinson, Liz Ashworth, Jacqueline Bellefontaine, Beverly LeBlanc, Susie Johns,
Tomaz Zaleski, Helen Barker-Benfield, Wendy Sweetzer, Kathryn Hawkins,
Fiona Burrell, Sue McMahon, Viv Gill, Nicky Sanderson de la Peña,
and Victoria Blashford-Snell

Proofreader John Skermer
Index Marie Lorimer

Thanks also to **Denby Pottery** for use of their products for photography
and to Jonathan Worth for hand modelling

Editor-in-Chief
Victoria Blashford-Snell first began cooking in pubs and restaurants in Bath and
Wiltshire. As a result of her zest for travel, she developed an imaginative variety of tastes,
from the Mediterranean to the Great Barrier Reef to the Himalayas. Today she runs
a successful catering business and teaches regular cookery courses in the UK.

Victoria has written several popular cookbooks, including *Canapés* and *Diva Cooking*, and has
co-authored six *Books for Cooks* cookbooks. She has also presented 30 programmes for
Carlton Food Network, UK, and appears regularly on several food shows in the US and Canada.